The Scapegoat

ALSO BY LUCY HUGHES-HALLETT

NON-FICTION

Cleopatra: Histories, Dreams and Distortions
Heroes
The Pike: Gabriele d'Annunzio

FICTION

Peculiar Ground
Fabulous

The Scapegoat

*The Brilliant Brief Life of the
Duke of Buckingham*

Lucy Hughes-Hallett

4th ESTATE • *London*

4th Estate
An imprint of HarperCollins*Publishers*
1 London Bridge Street
London SE1 9GF

www.4thestate.co.uk

HarperCollins*Publishers*
Macken House, 39/40 Mayor Street Upper
Dublin 1, D01 C9W8, Ireland

First published in Great Britain in 2024 by 4th Estate

1

A catalogue record for this book is
available from the British Library

ISBN 978-0-00-812655-1 (Hardback)
ISBN 978-0-00-812657-5 (Trade paperback)

Set in Minion Pro
Printed and bound in the UK using 100%
renewable electricity at CPI Group (UK) Ltd

MIX
Paper | Supporting
responsible forestry
FSC™ C007454

This book contains FSC™ certified paper and other controlled
sources to ensure responsible forest management.

For more information visit: www.harpercollins.co.uk/green

To Dan, Lettice and Mary
with love

Contents

A Note on Sources

IN the book that follows I refer often to the people who made it possible – those who set down their impressions during Buckingham's lifetime, or while his career was still within living memory. They are ambassadors, diarists, letter-writers, news-gatherers, proto-journalists, biographers, memoirists, historians, clergymen, statesmen, court recorders, poets, playwrights, politicians, gossips, Parliamentary clerks. Many of them are anonymous – including those who composed songs or wrote 'libels' (rhymes – usually scurrilous and satirical). Others are well known to history.

To have given them each a proper introduction in the course of my narrative would have overcrowded the story. Instead I list here the ones from whom I have drawn most.

George Abbot, Archbishop of Canterbury. A Puritan, inflexible in his detestation of Catholicism, Abbot was instrumental in bringing Buckingham to court, hoping to use him to influence King James into making war with Spain. For his character, see page 78.

John Aubrey. Aubrey was an archaeologist and architectural historian as well as being the author of *Brief Lives*. Born in 1626, only two years before Buckingham's death, he was able, thanks to his indefatigable pursuit of elderly contacts and recording of their reminiscences, to paint vivid pen portraits of a number of the luminaries of Buckingham's lifetime.

John Chamberlain. Chamberlain was a confirmed bachelor and popular guest who lived more in his friends' houses than his own. Endlessly curious about contemporary events and well connected, he kept up with all the latest news and passed it on in long letters, the majority of them to Sir Dudley Carleton. He died in the same year as Buckingham.

Roger Coke. Coke was born about the time of Buckingham's death but, as the grandson of Buckingham's great Parliamentary opponent Sir Edward Coke, he heard first-hand accounts of the Jacobean court and Parliament from his relatives and family connections. His *Detection of the Court and State of England* was published in 1696.

Sir Simonds D'Ewes. A devout Puritan, D'Ewes studied at the Middle Temple in the 1620s, keeping a diary in which he records his own doings alongside the news he picked up from conversations with fellow lawyers and from the pamphlets he read avidly. He became an MP and supported Parliament during the Civil Wars.

Sir John Eliot. Eliot first met Buckingham when they were both teenagers in France. He worked for him at the Admiralty, then entered Parliament in 1624. He repeatedly spoke out against his former patron, calling for Buckingham's impeachment. In 1629 he was imprisoned for the second time. In the Tower he wrote *Negotium posterorum*, his account of the 1625 Parliament, before dying there in 1632. For a fuller introduction, see page 462.

Albert de Fontenay. An envoy sent by Mary, Queen of Scots, from her English prison to Scotland in 1584 to treat with her son, King James, then aged eighteen.

Thomas Fuller. Clergyman and author. Only twenty years old when Buckingham died, Fuller records the testimony of people who knew him well. A royalist who kept his head down and survived the Civil Wars undisturbed, he is chiefly remembered for his compendium of biographical essays, *The Worthies of England*, posthumously published in 1662.

Godfrey Goodman, Bishop of Gloucester. Present at court through most of Buckingham's career, Goodman was at one time chaplain to Queen Anne, favoured by King James but much disliked by Puritans. His book *The Court of King James* was written in the 1650s, when he was

living in obscurity, his episcopal palace having been ransacked by
Parliamentary troops and his library destroyed. His purpose was to
refute Sir Anthony Weldon's account (see below), which Goodman
thought 'malicious-minded'.

Sir John Hacket. Royalist clergyman, chaplain to King James from 1623,
client and biographer of John Williams. Williams was an adviser to
King James who later became Archbishop of York, Lord Keeper of the
Great Seal from 1621 to 1625 and an opponent of Buckingham's war
policy.

James Howell. A clergyman's son who chose the footloose life of an
author and traveller. He wrote a novel and newsletters. He spoke a
number of languages and compiled dictionaries and grammars. Above
all, he was a prolific correspondent. Two years younger than
Buckingham, he was attached to the British embassy in Madrid when
Buckingham visited in 1623, and he was in Portsmouth when
Buckingham died there.

Edward Hyde, Earl of Clarendon. Hyde came to prominence after
Buckingham's death, but as Charles I's chief adviser from 1642 he had
ample opportunity to discuss him with the King. He went into exile in
1646, returning to England at the Restoration as Charles II's chief minister. He fell from power in 1667 and devoted his last years to revising his
History of the Rebellion, begun in the 1650s.

Sir John Oglander. MP, deputy-governor of Portsmouth, then governor of the Isle of Wight. Oglander was involved in preparations for
Buckingham's expedition to La Rochelle, and he was in Portsmouth
when Buckingham was killed. Ardently royalist, he was twice arrested
by Parliamentary troops during the Civil Wars. His memoir, commonplace book and diaries are vivid records of troubled times, combining a
wealth of practical detail with emotional openness. Some entries are
written in his own blood.

Francis Osborne. Buckingham's exact contemporary, Osborne was a
Parliamentarian and a republican. His hostile but illuminating account
of King James I's reign was published in 1658.

John Rous. Vicar of a Suffolk parish and a prolific correspondent, Rous kept a diary from 1625, in which he commented on public events as well as on crops and the weather and local gossip.

William Sanderson. A staunch royalist and secretary to Buckingham's friend and close associate Henry Rich, Earl of Holland. Like Goodman's, Sanderson's book written from exile in 1650 is framed as a riposte to Weldon's.

Count Leveneur de Tillières. French ambassador to England from 1621 to 1624. He considered the Jacobean court to be 'licentious … filthy and scandalous'.

Venetian State Papers. Throughout Buckingham's career, events at the English court were being observed by a sequence of Venetian ambassadors, whose reports constitute a detailed and dispassionate account of politics and personalities. They include Nicolò Molin, Antonio Foscarini, Girolamo Lando and Orazio Busino.

Sir Anthony Weldon. As Clerk to the Royal Kitchen, Weldon witnessed Buckingham's rise. He was subsequently dismissed, and his pamphlet *The Court and Character of King James* – satirical and salacious – was read by royalists as his revenge for his sacking. Modern historians argue it is more likely just disrespectfully truthful. He supported Parliament in the Civil Wars.

Sir Roger Wilbraham. Politician and lawyer and loyal monarchist. He was Solicitor General in Ireland in Queen Elizabeth's reign, and subsequently King James's Master of Requests. He kept a journal from 1593 to 1616.

Arthur Wilson. During the 1620s, the time of Buckingham's ascendancy, Wilson was secretary to the 3rd Earl of Essex (subsequently commander of the Parliamentary forces in the Civil Wars). He was a poet and playwright. His history, *The Life and Reign of King James*, published in 1653, describes many incidents to which he claims to have been 'eye and ear witness'.

Sir Henry Wotton. Diplomat, linguist, connoisseur, MP, treasured as a friend by distinguished contemporaries from John Donne to Isaak Walton. As ambassador in Venice and in The Hague over twenty years, he helped Buckingham assemble his art collection. Returning to England in 1624, he became Provost of Eton and wrote two biographical works about Buckingham. For more on him, see page 116.

For further information on these and all other sources, see the Notes and Select Bibliography at the back of this book.

A Note on Naming

GEORGE Villiers became the Earl of Buckingham in January 1617, later becoming Marquis and then Duke – always of Buckingham. I have occasionally found it convenient to refer to him as Buckingham when writing about a period before he held any of those titles.

Many of my characters were knights. I give them the 'Sir' on first appearance, but afterwards frequently leave it out.

Higher-ranking characters had multiple titles. To avoid confusion, I allow them only two names – their original surname on first appearance, and subsequently the highest title they attained. For instance, I introduce Robert Carr by that name and thereafter call him the Earl of Somerset, although for some of the period covered he was Viscount Rochester.

In some cases I ignore titles altogether. For instance I have called Francis Bacon by that name throughout, because it is the one by which he is best known to posterity.

I tend to refer to women by their given names alone – e.g. I call the Duchess of Buckingham Katherine or Kate. As a woman I regret this practice, but as an author I think that to write about two of my central characters as Buckingham and Buckingham would be awkward.

At the time I am writing about, Britain did not yet exist as a united state (dearly as King James I and VI wanted it to). The majority of the characters in this book were English. Of their kings, James was Scottish with a bit of French, while Charles was half Scottish-French, half Danish-German. I have used the words 'English' and 'British' carefully, but readers are warned that they do not exactly match reality.

INTRODUCTION

George Villiers, Duke of Buckingham:
drawing by Peter Paul Rubens, Paris 1625

HE was called a devil, a spotted monster, a comet that disrupted the natural order, scrambled social hierarchy and set the music of the spheres a-jangle. He was accused of being a traitor to his country, an enemy of the people and a regicide who poisoned the king who loved him.

To royalists, he was the vulgar upstart who dragged the monarchy into disrepute and weakened it fatally. To Puritans and republicans, he was the epitome of all the vices endemic at the degenerate court of the early Stuart kings. He was arrogant. He was greedy. His lust was insatiable.

Yet here are the words with which those who knew him well described him: modest, courteous, kind, obliging, affectionate, generous, gracious, loving and, again (this is the word that recurs most insistently), modest. By all reliable accounts, George Villiers, the Duke of Buckingham, was really very nice.

His beauty was extraordinary – even those who hated him, and by the time of his death they were legion, never denied it. He was called 'the handsomest-bodied man in Europe', and 'one of the handsomest men in the whole world'.

Three monarchs loved him. King James I of England (VI of Scotland) addressed him as 'Sweetheart' or as 'My sweet Child and Wife', shared his bed with him and told him that he would rather die than live without him. King Charles I worshipped him as a nervous adolescent worships an older and infinitely more glamorous brother. The Queen of France, Anne of Austria, told a confidante that if it were possible for an 'honest' wife to love anyone other than her husband, then Buckingham would be the man she chose. Many of her contemporaries believed that – honest or not – she had an affair with him.

*　*　*

This book is about Buckingham, but it is not about him alone. Buckingham was described by contemporaries as a meteor, a shooting star. In speaking of him, people turned to astronomy for their imagery because he seemed to them so grand, so brilliant. But he was not really a far-off heavenly body. His glamour was dazzling, but his life was shaped by the world he inhabited. His story forms the spine of my narrative, but – because no man is an island – it is also a book about a society; its pleasures and passions, its beliefs and its politics.

In early seventeenth-century England, punctilious good manners were juxtaposed with extreme violence. Letters were thickly laced with flattery, but a courtier might have his hand amputated for a breach of protocol.

It was a period of transition, in which the past and future jostled. Archaic political structures were challenged by world-altering novelties – the beginnings of print journalism, the increasing power of public opinion. The Middle Ages had yet to end. There were witches. Medicine was not so much a science as a symbolic code, as likely to kill as to cure. Meanwhile the Enlightenment had begun. Francis Bacon, Buckingham's mentor, was the great proponent of empirical scientific investigation.

Bacon is just one of the remarkable people who have a part in this story. John Tradescant designed Buckingham's parks and gardens. Ben Jonson and Inigo Jones collaborated on his party entertainments. Van Dyck and Rubens painted his portrait repeatedly. His political opponents included the great jurist Sir Edward Coke. William Laud, future archbishop and martyr, wrote his speeches.

Their world was both like ours and alien in surprising ways. The constitution and the laws under which British people still live owe much to the events of Buckingham's lifetime. The art and literature produced then still furnish modern minds, whether or not we consciously recognise it. We are Buckingham's successors, but there is much about his world that seems shocking now, and much that is entrancingly strange.

People wept more. Buckingham was often in tears, and we will see the chamber of the House of Commons full of strong men overcome with sobs. They spoke more fluently. It was a great age of drama and sermons and Parliamentary oratory. To read and write about England in the early seventeenth century is to be immersed in a flood of magnificent language. The language of court and Parliament – sonorous, grand

and lucid. The language of pamphleteers and libellers – sinewy and rude.

At the centre of my narrative is a web of love stories. Ageing king loves young man. Husband and wife love each other. Son loves father's male lover. Son loves mother. In these relationships we see love and family being redefined and gender roles subverted.

Buckingham was a man who lived a woman's life. There have been many royal mistresses. What makes Buckingham's career exceptional is that, because he was male, he was able to convert the influence of a favourite into the power of a chief minister. And because he was male, the way his physical beauty carried him to the highest place at court – something that would seem unremarkable in a woman's case – is rendered questionable.

This book is about big things – peace and war, Parliament and despotism. It is also about small things – babies, jewels, anemones. In it I interleave the big with the small, aiming to make a collage that conjures up a life in all its complexity.

Four years after Buckingham's death, the Puritan polemicist William Prynne published *Histriomastix*. The book is primarily an attack on the theatre, but Prynne's targets are many and various. In the preface he explains that he will be exposing the iniquity of the following: 'dancing, music, apparel, effeminacy, lascivious songs, laughter, adultery, obscene pictures, bonfires, New Year's gifts, grand Christmases, health-drinking, long hair, Lord's-days, dicing, with sundry pagan customs'.

I would add a few more headings – among them connoisseurship and the collecting of art, hunting, pacifism (which, to many people of the time, seemed interchangeable with effeminacy), same-sex love and landscape design – but, broadly speaking (I have nothing to say on dicing), Prynne's abominations correspond closely with the materials I have used to give substance to my picture of Buckingham and his world.

Buckingham's personal story is entangled with a public one. On the one hand, two kings struggling to assert their royal prerogative. On the other, lawyers and members of Parliament and preachers and polemicists doggedly striving to defend citizens' rights, in some cases sacrificing their own liberty to protect that of the people. In the middle,

Buckingham – identified as the 'grievance of grievances', the 'causing cause' of all the nation's discontents.

He was a favourite. We no longer use that word. But still, four centuries on, every president, every prime minister, has their chief of staff or their special advisers, their consultants and aides. Those people are not elected. They do not pass through the Civil Service selection process. They owe their power to the ruler's favour, and they are accountable to that person alone.

Their position is precarious. Francis Bacon warned Buckingham that often leaders, when the people begin to grumble, will sacrifice their favourites to placate the populace. When I began work on this book in 2020, large decisions about the way Britain was ruled were being made by one of the prime minister's staff, Dominic Cummings. He seemed to come, as Buckingham did, from nowhere. For a while he had power. But when the electorate became angry with the government, he was cast aside. He became a scapegoat, as Buckingham did four hundred years before.

In Buckingham's lifetime it was very hard to criticise a monarch. To do so, even in one's silent thoughts, might be treason, and treason was a capital offence. Twenty-one years after Buckingham died, the British people would kill their king, but first they took out their hidden unhappiness on his favourite, reimagining him as a monster and so opening the way to his death.

I

PEACE

St George's Day

23 April 1615. St George's Day, feast of England's patron saint. The Knights of the Garter process through the courtyards of Whitehall Palace, led by King James I. It is a solemn spectacle. An observer describes the King, princes, peers and 'worthies' marching together, 'amazing the beholders': they constitute 'one personal majesty, in one fellowship of honour'. It is also a social occasion: Lady Anne Clifford writes in her diary, 'There was such an infinite company ... as I think I shall never see the like.' The Garter Knights ride away to Windsor, for a lengthy service in the Chapel of St George, followed by a banquet.

The King loathes this kind of ceremonial, but he submits to it. At last, he withdraws to the Queen's private apartments, where a curious scene is acted out.

Queen Anne and the fourteen-year-old heir to the throne, Prince Charles, receive the King. Nearby, in adjoining rooms, there are, as always, a number of people in attendance. One of them is the Earl of Somerset, Robert Carr, the handsome blond Scotsman who came to England with King James when the latter inherited the English throne in 1603 and who has risen very high. The King has recently written to Somerset, assuring him 'my love hath been infinite towards you', but also telling him that their relationship has left him with 'a deeply wounded heart' and warning him that 'I have borne it as long as I possibly can'. Another of the bystanders is George Villiers.

Queen Anne has planned a little performance. At her signal, Villiers is called in to join the royal party. Prince Charles wears a sword. The Queen asks him to draw it and give it to her. Holding it, she kneels before the King and begs him 'to knight this noble gentleman, whose name [is] George, for the honour of St George whose feast he now kept'.

The King playfully pretends to be frightened when he sees the Queen coming at him with a naked sword. (Or is he only playing? He is notoriously fearful of assassins.) A courtier tells us he then granted the Queen's request and 'did it very joyfully; and it might very well be that it was his own contriving'. Eager as some powerful people were to see Villiers brought into the King's household, 'they were not so forward to promote [it] as the King to long to have it effected'. Taking the sword, signalling Villiers to kneel before him, James taps blade to shoulder, dubbing the young man knight.

Those who had the King's ear, including his wife, would often ask for honours for their protégés. The handing-out of titles and lucrative posts helped build the web of obligation that kept the monarchy secure. In the first year of his reign King James had created eighty-three earls, all of those titles being granted either to those who could pay well for them (the Crown was chronically short of money), or to those who had been recommended by the already-powerful who, in bringing on their friends, relations and clients, created smaller webs for themselves.

This knighting, though, had especial significance. It marked the public beginning of a career which amazed all contemporaries – prodigious for the rapidity of George Villiers's rise, the brilliance of his success, the catastrophe of his fall.

In 1615 King James I of England, VI of Scotland, was forty-eight years old. He was tough, and on horseback he was fearless and indefatigable. When out hunting (and it was calculated that he passed half his waking hours in the chase), he could spend all day in the saddle. But when standing on his own two feet, he was at a disadvantage. A congenital weakness of the legs meant that as he walked he staggered. 'His carriage is ungainly, his steps erratic and vagabond, even in his chamber,' wrote a French visitor to his court. Perhaps it was to disguise his defective limbs that he favoured wide breeches, 'in great pleats and full stuffed'. He would lean on favoured courtiers' shoulders, sometimes out of affection for them, but oftener because he needed support.

He was not, and had never been, a handsome man. He greatly disliked sitting for portraits, but enough of them were made to let us know that his nose was bulbous, his mouth small and pursed, and that by the time he came to England his cheeks were already sunken and his jowls sagged. Decades of hard drinking and hunting in all weathers had left his face mottled red. He wore a beard. Its style varied over the years, but it was always wispy ('scattering on his chin, and very thin,' said contemporary historian Arthur Wilson). There was something wrong with his mouth. Sir Anthony Weldon thought his tongue was too big. He spoke oddly, and when he drank he did so 'very uncomely, as if eating his drink, which came out into the cup on each side of his mouth'. Always on the watch for assassins to dodge or fools to ridicule, and celebrated for the pleasure he took in 'dissimulation', he had a shifty look. His clever eyes look warily out of portrait after portrait, lower lids drooping (Plate 2).

George Villiers, the twenty-two-year-old kneeling before him, was beautiful. He had the face, the King thought, of a youthful saint, or an angel. The Bishop of Gloucester, Godfrey Goodman, praised his 'lovely complexion'. Diarist Simonds D'Ewes admired his 'delicacy and handsome features', and his 'effeminate and curious hands and face'. His legs were celebrated for their length and fine shape. The earliest portrait we have of him, by William Larkin, dates from a year after this momentous St George's Day (Plate 1). It shows him standing in a dancer's pose, so that those legs become the focal point of the composition. Improbably slender and elongated, they are set off by the brevity of his puffed and slashed white satin breeches, by high-heeled white slippers and wrinkle-free white silk hose.

This exquisite creature had been trailed before King James as a piece of sexual bait. The King was married – though by this time he and Queen Anne lived largely separate lives – and had two living children, but everyone knew that he loved men. Physically imperfect, he was enchanted by male beauty, by masculine grace and fine clothes and courtly sophistication.

For seven years he had loved Somerset, but their relationship had become personally rancorous and politically untenable. Somerset had married Frances Howard, formerly Countess of Essex. Frances's father and uncles made up a powerful cabal at court. The Howards were friendly to Spain, and in favour of the toleration of Catholic worship. Protestant magnates, the Archbishop of Canterbury among them, saw the rift between the King and Somerset as an opportunity. They would be better able, they thought, to promote the cause of the 'true religion' (which meant Protestantism), bring forward their own friends and supporters and stir up an Anglo-Spanish war, if they could arrange for the King to fall in love with a new young man, a protégé of their own. There was nothing alien or distasteful to them about this idea. One of their number, the Earl of Montgomery, had himself once been a favourite of King James's. They looked about for a beautiful youth who could take Somerset's place in James's heart.

The King had first seen George Villiers the previous August. He was at Apethorpe – the palatial Northamptonshire home of Sir Anthony Mildmay, and one of the places he best liked to stay during his annual summer-time progress through his kingdom. A splendid hunt was laid on for him. Villiers was there. He had spent three years in France learning the art of the *manège*. He looked very well on a horse. It was noticed that the King had noticed him

We don't know who brought George Villiers to Apethorpe. Perhaps he joined the hunt as any local gentleman might have done. He was living with his mother only twenty-five miles away. Or perhaps it was his friend, another young man who had once been candidate for the role of King's favourite, Sir James Graham. Certainly Graham was soon acting as Villiers's agent and manager, soliciting money from those who might hope one day to profit from the benefits a new royal favourite could pass their way. Within a month Villiers was at court, with smart new clothes, serving as one of the royal cup-bearers. A courtier noted in a letter home that he 'begins to be in favour with His Majesty'.

There was a supper party that winter at the mediaeval palace of Baynard's Castle, the Earl of Pembroke's London home, on the river near old St Paul's. The historian William Sanderson was among those invited. As he made his way there along Fleet Street with one of his fellow guests, the other ordered his footman to throw dirt at a picture of Somerset displayed on a painter's stall. Sanderson asked why he did so. 'He told me that this meeting would discover.' Sure enough, listening to the conversation that night between a number of noble persons, Sanderson 'was acquainted with the design to bring in Villiers'. As Archbishop Abbot, who was among the guests, explained, they would use Villiers 'to drive out Somerset, as one nail drives out another'.

*   *   *

In March 1615 King James visited Cambridge. He was shown around one of the college libraries, where precious illuminated manuscripts were kept chained to their stands to deter thieves. King James made a joke. The books looked like prisoners, he said, but he loved reading so much that he would be happy to be imprisoned here with them. (James's jokes were often a little ponderous, but he was the King, so naturally everybody laughed.)

Later that day James attended a play staged by the students in his honour. He enjoyed the theatre, but this time he found it hard to concentrate. George Villiers was in the audience. Roger Coke reports that King James couldn't take his eyes off him, becoming 'confounded between his admiration of Villiers and the pleasure of the play'.

And then in April it was St George's Day, and the Queen made her surprising move.

Villiers was nobody special. He was the sixth child and fourth son of a Leicestershire gentleman. His father, also called George, had enough land to live decently on, but no more than that. He served as sheriff and was knighted by Queen Elizabeth for his services. Sir Henry Wotton would call the country-bumpkin Villierses a family 'without obscurity' but without 'any great lustre'. Villiers's mother, Mary, though, aimed higher.

She knew what her son was capable of. According to Wotton, she decided early that young George was no scholar. This need not be a handicap to greatness. Prince Henry, King James's heir, when taxed on his poor performance as a student, was to reply crossly, 'I know what becomes a Prince. It is not necessary for me to be a professor, but a soldier and a man of the world.' What was true for a prince was also true for a courtier. In later life, despite having spent three years in France in his teens, Buckingham was to claim he spoke French with difficulty and could not write it at all. (This may have been a lie: there were advantages to playing dumb when negotiating with foreign agents.) He had little Latin, the lingua franca of diplomats from all over Europe. His letters are engagingly artless, their syntax harum-scarum. When, in Spain with Prince Charles in 1623, he was obliged to be his own clerk, he did so with many apologies for his handwriting, and kept his letters brief.

He was to become a connoisseur of the visual arts, amassing a collection which rivalled that of his second king, Charles I, but there is no record of his having any literary enthusiasms. As one of the premier performers in court masques, and a commissioner of his own, he knew Ben Jonson. John Donne was his client. But he is not known to have commented on either's work. Thomas Middleton wrote a play about him (*A Game at Chess*): we do not know what he thought about it. But book-learning, as his mother knew, is not everything. George Villiers had other gifts.

His face was broad, his mouth and eyebrows wide and straight, his jaw cleanly cut. His skin was smooth and pale as ivory. He had dark wavy hair with auburn lights in it: when he grew a beard it came out tawny. And there were those legs. It is always hard, viewing portraits from the distant past, to see what distinguished a celebrated beauty from all the other good-enough-looking people around, but whatever beauty is – a combination of finely proportioned physical features, sex appeal, charisma and grace – Villiers had it.

His mother played to his strengths. She arranged for him to learn a little music: to be able to play and sing are attractive accomplishments. She taught him good manners. She 'chose', writes Wotton, 'to endue him with ornaments of youth, as dancing, fencing, and the like … to which lessons he had such a dextrous proclivity as his teachers were fain to restrain his forwardness'. His dancing, especially, was outstanding. Most importantly, she saw to it that he learnt horsemanship. She sent him to France, to the famous school in Angers, where he was trained to manage the celebrated breed of the 'Great Horse'.

An ambitious young man, hoping to rise at court, had first to acquire the desirable finish conferred by a smattering of cosmopolitan culture. When George Villiers came home from France, writes Thomas Fuller, he was 'one of the completest courtiers in Christendom, his body and behaviour mutually gracing one another'.

There is nothing unusual about a mother with a beautiful child grooming that child in readiness for a splendid match, teaching the child to make itself agreeable in the hopes of attracting a mate strong, rich and powerful enough to be able to guarantee the child's future security (and, incidentally, the mother's own). Such has been the practice of mothers of daughters throughout most of human history. For the mother of a son to do so seems stranger. For a young woman to be presented at court in the hope of catching the eye of a powerful protector or – better – a husband, would have been, in the early modern period, uncontroversial. For George Villiers's mother to have agreed that her boy should be paraded before a homosexual king, with a view to his becoming that king's erotic toy and intimate companion, was also ordinary enough to their contemporaries, but it is likely to make modern readers feel morally queasy.

The King's dinner was not only a meal. Served in the Presence Chamber, it was a public event – often the only moment in the day when a courtier could hope to lay eyes upon the monarch. It was also a ritual freighted with symbolic significance. Cooks, breadmasters, carvers and cup-bearers each played an appointed part in an elaborate performance. The service went far, far beyond the delivery of a plate of food to a hungry king.

Cookery was one of the plastic arts. Fowl was stuffed within fowl and decorated with candied fruit. Meat, ice, custard, sugar and pastry were the materials for sculptural artefacts. On occasion, a whole tableful of dishes would be laid out for the admiration of the company, before it was whisked away uneaten and another equally lavish feast brought out in its stead.

King James ate alone, in that no one else ate with him, but in company. He liked to talk with those who waited on him. The royal cup-bearers – Buckingham among them – served him at table, taking it in turns, one month on, one month off. They were low down in the ranks of courtly hierarchy, but they had more time with the King, when he was in easy mealtime mood, than many of the grandees who ran the country. 'He is very familiar with his domestics and gentlemen of the Chamber,' writes Sir Henry Wotton. 'With the magnates he is more serious and severe.' Standing at the King's elbow, ready to refill his glass, the cup-bearers had plentiful opportunities to enjoy his conversation and to impress him with their own. 'The dinner over,' wrote Wotton, King James's 'custom is to remain for a time, listening to jests and pleasantries, in which he takes great pleasure'.

Few people find it easy to engage in conversation with a head of state. James's manner was particularly disconcerting. King since babyhood, he had never been taught how to ingratiate himself, or had never seen the need to do so. 'His manners are aggressive and very uncivil,' wrote the French ambassador to Scotland when James was eighteen, and in middle age he was testy, given to making baffling interjections and disconcerting jokes. 'He had as many ready witty jests as any man living,' writes Weldon, 'at which he would not smile himself, but deliver them in a grave and serious manner.' The effect of his deadpan delivery was intimidating. How was a person, uncertain whether the King expected a laugh, to react?

He was suspicious. One of his courtiers reported that if a stranger came into his presence he would stare at the newcomer so fixedly that 'many for shame have left the room, as being out of countenance'. He couldn't be bothered with small talk: 'those ordinary ceremonies, which his variable and quick wit cannot attend'. He had a worrying disdain for decorum. He would curse and swear, taking the name of God in vain in a way that was shocking to seventeenth-century hearers. He also liked to talk dirty. One of his first actions, on coming to the English throne, was to call a great conference of divines to discuss the future of the Church of England, hoping to reconcile Puritans with high Anglicans. In that serious gathering of the godly, he let drop several asides so bawdy as to have caused choked silences. 'King James', wrote Sir Robert Moray, 'loved best of any discourse to talk of dirt and turds.'

Villiers dealt gracefully with all these off-putting regal characteristics. His letters show him playful and good-humoured, unafraid of the great people he dealt with, but polite and considerate. His often-praised skill in the art of pleasing included an ability to converse agreeably even with a gruff-and-glum king whose idea of entertaining mealtime conversation was a theological debate conducted in Latin. Buckingham does not, himself, appear to have taken much pleasure in intellectual exercise. The King was indulgent, being, as Clarendon put it, 'very flowing in affection towards persons so adorned'. Realising that his new cup-bearer had little to say on scholarly matters, James coaxed him instead to talk of what he had seen at the French court. Villiers 'could pertinently enlarge upon that subject, to the King's great delight'.

Others noticed that delight. Later Buckingham was to feel himself beleaguered by the resentment of the less lucky. Already, as he waited at the King's table, the spirit of Envy was lurking ready to trip him up.

There was a falling-out between Villiers and another cup-bearer. Villiers – whether purposely or out of ignorance – had taken the best position at the King's table when it was not his turn. The other cup-bearer had him removed, 'which was not done with over much kindness,' reports a fellow courtier, 'for indeed the other was Somerset's creature'. A little later this other cup-bearer spilt some gravy on Villiers's clothes. Clothes were expensive. Buckingham's sponsors had seen to it that he had a presentable suit, but it may have been his only one. He boxed the other's ears. The penalty for such unseemly violence in the King's presence was the cutting-off of the hand that had done the deed. Somerset, as Lord Chamberlain, master of the royal household, was responsible for ordering the amputation.

The King intervened, pardoning Villiers. In a direct confrontation between the soon-to-be-superseded favourite and the coming man, the King had made it clear that his loyalty was with the dazzling newcomer.

By November 1614 there were rumours that Villiers would soon be a Gentleman of the Bedchamber, one of the King's inner circle. The Queen herself had requested the place for him. Somerset kept him out by seeing to it that a nephew of his own was given the place instead. It did him no good. According to Archbishop Abbot, the King 'more and more loathed Somerset, and did not much conceal that his affection increased towards the other'.

Abbot's plan was to go by way of the Queen. It was the King's plan too, for as Abbot explains, King James had 'a fashion, that he would never admit anyone to nearness about himself but such a one as the Queen should commend unto him.' The point being 'that if the Queen afterwards, being ill-treated, should complain of this dear one, he might make his answer "It is 'long of yourself"'.' Canny and devious, King James, as Abbot notes, 'took delight in things of this nature'.

Queen Anne, according to the French ambassador, was 'an able woman' who had resigned herself to the knowledge that 'her husband cannot exist without a minion'. She baulked, though, at the Archbishop's plan. Abbot and his allies might see Villiers as a harmless pretty boy (Abbot called him 'a modest courteous youth … of a good nature') whom they could manipulate as they pleased. Queen Anne saw further. 'I do know your Master better than you all,' she told Abbot. 'If this young man be once brought in, the first person he will plague must be you that labour for him; yea, I shall have my part also. The King will teach him to despise and hardly intreat us all, that he may seem to be beholden to none but himself.' King James might choose to pretend to be swayed by his wife, but she understood he was using her as a puppet in a drama that, for her, could have no happy ending.

She gave in. And so, upon St George's Day, King James knighted his new favourite, granted him an income of £1,000 a year (he had been living on one twentieth of that) and made him a Gentleman of the Bedchamber, one of the group of intimate associates of the King who served him, and had his ear, night and day.

The charade enacted between King and Queen was a piece of theatre, and it had, accordingly, spectators. Somerset, standing in the next room, sent in a message to the King asking that Villiers should be only a Groom of the Bedchamber (a less prestigious role than Gentleman). Abbot, also listening by an open doorway, sent another message in to the Queen, urging her not to give way. Gentleman of the Bedchamber it was. The new-dubbed Sir George Villiers, according to Abbot, then 'went in with the King'.

A man in late middle age, physically unattractive but supremely powerful, resolves to take a 'dear one' for himself. His wife and his adolescent son are coerced into performing a sham ceremony which obliges them to accept complicity in the inception of this relationship. The new beloved is a man in his early twenties. The head of the Church of England, whose duty it is to safeguard the institution of marriage, to celebrate chastity and abominate sodomy, is busying himself assiduously, for the good of Holy Church, in the part of Pandar.

There are two ways of thinking about this. One is a shrug. The past is a foreign country: they do things differently there. The other is a question. If the beautiful young person had been female, would this scene have seemed more, or less, disturbing?

King James: Fear

'KING James I of England was the most cowardly man that ever I knew,' wrote Sir John Oglander, diarist of the Stuart establishment. 'How he tormented himself with fear of some sudden mischief may be proved by his great quilted doublets, pistol-proof … also his strange eyeing of strangers with a continual fearful observation.'

Poor James had good cause for fear. His early life in Scotland had been terrifying. He was the first and only child of Mary, Queen of Scots. While he was still in her womb, seven men with drawn swords burst into the small chamber where she was eating supper with her secretary and friend David Rizzio. Rizzio tried to shield himself by cowering behind the Queen, his arms around her pregnant belly. One of the intruders held a pistol to her chest as Rizzio was dragged into the next room and stabbed fifty-seven times.

Eight months after James was born, his father, Lord Darnley (who had been one of Rizzio's murderers), also died violently. The house in which he was staying was blown up. His corpse was found in the garden. The explosion was designed to seem accidental, but marks on Darnley's neck suggested he had been strangled, and his body dumped outside, before the gunpowder was lit. It was generally believed that the Earl of Bothwell had planned the murder, along with Queen Mary.

Three months later Bothwell and Mary were married, amidst rumours that he had raped her first and that she had wept bitterly on her wedding day. A group of noblemen rose up against the couple and defeated them in battle. Bothwell fled to Norway, where he was captured and then imprisoned in Denmark for the remainder of his life. Mary's baby son was taken away from her and sent to live at Stirling Castle under the guardianship of the Earl of Mar.

Perched on an isolated crag, with precipices falling away beneath it on three sides, the castle was an almost impregnable stronghold. Mar was ordered to dismiss all unnecessary attendants. James was to grow up in a tightly disciplined household, organised not for his pleasure but for his confinement. Queen Mary visited him once, the last time he ever saw her. After that she was forced to sign away her throne before escaping to England and twenty years of imprisonment. At the age of thirteen months, James was crowned King James VI of Scotland.

Throughout the rest of his childhood he was a trophy to be fought over by noblemen convinced that if they could get custody of his person, they could rule in his name. He had one regent after another. One after another they were killed. His uncle was murdered by an assassin. His grandfather was shot dead before his eyes, defending him from a group of armed men who had stormed into the castle intent on abducting him. His next regent was poisoned. The fourth quarrelled with his guardian, and repeatedly tried to break into Stirling Castle and carry him off. The child-King was spared none of this mayhem. On one occasion, when yet another band of would-be kidnappers had got into the castle by a ruse and were being fought off, with several men dead, little James, hearing the noise, ran out of his room, distraught with terror and tearing at his hair.

It would have been a traumatic start in life for the most robust child, but James was puny. The physician Théodore de Mayerne, who would attend him later, wrote that 'the King to the sixth year of his age was not able to walk, but was carried about, so weak was he from the bad milk of his drunken nurse'.

Even in the schoolroom he was abused and terrorised. When he was four, the celebrated scholar George Buchanan became one of his tutors. During the years he was serving as the child-King's mentor, Buchanan, an irascible anti-monarchist, wrote books in which he describes his pupil's mother as a 'vain, shallow, proud, ignorant, devious, conniving papist whore', and James himself as 'the true bird of the bloody nest from which he sprang'. Buchanan took pride in demonstrating his independence of mind by beating the lame young King frequently and severely. The Countess of Mar (whom James called Lady Minny, 'minny' being the seventeenth-century Scottish equivalent of 'mummy') remonstrated with him. Buchanan told her, 'Madam I have whipped his arse, you may kiss it if you please.' Four decades later James would say

of a gentleman at his court that 'he ever trembled at his approach, it minded him so' of 'his pedagogue' Buchanan.

Growing up didn't make James any safer. It only brought more oppressive responsibility. When he was not quite fifteen, the Earl of Morton was condemned to death for complicity in the murder of Darnley. James, who had known Morton as his regent, a figure of fatherly authority whom he should respect as well as fear, was required to authorise the execution. On the night Morton died, the King was seen to be in a state of extreme agitation. When Morton's last letters were brought to him, he declined to read them, but 'ranged up and down the floor of his chamber, clanking with his finger and his thumb'.

In Scotland, church and monarchy were at odds. The Presbyterian Kirk, whose founding father had been John Knox, taught a stern, pure

form of Calvinism. A king was not, as James believed, God's representative on earth. His authority was subordinate to that of the ministers of
the Kirk, subordinate even to the voice of individual conscience. Later,
in England, when presiding over a meeting of Anglican divines, James
was to shock those present by the fury with which he reacted to the use
of the word 'presbyter'. From the very beginning of his life he had been
aware that Presbyterians were his opponents.

A few months after Morton's execution, when he was still fifteen,
James was riding back from a hunting expedition when he was met on
the road by the Earl of Gowrie, with a thousand armed followers.
Gowrie was among the most prominent of the Presbyterian noblemen.
He 'invited' the young king to spend the night at his nearby Ruthven
Castle. (This incident would become known as the 'Ruthven Raid'.)
James, understanding that this was an invitation he couldn't refuse,
went along. The gentlemen of his guard were violently restrained from
following him. When he made to leave the following morning, he was
prevented from doing so. In tears, he begged to be allowed to go to
Edinburgh to rejoin his gentlemen there. It was forbidden.

For the following ten months he was effectively Gowrie's prisoner.
Even when he escaped he was still not free. A French emissary to
Scotland, Albert de Fontenay, sent home a perceptive description of the
young king. De Fontenay was full of praise for James's learning and
intelligence, but noticed that he did not 'dare to contradict the great
lords', having been 'nourished in fear'.

When James was twenty his mother was beheaded in Fotheringay
Castle. James was powerless to save her, or even to lodge any kind of
protest. When he was twenty-one he told de Fontenay that he had his
beard shaved with burning coals, 'fearing lest the barber should cut his
throat'. When he was twenty-five, recently married and staying at the
Palace of Holyrood with his new wife, the Earl of Bothwell (nephew of
the Bothwell Queen Mary had married) broke in, along with a band of
fifty armed followers, with the intention of carrying off the King. They
released some prisoners, set fire to the door of James's chamber and
tried to break through the young Queen's door with hammers. They
were chased off by townsfolk, but one of James's grooms was killed.

Six months later Bothwell, this time accompanied by three hundred
men, attacked the King and Queen in Falkland Palace, where James

loved to hunt deer in the surrounding forests and wild boar in the park. Bothwell's men broke down the gates with a battering ram. James shut himself into a tower, where he remained besieged until morning.

The following year, at Holyrood again, James heard a noise in the room next to his bedchamber. Half-dressed, he went out to investigate and found Bothwell kneeling, with a drawn sword laid on the floor beside him. James shouted for help, and tried to escape into his wife's room. Courtiers came to the rescue. Bothwell was banished from court.

It went on. It got worse. When he was thirty-four James was out hunting at Falkland again when he was approached by the Earl of Gowrie (son of the leader of the Ruthven Raid, who had been executed in 1584) and his brother Alexander Ruthven. According to James's version of the story, they offered to show him a pot of gold, which sounds suspiciously like a fairy story. Others suggested, then and later, that eighteen-year-old Alexander offered him sex. Whatever the inducement, James allowed himself to be tempted, and followed them to an isolated house. There, James claimed, the brothers led him upstairs to a small room. As they entered, Ruthven locked the door behind them. Alexander and another man tried to stab James to death with their daggers. Struggling against them, he managed to open a window and shout 'Treason'. His followers ran in to save him, killing Ruthven and Gowrie. The story – as James himself told it – is full of oddities and lacunae, but for the rest of his life, on the anniversary of the 'Gowrie Plot', James would order sermons read in thanksgiving for the saving of his life.

Two years later the English diplomat Sir Henry Wotton visited him in Scotland bearing warnings from the Grand Duke of Tuscany. The Grand Duke had recently exposed a conspiracy which included a plot against James's life. Wotton noticed that King James had 'a large number of gentlemen constantly about him, vigilant and alert', and that it was therefore 'very difficult for a foreigner to pass unnoticed, because immediately a new face arrives, they ask ... who he is, and what is his business'. By this time James's habit of wearing 'pistol-proof' quilted doublets was firmly established.

In 1603 Queen Elizabeth of England died. James, by this time thirty-six years old, inherited her throne. Leaving behind the competing Scottish warlords who had made his early life so turbulent, he came south with profound relief. Addressing his new subjects, he gave thanks to God – in words which convey the state of anxiety in which he lived for so long – for 'bringing him into this promised land' where he was treated with respect, 'not as before, elsewhere, a King without state, without honour, without order; where beardless boys would brave him to his face'.

In England, though, James was still not safe. In 1605 he narrowly escaped being blown up, along with almost the entire English ruling class, by the perpetrators of the Gunpowder Plot. Speaking in Parliament afterwards, he confessed that all his life he had felt beset by 'daily tempests of innumerable dangers'.

In 1610, four years before James met George Villiers, King Henri IV of France was stabbed to death in a Parisian street by the religious extremist François Ravaillac, making him the second French king in succession to die by an assassin's knife. On being given the news, the confirmation that his worst fears were well founded, King James of England was seen to turn as white as his ruff.

King James: Love

FATHERLESS from infancy, abandoned (however unwillingly) by his mother, intimidated and abused by his teacher, witness to and victim of repeated violent attacks, James grew up emotionally ravenous. He longed to be loved. He longed to be permitted to love.

In 1579, when he was thirteen, his cousin Esmé Stuart, Seigneur d'Aubigny, arrived in Scotland. Thirty-seven years old, described by a contemporary as 'a man of comely proportions and civil behaviour', d'Aubigny had been living in France at the court of King Henri III. To

the wary Scots noblemen and the elders of the Presbyterian Kirk it seemed likely he was an agent of the Pope and of international popery, or of the King of France. To James he seemed wonderful.

'No sooner did the young King see him,' wrote a contemporary, than, entranced by his 'ornaments of body and mind', he 'took him up and embraced him in a most amorous manner'. Francis Walsingham's agent in Scotland reported that James 'can hardly suffer him out of his presence', and that he was 'in such love with [d'Aubigny] as in the open sight of the people, oftentimes he will clasp him about his neck with his arms and kiss him'.

D'Aubigny was a married man with four children. It is unlikely he loved James as much as James loved him, but he was kind. He called James *'mon petit maistre'*. He brought with him a whiff of French sophistication, of the culture of the great European city where the King's mother had grown up. James was an excellent linguist. They spoke French together. They went hunting, which may have been the beginning of James's passion for the sport. A Presbyterian minister preached in Edinburgh's Great Kirk against the way the King's cousin 'laboured to corrupt him', and against his introducing into Scotland 'prodigality and vanity in apparel, superfluity in banqueting and delicate cheer, deflowering of dames and virgins, and other fruits of the French court'. Deflowering of dames and virgins would never interest James much but, starved as he had been in Stirling Castle of 'delicate cheer', the pleasures to which d'Aubigny was introducing him must have been intoxicating.

James may have enjoyed banqueting. He certainly appreciated 'vanity in apparel' in others, although he himself was often rather grubbily dressed. But most of his new-found pleasures were bookish and studious. James was a poet. Not a very good one, but what he lacked in talent he made up for in enthusiasm. Under d'Aubigny's influence he assembled a poetry-writing circle named the 'Castalian band'. He would set tasks for his fellow poets – translating verses by Petrarch or by the French poet Guillaume de Salluste du Bartas, to whom he wrote admiring letters. They composed sonnets. They debated poetic theory. It was all very far from the stern minister's visions of orgiastic debauchery.

*   *   *

By the following spring d'Aubigny was the Earl of Lennox. He was also Lord Chamberlain and First Gentleman of the Bedchamber – neither posts that had previously existed in Scotland. As Chamberlain he was creating a royal court, like the one he had known in France, and putting himself at the head of it. From being the quasi-orphaned ward in his guardian's household, a superior kind of prisoner, James now had a domestic establishment of his own, and Lennox was designing it for his pleasure. Controlling the King's household, he was also in control of the King.

The Scottish noblemen watched Lennox's rise with alarm and profound disapproval. So did the ministers of the Kirk. They seemed to be losing control of the King, and with him of the country. James raised Lennox yet higher, making him Scotland's only duke and therefore the second person in the kingdom.

It was to separate James from his over-mighty cousin that Gowrie and his Presbyterian associates seized the King. While he was Gowrie's captive, James was forced to issue a proclamation against Lennox, who was accused of holding him 'in a misty night of captivity and black darkness of shameful servitude'. Under extreme duress, James signed it in tears. One of his captors, unmoved, remarked that it was 'better that bairns should weep than bearded men'.

Intimidated and bullied, fearful of his church, and of Queen Elizabeth I of England, who was demanding Lennox be exposed as the French agent she believed him to be, James agreed to banish his beloved from Scotland. Lennox left, and died – apparently of natural causes – soon after. He had asked that his heart should be embalmed and sent to James, who wrote a poem in which the poet laments the hunting down of a beautiful phoenix by envious predatory birds. In a startlingly sexual image, the exotic bird, who is female, tries to shelter between the poet's legs while the attackers peck cruelly at them both. Still only sixteen, the King had lost his first love.

Other favourites followed. There was Alexander Lindsay, described by a contemporary as the King's 'minion and conceit' and 'his nightly bed-fellow'. There was the Earl of Huntly, only four years older than James. Huntly was, according to Lord Burghley's agent at the Scottish court, 'shallow-witted', but he had 'shrewd counsellors' who hoped to manipulate the King by means of him, and for a while he 'lodged in the

King's chamber and had place in the King's favour above all others'. This relationship ended painfully, with Huntly rebelling and taking up arms against the King. King James was 'in a great brangle, for he had great love to Huntly'. James had him arrested, but then invited him to dine and, according to the English observer, 'yea he kissed him to the amazement of many'. A few days later Huntly was sleeping in the King's chamber again. James, whispered his courtiers, must have been bewitched to be so tormented by this 'strange, extraordinary affection'.

'It is thought', wrote an English spy to Walsingham that year, 'this King is too much carried by young men that lie in his chamber and are his minions.' But be that as it may, a king must take a wife. James knew, as every Renaissance prince did, that his own marriageability was a card to be played carefully, for maximum advantage, financial (princesses brought large dowries) and strategic. When he was twenty-three he wrote an open letter to the Scottish people, in which he excused himself for having delayed his marriage so long (twenty-three was old for a royal bridegroom). He was aware, he said that, 'one man was as no man, and the want of hope of succession bred disdain.' Now, though, he was ready to do the right thing.

His bride would have to be Protestant. The sister of the King of Navarre was considered and rejected (too old, at thirty-one, to be sure of producing an heir). The King sought 'counsel of God by earnest prayer'. After fifteen days of consultation with the Almighty, he announced that God had guided him to marry Anna, the younger of the two eligible sisters of the King of Denmark who were the next most suitable contenders for his hand. Negotiations went well. In August 1589, when she was fourteen, Anna (to be known in her new countries as Anne of Denmark) married James by proxy at her father's court, and then set out to meet her husband.

James was solicitous of her comfort. He gave orders that shipbuilding should cease in Leith when her ship arrived there, so as not to 'unquiet her'. Turkish carpets and tapestries were to be laid wherever she walked, and there was to be no shooting allowed after she had gone to bed. Poor James knew all too well how distressing the sound of gunfire could be to a nervous teenager. He was doing his best to play the role of husband-to-be not only correctly, but with kindness.

Anna travelled to Norway and set sail for Scotland. On 12 September one of the ships accompanying her came into Leith, reporting that a great storm had scattered the fleet and 'it was feared the Queen was in danger upon the seas'. For over two weeks James stayed in a house overlooking the Firth of Forth, watching by the window for her. He ordered a general fast, in hope that God would be pleased and spare his bride. He sent another ship to Norway, carrying a letter ending with an assurance that he was praying with all his heart for her 'safe, swift and happy arrival', so 'that you can make proof of the entire affection of him who has vowed to you alone all his love'. He wrote sonnets reproaching 'cruel Cupid' for the 'ruthless rage' that had caused him such pain and sorrow. The English ambassador wrote drily that the King was playing with enthusiasm the role of 'a true lover' who 'thinketh every day a year till he see his joy and love approach'.

On 4 October James's emissary arrived in Norway, and heard that Anna's fleet had met with a sequence of disasters that had left vessels damaged and many men dead. It had therefore been decided to postpone her voyage until spring. The ship carrying the news back to Scotland took only three days. James decided, as he himself related, 'upon the instant, yea the very moment ... to make possible on my part that which was impossible on hers'. He appointed councillors to govern in his absence and set out for Norway, arriving safely a few days later.

The weather had turned wintry. The journey overland to Oslo, where Anna awaited him, took a further three weeks. James made his entrance at court in a red velvet coat stitched all over with golden stars and a black velvet cloak lined with sable. He strode straight up to Anna, not even pausing, as would have been usual, to take off his boots, and tried to kiss her, 'which she refused,' wrote one observer, 'it not being the form of the country'. Apologies, murmured explanations. All was soon smoothed over, and then came 'familiarity and kisses ... a joyful meeting'.

The couple travelled on to Elsinore. James stayed in Denmark until the following April, drinking, hunting, visiting scholars and accustoming himself to his relationship with Anna, whom he referred to as his 'new rib'.

Whether his passion, so ardent before he had laid eyes on his wife, matured into true love is debatable, but they got on well enough. Over the next thirteen years they conceived ten children (three miscarried, four died in infancy).

Afterwards they were together less and less, Queen Anne living at Oatlands Palace or in Greenwich, while for James, once he had moved south to England, there were other companions – James Hay, Philip Herbert – handsome young men, who each in turn basked in the King's favour for a while, after which he would arrange rich marriages for them and allow them to recede from his life.

He must have known that it was impossible for any of these men to put out of their minds the immense opportunities that his love opened up for them. Impossible for anyone to love a king disinterestedly. But James didn't want that. He enjoyed the inequality of the relationship. He relished his power over these handsome men, and one aspect of that power was his capacity to grant them tremendous favours, to make them rich and great and see them grateful. In return, some of them were kind to him – patient and affectionate and playful – and for that he, in his turn, was grateful to them.

And then, in 1607, the King fell deeply in love.

Robert Carr had come to England in his train. He was flaxen-haired, smallish and androgynous. Lord Thomas Howard records that he was 'straight-limbed, well-favoured, strong-shouldered and smooth-faced'. A more lyrical contemporary described Carr as 'fierce and gentle like the swift greyhounds of Teviotdale'. At first he was just one of several handsome young men who would run beside the King's coach as escort and ornament. He was required to read a Latin grace, and stumbled over it. He lost his place at court and went off to France to complete his education. Four years later, when he was twenty-three, he returned. It was then that he caught King James's eye.

There was a tournament to celebrate the anniversary of the King's coronation. Carr's horse stumbled, falling on him and breaking his leg. James always enjoyed fussing over an attractive invalid. One courtier wrote sardonically to another that Carr had better be properly grateful to his steed. 'If any mischance be to be wished, 'tis breaking a leg in the King's presence, for this fellow owes all his favour to that bout.' Carr was carried into a nearby house. The King called to commiserate with him 'and after, by his daily visiting him and mourning over him, taking all care for his speedy recovery, made the daybreak of his glory appear'.

When James fell in love, he fell hard. Godfrey Goodman, at this period Queen Anne's chaplain, wrote, 'I never knew any man who had

... such a violent passion of love as he had.' Now that passion flowed towards the handsome young Scotsman with his interesting injury. Anthony Weldon comments acidly that the English lords had been hoping that the King's next beloved might be one of their own kind, 'and to that end the Countess of Suffolk did look out choice young men, who she daily curled and perfumed their breaths'. Now, though, they 'left all hope ... Our young court-gallants are vanished like mushrooms.' Everyone was jostling to become friends with the new favourite, 'all adoring this rising sun'.

Over the next seven years James lavished gifts, honours and offices on Carr. When he came to the English throne, he had wisely left Elizabeth's first minister, Sir Robert Cecil, in place, relying on him to do the hard work of ruling, calling him 'my little beagle' and making him the Earl of Salisbury. But when Salisbury died, in 1612, the King took power into his own hands, making Carr his secretary, effectively the second man in the kingdom. Everyone who wanted access to the King had to apply to him. Each of them would give him a present – a dog, a horse, a jewel, a country estate.

By the summer of 1614, Carr was Earl of Somerset, Privy Councillor, Lord Keeper of the Privy Seal, Lord Warden of the Cinque Ports, Lord Treasurer of Scotland, Knight of the Garter and rich enough to be in a position to lend the King himself £20,000. The Venetian ambassador reported that it was he 'with whom the King decides everything and in whom His Majesty confides above all others'.

The King gave Somerset his picture, in a golden frame set with diamonds. He granted him Sir Walter Raleigh's confiscated estate, Sherborne Castle, with all its lands. In 1614 he made him Lord Chamberlain, and told the Privy Council, 'No man should marvel that he bestowed a place so near himself upon his friend, whom he loved above all men living.'

Later that same year, though, King James met another man whom he would love even more.

Dancing

OFTEN, of an evening, after King James had dined, his cup-bearers would perform before him. Godfrey Goodman records that 'the gentleman waiters ... did leap and exercise their bodies ... Buckingham of all others was the most active'. As the beautiful young man pranced, the King's eyes were on him.

The courts of Renaissance Europe were full of lords a-leaping. Henry Peacham, whose book *The Compleat Gentleman* was first printed when Buckingham's career was at its zenith, numbers excellence in 'jumping and leaping' among the 'most necessary commendable qualities concerning mind or body that may be required in a noble gentleman'. Baldassare Castiglione tells of an athletic young cardinal: 'When people come to see him, even if he has never met them before, he leads them into his garden, and insists against all protests that they should strip down and try to beat him at jumping.'

Castiglione's *The Book of the Courtier* was first published in 1528. Set at the court of the Montefeltro rulers of Urbino, it presents a group of gentlemen, and two ladies – all of them wittily argumentative – debating what is required of the perfect courtier. The book is an elegiac celebration of a society that Castiglione saw as being more or less defunct, but once it was translated into English by Sir Thomas Hoby in 1561, it was received in England as a blueprint for the future. Roger Ascham, the great Elizabethan educationalist, judged in 1570 that a diligent reading of it would benefit a young man even more than three years in Italy.

Italy had a curious position in the English world view. It was the home of popery and of poison, but it was also the home of scholarship, of courtly refinement and the arts. One of those arts was that of dance.

*   *   *

King James's 'gentleman waiters' weren't leaping out of simple exuberance. They were working on their dancing skills. The Puritan diarist
Sir Simonds D'Ewes reports disapprovingly in 1621 that his fellow law
students spent as much time at the dancing schools as they did in
fencing or riding. French dancing masters were especially sought
after.

Dancing was difficult. It was a noble pursuit, requiring the qualities,
all highly prized by Castiglione, of *'grazia'*, in which graciousness is
elided with physical grace; *'leggiadrezza'*, an airy lightness which trans-
forms the density and weight of flesh into something as delicate and
dainty as a fairy's wings; and *'sprezzatura'*. *Sprezzatura* means doing
difficult things and making them look easy. It means appearing to attach
no importance to one's own hard-won skill. For a dancer, it means
masking difficulty so that every gesture or move seems to have been
achieved, not by long practice and muscle-building exercise, but as
simply and naturally as the flight of a bird. It means winning a race and
then walking away, talking gaily, without breaking sweat. It means leaping higher than any of the other pushy young men at court, and doing
it with catlike fluidity, without apparent strain. A dancer, wrote
Castiglione, needs to be 'light on his feet and a master of time and
movement'. Buckingham was such a master.

He was shaped for dancing. Sir Henry Wotton comments on the way
the 'daintiness of his leg and foot' and 'freer delivery' stood out when he
danced among his peers. 'No man dances better,' wrote Arthur Wilson,
'no man runs or jumps better.' More: even when Buckingham was
simply entering a room or crossing a garden, in the way he walked or sat
or bowed to an acquaintance, he had what Peacham called that 'even-
ness of carriage ... without which our most graceful gifts are dead and
dull, as the diamond is without his foil'. 'From the nails of his fingers,
nay, from the sole of his foot to the crown of his head, there was no
blemish in him,' wrote a contemporary, but it was Buckingham's
deportment, the way he held himself and the way he moved, that consti-
tuted 'the beauty of his beauty'.

The Jacobean court's form of performance art provided the perfect
frame for displaying that loveliness. In 1614, as the Christmas season
came on, John Chamberlain reported that the King was rumoured to be
spending the enormous sum of £1,500 on a Twelfth Night masque. 'The
principal motive' for this lavish expenditure, writes Chamberlain, 'is

thought to be the gracing of young Villiers and to bring him on the stage'.

The masque was a very peculiar kind of performance. Its first flowering overlapped with the great age of English drama. Sometimes the two forms occupied the same spaces and played to the same audiences. King James and Queen Anne visited theatres and enjoyed what they saw there as much as they enjoyed the masques staged in their honour – so did many of their noble courtiers. The two types of performance employed similar talents, but they were as unlike each other as, in the twenty-first century, ballet is unlike football.

Like those two modern spectacles (both of which depend on the arduous training and athleticism of the performers, in both of which speed and strength and precise physical coordination are displayed, both of which are capable of bringing audiences to their feet roaring), Jacobean plays and Jacobean masques differed in their relationship with reality. The ballet dancer is impersonating a princess or a swan or a toy soldier in a story whose fictional nature is understood by performers and viewers alike. The footballer is engaged in a real contest – albeit a stylised one, governed by arcane conventions and existing solely for the entertainment of the onlookers – whose outcome will affect his personal career and his bank balance, and possibly even the economy of the city his team represents. Similarly, the actor in a Jacobean drama is playing a part, while the dancers in a masque are themselves. Their show, for all its extravagant strangeness, is a celebration of the real-world court of which they are part, and of the monarch who is at the centre of the performance.

'It is a true old saying', wrote King James, 'that a king is as one set on a stage, whose smallest actions and gestures all the people gazingly do behold.'

Monarchy was theatrical. If the King was God's representative on earth (and James I believed that he was), then he must occasionally make his quasi-divine person manifest. This James fully understood. He didn't enjoy it. 'Naturally he did not love to be looked on,' wrote Wilson. He could be rude about it. Once, when told the people wanted to see him, he replied, 'God's wounds I will pull down my breeches and they shall also see my arse.' But he accepted it as his duty. Once, when he was visiting a county town, his hosts offered him a coach. He said, 'I will have no coach, for the people are desirous to see a king, and so they shall as well see his body as his face.' He understood that a monarch must pass through the streets rather as, in Catholic societies, the effigies of saints are carried in procession on their feast days. He must confer the blessing of his appearance on his people, and receive in return the blessing of their reverence. He must permit them what a Hindu would call *darshan*.

As King James travelled south to claim his English throne in 1603 there was plague in London. The coronation was hurried through hugger-mugger, and once it was done the court moved precipitately to Winchester. But the following year James made up for it, riding through the capital with all due pomp and ceremony for the state opening of Parliament.

All London became the stage for a pageant. Seven triumphal arches were erected and adorned with shields and inscriptions and brightly painted carved figures, some of which were movable. Thomas Dekker wrote that these 'wonders of wood' climbed 'into the clouds': one arch was ninety feet tall. Each one became the setting for a live performance. There were musicians' galleries and stages high up in the arches' super-structure where actors appeared. As the King and Queen passed through the streets, they were repeatedly obliged to pause to watch allegorical scenes honouring them and admire elaborate tableaux on sets crafted by teams of skilled artisans, and featuring orations scripted by Ben Jonson or Thomas Dekker. Huge crowds turned out for the occasion. 'The streets seemed to be paved with men.' Children stood on the trestles usually used as market stalls. Women watched from every window.

In public celebrations like this one lay the roots of the curious mixed-media art of the masque – part drama, part ballet, part musical, part burlesque, part animated visual art whose moving parts were human, part solemn celebration of kingly power.

A Venetian ambassador, Orazio Busino, has left an account of what it was like to attend a masque in the early years of Buckingham's career at court. The setting on this occasion was the Great Hall of Whitehall Palace, laid out as a theatre, with two tiers of boxes along each side.

In the central space gentlemen promenaded. The boxes were filled with 'most noble and richly arrayed ladies'. Looking around him during the two hours he had to wait before the performance began, Busino was impressed by the plumes springing from their foreheads or attached to their fans, and by their brilliant jewels. He noted that the fashion for wide dresses was a blessing to those whose figures were less than perfect: 'any deformity, however monstrous, remains hidden'. He also noticed that not all the ladies needed or wanted such help. 'The plump and buxom display their bosoms very liberally.' (Jacobean ladies' breasts, nipples and all, were frequently on show.) At a court masque, the audience was as colourful as the goings-on onstage.

At last the King appeared, to the sound of trumpets. A star-spangled curtain was drawn aside. The set was revealed – an automated man-mountain: 'Atlas, whose enormous head was visible aloft under the very roof of the theatre; it rolled its eyes and moved itself very cleverly.'

The masques presented at the Jacobean court were beautiful, tedious, bizarre and deeply serious. Most of them were scripted by Ben Jonson and designed by Inigo Jones. They boasted effects that astonished their audiences.

Painted flats were whisked on and off to transform the space in the twinkling of an eye. Archways opened into great apparent distances. To spectators for whom perspectival drawing was brand new, such illusions seemed, in the most literal sense, magical.

In these dizzyingly strange artificial spaces appeared moving trees, chariots made of mother-of-pearl, sea monsters swimming on undulating oceans of blue-green silk, musicians dressed as mermaids or cherubs, playing underwater or above the clouds. There were gods and goddesses descending from the heavens.

The spectacle was lit by a multitude of candles, placed behind glass jars of coloured water so that they glowed like gemstones. When these coloured lights were lowered from the roof, they seemed to their audiences like a meteor shower. A golden mist descended from a suspended globe. Scented smoke billowed out from hidden censers.

All of this was amazing. Plays were normally performed on bare stages. Jones's designs were like nothing that had ever been seen in England before.

With a perspectival set there is only one perfect viewpoint. That is where the King sat. The ambassadors or councillors or high-court judges who sat on stools and benches around his throne basked in the glory of his presence. They could also see the show. Not so the noble courtiers in the boxes. Their view of the stage was sideways and partial. That was normal. That was acceptable. What mattered was that they could see King James. They had come to see the performance, yes, but they had also – and more importantly – come to see the King seeing the performance. The two spectacles were not clearly distinguished.

As King James I sat on his throne, red-faced, scrawny-bearded and shifting uncomfortably in his padded doublet and voluminous breeches, he was all too obviously imperfect. But a king is not only a physical being: the spectacle before him made manifest his other nature. He personified an abstraction which would hold its value (or so most people in England in the 1620s believed) for ever and ever – the idea of monarchy. In the masque being played out before him, that abstraction was made material. Watching it, he was contemplating his other self.

*   *   *

Most masques followed the same narrative structure.

First came the antimasque – comical, with knockabout action and visual grotesquerie. On one occasion the antimasque was fronted by a cook, who summoned up other actors representing vegetables or cuts of meat from a colossal cooking pot. In another, the leader was a great butt of wine, accompanied by a chorus of jolly bottles. The antimasque was funny, but it was also frightening. It represented disorder, darkness, mess and bad behaviour. Like the impossible creatures with which Hieronymus Bosch filled his visionary worlds – eggs with knives, jugs with mouths, fish with legs – the monsters peopling the antimasques were sinister instances of discord in nature.

The performers were professional actors. It would have been unseemly for a courtier to take the part of a bottle or a turnip. More – it would have been disgraceful. To appear in an assumed character was to dissimulate. No nobleman or great lady would want to be seen to do that.

While these inferior beings were tumbling around, making themselves ridiculous on the stage floor, the aristocratic dancers, in their sparkling costumes, waited their turn (Plate 8). At the pivotal moment, a tower would revolve, an island would float onstage or a mountain would be riven asunder, and the noble masquers would be revealed.

The antimasquers were banished. No more boisterous mechanicals. No more comedians imitating kitchen stuff. No more rowdiness and anti-hierarchical buffoonery. The dancers took the stage.

These were the great ones of the court. James didn't dance, but Queen Anne and their sons Prince Henry and Prince Charles all did. (Another difference between the masque and the drama was that women appeared in the former.)

The dances were vigorous. The ladies' dresses were daringly diaphanous, made of the finest gauze. Their skirts were above ankle length. The men wore their trunk-hose short, to reveal the outlines of their legs. The first masque in which Buckingham participated was the *The Golden Age Restored*. In it a choir sang, urging on the dancers:

> *Move, move then to these sounds.*
> *And do not only walk your solemn rounds,*
> *But give those light and airy bounds,*
> *That fit the Genii of these gladder grounds.*

The masquers worked hard to make their airy bounds seem as light, as *leggiadra*, as Castiglione required. Rehearsals went on for weeks or even months. Buckingham was one of the few acclaimed 'high dancers' capable of what a pamphleteer called those 'lofty galliards ... when men capered in the air like wanton kids ... and turned above ground as if they had been compact of fire or a purer element'. The practice required to attain such strength and skill was considered to be not only a physical training but a spiritual discipline.

Dancers moving together were like musicians in a consort, or like the constellations wheeling through the skies – each star on its divinely appointed course. Philosophers from Aristotle to Boethius had written of the silent music generated by the universe – the harmony of the spheres. Dancing together, each one brilliant but subordinate to the ensemble, the masquers were creating a *musica humana* reflecting the *musica mundana*. That harmony had a political dimension. 'Take but degree away ...' says Shakespeare's Ulysses, 'And hark what discord follows.' The antimasque represented that jangling out-of-jointedness. But once order was restored, the masquers, bathed in lights that glinted off their jewels, criss-crossed the stage, creating patterns pointing always towards the man at the centre of the show. King James might not take part in the dance, but he was willy-nilly part of it.

Inigo Jones contrived trails of torches radiating out from the throne, as though all this brilliance, this exquisitely kinetic geometry of moving stage scenery and leaping lords and coloured candlelight, emanated from the man whose inner being it made manifest. To those receptive to this kind of symbolic thinking, the masque and the monarch were as one.

Not everybody was so receptive. Busino was, by turns, sneery – 'spoiled as we are by the graceful and harmonious music of Italy, the composition did not strike us as very fine'; bewildered – 'they sang some jigs which we did not understand'; and utterly worn out – 'The story ended at half past two in the morning ... Should your lordships writhe on reading this document you may imagine the weariness I feel in relating it.'

He wasn't alone. Many in the audience looked forward impatiently to the moment when the dancers would choose partners from among the assembled courtiers and the revels began. Tight choreography gave way to looser, faster-paced brawls and *corrantoes*. Things became boisterous and, sometimes, pretty rough. Sir Dudley Carleton reports that *The Masque of Blackness* was succeeded by a scrum, with tables overturned, during which a couple were surprised *in flagrante* on the set.

It was unusual for a masque to be performed more than once, but in 1615 *The Golden Age Restored* found such favour that the King asked for it to be given again only a few days after the first show. The repetition was talked of as an unheard-of anomaly. It was generally understood as a clear indication that King James was by this time besotted with the talented masquer who had made his debut in it – young George Villiers.

Exit Somerset

THERE were nights, during the winter after King James first laid eyes on Villiers at Apethorpe, when the servants and courtiers who attended on the King could hear raised voices from within his bedchamber. The Earl of Somerset repeatedly visited James, and each time he launched into yet another of what the King called 'furious assaults'.

We know what was going on between the two of them because in the early weeks of 1615 James wrote Somerset a long reproachful letter. In it James describes Somerset's behaviour back to him, and pours out his own feelings.

Somerset believed there was a faction at court working against him, and trying to bring a new favourite in. The King said, no, there was no such faction. If he, James, had detected even a 'sparkle' of such a thing, he 'would have run upon it with my feet, as upon fire, to have extinguished it'. We know, though, that Somerset was right.

He thought that people were complaining that he had been given too much power. He believed that they were saying 'one man should not rule all, or that no man's dependence should be but upon the King'. It was true: they were saying that. They had been saying it for years, but Somerset, in his ascendancy, had been deaf to their whispers.

He sensed the King was less affectionate towards him than he had been. James had certainly doted on him once. Thomas Howard, describing the early stages of their relationship, records (with distaste) how he loved to touch and caress young Carr. He 'leaneth on his arm, pinches his cheek, smoothes his ruffled garment'. He was James's 'dear one', and according to Howard, the whole court therefore was jostling to flatter him. 'Will you say that the moon shineth all summer? That the stars are bright jewels fit for Carr's ears? … We are almost worn out in our endeavours to keep pace with this fellow.'

In those days Somerset, according to the French ambassador, Count Leveneur de Tillières, 'submitted entirely to the whims of his master, and he appeared to have no other passion than to second all his desires'. A ribald ballad of the period describes him as a stallion and 'a jolly sire' who set James's 'good grace a-fire'. As the years went by, though, their relationship shifted.

The time came when Tillières noticed that Somerset 'rejected with rudeness the caresses of the King'. In his letter of January 1615, James reproaches him for his 'long creeping back and withdrawing yourself from lying in my chamber, notwithstanding my many hundred times earnestly soliciting you to the contrary'. Somerset didn't like the competition presented by young Villiers, but he himself no longer wanted to spend his nights with King James.

James was hurt. In his letter he talks about how Somerset's recent behaviour had made him suffer 'the infinite grief of a deeply wounded heart'. He writes, 'God is my judge my love has been infinite towards you.'

'Has been' – that use of a past tense is significant. Each time Somerset came to the King's chamber at night and ranted and 'railed' he made himself less lovable in King James's eyes. He spoke in 'a strange frenzy'. He showed 'passion, fury and insolence'. He made James, his lord and master, feel like the scared, abused child he had once been, 'rebuking' him 'more sharply and bitterly than ever my master George Buchanan durst do'. And then he would go away.

Everyone saw and heard it. All the Gentlemen of the Bedchamber knew that Somerset no longer stayed the night, and how sad the King seemed, left alone after these scenes; how he was unable to sleep. It was humiliating. It was no way to revive a dwindling love.

'All I crave', wrote James, 'is that ... ye never think to hold grip of me but out of mere love, and not one hair by fear.' This was not about his dignity as a monarch. 'Consider that I am a freeman, if I were not a king.' It was about an abhorrence, rooted deep in James the man, of the stupid tyranny of the strong and furious over the mild and gentle. 'If ever I find that ye think to retain me by one sparkle of fear, all the violence of my love will in that instant be changed into as violent a hatred.'

*   *   *

Somerset was anxious and angry because he thought (correctly) that the King's desires were now directed elsewhere, but a greater calamity was about to overtake him than the loss of his place in the King's heart. That need have been no great disaster. James assured him that whoever else might be rising, Somerset – if only he would conduct himself more graciously – could keep his place in court, in power and in the King's affections. James would never allow another 'to rise in any degree of my favour except they may acknowledge and thank you as a furtherer of it'. This promise he kept. He sent George Villiers to Somerset. Villiers greeted the established favourite with respect, saying, 'I desire to be your friend and your creature.' Somerset was having none of it. He said, 'I will, if I can, break your neck.' Sir Anthony Weldon, who tells this story, believes that if the former favourite had been gracious to the coming man, the two could have coexisted amicably at court. But Somerset was already doomed.

The story of his downfall is complex and lurid and some of its details will remain forever uncertain. Here is its outline.

He had a friend – a very close friend – Sir Thomas Overbury. Overbury was the elder and the cleverer of the two. The Queen called

him the younger man's 'governor'. As Somerset rose in the King's favour, Overbury rose with him.

Somerset fell in love with a married woman, Frances, the Countess of Essex, who was the Earl of Suffolk's daughter and so one of the powerful Howard family. Frances was as scintillating personally as she was well connected. Arthur Wilson called her 'a beauty of the greatest magnitude in the horizon of the Court'.

Initially Overbury had no objection to his friend's amorous adventure, even helping him in the composition of his love letters. But then things grew serious. Somerset and Frances wanted to be man and wife. Frances had been married to the 3rd Earl of Essex (son of the ill-fated 2nd Earl, Queen Elizabeth's favourite) when they were fourteen and thirteen respectively, on the understanding that the marriage would not immediately be consummated. Essex went abroad, as young lords did, to complete his education. By the time he returned to claim his marital rights, Frances and Somerset were already in love. Divorce was near impossible. Frances asked for an annulment on the grounds that Essex had proved impotent. Essex was not inclined to grant it to her.

Thomas Overbury was dismayed by the way his friend had become embroiled in this scandalous affair. He blamed Frances. She knew it, and came to detest him. Overbury and Somerset quarrelled. King James, jealous of Overbury's hold over Somerset, was happy to oblige his favourite by getting him out of the way. He offered him various posts abroad – including the job of ambassador to Moscow.

Overbury refused to go. In April 1613, he was imprisoned in the Tower for 'contempt' of the King's wishes. There he fell ill. The illness was strange and virulent. Five months later he died.

His death might have been more discussed, had it not coincided with the beginning of the hearing to decide on the annulment of the Essexes' marriage. The case was the talk of the town. In order to establish whether their marriage had or had not been consummated, both parties were subjected to embarrassing questioning and physical investigations: Essex voluntarily lifting his nightshirt to display an erection; Frances being 'searched' in a lightless room to establish whether her hymen was still intact. It was declared that it was, but hardly anyone believed it: she and Somerset had been meeting 'privily' for two years already. Rumour had it that another woman, a genuine virgin, had been smuggled into her place in the dark.

Frances was accused of bewitching her husband. She counterclaimed that she and he both had been bewitched by some malevolent other who had made him impotent. When it was pointed out that Essex seemed capable of sex with other women, she refined her claim – the spell applied only to their marital relations.

The august commissioners (four bishops, four lawyers, two Privy Councillors) were disinclined to grant the annulment. King James intervened. He wanted Somerset, still his dear one, to have his desire. He appointed two further, more amenable, commissioners to gain a majority and force the annulment through.

Adultery, witchcraft, the sexual humiliation of an aristocrat, the perversion of due legal process – the case was scandalous but, with the King's support, Somerset and Frances were getting what they wanted. That Christmas, they were married at court, in the Chapel Royal, at the King's immense expense – Crown lands were sold to pay for the bride's jewels. Frances wore her long hair loose, as virgin brides did. John Donne wrote an eclogue celebrating the couple's radiance, their 'inflaming eyes' and 'loving hearts', and likening them to two suns who, rising, merge and become one.

The wedding masque by Thomas Campion, though, contained a sharply pointed line. The poet celebrates the 'affection between man and wife', but acknowledges that there were 'some' who 'friendship between man and man prefer'. Somerset might marry, but he was still King James's plaything.

Over the next two years talk spread about the strange circumstances surrounding Sir Thomas Overbury's death. In September 1615, the Lieutenant of the Tower, Sir Gervase Elwes, told the Secretary of State that Overbury had been poisoned. King James, on being informed, ordered Elwes to set down in writing all that he knew.

He wrote that in August 1613 he had become aware that one of the gaolers, Richard Weston, was giving Overbury poisoned food. He had confronted Weston, who told him he had 'been set on work' by unnamed others. Elwes took steps to ensure that food sent in for Overbury from outside would not be delivered. But Overbury was by this time in such a terrible physical state that medical help was needed. An apothecary attended. The apothecary's apprentice had been bribed to administer a poisonous 'clyster' (suppository). Elwes maintained that he did not know who had 'corrupted the servant', but he said that 'a principal actor' was one Anne Turner, who was said to be a witch. Turner was close to Frances Somerset, living in her household as a kind of servant-cum-companion and declaring the Countess was 'as dear unto me as my own soul'.

Suspicion fell on the Somersets. King James steeled himself. He ordered an investigation, to be led by the formidable Lord Chief Justice, Sir Edward Coke. Coke was known as the 'oracle of the law'. He was not one to bend the law to oblige anyone, however exalted. He told James, in response to a request from His Majesty, that, no, he would not be keeping the King informed of the progress of his enquiries. He began interrogating the witnesses.

One day in October, Somerset, who was with the King at his hunting lodge in Royston, set out early in the morning for London. On the road he met Coke. Coke had discovered that among the meals Elwes had thought poisoned were tarts and jellies sent to Overbury by his old friend Somerset. Coke was going to lay the evidence before the King. Somerset tried to persuade him to turn back. Coke refused.

The following day Somerset returned to Royston, only to leave again after a brief interview with King James. Sir Anthony Weldon, who was present, describes their parting. When Somerset kissed his hand, 'the King hung about his neck, slabbering his cheeks, saying "For God's sake, when shall I see thee again? On my soul, I shall neither eat nor sleep until you come again."' The two went down the stairs together and 'at the stairs' head, at the middle of the stairs, and at the stairs' foot' James continued to embrace Somerset and 'lament his departure'. Somerset rode off. The King, turning to those about him, said, 'I shall never see his face more.' When Somerset arrived back in London he was arrested, charged as an accessory to murder and imprisoned in the Tower.

Weldon presents this story of their last meeting as evidence of the King's viper-like 'art of dissimulation'. It can equally well be read as a scene of genuine pathos. Having heard Coke's evidence, King James knew what was coming. He was far too canny to suppose he could help his former favourite evade a murder charge. But there is no reason to doubt he was deeply distressed by their parting.

A series of trials began. Each hearing brought out more wild accusations and lurid fantasies. Witchcraft, poison of many kinds, an uprising of English Catholics, a Spanish invasion, plots to murder King James, Queen Anne and Prince Charles, the entire city of London to be set on fire. The court sessions induced public paranoia, while inflaming the public's appetite for sensational news.

First Richard Weston was found guilty and executed, then Anne Turner, then Gervase Elwes.

At last came the trials everyone had been waiting for, those of the Somersets. John Chamberlain hurried to the courtroom at six in the morning to get a seat, and it cost him the exorbitant sum of ten shillings. Frances was rapidly found guilty. She had already confessed to having poisoned Overbury, but she claimed that Somerset had not known about the plot. (This may be true – historians are still arguing over the extent of Somerset's complicity.)

Somerset's trial, on the following day, was more suspenseful. He had been increasingly distressed for several days, in a 'strange fit', and arrived in the courtroom two hours late. He had resisted all efforts to make him confess to Overbury's murder, even though King James had promised to pardon him and Frances if only he would do so.

Sir Francis Bacon, as Attorney General, was prosecuting. Speaking for several hours, Bacon alleged that Somerset had improperly allowed Overbury knowledge of state secrets 'of a high and dangerous nature', and that Overbury had used them to blackmail him – so the prosecution had a motive for murder.

Somerset, defending himself, was incoherent. 'His answers', wrote an onlooker, 'were so poor and idle as many of the Lords his peers shook their heads and blushed to hear such slender excuses.' He was found guilty.

On the day of the trial King James was at Greenwich Palace. He kept himself alone and apart, and refused all meals. According to Anthony Weldon he was dreadfully agitated, 'in restless motion' as he waited for news of the verdict, 'sending to every boat that came to the bridge, cursing all that came without tidings'.

Weldon thought he was on tenterhooks, afraid of what Somerset 'in passion' might say in court. During the trial two men stood behind the accused, ready to fling their cloaks over his head and muffle his words if he tried to say whatever it was that King James so dreaded the world hearing. What that was we may never know. Something about affairs of state perhaps; something about King James's collusion in the legally questionable imprisonment of Overbury; or – and this is what gossips were whispering with most relish – something, perhaps, about a sexual connection between Somerset and the King.

'Here may we see what a slave King James was to his favourites,' wrote an anti-monarchist later in the century. King James's depravity had been revealed, he wrote, 'by his agony till he heard that Somerset took his arraignment patiently and had told no tales'.

Somerset and Frances were both condemned to death. Their executions never took place. After six years' imprisonment in the Tower, they were released and allowed to live, under surveillance, in their house in Chiswick. According to Arthur Wilson, 'that love that made them break through all oppositions … grew so weak that it pined away and they lived long after (though in one house) as strangers to one another.'

* * *

'As soon as Somerset declined,' wrote Arthur Wilson, 'Buckingham mounted. Such is the court motion.' The King had once given Somerset a diamond necklace. On his conviction it was taken back. James gave it to Queen Anne, who passed it on to Buckingham. The new favourite wore it constantly. Buckingham was on his way to having all that Somerset had had – the diamonds, the power and influence and wealth, the King's love.

In August 1615, a few weeks before Somerset's arrest, King James had been on his summer progress through the countryside. Buckingham was with him. The court stopped at Farnham Castle in Surrey. Something happened between the King and his new favourite while they were in bed together there – something so intimate and delightful that for long afterwards they treasured its memory.

Buckingham was to write to James, after a day, years later, when the King had been especially affectionate towards him, that he wondered 'whether you loved me now ... better than that time which I shall never forget at Farnham, where the bed's head could not be found between the master and his dog'.

By 'his dog', Buckingham meant himself. He signed his letters to King James 'from Your Majesty's humble slave and dog'.

Showers of Love

GEORGE Villiers, wrote the Venetian ambassador Girolamo Lando, seemed 'natural, modest, affable, kind and courteous, and deserving of his good fortune'. Bishop Goodman agreed. Villiers didn't only have a 'lovely complexion' and a handsome body. He was respectful to his elders, 'his conversation so pleasing, and of so sweet a disposition'. Clarendon, whose uncles were both great men at the Jacobean court, had heard from them that Villiers 'was of a most flowing courtesy and affability to all men' and 'desirous to oblige'. He never lost his temper: Henry Wotton writes that 'there was in his natural constitution a marvellous equality'. He was a loyal and generous friend and a dutiful son. He was helpful to others in need of a sponsor at court. He had a 'sweet and attractive manner'.

To the King he seemed marvellous.

James was lonely. He and his wife hadn't lived together for nearly seven years. When Queen Anne visited Whitehall she kept to her apartments in the 'Queen's side' of the Palace, well removed from the all-male sanctum of the King's Bedchamber. The two got on, wrote Bishop Goodman, as well 'as man and wife could do, not conversing together'. (The word 'conversing' was then, like the word 'intercourse' now, ambiguous. It could be used of two people talking: or it could describe a sexual connection.) Four of James's children had died in early childhood. Of the three survivors, he lost two (to death or to marriage) in the two years before Buckingham arrived in his life.

In the autumn of 1612, Prince Henry, the Prince of Wales, fell ill. Henry's birth in 1594 had been one of the great events of King James's early life. To have fathered a male heir was, for a Renaissance monarch, a necessary achievement. It seemed to make the Stuart dynasty secure on the throne of Scotland. It brought the prospect of James becoming King of England a great deal nearer. In *Macbeth*, the play Shakespeare wrote three years after James came to England, Macbeth is devastated when the witches reveal that his offspring will not succeed him, while his friend Banquo will be patriarch to a line of kings. A crown was a hollow glory, unless one could hand it on to one's own descendants. On Henry's birth, James and his subjects rejoiced together. As a contemporary put it, the Scots people 'went daft for mirth'.

Self-confident and dashing as his father was not, Henry was athletic and strong (Plate 4). But that October, while playing tennis, he felt 'a small kind of giddy lumpish heaviness in his forehead'. Three weeks later he died of typhoid fever. He was eighteen.

His early death haloed his memory with pathos, and with the glamour of what might have been. John Webster and John Donne wrote elegies – Donne calling Henry 'the incomparable Prince' and Webster 'the greatest of the kingly race'. He was lamented as 'the delight of mankind, the expectation of nations, the strength of his father, and glory of his mother, religion's second hope'. King James had fewer, simpler, but more terrible words. One of his Councillors reports that 'even in the midst of the most important discussion he will burst out with "Henry is dead, Henry is dead"'.

The Prince's body was embalmed and lay in state in St James's Palace. On 7 December, over a thousand people followed the cortège to Westminster Abbey – taking four hours to cover that brief route – watched by thousands more. Poor men in black, recipients of the Prince's charity, led the procession, followed by servants and attendant nobles, priests and Privy Councillors, with black standards and regalia, and riderless horses draped in black.

On the hearse, Henry's effigy lay beneath an intricately carved and gilded catafalque, topped with a canopy of black velvet. Sir Isaac Wake, a future Secretary of State, describes scenes of hysterical grief. 'Under the canopy lay the goodly image of that lovely prince clothed with the richest garments he had, which did so lively represent his person, as that it did not only draw tears from the severest beholder, but caused a fearful outcry among the people as if they felt their own ruin in that loss.' Twelve-year-old Prince Charles, now heir to the throne, walked behind it alone as the chief mourner. His mother was not there. (Women didn't attend funerals.) King James was in bed, prostrated by grief.

Only weeks later, in February 1613, James's next child, Princess Elizabeth, married Frederick, the Elector Palatine. The wedding was a great event. The bride and groom glittered in cloth of silver. Elizabeth, sixteen years old and wearing an 'exceedingly rich coronet', made a charming picture. William Shakespeare and his players gave a perfor-

mance of *The Tempest*. The celebrations included a mock sea battle on the River Thames, between a ship of the English fleet and another carrying pretend Turkish infidels, for Princess Elizabeth's marriage was to be the first node in the mesh that would – so King James believed – hold the European union together, and make Christendom secure against unbelievers.

On the day of the ceremony James seemed frail and distraught. John Chamberlain thought him 'somewhat strangely attired' (he was wearing a cap and feather with a Spanish cape). When he was afterwards required to dub his new son-in-law Knight of the Garter he did so sitting up in bed, and muffed his lines, hanging the emblem of St George around Frederick's neck 'with few words'.

He was pleased with the match, but it left him even more isolated. Soon afterwards Elizabeth left England with her new husband. Waiting to embark in Margate, she wrote to her father, 'I shall perhaps never see again the flower of princes, the king of fathers, the best and most gracious father that the sun will ever see.' It was true. James had lost her. Her marriage would have a profoundly disturbing effect on the rest of his reign – complicating his foreign policy, bedevilling his relationship with his parliaments and his people – but father and daughter would never be reunited.

His only remaining child, Prince Charles, was as nervous and withdrawn as he himself had once been, and still living mostly with his mother. As his once-adored Somerset became progressively more 'insolent' and 'stubborn', James was in urgent need of kindness, companionship and a new love object. When sweet, amiable George Villiers came along, observers marvelled at how rapidly and absolutely 'the King's affection and favour' did 'flow so violently upon him'. Favours rained down on the King's new dear one, wrote Henry Wotton, not like 'sprinkling drops or dews', but thickly, in 'main showers'.

Older Women

READING and writing about the early Stuart establishment can feel lonely for a female author. Not one woman in Parliament or on the Privy Council or in the law courts or in the King's immediate circle. King James was notoriously misogynist. Under Buckingham's influence he was to modify his views, but he once likened women to war, as a 'necessary evil'.

But when one looks away from the official institutions, there were plenty of women around. Talented women, enterprising women, some of them in high places. Buckingham was promoted by them and depended on them. Clarendon thought that he lacked friends at the beginning of his career, but that may tell us more about the historian than about his subject. At the time of his first arrival at court, Buckingham had at least three people who supported and advised him. If Clarendon couldn't see them, that may be simply because, for Clarendon, women were invisible.

The first woman in Buckingham's life was his mother, Mary. Mother and son both looked back on his childhood with tender mock teasing. She called him, when he was an adult and prodigiously powerful, 'the same naughty boy George Villiers'. He said she had been endlessly tolerant with him when he was a little boy who 'did nothing else but unreasonably and frowardly wrangle'. Over the years she was to be his constant companion. Their relationship was possibly the most important in Buckingham's life.

She was the second wife of Sir George Villiers, Buckingham's father. Later, Buckingham's rivals would sneer at her for being of a 'mean family', and claim she had entered the Villiers household 'in a mean office'. Roger Coke tells a Cinderella-style story of how Mary served first in the kitchen. 'Her ragged habit could not shade the beautiful and excellent frame of her person,' writes Coke. Sir George saw her, and liked what he saw. He persuaded his first wife to make her a chamber-maid. The first wife dying, he 'became very sweet' on young Mary and gave her twenty pounds to buy a dress. Twenty pounds was more than enough to make a woman splendid. Seeing her transformed, George senior's 'affections', according to Coke, 'became so fired that to allay them he married her'.

Coke's story is misleading: Mary was a daughter of the Beaumont family, who were the Villierses' social equals and had intermarried with them before. It is unlikely that she ever skivvied in the kitchen. Rather, she was sent out of her own home to join another household, as young people of both sexes routinely were, to acquire some social polish and widen their acquaintance. When the mistress of the house died early – as women enduring the dangers of childbirth year after year frequently did – it was common for a widower, especially one with children (Sir George had three), to marry a woman who was already part of his household, be she his sister-in-law or, as in this case, someone more tenuously related. But though her origins were not 'mean', it is certainly true that young Mary Beaumont was to rise in the world, helped upward by her good looks.

Sir George died in 1606, his estate passing to his eldest son by his first marriage. Mary married again. Her second husband died within a few months. Her third was Sir Thomas Compton, whose brother was the Earl of Northampton and extremely rich. Compton helped her to send her two elder sons, John and young George – by this time aged sixteen – abroad to France.

At the outset of Buckingham's career, it was Mary who shaped and trained and groomed him. It was she who planned his education, as she explained, 'having had the care left me by the unfortunate loss of your dear father'.

When he first caught the King's eye, she so contrived it that he 'should appear with all the advantages his mother could set him forth'. When he joined the court, she followed him there. Later, she abetted him in abducting, and subsequently marrying, the richest girl in the kingdom. He saw to it that she became a countess in her own right. He named his daughter after her. She was with him in the Royal Bedchamber when King James was dying. When he was seeking to consolidate his position at the new King Charles's court, he requested and got for her the position of lady-in-waiting to the Queen. All his life he put up with being teased and scolded and put down by her, secure always in the 'more than ordinary natural love of a mother, which you have ever borne me'.

Mary made George Villiers what he was – a being who, when properly presented as she had been in her twenty-pound dress, could attract desire, and so gain wealth and influence. She was looked down on by the great ones at court – because she was not born an aristocrat, and because she sought to promote the careers, not only of her dazzling George, but of her other children as well. She was an upstart, a pushy tiger-mother. The Victorian historian S. R. Gardiner described her as 'unbearable'. Gardiner seems to have been impelled by the same kind of snobbery that drove her seventeenth-century critics. He doesn't use such words about, for instance, the Howard family, who manoeuvred even their most doltish nephews into prominent positions at court.

Those who knew her better enjoyed Mary's company. King James liked her. He took her out hunting with him, and always paid her marked attention when she appeared at great dinners. Henry Wotton called her a 'beautiful and provident mother'. She was to remain her glittering son's best friend, confidante and closest ally throughout his life.

Two other older women were instrumental in Buckingham's first step up the ladder of fortune. One of them was the Queen.

After 1606, and the birth of her last child (a girl who died in infancy), Queen Anne steered clear of Whitehall, where her husband's favourites were all too much in evidence. The Venetian envoy describes her as 'intelligent and prudent' and says that 'she might play as large a role as she wished. But she is averse to trouble; she sees that those who govern desire to be left alone, and so she professes indifference.' Rather than trying to lay claim to power, she established separate households for herself in Greenwich, at Denmark House on the Strand (where Somerset House now stands) and at Oatlands in Surrey.

In those places she gathered around herself a group of cultured, independent-minded women. Her ladies-in-waiting included the Countess of Pembroke, Philip Sidney's sister and a considerable poet in her own right, and her niece, Lady Mary Wroth, author of a lengthy and erudite prose romance. Anne herself wrote fluently in German, Latin, French, Scots, English and Italian, as well as her native Danish. Distancing herself from James's court, and from his policies, she became a patron of the arts. She employed Inigo Jones to beautify her palaces. She commissioned and danced in his first four masques (Plate 3).

She had her own opinions. King James was a pacifist. Queen Anne was not. At her prompting, Inigo Jones created masques celebrating warrior women. In one, Anne herself appeared as the goddess Athena, 'War-like Pallas, in her helmet dressed', carrying a lance and wearing a costume embroidered with 'implements of war'. In another, she was leader of a band of queens who have conquered foreign kings or murdered their own husbands to gain power. They are Amazons, viragos. In the playwright's notes, the queens 'wear armour, eat their victims, cut their hair, kill their men'.

Anne was as interested in painting as she was in performance. She commissioned portraits of her courtiers, and posed herself for Marcus Gheeraerts, Paul Van Somer and the miniaturist Peter Oliver. She befriended Alethea, Countess of Arundel, co-creator with her husband of a great collection of art and antiquities. Soon Queen Anne was buying too. One of her contemporaries wrote disparagingly of her preference for spending time with 'harmless pictures in a paltry gallery' when she could have been involving herself in intrigues at court. Now that choice seems admirable. The first connoisseur in the royal family, Anne left her collection of one hundred and twenty-five paintings to her second son, Charles, in whose hands it expanded to become one of the finest in Europe.

Her marriage had produced an adequate number of children, and by all accounts King James treated her – at least in public – with proper courtesy and respect, but it cannot have been very happy.

Probably, when she recommended young George Villiers to her husband on St George's Day, she did so sadly, but at least her relationship with the new favourite remained cordial, a fact which reflects well on them both. Polite and tactful as ever, Buckingham was to make himself so agreeable to her that within a year she was addressing him, with apparent affection, as 'my kind dog'.

*   *   *

The most brilliant of the group of women around Queen Anne was Lucy, the Countess of Bedford. She was the third of the older women who gave Buckingham his start in life.

Rich, beautiful and self-confident, Lucy Bedford shone. Just as, a decade later, Buckingham would be the outstanding dancer in the masques at Whitehall, so she was the star of the masques staged by Queen Anne in the first years of the reign. In *The Masque of Queens* (1609) she appeared as Penthesilea, Queen of the Amazons. Inigo Jones's sketch for her costume shows her in a magnificently plumed helmet and apparently bare-breasted, her fluttering skirts daringly short.

The Countess's family connections were socially exalted and intellectually distinguished. She was a relative of the Herberts and the Sidneys; and she was unusually well educated for a girl. Married at thirteen and

a mother by fifteen, she was still only twenty-four when Queen Elizabeth died. Her husband had joined Essex's rebellion and lost the royal favour. It was imperative to make a better impression in the new reign. Lucy skipped the old queen's funeral and raced north to Scotland, galloping horses to death in the speed of her going, to secure herself a place at the new court. It worked. She arrived days ahead of the dozens of other ladies travelling more decorously on the same mission. Queen Anne appointed her a Lady of the Bedchamber, and she travelled back south in the Queen's entourage.

On arrival in England, the royal family was divided. Princess Elizabeth was sent to live with Lucy Bedford's parents, Sir John and Lady Harington. Their son, Lucy's young brother John, joined Prince Henry's household and became his boon companion. Already close to the Queen, Lucy thus became close as well to her two eldest children.

She was a woman of many parts. Her husband, considerably older, made few demands on her, allowing her to pursue her interests and to establish her own small court. She was a pioneer in the art of garden design. She studied astronomy. At her estate in Twickenham, she combined both interests, commissioning a garden laid out according to the plan of the Ptolemaic universe, with concentric rows of trees and walks mirroring the orbits of the planets. She wrote about her other garden at More Park, 'I am still adding some trifles of pleasure to that place I am so much in love with.' She joked that if 'I were so fond of any man, I were in hard case'.

She wrote poetry and was a generous patron. John Dowland dedicated a collection of songs to her. Ben Jonson addressed her in his epigrams, and wrote a character based on her in a lost pastoral. Michael Drayton, Samuel Daniel and George Chapman were among her protégés. John Florio acknowledged her help on his translations of Montaigne's essays. John Donne made her godmother to his daughter and called her 'the first good angel ... that ever did in woman's shape appear'.

Queen Anne made the best of Buckingham's appearance at court. Lucy Bedford was one of those who had brought him there. Thomas Fuller tells us that when he first came to court it was the Countess, along with her cousin the Earl of Pembroke, who gave him financial support 'far above his patrimonial income' and 'led him by the hand'.

Sex

WHAT does it mean to say that King James loved men? Come to that, what does it ever mean when we talk about love? A mixture of physical desire with tenderness, with a euphoric happiness alternating with painful anxiety when things are not going well, with a longing to surrender all to the beloved, to be constantly with them, to cherish and protect them, to share jokes and secret language, to have them always in one's eye. A delight in pleasing them. An exaggerated estimate of their beauty and talent and kindness and good sense. A delicious ease in their company. A pleasure in feeling at one with them – coupled – relieved, so it feels, from the existential loneliness of the human condition. An impulse to give them whatever is to be given, be it the embroidered cloths of heaven or one's dreams, or a ring, or a horse, or melons from one's garden, or a grand manor house with all its rents, or a position at court (such as that which James gave Lennox and Somerset and Buckingham in turn) which will allow them to make a fortune from accepting backhanders and bribes. King James felt and expressed all of this.

Writing to Buckingham, he addressed him as Steenie (after St Stephen, who is said to have had 'the face of an angel') or as 'My sweet Steenie gossip'. When they were apart, he wrote wishing God would send his beloved 'a happy, joyful and speedy return into the arms of your dear dad'.

Here is part of a letter he wrote to Buckingham:

> My only sweet and dear child,
>   ... I cannot content myself without sending you this present,
> praying God that I may have a joyful and comfortable meeting
> with you and that we may make at this Christmas a new marriage
> ever to be kept hereafter; for, God so love me, as I desire only to live

in this world for your sake, and that I had rather live banished in
any part of the earth with you than live a sorrowful widow's life
without you. And so God bless you, my sweet child and wife, and
grant that ye may ever be a comfort to your dear dad and
husband.
  James R.

There is much that is unorthodox here. The way Buckingham, the physically perfect male, is feminised as a wife. The way James imagines himself in the role of 'widow' (the word 'widower' for a man was already in use – James's use of the female form is unusual). The way a parent–child relationship is overlaid on an erotic one. The way James's lover becomes his son.

In the relationship between the King and his favourite the boundaries between genders waver and dissolve. Familial love and sexual love merge with each other. The breaking-down of distinctions is liberating and dangerous. If Buckingham is both a child and a wife, then incest is implied, and so is paedophilia. If the King sees himself as a grieving 'widow', then the God-ordained order which places a man in authority over his womenfolk is threatened. Such a letter is transgressive, revolutionary. It is also generous and ardent. Whatever species of emotion is being described here – sexual or paternal, benign or abusive – it is certainly love.

In their correspondence it is generally King James who declares his feelings most openly, while Buckingham responds with 'thankfulness' or with affectionate teasing. Sometimes, though, he goes further. In an undated letter he tells the King, 'All and the least I can say is this, that I naturally so love your person, and upon so good experience and knowledge adore all your other parts ... that were not only all your people, but all the world besides, set together on one side, and you alone on the other, I should, to obey and please you, displease, nay despise all them.'

Another time he tells the King that what they share is 'more affection than between lovers in the best kind, man and wife'. 'I never yet', wrote Sir John Oglander, 'saw any fond husband make so much or so great dalliance over his beautiful spouse as I have seen King James over his favourites.' To James and to Buckingham, their relationship was as good as a marriage.

*   *   *

Not everybody thought so. Their hostile contemporaries – Puritan preachers or scurrilous pamphleteers alike – used a variety of disparaging words to describe the King's young love objects. They were 'minions', or 'catamites' or 'butt-slaves'. Such critics used equally disapproving words of the King. He was a 'buggerer'. He was a 'sodomite'. He was a ridiculous lecher: Weldon alleges that, as James walked unsteadily about, his fingers were 'ever in that walk fiddling about his codpiece'. To Roger Coke, writing in the next generation, James's 'way of lolling his arms about his favourites' necks and kissing them' was 'loathsome'.

In 1599 King James wrote *Basilikon Doron*, a book in the form of a letter of advice to his heir, Prince Henry, on how to be a good king. In it James declared that 'sodomy' was an 'abomination', one of the 'horrible crimes that ye are bound in conscience never to forgive'. He was not being hypocritical. He was probably not – in his opinion anyway – a sodomite.

The great jurist Sir Edward Coke called sodomy 'a detestable and abominable sin … committed by carnal knowledge against the ordinance of the Creator and order of nature'. It had been decreed a felony in the reign of Henry VIII. A person convicted of it should be 'hanged by the neck until he be dead'.

But there was uncertainty about what exactly sodomy was. Coke tends to use the word interchangeably with 'buggery', but he also suggests it might be something a woman could do with a baboon, and whereby she could get pregnant. It might be something men did exclusively to children: there were only six prosecutions for sodomy recorded in England between 1559 and 1602 – all but one involved the rape of very young boys. If sodomy took place between adult men, it was narrowly defined. Before a man is to be found guilty of it, wrote Coke, 'there must be *penetratio*, that is, *res in re*'. Coke's Latin cloaks a phrase that, even when translated into English, recoils from the explicit. *Res in re* – 'thing in thing'.

James's favourites slept with him. That was unremarkable. A monarch was very seldom alone. When James was a baby, he had seventeen attendants who took it in turns to rock his cradle. As an adult, he had grooms and Gentlemen of the Bedchamber who passed the night around him – some in adjoining rooms, some in his own room; some on pallets, some, his favourites, in his own bed.

Those favourites knew the smell of his hair, of his breath on first waking. They knew the feel of his skin. They heard him snore and mutter in his sleep. If he had nightmares, they were there to reassure him. His body warmed theirs; their bodies warmed his. They helped him to dress and undress. They assisted him when he bathed (which was probably not often), and when he defecated. They saw him naked or in his nightshirt, his weak, spindly legs unsupported by boots and unconcealed by hose. They knew how often he went to bed drunk (very often). They knew how, sleeping, he dribbled into his pillow.

Probably in the night he reached for them and held them, and they allowed it. Perhaps they welcomed it. Perhaps sometimes he pressed up against them, his penis erect. Perhaps he asked them to touch that penis, and stroke it until he came. Perhaps he did the same for them. Perhaps he did more.

We cannot know. The question of whether or not the royal penis was ever actually inserted into an orifice in the bodies of any of these men, or vice versa – whether 'thing in thing' took place – has exercised scholars for four centuries, but it is beside the main point, that point being that James had intensely intimate relationships with these men, and some of them he loved.

James's sexual orientation had been a matter of concern for his subjects from his early puberty. A monarch without an heir, as the Elizabethan English were discovering during James's youth, meant an uncertain future for the state. In the *Letter to the Scottish People* that James wrote just before his marriage, he declared he was taking a wife for his country's good, while 'as to my own nature, God is my witness I could have abstained longer'. This lack of eagerness for heterosexual sex was all too obvious to those around him. The King, wrote a contemporary observer, 'never regards the company of any woman, not so much as in any dalliance'. He knew that his single state 'bred in the breast of many a great jealousy of my inability, as if I were a barren stock'. That 'jealousy' would not be dispelled for a worryingly long time. Queen Anne was only fourteen when they married, but that didn't prevent wishful rumours that she was with child from circulating within weeks of the wedding. They were illusory. It wasn't until nearly three years later that her first pregnancy was announced.

James was capable of the necessary act, but his enthusiasm for it remained questionable. Henry Wotton was to praise 'the chasteness of his life, which he has preserved without stain ... contrary to the example of almost all his ancestors, who disturbed their kingdom with the great number of bastards which they left'. John Oglander was to call James 'the chastest prince for women that ever was, for he would often swear that he had never known any other woman than his wife'.

Men, though, he knew.

Sodomy, wrote Edward Coke, was so 'detestable' and 'abominable' that it was 'amongst Christians not to be named'. Priests dared not speak of homosexual acts, even to condemn them. Sinners could not confess to them. People who aspired to virtue could barely allow themselves to think about them. The poet George Wither was twice imprisoned, in 1614 and again in 1621, for publishing satires in which he railed against 'great men's darlings', but even he, when it came to talking about those darlings and the nature of their transgressions, drew back. All he could say was that they were 'base fellows (whom I must confess, I cannot find words able to express)'.

The most outspoken of many clergymen who attacked James for his 'corrupt concupiscence' was Thomas Scott. In 1622 he published a pamphlet entitled *The Belgicke Pismire: Stinging the Slothfull Sleeper, and Awaking the Diligent to Fast, Watch, Pray*. It was judged so excoriating that Scott was obliged to flee abroad to escape imprisonment, or worse. But even he equivocates. He fulminates against eating, drinking and dancing, but then takes refuge in circumlocution as he moves on to sins that 'abuse our bodies worse than beasts'. These sins, he writes, echoing Coke, are 'not to be named'.

The courtier Thomas Howard edges nervously towards the topic of King James's penchant for young men, and then as quickly backs off, employing an image into which he seems to have diverted all the sexual anxiety he didn't dare express. He could, he writes, say more, 'but silence and discretion should be linked together like dog and bitch, for of them is engendered security'.

*   *   *

In 1615, the year in which George Villiers joined the King's bedchamber and spent that memorable night with him at Farnham Castle, a book called *Corona Regia* (The Royal Crown) was published clandestinely abroad, and began to circulate in London. It was purportedly written by Isaac Casaubon, the eminent classical scholar who had died the previous year.

One of the leading lights of Genevan Calvinism, Casaubon moved to England in 1610. He was taken up by Archbishop Abbot and by the Bishop of Ely, the celebrated preacher Lancelot Andrewes. King James was mightily impressed with him, frequently summoning him to court so that they could discuss theology in French or Latin or Greek (Casaubon spoke no English). Casaubon found these interruptions to his researches irksome, but the King was delighted with him, and rewarded him with a pension. 'I will have Mr Casaubon paid before me, my wife, and my bairns,' he declared. If *Corona Regia* was the late scholar's tribute to his royal patron – as it purported to be – then nothing but good could be expected from that pen.

It was, in fact, nothing of the sort. Described by Sir Henry Wotton as 'a filthy false libel', the book was a satirical parody of the panegyric it purported to be. It presents a cruel caricature of King James, throbbing with prurience and furious homophobic revulsion.

The King it describes is physically misshapen, 'all things curved, twisted and wretched', and his crooked body is the outward and visible sign of his moral deformity. He is ugly, crass and ridiculous. He slurps and staggers and drinks until he vomits. He hides his sins behind a 'saintly veil' of 'righteousness and integrity', but his embarrassing secrets 'still burst through the cracks, so to speak, into the public eye'.

Those secrets have to do with his 'perverse tendencies'. The anonymous author looks to the ancient world for antecedents. Like Dionysius, the tyrant of Syracuse, James surrounds himself with boys. He is as unmanly as the Emperor Hadrian, who loved the beautiful Antinous and wept for him after his death 'like a woman'. Like these ancient 'pederasts', James shamelessly 'feasts [his] eyes with drunken pleasure at banquets, inciting desire with immodest words, caressing cheeks, stealing a kiss'.

These displays of lust are followed by consummation behind the closed doors of the bedchamber. Those private acts are cloaked in language borrowed from James's other passion – for hunting. 'You use a different kind of spear, you search through a different kind of under-brush, and you capture different kinds of pleasure.'

The author names names: Philip Herbert; Robert Carr; and finally 'a young man of incomparable beauty, George Villiers'.

Favourite

THERE is no guarantee, in a hereditary monarchy, that the occupant of the throne will be capable of good government, or of any government at all.

He may be an idiot. The practice of marrying near relations – notoriously frequent in the case of the Habsburg monarchs of seventeenth-century Spain, but common in royal families throughout Europe well into the twentieth century – can lead to disabilities of the intellect as well as of the body. He may be a serial killer, as King Richard III was widely believed to be. He may be a woman: in the century before King James's accession England had twice suffered that calamity, and Elizabeth I's remarkably successful reign had not been enough to persuade all doubters that a female on the throne could perhaps be a good thing. He may be a baby, as James had been when he became King of Scotland, or at best a young child: Edward VI was nine years old when he succeeded to the throne of England in 1547, and so was Louis XIII, when he became King of France in 1610.

Whatever else she/he may be, the chances of the monarch being a prudent manager, practised in statecraft, well versed in economics and the law, an astute politician and a subtle-minded diplomat, a tactful negotiator with Parliament and a patient controller of the greedy and belligerently competitive nobles who crowded Renaissance courts were never high. And even when such a paragon was cast up on the throne by genealogical good luck, it was most unlikely that he/she would want to devote all their time to the hard, tedious work of actually ruling.

Early modern monarchs needed people to undertake the troublesome task of running the country for them. In England the Privy Council, the group of elder statesmen who shared control of the various departments of state, helped with that, and so did the swarm of lesser officials who served them, but every monarch wanted his or her own people as well – advisers, secretaries, fixers and spies. And most picked out one special person whom they could trust to serve their interests faithfully, in whom they could confide and to whom they could delegate most of their work and a large part of their power. Such a man (in seventeenth-century England it was always a male) owed his place, and therefore would give his loyalty, solely to the king.

That person was not promoted by right of exalted birth, or by democratic election. He was a favourite.

By the end of 1615, wrote Sir Edward Sherburne, Buckingham was 'the man by whom all things do and must pass'.

He was King James's beloved. He was also the King's gatekeeper and chief executive and confidant. A contemporary observer explains: 'No suit, no petition, no grant, no letter, but he must have a hand in it; so that great rewards are bestowed upon him by suitors, and large sums of money by His Majesty.' To become a king's favourite was to become fortune's favourite as well. Somerset had grown immensely rich. Buckingham was about to do so too.

A character in one of John Marston's plays rhapsodises about the astonishing luck of being so picked out. 'What a delicious heaven is it for a man to be in a prince's favour! ... To have a general timorous respect observe a man; a stateful silence in his presence; solitariness in his absence; a confused hum and busy murmur of obsequious suitors ... petitionary vassals licking the pavement with their slavish knees ... O blessed state! What a ravishing prospect doth the Olympus of favour yield.'

Delicious indeed to receive such deference. But the favourite had no security, no independent status, no claim to power and honour but the King's will. King James liked it that way. 'He ever desired', wrote Weldon, 'to prefer mean men in great places.' He liked to 'make' his favourites. He trained them. When he took up with Buckingham, according to Clarendon, he delighted 'in indoctrinating his young inexperienced favourite, who, he knew, would always be looked upon as the workmanship of his own hands'. Sir Henry Wotton concurs: 'The King resolved to make him a masterpiece, and to mould him, as it were platonically, to his own idea.'

It was a commonplace of courtly discourse that everyone of high standing owed their position, even their very existence, to the King. In an entertainment he staged for the King's pleasure in 1621, Buckingham, playing a fortune-teller, said,

> *But why do I presume, though true,*
> *To tell a fortune, Sir, to you,*
> *Who are the maker here of all,*
> *Where none do stand, or sit in view,*
> *But owe their fortunes unto you?*

For favourites that was literally true. Somerset chafed at being treated as the King's made object, his artefact, but Buckingham – more tactful or more realistic – accepted the role, and profited by it. In one of the most loving letters he ever wrote to the King, he addressed James as his creator, without whom he would have been as nothing. 'I heartily and humbly thank you,' he wrote, for 'all I have'. He is overflowing with gratitude to 'my purveyor, my good fellow, my physician, my maker, my friend, my father, my all'.

Teacher/creator/monarch, student/creature/favourite – the parts could be shuffled and the relationship reversed. There is more than one kind of 'favourite'. In English history-writing the word has traditionally been used of people who owe their position to the monarch's emotional and erotic interest in them, like the handsome young men around the homosexual kings Edward II and Richard II. Buckingham, in the first years of his public career, was a favourite of that kind.

In his lifetime, though, there was a general understanding that every ruler needed someone to rely on – what a twenty-first-century American president might call a 'chief of staff', or what a seventeenth-century Spaniard would call a '*valido*' – and that that someone would generally be a partner in a monarch's work rather than a love object, not a student but a mentor. James's predecessor, Queen Elizabeth, had had favourites of the first kind: Leicester, Essex. But she had also had William Cecil, who effectively governed England on her behalf for forty years. He, too, could be described as her 'favourite'.

During his career Buckingham would meet and tussle with two such favourites – formidable, hard-working, serious statesmen whose power matched their great ambitions: the Count-Duke of Olivares in Spain and Cardinal Richelieu in France. Each of them was guide and chief executive to a very young king.

Eventually, after King James had died, Buckingham would be called upon to become that second kind of favourite. To begin with, though, he was amanuensis to a king who was older and cleverer and vastly more experienced than himself. He was a political novice. He made no claims to special knowledge, and pretended to no authority. He knew he had much to learn.

His 'ascent was so quick, that it seemed rather a flight than a growth', wrote Clarendon. It was 'as if he had been born a favourite'. To Clarendon this meant that Buckingham so swiftly outranked his peers and contemporaries that 'he never made a noble and worthy friendship with a man so near his equal, that he would frankly advise him for his honour and true interest'.

That is not quite true. George Villiers, aged twenty-two, was no seasoned statesman: his only proven talents were for dancing and dressage. But, displaying the 'modesty' for which he was often praised, he had the good sense to ask for help, and the charm to get it.

He had lost his father when he was still a boy. He set about acquiring some new ones. The first was the Archbishop of Canterbury. Abbot tells us that after Villiers was dubbed knight on St George's Day, he sought out the Archbishop in the Privy Gallery, embraced him and thanked him profusely. He 'professed that he was so infinitely bound to me,' wrote Abbot, 'that all his life he would honour me as his father'.

George Abbot came from a poor-to-middling family (his father was a cloth-worker), but he was, all the same, born to greatness. According to an eighteenth-century source, his mother, when she was pregnant, had a dream in which it was revealed to her that if she ate a pike, her child would become a prominent man. Not long afterwards, she was fetching water from the river when – lo and behold – she found a pike in her bucket.

She cooked and ate it. The story of the auspicious pike was 'reported to some gentlemen in the neighbourhood', and so 'they offered to stand sponsors for the child, and afterwards showed him many marks of favour'. Young George went to the grammar school and then joined the church, within which, as Thomas Fuller records, 'he did first creep, then

run, then fly into preferment'. He probably hadn't needed a magic fish to propel him upwards. One of his brothers became the Master of Balliol and Bishop of Salisbury; the other rose to be Lord Mayor of London and Governor of the East India Company. The Abbots may not have had rich parents, but they were clever, ambitious, masterful men.

George Abbot was an uncompromising Protestant. His parents had embraced Calvinism early and had been persecuted for their faith under Queen Mary. He referred to the Catholic Church as 'the Beast', and to the Pope as 'the Whore'. As Vice Chancellor of Oxford University (one of his steps on the ladder of preferment) he was an iconoclast. He had religious pictures burnt in Oxford's marketplace. When he saw a student beating his breast while contemplating a stained-glass window showing the crucifixion, Abbot had the window destroyed. He was an authoritarian. He demanded respect. He once had 140 undergraduates arrested for failing to take their hats off to him. He was a pedant and an obsessive. For five years, he preached a sermon every Thursday morning on a text from the Book of Jonah, which has only four chapters.

King James respected him. From 1605 he was one of the dominant members of the team of forty-seven clerics working on the translation

of the Bible. He was not above flattery. In one pamphlet he compared
King James not only to King Solomon (which was conventional), but
also to David, Josiah, Constantine the Great, Moses, the prophet
Hezekiah and the Emperor Theodosius. In 1611 he became archbishop.

Such a man had little in common with young George Villiers, but he
had a use for him. As long as the King's beloved Somerset was under the
influence of the Howards, he thought, the King would not be interested
in making holy war on Roman Catholicism in general, or Spain in
particular. Abbot wanted such a war. He and his associates, the Herberts,
apparently failed to understand how deep King James's pacifism ran.
They imagined that a new favourite, sponsored by them, might be
enough to lure the King into the pro-war camp. And so this irascible
prelate took upon himself the character of Daddy Coax, writing to
young George Villiers, 'And now my George because, out of your kind
affection towards me, you style me your father, I will from this day
forward repute and esteem you for my son.' He signed off, 'Your very
loving father, G. Cant.'

Throughout his life Buckingham would be noted for his politeness in
dealing with his elders, and for his readiness to be taught. In the Privy
Gallery that day he asked for 'some lessons how he should carry himself'.
Abbot gave him three instructions. The first was piously formulaic – to
say his prayers daily, asking God to bless the King and to give to himself
the grace to serve the King well. The second was more particular – he
was to 'do all good offices' between the King on the one hand and the
Queen and Prince Charles on the other. (It was in the hope that he
would do so that the Queen had conspired with Abbot to bring him in.)
Thirdly he was to 'fill his master's ears with nothing but truth'.

This last was more complicated. How could anyone be so audacious
as to speak truth to power, when the power in question was a man, like
King James, who believed himself to be God's representative on earth?
Who would dare risk the King's displeasure by contradicting him, when
all possibility of promotion depended on the King's favour? And yet,
however impossible in practice, such truth-telling was respected. What
princes 'lack most of all', wrote Castiglione, and what they most need, is
'someone to tell them the truth and remind them of what is right'.
Buckingham was being advised to become a kind of Shakespearean fool,
one whose nearness to the King and special relationship with him gave

him the freedom to say what was, for almost anyone else in the kingdom, unsayable. It was a daunting responsibility.

The next surrogate father to whom Buckingham turned for advice was
one of the cleverest people in England, the scientist and philosopher
(the two disciplines were not, at this period, distinct), Attorney General
and soon-to-be Lord Chancellor, Sir Francis Bacon.

Bacon's brilliance was widely acknowledged. He was always scintillating, always throwing off sparks. John Aubrey tells us that whenever
he dined with his friend the Earl of Dorset, Dorset would have an
'amanuensis' present, ready to record Bacon's bon mots. Bacon had his
own amanuenses too. When he walked in his garden, meditating, he
liked to have a secretary walk with him, so that when 'a notion darted
into his mind', as notions frequently did, he could dictate a note on the

spot. He kept those note-takers busy. The best among them – the only one, in his opinion, who could fully understand what he was saying – was the young Thomas Hobbes, the future author of *Leviathan*.

Bacon was sickly from childhood, and morbidly fastidious. When he was living in the Inns of Court his friend, the poet Sir Fulke Greville, supplied him with ale from his own kitchen because the brew served in Gray's Inn was not to his liking. All the same, before he went to bed, Bacon would drink strong beer as a way of slowing down the whirling of his restlessly enquiring mind, which otherwise kept him awake. He was greatly admired but not so much liked. 'He had a delicate, lively eye,' writes John Aubrey. To his fellow scientist William Harvey, the great anatomist and discoverer of the circulation of the blood, 'it was like the eye of a viper'.

His passion was for a new way of looking at and understanding the world – by scientific observation and scrupulous experimentation. He was an empiricist before the word was coined, and the father of the English Enlightenment. The poet George Herbert was another of the brilliant young men he employed and patronised. Herbert, as devout as Bacon was sceptical and sophisticated, wrote an encomium to him, in which he describes Bacon as 'Truth's High Priest; Nature's intimate Prophet; Philosophy's Treasury; Pine of Profundity and Elegance; Liberator of Science; Stupendous Arbiter of Reason and Sense', and so on and so forth through twenty-seven lines of Latin.

This intellectual dynamo hardly seems a likely friend for the young man whom Clarendon was to describe as 'illiterate'. (Buckingham could read and write perfectly well: Clarendon meant only that he hadn't studied classical literature or the law.) But Bacon would have had a variety of motives for cultivating the King's new darling.

Bacon was harassed by debt throughout his life. His connections were excellent. His father, Sir Nicholas Bacon, had been Queen Elizabeth's Lord Keeper of the Great Seal. But Francis was the second son of his father's second marriage, not his heir, and obliged to earn his own fortune. He always spent more than he could afford to – John Aubrey writes that when he was at Gorhambury, his house near St Albans, it 'seemed as if the court were there, so nobly did he live'. And Gorhambury wasn't enough for him: he wrote that as a gentleman should have different dwelling places for summer and winter, just as he had different clothes, and so he built Verulam House, only two miles from Gorhambury. He could drive from one to the other along three parallel roads wide enough for seven coaches to travel abreast and shaded by avenues of oak. A list of his household servants in 1618 reveals there were over a hundred of them. To maintain such an establishment, he needed far more money than he ever had.

The Earl of Salisbury, Secretary of State until 1612, was his cousin. But Bacon believed that Salisbury, jealous of his talents, obstructed rather than furthered his rise. He was admired as a brilliant advocate, but he wanted much more than that. He wanted one of the high offices of state, and years went by while he waited for such an appointment. In the meantime he cultivated those who might help him. When Somerset became the King's beloved, Bacon hastened to get close to him, describing himself as the favourite's 'creature and most intimate friend'. When Buckingham eclipsed Somerset, Bacon was prompt in switching horses.

Buckingham wrote to him, asking for guidance.

Bacon begins his reply by protesting that he is hardly ever at court, and really doesn't have much to say on the subject. He then goes on to give the lie to this by laying out, lucidly and in detail, how Buckingham should play his new role.

He defines the function of a favourite, which he describes as an 'office'. It is not just a personal relationship with the King. It is a job.

'It is no new thing for kings and princes to have their privadoes, their favourites, their friends,' he tells Villiers, 'for kings have their affections as well as private men.'

The favourite had the King's ear. Give the favourite something – not a paltry little present but a brooch set with large diamonds, a team of horses, a manor house with land attached, a painting by Titian, a marble statue unearthed from the Roman Forum – and he could give you something worth much more. Those offering these gifts wanted paid jobs or sinecures for themselves and their sons and their nephews and protégés, and they wanted high-born and/or rich husbands for their daughters. They wanted titles. They wanted land grants and lucrative monopolies. The King was worn out by what his son was to call the 'unnecessary pestering' of such demanding subjects. It was the favourite's task to receive requests, to filter out the undeserving and identify those who could really do the state some service. It was the favourite who transmitted royal favour on down the chain. The favourite could make or break a fortune, and so he was inundated, writes Weldon, with flattery and 'bounty'.

Now it was Buckingham's turn to become the recipient of that bounty. 'The whole kingdom hath cast their eye upon you, as the new rising star,' Francis Bacon told him, 'and no man thinks his business can prosper at court, unless he hath you for his good angel.' The favourite's job was time-consuming and arduous. It required tact and adroit management. It was immensely profitable. It brought adulation. It also attracted extreme hostility.

The nobility, who had grown up with the conviction that they – and they alone – were born to rule, greatly disliked seeing a favourite rise above them. From the very beginning of James's reign. they had been outraged at the way the King had devalued their status by distributing or selling titles too freely to his followers. Buckingham's advent distressed them further. 'Men of noble birth', explains Bacon, 'are noted to be envious towards new men when they rise. For the distance is altered, and it is like a deceit of the eye, that when others come on, they think themselves go back.'

Buckingham's sudden promotion disrupted the social hierarchy. Girolamo Lando, the Venetian ambassador, thought that the Jacobean noblemen couldn't 'endure that one born a simple gentleman ... should be the sole access to the court, the sole means of favour'. He reports that 'as a recreation', King James wrote some verses praising his new beloved and read them at a public banquet. 'This caused more comment than if he had done some great wrong to his kingdom.'

The nobility felt threatened by the King's favourites for reasons to do with the politics of class. Parliament deplored them for more mercenary reasons.

James loved to play the munificent father figure to his retinue of young men. He gave them land and titles, and paid off their exorbitant gambling debts. Forty thousand pounds slipped through his fingers this way in one year alone.

His generosity to the people of his immediate entourage, almost all of them Scottish, infuriated his new English subjects. Racism mingled with disapproval of the King's suspected homosexuality to make Parliamentary criticism of his extravagance venomous. In 1610 an MP complained that 'the King spent all upon his favourites and wanton courtiers'. In 1611 another asked what was the point of raising money by taxation, to fill the barrel of the King's wealth, 'if it shall daily run out thence by private cocks'. (The word 'cock' meant a kind of tap. It was also, then as now, a word for penis: the ambiguity was fully intended.) In 1614, the year King James first met George Villiers, a Parliament-man lamented that the 'great personages' at the King's court – the favourites – were 'their master's spaniels, but their country's wolves'.

Francis Bacon saw this kind of hostility as an inevitable consequence of a king's longing for a beloved partner – a friend. 'For princes, in regard of the distance of their fortune from that of their subjects and servants, cannot gather this fruit [friendship] except … they raise some persons to be, as it were, companions and almost equals to themselves.' To do so, warned Bacon, 'many times sorteth to inconvenience'. In allowing Somerset to imagine himself almost equal to the King, James had angered his subjects and made himself miserable. A favourite's position was always precarious. Buckingham should beware.

William Shakespeare was still alive when Villiers was knighted on St George's Day (he died on the same date a year later). He had probably been thinking of the Elizabethan Earl of Essex when he wrote his 25th sonnet, but its sentiments could as well have been applied to Somerset's rise and fall, or they could be read as a warning to Somerset's successor.

> Great princes' favourites their fair leaves spread
> But as the marigold at the sun's eye,
> And in themselves their pride lies buried,
> For at a frown they in their glory die.

Elizabeth's Essex beheaded, James's Somerset in the Tower – Buckingham didn't need to look very far to find sad stories of the fall of favourites. No wonder he felt in need of guidance.

Bedchamber

On St George's Day, 1615, after he had been knighted in the Queen's apartments, Archbishop Abbot tells us that the newly dubbed Sir George Villiers 'went in with the King'.

'Went in' where? Surely to the court's inner sanctum, a space from which nearly everybody (even the head of the Church of England) was excluded. Villiers had just been pronounced a Gentleman of the Bedchamber. It was to the Bedchamber that he would have followed King James.

The royal court was a complex organism in a constant state of flux and metamorphosis. Each succeeding monarch restructured it to suit his or her needs. It was made up of human beings, but it was conditioned by architecture.

Under the early Stuarts the labyrinthine sprawl of Whitehall Palace contained it. Bigger than the Vatican, bigger than any other palace in Europe until it was overtaken by Versailles, Whitehall had grown over seven centuries into a higgledy-piggledy complex of courtyards and colonnades and gardens and galleries and detached houses and inter-connected apartments and guardrooms and kitchens and sculleries and hidden passageways and privy chambers and banqueting halls and a chapel. It covered twenty-three acres and contained, according to one seventeenth-century source, a thousand rooms; according to another, two thousand. Hundreds of people lived in it. Thousands more strolled in and out of its public and semi-public spaces. It was designed for pleasure, and for business of the highest seriousness. It contained a tilt-yard and tennis courts. It was the location for masques and plays and weddings and ceremonial processions. It also contained the Council Chamber. From it the country was governed. It burnt down in 1698. Its only surviving part is Inigo Jones's Banqueting House, built in 1622, when Buckingham's career was at its zenith.

But the court had an existence independent of the palace that housed it. The court could be loaded onto carts and traipse around the country during the monarch's summer progress. It could be evacuated to Winchester or Oxford or Hampton Court in times of plague. It was immense and chaotic, but, looked at another way, it was very small and tightly contained. Fewer than twenty people had regular access to King James's privy lodgings. An awkward controversy over precedence arose when two noblemen found it impossible to squeeze past each other in one of the narrow, lightless corridors hidden behind the panelling of the Royal Bedchamber and neither would demean himself by stepping back to allow the other to pass.

The court was formal, its procedures rigidly codified. It was also as mutable as water. Under succeeding monarchs, new departments were added and others closed down. Its nucleus migrated. But however the relative importance of each compartment shifted, the court was always a set of spaces within other spaces, rooms within rooms, circles within concentric circles, boxes within boxes, dwindling in size but increasing in significance towards the centre.

The heart of it, under the first two Stuarts, was what King Charles I was to call the 'secret chamber', the little closet to which he withdrew, accompanied only by the Groom of the Stool, to defecate into the close-stool that was that official's special responsibility. The man who attended the King as he shat governed the Bedchamber (which was both a set of rooms and a group of people). Under King James, it seemed to many people that the Bedchamber governed the country. To be part of it, as Buckingham now was, was to be a made man.

'The courtier will never attempt to make his way into the private quarters of his master uninvited, even though he possesses considerable authority himself,' wrote Castiglione, 'for often when princes are by themselves, they enjoy the liberty of saying and doing just what they please, so they do not want to be seen or overheard by anyone in a position to criticise, and this is quite proper.'

That was certainly King James's way. He had grown up in a remote castle; he was not easy in a populous court. He preferred a small, tightly controlled household in which he could live secluded with a coterie of favoured and trusted men. When he first arrived in England they were nearly all Scottish, people whom he had known for years, and who, in the most literal sense, spoke his language. Many English contemporaries complain of how hard it was to understand the way the newcomers from the north spoke – the Scots thought the same of the English. What a relief for James, after hours of struggling to communicate with his new subjects, to be surrounded, when out of the public eye, by those with whom he could easily converse.

As years went by, more Englishmen became part of the King's intimate circle. To the Councillors who frequently found it hard to approach their royal master, this inner circle was to be envied and suspected.

In Buckingham's lifetime almost anyone 'of quality' might enter the outer courts and galleries of Whitehall Palace. Only 'ragged boys and unseemly persons' were to be turned away at the gate. The King's apartments, though, were harder of access. Those who sought entry had first to pass through the Guard Chamber, satisfying the keepers that they were desirable visitors. Next they would find themselves in the Presence Chamber. Here the King received official visitors and appeared on ceremonial occasions before his more distinguished subjects. The chamber was very large. Access to it was comparatively easy for those who had the right connections, and looked the part. Here, according to a Venetian ambassador, the nobles entered 'in confusion'.

Beyond lay the far more exclusive Privy Chamber. It was in the Privy Chamber that the King dined, and that George Villiers, when newly come to court, waited upon him as one of his cup-bearers. To enter it was a privilege. An invitation was required. For all but a few, the Privy Chamber would be the site of the closest encounter a person could ever hope to have with the King.

They could not approach too closely. It was forbidden to stand under the canopy (the cloth of state) that hung above his head, or to set foot upon his carpet. Only the cup-bearers and other waiters might approach within arm's length of his chair. A fortunate visitor might be summoned to stand within earshot and engage him in conversation. But those naive enough to imagine that, having penetrated so far, they had arrived at the seat of power were mistaken. After he had dined, and on occasion lingered to watch his young attendants leaping, the King 'went in'.

Beyond the Privy Chamber, and at a right angle to it, ran the Privy Gallery. Opening off it to the north was the Council Chamber. Members of the Privy Council had therefore the right, *ex officio*, to promenade in the Gallery. So did judges and bishops. It was there that George Villiers found Archbishop Abbot and thanked him for his wonderful promotion. In the Privy Gallery one was walking with some of the most important people in Jacobean England, very close to the hub of monarchical power. But not quite there yet.

To the south of the Gallery another door led to the Withdrawing Room, to which the King might invite someone – one of his great officers of state or an ambassador – with whom he wished to speak without too many watching eyes on them. Leading off the Withdrawing Room was the Lesser Withdrawing Room. Then came several 'closets' (small enclosed spaces which might be used for more private conversations, or for writing, or as cloakrooms, or for secret assignations), and at the end of this warren of rooms and concealed corridors and alcoves and annexes designed expressly for the withdrawal of the King from the public's gaze, at the very heart of the labyrinth, one arrived at a door kept locked, a door whose three golden keys, hung on a blue ribbon, were in the keeping of the Groom of the Stool. 'Princes of the blood' had the right of entry there, but no one else could pass through that door without the King's special invitation, which was not lightly given. Except, that is, for those Grooms and Gentlemen who served there. It was the door to the Bedchamber.

From now on, George Villiers would have the extraordinary privilege to pass frequently through that door, to go 'in with the King'.

Loving Buckingham

IN 1617, three years after they first met, King James became aware that it was being murmured that he was in thrall to his favourite. Some even said he had been bewitched. He didn't care. He felt himself uplifted by his love.

He decided to make things clear. Addressing his Privy Council, he told them, 'I, James, am neither a god nor an angel, but a man like any other. Therefore I act like a man, and confess to loving those dear to me more than other men. You may be sure that I love the Earl of Buckingham more than anyone else.'

He had begun by saying he was not a god, but he concluded by comparing himself to one: 'Jesus Christ did the same, and therefore I cannot be blamed. Christ had his John, and I have my George.'

James expressed that love by repeatedly promoting his 'dear one'. Here are the titles and offices that were the rungs of the ladder George Villiers scaled, lifted ever higher and higher by the doting King's favour.

APRIL 1615: SIR GEORGE VILLIERS, GENTLEMAN OF THE BEDCHAMBER

JANUARY 1616: MASTER OF THE HORSE

This office, along with Lord Chamberlain and Lord Steward, was not a governmental position, but one of the three highest at court. Somerset had wanted, but never achieved, it. As the Groom of the Stool was the King's constant attendant when he was in his own chambers, so the Master of the Horse was always with him when he was out and about. It was a title with ancient and glamorous antecedents: Mark Antony had been Julius Caesar's Master of the Horse. In the century preceding Buckingham's tenure it had been conferred on those to whom the monarch was especially close. Queen Elizabeth I's favourites, Leicester and Essex, had each held it.

APRIL 1616: KNIGHT OF THE GARTER

The Garter Knights were people of great individual distinction – Privy Councillors, military and naval commanders, high officers of the court. Associated both with the warrior-saint, George the dragon-killer, and with the orders of chivalry, the title had an aura of mingled sanctity and romance. Like an Arthurian Round Table knight, the Knights of the Garter (even though they were most of them, in reality, desk-bound middle-aged or elderly men) were touched by the dream of the stainless, venturous knight-errant, *sans peur et sans reproche*. It was to celebrate his induction into the Order that Buckingham posed for his portrait by William Larkin (Plate 1).

AUGUST 1616: BARON WHADDON AND VISCOUNT VILLIERS

These titles came accompanied by the property that would give substance to young Villiers's new status as a member of the land-owning aristocracy. He was given the Buckinghamshire estate of Lord Grey, who had died in the Tower. King James also offered him Sherborne, its lands, its castle and its fine new house, which had belonged to Sir Walter Raleigh and then to Somerset. Buckingham declined, 'praying the King that the building of his fortunes may not be founded upon the ruins of another'. He didn't want to follow too closely in Somerset's footprints. Instead the King assembled a portfolio for him of former royal properties from around the country, worth around £30,000.

SEPTEMBER 1616: LORD LIEUTENANT OF BUCKINGHAMSHIRE

JANUARY 1617: EARL OF BUCKINGHAM

The granting of this new title was celebrated by the court on what a contemporary observer sarcastically called 'a day of oblation and sacrifice', a quasi-religious ceremony in which 'the Viscount Villiers was adored with the title of the Earl of Buckingham'. Buckingham's rapid rise was engendering envy.

FEBRUARY 1617: PRIVY COUNCILLOR – ENGLAND

His admission onto the Privy Council, the committee of worldly-wise and immensely powerful elders who governed the country under the King's direction, normalised and ratified Buckingham's position in the state. Formerly a matter of private personal influence, exercised through his unparalleled closeness to the King, from now on it was official and overt.

That year a courtier wrote to tell a friend living abroad that no one in Whitehall 'can obtain grace except they vow and beseech at the shrine of the great one'.

MAY 1617: PRIVY COUNCILLOR – SCOTLAND

When King James revisited Scotland for the only time, Buckingham was with him. James appointed him to the Scottish Privy Council. When the King passed in procession through Edinburgh to open the Scottish Parliament, Buckingham rode with him, the only English peer so honoured.

JANUARY 1618: MARQUIS OF BUCKINGHAM

On first arriving in England, James had created forty-three new earls. Now he wanted to set Buckingham above this numerous throng. The French-derived title marked Buckingham as exceptional. John Chamberlain called it 'the greatest novelty'. Buckingham now stood at the pinnacle of the aristocracy.

1619: LORD HIGH ADMIRAL

One of the highest offices in the land. In an island kingdom with no standing army, to be commander of the fleet was to be the supreme commander of the nation's defence forces.

By this time Buckingham also held a number of lesser posts, including those of Justice in Eyre of the King's Forests beyond the River Trent, Keeper of Hampton Court, Clerk of the King's Bench. Each office brought with it privileges and perks, and opportunities to dispense favour in exchange for further large sums of money.

1623: DUKE OF BUCKINGHAM

Sir John Oglander wrote that Buckingham was 'the greatest subject that England ever had'. His new title confirmed that position. There were no other dukes in England outside of the royal family. From now on, if he performed in a masque, he would dance as an equal alongside the Prince of Wales. Only the King himself took precedence over him.

King James gave his Steenie honours and rank and power and immense riches. He also gave him love. He sent him a miniature of himself holding his heart in his hand, as though offering it to his beloved.

In a letter Buckingham wrote to him thanking him for his dukedom, he thanks the King as well for having given him 'more care than servants have of their masters, than physicians have of their patients', and for having repeatedly made expression 'of more tenderness than fathers have of children, of more friendship than between equals'. The letters that passed between the two of them are full of pleasure in the memories they share, and of yearning for their next meeting. Their relationship was doubly unequal. How could it not be, with one so much more powerful, the other so much more attractive? And yet they managed to find an equilibrium which kept their bond stable.

Courtiers confidently awaited Buckingham's fall. Powerful factions plotted it. In 1618 the Howard family picked out a promising young man, William Monson. They 'took great pains in tricking and pranking him up'. The Countess of Suffolk helping by 'washing his face every day with posset-curd'. James was having none of it. Monson's persistence irritated him. Several more would-be successors to Buckingham curled their hair and acquired new clothes and came hopefully to court, but year after year went by, and still King James doted exclusively on his dog Steenie.

1616. Viscount Fenton reports that 'His Majesty loves' Buckingham 'beyond measure'. Edward Sherburne confirms that Buckingham 'far exceeds the former [Somerset] in favour and affection'.

1617. George Gerrard writes, 'The King was never more careful, or did more tenderly love any that he hath raised than this Lord of Buckingham.'

The Venetian ambassador finds that Buckingham has almost regal authority. He can act for the King, who 'has given him all his heart, who will not eat, sup or remain an hour without him and considers him his whole joy'.

Arthur Wilson notes that by 1617 Buckingham reigned 'sole monarch in the King's affection … the King is not well without him, his company is his solace'.

1618. As Buckingham is created marquis, John Chamberlain tells Dudley Carleton that the King has given him the title 'for the affection he bare him, more than ever he did to any man'.

1619. A visitor from Italy attends the Twelfth Night masque at court. An antimasque featuring Bacchus and Silenus (both acting drunk) and a chorus of little boys dressed as frogs provides some knockabout fun. Actors playing personified virtues or Olympian gods declaim about the conflict between philosophy and sensual pleasure. Musicians sing 'some trills' and play the guitar.

The visitor is getting impatient, and so is King James, who suddenly shouts out, 'Why don't they dance? What did they make me come here for? Devil take you all, dance!'

It is embarrassing. What is required is a *deus ex machina*, like the divinities who come creaking down from Inigo Jones's painted heavens on swaying painted clouds, and who have the magical power to avert disaster and restore order. Fortunately there is just such a person to hand.

> The Marquis of Buckingham, His Majesty's favourite, immediately sprang forward, cutting a score of lofty and very minute capers, with so much grace and agility that he not only appeased the ire of his angry lord, but rendered himself the admiration and delight of everybody.

Simonds D'Ewes records that as Buckingham joined the dancing, the King cried, 'Begot [By God] George, I love thee dearly.'

1619. King James sends Buckingham to greet a newly arrived French envoy. The letter he carries assures the envoy that 'short of sending his heart', the King 'could not send him more than Buckingham'.

1622. Another of D'Ewes's diary entries: 'I was informed that the King hearing the Marquis was not well, went to visit him.' Buckingham had toothache. The barber was there ready to pull the tooth. (Barbers also served as dentists.) The King became frantic. He could not bear that his beloved was to be subjected to such a painful operation, one which would leave his perfect appearance marred. He ransacked the chamber, searching for the man's tools. 'Finding them, he threw them all away and swore that he would hang the barber, who hid himself under Sir George Goring's cloak.' James then appealed to Buckingham. '"Why man," quoth the King, "what doest thou mean to do, to spoil and kill thy self, and begot (swearing Scottishly) I shall not joy one good day after."'

Another occasion, also recorded by D'Ewes. The King, 'hugging him one time very seriously, he burst forth, "Begot man, never one loved another more than I do thee, and let God leave me when I leave thee."'

How had Buckingham won such love? His beauty can only partially account for it. He had charm as well – that elusive quality that has the precious power to make those who encounter it feel happier.

Castiglione writes that a courtier should (or at least should appear to) 'devote all his thought and strength to loving and almost worshipping the prince he serves'. He needs 'the discretion to discern what pleases his prince, and the wit and judgement to know how to act accordingly', so that 'whenever his prince sees him he believes that the courtier will have something agreeable to say'. He must be 'modest and reserved,' displaying always, 'and especially in public, the reverence and respect which should mark the attitude of a servant towards his master'.

All of these precepts Buckingham obeyed. As their intimacy increased, he teased James, but only privately, and always tenderly. He never lost sight of his position in relation to his master. To some he seemed a figure of vast, overweening magnificence, but better-informed observers praised the 'affection, faith and modesty' with which he treated the King. Over and over again he signed off his letters 'Your Majesty's humble slave and dog'. His doglike 'fidelity' to King James, thought Clarendon, was one of his best traits.

*   *   *

James was learned by any standards, and prodigiously so for a reigning monarch. By the time he was eight, he could swiftly and fluently translate a chapter of the Bible from Latin into French and then into English. As an adult he corresponded with scholars from across Europe. When he travelled to Denmark to collect his wife, he made use of his wedding tour to visit the great astronomer Tycho Brahe. On a visit to Oxford in 1605 he told his hosts that were he not a king, 'I would be a university man'.

Arrived in England, he promptly called a conference at Hampton Court to discuss dissension within the Church of England. Opening its proceedings, he thanked God for setting him 'among grave, learned and reverend men'. It was at that conference that the great project of retranslating the Bible into English was initiated – far and away the most ambitious and influential literary endeavour ever to have been sponsored by a British monarch.

He wrote and published essays on subjects ranging from witchcraft, through the horrid new habit of tobacco-smoking, to the nature of kingship. His political treatises were densely packed with classical references and philosophical argument. The poetry he wrote was sometimes playful, but his recreational reading was serious. His Bishop of Rochester, William Barlow, described him as a 'universal scholar, acute in arguing, subtle in distinguishing, logical in discussing'. Bishop Williams said that he was the 'most powerful speaker that ever swayed the sceptre of this kingdom'.

He didn't expect the young men he loved to be his intellectual equals, but he liked to teach, coaxing them gently towards greater understanding. In 1619 he made Buckingham what he considered the richest of gifts, dedicating to him his own commentary on the Lord's Prayer. It was, he wrote kindly, nice and short compared with most of his treatises. He hoped the younger man would not find it too difficult.

Most importantly, he was teaching him the art of government. Sir Henry Wotton thought that King James 'hardened and polished' Buckingham in 'the school of observance … and in the furnace of trial about himself (for he was a king could peruse men as well as books).' He was shaping the young man into a fit instrument for his use. 'I daily take care to better your understanding,' he told him, 'to enable you the more for my service in worldly affairs.' Buckingham, thought Francis Bacon, had in James 'the best tutor in Europe'.

Love and pedagogy. The eroticism of discipleship. The relationship between an older man with the wisdom of maturity and a young one whose mind is unformed but whose body is perfect. Now, in the twenty-first century, taboos surround that relationship, taboos that go back to the beginning of the Christian era. The Fathers of the Church warned anxiously against pederasty. But in the wake of the Renaissance, rediscovered classical texts permeated and shaped the ideas of all educated Europeans in Buckingham's lifetime – often in ways that tugged against Christian teaching – and in antiquity an erotic relationship between an older teacher and a young male student was idealised.

John Hacket referred to Buckingham as 'our English Alcibiades'. So did at least a dozen other seventeenth-century commentators. Alcibiades was the wayward aristocratic glamour boy of fifth-century BCE Athens. Rich and privileged, a charismatic commander and subsequently a traitor, he was as controversial as Buckingham was to be two millennia later. He is remembered now chiefly for his scandalous appearance in Plato's *Symposium*, accompanied by flute players and dancing girls, drunk and dazzling, wearing an ivy wreath aslant his brow like an avatar of Dionysus, or the personification of carnal love. Like Buckingham, he was famed for his beauty, but what made him seem to seventeenth-century commentators so especially like Buckingham was that he was Socrates's student and that Socrates loved him.

The two of them served together in the Athenian army, the stocky, pug-nosed, middle-aged philosopher – so the story goes – saving the exquisite young man's life in battle at great risk to his own. They shared a tent. The Romans had a word for that: '*contubernium*'. The word might refer simply to a group of soldiers who messed together. It could be erotically suggestive, describing the kind of sexual intimacy fighting men might enjoy with female camp followers, or with each other. It could also be used of a young man accompanying a general as his aide and apprentice. Comradeship, sex and the teacher–student connection overlap. In Greek and Roman culture such a relationship was an honourable one – with no guilt or shame attached – one from which a younger man could benefit.

Of all the ancient authors whose works shaped the mindset of Buckingham's contemporaries, Cicero was seen as the wisest and most authoritative. *De amicitia* was among his most influential works. First published in English by Caxton, it was retranslated in 1550 by Sir John Harington as *The Book of Friendship*. In it Cicero hymned male friendship in almost mystical terms. 'He that beholdeth his friend, doeth as it were behold a certain pattern of himself.' True friends merge – becoming one soul in two bodies. 'In friendship the absent be present, the needy never lack, the sick think themselves whole, and that which is hardest to be spoken, the dead never die.' 'Amor' and 'amity' spring from the same etymological root. For readers in Buckingham's lifetime love and friendship were not clearly differentiated, and they were expressed with equal fervour.

In 1617 a young man, James Howell, whom Buckingham would meet in Madrid six years later, wrote to his friend Richard Altham. He begins by thanking Altham for his letter full of 'such exquisite strains and raptures of love', and assures him 'that not a dram, nor a dose, nor a scruple of this precious Love of yours is lost, but is safely treasured up in my breast'. Their love is reciprocal. 'Mine to you is as cordial. It is passionate and perfect as Love can be.'

In modern colloquial English 'lover' nearly always means sexual partner. To say you are close to someone 'as a friend' means that you are not having sex with that person. Erotic love and friendly affection are kept apart. For the ancient philosophers, and for the Renaissance thinkers whose understanding of love derived from theirs, there was no such rigid distinction.

In 1613, a year before George Villiers came to court, John Florio published the second volume of his translations into English of Montaigne's *Essays*. In 'De l'amitié' Montaigne writes of his love for his friend Étienne de La Boétie. He considers Plato's description of love between older men and youths, like that between Socrates and Alcibiades. Montaigne objects that such relationships are flawed by 'a disparity of ages, and difference of offices between lovers'. To him, therefore, they are inferior to true friendship, rather as relationships between men and women are (because women, being dependent, can never be men's equals). But Montaigne believes there is hope for pairs like Buckingham and King James. That which begins with physical attraction can mature into something stronger and better. Sex can be the bait – delicious but ephemeral – that will land the big fish of friendship.

Friendship may include eroticism, but it is richer and deeper and stronger than erotic love. It is not tepid or circumspect. It is passionate and absolute. Thomas Churchyard describes it in his treatise *A Sparke of Friendship* (1588). Friendship is a mystery and a miracle. No one can 'tell from whence comes the privy and inward affection, that suddenly breeds in the breast, and is conveyed to the heart, with such a content and gladness, that the whole power of man leaps in the bowels of the body for joy at that instant'. Montaigne, writing about de La Boétie, concurs: 'If you press me to say why I loved him, I can say no more than because he was he, and I was I.'

This is love – joyful, overwhelming – the kind of love that ambushes at first sight. The kind of love to which King James succumbed when he first laid eyes on George Villiers. It might express itself through some form of sexual intercourse, or it might not – that doesn't much matter.

The not-mattering is alien to the twenty-first-century mind. We are accustomed to the question of who-does-what-to-whom-in-bed being one that defines relationships and shapes identities. In Buckingham's lifetime that wasn't necessarily so.

Peace

KING James 'could not endure a soldier or to see men drilled', wrote Sir John Oglander. 'To hear of war was death to him.'

Surrounded by violence from his earliest childhood, James grew up with a horror of it. He had learnt to mollify his enemies, to be circumspect and patient, to achieve his ends, not by bluster and severity, but by persuasion. In Scotland, as an adult king, he didn't punish his bullies and abusers; rather he absorbed them into his administration.

Vengeance didn't interest him. Nor did the concept of honour that glorified it. In 1614, when he first met George Villiers, he was in the midst of a campaign against duelling. That one man would kill another in response to a verbal insult seemed to him absurd and barbaric. He saw himself as an arbitrator. 'Those people were blest', he wrote, 'where a philosopher rules and where the ruler plays the philosopher.' He was pleased to be likened to Solomon, the wise judge-king whose name means 'Peaceful'. For him the purpose of wisdom was the settling of disputes by non-violent means. He told his Parliament, 'It is an unchristian thing to seek that by blood which may be had by peace.' The Venetian ambassador to London wrote, 'His Majesty is by nature placid, averse from cruelty … He loves quiet and repose, has no inclination to war, nay is opposed to it.'

His motto was *Beati Pacifici* – 'Blessed are the Peacemakers'. He called himself *Rex Pacificus*, 'the King of Peace'. When, in the masque *News from the New World*, Ben Jonson wanted to pull together veneration for a living monarch with a vision of sublime harmony, he imagined a race of beings who live beyond the moon, whose sole occupation is meditating, enraptured, on the greatness and virtue of King James. The dances gave material form to these extraterrestrial monarchists' consciousness – the intricate 'motions' whereby the courtiers in their spangled silken costumes traced serenely symmetrical patterns on the dance floor being 'formed to the music of your peace'.

When James arrived in England, peace talks between England and Spain were already in train. When the Earl of Essex, who had represented the belligerently anti-Spanish party in Elizabeth's time, had risen up in 1601, hoping to sweep the country back into war, he had lost the Queen's favour, and he had lost his head, leaving Salisbury the unchallenged leader of the government.

Pragmatic, clear-eyed, unimpressed by the romances of chivalry and patriotism, Salisbury opened secret negotiations with the Spanish. By the time King James acceded in 1603, the two nations were approaching an agreement. James was more than happy to allow them to proceed.

When he rode into London to claim his new crown, Thomas Dekker wrote that the Genius of the City welcomed him, saying,

> ... *soft-handed Peace so sweetly thrives,*
> *That bees in soldiers' helmets build their hives.*

To James, war was a waste of money and a waste of life. It was an absurdly inefficient way of resolving international disputes. It offended him financially, morally and intellectually.

His pacifism was not absolute. He told his first English Parliament that 'a secure and honourable war must be preferred to an unsecure and dishonourable peace,' and he was afraid that Europe's peace would always be 'unsecure' until the European powers joined together to form a defensive alliance against the Ottoman sultans of Constantinople. Sectarian strife between Christians seemed to him self-destructive and futile: a defensive war, though, to fend off an attack from Muslim 'infidels', he could sanction.

In 1589, before he became King of England, he had proposed the formation of a 'Christian League', to bring about 'the common peace of Christendom' and for defence against 'the Turk'. His plan was to begin by seeking alliances between Scotland, Denmark (hence his choice of a Danish princess as a wife) and the German Protestant states within the Holy Roman Empire. Ultimately, he hoped, his league would embrace the Catholic powers of France and Spain as well. James was not alone among his contemporaries in entertaining such a dream. In France the Duke of Sully, adviser to Henri IV, cherished an even more ambitious 'grand dessein' to put together 'a European Christendom of fifteen states, a Most Christian Republic, permanently at peace with itself'.

For decades James held to his vision of a European Union. When John Digby, the future Earl of Bristol, was going to Spain as England's ambassador in 1617, James instructed him to press for an alliance to enable 'a tribunal ... to decide the controversies, which may arise amongst the princes and estates of Christendom, without effusion of Christian blood'. So the 'common peace of Christendom' might be assured.

James's strategy was to bring all Europe together in shared loyalty to his family. He would marry his daughter Elizabeth to a Protestant prince. He would marry his heir to a daughter of one of the great Catholic powers – France or Spain. In this way he would become the father, not only of his own people, but of all Europe. His grandchildren would be the living emblems of a new golden age. All Christendom would stand as one, sectarian differences forgotten in familial bliss.

The King loved peace, but at the core of his palace lay a tiltyard, a place where war games were played.

A courtier, wrote Castiglione, must be proficient in 'all the physical exercises befitting a warrior'. He must be able to handle spirited horses, to tilt and joust, and be ready to 'handle expertly every kind of weapon'. A century later, in 1605, Miguel de Cervantes's great literary demolition of the code of chivalry by means of comedy and pathos, *The Ingenious Gentleman Don Quixote of La Mancha*, was published in Spain. An English translation of the first part appeared in 1612. To the most sophisticated minds of the Jacobean period, the cult of knightliness was an outmoded fantasy, a bit of a joke. But tournaments and jousts still provided a large part of the ceremonial of the court.

In the early years of James's reign, the parfit knight who shone at the centre of them was the heir to the throne.

Prince Henry was very much his mother's child. While James devoted his energies to uniting all Christendom, the French ambassador reported that Queen Anne 'says aloud, she hopes her son will one day overrun France as well as his ancestor Henry V'. While James deplored division and sought to create a net of diplomatic connections and dynastic marriages which would unite Europe, his wife and eldest son fostered a militant separatism.

In 1610 Prince Henry, not yet quite sixteen, commissioned and performed in a hybrid entertainment, 'Prince Henry's Barriers', a kind of tournament on foot in which masque and mock battle were combined. The themes were Arthurian. The Lady of the Lake appeared and conversed with the spirit of King Arthur. Merlin rose up from his tomb and joined the Lady in lamenting the decay of chivalry, but hoping that under the House of Stuart it might be revived.

Prince Henry, glittering in gold-chased armour, stepped forth ready to prove his prowess. Assisted by half a dozen other young noblemen, he took on fifty-eight challengers with pike and sword. The fighting lasted from ten o'clock at night until the following morning. A spectator records that 'the Prince performed … with wondrous skill and courage, to the great joy and admiration of all beholders'.

There was one beholder, though, who was less joyous – the Prince's father. When Henry wanted to stage a similar show the following year,

ILLUSTRISSIMI GENEROSISSIMIQUE PRI. HENRICI
MAGNÆ BRITANNIÆ ET HYBERNIÆ PRINCIPIS,
Vera Effigies.

King James forbade it. He was concerned for his son and heir's safety –
in Barriers, as in a tournament, real injuries were sustained. And
perhaps as well he recoiled from the entertainment's theme. The Rex
Pacificus had no wish to raise a son whose reputation rested on his willingness to fight all comers.

James was an intellectual; Henry thought study was for priests, not for
princes. James took part unwillingly in ceremonies and shows; Henry
loved to dress up as a Roman emperor or a fairy prince, and to show
himself in tournaments and masques. James had no mistresses; Henry
was pursued by all the ambitious young women at court, to several of
whom he gave generous presents, presumably in recognition of services
rendered. James was interested in religious differences, and non-parti-
san about them – he liked to have divines of all denominations about
him, Puritan or High Church alike, and to argue fiercely with them.
Henry was inflexibly Calvinist: he employed no Catholics, but had
twenty-four chaplains, who preached at him in rotation. James had a
rough tongue, and liked to shock; Henry, once he had his own court in
St James's Palace, imposed a high level of decorum on his followers,
fining them for swearing. James had little interest in colonies; Henry
supported the Virginia Company, and gave his name to a new-founded
American town, Henrico. He admired and protected Sir Walter Raleigh,
who dedicated his *History of the World* to him. James worked throughout his life for the unification of Christendom and the end of sectarian
conflict; Henry was an outspoken advocate for making holy war on
Spain.

It was said that the King was jealous of his handsome son. There was
a time when the two of them, each separately out hunting, met on
Newmarket Heath. Prince Henry had numerous aristocratic companions with him; James only a few, 'and those mean persons'. When Henry
and his troop moved off, King James's fool, the dwarf Archy Armstrong,
began to mock him because his following was so comparatively small.
Archy's taunts reduced the King to tears. He got over it, and scolded
Archy, but the jester had touched a raw spot.

It wasn't that James envied his son's grander entourage – that was his
for the asking if he wanted it. More importantly, Henry's lack of sympathy with his political aims was a looming anxiety. Henry's admirers
called upon him to fight. 'Up then, brave Prince,' wrote one, 'the eyes of

all Christendom are now cast upon you, to see you begin.' Another prayed that he might 'live to march over the Alps and to trail a pike before the walls of Rome, under Your Highness's standard'.

The King had cause to fear his own child. Would Henry, succeeding him, undo all that he himself had worked for? Would the web of political alliances and dynastic marriages with which he hoped to bind Christendom together survive his death? Would Henry render his life's work futile by going to war? The answer is that, yes, if he had lived long enough, very probably he would have done.

It was to scotch the King's peaceful aims that George Villiers had first been introduced to him. To the Protestant interest (led by the Earls of Pembroke and Montgomery and their cousin Lucy Bedford, and Archbishop Abbot) a willingness to live amicably alongside the earthly supporters of the Catholic Church was craven. Surely, once the King's heart had been won by a beautiful youth whom they imagined they could manipulate at will, James could be persuaded that his preference for peaceful coexistence with the Antichrist (the Pope) and his myrmidons (the armies of Catholic Spain) was a shame and a sin.

So they reasoned, but the King's detestation of war ran deep, and Buckingham's loyalty to his sponsors was shallow. The Queen was right. Once he had been helped to his place at court, he forgot his helpers. Far from being the pretty puppet they had supposed him to be, he had his own opinions and his own allegiances. His loyalty was to no one but the King – his maker, his master, his dear old Dad.

Horses

NOTHING, wrote the author of a seventeenth-century manual of horsemanship, could be more admirable than the art of equitation. 'Does any earthly thing breed more wonder?'

It was when he rode in a tournament that Somerset had first caught King James's eye. It was when he was mounted for the hunt at Apethorpe that George Villiers had made an equally indelible impression on the King.

When Buckingham became Master of the Horse in January 1616, he acquired not only an august title but also a job. It was one for which he was well equipped. The earliest description of him that we have is from a friend who saw him in 1612, before his great ascent began, at a day's horse racing near Newmarket. He was wearing what was then his one and only suit – black, 'broken out in divers places'. He hadn't found, or couldn't afford, a room at the inn, so he spent that night on a 'trundle bed' (the kind a servant might sleep on) in the corner of another man's room.

The story is told for its piquancy in the light of what was to come. Imagine that great Buckingham was once poor and shabby! It carries as well another message: Buckingham cared enough about horses to put up with discomfort to watch them race.

As Master of the Horse, he was responsible for all the King's horses and coaches, and the management of the royal stables. He had a staff of two hundred people. He had a suite of twenty rooms in Whitehall Palace. (No more dossing down in the corner of someone else's chamber.) He could take for himself any horse the King no longer needed (and he was the sole judge of that need). He had a salary, augmented by a 'diet' of sixteen 'courses', which meant he could have himself and his friends fed at the King's expense when he was at court, or he could sell the privilege, thus greatly increasing his income.

He was a part of the royal household rather than of the national government, but the nature of his position, and the enthusiasm he brought to it, meant that his work had an effect felt far beyond the court.

Plough horses, carthorses, saddle horses, coach horses, warhorses, post-horses, racehorses, hunters and hacks – in seventeenth-century England horses were omnipresent. To be Master of the Horse was to be the minister for transport, for military procurement and for energy. It also brought involvement in agriculture, in trade (the only haulage was horse-powered), in arts and entertainment (races, tournaments, jousts) and in the food supply. Hunting on horseback was recreation, but it also provided those who could afford it with meat. Horses were essential to every aspect of the nation's economy.

The breeding of horses was a publicly beneficial practice. For those of a certain class it was compulsory. All owners of parks were required to keep a prescribed number of brood mares, all to be at least thirteen hands tall. The nobility and clergy had to keep stallions as well – one for a gentleman whose wife wore a silk gown or a velvet bonnet, seven for a duke. Those stallions might each service scores of mares. The loan of a stallion was offered as a generous favour. In households great or small, the birth of a promising foal was an occasion to be celebrated.

As Buckingham assumed his new role, there was work to be done. English horses were not highly regarded. It was no coincidence that ambitious young men like the Villiers brothers went abroad to learn how to ride well. Intent on improving the nation's bloodstock, Buckingham dispatched agents to Spain and Italy to buy. He asked the Spanish ambassador to send him four Spanish mares and four Barbary (Arab) mares from which he could breed. The three 'foundation stallions' from which – by Jockey Club rules – all modern racehorses must be descended if they are to be designated 'thoroughbred' were brought to England in the eighteenth century. They were comparative latecomers. Over a hundred years before their arrival, in December 1616, for the extravagant sum of £154, Buckingham imported an Arab stallion for the royal stud.

The results were excellent. King James followed the breeding programme with excited approval. When Buckingham was away in

Spain, in 1623, James wrote to him with the best of the recent news: 'Your bay Spanish mare with the black mane and tail hath an exceeding fair and fine horse-foal of ten days old.' The King rejoiced. He thanked God and the Master of the Horse for providing him with 'such a number of fair, useful' animals. 'I profess I never was master of such horses.'

To be on horseback was to be virile, glamorous and commanding. Titian's great portrait of Charles V at the battle of Mühlberg, painted in 1548, shows the Holy Roman Emperor calmly in control of a black charger that seems about to break into a gallop. Encased in gleaming gold-chased armour, he peers, thoughtful but undaunted, into the distance.

Charles V was a sedentary man who was severely lamed by gout. At Mühlberg he was actually carried about the battlefield on a stretcher, but Titian ignored that fact. To be a victor, a hero, a man needed a horse between his knees. So, in the year King James came to the throne of

England, Peter Paul Rubens painted the Spanish king's favourite, the Duke of Lerma, riding a white horse towards the viewer as though he was about to trot out through the surface of the painting.

Buckingham was to see both paintings in Madrid in 1623 and, inspired by them, in 1625 he would commission Rubens to paint a portrait of himself in a similarly heroic pose. Buckingham had yet to ride into battle, but, humouring him, Rubens portrayed him in full armour as though ready for combat, seated atop a glossy bay horse.

The painting was destroyed in a fire in 1949, but a sketch for it survives (left). The pose Rubens chose is the 'levade', one of the hardest moves in the art of the *manège*. It requires the horse to squat on its haunches, sustaining its whole weight, and its rider's, on its back legs. In Rubens's painting, an angel with a trumpet flies above the figures, as though proclaiming a victory. The horse's mane and tail flutter; eyes glitter; nostrils flare. Buckingham, composed and triumphant, looks out at us. The horse's raised front hooves flail at the allegorised foes (a naked woman and a Triton), who cower in awe, overwhelmed by the splendour of Buckingham astride.

The Arts of Peace

WHEN Balthazar Gerbier and Buckingham first met, the latter was in bed, lolling on pink silk cushions. It was 1616. They were both twenty-four years old. Buckingham was receiving suitors in his chambers in Whitehall Palace. Gerbier had recently arrived in London in the entourage of the Dutch ambassador and he was looking for a patron.

Gerbier had plenty to offer. He was enthusiastic and bumptious. Born in Holland to French Huguenot parents, he spoke several languages, English included. He had lived in Gascony, Bordeaux, Antwerp. He knew how to find his feet and fit in. Obliged to be self-reliant since his father, a cloth merchant, had died a bankrupt when he was six years old, he could do all sorts of things. He was a calligrapher and illuminator at a time when official documents were artworks, written and decorated exquisitely by hand. He had already been employed in that capacity by Prince Maurice, the Stadtholder of Nassau, but he was not only a 'penman'. By his own account, he also excelled 'not a little in the mathematics, as geometry, architecture, fortifications, and in the framing of warlike engines'. He was an accomplished horseman. He had a flair for 'contriving scenes, masques, shows, and entertainments for great princes'.

He was to make good on all of these boasts. In cataloguing his many talents he didn't even mention those for which he was to become best known. He is remembered as an architect, as a portrait painter and, above all, as the creator and curator of a great collection – Buckingham's.

By the time he met Buckingham, only weeks after first setting foot in London, Gerbier had already drawn a portrait of the sixteen-year-old Charles, Prince of Wales. He was an adventurer, a hustler, a dealer, a fixer, a go-between, someone whose nose for a bargain and whose eye for the main chance were both exceptionally keen. He could make his way into the most exclusive circles, whether invited or not. He could talk great aristocrats into selling things they hadn't intended to sell. He could flatter and cajole and defer. When he glimpsed an opportunity, he could be very swift to pounce. He was a diplomat – discreet and subtle – who made himself most useful in covert negotiations when his role was not officially acknowledged. He could keep secrets.

With all this, there was a kind of innocence about Gerbier. His portraits show him more lively than forceful. Wily and acquisitive, he yet ended up owning almost nothing. For all his gifts, he failed to impress. Bustling and resourceful, in the late 1620s he came close to brokering a peace deal that might have saved all Europe from the horror of the Thirty Years War. He failed largely because he didn't have the social status or the perceived gravitas to persuade those in power to take him seriously.

Towards the end of his life he would write that the 'many secrets I had gathered from divers rare persons' made him useful, and 'pleasing

to Great Ones'. Others whose careers ran parallel with him – Endymion Porter, his fellow courtier in Buckingham's household, or Peter Paul Rubens, his fellow artist and collaborator in covert diplomacy – became Great Ones themselves. Gerbier was only ever the servant of greatness. He was 'Buckingham's man'.

At that first meeting in his bedchamber, Buckingham was amused by Gerbier, but he didn't immediately trust him. There were workmen about, busy remodelling the new Master of the Horse's quarters. Buckingham told Gerbier to look behind a bolster. There Gerbier found a package containing 500 livres. Buckingham asked him to pay the workmen with it. It was a test, and Gerbier knew it. Instead of doing as he was told, which would have been irregular, he gave the package to Buckingham's steward, instructing the man to lock it up until the builders presented their bills. Buckingham was pleased. He laughed. He took Gerbier into his household.

Gerbier was the favourite's favourite, the secretary to whom Buckingham entrusted the correspondence, often in cipher, by which he maintained contact with his agents abroad. He became one of those agents. He travelled. He tells us that Buckingham and King James used him for 'secret messages'. Between his first meeting with Buckingham and the latter's death twelve years later, Gerbier was seen in the Netherlands, in Italy, in France, in the princely states of Germany, in Spain. He was gathering intelligence, assessing the mood of England's potential enemies and allies. He was also keeping an eye out for opportunities to buy artworks.

Picture-hunting was sometimes a cover for more politically delicate activity. As Gerbier was to write, wherever he travelled, 'malicious ignorant persons' would speculate about what his secret mission might be. It was useful to be able to point to the politically innocuous business of acquiring art for his patron. But buying beautiful things was also his real passion. Well informed, quick on the uptake, as knowledgeable about old masters as he was about the coming painters, he was outstandingly good at it.

Buckingham was interested in art too. In the twelve years of his ascendancy, he sat for his portrait dozens of times. He was happy to provide the funds for the collection Gerbier aspired to build for him.

In 1619 Gerbier was in Flanders, on a covert diplomatic mission whose details his memoirs don't reveal. (In his letters he overflows with puppyish ebullience, but he knew when to hold his tongue, or his pen.) While in Hainault, he got wind of a rumour that the Duke of Aerschot was in financial difficulties. Gerbier knew that Aerschot owned nine large canvases by Veronese. He made the Duke an offer. He bought the paintings for Buckingham. In recognition of Gerbier's coup, Buckingham appointed him 'keeper of my pictures and other rarities'.

That purchase was to be the beginning of one of the three great English collections of the era, the other two being those of King Charles I and of the Earl and Countess of Arundel.

Thomas Howard, the Earl of Arundel, was described by Peter Paul Rubens as 'one of the evangelists of our art'.

Arundel was everything that Buckingham was not. Buckingham was an upstart; Arundel was not only a leading member of the aristocracy, he was also to become Earl Marshal, which made him the official representative of that caste and the custodian of its honour.

Buckingham was the cynosure of all eyes, displaying his exquisite body bejewelled and upholstered in satin and brocade. Arundel's appearance was sombre – as a young man he was censured for making insufficient effort to deck himself out for Prince Henry's Barriers, for which courtiers were expected to make themselves 'rich and dainty'. He always dressed for preference in black.

Buckingham loved horses and dancing, and couldn't find the time for much book-reading. Arundel was scholarly. His close friends included the historian William Camden and Sir Robert Cotton, the antiquarian to whom we owe the preservation of the sole surviving manuscripts of *Beowulf* and *Sir Gawain and the Green Knight*. Buckingham was known for his 'overflowing courtesy ... prone to gratify all strangers'. Arundel, writes Clarendon, 'was a man who lived always within himself'.

The Howards were possessors of many estates and holders of multiple titles, but under Queen Elizabeth they had suffered for their staunch Catholicism. Arundel would have been the Duke of Norfolk, England's premier peer, but that his grandfather, the 4th Duke, had conspired to free Mary, Queen of Scots, to marry her and to drive Elizabeth off the throne of England. The plot was discovered. The Duke was imprisoned in the Tower, and then beheaded.

His son, Arundel's father, had fared no better. Another devout Catholic, he was suspected of treacherously conspiring with Spain. He passed ten years in the Tower and died there in 1595, to be subsequently canonised by the Pope for his heroic refusal to convert to Protestantism. Arundel, born after he was imprisoned, never met him. Small wonder, with such antecedents, that he grew up reserved and gloomy.

Arundel was nineteen when Queen Elizabeth died. His childhood had been shadowed by his grandfather's and father's disgrace and he had lived – by Howard standards – a life of scrimping obscurity and loneliness. The accession of King James changed that. Two of Arundel's Howard uncles – the Earls of Northampton and Suffolk – became great men at the Jacobean court. With their assistance he set about reclaiming his forebears' estates and titles. In 1605 he married an heiress, Alethea Talbot, daughter of the Earl of Shrewsbury and granddaughter of Bess of Hardwick. Her inheritance made him as rich as he felt he always ought to have been.

She was also to become his active partner in the prime project of his life, the accumulating of a great collection. Historians have tended to ignore her contribution, but it was mostly her money that paid for the wonderful things the Arundels came to own. She was said to have a 'mania' for travel. She was also a true connoisseur. The portrait Rubens painted of her in 1621 shows her magnificently dressed and enthroned, accompanied by a tiny dwarf and an enormous dog, while Sir Dudley Carleton, the art-dealing ambassador to the Netherlands, stands behind her chair. This was a woman respected and deferred to in a man's world.

With the war against Spain concluded at last, the English could explore continental Europe in a way that had been impossible for decades. English boys like George Villiers and his brother could go to France to finish their education. English art lovers could go to Italy and feast their eyes on the buildings of Ancient Rome, of mediaeval Venice or Renaissance Florence (although that city was not yet a favourite among them). They could acquaint themselves with splendid architecture and take home ideas for the embellishment of the stately homes of England. With the help of the *ciceroni* and scholars and fixers who fluttered eagerly around them, scenting money, they could shop for artworks, ancient and modern.

The Arundels were among the most avid buyers. In 1612 Arundel went to Antwerp, where he met Rubens and posed for a portrait, then travelled south to Italy. News of Prince Henry's death sent him homeward, but early in 1613, he and his wife, taking Inigo Jones with them, set out on a comprehensive nineteen-month tour of Italy. They were serious and ascetic. Arundel and Jones would post ahead to look for lodgings, once sleeping in a 'vile *ostaria*', where Arundel reported there was 'one mattress, one blanket, no bolster or anything else'. They were learning by looking, and buying as they went. By the time of Arundel's death they owned 700 pictures.

Arundel was, for a while, the supreme art collector in England. He would be matched and subsequently outdone by Charles I, but before Prince Charles began to buy, Arundel's great rival for the role of the English Maecenas was someone whose position at court was deeply offensive to his conservative sensibilities – that nobody from nowhere, Buckingham.

Instead of sending armies abroad, King James sent diplomats. There had been ambassadors before. There were foreign ambassadors at Henry VIII's court, like those in Holbein's magnificent portrait of two Frenchmen. In Elizabeth's reign, there were English ambassadors scattered across Europe, but in James's reign diplomacy acquired a new status.

He established permanent embassies where there had been none before, or where they had been abandoned when Henry VIII severed links with Rome, condemning England to seven decades of insularity and isolation. James invited fellow monarchs to send envoys to his court. In the twenty years of his reign he received more than 250 delegations from over thirty different states.

People joked about it. James Howell, who served in the British embassy in Madrid, reports a quip that was going around in the early 1620s, when the Elector Palatine was in need of help: 'The Danes send 100,000 red herrings, the Dutch 100,000 cheeses, and the English 100,000 ambassadors.' A joke, but speaking seriously as he looked back over his long life four decades later, the same James Howell wrote, 'If it were not for ambassadors, wars would be endless and enmities everlasting.'

*   *   *

Clever, cultured, independent-minded men filled the new ambassadorial posts. Ambassadors ran spies and fostered trade. They entertained distinguished English visitors, and kept a sharp eye, through their networks of secret agents, on those of them who might be suspected of conspiring with foreign enemies – Jesuits in particular. In an age when communications were so slow that an ambassador could never be certain whether the sovereign he represented was dead or alive, they made policy. Living abroad, often for decades, they used their time to become historians and connoisseurs.

Several of these ambassadors were to become associates of Buckingham's. Outliers from the English establishment by the nature of their employment, they seem to have been congenial to him. They were also useful – useful in their official capacity as informants about foreign affairs, equally useful in helping him buy art.

Three in particular were to become his friends and protégés. One of them, Sir Henry Wotton, would be the first person to write his biography.

A generation older than Buckingham, Wotton was a poet, a scientist, an authority on classical architecture and a linguist so proficient that he once lived for three months in Scotland under the assumed persona of an Italian without his true nationality being detected.

He was a cosmopolitan, convivial man with a witty turn of phrase, whose company was treasured. At Oxford his friends included John Donne, who celebrated their friendship in verse, and the jurist Alberico Gentili, then beginning his pioneering work on international law. As a traveller in his twenties, Wotton studied at Altdorf in southern Germany, lodged with the great classicist and theologian Isaac Casaubon in Geneva, and was made welcome in several of the Italian courts. The Earl of Essex employed him as a news-gatherer – a set of eyes and ears sharp and quick enough to pass back trustworthy information from across Europe.

He first came to King James's notice when the latter was still in Scotland. The Grand Duke of Tuscany had uncovered a conspiracy against James's life. He chose Wotton (then living in Florence) to travel to Edinburgh to warn James and – just in case the warning came too late – to present him with an antidote to poison. Wotton pleased the King so well that when he became King of England the following year, James

offered him the choice of the two most important embassies in Europe – Paris or Madrid.

Wotton declined both. As a younger son he could not afford such prominent postings. (Ambassadors were expected to entertain in grand style at their own expense.) Besides, the work would be onerous. More than power and prestige, Wotton wanted a pleasant life. In one of his most famous poems he writes of the happiness of one 'that serveth not another's will'. A less politically vexed, less expensive embassy would suit him better, one where 'another's will', the authority of King James, would be less bothersome. He chose Venice, and lived there, on and off, for the next twenty years. He kept open house for distinguished travellers from England, and made himself into the first great English *cognoscente* of Italian Renaissance art.

He rented a palazzo in the out-of-the-way district of Cannaregio. He decorated it with arrases and gilded leather wall hangings, and filled it with paintings and armour, and furniture hired from the Jewish dealers who had their businesses in the neighbourhood (the Ghetto was nearby). He also had a villa at Noventa, along the Brenta canal, where he drank wine from his own vineyards and cultivated his garden. He sent the King melon seeds (melons were highly prized) and cuttings from his rose bushes. To the great plant collector John Tradescant he sent fennel – a vegetable unknown in England – with instructions on how to cook it.

Unmarried, he filled his household with young Englishmen – nephews, students, sons of old friends. With them, he read philosophy, carried out experiments in chemistry and made music: he played the viol da gamba. He kept a pet ape, which once got him into trouble with his neighbours by biting a child. In winter he would go out on the lagoon in his gondola, warmly wrapped in furs, to shoot duck 'on the wing', a sport then unknown in England. As the representative of a Protestant nation, he played no visible part in the ceremonies of the church, but he liked to attend them incognito. He went frequently to hear the singing in the nearby church of San Girolamo, and one Christmas he climbed into the organ loft in St Mark's for the best view of the celebrations.

Wotton is credited with having initiated the fashion for English collectors to buy Italian paintings, and particularly those of the Venetian school. He himself collected Palladio's drawings and wrote a treatise on architecture. He employed an artist as his picture-finder (as Buckingham employed Gerbier), sending the man travelling around the country hunting for works that could be bought. Without Wotton, Buckingham's collection could not have been as magnificent as it was to become.

Between 1604 and 1624 he was the English ambassador in Venice, then in The Hague, and then in Venice again. Back in England, he became provost of Eton and accepted a commission to write a history of England. He never got down to it. He was too busy fishing with his new friend Izaak Walton (author of *The Compleat Angler*) and generally enjoying himself, something he had always been good at doing. He did find time, though, to write two kindly word portraits of Buckingham, who had been his patron and friend.

Thomas Roe, with whose help Buckingham was to obtain quantities of classical statuary, was a more adventurous traveller. Like Wotton, he was sociable. He called himself a 'very merry man' and was described as one 'who goeth among the company of the wits'. John Donne and Ben Jonson were among the friends of his youth. On King James's accession, he joined the household of Prince Henry. In 1610 he was the commander of an expedition to Guiana, sponsored by Walter Raleigh from his prison in the Tower. Roe established two settlements near the mouth of the Amazon, and then travelled on, venturing three hundred miles upriver, searching for El Dorado.

He was subsequently a soldier and a member of Parliament, but then gave up both callings to become the first English ambassador to India, sent by the East India Company in 1615 to the court of the Mogul Emperor Jahangir. He got on well with the Emperor, who received him with 'a free and noble jollity' – perhaps induced by the beer-drinking to which Roe had introduced him – and he succeeded in securing permission for the establishment of an East India Company factory in Surat.

He would travel with Jahangir when he went on a progress. Each night the court would be housed in a camp that extended for six miles – hundreds of elephants, thousands of horses, silken tents in gorgeous clashing colours as far as the eye could see.

Returning to Whitehall, which must have seemed rather drab by comparison, Roe presented the Emperor's gifts to King James. John Chamberlain records that they included 'two antelopes, a strange and beautiful kind of red deer, a rich tent, rare carpets, certain umbrellas and suchlike trinkets from the Great Mogul'. After another spell in Parliament, Roe moved to his next posting, in Constantinople. There Buckingham would bombard him with requests for beautiful ancient things.

The person to whom John Chamberlain addressed that letter about Jahangir's gifts, and most of the rest of the several hundred newsletters he wrote, designed to keep an expatriate up to date on doings in the metropolis, was the third ambassador who was to play a notable part in Buckingham's life and picture-collecting – Sir Dudley Carleton. Carleton followed Henry Wotton as ambassador in both Venice and The Hague, before returning to England to join the Privy Council. If Wotton was the cosmopolitan connoisseur and Roe was the adventurer, Carleton was the dedicated politician and devout Calvinist who cared – deeply and seriously – about international politics and about the religious differences that shadowed the era.

Wotton adored Venice. Carleton, for almost exactly the same reasons, was bored and frustrated there. It was too strange, too Catholic, too far from home. The Hague was much more to his liking. It was also, as Buckingham was to find to his advantage, handy for Antwerp, home of Peter Paul Rubens, who was almost as prodigiously busy and successful as an undercover diplomat and art dealer as he was as a painter.

Buckingham, Gerbier, Rubens, Carleton, Wotton – all together or separately, they would frequently meet again. After Buckingham's death, Rubens would visit London for the first time, and view Buckingham's collection, which contained over forty of his own paintings, and conclude that it was the finest in Europe.

Work

WHEN King James dedicated his commentary on the Lord's Prayer to Buckingham, he apologised for giving his favourite little leisure for reading. He knew Buckingham was busy day and night with 'your continual attendance upon my service, your daily employments in the same' and that he was plagued by 'the uncessant swarm of suitors importunately hanging upon you without discretion'. Buckingham's detractors imagined him as a pampered pet living a life of luxurious indolence. In fact, as the King his master acknowledged, he was working like a dog.

Francis Bacon, in his letter of instruction, had written that the more accurate title for the role he had been called upon to perform was not 'favourite' but the one the Romans used: '*participes curarum*' (sharer of cares). Buckingham was King James's secretary, his stand-in, his deputy and special adviser and chief of staff. His task, said James, was 'keeping my back unbroken with business'. He shared the King's cares. He did most of his work.

When in London, King James barely dared go out. Wilson writes that 'those formalities of state, which set a lustre upon princes in their people's eyes, were but so many burthens to him'. It wasn't just that he was impatient of ceremony and bored by the speeches and tableaux and triumphal arches with which his people tried to please him. Always fearful of assassination, he was scared by the crowds who jostled around him when he showed himself in public. Wilson writes that when visiting the Tower, 'he took pleasure in baiting lions, but when he came abroad, he was so troubled with swarms that he feared to be baited by the people'.

The English were known for gawping at royalty. A generation after Buckingham came to court they would turn out to see a king killed – the most sensational royal spectacle imaginable – but in his lifetime their curiosity still looked, most of the time, like love. Nicolò Molin, who, in his role as Venetian ambassador to England, represented a thousand-year-old republic, was bemused to observe how they 'adore their sovereigns, and if the King passed through the same street a hundred times a day the people would still run to see him'. James, sceptical of that fickle adoration, kept to his palaces. Even there he was pestered and harassed. Courtiers – forever seeking to ingratiate themselves or to beg for advancement – were as bothersome as *hoi polloi*. 'The throng at court … evermore swarmed about His Majesty at every back gate and privy door, to his great offence.'

To get away from them, James left town, frequently and for long periods. For many months of every year he would be in Theobalds, the magnificent prodigy house in Hertfordshire that Salisbury had given him (to be rewarded with Hatfield in exchange), or at his hunting lodge in Newmarket. Or he would go to the one at Royston, which was no more than a couple of converted village houses knocked together, and was so lacking in basic comforts that the Queen refused to visit it, and where he lived so modestly that visitors were shocked.

While he secluded himself, the business of government went on. Someone had to watch over it on his behalf. Someone had to keep him informed of every political shift, of every argument in the Privy Council, of every ambassador's report, of every worrisome public expense. Someone he could trust, the sharer in his cares.

The Count of Gondomar, the Spanish ambassador who was to play a prominent role in Buckingham's story, reports that the King 'shows him everything and gives him account of everything, desiring to keep him informed and make him capable of handling negotiations; and so the Marquis gives him all the letters he receives and the King gives him the minutes of the replies he has to make'. The two of them worked as closely together as a rider with his horse, a swordsman with his weapon. In 1618 Lord Fenton wrote that King James 'imparts to no one but the Marquis of Buckingham'.

Buckingham learnt fast. Bishop Goodman testifies that 'truly his intellectuals were very great; he had a sound judgement and was of a quick apprehension'.

He needed to be quick. Francis Bacon, briefing him for his job, explains that, as the favourite, he will be the conduit through which the

King gets his information. He must filter that information, sifting out malicious gossip and false rumour. He must be 'a continual sentinel, always to stand upon your watch, to give him true intelligence'.

Everyone will be trying to communicate with the elusive King, and the only way to do so will be by way of Buckingham. Everyone will be wanting something from him, offering him inducements of which he should be wary. He must learn to distinguish between true friends and 'sycophants, the bane of all courts. They are flies who will not only buzz about in every ear, but will blow and corrupt every plate where they light.' Everyone will be flattering and cajoling him. Some will be scheming to bring him down. People will be waylaying him in the street and trying to take him aside in palace corridors. Even in his chamber, he will be pestered by those asking for support for their business plans or overseas adventures. They will make his time 'a purgatory'.

His workload will be immense. Bacon gives some excellent advice as to how he is to manage it:

1. Buckingham will be inundated with 'suits'. To limit the pestering, instruct all petitioners to put their requests in writing and tell them when they can expect an answer. 'So shall you be eased of the suitor in the meantime, and he rest quiet till the day appointed.'
2. Seventeenth-century business letters tended to be prolix. Bacon himself, on becoming – with Buckingham's help – Lord Keeper of the Privy Seal, wrote to thank him, saying, 'You are the truest and perfectest mirror and example of firm and generous friendship that ever was in court. And I shall count every day lost wherein I shall not either study your well doing in thought, or do your name honour in speech,' and so on and so forth for several paragraphs. Bacon knew convention required one to write such guff. He also knew what a waste of time reading it could be. So he advises Buckingham to employ a secretary to wade through the compliments, clichés and circumlocutions and underline the 'matter, which always lies in a narrow room'. Set apart an hour or so each day for reading the underlined passages. Respond immediately to straightforward requests.

3. Some petitions will raise complex questions. Choose expert advisers, two or three to cover each area. Send them copies of petitions, asking for guidance within twenty days. Set apart an hour or two each week to reread the petitions, with your advisers' various responses. You will soon be able to 'return answers to petitions of all natures as an oracle'.
4. If you are going to say no, say it firmly, and at once. Remember that 'a reasonable and a fair denial' is acceptable, while delay and indecisiveness breed resentment.

Buckingham won't be dealing with trivia. Bacon lists eight topics he will have to consider. His role is primarily that of handing out jobs – of patronage. He needs to know how to judge a man's capacity, his motives and allegiances, his loyalty and his good sense. (It would be a man – no woman was ever considered for an official post.)

I. RELIGION AND CHURCH-MEN, OR CHURCH-MATTERS

This was a time when Christendom was riven by doctrinal disputes that escalated with terrifying ease into persecution, torture and warfare. Church matters were politically inflammatory.

II. THE LAWS AND THE PROFESSORS THEREOF

The right kind of judges, says Bacon, will not only resolve legal disputes. They can also report on the mood in the country, which, travelling the land on their circuits, they know far better than anyone in Whitehall. Bacon advises that judges must be chosen 'only with an eye upon the public good', for their deep knowledge of the law, their prudence and discretion.

The advice is unimpeachable but, read with hindsight, it carries a tang of irony. Both Bacon and Buckingham would eventually face impeachment. Bacon, a judge, was to be accused of accepting bribes; Buckingham of selling offices and of nepotism.

III. THE PRIVY COUNCIL AND MATTERS OF STATE

Matters of state 'are *secreta & arcana*' not to be talked about. 'I dare not take upon me to say much,' writes Bacon, who had become a Councillor, thanks to Buckingham's intercession with the King, in June 1616. As usual, though, he does in fact say plenty.

The Council should never be 'sudden'. They should deliberate, reflect and then deliberate again before arriving at a decision. The King should not attend their meetings too often, lest he 'overawe' the Councillors. He should be 'attentive' to their advice (which is not to say that he must follow it).

Buckingham became a Privy Councillor in February 1617, when he was twenty-four. When matters of state were debated by the highest in the land, he was in the room. Whatever was said there he could report back to King James.

IV. NEGOTIATION WITH FOREIGN PRINCES OR STATES

Again, Bacon's advice dwells on the wise appointments of ambassadors. There is a use for rich young noblemen, whose social status fits them to represent the monarchy, but they must be partnered with 'persons of great judgement and known experience'.

As we have seen, Buckingham would come to know and value some such persons.

V. WAR BY SEA OR LAND

The King loves peace, writes Bacon, but 'the best way to continue a secure peace, is to be prepared for a war'. 'Let arms and ammunition of all sorts be provided and stored up, as against a day of battle; let the ports and forts be fitted so, as if by the next wind we might hear of an alarum.' As Lord Admiral, Buckingham would attempt to act on this advice.

VI. FOREIGN PLANTATIONS AND COLONIES

This was a topic of great interest to Bacon, who had had a part in establishing the colonies in Virginia, Newfoundland and the Carolinas, but not to King James. The beginnings of British colonialism can be seen in retrospect to be one of the most significant developments of the era, but it was driven by private enterprise, not by royal policy. Buckingham would have little to do with it.

VII. MATTER OF TRADE

Trade, wrote Bacon, was not his profession, but of course he had thought about it.

Some of his advice is uncontroversial. Exports must exceed imports. Remember that navigable rivers are essential for the circulation of goods. Agriculture must be supported. So must fishing, which is to this island-nation a mine of 'Indian wealth'. Establish a separate council to oversee trade.

Bacon's most emphatically made point, though, is that luxury is deplorable and deleterious to the economy, in that it often involves spending British money on goods from overseas. The rich must be discouraged from importing 'apes and peacocks' and foreign wines. 'If we would needs be drunk ... we might be drunk [on British ale] with half the cost.'

Excessively expensive clothes were especially ridiculous. 'If we must be vain and superfluous in laces and embroideries,' he writes, then at least let these fripperies be British-made.

Buckingham, with his ropes of pearls and his diamond-encrusted satin suits, his Barbary mares and his collection of Flemish and Italian paintings, does not appear to have taken this advice very seriously to heart.

Nor, as it happens, did Bacon himself, who was known, according to John Aubrey, for the gorgeousness of his servants' liveries, and for the fact that he required them all to wear boots made of Spanish leather – British leather, in his opinion, having a horrid smell.

VIII. THE COURT OR CURIALITIE

Buckingham is now too important to bother himself, says Bacon, with court appointments. 'This would be too low for your thoughts.'

As it turned out, helping his friends and relations to positions at court was a major strand of Buckingham's working life.

These eight topics, writes Bacon with superb understatement, will probably be enough 'to take up your time'.

In 1625 Buckingham, through Balthazar Gerbier's agency, would acquire Titian's double portrait *Cardinal Georges d'Armagnac and his secretary Guillaume Philandrier*.

Titian's painting shows the Cardinal, an imposing figure in voluminous black clothes, with a letter in his hand, gazing pensively over the viewer's right shoulder. Placed a little lower, and looking up at him, sits his secretary, pen poised. The secretary is richly dressed but subordinate. His pose speaks of energy, harnessed but ready. Whatever his master wants done, he will do it. He watches him as intently as a dog watches his handler, waiting for the command.

Gerbier bought the picture in Paris. When he got it back to England and showed it to his employer, he was disappointed in Buckingham's response. 'I beg Your Excellency to look at it a little more at your leisure. Inigo Jones almost went down on his knees before it.' (Jones's approval mattered to Gerbier – he often quotes him as arbiter.)

The painting is indeed wonderful – rich in colour, charged with the emotional drama between the two sitters. It is also extraordinarily apt that it should have come into Buckingham's possession. The relationship it depicts – one in which personal intimacy and shared work are combined – mirrors that between him and King James.

The Law

THE King held court in Whitehall Palace. Half a mile to the south was another palace, containing courts of another kind.

The Palace of Westminster was a cluster of buildings that had grown haphazardly over hundreds of years, sprawling along the west bank of the Thames. At its centre was Westminster Hall. In that immense structure, already six centuries old when Buckingham knew it, with its hammerbeam roof that still, even to twenty-first-century eyes, seems like the work of Titans, the law courts met. The King's Bench, the Court of Common Pleas, the Court of Chancery, each in its allotted part of the vast unpartitioned space. Impossible to light such a room. Impossible to heat it. It was always dim, always draughty. In term-time, when all the courts were sitting, when lawyers and clerks and petitioners jostled through, when prisoners were brought in under guard, when the public came to gawp at notorious criminals or to savour the performances of noted orators, when news-gatherers and courtiers crowded in to keep abreast of the latest scandal or the latest shocking crime, the hurry and the din must have rivalled that of Pandaemonium.

There were other rooms in the palace of equal significance. The Parliament Chamber, where the House of Lords sat, was adjacent to the great Hall. To the other side was St Stephen's Chapel, which served as the Commons chamber, where the members sat in the choir stalls, facing each other across the aisle. But King James dissolved Parliament in 1614, shortly before he first met George Villiers. He didn't recall it for the next seven years. For the first half of Buckingham's life as a courtier, Westminster was not the seat of government. That went on in Whitehall – unofficially in the Bedchamber, or officially in the Chamber of the Privy Council. Westminster, meanwhile, was the seat of law.

*   *   *

Two remarkable men dominated the Jacobean legal establishment. One, Sir Francis Bacon, presided, as we have seen, over the beginning of Buckingham's public life. The other, Sir Edward Coke, precipitated its end.

They were polar opposites. Bacon was subtle and diplomatic ('slippery', said his enemies). Coke was quick to anger and intransigent in his dogged defence of principle. Bacon was a flatterer: he told King James that his book *Basilikon Doron* 'filled the whole realm as with a good perfume or incense'. As a barrister he was suave and sarcastic – the smiler with a knife. Coke was brusque at home and rudely aggressive in court. As Sir Walter Raleigh's prosecutor, tasked with getting a popular hero convicted of treason on highly questionable evidence, Coke resorted to abuse, calling Raleigh 'a spider of Hell', 'a monster', the vilest viper on the face of the earth and 'the most execrable traitor that ever lived'. John Aubrey thought his performance in the trial was 'too clownish and bitter'.

Bacon was a polymath, as interested in physics and astronomy as he was in legal matters, one whose hyperactive mind darted freely from alchemy to the constitution of the Roman republic, who had something to say on everything: on friendship, on envy, on empire, on the most appropriate shrubs to plant in shade. Coke was a single-minded jurist: 'wonderful painstaking,' says John Aubrey. He rose every day at 3 a.m. and worked ceaselessly. He was choleric, deeply learned in the law, of inflexible integrity. King James said he was 'one who seemed to eat, drink and evacuate nothing but law'.

People were intimidated by Bacon; they made fun of Coke. Courtiers cracked snobbish jokes about his name, which was pronounced 'cook', as though he might have been descended from a domestic servant. A comedy performed before the King in Cambridge featured a character called Sir Ignoramus played by an actor dressed and bearded like Coke and imitating his voice.

Bacon grew up in one of the palatial houses between the Strand and the River Thames that were the grandest residences in London. He sneered that Coke, whose origins were less exalted, was 'neither liberal, nor affable, nor magnificent'. But financially Bacon was on the way down while Coke was on the way up. His father was a lawyer who earned enough to buy himself into the ranks of minor country gentry, and Coke himself, by dint of hard work, became a very wealthy man.

Bacon's household was full of young men. Even after his marriage he lived like a bachelor, whether at Lincoln's Inn or at his house in Gorhambury. Coke was a paterfamilias who bullied and domineered over his wife and daughters as though by masculine right. Bacon's speeches, in court or in Parliament, were mellifluous, subtly argued and erudite. Sir Dudley Carleton called him 'the best orator that ever sat' within the walls of the Palace of Westminster. Coke spoke plainly and like a lawyer, chiselling down his words until there was no room for ambiguity or misinterpretation, and piling precedent upon precedent until his hearers were exhausted.

Most importantly, the two men's politics, and therefore their views of their role as jurists, were opposed. Buckingham's life story was to become tangled with a great debate between royal absolutism and a more nuanced view of the role of the monarchy, one in which a King's authority was balanced by the powers of the judiciary and legislature.

Bacon saw the judges as the 'lions beneath the throne' – formidable beasts but subservient to royal authority, which they must not 'check or oppose'. The monarch was above the law. Coke disagreed. To him the law should correct and curtail the monarch's power for the protection of the people's rights. As Attorney General (the state prosecutor) he had served the monarch loyally, rooting out treason and guarding the throne. But once he became Chief Justice in 1606, his mission would be to defend the principle that even the King, to whom the whole nation was subject, was subject to the law.

Bacon and Coke had risen alongside each other, always acquainted but never friendly. They studied at the same college in Cambridge (not simultaneously – Coke was nine years the older). They were frequently together in courts of law, sometimes supporting, often opposing each other. They jostled each other for high office. They were each in turn Solicitor General and Attorney General. Coke held both titles first, and he was the first to become a Privy Councillor and Lord Chief Justice, but eventually Bacon leapfrogged over him, rising in 1618, as Coke never did, to the supreme legal rank of Lord Chancellor.

They were rivals privately and matrimonially as well as publicly and professionally. They wanted the same woman as a wife. Elizabeth, née Cecil, was Lord Burghley's granddaughter. When her first husband, Sir William Hatton, died she was left a twenty-year-old widow with a great fortune. Bacon, who was her cousin, came courting, but it was Coke – by this time the richer of the two men – who carried her off.

Both men were to be linked to Buckingham. While Bacon appointed himself the favourite's avuncular mentor, and Buckingham rewarded him with a place on the Privy Council, Coke initially kept his distance. What business did a serious person like him have with the kind of prancing popinjay Buckingham appeared to be? There came a time, though, when he needed Buckingham's help.

In 1616 King James asked the judges of the King's Bench to approve an archaic legal instrument known as a 'commendam', granting the income and privileges of a bishopric to one of his protégés while excusing the man from actually performing any episcopal duties. The Bench was led by the Lord Chief Justice, Edward Coke.

Coke was not the man to nod through such an abuse. He ruled that the commendam was illegal, and prevailed upon his fellow judges to write to the King, declaring that whenever they received instructions that were contrary to the law – even if they came from His Majesty himself – they would ignore them, 'and go forth to do the law notwithstanding'.

James summoned the judges into his presence. He berated them furiously, holding their letter in his hand, and then ripped it up. The majority of the judges fell to their knees and prayed for pardon. Only Coke staunchly defended his position, telling the King that when the case came before him, 'I shall do that which shall be fit for a judge to do.'

He was not forgiven. Over the next year Coke was excluded from the Privy Council and dismissed from his post as Lord Chief Justice.

For nearly half a century, ever since he had embarked on his legal career, he had been recording all the legal cases in which he had participated or that had struck him as worthy of attention. Those 'Reports' – all thirteen volumes of them – are among the foundational documents of British Common Law, still essential reading for practising lawyers. The King ordered him to make use of his enforced leisure to revise them, 'expunging and retracting' the 'errors and offensive conceits' with which, in James's opinion, they were riddled.

Those errors and conceits were passages in which Coke seemed to question the powers vested in the sovereign by long tradition and known as the royal prerogative. The prerogative powers allowed a monarch to begin and end wars, to grant honours and pardons, to appoint judges and to prorogue Parliament – all without Parliamentary approval. King James and his son King Charles both jealously guarded their prerogative. Disputes over it would punctuate Buckingham's life.

In 1617 Buckingham – with his mother's encouragement – turned his mind to finding a suitable wife for his elder brother, John Villiers. John suffered from an intermittent mental illness, during which his mother would have him confined to an asylum. Between alternating bouts of mania and depression, though, John made an adequately presentable suitor. Buckingham was loyally fond of him, declaring he 'had more wit and honesty than all the kindred beside', and (not yet married himself) he had made John his heir. The King had promised to ennoble him. Sir Edward Coke had a daughter, Frances, aged fourteen. Buckingham proposed a match.

Coke was not immediately taken with the idea. The problem was not his proposed son-in-law's mental health. He baulked at the huge dowry requested. But since the row over the commendam, his legal career seemed to be over. Perhaps Buckingham would intercede for him with the King. He gave his consent.

Coke's wife, however, refused hers. In most families this would have been unimportant, the father being within the family – as King James had several times pointed out – as a king is in his kingdom. But the Coke family was different. Elizabeth was not a docile woman or a dutiful wife.

She was twenty-six years younger than Coke, but she was formidably articulate and independent-minded. She persisted, even after marrying Coke, in calling herself Lady Hatton. She was required to do so under the terms on which she had inherited her first husband's fortune, but to her contemporaries it seemed that she was thereby publicly proclaiming her unwifelike independence.

She was rich, and, instead of submissively handing over all she had to her lord and master, she insisted on managing her own property. When Coke tried to assert his ownership of it, she fought him through the courts. The dispute was public, bitter and irresolvable, until the King himself intervened. The couple were never fully reconciled. At Coke's funeral, Elizabeth is said to have remarked, 'We shall never see his like again, thanks be to God.'

In 1617 she defied him over their daughter's marriage. No, she said, she did not consider the 'lunatic' John Villiers a satisfactory prospective son-in-law and, anyway, she had promised Frances to someone else. Her recalcitrance mattered, not because a mother might expect some say in determining her child's future, but because it was Lady Hatton's fortune, the prospect of a large dowry drawn from it and ultimately a rich inheritance, that made Frances such a desirable bride.

What Frances herself thought of the marriage proposed for her, nobody recorded. What we do know is that between January 1617, when the wedding was first discussed, and September of that year, when it finally took place, she was the bone of contention in a vicious dogfight between her parents – repeatedly abducted, hustled from place to place and imprisoned.

First round. Lady Hatton, without informing Coke of her plans, left London, taking Frances with her. They went secretly to a borrowed house near Oatlands, probably because Lady Hatton hoped for the protection of Queen Anne.

Second round. Coke, enraged by his wife and daughter's disappearance, was initially clueless as to their whereabouts, but when someone indiscreetly disclosed the secret, he applied to Lord Chancellor Bacon for a search warrant. Bacon – who had already advised Buckingham against promoting the match – refused. Coke applied instead to the Secretary of State, Sir Ralph Winwood. Winwood complied.

Third round. Coke rode to Oatlands with a band of armed men. Arriving at the house, he called upon his wife to let him in and hand over Frances. When she refused, he ordered his men to batter down the door. Once inside, they grabbed Frances and carried her off. Over the next few weeks Coke kept Frances locked up and hidden away in various friends' houses, while her mother tried to find her.

Fourth round. Lady Hatton turned to the Privy Council, asserting that her husband's break-in was a criminal act and demanding he should be brought to justice. Initially the Councillors were inclined to support her, but then two all-powerful new players entered the contest. The King and Buckingham had been in Scotland. Receiving letters from Coke as they travelled back south, they stepped in. The King wrote reprimanding the Privy Council for obstructing a marriage that was pleasing to Buckingham and therefore to himself.

Fifth round. Lady Hatton was placed under house arrest at the home of a London alderman.

Sixth round. Frances, perhaps by now ready for any alliance that would secure her freedom from her warring parents, formally consented to marry John Villiers because, she said pathetically, 'I think it will be a means of the King's favour to my father,' and because, after all, Villiers (whom she had not met) was 'not to be misliked; his fortune is very good; a gentleman well born'. The marriage took place in September at Hampton Court. The King gave away the bride. The bride's mother, still locked up, was not present.

Seventh round. The marriage signed and sealed, Buckingham, accompanied by a splendid entourage, went to release Lady Hatton from her confinement. She was received back at court. The Cecil family gave a 'great supper for reuniting' themselves with Buckingham's family, and especially to celebrate the coming-together of Buckingham's mother and Lady Hatton – now co-mothers-in-law. A few days later Lady Hatton, putting a brave face on her defeat, reciprocated with a feast to which the King and all the Villiers family were invited. King James was very gracious 'and made four of her creatures knights', but his 'principal graces and favours lighted on the Lady Compton [Buckingham's mother] and her children; whom the King praised and kissed, and blessed all those that wished them well'.

The wedded pair were not happy. John's sanity became increasingly precarious. There was an occasion when he appeared at the window of Buckingham's London house and, according to John Chamberlain, 'beat down the glass windows with his bare fists and, all bloodied, cried out to the people that passed by'. Four years after their marriage, Frances, still only nineteen, ran off with Sir Robert Howard. Buckingham, angry on his cuckolded brother's behalf, had the lovers charged with adultery (a criminal offence). Howard was jailed for months in the Fleet prison, and excommunicated. Frances was also given a prison sentence, but evaded it by fleeing abroad.

The marriage failed to restore Coke's position. Buckingham did nothing to help him. His legal career was over. It had also done Sir Francis Bacon no good.

While Buckingham was absent in Scotland, Bacon had written to him, advising him against the match. Buckingham's reply was sharp: 'In this business of my brother's that you over-trouble yourself with, I understand that you have carried yourself with much scorn and neglect, both towards myself and friends.' Bacon, unlike Coke, knew how to smooth things over. There were apologies and a reconciliation. For four more years they worked amicably together, but the bond between the young favourite and his brilliant adviser had been weakened.

Young Women

THE Jacobean court was notorious – then and later – for louche behaviour. A contemporary pamphlet fulminates against the way 'the holy state of matrimony was most perfidiously broken' there, and 'even great persons prostitute their bodies ... and consume their substance in lascivious appetites of all sorts'. A generation later the Puritan poet and biographer Lucy Hutchinson described it in retrospect as a 'nursery of lust and intemperance' where 'vice and lewdness' reigned. These are the voices of disapproving outsiders, but even insiders were shocked. Sir John Harington wrote to a friend, 'We are going on, hereabouts, as if the Devil was contriving every man should blow up himself by wild riot,' and Lady Anne Clifford noted in her diary 'how all the ladies about the court had gotten such ill names that it was grown a scandalous place'.

Buckingham was a beautiful man. He was charming. He was rich. As the King's favourite he wasn't exactly unattached, but he was technically single, and James was often out of town. He didn't marry until he had been at court for seven years. His wife was later to write of his 'one sin ... loving women too well'. He was said to have had a number of lovers in those years.

One of them was the Countess of Salisbury, born Catherine Howard, whose sister Frances – murderer of Thomas Overbury – was the most notorious woman in London. Others, more transient, remain nameless. According to Arthur Wilson, Buckingham was shamelessly promiscuous. When he desired a woman, his friends would lure her to a respectable house with what sounded like a harmless invitation. Buckingham would arrive 'as by accident' and set about charming her into bed 'while his train attended at the door as if it were an honourable visit'. To some people – then and later – this made him a vile seducer and a misogynist. 'He looks upon the whole race of women as inferior things, and uses them as if the sex were one, best pleased with all.' To others it seemed like normal behaviour for a single man in his twenties.

His name was to be linked with those of a number of ladies who were involved in sexual scandals. It is as though, in the public imagination, any woman who was known to be anything other than a chaste and obedient wife would be bound to have succumbed to Buckingham's charms, which he would be equally bound to have tried out on her. Even Buckingham's own sister-in-law Frances, née Coke, the unhappy wife of his poor half-crazed brother John, was alleged – implausibly – to be among his mistresses.

More persuasive hints suggest, though, that Buckingham did have one long-running love affair, beginning before his marriage and possibly continuing thereafter. The woman in question was Lady Lucy Percy, the second daughter of Henry, Earl of Northumberland.

Northumberland had been imprisoned at the time of the Gunpowder Plot. Although his guilt was never conclusively proved, he was held in the Tower for the next sixteen years. There, like Walter Raleigh, with whom he smoked tobacco and talked science, he made himself comfortable (he was allowed twenty servants) and used his time in scholarly pursuits, conducting experiments and reading the books in the extensive library he assembled. He became known as the Wizard Earl. His daughter seems to have been as unconventional as he was.

In 1617, when she was eighteen, Lucy married James Hay, subsequently Earl of Carlisle, a Scot who had come south with King James and been his favourite for a while. Carlisle, who was to become one of Buckingham's inner circle, was twenty years older than her. He was odd-looking. Princess Elizabeth had nicknamed him Camel-face. But he was sophisticated and witty. Balthazar Gerbier describes him as 'a devotee of gallantry, of ballets, clothes and excessive fanfare'. He was known for his extravagances – for his masques and banquets. He knew how to keep a young wife amused.

Initially his marriage to Lucy seemed to be passionate and happy. Just over a year later, though, King James sent Carlisle abroad on a diplomatic mission to Germany. John Chamberlain reports that Lucy parted from him with 'long *congées* and leave-takings', and followed him to

Gravesend to wave him off in tears, saying she 'would not forsake him' until he was actually under sail.

Carlisle was gone for six months. His mission achieved nothing. By the time he returned it was being said that its ostensible purpose was a blind. The French ambassador reported that he had been got out of the way 'to consummate a love that the Marquis of Buckingham has for someone very close to him'.

Lucy was a famous beauty. In the next decade she would inspire Sir John Suckling's dialogue poem 'Upon My Lady Carlisle's Walking in Hampton Court Gardens'.

In the poem, the first speaker rhapsodises romantically:

> *Heardst thou not music when she talked?*
> *And didst not find that as she walked*
> *She threw rare perfumes all about,*
> *Such as bean-blossoms newly out,*
> *Or chafèd spices give? –*

The other speaker (J. S. – Suckling himself) responds more earthily. He has been mentally undressing her, he says:

> *I was undoing all she wore,*
> *And had she walked but one turn more,*
> *Eve in her first state had not been*
> *More naked or more plainly seen.*

As well as being distractingly sexy, and fragrant as bean-blossom, Lucy was independent-minded, brave and unafraid of scandal. Later she was to have affairs with both the royalist Thomas Wentworth, Earl of Strafford, and the Parliamentarian John Pym. During the Civil Wars she was a double agent, passing information for both sides. She endured imprisonment in the Tower (in circumstances far less comfortable than her father had enjoyed) and was threatened with torture. It is perfectly credible that she would have been reckless enough, even as a teenaged newly-wed, to say yes to Buckingham's advances.

The Carlisles' marriage survived. Many romancers have imagined that Lucy's affair with Buckingham continued after her husband's return from abroad, but the only sure information we have about their ongoing relationship is that once, after dining at the Carlisles' house, Buckingham (by this time married) had a nasty stomach upset.

In fiction, though, they remain forever linked. The Duke of la Rochefoucauld includes in his memoirs (first published in the 1660s) a story he had heard from the Duchess of Chevreuse, who knew Buckingham well.

He relates that King Louis of France gave his wife, Queen Anne, some diamond studs. Queen Anne gave them to Buckingham, with whom she was in love. Back in England Lucy Carlisle stole them out of jealous pique because Buckingham 'had loved her before he loved the Queen of France'. King Louis asked Queen Anne why she wasn't wearing the studs. To allay his jealous suspicions, she needed to recover them.

Centuries later the story of how she got them back formed the backbone of the plot of Alexandre Dumas's novel *The Three Musketeers* (1844), in which Buckingham appears as a dashing romantic hero, and there is a bold, bad, beautiful woman known as Milady de Winter, modelled on Lucy Carlisle.

Hunting

In making Buckingham his Master of the Horse, King James had associated his George with hunting, which Sir Roger Wilbraham tells us was 'the sport he preferreth above all worldly delights and pastimes'. Over the next decade the two of them would hunt together hundreds of times.

James's first English favourite was Philip Herbert, later Earl of Montgomery, who could 'pretend', wrote Clarendon, 'to no other qualification than that he understood horses and dogs very well'. For James, this was enough of a bond. Horses and dogs brought the King his greatest pleasures. Those surprised by the fact that he had called Salisbury – that subtle-minded statesman – his 'little beagle', or by Buckingham's referring to himself as 'your dog', should bear in mind that James was known to have considerably less respect and affection for most of his human companions than he did for his hounds.

In 1620 a diplomat with urgent news joined him, as many statesmen and ambassadors were obliged to do throughout his reign, on a day's hunting, and found him surrounded by 'beagles, spaniels, greyhounds, sparrowhawks and goshawks', looking like 'a *Gran Cazador*', a great huntsman. This was King James at his happiest.

Shortly before Mary, Queen of Scots was beheaded, a Scottish visitor to the English court assured Queen Elizabeth that, though Mary's son (then the twenty-year-old King of Scotland) would be obliged to rage against Elizabeth publicly if she were to kill his mother, he would do so only to please his subjects, and he could anyway be placated without undue trouble. Elizabeth might 'easily satisfy him, in sending him dogs and deer'.

It was true that this was James's favourite kind of present. He once stayed with Sir Oliver Cromwell (whose nephew of the same name would prove a scourge to the Stuart monarchy). Sir Oliver the elder, who had no objection to royalty, gave his visitor 'some goodly horses', a pack of 'fleet and deep-mouthed hounds' and 'divers hawks of excellent wing'. It was a well-chosen gift. Twenty years later King James was to write to Buckingham in Spain, advising him not to bother with offering jewels or diamond-encrusted swords or any other precious knick-knacks to the Count-Duke of Olivares. Far better for 'horses, dogs, hawks, and suchlike to be sent to him out of England'. That, thought James, 'will be a far more noble and acceptable present to him'.

'Hunting', wrote Castiglione, was 'the true pastime of great lords' and 'a suitable pursuit for a courtier'. Hunting was a kind of military training. It prepared young men for warfare. Hunting, men learnt to endure 'heat, cold, hunger, thirst, to rise early, watch late, lie and fare hardly'. Hunting was a discipline – physical and moral – but it was also exhila-ratingly pleasurable. King James, who had no wish to make a warrior of himself, adored it.

His passion for hunting had begun early. 'He loves the chase above all the pleasures of this world,' wrote the French ambassador when he was in his early teens. He lives 'in the saddle for six hours on end, running up hills and down dales with loosened bridle'. He was still an enthusiast when he inherited the English crown. As he travelled south through his new kingdom in 1603, he repeatedly paused or turned aside to enjoy the hunting.

Reaching London at last, he stayed initially in the Tower, slipping out secretly, with a few attendants, to explore his new 'houses, castles, forests and chases', and 'therein took high delight, especially to see such store of deer and game in his parks for hunting'. He later said that on arrival in England he had felt that 'every day was Christmas'. These forests and chases were his very best presents.

For months on end, James would be away from London. Theobalds was a palace, three storeys high, with a grand facade a quarter of a mile wide, all glinting with glass, and enclosing five courtyards. There were towers surmounted by golden lions holding weather vanes aloft. The ceiling of the double-height great hall was decorated with signs of the zodiac, ingeniously lit at night so that each sign seemed to be attended by the 'stars proper to each'. There was a minstrels' gallery, and a great fireplace of blue marble. The walls were decorated with heraldic devices. On each side of the hall stood six wooden pillars carved to look like trees with 'the natural bark so artfully joined with birds' nests and leaves as well as fruit upon them' that 'when the steward of the house opened the windows, which looked upon the beautiful pleasure garden, birds flew into the hall, perched themselves upon the trees, and began to sing'.

Sometimes Queen Anne would join her husband there. Their most harmonious times seem to have been on the hunting field. In 1607 a courtier reported that 'the Queen doth every day ride in the coach with the King and there they both do take their horses to hunt'. Anne had a diamond brooch in the shape of a crossbow that she would wear in her hair.

She posed for her portrait by Paul Van Somer, dressed in a green damask hunting costume adorned with carnation-coloured rosettes and row upon row of lace. Her fashionably frizzled blonde hair is piled high, and topped with a tall plumed hat. She has dismounted from her horse, which stands behind her, held by a black groom. She has two greyhounds on leashes – token of her regal authority – while others sit at her

feet or gaze adoringly up at her. And Anne didn't only pose as a huntress. In 1613, in the course of a hunt in which she was playing an active part, she accidentally shot and killed one of the King's favourite dogs, Jewel. Hounds might be loved by their masters, and they were also – if pure-bred and fully trained – extremely valuable. James was furious, until he was told that the culprit was the Queen. Graciously, he not only forgave her, but sent her a punning peace token, a jewel worth £2,000, 'as a legacy from his dead dog'.

James was unapologetic about his long absences from the capital. He told his Privy Council that hunting was necessary to his health, on which depended 'the health and welfare of us all'. He asked the Councillors therefore 'to undertake the charge and burden of affairs and foresee that he be not interrupted nor troubled with too much business'. To Salisbury, he argued that he spent no more time hunting 'than other kings will consume upon their physical diets and going to their whores'. When the season for stag-hunting ended, he would have a hundred hares released and hunt them instead. Sometimes his companions despaired of ever returning to court. 'We are all become wild men wandering in a forest.'

King James claimed that even when he wasn't present in Whitehall or Westminster, he knew very well what was going on there. That was thanks to Buckingham. Day after day, month after month, the favourite travelled, by coach or on horseback, back and forth over the roads leading north and north-east out of London, bringing his royal master news of what was being said and done at court, in the Council Chamber or in Parliament.

The huntsman's usual prey was the male fallow deer (the buck) or the male red deer (the stag or hart) – the larger and the more grandly antlered, the better.

Hunting could be a static sport. Deer reared for the purpose would be confined within the high walls of a park. On the appointed day they would be driven, by dogs and beaters, past a stand, which might be a temporary timber structure or an exquisite stone building: some hunting pavilions looked like palaces in miniature. From their parapeted roofs or balconies, ladies and gentlemen could shoot at the driven deer with their crossbows, before retreating indoors for refreshments.

To James, shooting at driven deer was better than nothing, but it was artificial. It was tame. Without the chase there was no physical exertion, no thrill. The use of the crossbow set a distance between hunter and prey. In *Basilikon Doron* he advised Prince Henry to hunt 'with running hounds, which is the most honourable and noblest sort thereof'. That was the real thing: fast, bloody, dangerous and exhilarating.

Hunting was an ancient art with long-established rituals and ceremonies. In the previous generation, George Turberville – poet, bishop's son, diplomat and traveller to Russia – had laid out in his book *The Noble Art of Venerie* how it was to be done.

The evening before a hunt, the Chief Huntsman (who, at King James's court, was a highly respected person) would visit the Master of the Games in the latter's chamber to learn where the King wished to hunt the following morning. Then he went early to bed.

Before dawn, he and his men were up again, filling their leather bottles with wine and rinsing their hounds' nostrils with vinegar to make their sense of smell the keener. The long day's sport began.

It progressed through eight stages.

THE QUEST

While the gentlemen are at breakfast, the Chief Huntsman takes his 'lymer' (usually a bloodhound with a particularly acute nose) to search the chosen area, on the lookout for droppings ('fewmets') or tracks, hoping to sight a stag but taking all possible care not to disturb it prematurely.

THE ASSEMBLY

The King and his friends, on horseback, gather ready for the chase to begin.

THE RELAYS

The Chief Huntsman, having discovered where the stag is, can predict in which direction he will attempt to escape. Huntsmen, each with several hounds, station themselves along the route he is expected to take.

THE MOVING, OR UNHARBOURING

The first hounds are loosed into the thicket where the stag is hiding. It races away. The hounds pursue it, giving tongue.

The sound they make is musical, and highly valued by connoisseurs. Shakespeare's Queen Hippolyta says that she has hunted with Hercules and never did she hear elsewhere 'so musical a discord' as the baying of the hero's hounds. Her husband Theseus, nettled, insists that his hounds are more harmonious, having been chosen expressly for the timbre of their voices, 'matched in mouth like bells, each under each'.

This was no poet's fancy. Gervase Markham, author of *Country Contentments* (1615), suggests selecting hounds as you might assemble a choir. A kennel, he writes, should include 'some large dogs that have deep solemn mouths' to provide the bass line. 'Then a double number of loud ringing mouths which must bear the counter tenor.' Then come some 'plain sweet mouths' to 'bear the middle part'. The consort is completed by 'a couple or two of beagles, which as small trebles may warble amongst them'.

As the canine music begins, the horns sound the call for 'Gone away'. The sportsmen put their horses to a gallop and follow the pack. The chase is on.

THE BAYING

When the stag can run no further, it turns, desperate, to defend itself with its antlers. As the dogs circle it, the huntsmen step forward and kill it with their swords.

THE MORT

The huntsman sounds a single piercing note on his horn. Then, as Turberville tells us, 'the huntsman on his knees handed the hunting knife to the King, who stabbed the hart's carcass as if he were killing the hart'.

This was King James's moment. According to the Venetian ambassador, 'On His Majesty coming up with the dead game, he dismounts, and cuts its throat.'

THE UNMAKING

The stag is cut open and disembowelled (King James and his fellow Scots would have called this the 'gralloching').

At this point King James habitually does something that foreign visitors find revolting. 'On Saturday last,' wrote a contemporary observer, 'the King killed a buck in Eltham Park and so soon as it was opened stood in the belly of it and bathed his bare feet and legs with the warm blood; since which time he has been so nimble that he thinketh this the only remedy for the gout.'

The carcass is cut up, and the meat packed into a cart or slung over poles for transport back to the royal kitchens.

THE CUREE

Once the best parts of the meat have been removed, the hounds are rewarded with the offal. All of those horsemen who have ridden hard and long enough to be in at the death are honoured by being marked on the forehead with a dab of the dead creature's blood.

*   *   *

There were times when, if the King didn't choose to return to court, the court came to him. James would plan a great hunt and invite foreign visitors to take part. A Spanish ambassador described one such occasion as a 'Noble and magnificent entertainment' such as he had never 'seen the like before'. At other times diplomats determined to get an audience with the elusive king would order their tailors to make them special hunting outfits and follow him into the country uninvited. These visitors were not allowed to remain mere spectators. However exhausted or terrified they might be, they had to join the chase. The Spanish Count of Gondomar was particularly plucky. A rival ambassador commented, 'He tries to conform in all things to the inclination and taste of the king.' He 'vies with him in putting his hands in the blood of bucks and stags, and doing cheerfully everything that His Majesty does'. It worked. 'In this way he acquired his favour.'

It was harder for courtiers to approach King James when he was in his hunting lodges, but country people saw a great deal of him – more than they wanted. Hunting parties trampling the crops and damaging hedges have never been welcome to farmers, and people who depended on being able to gather firewood or trap rabbits in the royal woods suffered when the King's huntsmen were patrolling those woods in preparation for the King's sport.

Once one of James's hounds – a favourite called Jowler – was missing at the end of the day. The following morning it reappeared with a note attached to its collar. 'Good Mr Jowler,' it read, 'we pray you speak to the King, for he hears you every day as he doth not us.' The message Jowler was to convey was that the King should go back to London. Hardly a welcoming one, but the King was amused.

Because James hid himself away from the public gaze, people imagined he must have a guilty secret, a shocking vice.
A rhyme appeared:

> King James loves to be merry ...
> At Christmas he hath dancing.
> In the summer tide
> Abroad will he ride
> With a guard about him prancing ...

At Royston and Newmarket
He'll hunt till he be lean.
But he hath merry boys
That with masks and toys
Can make him fat again.

Those last three lines have repeatedly been read as coded references to sex.

There was talk of 'bawdy songs' and 'antic dances', of the King's 'jovial boys' dancing 'until they stink of sweat', and singing 'scurrilous and base stuff'. Francis Osborne wrote that the King's kissing his favourites 'after so lascivious a mode in public, and upon the theatre, as it were, of the world' gave rise to suspicions of 'some things done in the tiring house'. As a tiring house (dressing room) is to a theatre, so James's hunting lodges were to the court – places where he was offstage, at ease. Those unspeakable 'things' Osborne alludes to – that he says, primly, are beyond his powers of expression – are sexual acts. Anthony Weldon, ears always pricked for any whisper of scandal, thought that James's reason for spending so much time in the country was 'rather that he might enjoy his favourite with more privacy, than that he loved the sport'.

James enjoyed watching his young male attendants dancing. He enjoyed drinking. But the hostile commentators who imagined him giving himself over to dissipation in his rural retreats exaggerated. A visiting ambassador notes that the King was keen on 'spending all the time he can upon hunting and studies' – the latter taking up more of his time than the former. John Hacket wrote that James 'went not out with his hounds above three days in the week, and hunting was soon over. Much of the time His Majesty spent in state contrivances, and at his book.'

While he hunted, he was riding horses Buckingham had bred for him, and he often thanked Buckingham for them. When he bent his mind to 'state contrivances', Buckingham was at hand to help him. They might be away from the centres of power, but their work went on.

Family

IN June 1618 Buckingham gave a party. Its ostensible purpose was to be the reconciliation of King James and Prince Charles, who had had a falling-out. Buckingham, modest as ever, called it 'The Prince's Feast', but Charles renamed it 'The Friend's Feast', Buckingham being by then, to both father and son, not only a friend, but The Friend.

The eating and drinking spread itself over two days, beginning on Friday and culminating in a splendid dinner on Saturday. The King and Prince sat beneath a canopy of state at a table apart, but in the same room a second board was spread. There were placed Buckingham's mother, his sister Susan, Lady Feilding, his brother John Villiers and his wife, and – as another guest reports – 'divers others of the same race'.

King James 'declared himself very highly in favour' of Buckingham. He then toasted each of the Villiers family in turn. He sent them 'secret messages'. At last, dinner over, he rose 'and came personally to the table, and drank a common health to all the noble family'. He proclaimed his intention of advancing Buckingham's relatives 'above all others'. He declared, 'I live to that end.' He assured the assembled Villierses that even after his death, his 'posterity' (there present in the person of Prince Charles) would remember his commandments and continue to promote their interests.

The King kept his promises. A year later John Villiers was made Viscount Purbeck. Susan and her husband became the Earl and Countess of Denbigh. Buckingham's younger brother, Christopher or Kit or Kester, became Earl of Anglesey. Their mother was created Countess of Buckingham in her own right. The whole Villiers clan were rising along with their George.

A rhyme circulated about the way the Villiers brothers helped each other come up in the world:

Above in the skies shall Gemini rise
And twins the court shall pester:
George shall call up his brother Jack,
And Jack his brother Kester.

Later Buckingham was criticised for helping his relatives. But before public opinion turned ferociously against him, his carrying his family upwards with him seemed to many right and proper. It was a fortunate man's bounden duty to share his luck with his relatives. John Chamberlain praised Buckingham's 'good disposition in doing good to his kindred and friends'.

As a boy King James had keenly felt his lack of near relations. 'I was alone, without father or mother, brother or sister,' he wrote. It was partly because Esmé Stuart (latterly Earl of Lennox) was his cousin that he welcomed him so warmly. Here was not only a handsome man he could dote upon; here was also the kindly big brother he had never had. When James resolved to marry, despite his avowed lack of enthusiasm for marital sex, he eagerly adopted the roles of wooer and ardent young husband. He longed for a companion, and for a family. Once he had a wife and children, though, he seemed not to know what to do with them.

Those who have been unloved as children may have difficulty creating happy childhoods for their offspring. We have seen that James had been separated from his mother while still a baby and had spent his boyhood as a virtual prisoner within the walls of Stirling Castle. When his first son, Prince Henry, was born he could think of no better way of rearing him than by replicating the process. Henry was taken from his mother when he was only a few days old. He was sent to Stirling Castle, and there he passed his early childhood under the guardianship of the Earl of Mar, whose father had been his father's guardian.

Queen Anne was given no choice in the matter. Here is James's advice to a husband: 'Treat her as your own flesh, command her as her Lord, cherish her as your helper, rule her as your pupil, and please her in all things reasonable; but teach her not to be curious in things that belong to her not.' Those 'things', apparently, included the care of her own baby.

Given the dangers surrounding the royal family (this was the period when the Earl of Bothwell repeatedly broke into their palaces with murderous intent), James's decision to confine his heir in an impregnable stronghold did have some justification, but Anne found the confiscation of her child unbearable. She fought against it, without success. The marriage was badly damaged by it. 'No good can come between the King and Queen till she be satisfied anent the Prince,' wrote a Scottish courtier at the time. 'There is nothing but lurking hatred disguised with cunning dissimulation betwixt the King and the Queen,' wrote another.

In 1603, before James went south to England, he wrote to Henry, still in Stirling, promising the nine-year-old boy that he would eventually be sent for and enjoy 'continual residence with me ever after', but not naming any date. He then set out for his new kingdom, instructing Queen Anne to follow a month later with their two younger children, Princess Elizabeth and Prince Charles. The Queen was not prepared to leave Henry behind. She went to Stirling, with a band of noblemen and their armed supporters, and demanded to see her son. The Countess of Mar – following the King's instructions – told her she could visit but her armed followers were forbidden to come within ten miles of the Prince. The Venetian ambassador reports that Anne 'flew into a violent fury, and four months gone with child as she was, she beat her own belly, so that they say she is in manifest danger of miscarriage and death'. She survived, but the child she was carrying did not.

James capitulated. Queen Anne was allowed to take Henry south with her along with Princess Elizabeth. Little Prince Charles – aged two and half, just beginning to say a few words, but according to his guardian 'a very weak child of his body and feet' – was left behind for the time being. Perhaps the Queen gave up on him, agreeing with the courtier who wrote that he was 'not likely to live'. It was over a year before he joined his parents in their new kingdom.

Two more children were born to James and Anne in England – girls who both died in infancy. By the time King James fell for Somerset in 1607 the sexual side of the royal marriage had petered out, and the couple were seldom together. 'I thank God, I carry that love and respect unto you which by the law of God and nature I ought to do my wife and mother of my children,' he wrote to Anne. He loved her according to his bond. No less. No more.

*   *   *

When Buckingham came into King James's life, the effect – surprisingly enough – was to ease relationships within the royal family. Queen Anne had told Archbishop Abbot that she expected the new favourite to 'plague ... despise and hardly treat' her, but the reverse was true. Anne and her children found him to be a helpful mediator between themselves and the King.

Princess Elizabeth, living far off in central Europe with her husband, the Elector Palatine, asked Buckingham to be godfather to her child and, when she wanted her father's military support for her husband's cause, it was to Buckingham she wrote, asking him to intercede. When Queen Anne hoped to save Sir Walter Raleigh, it was Buckingham she approached, begging him to make her case to the King. When Prince Charles found that he had unintentionally annoyed James, it was Buckingham whom he commissioned to convey his apologies to his father. 'I pray you to commend my most humble service to His Majesty, and tell him that I am very very sorry that I have done anything [that] may offend him, and that I will be content to have any penance inflicted upon me so he may forgive me, although I had never a thought nor never shall have to displease him.'

Fathers were intimidating: a kingly father doubly so. Charles was nervous and awkward (Plate 13). In May 1616, when he was still a gauche fifteen-year-old, he was in the garden of Greenwich Palace with Buckingham and the King. 'Being merrily disposed', Charles called Buckingham over as though to show him some interesting plant, and then, once Buckingham was in position, the Prince switched on a concealed fountain, wetting him. The 'jest' misfired. Hidden waterspouts were a fashionable feature of seventeenth-century gardens, but they were much more amusing for the people doing the squirting than they were for the squirted. Buckingham – expensively dressed and carefully groomed – couldn't hide his annoyance. Seeing it, the King, taking his favourite's side against his own child, boxed Prince Charles's ears.

The son might well have been jealous of the man who called the King 'Dad' and who was so evidently better loved by his father than he himself was. Once Buckingham and Charles had formed a bond, though, the King's affection for his favourite spilt over onto his own child. The Friend's Feast celebrated the new harmony between the three of them. Together the younger two became James's 'sweet boys' and the

1. *George Villiers* William Larkin, 1616

1609

2. *King James I*
John de Critz

3. *Queen Anne dressed for a Masque*
Isaac Oliver

4. *Henry, Prince of Wales on the Hunting Field*
Robert Peake the Elder

5. *Princess Elizabeth, future Electress Palatine and Queen of Bohemia*
Robert Peake the Elder

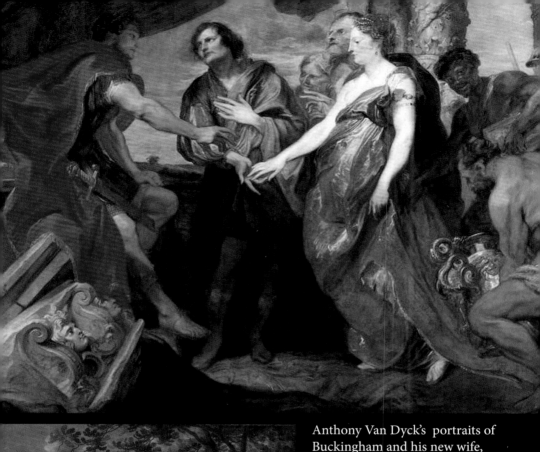

Anthony Van Dyck's portraits of Buckingham and his new wife, Katherine, 1621

6. Above *The Continence of Scipio*

7. Left *The Duke and Duchess of Buckingham as Venus and Adonis*

8. Costume designs for
masques by Inigo Jones

Buckingham as a collector
9. Above left *Ecce Homo* Titian
10. Above right *Venus and Mars* Paolo Veronese
11. Below right *Pietá* Andrea del Sarto
12. Below left *St John* and *St Peter* Adam Elsheimer

13. *Charles I when Prince of Wales*
Hendrick Van Steenwijk circa 1620

timid youth he had neglected and scolded became, in his twenties, his father's dear 'Baby Charles'.

Buckingham was embraced by the royal family, but he never neglected the family he came from. When he moved into Whitehall Palace, his mother came with him. Mary's third husband, Thomas Compton, was, as she put it, 'not well in his head', a 'distemper in his brain', aggravated by wine and tobacco, giving rise to manic periods of 'overjoying', when he talked unstoppably, making no sense. She sent him to a Mr Napper, who kept an asylum hidden away in Whittlewood Forest, where her eldest son, John, had also been secluded for a while. Thus relieved of her unhappy marital responsibilities, the new Countess of Buckingham followed her dazzling second son to court.

Both before and after his marriage she was constantly with him. She hunted with him and entertained the King with him. James was once driven to ask her to refrain from meddling in state affairs, but so long as she observed the boundaries the King set, he showed her great favour. He included the Countess in his invitations, and sent her melons from his greenhouses. In 1621 Simonds D'Ewes noticed that as the King rode from Whitehall to Westminster, 'the windows were filled with many great ladies', but he 'spoke to none of them but to the Marquis of Buckingham's mother'.

The King smiled upon Buckingham's family. There were those among his subjects who did not. In 1621 a scurrilous verse appeared in which the poet jeers at Buckingham's relatives.

> [They] drink and play
> In court still busy
> They will sup at the cup
> Till their brains dizzy.

The Villierses were said to be too numerous, too vulgar and grasping, over-promoted, over-sexed and over-rich. In letters and pamphlets and popular rhymes they are referred to as 'the kindred' or 'the tribe'. Weldon reports that they all hurried to court once their George was established there, but struggled to learn how 'to carry themselves in a court-like garb', and that they were insufficiently refined to master the intricate measures of the courtly French dances, so that, to oblige them, all the courtiers had to be content with country dances suitable only for clodhopping bumpkins.

As well as his full brothers and sister, Buckingham had half-siblings and cousins and nephews and nieces. There weren't, in fact, so very many of them, but they were written about as though they were a swarm, an infestation. The way to advancement in King James's England, said the gossips, was to marry them. 'He had a numerous and beautiful female kindred,' wrote Thomas Fuller, exaggerating for comic effect. 'There was hardly a noble stock in England into which one of these his scions was not grafted.' Normally a girl's parents needed to offer a dowry in order to get a good marriage for her – not so for the Villierses. 'Most of his nieces were matched with little more portion than their uncle's smiles, the forerunner of some good office or honour to follow on their husbands.'

The rhymers seized upon these unions, leering and sneering.

Snobbish contempt for the upstart Villierses shades into salaciousness. It is as though the sexual unease that Buckingham's relationship with King James arouses – and which cannot be spoken of for fear of charges of lese-majesty – is being transposed laterally onto the relationships of his family members. 'They get the Devil and all' that 'swive the kindred', writes a rhymer. The 'tribe' are all sexually voracious money-grubbers. Buckingham's mother is alleged to be having sex with Bishop Williams, Lord Keeper of the Great Seal, who had begun his career as her chaplain.

> Old Beldame Buckingham,
> With her Lord Keeper,
> She loves the fucking game,
> He's her cunt creeper.

Lionel Cranfield, the future Lord Treasurer, is married to Buckingham's cousin, Anne Brett. According to the rhymer's wildly improbable allegation, she is being 'used you know how' by the Earl of Arundel, but Cranfield's complaisance has been bought.

These be they, go so gay
And keep the money,
Which he can better keep
Than his wife's cunny.

This verse was particularly nasty, but it was one of many 'libels' (the ribald anonymous poems that circulated in London) slinging mud at Buckingham and his clan. Most of them he ignored, but this one he took seriously. It was published anonymously. He offered a large sum – a thousand pounds according to one source – to anyone who could identify the author. Attacks on himself he could rise above. An attack on his family hurt him.

The time came when Buckingham wanted to start a new family of his own.

King James never begrudged his favourites the chance to marry. On the contrary, he delighted in the idea of their domestic happiness, the 'comforts' of their 'sanctified bed', their 'licensed joys', and most of all, their generation of youthful copies of themselves.

Five years before King James met George Villiers, William Shakespeare's Sonnets were published. The first seventeen are addressed to a beautiful young man, and in each one the poet is calling upon the 'fair youth' to marry and produce children. Over and over again he reproaches the young man as a 'niggard', a 'glutton', an 'unthrift' because he has hung back from procreation. Beauty is lent not given. Nature requires that it be used and reproduced.

She carved thee for her seal, and meant thereby
Thou shouldst print more, not let that copy die.

King James would have endorsed Shakespeare's argument. That a glowing, godlike young man was duty-bound to beget new versions of himself, to gladden the world with his younger simulacra, would have seemed to him entirely right.

When Princess Elizabeth married Frederick, the Elector Palatine, in 1613, King James went to visit the bride and groom in their bedchamber the following morning. They were both aged sixteen and, according to

John Chamberlain, Frederick was 'much too young and small-timbered' for marriage. But this was not to be one of those royal unions whose consummation was delayed. James was impatient to ascertain what had passed between 'these young turtles that were coupled on St Valentine's Day'. He asked Frederick 'whether he were his true son-in-law'. Frederick assured him that he was. Elizabeth confirmed it by giving birth to James's first grandchild only eleven months later.

An unconsummated marriage could all too easily be annulled, and it was essential to King James's plan for Christendom that this one should hold firm. The purpose of a dynastic marriage was to produce heirs, and the recent death of Prince Henry must have made James impatient for spares – Prince Charles being so puny. All the same, James's eagerness to be informed about Elizabeth's wedding night has seemed to historians ever since at best tactlessly intrusive, at worst creepy.

As with his daughter, so with his favourites. To James a marriage didn't open up a private sphere from which he was excluded. Rather, it extended the circle of his intimates. He repeatedly inserted himself – a formidable kingly cuckoo – into the nests of the young people around him. When his first English favourite, Philip Herbert, married Lady Susan de Vere in 1604, James gave the couple a substantial estate but allowed them little time to be alone together. They were still in bed, on the morning after their wedding, when the King, 'in shirt and night-gown', appeared in their room in Whitehall. He 'spent a good time in or upon the bed with them'. Shortly thereafter he summoned Herbert to come away with him on a hunting trip – there were to be no honeymoons for the King's dear ones.

Somerset's marriage to Frances Howard was the occasion for another such morning-after visit. The celebrations at Whitehall, with feasting and a masque, lasted until two in the morning. John Donne, in his epithalamium, imagined that Frances would have no rest that night, but rather must offer herself as a 'new banquet' to her bridegroom, 'And do all this day's dances o'er again'. Be that as it may, she and Somerset were given no time to sleep in, or to enjoy the first morning of their long-deferred marriage in private. King James was in their bedchamber before they were up – tactless certainly, prurient perhaps, but at least generous. He was bringing with him a further lavish wedding present, a jewel worth £3,000.

Rather than allowing their marriage to interrupt his relationship with Somerset, he simply included Frances in it. Arthur Wilson said that she was 'the King's favourite, as well as her husband'. He would give the pair whatever they wanted, except time to be together without him.

By 1619, Buckingham was a tremendous catch. He was twenty-seven, a marquis and a very rich man. Several high-born ladies had been proposed as suitable wives for him, but the one he wanted was Katherine Manners, the seventeen-year-old daughter of the Earl of Rutland.

Katherine was not a beauty. Her portraits show a heavy-set young woman who sits or stands stolidly, confident and poised, but with none of the grace and *leggiadrezza* of her dancer husband. She has a low brow and a long nose. She was very rich, and would become richer. She had already inherited her late mother's property. In the spring of 1620, the second of her two younger half-brothers died. So Katherine became heiress to much of her father's estate as well. But Buckingham's choice was not a straightforwardly pragmatic one. Katherine was Catholic, which meant that to be connected with her might be a hindrance to his ambitions. He was undeterred. The couple's letters suggest that they were truly fond of each other.

King James would not sanction the marriage unless Katherine converted to Protestantism. She refused. Representatives of both religious denominations became involved. For Protestantism, John Williams, at this time the King's Chaplain, negotiated with Rutland on Buckingham's behalf. The Earl, owner of vast estates that had been in his family for generations, was not impressed by Buckingham's position at court, so precariously dependent on the King's love. Katherine was his only daughter: she was not to be lightly disposed of. Williams 'brought the Earl about ... dextrously with his art and pleasant wit', but an agreement remained elusive. Rutland was reluctant to hand over the immense dowry Buckingham was demanding.

For the other side, the Count of Gondomar, the Spanish ambassador, watched the negotiations beadily. For the royal favourite to be married to a Catholic would have been good news to the Most Catholic King of Spain. In March 1620 Gondomar reported that Katherine was holding fast to her faith.

Buckingham's mother intervened. Always her George's most constant supporter, she called on Katherine and invited the girl to come back to her own apartments for supper. Katherine did not tell her father where she was going. Buckingham was also at his mother's that evening. Katherine stayed the night – perhaps, as one source says, because she was taken ill, perhaps for other reasons. When she tried to go home the following day Rutland, irate, refused to take her in. She went to her uncle's instead while her father and her suitor wrangled over her future.

Rutland wrote Buckingham an incoherent letter in which there is much talk of honour – Katherine's honour, his own honour, Buckingham's honour. All, he suggests, have been besmirched by the overnight stay. He is angry with Katherine, who has gone behind his back, as though, he writes, she has no affection or esteem for him, but 'I must preserve her honour if it were with the hazard of my life.'

He implies that Buckingham has taken her virginity. To do so amounts to theft. As a contemporary pamphleteer put it, 'Children are so much the goods, the possessions of their parent, that they cannot, without a kind of theft, give away themselves without the allowance of those that have the right in them.'

Thus robbed, Rutland is angry, but his blustering reveals that he doesn't know what to do about it. Should he tell Buckingham to be gone, or should he bind him firmly into his family? He demands to be told whether 'she is yours'. He reminds Buckingham that the latter has made 'noble offers'. Now he requires 'real performance'. He seems to be saying that the only way for Katherine's honour to be preserved is for Buckingham to marry her, in which case he – Rutland – will no longer oppose the match. 'Then you shall find me tractable to deal like a loving father.'

Buckingham was stung. To compromise a woman's reputation as a way of obliging her family to accept an otherwise ineligible suitor was the kind of trick a penniless fortune-hunter might play. It seems pretty clear that he and his mother had played it, but, all the same, he was offended by the allegation.

Writing back to Rutland, he haughtily points out that 'considering of the favour that it pleaseth His Majesty, though undeservedly, to bestow upon me', he is a very desirable son-in-law. He has no need to go 'stealing of a wife against the consent of her parents'. As a way of reminding the Earl how close he is to the King, he reveals that he has hastened to

Hampton Court, and thrown himself at James's feet, 'confessing freely unto him all that has passed in privacy between your lordship and me concerning your daughter's marriage'. The King is sympathetic. But, Buckingham goes on, now that communications between the two families have taken this ugly turn, he has abandoned his 'former resolution' to marry Katherine. He has been insulted: he will not submit to being ordered about. 'Your harsh usage of me and your own daughter' has put him off. He wants nothing more to do with the match. He denies seducing Katherine. 'She never received any blemish in her honour but that which came by your own tongue.' Let her father marry her off to whomever he pleases.

More high words about honour. More arguing about the marriage portion. More religious persuasion. But perhaps all of this was mere posturing – moves in a negotiation for which both parties wanted success. According to Wilson, who gives a more overtly scandalous account of the courtship in which Buckingham himself carries Katherine off to his lodgings in Whitehall and 'keeps her there for some time', the two men eventually laid aside their pride and 'quickly salved up the wound, before it grew to a quarrel'.

In May, two months after the entrapment – or abduction/seduction, or lovers' tryst, or innocent supper party, or whatever it was – Buckingham and Katherine were married. The wedding, in Rutland's London house near Tower Hill, was a quiet one by comparison with the feasts and masques that had marked Somerset's ill-fated union. The dowry was fixed at half what Buckingham had originally demanded, but it was still substantial. Katherine had converted to Protestantism. Her devotion to Roman Catholicism had given way, said her husband ungallantly, to her 'lechery'. The handsomest man in Europe was, it turned out, worth more to her than a Mass.

It wasn't an easy marriage. There were three people in it, one of whom, King James, was all-powerful and extremely demanding. Buckingham was frequently called away to dance attendance on him, and the King was not Katherine's only rival. She had to endure much jealousy. Things between husband and wife, as Buckingham once wrote, could get 'something stormy'. But three years later, when Buckingham was absent in Spain, Katherine wrote to him, 'Never woman was so happy as I am, for never was there so kind a husband as you are; and

God make me thankful to Him for you ... I cannot express the infinite affection I bear you; but for God's sake believe me that there was never woman loved man as I do you.'

King James was delighted by his Steenie's marriage. He didn't join the newly-weds in bed the following morning. The wedding having taken place in Rutland's house, he could hardly stroll in on them *en déshabillé* as he could into a marriage chamber in his own palace. But though he wasn't with them in fact, he was with them in spirit, and wrote to tell them so. The following morning-after letter was delivered to Buckingham:

My only sweet and dear child,
Thy dear dad sends thee his blessing this morning and also to his daughter. The Lord of Heaven send you a sweet and blithe wakening, all kind of comfort in your sanctified bed, and bless the fruits thereof that I may have sweet bedchamber boys to play me with, and this is my daily prayer, sweet heart.

Once his 'sweet child' Buckingham was a family man, King James insisted on becoming part of that family. The young couple and their future progeny were all the King's – his children, his playthings, his sweet companions. So abundant was his love for Buckingham, it could even overflow to include his dear one's tetchy father-in-law.

Simonds D'Ewes reports a cosy scene at court the following Christmas. Buckingham and his wife and mother were playing cards with Prince Charles and the Earl of Rutland. 'The King looking on, he openly professed: "Here is a father and a son (meaning himself and the prince), a father and a daughter (meaning Rutland and his daughter) and a son and mother (meaning Buckingham and his mother). The Devil on me if I know which I love best."'

Actually it was not hard, for James or anyone else, to know who was his best-beloved. He might welcome Katherine as his new 'daughter', but he was not going to give up his Steenie to her for more than a few hours. His wedding-morning letter continues with an instruction that Buckingham, on rising, should not allow himself to be detained by troublesome petitioners but should come, smiling, straight to the King, 'that at meeting I may see thy white teeth shine upon me'. Later that day, however much he might wish to spend a little more time with his bride, Buckingham must ready himself 'to bear me comfortable company in my journey', leaving his new wife behind in London as, humble slave and dog that he was, he followed his master out of town.

James's wish for 'sweet bedchamber boys' with whom he could 'play me' has an ugly sound, but there are no other grounds for suspecting the King of paedophilia. He was drawn to strapping young men. All of his known favourites were in their twenties by the time he took them up. Rather than signalling any transgressive sexual interest in children, James's eagerness for Buckingham to have babies was of a piece with his new-found enthusiasm for family life.

His own life as a husband and father had been a dutiful but joyless exercise in heir-creation. He was, wrote Weldon, 'not very uxorious', in reply to which Bishop Goodman, who generally tries to defend James against Weldon's snide innuendo, could only say, 'There was little in the Queen to make him uxorious.'

It wasn't just that James was not sexually attracted to women. Before Buckingham came into his life he was hostile to them in a way that went well beyond the casual sexism of the time. As a young man he wrote 'A Satire against Women'. In this poem he declares that, just as all goats climb and all chicken cackle, all hounds chase hares and all magpies steal (and so on and so forth – there are forty-two instances of such biologically determined behaviour), 'just so are women all by nature vain'. Women cannot keep secrets; they bear grudges; they gossip. They are greedy 'for every gilded thing'. They scheme to 'to win a noble name/ By false affection and by flattering'. They are crafty, but they are 'all fools'.

Misogynist invective of this kind was not uncommon in Scotland in James's youth. But his railing against women went far beyond the conventional. The French ambassador was unpleasantly struck by it. He 'piques himself on great contempt for women … and scoffs with great levity at all men who pay them honour'. There is no record of James's ever having had a female friend.

But 'here was a strange change', writes Weldon. James, who 'naturally in former times hated women', who sent his own children away to be brought up by guardians and, once they were of age, set them up in separate households of their own, discovered, under Buckingham's influence, the pleasures of family life. Whereas once he 'would not endure his queen and children in his lodgings, now you would have judged that none but women frequented them'.

James was not abruptly transformed from a woman-hater into a respecter of women. In writing to Buckingham he several times refers to the latter's wife, sister and mother as 'your cunts'. Historians have tried to persuade themselves that he means 'your countesses', but Katherine became a marchioness on her marriage, and then a duchess, and James was careful about titles. His handwriting is perfectly legible, and his spelling – 'cuntes' – leaves little room for doubt. But however crudely he might talk about the Buckingham ladies behind their backs, in addressing them he was kind.

When Katherine was first pregnant, he wrote repeatedly to Buckingham, fussing over her welfare as he never had over that of his own daughter. (Elizabeth had by this time given birth to five of the thirteen children she would eventually bear.) 'Let her never go in a coach on the street' ... 'Let your mother keep all hasty news from coming to her ears' ... 'Let her not eat too much fruit.' Perhaps, at first, he was solicitous not so much of Katherine herself as of the incubator of his favourite's baby. He also wrote, 'The Lord of Heaven bless thee this morning and thy thing my daughter, and the sweet little thing that is in her belly.' But it wasn't long before Katherine and baby alike had ceased to be his George's 'things' and become King James's own dear ones. 'God bless thee, sweet Kate,' he writes, 'and little Mall [Mary, the Buckinghams' first child] to the comfort of thy dear dad.'

Soon Mall and her brothers and cousins would be habitués of the innermost chambers of the court, softening and enlivening what had once been an unrelievedly masculine household. Wilson writes that 'the King, that never much cared for women, had his court swarming with the Marquis's kindred, so that little ones would dance up and down the privy lodgings like fairies'.

Here are some lines from *The Two Noble Kinsmen*, by William Shakespeare and John Fletcher, first performed in 1614, the year King James and Buckingham met, and revived for a performance at court in the year Buckingham married. The play has two heroes. Here one of them, Arcite, is addressing his beloved friend and cousin, Palamon:

We are an endless mine to one another:
We are one another's wife, ever begetting
New births of love; we are father, friends, acquaintance;
We are in one another, families.

Homophobic rhetoric, from Buckingham's lifetime to our own, has opposed same-sex love to familial happiness, as though the two were irreconcilable. King James, the unloved orphan growing up lonely and in fear, had found quite otherwise. His marriage had been troubled and distant. As a father he had been overly authoritarian and unsympathetic. In loving Buckingham, he had acquired – however unorthodox the means – a happy family of his own at last.

Portraits of a Marriage

WHILE Buckingham and his wife were enjoying their first winter as a married couple, Anthony Van Dyck, twenty-one years old and prodigiously talented, came to London for the first time. 'His work is beginning to be esteemed hardly less than that of his master,' wrote the Earl of Arundel's secretary. That master was Peter Paul Rubens, who called Van Dyck 'the best of my students', and who had sent him to London with letters of introduction.

When he returned to London twelve years later, after a long sojourn in Italy, Van Dyck was to become the supreme artist of pre-revolutionary Stuart England. He was so fashionable that his paintings defined fashion. His name was attached to hats and hairdos and beards and lace collars. He depicted all the great ones of the court, lending his subjects a glamour and a tenderly rendered humanity that was all his own. He even made anxious, stiff-mannered little King Charles I look noble and romantic. His representations of Charles's court became, after the onset of the civil wars and the Commonwealth, royalist political icons – images of the grace and vulnerability of a culture gone with the wind.

In 1620, though, he was a newcomer with a name to make and an approach to art that most of the English found outlandish. In the course of the few months he spent in London he would paint the Earl of Arundel's portrait and make a chalk drawing of King James, who granted him a pension of £100 per annum. But the most important works that resulted from his first English visit were both celebrations of Buckingham's marriage.

*   *   *

One of them is a history painting, *The Continence of Scipio* (Plate 6). Scipio was a Roman general, hero of the second Punic war, Hannibal's great opponent. Van Dyck's painting depicts an incident recorded by Livy.

A young Carthaginian noblewoman has been captured by the victorious Romans and granted as a trophy to Scipio. Her parents offer a load of treasure to buy her freedom. Her betrothed, a Carthaginian youth named Allucius, comes with them to the Roman camp to plead for her freedom. Scipio is merciful. Instead of making her his concubine, as would have been expected, he hands back the young woman with assurances that she is untouched and her virtue undefiled. All the precious objects that her parents have offered him for a ransom, he gives to the young couple as a wedding gift.

Many artists, from Bellini to Reynolds, have treated the edifying subject – Scipio self-denying, chaste and generous, the lovers grateful.

The circumstances surrounding Buckingham's marriage were being picked over by the scandalmongers. The most prominent man at court, the greatest heiress in the land – how come such a couple had not been wed with days of feasting, with masques and epithalamia such as had greeted Somerset's marriage, with a great ceremony in Westminster Abbey, the bride weighed down with cloth of silver and sparkling with gemstones? People said Katherine had been tricked into marriage, or perhaps raped. Or, besotted with beautiful Buckingham, she had absconded from her father's house. Something had made it necessary for the pair to be married hurriedly, and without the normal to-do. The story gave an impression of shiftiness and making-the-best-of-things that needed to be erased.

The King and Buckingham were suspected of sexual depravity, but James was also known to be 'the chastest prince for women'. Would this not be a good moment to celebrate that chastity? To honour the King in the guise of the admirably 'continent' Scipio, to show him magnanimously refusing improper sexual pleasures that a lesser man would have taken as his due? To emphasise how benignly the King sanctioned the marriage of an unsullied bride and her devoted groom?

In Van Dyck's painting the Carthaginian maiden, who stands with demurely downcast eyes, as passive as the precious rugs and vessels and sculpted marbles that are being offered as her ransom, is unmistakably

Katherine. Long straight nose. Softly rounded jawline. Creamily solid shoulders. Next to her, at the centre of the picture, stands Allucius, a portrait of Buckingham. He turns his face up to gaze at Scipio, in a posture of submissive gratitude. Scipio, enthroned beneath a canopy, is shadowed, his face (seen from below and in profile) hard to read. While attendants and onlookers jostle around them, the two men appear frozen, their gazes locked.

The heart of the composition is an intricate arrangement of hands. Allucius's two hands cross over, one pointing tentatively towards his lady-love, who reaches out to touch it with one of hers, the other laid on his heart and gesturing towards the kingly Scipio, whose powerful right arm completes the knot.

Van Dyck's English was not good. He is cruelly caricatured in Ben Jonson's *Masque of Augurs* as 'Van Goose', a gibberish-speaking Dutchman who advocates a dangerously novel kind of art. 'De more absurd it be, and vrom de purpose … it is de more art'. (Philistine jokes about artistic innovation have varied little over the centuries.) But he would certainly have heard enough tittle-tattle to understand the complexity of the Buckingham marriage.

Some scholars believe that *The Continence of Scipio* was commissioned by Arundel as a present for Buckingham. John Chamberlain wrote that year that Arundel was perpetually plying the Marquis of Buckingham with gifts. Buckingham was the route to preferment, and Arundel wanted to be Lord Treasurer.

Or perhaps the patron was King James, and the picture was his wedding gift to the young couple. Or perhaps it was Buckingham himself who commissioned the work. Gerbier, with his Flemish connections, would have urged him to snap up a work from the promising young artist. But whoever ordered and paid for the picture, Buckingham must certainly have sat for it, and approved its composition.

The *portrait historié*, in which a real-life sitter appears as a historical or mythological figure, was a new genre (it wouldn't even get its name until the eighteenth century). No one in England had ever seen such a thing before. The majority of English patrons wanted themselves to be recorded for posterity in all their pomp, in static dignified postures, their jewels and clothes all shinily in place. But Buckingham forsakes realism and embraces legend. He is not showing off his real-world status; he is an actor in fancy dress. He is not insisting on his dominance; he presents himself as a supplicant. He allows himself and his wife to be shown scantily draped. He inserts himself into a tableau with the glamour of classical antiquity, while delicately and knowingly exploring the complexities of a triangular relationship between a regal benefactor, a grateful younger man and the bride the former was graciously giving to the latter.

The painting was to hang in the great hall of Buckingham's grandest home, York House, a constant reminder of his dependency on King James. Allucius/Buckingham, gazing, hand on heart, at the shadowed Scipio as he presents his brightly illuminated betrothed to him, seems to be miming his assurance that – wife or no wife – he will be the King's for ever. The 'humble slave and dog' presents his Carthaginian-style Katherine to his master as a well-trained retriever lays a hare at his master's feet.

The Continence of Scipio was unorthodox to early-seventeenth-century English viewers. Van Dyck's other portrait of Buckingham and his Kate (as he was by now calling her) was mind-blowing – sexy, dynamic, brilliantly coloured, outrageously strange. To look at William Larkin's portrait of Buckingham, painted in 1616, and then at Van Dyck's *The Duke and Duchess of Buckingham as Venus and Adonis*, painted less than five years later, is to have the dizzying experience of a ride in a vastly accelerated time machine (Plate 7).

Larkin's approach to figure-painting is not substantially different from that of the artists who painted Queen Elizabeth in the previous century. A stationary figure, hieratically posed. Costume designed to signal the wearer's status and display his or her wealth. An indoor setting artfully dressed to convey messages about the subject's claims to respect. Immobile faces. Bodies arranged according to long-established iconographic tradition. Everything still. Everything stiff. Then turn to Van Dyck. The baroque has blown in across the Channel, shaking the windows and rattling the walls.

The couple are outdoors, beneath a sky over which clouds race. Buckingham wears nothing but a pair of sandals and a billow of kingfisher-blue silk that just – only just – covers his crotch. The drapery flares out behind him. He, the great dancer, is on his toes, in motion. His arm is around the shoulders of his wife, his Venus. He leans in to her solicitously, tenderly, hand on heart again, his eyes seeking her face.

She is more rooted, more proud. Serenely, she gazes out at the viewer. Her wrap is a length of golden-orange satin. It has slipped down to her waist, leaving her upper body, including her pearly-pale breasts, entirely exposed. She holds it carelessly. It will soon slip further. Both of them are solemn, concentrated, because the joy of love is majestic, awe-inspiring, a distinguished thing.

The long poem *Venus and Adonis* was William Shakespeare's first published work. Written in 1593, when an outbreak of plague had closed the theatres and left the actor/dramatist with time on his hands, it was repeatedly reprinted. Its sixteenth edition had just appeared when Van Dyck came to England in 1620. A version of a story from Ovid, it tells how Venus, goddess of love, looks down from Olympus and sees Adonis, a young man of such dazzling beauty that she immediately descends to earth to make him her lover.

She finds him just setting out for a day's hunting. Forget the chase, she says. She has greater pleasures to offer. Adonis is reluctant. He loves to hunt. He is scared. He is too young, he tells her. Fruit 'being early plucked, is sour to taste'. He feels insecure, immature: 'Measure my strangeness with my unripe years.' He is altogether unready for sex with a woman: 'Before I know myself, seek not to know me.'

Venus won't take no for an answer. (Shakespeare's poem is comic.) She persuades Adonis to lie down with her.

> *'Fondling' she saith, 'since I have hemmed thee here*
> *Within the circuit of this ivory pale,*
> *I'll be a park, and thou shalt be my deer.'*

A 'pale' might be a fence, but here it is Venus's ivory-coloured arms. She urges him to enjoy himself.

> *Feed where thou wilt, on mountain or in dale;*
> *Graze on my lips, and if those hills be dry,*
> *Stray lower, where the pleasant fountains lie.*

The goddess of love is freely offering herself. Adonis breaks away and goes to his horse, but the horse gallops off in pursuit of a mare. All nature – except for virginal Adonis – is sexually aroused. Venus continues to plead and wheedle. Adonis remains cold. She faints. Afraid he has killed her, he holds her until she comes back to life, then tears himself away again. Will I see you tomorrow? she asks. No, he says, he has plans. He will be hunting boar. Venus, who is getting seriously annoyed, has a vision of the boar killing him.

The next day, sure enough, Adonis is gored to death by the boar he is pursuing. Flowers bloom where he falls, purple and white like the blood running down his marmoreal limbs.

It is hardly a happy story with which to celebrate a marriage, but Van Dyck turns it around. Titian, and Van Dyck's own mentor Rubens, had both painted the subject. In Rubens's version (now in the Hermitage), Venus, naked and voluptuously plump, clings to Adonis. He tries to shake her off. A hound leaps beside him, turning to look up at his master as though urging him to stop wasting time and begin the hunt. That hound must have been painted by Rubens's pupil, Van Dyck, and it appears again, exactly reproduced, in Van Dyck's own treatment. This time, though, rather than striving to be off and away with his dog, Adonis ignores him.

Van Dyck's Buckingham/Adonis is no frigid adolescent. Buckingham has grown up and bulked out. His thighs, so wand-like in Larkin's painting, are tremendously muscled. He has a beard, and a broad chest and wrestler's arms. He is a mature man delighting in his wife. The dog's genitals, exposed by its leaping pose, remind us of what is so insecurely hidden beneath the couple's drapery. Van Dyck's *Venus and Adonis* is a painting, not of love rejected, but of consummation. Katherine/Venus's look – satisfied to the point of smugness – bears unmistakably the lineaments of gratified desire.

Hidden away in private collections, the painting was all but unknown to art-historians until it came up for auction at Christie's in 2018. We do not know where it was placed in the Buckinghams' house. Let us imagine it hung above their bed.

The Spanish Match

THERE was another marriage to be arranged, that of Prince Charles.

From the very beginning of his English reign, James had been considering marrying his heir (first Henry and subsequently Charles) to a Spanish princess.

Talk of such a marriage formed a part of the Anglo-Spanish peace conference in 1604. The Spanish envoys suggested it, but on condition that Prince Henry, then aged eight, convert to Catholicism forthwith and be sent to Madrid to grow up at the Spanish court. That was out of the question. But perhaps with the passage of time more acceptable terms might be agreed upon. Royal marriage negotiations, especially those in which the couple concerned were still so young, were moves in a diplomatic game. Children died, alliances shifted, better offers might be forthcoming.

James continued to hope that the 'Spanish Match', as it came to be known, might one day be made. It formed part of his grand plan for the unification of Christendom. It was with its prospect in mind that James betrothed his daughter Elizabeth to the Elector Palatine, foremost among the Protestant princes within the Holy Roman Empire. The necessary next knot would be tied once James's son had married into the royal family of one of the great Catholic powers – the most likely one being Spain.

Henry died. The princess who had been intended for him, the Infanta Ana, married Louis XIII and became Queen Anne of France. But she had a younger sister, the Infanta Maria. Diego Sarmiento de Acuña, Count of Gondomar, the Spanish ambassador to London, suggested that Maria might perhaps, one day, marry the new heir, Prince Charles.

* * *

Gondomar was Spanish ambassador at the court of King James for nine years (with intermissions) from 1613. Throughout that time he continued to promote the Match.

Gondomar was sophisticated and subtle-minded. He was to become a hate figure for all those anti-Catholic, anti-Spanish English people who detested the idea of closer association with their old enemy. They saw Gondomar as devious and duplicitous. It was to describe him that the word 'Machiavellian' was first used, pejoratively, in English. They mocked him cruelly for his physical disabilities. (He suffered from some sort of painful and embarrassing condition – perhaps an enlargement of his testicles or an anal fistula.) King James, on the other hand, got on with him very well.

The two of them conversed, as was normal among diplomats, in Latin. Gondomar paid James a nicely turned compliment that flattered them both. He told the King that he spoke Latin well, 'like a scholar', while he – Gondomar – spoke Latin badly, 'like a king'.

The English Parliament was generally hostile to Spain, and unenthusiastic about the peace agreement sealed at the beginning of James's reign, but in 1614 King James dismissed Parliament, and didn't recall it for seven years. Meanwhile he and Gondomar worked to construct a newly cordial relationship between their two countries.

They became friends, or anyway mutually appreciative sparring partners. They were almost the same age and had almost the same name.
They called themselves the 'two Diegos' (Diego being one of the Spanish
equivalents of James) and toasted each other as such, drinking from the
same bottle. When Gondomar was recalled to Spain in 1622, King James
wrote, 'On account of his desire for universal Christian peace and our
friendship and that of our realms, I have never treated with another
prince's ambassador with greater love.'

Gondomar's chief aims, as ambassador to England, were to discourage
any alliance between the English and the French, and to ensure that the
English would not be tempted to intervene in the conflict in the
Netherlands between the Spanish and the breakaway Dutch Republic.

In each case the prospect of a royal marriage was useful. While the
Spanish Match remained a credible possibility, Charles would not be
married to a French princess. Nor would James want to antagonise his
son's future father-in-law by meddling on the side of the Dutch.

And then there was the question of religion. The Roman Catholics of
King James's kingdoms were no longer persecuted as ferociously as they
had been under Queen Elizabeth, but they were still subject to numerous prohibitions and penalties, and they were not allowed to celebrate
Mass in public. Gondomar believed that the prospect of the Spanish
Match gave him leverage to negotiate a better deal for them. If he won
them the right to worship freely, he would have done glorious service
not only to his King, but also to his co-religionists and his God.

There was a problem. King James and Gondomar might believe their
peoples could be friends. They underestimated how deeply and fiercely
a substantial proportion of the English population, and of their
Parliamentary representatives, hated Spain.

For twenty years before James came to the throne, the English had
been in a state of undeclared war with Spain. That war had generated a
great body of hostile propaganda (later termed the 'black legend'). Here
is the Elizabethan patriot author Robert Ashley writing in 1589, the year
after the Spanish Armada's attempted invasion. To Ashley the Spanish
are 'scum of Barbarians'. The entire nation is 'unfaithful, ravenous, and
insatiable'. In a Spaniard's nature 'may be seen together incorporated, a
crafty fox, a ravenous wolf, and a raging tiger'. He is 'an unclean and

filthy swine, a thievish owlet, a proud peacock ... a legion of devils'. The Spanish are so cruel as to make the ancient Scythians seem mild by comparison. They are lustful and perverted. Their pretence at valour is all just 'brags and boastings'. Spain 'is and ever hath been the sink, the puddle, and filthy heap of the most loathsome, infected, and slavish people that ever yet lived on earth'.

That deeply ingrained racism would not easily be erased. There were British Hispanophiles, but they were exceptional. James Howell, an English diplomat in Madrid, wrote to a friend in London that he was sorry to hear how uncivilly the Spanish ambassador had been treated in England: 'What ballads and pasquils and fopperies and plays were made against Gondomar' when he was just 'doing his master's business'.

Buckingham saw no reason to hate Spain. Gondomar got to know him well. He became very friendly with Buckingham's wife and mother. He and Buckingham would meet sometimes, privately, at his residence near Holborn to talk about things that the King could not discuss publicly, so infuriating would his ultra-Protestant subjects have found them. One of those matters, Gondomar's grand project, the Spanish Match, would become the occasion for the most surprising adventure of Buckingham's life.

Magic

WHEN Prince Henry was dying in 1612 he was attended by six of the most learned physicians in the land. They tried tisanes and broth. They tried a purge (a laxative) and a clyster (an enema). They tried bleeding. They administered a panacea, sent by Sir Walter Raleigh from his imprisonment in the Tower. (Henry was a supporter of Raleigh's; Raleigh knew that his own life might well depend on the Prince's being saved.) Finally, they tried birds.

Henry's head was shaved and dead pigeons were laid on it. To no avail. On the following day a cock was killed,and slit down the back to open it out, spatchcock-fashion. It was then placed against the soles of the prince's feet. Two days later Prince Henry died.

In Buckingham's lifetime the Middle Ages were not yet over, but the Enlightenment (which would not be so named for several more decades) had already begun. There were witches and witch-hunters. There were also diligent, scholarly rationalists. Buckingham was fortunate to have as a mentor Francis Bacon, whose scalpel-sharp mind could be turned to almost any purpose, who advised him on how to conduct himself at court and in government, but who was also the father of empiricism and the instigator of a strain of thinking which would eventually come to be called 'scientific'.

Dead-pigeon magic and experiment-based science – both were current, both were deadly serious.

Buckingham's entourage included one Dr John Lambe. Buckingham had first contacted Lambe for advice about his elder brother John, Viscount Purbeck. Purbeck was intermittently mad – he would probably now be categorised as bipolar. Buckingham consulted a number of healers on his behalf. There was someone Buckingham described as a 'man that offered him a strange way of cure for himself and his brother'. There was the 'astrological-physician' Dr Richard Napier, whose methods blended Galenic medicine with magic. Napier, in one month in 1614, cast twenty-seven horoscopes. Often he would prescribe treatment without even meeting the patient, simply from reading the stars. When he did make a home-visit, he would begin by conjuring up the Archangel Raphael, who would tell him whether the patient had been bewitched.

And then there was Dr Lambe.

Lambe was a wizard. We know quite a bit about him, not only from a contemporary account of his life, but also because he was frequently in trouble with the law, so the charges against him have been preserved in court records. He told fortunes. He could discover who was, or wasn't, a witch (perhaps because he was one himself). He could find things that were lost. He had a crystal ball in which those who paid for the privilege could see the face of the man or woman they were going to marry. Like Marlowe's Doctor Faustus, he could conjure up spirits.

So far, perhaps, so harmless. But Lambe used his arts for devilish ends. He naughtily bewitched (or drugged) a young woman so that she

became delusional and – imagining herself to be walking through deep water – hitched her skirts up to her waist to keep them dry, thereby revealing her nakedness while male onlookers leered and sniggered. He was believed to be able to 'intoxicate, poison, and bewitch any man' to make him impotent. He could also, if properly rewarded, see to it that a person peaked and pined. He was found guilty of 'maliciously, and feloniously' consuming 'the body and strength' of a certain Lord W. by means of his 'evil, devilish, and execrable arts'.

Lambe did time for these practices in several different prisons, including the King's Bench. There he lived surprisingly comfortably, playing the virginals, with a servant to wait upon him, entertaining friends and plucking bottles of sack out of thin air to pour drinks for them.

Some people thought him amusing. When he was at liberty well-to-do people invited him to their houses and laughed at his tricks. No one could be sure whether he was a fraud and a scallywag, or a dangerous sorcerer. People wondered why, if he was really as well-versed in the dark arts as he claimed, he seemed 'to be altogether unlearned, and silly of discourse'. Others thought he made light of his science because it was safer to be thought 'an impostor' than to be known to be 'truly and guiltily learned in those wicked mysteries'.

Buckingham seems to have been half-entertained, half-impressed by Lambe. He referred to him as 'my devil'. A rhyme circulated in which he was imagined boasting that he had commissioned Lambe to make love potions for him, using 'Lambe's philtres to incite/Chaste ladies to my fowl lust's delight'.

Buckingham employed a wizard. His wife's family had been devastated, they believed, by witches.

Katherine was the Earl of Rutland's only child by his first marriage. After her mother's death (smallpox) Rutland married again. With his second wife, Cecilia, he had two sons. Katherine had inherited her mother's fortune, but being female, she would receive no more from her father while her half-brothers lived. Rutland's great houses at Belvoir and Haddon, and the bulk of his estates in Yorkshire, Derbyshire and Northamptonshire, would go to Lord Henry Manners, the eldest of the two, with a lesser share being granted to Francis, the second son.

There were three women – Joan Flower, and her two daughters, Margaret and Philippa – who lived in the nearby village and worked as cleaners or kitchen maids at Belvoir Castle. By the time they enter the historical record, Joan's husband was no longer with her. None of the three women went to church. Neighbours said they kept a 'bawdy house'. Joan was 'a monstrous malicious woman, full of imprecations irreligious'. Margaret and Philippa were said to be 'abandoned and profligate women, who scrupled not at the means by which to satisfy their inordinate desires'. A ballad circulating soon after their deaths described Philippa as a 'well-known strumpet lewd'.

Through the fear and disgust the three were eventually to inspire, one can dimly make out three women living in the financially precarious and reputationally unsafe condition of those without a male protector. Joan was loud-mouthed and combative, a complainer and a grudge-bearer, not an easy neighbour. She was knowledgeable about medicinal plants and herbs, and made a bit of money by selling remedies. Her daughters supplemented the income they earned from drudging at the castle by selling sex.

In 1613 some of the other servants at Belvoir Castle told the Countess that Margaret Flower was stealing food. Soon afterwards Margaret was accused of 'undecencies'. The Countess dismissed her. Joan Flower, furious on her daughter's behalf, made a noisy scene. She protested loudly and 'terrified them all with curses and threatening of revenge'.

This is how a great many witch-hunting stories begin. An angry or desperate woman rants and yells. No one pays much attention at the time, but later those threats and – most particularly – those curses are remembered.

Later in the same year the Rutlands' elder son, Henry, fell ill. No one could decide what was wrong with him. An account of the story written in 1620, and entitled *The Wonderful Discoverie of the Witchcrafts of Margaret and Philippa Flower, daughters of Joan Flower*, tells us that he 'sickened very strangely' and 'did lingering, lie tormented long'. In September he died. He was less than six years old.

A little later the rest of the family fell ill. Katherine, the eldest child, and her father and stepmother all suffered 'sickness and extraordinary convulsions'. They recovered, but the surviving boy, Lord Francis, now Rutland's heir, did not. He was 'most barbarously and inhumanely tortured' by his illness. From descriptions of his symptoms it is clear that he had epilepsy – which was one of the conditions that Robert Burton, author of *The Anatomy of Melancholy*, lists as completely baffling seventeenth-century physicians. Epilepsy was strongly associated with witchcraft. The sufferer, struggling in fits, seems to have been possessed by an external power – a devil perhaps.

Doctors were summoned. The 'astrological-physician' Richard Napier was among them. So was Dr Francis Anthony, who had been reprimanded by the Royal College of Physicians for his use of an alchemical remedy called 'essence of gold' that he claimed was a universal panacea. No one could help poor little Francis.

It was soon being said in the neighbourhood that Joan Flower, 'the old malicious fiend', had brought down this calamity on the Rutlands and their children when she cursed them. People came forward with other sinister stories of supernatural goings-on in the Flowers' household. A local man who had been visiting Philippa at night said she had bewitched him so that 'he had no power to leave', being 'marvellously altered both in mind and body'.

Initially the Rutlands ignored the rumours, but when, after five years of suffering, Francis was no better, *The Wonderful Discoverie* tells us 'their hearts began to breed dislike and greatly grew afraid' of the Flower women. Early in 1619, Joan, Margaret and Philippa were arrested on suspicion of murderous witchcraft. They were taken on foot, in midwinter, to Lincoln. Joan died on the way, perhaps of exposure, perhaps

choking to death on a piece of bread designed to be a test of her guilt. In Lincoln, Margaret and Philippa were interrogated for five weeks in a prison tower known as the 'witch-hole'. They insisted on their innocence for as long as they could withstand their interrogators, but eventually Margaret confessed to having helped her mother bewitch the Rutlands and their children. Her confession is confused and phantasmagorical. She says that four devils visited her in her cell. One of them had 'a black head like an ape'. Another was her mother's cat Rutterkin. It sounds as though, sleep-deprived and terrified as she must have been, her sanity was giving way.

The women's trial took place at the next assizes. The Earl of Rutland attended. On the strength of Margaret's confession, she and her sister were found guilty of entertaining and employing 'evil and wicked sprits'. They were hanged before a crowd who, according to *The Wonderful Discoverie*, were terrified to behold 'such dissolute and abominable creatures'.

Ever since Henry died and Francis first fell ill the Rutlands had been hoping other children might be born to them, but none came. They had hoped that the witches' wicked power might relax its grip after their death and that Francis might recover. It didn't happen.

By June 1619, a few months after the Flowers' executions, Buckingham approached the Earl of Rutland, asking to marry his daughter Katherine. Negotiations continued for the rest of that year. One of Buckingham's demands was that if Katherine's little brother 'should fail', making her her father's sole heir, her dowry should be doubled. By January 1620 it was reported that the couple were 'contracted'.

Two months later Francis died. John Chamberlain writes that he had been killed 'by witchcraft (as some will have it) but in all likelihood of the falling sickness', and that he was generally 'a weak child'. The credulous majority, though, felt certain the 'Belvoir Witches', as the Flowers were known, were responsible.

The boy's death made Katherine the richest heiress in the country. Chamberlain had reported that talks about the marriage had been broken off because of Buckingham's 'exorbitant demands'. But with Francis gone, writes Chamberlain, 'his death may chance bring on the match again'. A month later, Katherine and Buckingham were wed.

There is absolutely no reason to suppose that Buckingham had any hand in Francis Manners's death. It is certainly true, though, that he profited by it. Later, when he was being accused of killing King James, the death of the boy who should have been his brother-in-law was remembered, and brought up against him as another crime in which he was implicated.

The boy's father, certainly, never suspected him. On the Earl of Rutland's tomb there are two stone-carved figures of small boys, kneeling, each clutching a skull. The inscription explains that they are Henry and Francis, 'both who died in their infancy by wicked practice and sorcery'.

Apocalypse

In May 1618 three emissaries of the Holy Roman Emperor were thrown out of a high window in Hradčany Castle in the Bohemian capital of Prague. They survived. According to Catholic sources they were caught in the arms of angels, who set them down gently on their feet. Protestants relate that their fall was broken when they tumbled into a dungheap. Their defenestration is conventionally identified as the beginning of the devastating sequence of overlapping conflicts known as the Thirty Years War.

There was, at that time, small reason why anyone in England should concern themselves with the clashes between the Holy Roman Empire and the Protestant nationalist nobility of Bohemia. In the following year, though, the Bohemians dismissed their elective king, a Habsburg and a Catholic, and invited Frederick, the Elector Palatine, King James of England's son-in-law, to take his place. Frederick accepted, and set out to take possession of his new kingdom, thereby making an inveterate enemy of the displaced King Ferdinand, who was about to become Holy Roman Emperor.

Frederick's supporters framed his bid for power in Bohemia as an apocalyptic battle between (Protestant) good and (Roman Catholic) evil. Edward Herbert, ambassador in Paris, exulted in 'the apparent way His providence hath opened to the ruin of the papacy', while in England Archbishop Abbot wrote, 'Methinks I do in this … foresee the work of God.' Abbot prophesied that Frederick's move would trigger anti-Catholic uprisings across Europe. 'By piece and piece, the Kings of the Earth that gave their power unto the Beast … shall now tear the Whore, and make her desolate, as St John in his revelation hath foretold.' A pamphlet published in Amsterdam in praise of Frederick was entitled *The Messiah Already Come*.

King James was not pleased. As a reigning monarch, and an apologist for monarchy, he could not be expected to think well of deposition. More – when he had wedded his daughter Elizabeth to Frederick, the two of them gleaming in cloth of silver, he had seen their union as one of the ties in the great web he was weaving to bind all Christendom together. He had been sure that Elizabeth would play her part in bringing about the golden age of pan-European peace that was to be his life's work. And now here was her husband stirring up a sectarian conflict at the heart of the continent.

Frederick and Elizabeth reigned in Prague for only a few months before the Emperor Ferdinand moved to expel them. In November 1620 their forces were decisively defeated by the Imperial army at the Battle of White Mountain near Prague. Spanish troops in league with the Empire occupied most of Frederick's original realm of the Palatinate. He and Elizabeth were now throneless refugees. As they began their life in exile, with the peculiar English love of losers operating in their favour, Elizabeth and Frederick were reimagined in Elizabeth's home country as romantic figures – the Winter King and the Winter Queen.

The anti-Spanish party called loudly on the King to take up arms on their behalf, for the sake of family ties, for the sake of that dangerously nebulous concept 'honour' and for the sake of 'true [i.e. Protestant] religion'.

Voices prophesied war. 'Let all our spirits be gathered up to animate this business,' preached Archbishop Abbot, 'that the world may take notice that we are awake when God calls.'

Abbot and his confederates had brought Buckingham to court precisely so that when God called there would be someone close to the King through whom they could speak up for an anti-Catholic, anti-Spanish war. It did them little good. Before the Battle of White Mountain William Trumbull, English ambassador in Brussels, heard tell that Buckingham had declared he would be glad to spend all the 'bounty' he had received from the King in Frederick's cause. But Buckingham was the King's instrument, not an independent policy-maker, and James, at that point, had no intention of aiding and abetting his son-in-law's bid for Bohemia.

The Spanish occupation of the Palatinate, though, was another matter. That was obnoxious to James, not only because of his family connection to Frederick, but also because it was an assault on the rights of a legitimate ruler. The King sent messages to Frederick and Elizabeth, in exile in The Hague. He didn't offer them sanctuary and a home in England – that, he thought, would be to provoke the Habsburg powers too far. But he assured them he would help them regain their own territory (but not Bohemia), by use of force if necessary. The messenger was Buckingham's half-brother, Sir Edward Villiers. At the same time James authorised the collection of a 'benevolence' – financial aid for Frederick to help him evict the Spanish invaders. Buckingham personally contributed the huge sum of £5,000.

However reluctantly King James contemplated the possibility of war, Buckingham, it seems, was ready for it. He began to take lessons in swordsmanship.

The predicament of the Winter King and Queen was to complicate King James's foreign policy and destabilise his government for the rest of his life. It brought his obligations as a monarch and a father into direct conflict with his pacifism and his vision of a united Europe. It angered and saddened him. It was eventually to cause a rift between him and the two people he loved best in the world – his 'sweet boys', Prince Charles and Buckingham.

More immediately, it forced him to engage with Parliament – something he never liked doing. He had told the Spanish ambassador he was 'surprised that my ancestors should ever have permitted such an institution to come into existence'.

For seven years he had been getting by without it, his government feeding, as he puts it, 'like a shellfish upon his own moisture'. But now, if he was to be called upon to send a task force to restore Frederick and Elizabeth to the Palatinate, or – worse – if it became necessary to make war on Spain, he was going to need a great deal of money. He could not tax his subjects without their consent, given by their representatives in Parliament. Parliament must grant him subsidies.

Corruption

IN the six years Buckingham had been at court, King James's fantasy of divine kingship – archaic as it was – had been unchecked by the realities of the English constitution. Wielding power as his lord and master's assistant, Buckingham had operated within what seemed to be an absolute monarchy. In 1621, speaking in the House of Commons and exaggerating his former naivety for rhetorical effect, he told the assembled members that he had known nothing of parliaments, but that he was resolved to 'be a scholar', to study this strange new world in which a monarch was obliged to beg for his subjects' support.

King James, early in his English reign, had defined the relationship between Parliament and himself. Kings, he said, were 'God's lieutenants'. More than that, they 'were justly called gods, for that they exercise a manner or resemblance of divine power'. As King, he elaborated, he was like a father – his people being his children. He was like a head, the rest of the nation being the body, each part of which was governed by the head's commands.

Parliament was to know its place. It was not there to initiate legislation, but to endorse those laws upon which the King and Council had resolved. Its members should not presume to 'meddle with main points of government', explained James, since 'that is my craft'. They should not entertain 'complaints against your King'. Nor should they concern themselves 'with the church, nor with state matters, nor with princes' prerogatives'. Any 'unquiet spirit and busybody' who tried to do so should be shunned as a 'spirit of Satan'.

Parliament was the King's partner, but subordinate to him, as a wife is to her husband. He was bound, as a husband is, 'to cherish his wife, to entreat her kindly … and procure her love by all means'. In return for his kindness, Parliament, like a good wife, should serve him as an obedient helpmeet, not waste time quibbling about its rights and privileges. Parliament existed to 'make laws and reform abuses' (at the King's prompting and subject to the King's approval). Most importantly, it was to keep the King supplied with money. Like a husband calling for his dinner, 'the King is to open himself in his wants', and like a good wife hurrying to set her man's favourite dish on the table, 'the people' (represented by Parliament) were to 'supply' those wants.

It is worth recalling at this point that Queen Anne had chosen to live apart from her husband.

The 1621 Parliament began smilingly. As he rode towards Westminster, King James was observed to be 'very cheerful all the way'. It was exceptionally cold. The Thames had frozen over, its surface strewn with chunks of ice 'like rocks and mountains, with strange and hideous aspect'. But his people had braved the wintry weather to stand three-deep along his route, crying out, 'God bless ye! God bless ye!', and James, who was often impatient with crowds, 'spake often and lovingly' to them.

When the King wished to address his entire Parliament, they would assemble in the Parliament Chamber, the Lords seated, the Commons standing tight-packed behind the balustrade – the Bar – that fenced off the part of the hall furthest from the throne. On this occasion James kept the duration of his speech to a modest one hour, for fear, he said, of wearying the members (he was easily capable of speaking for five times as long). He spoke of all the prudent economies he had made (or that Lord Treasurer Cranfield had made for him), and assured them how well managed his Exchequer now was. He spoke of the Navy, and how effectively Buckingham as Lord Admiral, 'albeit he was young and inexperienced', had reformed it, so that more ships were now being built at less expense. The Commons should not fear, he said, to entrust further funds to him. If they voted him 'supply' – in other words, authorised a programme of taxation – 'they should not put their money into a broken purse, but might be right well assured to have it well and husbandly disposed of'.

The Commons responded by granting him 'two subsidies' amounting to £160,000 – nothing like enough to fund the kind of aggressive war-making for which Archbishop Abbot and the rest of the anti-Span-

ish faction were calling, but evidence of goodwill at least. The King thanked them for 'their free, noble and not merchant-like dealing' (not the most tactful wording for a speech addressed to an audience including a substantial number of merchants, but intended kindly). The Speaker said what a 'comfort' it was 'to see those mists that in other parliaments darkened the sun of our sovereign' break apart to reveal the King's 'wonderful grace'. James agreed: 'Nothing more rejoiceth me.' Finally, to round off the happy exchange, James ventured a bit of play-acting of the kind that made his company so disconcerting. He drew a bystanding lord's sword (he seldom wore one himself). 'I mean to kill your Speaker,' he said, 'in remembrance of this day's work.'

Just a bit of fun. Actually he made use of the sword to dub the Speaker knight. But a discordant reminder, amidst all this concord, that Parliament's very existence depended, in his view, upon the King's consent. Its members, he would remind them in the course of this session, 'derived all matters of privilege from him, and by his grant'. Most of them would have heartily disagreed with this reading of the constitution, but it is what James sincerely believed.

The comfort and joy were short-lived. Dark mists once more obscured the sun. King James had asked voters not to elect 'discontented persons that cannot fish but in troubled waters'. Some of his new MPs turned out to be persons of that kind. Many of them were Puritans, and King James had said he detested a Puritan as much as a Catholic, in both cases not for doctrinal reasons but because they were not sufficiently deferential to the Crown. The members of the 1621 Parliament, before they would approve the raising of the money he needed, were determined to express their disapproval of the way he was ruling his kingdom.

For seven years, James had financed his regime by means that bypassed Parliamentary sanction – not by taxation, but by selling titles and offices and – most controversially – selling monopolies.

The purchaser of a monopoly acquired the exclusive right to control production and trade in a particular commodity, issuing licences to manufacturers and merchants, who had to pay dearly for them. Patents, covering services or technological innovations, operated in similar fashion. The system benefited the Exchequer, but to the shopkeepers and artisans who had to buy licences they felt like a form of extortion, whereby the rich and idle screwed money out of the hard-working lower orders. To the majority of Parliamentarians they seemed unfair, probably illegal, and definitely corrupt. In making the Crown financially independent of Parliament, they disrupted the balance of power within the state.

By the time the new Parliament assembled, wrote John Chamberlain, the King's 'impositions and patents are grown so grievous that of necessity they must be spoken of'.

Buckingham had granted his brother Kit Villiers a patent allowing him to rake off fees from the probate of wills. He had seen to it that Kit and their half-brother, Edward Villiers, had shares with their cousin, Sir Giles Mompesson, in the patent regulating inns. Edward Villiers also held the monopoly on the manufacture of gold and silver thread. Several of Buckingham's nephews and cousins and brothers-in-law enjoyed similar perks. 'The Lord Marquis', wrote John Hacket, 'was of a kind nature ... not willing to deny a suit, but prone to gratify all strangers, chiefly if any of his kindred brought them in their hand.'

None of these arrangements was unusual or, by the standards of the Jacobean court, egregiously extortionate. It seems not to have occurred to Buckingham that they might be censured.

King James had hoped that Parliament would not contain too many 'wrangling lawyers'. He was right to fear it.

Edward Coke, his legal career finished by the row over the commendam five years previously, was sitting in the Commons. He was about to turn seventy, as irascible and domineering as ever. He had been an authoritative judge. In his second career as a Parliament-man he would be a juggernaut of righteous conviction armed with a vast magazine of legal knowledge.

Days after the session began, Coke enquired about the patent of inns. In the ensuing discussion it came out that Sir Giles Mompesson, the principal patentee, had granted the licence for an inn in Devonshire to a suspected murderer, ignoring the advice of local magistrates. Had he been bribed to do so? Mompesson was called in for questioning. He protested his innocence of any corrupt dealing, but then appeared to confirm his guilt by going into hiding.

Buckingham was required to attend a Parliamentary conference on the case. He told the assembled company that, now that it appeared that his relative, Mompesson, had offended, he – Buckingham – would be 'the chiefest and forwardest against him'. He didn't seem intimidated. He didn't even seem much concerned that his two brothers and his cousin were implicated in what looked at best like negligence, at worst like corruption. Badly misreading the nature of Edward Coke, he tried to lighten the atmosphere with a flippant joke, implying that Mompesson, in having 'taken [to] his heels', had proved himself no fool.

Surely, Buckingham must have thought, this trivial dispute about a Devonshire innkeeper could not touch him, the human meteor, the best-beloved of the godlike King? Parliament was there to grant the King supply. He was impatient for them to get on with it. Why were they wasting time with these petty complaints?

It got worse. Edward Villiers had paid £4,000 for his monopoly on gold and silver thread, but it was hard to enforce. Manufacturers refused to apply for the licence and pay the fee. They were supported by the

Worshipful Company of Goldsmiths, one of the great City livery companies, who thought the monopoly encroached on their own long-established authority. Edward Villiers appealed to the Attorney General, Sir Henry Yelverton, saying 'the cause now lay ableeding', and unless the law intervened, 'all was lost'. Yelverton agreed to help the monopolist. Some of the recalcitrant gold thread-makers were imprisoned.

Outrage in the manufacturing community. The City authorities appealed to the King. James ordered that the thread-makers be released. He would not, he said 'govern his people by bonds'. But, how, in that case, were the monopolies to be made to work? When, in March 1621, the case was discussed in Parliament, the answer seemed to many obvious. They should not work at all.

Buckingham had been warned. In November 1620, as it became clear Parliament would soon be summoned, Francis Bacon had written to him. He advised Buckingham to suspend all the patents held by his family members. So, wrote Bacon, he could 'put off the envy of these things (which I think in themselves bear no great fruit) and rather take the thanks for ceasing them'.

Buckingham took no notice. A couple of months later the Dean of Westminster, John Williams (a good friend to the Villiers family), gave similar advice. Buckingham should send his brother Edward abroad, he said, maybe on 'an embassage to some of the princes of Germany'. (Edward, alarmed by the storm that seemed about to break over him, had already gone.) Williams went on: 'My sentence is, cast all monopolies and patents of griping projections into the Dead Sea.' Again, Buckingham did nothing.

Now the danger was mounting. Sir Edward Giles, MP, called upon his fellow Parliamentarians to act against these extortionate 'devices'. Monopolists were 'bloodsuckers of the kingdom and vipers of the commonwealth', he said. 'Let no man's greatness daunt us.' He was thinking of Edward Villiers's all-powerful brother.

This time both James and Buckingham realised the controversy was no joking matter. The King came to Westminster to shield the favourite. He spoke at length. He was ashamed to have such rottenness discovered at the heart of his government: 'It makes my hair stand upright.'

Buckingham, he said, had 'moved me many times in things of this kind', always explaining how the monopolies and patents he proposed would benefit the kingdom, while demonstrating his honourable disinterest by saying, 'For myself, I will have none of them.' (This was not quite true: Buckingham himself held the monopoly on saltpetre, an essential ingredient of gunpowder – a commodity that, with a war impending, was likely soon to be greatly in demand.) James asked Parliament to imagine how Buckingham was ceaselessly 'pestered and troubled at his chamber' by 'projectors', until 'his time hath been a purgatory to him'. If some of those 'projectors' turned out to have been dishonourable, Buckingham could hardly be blamed, the King seemed to be saying, for failing to foresee it.

At this point King James and Buckingham enacted a little scene together, one they had clearly rehearsed. Earlier in the session Edward Coke had used the image of a 'white crow' to describe someone whose outward appearance was pure as the driven snow but who was black-hearted, 'oftentimes craving and acquiring'. Now King James said that if Buckingham 'prove not himself a white crow [meaning blameless], he shall be called a black crow'. Buckingham stepped forward. He fell to his knees before the King. He declared that if he could not clear himself of all suspicion, he would be 'contented to abide Your Majesty's censure' and be called a 'black crow'.

The charade had its effect. It was not Buckingham whose political career was about to be sacrificed to appease Parliament.

Buckingham and his supporters had been working to divert Parliament's accusatory attention away from him, and therefore away from the King. His protégé Edward Sackville reminded the House that before the King approved a patent, he sought the opinion of people 'of place and trust about him'. If any patent or monopoly seemed improper, then the fault lay with those 'referees, who misled His Majesty'.

Cranfield, Buckingham's right-hand man in the Treasury, took up the theme, asking that 'the referees of all patents of grievances' should be 'examined for His Majesty's honour, who by them hath been abused'. In many cases the referee was – by natural consequence of his high offices – the former Attorney General and present Lord Chancellor, Francis Bacon.

It's unlikely that anyone – Sackville, Cranfield or Buckingham himself – foresaw the consequences of their strategy. They did not expect the Commons would be so bold as to attempt to disgrace one of the King's great officers. A few days after his first intervention Cranfield, nervously backtracking, told Bacon apologetically that though he had 'been the trumpet' against the referees, he had raised the question only to protect the King and 'did now incline ... not to have the referees meddled with'. Too late. Edward Coke – implacable in his pursuit of legal rectitude, no friend of Bacon's – had taken up the case.

On 14 March two gentlemen presented petitions to the Commons, alleging that Bacon was guilty of bribery and corruption. Further accusers came forward. Coke had found an all-but obsolete legal instrument – that of 'impeachment' – which had not been used since 1459 but would serve its purpose now. On 19 March Bacon was formally accused of taking bribes, a criminal offence. He would be tried by his peers in the House of Lords.

That evening the King sent Buckingham to visit Bacon at home, twice. Buckingham found his former mentor 'very sick and heavy'. He said, 'With respect to this charge of bribery, I am as innocent as any man born on St Innocent's Day.' The following day he asked for time to prepare to meet his accusers. His request was granted. His trial was deferred until after the Easter recess. But when it came, on 3 May, he offered no defence.

Why didn't Bacon defend himself? He initially intended to do so. Over Easter he wrote to Buckingham, 'I know I have clean hands and a clean heart.' He didn't pretend that he never received gifts or favours from suitors. Of course he received them. Everybody with power and influence did. King James told the Venetian ambassador, 'If I were to imitate the conduct of your republic and begin to punish those who take bribes, I should soon not have a single subject left.' How else had Edward Coke, Bacon's attacker, become so rich? How else had Buckingham acquired so many beautiful houses, and works of art, and the priceless gewgaws that made it seem he went 'manacled, fettered and imprisoned with jewels'?

Bacon was careless about money – careless about spending it, incautious in receiving it. People had given him gold, wine, jewelled buttons, a cabinet, ambergris, a diamond ring. Always assuring him that they expected nothing in return, that what they gave were simply tokens of their esteem. What mattered, as Bacon saw it, was that he hadn't allowed his acceptance of gifts to influence him in the performance of his judicial duties. 'I never had a bribe or reward in my eye or [my] thought when pronouncing judgment.'

It was probably true, and it is probably precisely his probity that brought Bacon down. Disappointed, those who had thought to buy him, and were angry to find that he was not to be bought, became vengeful.

The mere acceptance of a bribe, though, makes a man guilty. Bacon knew that Coke, and his other accusers, would look not at his thoughts but at the rich gifts that had come his way. 'Job himself,' he told the King, 'or whoever was the justest judge, by such hunting for matters against him as hath been used against me, may for a time seem foul.'

Already the pamphleteers and libellers were jeering. His name was an easy one to twist into a cruel joke. Now he was described as a 'hog well fed with bribery'. He was finding, as Buckingham would too, how envy follows success. He knew how many people disliked him. He knew how slippery was the peak of power on which he stood. 'Greatness is the mark,' he wrote, 'and accusation is the game.'

The chase was on. Bacon was prey. Coke would be a relentless huntsman. Perhaps Bacon just refused the sport. He wasn't well. He had always been nervous – inclined to be prostrated by anxiety. He took to his bed, saying, 'It is no feigning or fainting but sickness both of my heart and of my back.' He despaired. Chamberlain reports that he ordered his attendants 'not to take any notice of him, but altogether to forget him and not hereafter speak of him, or remember there was ever such a man in the world'.

Buckingham told the Lords that Bacon was unlikely to live long. In fact he survived another five years, but he may have been already too weary to fight. In April he wrote, 'I am ready to make an oblation of myself to the King.' He himself had described to Buckingham how this worked. Favourites, he had written, can be 'offered as a sacrifice to appease the multitude'. So can Lord Chancellors. Bacon was a decoy to draw the hounds away from the throne. He would bear the opprobrium that would otherwise fall on Buckingham or on the King.

Ganymede

IT is not clear why the Commons turned on Bacon so suddenly and savagely. It is equally unclear why he submitted so meekly. The twenti-eth-century scholar Conrad Russell, one of the most knowledgeable of modern historians of the period, wrote, 'The case remains remarkably obscure.' That obscurity hints at a hidden subtext. The story has a theme that was not made explicit in Parliament.

It is possible Bacon allowed the allegation of bribe-taking to stand because he had been threatened with another, more dangerous charge. John Aubrey defends him on the first count – 'His Lordship always gave judgment *secundum aequum et bonum* [according to what was fair and good]' – but also hints at a second one. Whatever Bacon himself did or didn't do, writes Aubrey, there were people around him who took bribes. Those people were 'his Ganymedes and favourites'.

While Parliament sat in 1621, the French ambassador to London, Count Leveneur de Tillières, was reporting to his masters back in Paris. He was doing his best, he wrote, to find 'the most decent expressions' to describe the culture of the English court but, really, there was nothing decent about it. It was 'infamous, licentious … filthy and scandalous'. King James was 'as good for nothing as possible'. Buckingham dominated and manipulated him. James 'suffers himself to be walked in leading strings like a child'. He was 'lost in pleasures'. He was 'plunging himself deeper into vice'.

That 'vice' was attracting comment. Tillières reported that 'audacious language, offensive pictures, calumnious pamphlets … are common here'. A handwritten tract entitled *Tom Tell Troath* was circulating. The anonymous author wrote, 'It is a part of supremacy, not to have your darling sin laid open.' Things that could not be said openly, though, could nonetheless be implied. 'Tom' tells of an unnamed king, 'notoriously wicked in his person', who 'kisses his minions without shame' and makes 'his grooms his companions without danger'.

Simonds D'Ewes sat up late with friends talking about three books (one of them probably *Corona Regia*), all 'terrible and wholly against the King himself, accusing him of atheism, sodomy, etc.'. On another occasion they talked about 'things … that were secret', like, for instance, 'the sin of sodomy … how frequent it was in this wicked city'. D'Ewes thought that 'if God did not provide some wonderful blessing against it, we could not but expect some horrible punishment'. The worst of it, he goes on, 'being as we had probable cause to fear' that sodomy was 'a sin in the prince'. By 'prince' he meant the King.

D'Ewes was talking in private, with trusted friends. Parliamentarians could not speak so openly about what many of them saw as the outrageous impropriety of Buckingham's relationship with King James. Thought, though, is like water. Eventually it will find its way under or round or through any obstacle.

One way of speaking about the unspeakable was to transpose it into the realms of mythology.

An anonymous poem called *The Warres of the Gods* appeared. It told of an uprising of the lesser Olympian deities against 'him that rules the thunder' – Jove, their king. They fume at the way, drunk with forbidden nectar, he neglects his responsibilities and 'lies playing' with Ganymede, a 'white-faced boy' whose 'ivory forehead' recalls Buckingham's. They feel that this relationship has disrupted the harmony of the spheres. The 'glorious starry border' of the heavens is disordered. King Jove must be displaced 'for loving so against nature'. The rebels are ready to 'rend the heavens asunder'.

> *They threaten without mercy*
> *To have him burned*
> *That thus have turned*
> *Love's pleasures Arsey Versey.*

Ganymede was a Trojan youth, 'the loveliest born of the race of mortals', says Homer. His beauty so tempted the gods that they stole him away to Mount Olympus. His story was told by numerous ancient poets. In some versions he is a hunter, and as he is abducted skywards his companions stare sadly up at their disappearing friend while his hounds bark themselves hoarse to see their master so snatched away from them. In others he is tending his sheep on Mount Ida, not far from Troy, when an eagle – Jove's emissary, or Jove himself in disguise – swoops down and carries him away. Arriving in Olympus, he is granted immortality, and supplants the goddess Hebe, taking over her role as cup-bearer – in some versions to all the gods, in others solely to Jove, who loves him passionately.

Artists, notably Michelangelo and Rubens, show Ganymede struggling in the gigantic eagle's embrace – his pale, perfect body tightly restrained by its black wings, his legs pinioned by its cruel claws. Feathery and scaly, the eagle is fearsome, its snaky neck and head unmistakably phallic. But Ganymede seems more amazed than afraid. This is a rape, in the seventeenth-century sense of the word, which was more capacious than the modern one. It includes the idea of sexual assault, but also more generally of being carried away – emotionally as well as literally. Ganymede, seized and lifted heavenwards, is enraptured.

So much for artists' visions. To the earthier-minded gossips of seventeenth-century Britain, a 'Ganymede' was a young man who had sex (usually as a passive partner) with an older one. The mythical youth's Latin name was Catamitus. A 'catamite' was the common term for what was more rudely called a 'butt-boy'. A lovely youth snatched up from an ordinary human existence to become cup-bearer to a king – the fit between the Ganymede of myth and the Buckingham of fact was perfect, and the authors of 'libels' soon seized on it. One offered up a mock pious prayer:

> Thou wilt be pleased, great God, to save
> My sovereign from a Ganymede.

He begs that the King be helped to resist the temptations offered by 'whoreish breath', kissable lips, and 'a smooth and beardless chin/As may provoke or tempt to sin'. Just such breath, such lips and such a chin had Buckingham.

*   *   *

Buckingham was reimagined as Ganymede. But Buckingham was still untouchable. To accuse him of any kind of sexual transgression was to accuse the King along with him. No member of Parliament, in 1621, was ready to do that. But Francis Bacon, says Aubrey, kept 'Ganymedes' in his household. And Bacon could be brought down.

Aubrey wasn't the only seventeenth-century gossip aware of Bacon's 'Ganymedes and favourites'. Simonds D'Ewes wrote that Bacon had 'stupendous and great vices', notably 'the most horrible and secret sin of sodomy'. Bacon surrounded himself with young men and showed little interest in women. He wrote that 'the best works, and of greatest merit for the public, have proceeded from the unmarried or childless men'. His own late marriage produced no children. His wife – who was thirty-two years younger – seems to have been chosen for the size of her dowry. His chaplain wrote that he treated her initially with 'much conjugal love and respect'. Later, though, he disinherited her, probably because he had found out about her affair with Sir John Underhill, whom she married only eleven days after Bacon's death. He kept a manservant – 'one Godrick a very effeminate-faced youth' – who was, writes D'Ewes, 'his catamite and bedfellow'.

Bacon was not being charged with sodomy or anything like it, but because, like King James, he was known to be attracted to 'Ganymedes', he could be treated as James's whipping boy. He was a decoy, deflecting hostility – homophobic hostility as well as indignation about financial misdemeanours – away from James and Buckingham and onto himself. And perhaps he understood so much, and that is what he meant when he talked about making himself an 'oblation' to the King.

Despenser

On 3 May 1621, the case against Francis Bacon was heard in the House of Lords. Bacon was not present. He was ill in bed. When the Lords pressed him to respond to the charges (there were now twenty-eight of them), he sent a scroll on which was written 'I am guilty of corruption, and do renounce all defence.' The Lords were nonplussed. They sent a deputation to him, asking for confirmation that the scroll was genuine. Bacon said, 'My Lords, it is my act, my hand, my heart. I beseech your Lordships, be merciful to a broken reed.'

The philosopher and scientist whose 'new Atlantis' would be revered, two generations on, by the members of the Royal Society; whom Voltaire, in the next century, would acclaim as the father of the scientific method; the brilliant polymath whose restless mind was among the most valuable intellectual assets of the Jacobean state; whom Ben Jonson called 'one of the greatest men and most worthy of admiration that had been in many ages'; was to be dismissed from his post as Lord Chancellor, fined the colossal sum of £40,000, barred for ever from taking his seat in Parliament or holding any government office, forbidden to appear ever again within twelve miles of the court, and imprisoned (albeit briefly) in the Tower of London.

Four Lords came to his house to inform him of the sentence. Bacon lay and watched as they took the Great Seal from its place near his bed. 'By my own fault I have lost it,' he said.

Buckingham had visited the beleaguered Lord Chancellor repeatedly during the Easter recess and Bacon had written gratefully, calling him 'my anchor in these floods'. But the favourite couldn't save him. Buckingham, for so long armoured by the King's love, was no longer invulnerable.

King James had told Parliament, just before its adjournment, that 'so precious unto me is the public good' that he would not compromise his commitment to it for any 'private person whatsoever, were he never so dear unto me'. No one could doubt which dear person he had in mind. During the recess, as they waited to hear Bacon's fate, the French ambassador reported that Buckingham and his friends were seized by 'a great melancholy'. Rumours were circulating that Buckingham would soon go the way of Somerset, cast off by the King when he became an embarrassment; that it could be shown that Buckingham worked always for his own 'private ends'; that when Parliament reconvened, the Commons would begin to investigate Buckingham's financial affairs, and that the King had authorised them to do so; that on Easter Day Buckingham absented himself from the great feast at court to attend a horse race; that, no – on the contrary – on Easter Day Buckingham was at the palace but 'the King sent no meat from his table to the Marquis, which is the strangest news of all'.

Those rumours didn't grow by themselves. They were planted and nurtured and propagated by Buckingham's enemies. One of them was the Earl of Southampton, who said that year that 'there would never be good reformation while one did so wholly govern the King'. Buckingham was being keenly watched by those who hoped for his downfall, and he was watching his watchers. He had agents to keep him informed of what was being said around town. One of them reported that 'your adversaries continue their meetings and conferences', where they discuss 'how to give His Majesty some foul distaste of you, as making you the only author of all grievances and oppressions whatsoever'.

In May, Francis Bacon's case having been disposed of, Parliament turned its attention to another senior member of the legal establishment, Sir Henry Yelverton. In 1617 King James had appointed Yelverton Attorney General without consulting Buckingham, to the latter's annoyance, making him one of the few holders of high office who did not owe his position to the favourite's patronage. Yelverton believed that Buckingham had been hostile to him ever since.

In 1620 Yelverton had been accused of an improper transaction relating to some Crown lands. He was found guilty, fined, stripped of his office and imprisoned briefly in the Tower. John Chamberlain, reporting the case, gave his opinion that Yelverton had been brought down because 'he is not, nor seeks to be, in favour with the favourite'. Yelverton agreed.

Now Yelverton had become embroiled in the story of the Villiers family's monopolies, and was being examined by the Lords. It was Yelverton who had ordered the imprisonment of those thread-makers who would not buy their patents from the Villiers brothers, Edward and Kit. Now he told the Lords he had only done so out of fear, because 'my Lord of Buckingham was ever at His Majesty's hand, ready upon every occasion to hew me down'. He had also authorised the sale of the patent for inns to George Mompesson. Now he alleged he had been warned that if he didn't allow it to pass, Buckingham would cause him to lose his place.

He was admitting to having done wrong in the past to save his own position. But now, having already lost that position, he was ready, even though Buckingham was present, to speak out. A contemporary news-writer says that he spoke 'rashly or madly', making 'bitter speeches against Lord Buckingham' and 'thus wonderfully offending His Majesty'.

What Yelverton said was: 'I dare say if my Lord of Buckingham had but read the articles exhibited in this place against Hugh Spencer ... he would not have pursued me with such bitterness.'

The name Yelverton had spoken reeked of transgressive politics and forbidden sex. It conjured up visions, horrid to the kingly mind, of uprisings and regicide. To those concerned about good government, it epitomised the dangers of vesting too much power in a royal favourite. The dramatist and historian Elizabeth Cary, Viscountess Falkland, wrote that it provided 'a perfect mirror ... how full of danger and hazard it is, for one man's love, to sell the affections and peace of the whole kingdom'. To Puritans it stood for the unmentionable sin.

Hugh Spencer, more usually known as Hugh Despenser, was one of the favourites of the fourteenth-century monarch King Edward II.

English theatregoers knew Edward II's story well, if not entirely accurately. Christopher Marlowe's play *The Troublesome Reign and Lamentable Death of Edward the Second* was first performed in 1593 and repeatedly revived into the 1620s. It tells how King Edward becomes bewitched by 'a sly inveigling Frenchman', Piers Gaveston, who surrounds the young king with 'wanton poets' and 'pleasant wits'. Edward is 'love-sick for his minion'.

Marlowe was probably thinking of James, King only of Scotland at the time of the play's writing, and his relationship with his handsome French cousin, d'Aubigny. Certainly the play's audiences drew the parallel, and so did those who read Michael Drayton's long poem *Piers Gaveston*, first published the same year as Marlowe's play.

The chronicles relate that nobles, church and Parliament alike detested Gaveston for his extravagance, his contempt for law and tradition, and the inordinate amount of power the King's favour gave him. Twice Edward gave in to pressure from the barons and sent him into exile. Each time he returned. Each time there were further uprisings. The kingdom became a battlefield in a protracted civil war in which Gaveston was the *casus belli*. Eventually he was summarily killed, to be replaced as Edward's favourite, a few years later, by Hugh Despenser.

In Marlowe's play, Despenser is a less prominent character than Gaveston, but the chroniclers tell us he was hated for all the reasons Gaveston had been, and more besides. He was greedy and rapacious. He was said to be a murderer who had dishonourably killed a hostage entrusted to his keeping. He was called a pirate, 'a sea monster, lying in wait for merchants as they crossed the sea'. His relationship with King Edward was shocking. A scribe in Newham Abbey described the two of them as 'the king and his husband'. The Bishop of Winchester denounced them from his pulpit as a pair of 'sodomites'.

Edward's wife, Queen Isabella, and her lover, the Earl of Mortimer, invaded England from France. King Edward and Despenser were both captured in the Welsh borders. Despenser was hanged, drawn and quartered. That horrible death was made even more ghastly by the fact that before he was chopped up, Despenser was displayed, still alive, lashed high up on a ladder so that the crowd could enjoy the spectacle as his penis and testicles were cut off and flung into the fire.

When Yelverton spoke Spencer/Despenser's name in 1621 it caused an uproar. The heir to the throne on his feet protesting: Prince Charles said he could not 'sit quiet' to hear 'his father's government so paralleled and scandalised'. The Lord Treasurer rebuking Yelverton: 'Let him stick to the point.' Buckingham, as usual, cool.

Repeatedly, over the next years, as attacks on him multiplied, Buckingham was to say he wanted to answer his critics, not to silence them. Yelverton had suggested that he was like Despenser – a murderer, a pirate, a sodomite and a monster. He didn't fume or rage. He said, 'Let him proceed. He that will seek to stop him is more my enemy than his.'

Yelverton had no more to say, so Buckingham went on. He was content, he said, to overlook the slander against himself. But Yelverton had impugned the King's honour. Should he not therefore be sent to the Tower? More angry argument. Several peers asserted that Yelverton's implied insults were directed solely at Buckingham: the King's honour was untouched. But when the exchange was reported to him, King James saw what Buckingham had seen.

After Despenser's execution, Edward was forced to abdicate. He signed his agreement in tears. He was moved to Berkeley Castle and there he was murdered.

There is no historical evidence to support the popular belief that his assassins killed him by thrusting a red-hot poker into his anus. Nor, in the early published texts of Marlowe's play, is there any stage direction describing such an act. All the same, that is how Edward was generally believed to have died and that is how, in nearly every production of the play from Buckingham's lifetime to our own, his story ends.

When King James was told what had been said in Parliament that day he said, 'If he [Buckingham] be Spencer, I am Edward II.' He knew what Yelverton meant. There was sodomy, the sin that dare not speak its name, and Edward's infatuation with his favourites, but there were other things that, from James's point of view, were even worse. Edward couldn't control his barons. He allowed his personal feelings to distort his political judgement. He was chased off his throne. He died ignominiously (poker or no poker). 'To reckon me with such a prince is to esteem me a weak man,' said James. 'I had rather be no king than such a one as King Edward II.'

A few days later Yelverton was examined by his successor as Attorney General, who ruled, 'The abuses of Hugh Spencer are fastened upon the Lord of Buckingham. They reflect upon the King because Lord Buckingham is so near the King.' Yelverton was sentenced to imprisonment at the King's pleasure, and, to compensate for his insult, he was ordered to pay a fine of 5,000 marks to Buckingham.

Buckingham had won a round against his opponents. It had been demonstrated that to attack him was tantamount to treason against His Majesty. He had displayed his strength. He went on to display his sweetness. As though as a tacit rebuke to those who would compare him to the rapacious Despenser, he remitted Yelverton's fine. He had come through.

On 28 May, King James adjourned Parliament. The Earl of Southampton, who led the opposition in the Upper House, was arrested and imprisoned for being more careful of the 'liberties of the Parliament than became any Privy Councillor', and perhaps also because he was known to be hostile to Buckingham. He had said that he did not like attending the Council 'because there were so many boys and base fellows' there.

Houses

IN the summer of 1621, with Parliament adjourned, Buckingham and his wife moved into their newly acquired house, at Burley-on-the-Hill in Rutland.

Recently built for Buckingham's early sponsor, the Countess of Bedford, the house was splendid in the fashionable neo-Palladian style, 'built *à la modern*', as John Evelyn put it when he visited it in the 1650s. It stood on the brow of a hill, visible from miles around and looking south over the river valley that is now Rutland Water. The grounds were grandly laid out. A double avenue led up to the forecourt. There was a bowling green and an artificial 'mount'. Three rows of terraces descended the hill, from which four further avenues provided vistas into the park and the countryside beyond. Even the stables were magnificent. Designed for Buckingham by Inigo Jones, they could accommodate forty horses: Thomas Fuller thought them superior to any other stable in the country. If the horses' food, he wrote, was as plentiful as their housing was 'stately', they were 'the best accommodated in England'.

Buckingham set about improving the park, with a view to making it a place where the King could happily hunt. He planted over a thousand walnut trees, a gift from the Earl of Northumberland, and he asked the Earl of Mar to send him 'four or five thousand' Scottish fir saplings, as though he was hoping to recreate the landscape of James's youth. The park was walled around and filled with deer.

When King James paid his first visit to Burley in August 1621 the porter greeted him with some lines of verse signalling that the King was not to suppose – as he took in the grandeur of the place – that his favourite was getting above himself. Rather Buckingham was constantly and gratefully aware that all the splendour of his current position, made concrete in his new home, he owed to the King.

Welcome, O welcome then, and enter here
The house your bounty hath built ...
The master is your creature, as the place
And every good about him is your grace.

Buckingham staged a masque to celebrate James's arrival.

The Gypsies Metamorphosed was highly unorthodox. It was written, as usual, by Ben Jonson, but, in contravention of the normal conventions of the masque, Buckingham had required Jonson to give him a speaking part. He was playing First Gypsy. The other 'gypsies' were his brothers and his good friend Endymion Porter. They were acting, and even more shocking, they were acting as thieves and charlatans.

They mingled with the audience, pretending to pick pockets. First Gypsy Buckingham offered to read people's palms and tell their fortunes. He looked at the King's hand. He pretended to be thunderstruck. He announced that he could read in the lines of the King's hand that this was a great man, the godlike father and 'maker' of them all.

Buckingham had not been homeless before he bought Burley. The King had given him a whole portfolio of houses and land. Some of his petitioners traded real estate for the favours or titles he granted them. Here are some of the properties he acquired during his years as favourite.

1616. His quarters in Whitehall Palace. As Master of the Horse, Buckingham was assigned a magnificent apartment in a timber-framed building standing on four great pillars, overlooking the Privy Garden, which formed part of the additions to the old palace designed by Inigo Jones. Buckingham commissioned Jones to design a new ceiling for his dining room.

1617. Whaddon Chase. A forest in Buckinghamshire, well stocked with game.

1617. Dalby. A fine house in Leicestershire, bought for £29,000 and a title for the vendor, Sir Edward Noel, henceforward Baron Noel.

1618. Wanstead. A great house in Essex, former home in turn of Queen Elizabeth's two favourites – the Earl of Leicester and the Earl of Essex. Buckingham was given it by Mountjoy Blount (who subsequently married his niece) in exchange for an Irish baronage.

Wanstead had excellent hunting. In June 1618 Buckingham entertained the King there for a feast. Part of the entertainment took place in the open air, served in what one of the guests describes as 'an extremely well-devised artificial wood, which was planted like a palace, having its hall and presence chamber, bedroom, drawing room, cabinet and so forth, formed by drawing the hangings from one tree to another'.

1619. Wallingford House. A grand London mansion, with a wide facade overlooking St James's Park, on the site where the Old Admiralty Building now stands. Next-door neighbour to Whitehall Palace, it was the ideal home for the greatest man in the country after the monarch. Buckingham rented it, and set Inigo Jones to work on its renovation. It became his London base, and the office where his personal staff worked.

1621. The purchase of Burley-on-the-Hill. But Buckingham's list of houses would not end there.

June 1622. New Hall, near Chelmsford in Essex – conveniently close to London and to the King's hunting grounds at Newmarket. It was built for Henry VIII, lived in by Queen Mary and given by Queen Elizabeth to the Earl of Sussex, who extended it in late Tudor style, with ornate brickwork and broad staircases and immense bay windows.

New Hall was palatial enough to make a fit country home for Buckingham. He bought it for £20,000, and at once began to make a deer park around it, writing gleefully to the King, 'I have found this morning another fine wood that must in with the rest, and two hundred acres of meadows, broom closes and plentiful springs running through them, so that I hope Newhall shall be nothing inferior to Burley.'

He commissioned Inigo Jones to alter the house 'according to the modern fashion'. Jones designed elaborate baroque gateways and coffered ceilings and a Palladian-style chapel, making the house so desirable that two decades later Oliver Cromwell took it for himself. John Evelyn was impressed by the garden and grounds, the walks and water features, the 'wilderness' and tennis courts and terraces, and above all by the 'ample shady and venerable trees'. King James had ordered a thousand oak trees to be sent to New Hall from his woods in Kent. Later, when he became King, Charles added another five hundred. Best of all, thought Evelyn, was 'the sweet and fair avenue planted with stately lime trees in four rows for near a mile in length.'

New Hall still has a stately avenue. The house was partly demolished in the eighteenth century, but enough still stands to show how splendid it must have been. It is the only one of Buckingham's houses to have even partially survived. Its remaining wing is now a boarding school.

1627. Chelsea House. The beautiful old house by the Thames that had once been home to Thomas More. With its two courtyards, its gardens and orchards, it was described by Evelyn as 'a spacious and excellent place for the extent of the ground and situation, in a most sweet air'.

Adding it to his holdings just a year before his death, Buckingham used it only intermittently, but it was where he stored and displayed much of his sculpture collection. His mother lived there, and after Buckingham's death his widow Katherine frequently joined her. Beaufort Street runs through what were once its gardens, bounded to one side by the King's Road, to the other by the river.

More important, though, than any of these, was the great house on the Strand, known as York House, that was to become the showcase of Buckingham's magnificence.

York House stood where commuters now jostle and hurry on the platforms of Charing Cross station, its gardens and stables extending over streets subsequently named after their once-upon-a-time owner. (George Street, Duke Street and Of Alley have been built over, but Villiers Street and Buckingham Street still stand.)

In Buckingham's time it was the westernmost of the palatial houses lined up between the River Thames and the Strand. One of its neighbours was Arundel House. Another was Denmark House, where Queen Anne lived when Buckingham first came to court, and which was subsequently granted to Queen Henrietta Maria. The grounds of York House extended into what is now Victoria Embankment Gardens, where the baroque Watergate erected during Buckingham's tenure still stands, the only remnant of the house's seventeenth-century splendour.

York House belonged to the diocese of the Archbishops of York. For several generations it had been leased out to the Lord Chancellor or Lord Keeper of the Great Seal, becoming by custom and tradition a kind of official residence. Sir Nicholas Bacon, Queen Elizabeth's Lord Keeper, had lived there. His son, Francis Bacon, on becoming Lord Keeper himself in 1617, took a twenty-one-year lease, rejoicing because it was 'where my father died and where I first breathed, and there will I yield my last breath, if it so please God, and the King will give me leave'.

It did not, as it turned out, please God or the King that he should do so.

When a great man falls, good things come the way of bystanders swift and determined enough to snap them up.

Bacon had been banned from coming near the court. He could no longer use a London residence. He needed money to pay his stupendous fine. Buckingham saw an opportunity. An opportunity to help out an old friend (or so he told himself) that was also an opportunity for himself to become master of one of the grandest houses in London. Wallingford House was all very well, but it lacked that all-important river frontage. It was Buckingham's headquarters, where his secretaries and agents met to serve him, and it would continue to be his family's home, but York House, once rebuilt and lavishly refurbished, would be the stage on which his magnificence could be displayed. Buckingham offered to take the remainder of the lease on York House off Bacon's hands.

Bacon, still ill, still shocked and smarting, was not grateful. He did not think Buckingham was doing him a favour. On the contrary, what he saw was Buckingham's vulture-like eagerness to profit by his misfortunes. He thought it greedy and heartless. He was in no hurry to part with his beloved home.

Buckingham, in turn, took umbrage. He had done as much as he could for Bacon, he thought. When the Lords had debated his impeachment, only one of their number voted in Bacon's favour. That lone voice was Buckingham's. He had persuaded the King to release Bacon from the Tower as soon as it could possibly be done. He had tried to obtain a full pardon for him – unsuccessfully as it turns out, but he had done his best. Now he was exasperated. What did Bacon want to keep York House for, since he was forbidden to come to London?

Bacon's wife wrote a placatory letter and came to see Buckingham. Tempers cooled. Courtesies were exchanged. Buckingham didn't exactly apologise, but he admitted it was 'unreasonableness to desire that which is another man's'. Bacon didn't exactly apologise either, but he wrote, 'I was ever resolved that your lordship should have had it, or no man.' The deal was done.

Matters of State

TROUBLE in Parliament; trouble abroad. King James's vision of a peacefully united Europe was unravelling.

When Emperor Ferdinand drove the Winter King and Queen out of Prague in November 1620, the Emperor's cousin, the Spanish King Philip III, saw an opportunity. The two great Habsburg powers – the Holy Roman Empire and Spain – operated independently of each other, but there were times when their interests coincided, and this was one of them. Frederick's effrontery in laying claim to Bohemia provided the pretext for a retaliatory attack. Seven thousand men from the Spanish army of Flanders, led by the celebrated General Spinola, invaded the Palatinate. So did Duke Maximilian of Bavaria, leader of the Catholic League (a loose association of Catholic states within the Empire).

The Palatinate lay in the south-west of the Holy Roman Empire, of which it was one of the numerous constituent statelets. Straddling the Rhine, it was made up of a number of parcels of territory, the westernmost lying along the border with Alsace and Lorraine, those further east surrounding the cities of Mannheim and Heidelberg. It was a comparatively small, fragmented state, a land of forests and mountains. Two considerations, though, made it more important than it might look on the map. One was that it lay across a convenient route from Spain to the Spanish Netherlands: if Spinola could gain control of it, the Palatinate would be a strategically useful base for Spanish forces attempting to subdue the rebellious Dutch Republic. Another was that its ruler, by centuries-long tradition, was one of the seven prince-electors who appointed the Holy Roman Emperor. For several generations the emperor had been a Habsburg, the title having become effectively (though not officially) hereditary within that family, but the Protestants of the Empire dreamed of a change. While Frederick remained the

Elector Palatine, he might one day be in a position to choose a Protestant emperor, even perhaps to become one himself.

Frederick fought to defend his territory. Volunteers from England, Scotland and Wales – inspired by anti-Catholic fervour, by sentimental devotion to their own Princess Elizabeth or simply by a restless hunger for military action – set out to support Frederick, in such numbers that King James felt obliged to appoint a commander to lead them, Sir Horace Vere. For all the King's determination not to send a British expeditionary force, one had come into being.

In March 1621, King Philip III of Spain died. His successor, Philip IV, was sixteen years old. In April King James dispatched the veteran English ambassador John Digby on a five-month ambassadorial tour to Brussels, Vienna, Munich and Heidelberg. His mission was to pacify Frederick and to prevail upon the Emperor and the German Catholic princes to rein back their armies and negotiate. He was also instructed to hasten the protracted negotiations for the marriage between Prince Charles and the Infanta, sister to the new Spanish king.

The Spanish Match, King James believed, could make him financially independent of Parliament and its niggardly subsidies: the Infanta's dowry would be munificent. He intended to make it a condition of the marriage contract that the Palatinate be restored to Frederick, while he undertook to persuade the latter to relinquish his claim to Bohemia. And so as father-in-law to Frederick, the most belligerent of the German Protestant princes, and to a Habsburg princess, King James, Rex Pacificus, would join all Europe together as part of his happy family and save all Christendom from the escalating war.

In October, Digby, by this time Earl of Bristol, came back from his five-month diplomatic tour, bringing heavy news. He told the King and Privy Council that a peaceful solution was impossible. If the Palatinate was to be saved, money and troops must be found to support Frederick. Parliament would have to be recalled. When it was, Bristol would tell it that unless the King was ready to 'abandon his children and the Palatinate', he must 'declare himself for war'.

That night Buckingham visited the Count of Gondomar and told him the substance of Bristol's advice. The ensuing conversation (recorded by Gondomar) shows us one of the ways in which Buckingham made himself useful to the King. When the favourite spoke with the Spanish ambassador of an evening, in his private lodgings, things could be said in the knowledge that they would be passed back to Madrid but would not reach the English Parliament. And because Buckingham was the King's mouthpiece, words that the King himself was too careful ever to utter would be understood, nonetheless, to have come from him.

This was what Buckingham had come to tell Gondomar: the King needed money. Parliament would almost certainly grant him generous subsidies if MPs believed those subsidies were to be used for a war against Spain. But the ambassador was not to suppose, for all the loud talk of war that would soon be sounding through the land, that such a war was really imminent. King James was as peaceably disposed as ever, and as eager to marry his son to a Spanish princess. There would be no sudden change of policy. The Spaniard would be kept fully informed. 'The King', noted Gondomar, 'trusted no one so entirely as him [Buckingham] and myself, because he knew that we had no other goal but peace and the common good.'

The next day Gondomar visited Whitehall Palace and met with King James, who led him to a window embrasure where they would not be overheard. Buckingham joined them there and said something enigmatic, once more suggesting to Gondomar that whatever funds Parliament voted, those funds would not – whatever might be said in Westminster – be used in a way hostile to Spain.

The conversation was jocular and ambiguous – as confusing as James's stated policy. He would ask his Parliament to subsidise war-making against an unnamed enemy who must surely be Spain, while continuing to negotiate for a marriage between his son and the Infanta Maria. He would approach Spain – as his representative was to tell the Commons later that month – 'with a sword in one hand and a treaty in the other'.

Parliament reconvened in November. Prince Charles took his seat in the Lords. King James and Buckingham were absent. They had gone to Newmarket, where they could hunt, and where James would not be pestered by Hispanophobe Puritans and other troublemaking people. Prince Charles – now of age – had stayed behind in London, 'with a secret commission' to dissolve Parliament if the members tried to 'meddle' in things that did not concern them.

In the King's absence, the Lord Keeper of the Great Seal was his mouthpiece. Francis Bacon had been replaced in the role by John Williams, by this time Bishop of Lincoln. King James trusted Williams as one who 'knew his mind and would do his bidding'. Speaking for the King, he informed Parliament that 'matters of state' were not to be raised. As Francis Bacon had told Buckingham years before, *'arcana imperii'* were to be discussed only by the King and his Councillors. Parliament's sole business was to vote through subsidies so that their king would be ready, if necessary, for war.

King James's vision of a European union was not shared by the majority of his people, or by their representatives in the House of Commons. In the seven years he had run the country without consulting Parliament, he had been able to ignore that fact. No longer. In 1621 the clash between his foreign policy and his people's desires was made unmistakably evident. English patriots hated Spain. English Protestants hated the Roman Catholic Church. English Puritans, who were strongly present in the Commons, hated even those aspects of Anglican worship that smelt to them of Catholicism, and they detested equally, on political and egalitarian grounds, the hierarchy within the church (topped by the bishops) that seemed to reflect and endorse the inequalities of secular society.

To think of Parliament as a collective is problematic. A large proportion of MPs took their seats only infrequently. Of those who did attend, the majority never spoke. The kind of politically engaged 'turbulent spirits' whom James disliked dominated proceedings. We cannot know what the silent backbenchers thought in 1621. We do know, though, that those whose words have come down to us were extraordinarily united in their views.

They detested the prospect of the Spanish Match for Prince Charles. They wanted to recover the Palatinate. They also wanted a larger war with Spain. They wanted a confrontation with the King who sought to limit their right to discuss such things.

In the Commons, on the first day of this Parliament's third and final session, member after member rose to express their hostility to Roman Catholicism, and to Spain in particular.

On the second day Sir Edward Coke had his say. His speech was an anti-papist, anti-Spanish tirade. He had been Attorney General in

Elizabeth's day, when the Pope had excommunicated the Queen of England, sanctioning her assassination. To Coke then (and in this he spoke for the majority of Elizabethan English people), 'simply to be a Catholic was to be a traitor'. He was still of that mind. He spoke now of assassins sent by Spain to murder Queen Elizabeth, who was 'the flower of Queens as the rose is the Queen of flowers'. He spoke of a Spanish 'plague' that was killing sheep. Of syphilis, imported into England by Spaniards. Of Guy Fawkes and his fellow conspirators in the 'Powder Treason' – all of them, in Coke's view, tools of Spain. On and on it went. Coke's refrain was 'Remember the Armada!'

Others joined in the chorus. Sir Robert Phelips inveighed against 'Spain's falsehood' and 'the great Roman monster'. Another member dwelt on Queen Mary I's marriage to King Philip II of Spain, 'which was the shortening of her days, the loss of Calais and exhausting of our treasure'. Another recalled how a loyal minister had preached against the Gunpowder Plotters, and afterwards been set upon and beaten nearly to death by papists. Another complained that even now English Catholics in their hundreds were flocking to the Spanish ambassador's residence to join Gondomar in the Mass. Another said that if Prince Charles married a Spanish Catholic princess, then 'the passing bell tolls for religion'.

More grievances. More angry anti-Catholic rhetoric. More demonising of the Spanish. Remember the Armada! Remember the Armada! Remember the Armada!

It was as though members were lashing themselves into a state of indignation that would embolden them to confront the authority of their king. When the House was sufficiently heated, sufficiently furious, Coke summed up. 'Every man's heart here concurreth. But the King not knowing our hearts, we must do it by words.'

King James and Buckingham had seen this coming, but it was alien to them. James had been still in Scotland when the Armada made its failed attempt at an invasion in 1588: he didn't share the memories of fear and anger to which Coke was appealing. King James's mother, Mary, Queen of Scots, was a Catholic and, in many people's opinion, a martyr for the Catholic faith. One of his first important acts as King of England had been to ratify the peace treaty with Spain. The Gunpowder Plot of 1605 had shaken him, but he saw it politically – he abhorred the conspirators because they were terrorists and they had tried to kill him, not because of their creed.

As for Buckingham, he could not possibly remember the Armada. It had sailed up the Channel four years before he was born. He was a Protestant, but he had been educated in Catholic France. He was married to a woman from a notable Catholic family who had converted only recently, and for transparently opportunistic reasons. He didn't hate or fear the Roman Church, nor did he hate or fear Spain. He got on well with Gondomar. As Parliament reconvened, Balthazar Gerbier was travelling on Buckingham's behalf in Italy, visiting Rome (home of the Antichrist, to the more extreme Puritan mind) and bringing back images of the Virgin Mary and the saints to furnish Buckingham's houses with pictures certain MPs would have considered idolatrous.

Both king and favourite understood that their easy-going approach to religion was not shared by the majority of the English. They were aware of how unpopular the Spanish Match would be with Parliament. It was for that reason they were hiding out in Newmarket as the Commons raged.

On 1 December, guided by Sir Edward Coke, the Commons drew up a petition to be presented to the King. They called on him to 'speedily and effectually take your sword into your hand' against Spain. They asked him to enforce penal laws against British Catholics. They requested that Prince Charles 'may be timely and happily married to one of our own religion'. They would, they said, grant a subsidy, but on their own terms. The money raised was to be used 'for the relief of the Palatinate only'.

Even before the House had formally agreed that the petition should be sent, a copy of it had reached King James. He was outraged. It was for Parliament to support him, not to order him about. It was for him to decide when and with whom he went to war; to whom he married his son; how he treated his Catholic subjects. 'Those Puritans and malcontents would have me die a miserable death,' he said.

In a letter handed to the Speaker on 4 December he wrote that he had heard of the existence of such a petition, but 'we will not deign the hearing nor the answering of it'. He accused the members of being 'fiery and popular spirits'. They reminded him horribly of the 'Puritan Ministers of Scotland' who had made his early life so difficult. He accused them of concerning themselves improperly 'with matters far above their reach and capacities'. He commanded them 'not to meddle henceforth with any thing concerning our government or deep matters of state'. His son's marriage especially, he informed them, was none of their business. In presuming to question such things, 'you usurp upon our prerogative royal'.

The Speaker read out the King's letter. The members were awed. The King's displeasure was intimidating. Many of them wanted to withdraw their defiance. Some of them sought to persuade themselves that it was not the King that was their opponent, but some sinister other. They didn't name Buckingham, but they said, 'The King is misled by some about him.' Already Buckingham was becoming the object of hostility deflected away from its true target.

The Commons redrafted their petition. Twelve knights carried the revised petition to Newmarket. James laid it aside unread. Three days later his reply reached the Commons. 'We are an old and experienced King, needing no such lessons,' he wrote. The Commons had invoked their rights of freedom of speech and immunity from arrest. He told them that those were not 'rights', but favours they owed to the Crown. 'Your privileges were derived from the grace and permission of our ancestors and us.'

The Commons had been concerned about the Spanish Match, about Catholics. No longer. Now they were concerned for their existence as an institution. Many of them were dismayed into silence. Not so Sir Edward Coke. He declared ringingly, 'The privilege of this House is the nurse and life of all our laws, the subject's best inheritance.' He trumpeted his respect for Magna Carta. He sounded the alarm. 'This strikes at the root.' He flattered and fired his listeners in the House, as a commander must before a desperate battle. He told them how great they were, how brave. He told them how tremendous was the significance of the conflict in which they were engaged. They were few, as Henry Vs 'happy few' had been, but like that 'band of brothers', they served 'for thousands. For tens of thousands.'

They drafted a protestation. It was not sent to the King. There was no guarantee that he would read it. Instead it was entered into the Journal of the House of Commons, the book of record in which the clerks' accounts of proceedings were preserved. Once more it asserted that members of Parliament were entitled to discuss matters of state, and that their right to do so was the 'ancient and undoubted birthright and inheritance of the subjects of England'. It was for them, not the King, to decide what they could or could not discuss. Once more it insisted that 'every member of the House of Parliament hath and of right ought to have' freedom of speech and freedom from arrest for anything done or said in Parliament.

So began a dispute between the Crown and Parliament that would continue for the rest of Buckingham's life, and to which his own person would become increasingly central. On the one hand the law – Edward Coke and others speaking up for the rights enshrined in Magna Carta. On the other King James, and subsequently King Charles, defending their royal prerogative. It was a debate that would be silenced a year after Buckingham's death, when King Charles dissolved Parliament and embarked on his 'personal rule'. Eleven years later it would break out into war.

King James, hearing of the protestation, returned to London accompanied by Buckingham. On 18 December he summoned members of the Commons to the Council Chamber. He demanded to see the Journal. While they watched, he took hold of it and tore out the page on which the protestation was written, saying it should be 'razed out of all memories and utterly annihilated'. He was too late – printed copies of the text were already circulating throughout the kingdom.

Parliament was adjourned. Sir Edward Coke was summoned before the Privy Council and told, 'You have forgotten the duty of a servant, the duty of a Councillor of State and the duty of a subject.' He was expelled from the Council and taken under guard to the Tower of London. In order to avoid an argument about the legitimacy of arresting a member of Parliament, he was charged with an offence that had nothing to do with politics – the non-payment of a debt incumbent on his wife's estate.

Earlier in the year his great rival, Francis Bacon, had been released from the Tower after only a few days. Coke was held there for seven months, during which he turned seventy. He was allowed no exercise, no visitors and no books. He wrote Latin verses on the wall of his cell with a piece of coal. Meanwhile his rooms in the Temple were searched for evidence of treason. None could be found.

Eventually his case came up in court. The Attorney General refused to take part in the prosecution. 'Let my tongue cleave to the roof of my mouth, whenever I open it against Sir Edward Coke,' he said. The three justices agreed there was no case to be answered. In August Coke was allowed to go home.

Gerbier in Italy

WHILE Parliament was sitting in 1621, Buckingham was thinking about art as well as politics. The Veroneses Balthazar Gerbier had acquired for him in the Netherlands, the Van Dyck marriage portraits – he had already the beginnings of a collection. Now he wanted more. He sent Gerbier to Italy, with money (200 livres) in his pocket.

Gerbier went first to Rome, where he visited the villas and palaces 'all beset with rare antique statues and within garnished with many rare pictures'. He was getting his eye in. On his return, as architect, interior decorator and custodian of York House, Gerbier would be creating for Buckingham a palace similarly beset and garnished.

He played the tourist assiduously. He admired Michelangelo's work in the Sistine Chapel, and 'the matchless pictures of Raphael d'Urbin'. He sketched the most celebrated of the ancient sculptures in the Vatican, especially the *Laocoön*, which was the artwork every connoisseur of the time had to see. He was improving his knowledge of past masters; he also had a sharp eye for new talent. He bought a painting – 'a great piece of the Four Seasons' – by the newly fashionable Guido Reni, and had it crated up and shipped back to Buckingham. He befriended the Netherlandish artists who congregated around the Spanish Steps. Always liking to be busy, he compiled a guidebook for English visitors, listing the Eternal City's unmissable sights.

He travelled north, stopping off at Bologna and Padua, and passing along the Brenta canal, admiring 'the ravishing palaces and gardens' with which it was lined. Arriving in Venice at last, he made contact with ambassador Henry Wotton and with the Dutch fixer and dealer Daniel Nys. Nys's honesty was questionable, but he could open doors, expedite deals, lend money (at interest, naturally). Gerbier made use of him.

He went everywhere, saw everything, soon concluding that, though Roman artists were more skilled at drawing, the Venetians surpassed them in their use of colour. He visited churches and palazzi. With Wotton as his sponsor, he met the right people. He began shopping for Buckingham. A *Christ and the Woman Taken in Adultery* by Jacopo Tintoretto. *The Adoration of the Shepherds* by Jacopo Bassano and two further works by his son Francesco. A number of smaller works, and – Gerbier's great coup – Titian's *Ecce Homo* (Plate 9).

A swirling composition nearly eight feet high and twelve feet wide, full of rich colour, turbulent action and solemn drama, the *Ecce Homo* was a tremendous thing to have acquired. Its composition is boldly dramatic. Christ, in his crown of thorns, stands humbled in the upper left-hand corner. Pilate, showily dressed with sky-blue ribbons on his buskins (Titian's model was the poet and pornographer Pietro Aretino), displays him to the crowd. All the power and glory of the world is crammed into the centre of the pictorial space – the Emperor Charles V on horseback, the Pope in a scarlet robe, the Sultan in an immense turban – but the composition is held by a young woman in white, who looks quietly out at the viewer, her child leaning against her. Titian himself is there, a bearded face, half-obscured. At bottom left a beggar, apparently the only person present to have comprehended the horror of the impending crucifixion, emits a silent scream.

As Gerbier recognised, it is one of the world's great paintings, the kind of masterpiece whose ownership would, at one stroke, admit his master to the art-collecting elite. (It is now in Vienna, in the Kunsthistorisches Museum.) To get it, Gerbier paid 275 livres, five times the price of the smaller but also impressive Tintoretto. He had already exceeded his budget: he had to borrow from Nys.

It was a bold purchase, and a shrewd one. On seeing the *Ecce Homo*, when it arrived back in London, Inigo Jones (Gerbier's rival as artistic adviser to Buckingham, and probably the possessor of the finest eye then in England) is said to have kissed the canvas. Even more gratifying for Buckingham, a beginner in the collecting game, the Earl of Arundel promptly offered him the astronomical sum of 7,000 livres for it. Buckingham (politely, of course) declined.

*   *   *

To buy a painting was one thing. To get it home was a far more arduous task. Gerbier had carved and gilded frames made for his greatest prizes. All the canvases were wrapped in baize and then in water-resistant wax-impregnated 'cere-cloth', and loaded into made-to-measure crates.

There were two possible ways of transporting them home. They could go by sea, but ships could sink, and even if they didn't salt water could penetrate even the most careful wrappings. The alternative, which Gerbier took, was to load his precious purchases on ox-carts and have them hauled slowly and laboriously westwards across the northern Italian plain. From Turin they began to ascend the Alps. Paintings were strapped onto mules' backs, or, when the paths were at their narrowest, human porters carried them. Mud, snow, ice, swollen rivers, rockfalls. At every stop along the way there were payments to be made – 'customs duties' or frankly demanded bribes or the buying-off of bandits. Weeks of anxious and uncomfortable travel. The Channel to be crossed. But then, at last, the triumphant uncrating.

There are stories about the arrival of artworks from abroad which nicely convey the anxiety, wonder and bewilderment with which they were received. Buying art was an unpredictable business. So few English purchasers had travelled, they were unlikely to know anything at all about the artists whose works they were acquiring. Collectors had to trust their agents absolutely. Later, once Prince Charles had also begun to buy, he liked to make a guessing game of new arrivals. In flickering candlelight (a conservator's nightmare: the greasy smoke, the soot, the dripping wax), the canvases were taken from their crates. The assembled courtiers would be asked to guess at attributions – a cruel game given how few of them had ever seen the works of continental artists. But perhaps they all knew anyway that it was wiser to allow the Prince to be the first to say the right name.

The Arundels were unusual among aristocratic collectors in having visited Rubens in his studio, and travelled across Europe, and learnt by looking to understand and appreciate Italian renaissance painting. Buckingham used to visit Arundel's collection – he once tipped the curator a generous twenty-two shillings for showing him round – but he himself would not travel beyond France until 1623. He would never see Italy. The pictures Gerbier brought home for him must have seemed astonishing.

*   *   *

There is a long-established, obnoxiously snobbish tradition – which had its beginnings in Buckingham's lifetime and was still shaping art-historical comment in the mid-twentieth century – that suggests that while Arundel, great nobleman that he was, was a serious art lover and scholar, Buckingham, the upstart splashing out his new money, was too vulgar and frivolous to understand what he was buying.

According to this line of thought, Arundel, who posed for his portrait soberly black-clad in his picture gallery, was a proper connoisseur. Buckingham, whose portraits show him astride a prancing horse or dressed to dazzle in slashed silk brocade and pearls, or scantily draped in the role of a mythological lover, was too intellectually lightweight, too preoccupied with appearances, to appreciate the profound significance of the things he was acquiring.

But what is a picture, if not an appearance?

In his art-collecting, as in his clothes, his horses, his houses, his gardens, Buckingham recognised, wanted and delighted in beauty. His contemporaries, anxiously demonstrating their seriousness by talking about exemplary antique virtue, verisimilitude or historicity or religious symbolism, may have been puzzled by the apparent frivolity of his attitude to art, but to the modern mind there is nothing strange or reprehensible about valuing an artwork primarily for its beauty. The word 'aesthetic' would not acquire its present meaning until two hundred years after his time, but Buckingham was an aesthete nonetheless.

By the time Gerbier and his precious cargo arrived back in London, Buckingham was master of York House. He appointed Gerbier its Keeper. Over the succeeding years the two of them transformed the rambling mediaeval building into a palace in the Italianate Renaissance style that Gerbier had learnt to admire and which he had so carefully studied. They bought (Gerbier doing the legwork, Buckingham finding the money) 'rarities, books, medals, marble statues, and pictures great store'.

They created a great collection. Both still in their twenties, both enjoying worldly success beyond anything they could have imagined as children, they write to each other with uninhibited zest. Others among Buckingham's correspondents exhibit a deference in which sycophancy is mingled with fear. They address him as 'Gracious patron' or

'Excellency' or even 'High and illustrious prince'. They beg for favours. They disguise their begging with compliments. Gerbier does none of this. He addresses Buckingham briskly as 'My lord' – or, when he's feeling bumptious, 'My sweet lord'. He writes to him as to an employer, certainly, but one with whom he is engaged, to the great enjoyment of both of them, in a thrilling endeavour.

Effeminacy

In *Basilikon Doron*, King James advised his son to 'especially eschew to be effeminate in your clothes, in perfuming, preening, or such like'. He was speaking to the public, and to posterity. Privately, though, effeminacy pleased him. Francis Osborne noted that Somerset had a fair complexion, 'equally sharing the beauty of both sexes'. Buckingham's hands and face struck Simonds D'Ewes – likewise – as being 'full of delicacy … especially effeminate and curious'. The King loved the two of them in turn, according to Osborne, 'as if he had mistaken their sex, and thought them ladies', which the two favourites 'laboured to resemble, in the effeminateness of their dressings'. The Count de Tillières thought King James lost interest in Somerset when he acquired 'a manly beard'.

To James's Puritan subjects, 'effeminacy' was abhorrent. In the year Buckingham came to court, one Barnaby Rich wrote a pamphlet inveighing against those degenerate courtiers who 'will so curl their hair, pick their brows and metamorphosise themselves … that they rather make show to be demi-harlots than men'. Sexual indeterminacy was threatening and repellent. The minister and schoolmaster Thomas Beard wrote a book, one of whose chapters was entitled 'Of Effeminate persons, Sodomites, and other such Monsters'.

Such monsters were the polar opposites of the soldierly men of action who were imagined to have made Elizabethan England great. Those were the days, wrote Fulke Greville in 1612, when true-born gentlemen dared to undertake 'heroical enterprises abroad' – how deplorably different was this new 'effeminate age'. The poet Richard Brathwaite agreed. He compared an admirable soldier, at ease among cannons and clattering armour and battlefields, with an effete 'carpet knight', associated with perfumes, powders, 'nimble capering' and 'the voice of amorous Ganymedes'. It's not hard to guess at whom Brathwaite was aiming. His poem appeared in 1615, the year George Villiers, the King's cup-bearer and Ganymede whose 'nimble capering' was so much admired, received his knighthood.

In 1609 Queen Anne danced in *The Masque of Queens* at Whitehall Palace. She appeared in the persona of Bel-Anna (a pun conflating Bella Anna – beautiful Anna – with Bellona, goddess of war). Before she and her ladies appeared, though, came 'a spectacle of strangeness'. A group of 'hags' or witches performed 'a magical dance, full of preposterous change and gesticulation'. Their chief says,

> *I hate to see these fruits of a soft peace,*
> *And curse the piety gives it such increase.*
> *Let us disturb it then, and blast the light.*

By 1622 there were many people in England who, without being wicked witches, itched to disturb the peace.

King James declared that 'his subjects were as dear to him as his children, and therefore he would not embark them in an unjust and needless quarrel'. Many of those 'children' were ungrateful for his fatherly care.

Peace was dull. Peace was debilitating. It was a 'lullaby', wrote the preacher and polemicist Thomas Scott, that rocked the sluggard England asleep. Peace 'hath made us drunk with ease and carelessness', wrote Bishop Goodman, and so 'we fell to luxury and riot'.

Peace allowed discontent to fester. Looking back on James's reign, Arthur Wilson wrote, 'Peace was maintained by him as in the time of Augustus; and Peace begot Plenty, and Plenty begot Ease and Wantonness, and Ease and Wantonness begot Poetry.' This latter development did not strike Wilson as desirable. Poets were the enemy of established authority. 'Poetry swelled to that bulk in his time that it begot strange monstrous satyrs against the King's own person.'

The long peace that King James had brokered, and steadfastly preserved against the hawks with whom he was surrounded, had brought England unprecedented prosperity. A whole generation of young men had been spared the horrors of the press gang and the battlefield. All the same, wrote Thomas Scott, peace was an 'iniquity'.

* * *

King James's pacifism was connected, in many of his subjects' minds, with his questionable sexuality. Warmongering was manly. William Trumbull, his envoy in Brussels, described a bellicose policy as being 'vigorous and masculine'. But King James, wrote the Tuscan ambassador, was 'timid' and 'lenient, and averse to the shedding of blood'. These were feminine weaknesses. James lacked the essential quality of *virtù* – a word in which the etymological root of 'virtue' overlaps with that of 'virility' – the strength and courage that was seen as being quintessentially male.

King James was physically brave. Out hunting he took risks that appalled his courtiers. Once he was nearly killed when his horse stumbled and he was tossed into a river. He scrambled out, remounted, still sopping wet, and rode on. No matter: hunting was one of the pleasures of peace, and therefore no test of masculinity. In a pamphlet from 1622 inveighing against the degeneracy of English manhood, the author lists hunting and hawking as ways in which men squander their time when they should be busy with 'shooting, running, wrestling and the like strenuous and manly sports'. However intrepid a horseman James may have been, to contemporary commentators his dislike of violence convicted him of 'mere impotency, and baseness of mind'. He was unworthy of his high estate – to be noble, in this world still saturated with the ethos of feudalism, was to be a fighting man.

Few of King James's contemporaries recognised that international disputes might be more efficiently settled without bloodshed. A monarch who sought to keep the peace was seldom admired for his statesmanship or thanked for the tremendous benefits he thereby conferred on his people. He could only be seen as a coward. James 'was infinitely inclined to peace, but more out of fear than conscience', wrote Anthony Weldon. Count Gondomar reported that 'fear alone guides the King'. Sir John Oglander, a royalist who otherwise admired him, thought, 'King James I was the most cowardly man that ever I knew.'

Unlike his predecessor, Queen Elizabeth, who declared in her Tilbury speech that despite her biological sex she was ready to take up arms, James had the 'heart and stomach', not of a king, but of a 'weak and feeble woman'.

*   *   *

James held steadfastly to peace. When his daughter and son-in-law were driven out of the Palatinate, he relied on his network of ambassadors and envoys and secret agents to work towards a negotiated settlement. Anthony Weldon complained that 'he had rather spend 100,000 livres on embassies to keep or procure peace with dishonour' than spend one-tenth of that sum on an army 'that would have forced peace with honour'. James would have queried Weldon's accounting, but it was true that he cared nothing for the sort of 'honour' warfare brought.

As he continued to stall, the frustration of the war party, and the allegations of unmanliness, intensified and reinforced each other.

Effeminacy and homosexuality were not invariably linked. It is heterosexual passion for Cleopatra that unmans Shakespeare's Antony. Their love, making him the helpless subordinate of a dominant woman, scrambles gender so that Antony, poor besotted fool,

> *... is not more manlike*
> *Than Cleopatra, nor the queen of Ptolemy*
> *More womanly than he.*

But if a man who loved a woman too much risked taking on some of her womanly weakness, it was still more dangerous to his masculinity for a man to love one of his own sex. In King James, the man-loving king who preferred disputation and diplomacy to jousting and battle, those who equated proper desires with a proper zest for licensed violence found their doubly dubious bugbear.

It was a troubling time for those made uncomfortable by gender fluidity. D'Ewes wrote queasily of boys 'grown to the height of wickedness' who painted their faces like women. Michael Drayton wrote a poem, *The Moon-Calf*, in which the Devil fathers 'monstrous twins ... a feminine man, a woman masculine'. The former bathes in milk and takes his 'beastly, outrageous' pleasure with a 'smooth-chinned, plump-thighed Catamite'.

Two tracts appeared. They were entitled *Hic Mulier* (The He-Woman) and *Haec Vir* (The She-Man). In the first the anonymous author complains that 'since the days of Adam women were never so masculine'. Women had grown unmanageable; they were cutting their hair short, and exchanging their proper implement, the needle, for the sword. The second, apparently written by the same male author but in the voice of a woman, suggests that this is the fault of men. How can they expect their women to be womanly, when they themselves are so unmanly?

The trouble is that men are no longer warriors. 'You have demolished the noble school of Horsemanship … hung up your arms to rust, glued up those swords in their scabbards that would shake all Christendom with the brandish, and entertained into your minds … softness, dullness and effeminate niceness.' So, in the opinion of this imaginary woman, they have forfeited their women's respect. Only when they take up arms will the proper relationship between aggressive males and submissive females be restored. 'Then will we love and serve you; then will we hear and obey you.'

In 1620 Thomas Scott wrote *Vox Populi: or News from Spain*. Writing as though in the voice of the Count of Gondomar, he assured the Spanish they had nothing to fear from the 'effeminate and cowardly' English because 'their bodies by long disuse of arms were disabled and their minds effeminated by peace and luxury'. In another pamphlet two years later Scott elaborated on the theme. Englishmen were 'degenerate', preoccupied with 'effeminate fashions and mollifying pleasures'. Many agreed with him.

The preacher John Everard thundered against 'these wanton and womanish times' in which Englishmen, like the inhabitants of ancient Nineveh, were 'proud as women, foolish and void of council as women, fantastical and new-fangled as women, fearful and coward-like as women, nice and effeminate as women'.

Only war could restore their manhood.

Having dissolved Parliament so abruptly in December 1621, without subsidies having been granted, King James was in no position to make war. Nor did he wish to. Throughout the summer and autumn of 1622 the Imperial general, Count Tilly, was in the Palatinate, along with Maximilian and the armies of the Catholic League, besieging cities, and taking them one by one. Heidelberg fell in September. Mannheim in November. Frederick and his family fled to the Netherlands. Sir Horace Vere's troop of English volunteers held out in Frankenthal, but their cause was all too evidently lost.

In November 1621, when Parliament was calling for King James to take up his sword and declare war on Spain, Gondomar told Buckingham, 'If I were not so certain of the King's word and his goodness, that he would punish his Commons and set things right with the speed and severity that was called for, I would have left his Kingdom without waiting a third day.' In December, though, after King James tore up the Commons' protestation, Gondomar wrote home jubilantly. 'It is certain the King will never summon another Parliament,' he said. He thought this was excellent news for Spain.

The negotiations over the Spanish Match resumed.

In Rome, in July 1622, an assembly of cardinals, presided over by Pope Gregory XV himself, met to consider the Anglo-Spanish Match. The Spanish had made it plain from the outset that the marriage between the Catholic Infanta Maria and the Protestant Prince Charles could not go ahead without a papal dispensation.

The Pope and his cardinals decided that before they could give the union their blessing, King James must commit himself to repealing the penal laws against his Roman Catholic subjects.

Furthermore, the cardinals suggested not only that should Prince Charles convert, but that King James himself should declare himself a Catholic. Scholar that he was, he must surely have realised that the Roman Catholic faith was that 'true and ancient one' in which 'he could find salvation'.

The cardinals' ruling was a provocation. In England, exasperated Protestant preachers invoked the Book of Exodus, which told them 'The Lord is a man of war'. King James, a man of peace, ignored them. He ignored protocol. He ignored the concept of manliness that valorised pride and disdained a polite petitioner. Instead of indignantly rejecting the demands from Rome, King James turned to the person many of his subjects saw as the Antichrist, but whom he addressed as 'Most Holy Father'. He wrote personally and privately to the Pope.

It was a most unconventional move. James wrote as though from another century, from another planet. He wrote as though England's defection from the Roman Church had never caused its great rift; as though the Inquisition, which had made it dangerous for any Protestant to travel in Spain or Italy for nearly a century, had never been; as though all the people tortured or killed for their faith under England's Tudor monarchs (Protestants under Mary, Catholics under Elizabeth) had never suffered; as though the German lands were not at that moment being plunged into what would turn out to be three decades of sectarian conflict. His letter was naive, unrealistic and entirely reasonable. He wrote as Jesus might perhaps have done.

He opens his letter by acknowledging the strangeness of it. There was no direct communication between the Vatican and the English court. A Pope cannot correspond with a Protestant. James wrote, 'Your Holiness will perhaps marvel that we, differing from you in point of religion, should now salute you with our letters.' But desperate times call for unprecedented measures. 'Such is the trouble of our mind for these calamitous discords and bloodsheds, which for these late years by-past have so miserably rent the Christian world ... as we could no longer abstain.'

He makes the breathtakingly heretical suggestion that heresy is a triviality. He reminds Gregory that 'we all worship the same most blessed Trinity' and all 'look to Jesus Christ for salvation'. He asks the Pope, 'friendly and seriously', to set aside sectarian disagreements, and that he 'would be pleased, together with us' to put his hand to halting the escalating war in Europe and to reconciling the warring parties. After all, he goes on, the two of them have a common cause, the preservation of 'the state of Christendom'. Why should they not collaborate on 'so pious a work, and so worthy of a Christian prince' as the keeping of peace?

The Pope never replied to the letter. We do not know what he thought of it. We do know that the armies of the Catholic League, this time commanded by Count Tilly, won victory after victory that year with papal backing. In one of those battles, Tilly's forces faced an army numbering 15,000. By the day's end some 13,000 of those men lay dead on the battlefield. Such was the pious work His Holiness chose over the peacemaking James proposed.

The fighting transformed much of the Continent, in the words of an English preacher, into 'a Golgotha, a place of dead men's skulls ... a field of blood'. Twenty years after James's failed peace initiative – two decades of almost continuous warfare – a traveller through Germany reported, 'One may travel ten miles without seeing man or beast. In all the villages the houses are filled with corpses, carcasses intermingled, slain by pest and hunger and partially devoured by wolves, dogs and carrion crows, because there is no one left to bury them.'

James's letter, reaching out – defiant of all sacred and secular convention – to the only person on earth whose authority might have been sufficient to arrest that ghastly process of destruction, seems in retrospect visionary and courageous.

Had his English critics read it, they would have thought it effeminate in the extreme.

Prince Charles

THERE was a time, early in 1622, when King James appeared in the Presence Chamber, ready for his dinner, to find that Buckingham was not there. Simonds D'Ewes, who tells the story, relates that James declared he would not eat until Buckingham joined him. Buckingham was playing tennis. Tennis (then a game played indoors and resembling the modern game of squash) was a favourite pastime for young men at the Jacobean court. It was a spectator sport. Castiglione writes of how, in playing tennis, a courtier can display to an appreciative audience 'how well he is built physically, how quick and agile he is in every member'. When Buckingham played in the palace courts he would have drawn a crowd.

A messenger was sent to summon him. The messenger returned alone. Other messengers were sent. Still no Buckingham. At last the King himself 'arose and called into the tennis court to him, "Come away, come away, Buckingham, for the King hath vowed not to eat a bit until you come."'

There was another time when King and favourite attended a service in the palace chapel. Afterwards King James was ready to leave, but Buckingham was not. The King 'tarried a long time, calling him to go with him'. Buckingham took no notice. 'He strode carelessly talking with another lord and that a good while.' When at last he deigned to join the King, James didn't reprimand him for so disrespectfully keeping his monarch waiting. Instead James 'fell upon his neck without saying any more words'.

D'Ewes tells these stories as illustrations of Buckingham's 'greatness'. They are also suggestions that the balance of power within the relationship was shifting. James was becoming clinging and needy, Buckingham confident and careless. No longer was he a docile Ganymede, serving his lord and master with alacrity. He was nearly thirty, a married man with a child on the way, with his own houses and interests and work to do.

The King was his master still, of course, but there were others making demands on his time. When they were apart he didn't write as frequently as the King would like him to. He says that he can't commit himself to an exact date for their next meeting. 'I fear before Wednesday I shall not be able to get out of this beastly town.' He forgets to ask the King for his blessing, and doesn't seem to care much about it. He still signs himself 'Your Majesty's humble slave and dog', but he is no longer quite so humble, and his devotion is less doggily exclusive. He has other allies, other friends.

One of those others was the Prince of Wales.

As a child Prince Charles was sickly and withdrawn. According to a contemporary biographer, he 'was exceedingly feeble in his lower parts'. Like his father, he had something wrong with his legs, which grew 'not erect, but rapandous and embowed'. And, like his father, he had something wrong with his tongue. James's problem seems only to have affected his table manners, but Charles's made it hard for him to talk. To master his impediment he took to speaking slowly. 'The best and surest way is to take good deliberation first, and not to be sudden of speech,' he wrote. The child of a garrulous father and a mother who loved to dress up and dance in public, he was quiet, tentative, unsure.

For the first twelve years of his life he was eclipsed by his glamorous elder brother. 'The gallantry of Henry's heroic spirit tended somewhat to the disadvantage, and extenuation of Charles his glory,' wrote a contemporary. Henry was 'forward and enterprising'; Charles was 'of a studious and retired spirit'.

Henry was not very kind to him. The Venetian ambassador records an occasion when King James, exasperated by Henry's refusal to study, threatened to cut him out of the line of succession, leaving the crown to Charles, 'who was far quicker at learning and studied more earnestly'. Henry snapped back, 'If my brother is as learned as they say, we'll make him Archbishop of Canterbury.' Kingship, in other words, demanded more dashing, virile qualities than Charles possessed.

When Henry died, and only a month later Elizabeth married and left England for ever, Charles – just twelve – was suddenly thrust forward. He had to cope not only with his grief, but also with the terrifying ordeal (for a frail, anxious boy) of officiating as chief mourner at his brother's lugubriously theatrical funeral. His parents were living apart. He was, effectively, the only child of a troubled marriage. An enormous weight of new responsibilities fell upon him as heir to the throne (Plate 13). He was scrutinised, discussed, appraised and – as he would have been all too well aware – frequently found wanting. He had a great destiny, but an onerous one. His father told him he 'must not expect a soft and easy crown, but a crown full of thorny cares'.

When he was fifteen – a self-conscious, unusually small adolescent (he never grew much taller than five foot) – his father fell in love with a man who was as graceful and confident and athletic as he was awkward, a man only eight years older than himself.

The relationship between favourite and heir did not begin well.

In March 1616 Prince Charles admired a ring (probably a gift from the King) that Buckingham was wearing. Charles asked to try it, and slipped it onto his own finger. The next day Buckingham asked for it back. Prince Charles said he could not find it. Buckingham appealed to the King, who told off the Prince and 'used such bitter language to him as forced His Highness to shed tears'.

Then there was an occasion when Buckingham was wearing the heavy tennis 'glove', a flat paddle or bat, made of canvas and leather and strapped to the player's hand. Prince Charles did or said something that irritated Buckingham so extremely he raised his hand. Onlookers were shocked to see that he only just managed to restrain himself from hitting the Prince of Wales. Another time he was heard to tell Charles to 'kiss his arse'.

Gradually, though, things got better. Prince Charles had been spending most of his time with his mother. As he approached adulthood the King made efforts to bring him closer. In the autumn of 1617 Charles was with James in the country. The Prince rode well. The King told him that his horsemanship and his fondness for hunting proved that he was his father's 'true and worthy son'. A watchful ambassador wrote that their newly cordial relationship was 'a danger for some other great person'. He meant that if father and son were to become more affectionate, Buckingham's hold over the King would be loosened.

Probably Buckingham saw the danger. He must have reflected that the King would not live for ever and that for his own future security he needed to befriend the heir. Many observers thought so. Perhaps he set out to enchant the gauche teenage prince for careerist reasons, but perhaps he was not acting cynically. Perhaps he felt sorry for the earnest boy whose attempts to be playful only succeeded in being annoying, who struggled to speak and found it so hard to get on with his irascible father. Perhaps it was pleasant for him to have another young person around when he was attending on the King. Perhaps being charming came so easily to Buckingham that he barely thought what he was doing as he set about winning over the Prince of Wales.

By the summer of 1618 any coldness between the two of them had vanished. Prince Charles wrote to Buckingham asking his advice on how to smooth over a misunderstanding between himself and King James. He addressed the favourite by his father's pet name for him, 'Steenie', and signed himself 'your true, constant, loving friend'.

Four years later, in March 1622, King James told his Privy Council – some of whom demonstrated their devotion to him by openly weeping – that he was feeling his age. He was still in his fifties, but he felt vulnerable. He was planning his succession. He announced that in future he would be sharing his power with his son because the burden of kingship was too much for him to bear alone.

This shift was no threat to Buckingham, who was by this time as easy with the heir as he was with the King. He teased Charles fearlessly, as a fellow member of the unusual little homoerotic family of three they formed with King James. At the end of a letter to the King, Buckingham added a postscript: 'Baby Charles, I kiss thy warty hands.'

Buckingham's other family was increasing. In March 1622 Katherine gave birth to their first child. That the baby was a girl was disappointing – any seventeenth-century nobleman hoped for a male heir to whom to leave his estates and titles – but it didn't prevent her parents doting on her. She was named Mary, after her grandmother, the Countess of Buckingham, and was usually known, as the Countess was, as Mall.

A growing family, a growing number of houses. In February 1622 Buckingham finally got possession of Bacon's York House and set Gerbier to remodel it. His purchase of Wallingford House, in which he had already been living for two years, was completed. Inigo Jones, not to be excluded from the grand project of providing magnificent homes

as a setting for the glitter of Buckingham's brilliance, set to work planning a gatehouse here, a stable block there, a coffered ceiling in the
other place. In July Buckingham went to Essex with his mother to view
New Hall, and immediately decided to take it.

James wrote to Lord Treasurer Cranfield, instructing him to promptly
find money for Buckingham to cover the costs of his new houses and
their furnishing. To Buckingham himself he sent melons and peaches
and grapes and partridges and leverets (hares) and a kid and so many
other good things that Buckingham declared he could not list them all
in his thank-you letters. They wrote to each other whenever they were
apart, teasing and joking and then abruptly lapsing into love talk.

Buckingham to James:

> How can I but write merrily [to the one] I so love best and beyond
> all the world.

A young man called Arthur Brett came to court. He was a cousin of
Buckingham's, and his sister was married to Lord Cranfield. He was
very handsome. Maybe this time Buckingham had been unwise to help
bring one of his relations forward. The Earl of Kellie wrote to a friend in
Scotland that it was being said that 'His Majesty should begin to love
and favour one young man called Brett'. Perhaps Buckingham briefly
felt threatened by Brett. He arranged for him to be knighted, and then
sent off on travels abroad. By the end of the year it was once more
certain he had no need to fear any rival.

King James to Buckingham:

> My only sweet and dear child, I pray thee haste thee home to thy
> dear dad by sun-setting at the furthest ... and so Lord send me
> comfortable and happy with thee this night.
>   James R.

II

SPAIN

The Plan

IN January 1623 Buckingham and Prince Charles came up with a plan. The plan was so risky and peculiar that it has bewildered people from that day to this. At the time the Venetian ambassador to London, Alvise Valaresso, called it 'an abyss of marvels, a monster among decisions; a labyrinth without head or way out'. Nearly four hundred years later Thomas Cogswell, among the foremost twenty-first-century historians of Jacobean England, called it 'one of the most mysterious episodes in early modern English history'.

The plan was that the two young men would travel together all the way to Madrid. They would go disguised and incognito. They would take only two or three companions. They would travel by public transport (post-horses). Once arrived in the Spanish capital, they would reveal themselves and somehow, by the sheer power of their presence, cut through all the difficulties that had kept the negotiations for the Spanish Match deadlocked for years. They would bring home the Infanta Maria as Charles's bride.

They tricked King James into giving his consent. When he understood how they had hoodwinked him, the King 'fell into a great passion of tears' and told Buckingham and Prince Charles – the two people he loved best in the world – that they were breaking his heart.

We know how it was done from Edward Hyde, Earl of Clarendon, the royalist statesman and historian of the next generation, who could have heard the story from Charles himself.

According to Clarendon, Buckingham began to talk to Charles about how unfortunate princes were in that they had so little part in the choosing of their wives. (Given that Buckingham himself was recently wed, it is not hard to imagine how this topic might have arisen.)

'From hence,' goes on Clarendon, the two 'discoursed how gallant and how brave a thing it would be, for His Highness to make a journey into Spain, and to fetch home his mistress'. They imagined how the 'slow progress in all things of ceremony' would 'be in a moment removed by his own presence'. The Infanta would be honoured and touched that her suitor had come so far to seek her. The King of Spain must surely feel gratified, and might be persuaded to intervene in the Palatinate to please the Prince of Wales, as he never would for a mere ambassador. 'These discourses made so deep impression upon the mind and spirit of the prince,' writes Clarendon, 'that he was transported with the thought of it, and most impatiently solicitous to bring it to pass.'

Charles and Buckingham were fully aware how outrageous their plan would be seen to be. The heir to the throne of a major European power could not go gadding around the world as any other young man might. There were protocols to be observed. There were very real risks to be considered – shipwreck, robbers, assassins, a horse stumbling on a mountain road. They were also aware that all of James's advisers would be opposed to the idea, and that the King, being cautious, would thankfully take his Councillors' advice and veto the plan. So they came up with a strategy.

Prince Charles would tell his father that there was something he wanted very badly, an 'earnest desire and suit'. He would not reveal what it was until James had sworn not to consult anyone else about it, but to make his own decision unaided. King James, who prided himself on his wisdom and was confident he could make his own mind up about this mysterious suit, 'cheerfully consented' to the condition.

The three men were alone together. Prince Charles went down on his knees and made his proposal. He didn't go into detail. He just said he wanted to go to Spain to bring home his bride. The King didn't immediately refuse. He hesitated. He looked to Buckingham, as though for support, but Buckingham offered no guidance. He merely said how upset Charles would be if his request was refused. Charles followed up by insisting that this was the best way to bring the long-sought Spanish Match to its conclusion, and saying that, once in Madrid, he would 'in a moment' persuade the Spanish king to restore the Palatinate to Elizabeth and Frederick.

King James didn't immediately see the suggestion as being as dangerous as those around him would. After all, he had himself sailed over stormy seas to fetch home his wife. He said they could go.

Probably, as Clarendon suggests, he reflected that the preparations for such a journey would take up much time. He would have been thinking of a fleet of ships, of a great train of courtiers, of costly presents, of jewels being withdrawn from the royal jewel house to be presented to the bride and her family, of troops to guard the Prince, of gorgeous clothes to be made and transported, of the fixtures and fittings of an entire court lumbering on carts across Europe or being tossed about in the rough seas of the Bay of Biscay.

It would all be dreadfully expensive, of course, but with any luck it wouldn't actually happen. James would have reflected that if the land route was chosen, the King of France would have to be asked for permission for the princely party to pass through that country, permission which might well not be forthcoming, given how little the French were likely to be pleased by an Anglo-Spanish alliance. He would have considered that all these time-consuming preparations would allow plenty of opportunity for rethinking, and perhaps retracting. And so he 'gave his approbation, and promised that the Prince should make the journey he was so much inclined to'.

The trap the two young men had set snapped shut. Once they had the King's promise – which, from a man of honour, was irrevocable – they told James that the success of the trip depended on speed and secrecy. It was not to be the cumbersome royal progress he envisaged. They had discussed their plan, they said, with no one but each other. They wanted no pomp and circumstance, no retinue of attendants. They would go 'suddenly' – within a few days – with only two companions, and even those two would not be told their destination.

James was dumbfounded. This was a completely unexpected twist. He had been inveigled into giving his consent before he understood what he was consenting to. Buckingham and Charles told him that they would come back the following morning to discuss the final details. Meanwhile, in accordance with his original promise, the King must speak to no one.

Clarendon imagines that James passed a terrible night. 'A thousand difficulties and dangers occurred to him, and so many precipices which could hardly be avoided in such a journey.' He thought of all the risks they would be running. He thought that Charles was his only son, and the nation's hope. He thought how angry his people would be that their prince was delivering himself into the hands of the hated Spaniards – and how much angrier if 'any ill accident' should happen.

He thought how stupid and undignified the whole adventure would look to foreign powers. He saw, with dreadful clarity, how Charles's arrival in Madrid would be seen as a capitulation to all of Spain's demands and an acceptance of all Rome's conditions for the Spanish Match. He guessed how gleefully the Spanish would insist on rewriting the marriage contract, so near to completion after years of patient negotiation, once Charles arrived in Madrid, a self-surrendered hostage.

He wondered how he could have been so weak as to consent, 'contrary to the light of his understanding, as well as the current of his affection'. He didn't sleep.

The Match

THROUGHOUT 1622, the year before that painful conversation, King James and Buckingham had continued to work with Gondomar towards realising the Spanish Match.

In the spring, the Earl of Bristol set out for Spain, where he was to resume his post as the English ambassador. He would work alongside Sir Walter Aston, who was already *en poste* in Madrid. As an experienced Spanish hand who knew very well how the diplomatic game was played in Madrid, Bristol was being sent back there expressly in order to expedite the Match.

May. A few weeks after Bristol's departure, Count Gondomar also left London for Spain. On his arrival, James Howell, an aide in the British embassy in Madrid, wrote home, 'Count Gondomar doth strongly negotiate a match twixt our prince and the Infanta of Spain.'

August. Bristol reached Madrid. There was a new king in Spain. The effective ruler was the Count-Duke of Olivares, young King Philip's mentor and favourite (the Spanish term was *privado*).

Bristol reported to King James that he had been given a warm welcome and that he now believed that Philip IV, 'merely to gratify His Majesty [King James], would not make the match without resolving to restore the Palatinate, nor restore the Palatinate without resolving to make the match'.

Bristol does not seem to have noticed the negatives hedging this promise.

Early October. Francis Cottington, former ambassador to Madrid, returned to London, having handed over to Bristol and Aston. He reported the good news that Gondomar was one of the commissioners appointed to treat with Bristol; that the commissioners had expressed their disapproval of the cardinals' additional requirements; that King Philip would write to the Pope asking him not to insist upon them. Bristol had had an audience with King Philip during which the King 'expressed an earnest desire that the match should be concluded, and that therein no time should be lost'.

Late October. Gondomar wrote to Buckingham, 'The decision has already been made here, and with very great enthusiasm, that the Prince of Wales should mount Spain.' The phrasing was disrespectfully lewd as a way of speaking of two royal persons, but friendly in playing on Buckingham's expert interest in horse-breeding.

Late October. Endymion Porter arrived in Madrid. Porter had a Spanish grandmother and had grown up in Spain, serving as a page in the household of Olivares's father, before he came to England and became a protégé of Buckingham's. By this time he was Prince Charles's Master of the Horse. Annoyingly for Bristol, Buckingham had sent Porter out to see if he could use his personal connection to bypass the ambassador and speed matters up.

Olivares received Porter graciously, as a man whom he had 'tended and favoured' when they were both children. They had a private conversation. Porter brought up the question of the Match and asked Olivares to confirm that Spanish troops would be used to restore Frederick to the Palatinate. Olivares lost his temper and said sharply, 'I know nothing of it,' and 'as for the marriage, I know not what it means.'

Porter reported the exchange to Bristol, who demanded an explanation from Olivares for this apparent backward step. Olivares explained he had not wanted to discuss matters of state with a mere envoy. Bristol believed him.

November. One of Bristol's aides wrote that the 'general voice runs through Madrid that the match with England is concluded'. Buckingham, as Lord High Admiral, asked the Lord Treasurer for money to pay for a fleet because, he declared, 'in the spring we shall go for the daughter of Spain'. He and Prince Charles both began taking Spanish lessons.

2 January 1623. Endymion Porter arrived back in London bearing letters from Bristol to King James with the 'good and gladsome tidings' that the Infanta could be on her way to London 'by the spring'. Later Buckingham was to say that the dispatches Porter brought were 'fraught with generalities, without any one particular or certainty at all'. At the time, though, he overlooked that troubling vagueness. The Infanta could be married by proxy, and set out for her new home, just as soon as the Pope gave his dispensation.

Few people in London seem to have understood that the dispensation might never be forthcoming. The Venetian envoy wrote that the Spanish Match was 'an accomplished fact'. Porter's news, writes John Chamberlain, left King James 'very merry and jocund'.

So why, a month after Endymion Porter's return with the 'gladsome' (if misleading) news, did Prince Charles and Buckingham decide they could no longer wait for the diplomatic process to deliver the Infanta to her bridegroom? Why break the King's heart by embarking on their wild adventure?

It wasn't a sudden impulse. Later, after the adventure had turned into a fiasco, Buckingham was widely blamed for leading the Prince astray, but the record suggests it was Charles's idea, and that it had been on his mind for months.

In May 1622, when Gondomar was leaving London, Charles had said to him that, if necessary, he would travel secretly, in disguise, to Madrid to claim his bride. On arriving in Spain, Gondomar duly told King Philip IV that 'this prince has offered, in great confidence, and secretly,' to come to Madrid 'incognito with only two attendants'. When Endymion Porter went out to Madrid in October, he carried secret letters from Charles to Gondomar, reiterating the offer and asking Gondomar how he thought his sudden apparition in the Spanish capital would be received. Neither Porter nor Gondomar mentioned the Prince's proposal to Bristol, who said afterwards he would 'directly have protested against it'.

With hindsight, testifying to Parliament in 1626, Bristol was to describe these letters as being a 'treacherous' correspondence between

Buckingham and Gondomar, the makings of a plot whereby the former, with Porter as accomplice, would deliver Prince Charles to Madrid. There, Gondomar hoped, Charles could be persuaded, or even coerced, into converting to Catholicism – a great coup for the Roman Church.

Why Buckingham would have wished to enter into such a conspiracy Bristol couldn't say.

As Lord High Admiral, Buckingham was preparing a fleet to fetch the Infanta to her marital home with all due ceremony. It is true that he was thinking of taking Charles along: he wrote to Gondomar in October 1622 that he 'intended to take his friend with him in secret, to bring back that beautiful angel'. Rumours of that plan spread. John Chamberlain wrote that he had heard 'that the Prince himself goes in person'. But Charles's sailing out on the flagship of an imposing fleet, to fetch home a bride who was already married to him by proxy, is a very different scenario from his galloping all the way to Madrid. The enthusiasm for that wild ride was Charles's own.

The Codpiece Point

CHARLES was twenty-two. When Gondomar first proposed he might marry the Infanta Maria, he was in his early teens. It was just the kind of marriage (dynastic, pragmatic) to which he was doomed. But as years and years went by, he became impatient. Sitting in on the acrimonious debates in the 1621 Parliament, he heard the Match being discussed with no concern for his personal happiness. He wrote wretchedly to the King about how it distressed him to hear 'my marriage so much prostituted in the House'.

He was of more than marriageable age. Buckingham wrote to Gondomar, 'The Prince is full ripe for such a business.' He was six years older than his brother-in-law, the troublesome Elector Palatine, had been on his wedding day, almost as old as James had been when he married – and James had felt obliged to apologise to the Scottish people for being so slow in giving them a queen.

Charles was shy sexually. According to the Venetian Ambassador, Lando, he 'blushed like a modest maiden if he heard talk of shameful things'. And so, Lando goes on, the court beauties who had followed Prince Henry around, intent on seducing him and subsequently getting money from him, didn't even try to tempt the younger brother, seeing that it was hopeless. But by 1622 Charles was tired of celibacy. What the King called 'the codpiece point' was pressing urgently upon him. He wanted his wife.

Charles had initially been under no romantic illusions about his proposed marriage. He once remarked to his courtiers, after viewing a portrait of the Infanta, 'Were it not for the sin, it would be well if princes could have two wives; one for reason of state, the other to please themselves.' But somehow, in the months before he set out for Spain, he succeeded in persuading himself that the Infanta Maria could be the one to please him. He decided he was in love.

Those who favoured the Match were fanning the flames. Bristol wrote to him in December 1622 describing a court entertainment where the Infanta had 'danced as well as any ever I saw'. Afterwards she sat next to her brother, King Philip, and 'it was an hundred times repeated that night, "If only, please God, the Prince of England could see her! How exquisite, how beautiful, how like an angel she is."' Charles took the bait. Bristol wrote again archly that it was clear 'the little god [Cupid] has been somewhat busy with you'.

Charles ignored the teasing, and wrote solemnly, 'If you wonder how I can love before I see, the truth is I have seen her picture and heard the report of her virtues by a number whom I trust, so as her idea is engraven in my heart where I hope to preserve it till I enjoy the principal.' His longing for that enjoyment was becoming ever more urgent. He could not wait much longer.

Companions

FEBRUARY 1623. The morning after King James had so unwisely promised to let them go to Spain, the Prince and Buckingham presented themselves again in his bedchamber. On seeing them, the King burst into a 'storm of weeping'. Once he had recovered himself, he told them he was withdrawing his consent to their journey and explained, point by point, why their idea was such a disastrously bad one.

It was bad for himself, because it imperilled his son, 'with whom his life was bound up'. He was talking of his personal life as a father, but also of his life as a monarch and father of his people. Should Charles be killed or kidnapped along the way, or held against his will in Madrid, the whole nation would suffer.

It was bad for Charles, whose marriage – which might, with a little more patience, soon come off – would almost certainly be put out of reach. 'The Prince should no sooner arrive at Madrid, than all the articles of the treaty should be laid aside, and new matters be proposed which could never be consented to.'

It was bad for Buckingham, whose 'enemies … amongst the greatest persons of the nobility' would 'make such use of this occasion, that it would not be in His Majesty's power to protect him'. The people would hate him for taking their prince to Spain. His 'ruin' would be inevitable.

It was bad for all Europe. The 'rash action' of the young men's journey would 'irrecoverably break' the Spanish Match, which in turn would destroy King James's hopes of a peaceable solution to the problem of the Palatinate.

All of these arguments were sound. Charles and Buckingham didn't bother to challenge them. Instead they railed against the King. Buckingham accused him of having broken his preliminary promise to consult nobody. Surely his second thoughts had been prompted by 'some rascal, who had furnished him with those pitiful reasons'. Forced onto the defensive, James pitifully swore 'with many oaths' that he had not 'communicated the matter with any person living'. He continued to beg – 'with sighs and tears', with 'disorder and passion' – to be released from his promise.

While he pleaded and wept, Buckingham, instead of leaping to his master's defence as a good dog should, was 'standing a long time by, without saying a word'. Charles – giving evidence of the stubborn inflexibility which was eventually to be the death of him – was adamant. He reminded his father 'of the promise he had made, which was so sacred that he hoped he would not violate it'.

When at last Buckingham spoke, it was in 'rougher dialect' than the Prince had used. He told the monarch, whose 'humble slave' he still claimed to be, that 'nobody could believe anything he said, [if] he retracted so soon the promise he had so solemnly made'.

Something had changed. The King was being bullied. His 'sweet boys' were now in league against him. Clarendon praises Buckingham elsewhere for his 'flowing courtesy and affability', yet here was this paragon of good manners rudely ignoring the King's wishes. Acting as though all James's wise advice was so much inconsequential blather, he and the Prince proceeded to outline their plans.

They would be ready to set off in two days' time, they said. They would leave London at once – Charles ostensibly to hunt at Theobalds, Buckingham to 'take physic' at Chelsea. From those two pretend destinations, they would each travel on to Buckingham's house in Essex, New Hall. They had chosen their companions – Francis Cottington and Endymion Porter.

At last something of which the King could approve. These two were excellent choices.

Porter's relationship with Olivares was useful, and he had a wide circle of Spanish friends (who knew him as Don Antonio). When he came to England he had joined Buckingham's entourage as a favoured friend. He shared Buckingham's interest in art. Soon he married Buckingham's niece and became part of his family. In 1621 he performed in the masque *The Gypsies Metamorphosed*, along with

Buckingham's brother and his brother-in-law. In 1622 he moved to Prince Charles's household and long remained one of Charles's most trusted associates.

According to Anthony à Wood, the antiquarian of the next generation, Porter was 'beloved by two kings: James I for his admirable wit and Charles I for his general bearing, brave style, sweet temper, great experience, travels and modern languages'. He was comically ill-named: according to classical legend Endymion was a youth so beautiful that the moon goddess Selene fell passionately in love with him. A double portrait of Porter with Van Dyck, painted by the latter, shows him stocky of body and puffy of face. But though he was no beauty, many of his contemporaries found him a delightful friend.

Francis Cottington was less amiable. Clarendon writes, 'He left behind him a greater esteem of his parts than love of his person.' But he was a good man to go to Spain with. He had been consul in Seville as well as ambassador in Madrid. Simonds D'Ewes refers to him as a 'Hispaniolised Englishman'. King James had appointed him secretary to the Prince of Wales, in the expectation that – as the negotiations over the marriage contract proceeded – he would be able to guide Charles through the complexities of Spanish court life and Spanish diplomacy.

It was Buckingham and Charles's plan, in keeping with the spirit of boyish derring-do in which they had proposed their escapade, that these two would not be told where they were going until they were about to board ship. But King James pointed out that it would be wise to make use of their knowledge of Spain immediately. They had both travelled there and back frequently: 'many things would occur to them, as necessary to the journey'.

Cottington was at hand, waiting in an outer room. James had him called in, and cautioned him that he was not, 'upon his life', to disclose what followed 'to any man alive'. James then said, 'Cottington, here is Baby Charles and Steenie … who have a great mind to go by post into Spain to fetch home the Infanta, and will have but two more in their company and have chosen you for one. What think you of the journey?'

Buckingham whispered in Prince Charles's ear that Cottington would oppose the journey. Charles whispered back, 'He durst not.'

It is true that Cottington was afraid. He often told Clarendon, afterwards, that 'when he heard the King, he fell into such a trembling, that he could hardly speak'. He had been assisting the Earl of Bristol, as together they inched towards an agreement on the marriage contract. He must have foreseen, at least as clearly as James did and with a great deal more insider knowledge, how this crazy scheme would nullify all their patient diplomacy. He also saw how the balance of power was tilting away from the monarch and towards the coalition of the favourite and the heir. He could not answer James's question without irritating, perhaps infuriating, either his present or his future king.

Speak he did, though, with a forthrightness that demonstrates his integrity. Once the Spaniards had Prince Charles in their hands, he said, 'they would make new overtures,' especially insisting on absolute freedom of worship for British Catholics, a condition King James could not accept. In short, the journey 'would render all that had been done towards the Match fruitless'.

At this point Buckingham turned on Cottington 'with all possible bitterness of words'. He accused him of pride, of jealousy. He put him down cruelly. He told Cottington that he had been asked only for information as to the best route, but the former ambassador had had the presumption to give his advice upon 'matter of state'. He said Cottington would repent of giving his uncalled-for opinion 'as long as he lived'.

James was shocked. With more tears, he pointed out that Cottington had only endorsed what he himself had already said. Buckingham didn't care. He heaped 'a thousand new reproaches' on Cottington while King James listened in 'agony', protesting, mildly and too late, 'Nay by God, Steenie, you are very much to blame to use him so.'

The King was defeated. The scene ended with him throwing himself onto his bed and falling 'into a new passion and lamentation'.

The journey was decided upon, and 'all directions given accordingly to Sir Francis Cottington', who was thus obliged – poor man – not only to join what he knew was a stupid adventure, but also to travel across Europe in extremely uncomfortable circumstances, along with a man who had humiliated him before their master.

Buckingham and Charles had prevailed. Their plan would take them abroad for months, and when they returned they would – together – repeatedly challenge James's authority and oppose his policies. Buckingham's allegiances had shifted. But James was still in love. Buckingham had made him cry, had defied him and spoken to him rudely, but later on that day, James wrote to him as follows:

> *My only sweet and dear child,*
> *I am now so miserable a coward, as I do nothing but weep and mourn; for I protest to God I rode this afternoon a great way in the park without speaking to anybody and the tears trickling down my cheeks, as now they do that I can scarcely see to write.*

His only recourse while Buckingham is away, he writes, will be to 'pry into thy defects with the eye of an enemy' and so harden his heart. But he knows such a mind game will be useless, 'for as it proceeds from love, so it cannot but end in love'. In the meantime he is longing for one last meeting.

Sweet heart ... Cast thee to be here tomorrow, as near about two in
the afternoon as thou can, and come galloping hither. Remember
thy picture and suffer none of the Council to come here. For God's
sake write not a word again and let no creature see this letter ...
thy dear dad and Christian gossip.
    James R.

Two days later, three men on horseback took the ferry across the River
Thames from Tilbury on the northern (Essex) shore to Gravesend in
Kent. Two of them – one strikingly handsome with a magnificent
physique, the other nervous-looking and very short – were wearing false
beards. The beards were no more natural-looking than such things
generally are.

Reaching the Kentish side of the river, the three fumbled for a coin to
pay for their passage. They could come up with nothing smaller,
between them, than a gold piece worth several hundred times the
normal fare.

Chivalry

WHEN it became known that Prince Charles and Buckingham had absented themselves from court, the Privy Councillors rode in a body to Newmarket to ask King James what was going on. The King told them, adding that the adventure had been undertaken partly 'to give a final end to that business [the Match] that had distracted His Majesty's other affairs for so long a time', and partly because Prince Charles had such a 'passion' and such 'an earnest desire to see his mistress'.

There are ways of thinking about a man besotted with a woman he barely knows or doesn't know at all; who becomes obsessed with that woman; who determines that he must have her as his lover or wife; who follows her around, in this case making a long and perilous journey in pursuit of her; who swears that she is the only one for him.

One way, the modern one, would be to call the man a stalker, and warn the woman to stay clear. Another, adopted by several of the seventeenth-century observers who recorded the journey to Madrid, was to make a bawdy joke of the whole silly codpiece-driven business. Boys will be boys. But there is another way of thinking that etherealises the man's passion and glorifies his pursuit.

The never-never land of chivalry and the fantasy of courtly love have been entrancing and confusing Europeans for over a thousand years. In the 1620s those intertwined systems of illusion were at once obsolete and still potent.

Shakespeare had written about the chronicles 'of wasted time' in which one could read of 'ladies dead, and lovely knights'. The culture the old romances celebrated was past (if it had ever existed). It was 'wasted', worn out, its ideology thin, its beauties faded, their value gone. To pay too much mind to it was to waste one's own time.

Dead or not, though, the chivalric ideal was still influential. Thomas Malory's compendium of the Arthurian romances, *Le Morte d'Arthur*, first published by Caxton in 1485, remained popular: a further edition would appear in 1634.

Chivalry glamorised warfare. It validated the code of honour that kept duelling alive. It was profoundly uncongenial to King James, the Rex Pacificus, but even he, when his sweet boys defied him and set off for Spain, consoled himself by invoking its archaic language: when he wrote to them after their departure, he addressed them as 'dear venturous knights, worthy to be put in a new romance'.

Knights-errant tended to encounter distressed damsels. When they did so, it was incumbent upon them to challenge whichever evil being – knight-gone-wrong, sorcerer, ogre – had caused her unhappiness.

After the Battle of White Mountain, King James's daughter, Elizabeth, who had become, so briefly, the Queen of Bohemia, came to be seen as just such a pathetic victim in need of chivalric support. Elizabeth was a wife, the mother of numerous children, and a political operator at least as forceful and determined as her husband, but in England she was generally talked about as if she was a frail, defenceless girl, alone in a sea of troubles.

At a Christmas dinner at the Middle Temple, just a few weeks before Prince Charles and Buckingham set out for Spain, one of the assembled lawyers 'took a cup of wine in one hand, and held his sword in the other, and so began a health to the distressed Lady Elizabeth, and having drunk, kissed his sword, and laying his hand upon it, took an oath to live and die in her service'. The sword and cup were then passed around and, one after another, the other diners pledged themselves as well. It was as though they imagined themselves seated at the Round Table in Camelot.

According to the romances, a mediaeval knight, bound by his duties as vassal to fight for his master, would beautify the obligations feudalism laid upon him by imagining himself in love with his liege-lord's lady, ready to lay down his life for her.

The potency of that emotional fantasy long outlived vassalage. Here is Edmund Burke reflecting on Marie Antoinette in 1790, the year after the storming of the Bastille, three years before her decapitation. Burke had seen and adored her many years earlier when she was newly arrived at Versailles, 'glittering like the morning star'.

> Little did I dream that I should have lived to see such disasters fallen upon her in a nation of gallant men, in a nation of men of honour and of cavaliers. I thought ten thousand swords must have leaped from their scabbards to avenge even a look that threatened her with insult. But the age of chivalry is gone. That of sophisters, economists, and calculators, has succeeded; and the glory of Europe is extinguished for ever.

This much anthologised passage made it into print against the forceful advice of Burke's friend and mentor Philip Francis (aka the pamphleteer 'Junius'). Francis pointed out that Burke had not even tried to demonstrate that Marie Antoinette had any 'moral merits'. He had merely gushed – lover-like – over the 'delightful vision' she presented. 'In my opinion all that you say of the Queen is pure foppery.'

King James, could he have read Junius's criticism in 1622, would surely have agreed with him. He was working for a peaceful solution to his daughter's problems. The idea of ten thousand swords leaping from their scabbards to avenge her 'insult' would have seemed to him futile, politically counterproductive and diplomatically crass. He had written playfully about 'venturous knights', but he knew the difference between romance and realpolitik. When he heard of the oaths taken at the Temple dinner, he was, according to the letter-writer who recorded it, 'highly displeased'.

The Journey

Tuesday, 18 February 1623. Early morning. New Hall, Buckingham's mansion in Essex. Prince Charles joins Buckingham. They lay aside their illustrious identities and assume the pseudonyms of Tom and Jack Smith, along with their false beards.

Buckingham's Master of the Horse, Sir Richard Graham, is going with them. Thanks to Sir Henry Wotton's detailed account of the journey, we can track them almost hour by hour.

All three travellers are fast riders. By midday they are boarding the ferry to cross the Thames at Tilbury. Disembarking at Gravesend, they gallop on for Dover, leaving the bemused ferryman wondering over a gold coin.

Gravesend. The ferryman is no fool. Passengers into Kent are frequently bound for Dover, to take ship for France. Young gentlemen travelling incognito are likely to be going abroad in order to settle a quarrel – duelling having recently been outlawed in England by the peace-loving King James I. Gentlemen so rich they carry gold, and only gold, and so shady as to go disguised, will be of interest to the authorities.

The ferryman sees his three passengers on their way and then – hoping for a reward – reports them to the town's officers. The officers set off in pursuit.

Rochester. The officers from Gravesend arrive too late. The mysterious gentlemen have already changed horses and galloped on. The officers turn back. But on the next hill, the travellers once more narrowly escape exposure. The French ambassador is coming up the road from Dover, riding in the King's coach with numerous attendants. The Smith brothers and Graham 'teach post hackneys to leap hedges', forcing their hired horses to leave the road in a hurry and detour through fields.

Canterbury. By this time, fast as they are riding, rumours of the trio's progress are preceding them. The mayor waylays them at the posting inn as their next mounts are being led out. Clearly there is something rum about them. (Those beards!) The mayor has no legal authority to stop them travelling on, but he feels he should try. He blusters and fibs. He says he has warrants for their detention from the Privy Council. They refuse to believe it. No, not the Privy Council, he admits, but from the Master of Ceremonies. Really? Well, actually no: from the Lieutenant of Dover Castle.

The 'confused fiction' makes the travellers laugh. Realising the poor mayor will not be put off, Buckingham removes his beard and declares himself. The thing is, he explains, that as Lord Admiral he has a fancy to inspect the fleet moored in the Channel, and to do so incognito, so that he can assess its true state of readiness.

'Tom Smith', the smaller, less noticeable of the two supposed brothers, keeps his beard on. No one asks who he might be. The mayor is placated. The travellers ride on. But almost immediately another sharp-eyed observer comes close to spoiling their adventure. The 'baggage post-boy' has been in Whitehall (people come and go freely in the palace's outer courtyards) and he is neither as literally deaf nor as figuratively dumb as they suppose. The Smiths seem familiar to him. Something about their conversation gives him a 'glimmering' as to who they are. 'His mouth was easily shut,' writes Wotton (another gold coin?).

Dover. They arrive at six o'clock of a dark winter's evening. Francis Cottington and Endymion Porter are there to meet them, with a vessel ready for their Channel crossing. They hoped to embark at once, but the night is tempestuous. They put up at an inn.

Wednesday. They sail at first light, landing at Boulogne six hours later, both of the Smiths having been horribly seasick. They ride on to Montreuil.

Buckingham (generally admired for his horsemanship) falls seven times as they gallop towards Paris.

One of the most striking things about their journey is how admirably efficient it shows the Europe-spanning network of posting inns to be. All the same, the horses for hire are not as well schooled as those the King of England's Master of the Horse is accustomed to riding. The risks the travellers are running are not only political. Writing to King James the following day, Buckingham describes Charles's mounts stumbling repeatedly, but declares the Prince 'so much more stronger' than he used to be, holding 'them up by main strength of manhood' while he cries, 'On. On. On.'

Letter from King James, undated but probably written the day Buckingham and the Prince left New Hall:

> *Sweet boys,*
> *The news of your going is already so blown abroad as I am*
> *forced for your safety to post this bearer after you, who will give his*
> *best advice and attendance on your journey. God bless you both,*
> *my sweet babes, and send you a safe and happy return.*
> *James R.*

We do not know who the King's 'bearer' was, or whether he caught up with the pseudo-Smiths before they sailed. But we do know that the French ambassador was curious to know the identity of the horsemen who had so recklessly leapt their horses over the roadside hedges rather than meet him on the road. He sent a man back to Dover to investigate. That man found the port, and all the others along the south coast, closed to all shipping, on the King's orders.

James was doing his best to allow his 'sweet babes' to get away undetected and unpursued. He knew, though, how rumour could 'make the wind [its] post-horse', and how – close the ports as he might – there would always be a blind creek from which a boat could slip out unmarked.

The next morning he wrote again. 'I thank you for your comfortable letters, but, alas, think it not possible that you can be many hours undiscovered.' Questions were already being asked at home about the absence from the English court of the heir and the favourite. Those questions, and the lack of satisfactory answers, would be relayed to the Continent. James judged that his fellow monarch, King Louis XIII of France, would soon be aware of the presence of the Prince of Wales in his kingdom. So he wrote to the French king 'with a short letter of my own hand to show him that respect, that I may acquaint him with my son's passing unknown through his country'.

For a prince to travel through the domain of a fellow monarch without paying his respects was shockingly discourteous. It was underhand. It was diplomatically clumsy. It smacked of conspiracy. It was unworthy of the dignity befitting a royal personage. It made a silly game of royalty itself. In a continent at war, at a time when Anglo-French relations were not particularly cordial, it might also be dangerous.

Charles and Buckingham didn't care. If King James's letters reached them (they probably didn't), the young men ignored his warnings.

By all accounts the party consisted solely of the two Smiths and their three companions. Graham, Porter and Cottington were distinguished gentlemen. They might all be described as the King's 'servants', but that doesn't mean they were accustomed to taking care of the laundry or lugging water from the pump for the horses. But travellers using public transport (post-horses) and eating and sleeping in inns can do without a household of their own. Perhaps there were temporary attendants picked up along the way – like the 'baggage post-boy' who had recognised them in Kent – but Wotton assures us that the five named were 'the whole *parada* of this journey'.

They hurried on at breakneck speed.

Thursday. Paris. At a posting inn just short of the city, a party of German gentlemen, recently returned from England, stare at them. The Germans have visited Newmarket, and there they saw the Prince of Wales and the Marquis of Buckingham riding with King James in his coach. Now they feel sure they are seeing the former two again. No, no, Richard Graham assures them, they are mistaken. Eventually the Germans are persuaded, 'which is no very hard matter,' writes Wotton, 'for the very strangeness of the thing itself, and almost the impossibility to conceive so great a prince and favourite so suddenly metamorphised into travellers with no greater train, was enough to make any man unbelieve his five senses'.

Arrived in the great city, the 'Smiths' and their friends take rooms at an inn.

* * *

Paris was crowded, stinking, filthy and exhilarating. James Howell, whom Buckingham and Charles would soon meet in Madrid, called it a 'huge magazine of men, the epitome of this populous kingdom and the rendezvous of all foreigners'. Howell writes of the peculiarities of Parisian mud – ''Tis such a dirt, that by perpetual motions is beaten into such black unctuous oil, that where it sticks no art can wash it off' – and Parisian traffic jams. In the narrow mediaeval streets, 'sometimes one shall meet with a stop half a mile long of coaches, carts and horses that can move neither forward nor backward'.

The number of Parisian 'night-rogues' shocked British visitors. A gang operating around the Pont Neuf, armed with pistols and swords, stole pedestrians' cloaks and hats, taunting their victims by showing a fake document claiming this was a legally sanctioned tribute. Howell writes, 'There is never a night passes but some robbing or murder is committed in this town.'

Friday. After a night's rest, the travellers resolve to devote a day to pleasure before pushing on southwards. And what a king-in-waiting wants to see, naturally enough, is how a monarch of almost his own age (Louis XIII is twenty-one to Charles's twenty-two) conducts himself at his court.

The beards having proved inadequate as disguises, Jack and Tom Smith visit a wig-maker and buy themselves full-bottomed periwigs (as yet not much worn in England but *le dernier cri* in France since King Louis has taken to wearing one) and set out for the Louvre.

Charles had never left the British Isles before, but Buckingham had spent three years in France. When he first became King James's cup-bearer, one of the topics of their conversation was the French court: the King, whose mother had once been Queen of France, who had so loved his French cousin when he was a teenager, was eager to hear everything young Villiers could tell of what he had seen there. Buckingham had been nobody of consequence back at the time of his first French visit, but he knows his way around.

The French court, like the English one, has its private chambers to which only the privileged have access, but it also has its semi-public spaces. Someone who looks right can gain the *entrée* to its outer rooms, where the King and his family appear before their people. Charles and Buckingham, still incognito, are able to watch King Louis 'solacing himself with familiar pleasures' before a crowd of courtiers in one of the palace's galleries. They are among the observers standing by while the Queen Mother, the redoubtable Marie de Médicis who has ruled France for fifteen years as Louis's regent, eats her dinner. In both places they are alarmed to see Monsieur de Cadinet, who has been the French ambassador in London and knows them both well by sight, but their false hair protects them – Cadinet gives no sign of having recognised them.

They overhear two gentlemen talking about a court ballet in which the royal ladies will be dancing. Seizing the moment, they follow those gentlemen, joining the press of courtiers hoping to spectate. The Lord Chamberlain lets them pass, perhaps, as Wotton supposes, 'out of humanity to strangers', perhaps because Rumour has already hinted to him who they might be, perhaps simply because Buckingham (who, as the older and so much the more confident and physically impressive of the two, is presenting himself as his companion's master) seems to him such a fine specimen of an English milord.

They are ushered to seats from which they have an unimpeded view. Among the dancers is Queen Anne, elder sister of the Infanta whom Charles is hoping soon to wed. Charles thinks Anne 'the handsomest' of the nineteen 'fair dancing ladies'. The sight of her, he writes to his father afterwards, 'hath wrought in me a greater desire to see her sister'.

Neither of the Smiths makes any comment on Charles's first sight of the fourteen-year-old French princess, King Louis's younger sister Henrietta Maria, who is among the dancers and who, just over two years later, will become Charles's wife.

Buckingham writes to tell King James that their incognito visit to the French royal palace is 'a great tickling to add to the history of our adventures'.

Saturday. By three the next morning, the Smiths are on the road again. At this point we lose sight of their day-to-day schedule, but we get repeated glimpses of their progress.

In Bordeaux they buy new riding coats, all of the same colour, and of a 'kind of noble simplicity'. There Francis Cottington has a hard time refusing the pressing hospitality of a local grandee, the Duke of Épernon, who is insistent that the travellers from abroad should allow him to entertain them. Épernon is a man of the world, who might well guess their identities. It would never do, explains Cottington. The Duke must excuse his companions. They are 'gentlemen of mean degree' who are yet 'formed but little to Courtship'. They will feel more at ease in the inn.

At ease, perhaps, but not well fed. It is Lent. In Catholic France meat is not being served. They begin to crave it.

As they approach the Spanish border they encounter a herd of goats. Graham suggests they help themselves to a kid. Prince Charles teasingly rebukes him for acting like one of his cattle-rustling Scottish forebears, whereupon Graham gives the goatherd some money. There are things, though, that money can't buy, a young goat's compliance in his own slaughter being one of them. Buckingham and Graham together chase the poor creature several times around a haystack before Charles, firing from the saddle, finally kills it with a pistol bullet to the head. They skin it and chop it up and grill its meat over the fire at the next inn.

What larks the two Smiths were having! For all the hundreds of days King James's son and his favourite had spent attending him out hunting, neither had ever had to hunt in earnest for his own food. A prince playing at being a pauper. A favourite relieved of the complexities of courtly intrigue and international diplomacy, and the emotional demands of mother, wife, baby and doting King. Both of them exhilarated by the freedom and the perils of being far from home and out on the road.

For their companions, though, and especially for Cottington, the most experienced and least willing of the party, the responsibility of keeping them safe on their crazy progress must have been nightmarish.

At Bayonne, the last city on French territory, the governor tells his officers that he feels sure the travellers are 'of more worth than their habits betrayed', but, tactful or unwilling to get involved in what might be a dangerous intrigue, he lets them pass on unquestioned. (Only hours later, he gets news of their identity.) As Buckingham writes triumphantly to King James, they have ridden the length of France 'undiscovered by any Monsieur'.

At the next post after Bayonne, they meet a compatriot, Mr Gresley, going the other way. Gresley is an aide to the British ambassador in Madrid – who is still utterly unaware of the visitors who are about to descend on him – and he is carrying letters to King James. Buckingham writes jocularly to James, 'We saucily opened your letters,' and declares that they saw nothing in Bristol's report that 'made us repent our journey'. In fact they couldn't read it at all. It was encrypted, as diplomatic reports routinely were, and no one had thought that the Prince and Buckingham might need the code. They send the letters on – seals broken – with poor Gresley. 'We thought it fit he should go forward to bring you certain news of your boys.'

As they set out into the mountainous borderlands, it is Cottington's turn to play at being master, while his 'servants' Charles and Buckingham ride ahead. The passes through the Pyrenees are infested with bandits and – carrying between them about £1,000 in gold, a colossal potential haul – they are a bandit's dream prey. They have left no record of this part of the journey, but Sir Richard Wynn, one of the numerous English courtiers who would soon follow them out to Spain, has done.

Wynn and his companions arrived in Spain a month later, by ship to Santander, so his route to Madrid was to the west of the one the Smiths' party would have taken from Bayonne. Wynn describes mountain slopes cloaked with snow, looming above a 'country infinitely rocky, covered with firs and juniper trees'. There were few human settlements. In thirty leagues (approximately ninety miles) Wynn saw 'but one castle and a poor village'.

Poor it was. James Howell, passing through the Pyrenees a few years earlier, reports that country people 'live no better than brute animals in point of food, for their ordinary commons is grass and water'. The 'grass' or 'herbs' are dressed with oil and vinegar – but to a British traveller a green salad did not make an adequate dinner for a man.

In Santander, a busy port, Wynn saw 'neither glass windows nor chimneys'. The townspeople lodged them in their own homes and did their best to entertain them, but Wynn complains that he and his fellow courtiers were expected to eat, not seated comfortably around tables, but from a 'plank set up', with not so much as a stool to sit upon. Lent being past, they were given meat, 'a kid held above a fire until it was burnt black', but 'table cloths nor napkins was there none'.

Once Wynn and the rest of the British courtiers set out for Madrid, these domestic inadequacies were eclipsed by the rigours of the journey.

They travelled by 'the most wicked ways and country that ever Christians passed'. Sixty mules had been found for them, and 'I believe no other beasts in the world could have passed ... the terrible stony hills we climbed, and the steep downfalls we descended.' For miles together they traversed 'a narrow passage of two foot broad, all made like stairs, lying a hundred fathoms above a great river, whose roaring amongst the stones was such, that we could not hear one another speak'. They could see snow lying high above them, but 'the heat between these hills was such, that we thought ourselves in stoves'.

The first night, they slept in a refuge in which, so the muleteers told them, King Philip and his queen had once passed a night. It was windowless, 'yet we wanted no air, for there was not a foot of that royal room that wanted holes'. They travelled on through woods inhabited by bears and wolves. At night the muleteers lit fires to scare off wild beasts. They said that a man had been killed and left in pieces a few days before.

A few weeks earlier Buckingham, Prince Charles and the rest of their *parada* had passed through similar terrain, sheltering by night in equally spartan lodgings, and eating – the Lenten fast still being observed – even more frugally. But whether because they didn't want to alarm King James, or because the excitement of their adventure inured them to hardship, they made no complaints in their letters home.

'The great business of the Match was tending to a period,' wrote James Howell, then an aide to the British ambassador in Madrid, 'and there wanted nothing to consummate all things, when, to the wonderment of the world, the Prince and the Marquis of Buckingham arrived at this court on Friday last, upon the close of the evening.'

Their journey had been accomplished in just over two weeks. They had left Porter and Cottington behind, galloping ahead and reaching the Spanish capital attended only by Richard Graham. At eight o'clock in the evening they were at the door of the House of the Seven Chimneys, the residence of the Earl of Bristol.

Buckingham went in first. He introduced himself as Mr Smith and said he had come to inform the ambassador that his emissary, Gresley, had 'fallen into thieves' hands' and 'had all his letters taken away'. He was invited to come up and give Bristol the news in person. No, he said, he couldn't do that. He had hurt his leg and couldn't climb the stairs. Would the ambassador be so kind as to come down and meet him at the door? (Buckingham must have been reluctant to take his eye off Charles, waiting outside.) Bristol sent his nephew to see who this importunate stranger might be. The young man recognised Buckingham. Bristol, 'in a kind of astonishment', went down and found not only the favourite but also the Prince of Wales, 'who stood all this while in the street with a postilion' and 'brought them ... handsomely up to his chamber'.

Howell, looking back on that memorable night, was struck above all by the fact that he had seen the great favourite (already a marquis, soon to be a duke, the richest and most powerful non-royal person in Britain) carrying his own luggage. Buckingham had entered the ambassador's residence – this was all but unthinkable – 'with a portmanteau under his arm'.

'The coming of the illustrious Prince of Wales into these kingdoms,' wrote the Spanish reporter Andrés de Almansa y Mendoza, 'was the strangest occurrence that the world hath for many ages seen ... It astonished whole nations.' Before the travellers had even arrived in Madrid it was already the talk of Britain and of France. As they revealed themselves to Bristol they were aware that the news of their journey was galloping after them. 'We found posts making such haste,' wrote Buckingham, 'that it would be discovered within twelve hours after.' It was essential they should declare their arrival to the Spanish authorities before Rumour pre-empted them.

A messenger was sent at once to the Count of Gondomar, telling him that Buckingham was in Madrid. No word about the Prince, but Gondomar knew within two hours of the pair's arrival that Charles was there too. (Before the night was out, wrote Howell, 'dark rumours ran in every corner how some great man was come from England'.)

Early on Saturday morning, Gondomar hurried over to the embassy to pay his respects to the Prince and to Buckingham. He then went on to the royal palace, the Alcázar, to request an immediate audience with the all-powerful Count-Duke of Olivares, King Philip IV's favourite.

Olivares had heard the rumours. He asked Gondomar, 'Has the King of England arrived?' 'If not the King,' said Gondomar, 'at least I have the Prince.'

Olivares

DON Gaspar de Guzmán, the Count-Duke of Olivares, was officially just one of the King of Spain's ministers. Actually he was supreme.

When the previous king, Philip III, fell ill, Olivares is reported to have said, 'Now everything is mine.' As Gentleman to the sixteen-year-old heir to the throne, he had established absolute dominance over the young prince. 'Everything?' asked another courtier. 'Yes,' replied Olivares, 'without exception.'

When his boy-master became King Philip IV, he made good his claim. The English resident in Spain called him 'the sole minister of the king and kingdom; the maestro who moves all the wheels of that great clock'. A poet described him as a modern Atlas, holding up the world – or at least that large part of it straddled by the Spanish empire – on his own shoulders.

They were tremendous shoulders – literally as well as figuratively. A year after Buckingham and Prince Charles visited, Olivares's portrait was painted (for the first of many times) by Diego Velázquez, who had come to Madrid under his patronage (Plate 14). The portrait is six and a half feet high, four and a half feet wide, and the massive figure of the Count fills the picture space almost entirely. His bulk is not gross. It is grand.

His clothes are sombrely magnificent – black velvet, black satin, dark puce for his voluminous breeches. The only accents of bright colour are the scarlet insignia embroidered on his chest that proclaim him a commander of the Order of Calatrava, a heavy gold chain slung across his torso, and the weighty golden key and golden spurs tucked into his belt that identify him, respectively, as the King's *sumiller de corps* (equivalent of the Groom of the Stool) and as Master of the Horse. His right hand, magnified by the unusual perspective to the size of a giant's, grips the edge of a velvet-draped table. His head, atop his imposing body, is curiously small, as though we spectators, peering up at his face, are way, way beneath him.

But though we see him as from afar, Olivares looks at us directly. He is ugly, with a long pendulous nose, cheeks that hang in swags of puffy flesh and a broad chin masked by an inadequate beard, but his eyes are commanding. The Genoese ambassador wrote, around this time, that Olivares was '*odiatissimo*' – most hateful – but the President of the Council of Castile describes him putting aside dissent calmly, laughing, 'as was his habit, because he was suave by nature'.

In 1623 he was thirty-six, six years older than Buckingham. He was a favourite of a very different stamp. Not the amanuensis and disciple of an experienced and scholarly king, but the mentor of a callow young one. Not the kind of loving, teasing, playful friend who could address his king as 'dear Dad and Gossip', but a conscientious royal servant who occasionally found it necessary to remind Philip (who preferred hunting to committee work) of the necessity of spending hours and hours of every day poring over state papers. Not a lovely youth who made his way to influence and power by beauty and easy good manners, but a strong-willed, phenomenally hard-working, deeply serious man, prone to bouts of grim depression and outbursts of rage.

Castiglione wrote that a courtier should 'encourage and help his prince to be virtuous'. Few of a prince's friends will speak frankly to him, and so 'from being friends they become flatterers'. The ideal courtier, though, is braver. He demonstrates his loyalty by 'leading his prince along the stern path of virtue, adorning it, however, with shady fronds and strewing it with gay flowers to lessen the tedium of an arduous journey'. That was the kind of courtier Olivares strove to be. Strewing gay flowers was not his forte, but he was a resolute walker on the stern path of virtue, and his loyalty was absolute. When young Philip was snappish with him one day, instead of reproaching him, Olivares solemnly kissed the royal chamber pot (which he happened to be carrying, in his capacity as the King's most intimate body servant) before offering to resign if the King no longer valued his service. His resignation was not accepted.

All through the summer of 1623 Buckingham and Olivares (when he could spare the time) were to be locked in a weirdly slow-motion battle of wits from which a clear outcome seemed ever more elusive.

Buckingham was to find that negotiating with his Spanish counterpart was frustrating, infuriating and sometimes – when the Count-Duke unleashed his temper – very frightening.

Olivares could make things happen. In Spain it was he who decided, as Buckingham did in England, who gained access to the monarch. 'He speedily got me, your Dog Steenie,' wrote Buckingham to King James, 'a private audience of the King.'

On the afternoon of Saturday, 8 March, his first full day in Madrid, Buckingham, accompanied by Gondomar and Bristol, was taken in a closed carriage to the Alcázar, the immense and much remodelled Moorish castle at the western edge of the city which was both the royal palace and the seat of government. The carriage drew up in a courtyard. Olivares climbed into it. He and Buckingham talked for an hour, the two ambassadors interpreting.

Olivares liked to talk in carriages. Fully aware that palace walls have ears, he would often invite those with whom he wished to speak confidentially to join him on a drive.

He could be charming. He could be elaborately courteous. He could be jocular. And then he could abruptly extinguish the smiles and erase the lightly given promises as though they had never been. A Genoese ambassador wrote that 'his character is dangerous because of his sudden outbursts of anger, his love of novelties and of dangerous counsels'. At that first meeting with Buckingham he was jovial, and apparently compliant. Buckingham reported back to King James that he had declared that if the Pope would not grant a dispensation permitting the marriage, the Spanish would give the Infanta Maria to Charles anyway 'as his wench'.

It seems extraordinary that Olivares would have said such a thing, even as a joke. Perhaps an interpreter stumbled. More likely something Olivares intended as an elaborate compliment was understood by Buckingham in too literal a spirit. If so, it was the first of a sequence of misapprehensions that would leave the two favourites – by summer's end – furiously opposed to each other.

Their initial interview concluded, Olivares led Buckingham and his companions up to the top floor of the palace, where the royal family had their apartments. He presented Buckingham to King Philip IV (Plate 18). The meeting was a great success. Buckingham, on terms of easy intimacy with one monarch, was not going to be intimidated by another one. He was thirty, still beautiful, and now sophisticated, confident. Philip, about to turn eighteen, succumbed to his charm at once. He welcomed the visitor, according to Bristol, 'with so much alacrity and freeness that I never saw the Spanish gravity so laid aside before'.

The audience over, Olivares returned with Buckingham, announcing that he wished to 'salute the Prince in the King's name'. This he did kneeling: it is piquant to imagine that portly body lumbering to the floor before the diminutive prince. Endymion Porter – who had arrived in Madrid, along with Cottington, that morning – interpreted. Olivares revered royalty, regardless of the shortcomings (arrant heresy, in this case) of the person in whom it was incarnated. He kissed Charles's hands and embraced his thighs after the extravagant Spanish fashion. Along with 'other high compliments', he declared 'how immeasurably glad His Catholic Majesty was of his coming'.

Things seemed to have begun well.

King James and Buckingham believed in the Match. Prince Charles believed in it. So did Gondomar and Bristol. We know now – thanks to the efforts of modern historians – that the Match was a chimera. For all the 'high compliments' with which Buckingham and Prince Charles were being greeted, there was no possibility of their getting what they had come for.

Back in 1613 there had been talk of another infanta, King Philip III's niece, marrying the Prince of Wales. Philip summoned a committee (a *junta*) of theologians to consider the matter. Four out of six of them concluded that, in their opinion, even to consider such a union was a mortal sin. When, in the following year, Gondomar began to urge the match between Charles and the Infanta Maria, King Philip III had one of his representatives enter into a secret, arm's-length correspondence with representatives of Pope Paul V to enquire what His Holiness would think of such a marriage. The Pope's judgement was unequivocal. He would give no dispensation for a Spanish infanta to marry a Protestant prince of England, unless the prince converted to Catholicism.

This ruling was not made public. The British ambassador was allowed to keep calling for the marriage. The Spanish king and his councillors allowed him to believe it was still feasible. They made encouraging concessions. In 1615 a treaty of marriage was drafted. In 1617 Gondomar reported back to the Spanish Council of State from London that the English Privy Council had 'voted that there was nowhere in the world a marriage or alliance more suitable for the prince'. In 1618, in Madrid, Bristol negotiated the proffered dowry up from 500,000 to 600,000 livres, and wrote to tell King James that King Philip III 'professeth an extraordinary desire to make the Match, and is resolved on it if the point of religion can be accommodated'. In 1621, the King of Spain hinted to Gondomar that perhaps the papal dispensation, though desirable, might not actually be necessary.

It all looked hopeful. But the hopeful developments were meaningless. The Spaniards had no more intention of concluding the contract than Odysseus' wife Penelope had ever had of completing her tapestry.

In 1621, King Philip III fell ill. Aware that he was dying, he summoned his heir. The conversation between dying father and son was not recorded, but in the following year the son, by this time King Philip IV, told Olivares what his father had said to him on his deathbed. Philip III had told the younger Philip that he should never permit the marriage between the Infanta Maria and Prince Charles unless the British would agree to all Spain's demands – including the Prince's conversion and the repeal of all anti-Catholic legislation in James's kingdoms. Philip III had understood those concessions could never be granted, and so his ministers also 'understood, and so treated this match ever with an intention to delay it'.

The time was coming, though, now that Charles was of an age to marry, when delaying could not continue indefinitely. Buckingham wrote frankly to Gondomar, 'The King our master longs to see an issue proceed from his loins.' A decision had to be made in Spain, and it was made in the negative. Philip IV told Olivares that his fifteen-year-old sister, of whom he was very fond, was 'averse' to the match and so, for that reason and all the others, 'it is time to seek some means to divert the treaty, which I would have you find out'.

Gondomar, who would be the British negotiators' main contact in Madrid, was not informed of the King's decision to 'divert' the Match. He would continue to assure the British – in the good faith of his ignorance – that it might yet go forward. It would be for Olivares to prevent its doing so. He was to do it nicely, if possible. The Match must not take place, Philip IV instructed him, unless, of course, Prince Charles converted, but neither King nor *privado* believed that was likely. But means must still be found to somehow give 'satisfaction to the King of Great Britain, who hath deserved very much'.

If the British trying to negotiate the Match, from King James downwards, misunderstood the Spaniards' true intentions, it is not because they were obtuse or ignorant. They were baffled by Philip IV and Olivares's impossibly self-contradictory secret policy of giving them 'satisfaction' while ultimately, always and for ever, denying them that which they wanted.

Olivares had been in power for only two years. He was strong (he prided himself on his horsemanship) but he was not healthy. As well as his bouts of depression and his sudden rages, there were physical problems. He suffered from what he described as 'gigantic' headaches, from insomnia, from gout, from sciatica. There were days when he was not well enough to carry out his duty, as *sumiller de corps*, to hand the King his clean shirt in the morning. There were other days when he had to be carried around in a chair. The pain with which he lived affected his temper. 'My disposition', he confessed, 'is not a very good one.' He drove his secretaries to work almost as hard as he did, and he habitually worked eighteen hours a day. He had no patience with his critics. A Genoese ambassador describes him beating his fists against a window frame in his fury when crossed.

Buckingham, while in Spain, was preoccupied with the Match. Olivares had many other things on his mind. When Olivares was evasive, when it seemed the negotiations had ground to a halt, Buckingham fumed. It was hard for him to comprehend the fact that for Olivares the Match was a comparatively minor concern.

The task Olivares had assumed on the accession of his king was immense. Here are some of the issues with which he was preoccupied.

The twelve-year truce with the Dutch Republic had come to an end in 1621. It was for Olivares to decide whether to resume the conflict or to let Holland go.

The Spanish treasury was close to empty. The national debt was colossal. There seemed no possibility of servicing, let alone repaying it, without radical fiscal reform. Olivares was determined to halt the flow of money out of the royal purse. He wanted Spain to be efficient and businesslike and much less wasteful.

The members of the Cortes, the Spanish Parliament, were increasingly restive under the autocratic rule of the Habsburg monarchs and their favourites. Throughout the months of Buckingham and Prince Charles's sojourn in Madrid, Olivares was wrestling with a major constitutional conflict as the Cortes challenged the monarchy, much as the English Parliament was about to do.

The wealth flowing into the Exchequer from the silver mines of South America had slowed. The captains of the treasure ships routinely under-declared the quantity they were carrying by up to 80 per cent. On arrival in Spanish ports, the unregistered portion of their precious cargoes was unloaded secretly, by night, before customs officials could make their inventory. The dispersal of bribes (another bottomless financial drain) sustained the fraud.

Trade and industry were faltering, and needed to be stimulated.

The countryside was becoming depopulated – something had to be done about that in order to secure the food supply. Olivares was ordering the nobility back to their country estates, and banning country people from moving into cities. He encouraged foreign workers to immigrate (provided they were Catholic). He restricted the establishment of grammar schools in country towns: he wanted illiterate agricultural labourers, not discontented clerks.

The state supported a plethora of petty municipal officials, many of whose positions were hereditary, passing from father to son. Olivares proposed to abolish two-thirds of their jobs, and prevailed upon the King to promise he would never create new ones.

All of these measures met with fury, stubborn obstructionism or despair. That opposition became even fiercer when Olivares established a committee, the Junta Grande de Reformación, whose members included all the senior Councillors, and announced they would work with him seven days a week on a great project.

In February 1623 (just weeks before Buckingham and Prince Charles arrived) Olivares presented the resulting 'Articles', in which he proposed a thorough revision of Spanish society. The articles were comprehensive, covering everything from the profound to the superficial, from the extirpation of deeply rooted corruption and the establishment of new systems of taxation and banking, to the limiting of extravagant spending on fashion, on unnecessary servants, on dowries. Olivares forbade the import of foreign manufactured goods (excepting only Flemish tapestries). He introduced draconian sumptuary laws, including the banning of the ruff in favour of the less expensive starched collar, the *golilla*. He announced that brothels would no longer be tolerated.

When the two visitors arrived from England he was really very, very busy.

Invisible

CHARLES would never win his bride. A visiting prince, though, had to be deferred to and entertained. The ancient code of hospitality required it, and the need for Spain to demonstrate its magnificence (even as its wealth dwindled away) made it imperative. However dismayingly unconventional the arrival of the visitors from England had been, they must be given a properly ceremonious reception as soon as it could be organised. Meanwhile, they must be humoured.

Buckingham told King James jubilantly that he found Olivares 'full of real courtesy' and 'overvaluing of our journey', to such an extent that he declared King Philip 'can deny nothing that is in his kingdom'. And all that Charles wished for, so Buckingham gave Olivares to understand that first afternoon, was a glimpse of his intended bride.

Prince Charles could not appear before the Spanish people until he had made his formal entrance into the city of Madrid. Arriving as he had done, without any of the fitting pomp and circumstance, he was a wraith, an embarrassment, an offence against the institution of monarchy.

If a future King of England could be called Tom Smith; if he could turn up after dark, with just a couple of companions, at the ambassador's residence and be kept standing in the street because his arrival was unheralded; if he could be seen wearing an ordinary riding suit, run up for him at short notice by an ordinary tailor in Bordeaux; if, in short, he was a man like any other, then the mystique of monarchy, the divinity that doth hedge a king, was dimmed. The Spanish king could not recognise him publicly for fear of suggesting that he too – King Philip IV, Most Catholic King, a being revered throughout his empire in much the same way that saints and martyrs were revered – was also a mere mortal.

The grand entrance of the Prince of Wales into the city was set for the following week. But meanwhile, yes, it could be arranged, because Philip had promised to deny him nothing, that Charles could see the Infanta, but on no account might she, or any other of the great ones of Spain, be seen to see him.

The encounter, or one-way viewing, took place on Sunday in the Pardo, a park outside the city where King Philip frequently went to hunt. The visitors were driven to the appointed place in what Buckingham, describing the scene to King James as a great joke, called 'an invisible coach'. The streets it passed through as they left the city were crowded, but 'nobody was suffered to take notice of it, though seen by all the world'.

Arrived at the appointed spot, they waited, with the window blinds closed. A long line of carriages appeared, and passed them by three times. In the carriages rode the Papal Nuncio, the Imperial ambassador, the French ambassador, the 'best of the nobility' and, separately, the ladies of the court. Last came the royal family.

Peering beneath the blinds of the invisible coach, Buckingham and Charles saw the King's two young brothers, Don Carlos and the Cardinal-Infante. Then came the Queen. Then, at last, came the carriage containing the King and, seated beside him, Prince Charles's intended bride, the Infanta Maria. She wore a blue ribbon round her arm – a prearranged signal so that the Prince might know which, of the many ladies processing past him, she was. He had been declaring for months that he was in love with her, but he was now laying eyes on her for the first time.

He saw. He loved. Buckingham, writing to James that night, reported, 'Baby Charles is so touched at heart, that he confesses all he ever yet saw is nothing to her and swears that if he wants [i.e. doesn't get] her, there shall be blows.'

After passing three times before the invisible coach, the royal procession drew away. Olivares joined the Englishmen, and escorted them back to the House of Seven Chimneys, telling them, according to Buckingham, that King Philip so 'longed and died for want of a nearer sight' of the Prince that their first meeting was to take place that very day.

For reasons of diplomatic protocol, it was out of the question for Philip to come to the embassy. For reasons of monarchical decorum, it was equally impossible for Charles to visit him in the royal palace with-out a properly kingly retinue. The rendezvous would have to take place in private and on neutral territory.

The streets around the House of Seven Chimneys were now packed with people who had got wind of the Prince's presence there. More diversionary manoeuvres. A coach drew up. One of the gentlemen of the embassy, acting as decoy with his hat pulled well down, got into it and was driven off. The crowd, assuming he was the Prince, hurried after. Two more closed coaches arrived. One of them contained Olivares, who took Buckingham to where King Philip was 'walking in the streets, with his cloak thrown over his face, and sword and buckler by his side'. Philip leapt into the coach. Meanwhile Charles, in the other coach, had been escorted back to the Pardo Park. There the others joined him. The Spanish King and the English King-to-be met at last, and exchanged 'kindness and compliments'.

It still appeared that things were going well.

Separation

As his sweet venturous boys were galloping across France, untrammelled by ceremony, free of the social requirements of court and unhindered by the lumbering cartloads of fittings and furnishings normally attendant upon a royal progress, King James, in bed with a sore knee, was busy encumbering them again.

By the time they arrived on Spanish soil, back in England courtiers were clamouring for the privilege of joining the train that must surely soon follow them. 'Noblemen you will have enow, and too many,' wrote the King. 'Carlisle and Mountjoy already gone, Andover goes presently and Rocheford by land, Compton goes by sea, and I think Percy and Arran and Denbigh go by land.' Prince Charles had left a list of the servants he would like to have with him, but the principal officers of his household found the list far too short. King James added the extra names proposed, 'and then every man ran upon me for his friend so I was torn to pieces amongst them'.

Three ships were being prepared: 'Fewer ships I durst not hazard for fear of pirates.' People were coming. So was a great deal of stuff, some of it immensely valuable. The King was sending 'Georges', the insignia of the Order of the Garter, to be presented to King Philip and other Spanish dignitaries. He was also sending Charles and Buckingham their Garter robes, so that they could wear them on St George's Day, 'for it will be a goodly sight for the Spaniards to see my two boys dine in them'.

There would be many more clothes in the cargo, gorgeous garments fit for a prince and his companion. The King was also sending 'tilting stuff ... bravely set forth and fit for a wooer', but he wasn't happy about it. 'In good faith the weather will be so hot there before ye can use it, that I would wish you rather to forbear it, for I fear my baby may catch a fever.' He fussed over them as tenderly as any mother sending a child away for a first sleepover. 'My sweet babies, for God's sake and your dear Dad's, put not yourselves in hazard by any violent exercise.' Nonetheless he was sending horses and hounds, some for his sweet babies to use, some to be presented to Olivares, who would appreciate them, James thought.

The ships would also be carrying some of the finest jewels from the royal collection. There were rings and watches to be given to Spanish courtiers, and alongside these minor trinkets, there were pieces of fabled magnificence:

A hand-sized jewel called 'The Three Brothers', incorporating a blue diamond, pearls and spinels, which had belonged to the fourteenth-century dukes of Burgundy, then passed through the hands of the great Renaissance banking family, the Fuggers, before becoming one of the English Crown Jewels in the reign of Edward VI (Fugger having turned down an offer for it from Suleiman the Magnificent). It appears in two portraits of Queen Elizabeth; King James himself wore it in his hat when he posed for John de Critz.

A diamond known as 'The Mirror of France', for Prince Charles to wear in his hat 'with a little black feather'.

The great diamond chain that the King had given Buckingham's wife, and that she now sent on to her husband as having, for the present, the greater need of it.

A rope of pearls, a collar set with thirteen great rubies and thirteen 'knots or cinques' of pearls, a headdress decorated with twenty-two 'great pear pearls', three pear-shaped diamonds for the Infanta to wear – two as earrings and the third hanging in the middle of her forehead.

Of these treasures, 'my baby is to present some to his mistress and some of the best he is to wear himself, and the next best he will lend my bastard brat to wear'. The 'bastard brat' was Buckingham. It seems that the more these men loved each other, the more they teased and mock-abused each other.

The King had intended to include a particularly brilliant and intricate jewel among those pieces for his son's 'mistress'. It had 'two fair long diamonds set like an anchor, and a fair pendant diamond hanging at them', but then he changed his mind. The anchor-shaped piece was 'fit for an admiral to wear', and so he instructed Charles to give it, not to the Infanta after all, but to Lord Admiral Buckingham. And from himself he sent for his 'sweet Steenie' a large diamond that the favourite had once before refused as being too splendid for a mere commoner. 'And I have hung a fair pear pearl to it for wearing in thy hat.'

King James's letters are full of yearning affection. He is not interested in any of the young men who might have hoped to console him in Buckingham's absence. At the end of March, Sir William Beecher writes that 'we have not had so much as a whisper of a new favourite'. Each of James's letters ends with a wish for his sweet boys' 'comfortable and happy return to your dear dad'. Gerbier reports that King James has sent for the miniature that he – Gerbier – painted of his master. The King confirms it. 'I wear Steenie's picture on a blue ribbon under my waistcoat next my heart.'

Buckingham responded with extravagant presents. The King liked natural curiosities – dead or, better still, alive. Buckingham sent him four asses, five camels and an elephant. When they reached London, after a long trek to Santander and a sea voyage, the city streets were lined with onlookers who had waited up past midnight to see the strange beasts plodding slowly into their new home in St James's Park.

He wrote that Prince Charles had gone hunting in the Pardo with King Philip but he had chosen to stay behind. 'Here am I, now in a chamber alone, enjoying and reading over and over your sweet cordial letters. I stayed for this purpose only.' He resolves 'never to lose sight of that I love so preciously again'. He writes to thank James repeatedly 'for your innumerable favours and cares of me'. He commiserates when he hears that James is ill in bed. He hopes that soon the King will be 'marching upon your well-shaped legs again' (an affectionate tease – James's legs were famously misshapen).

He also writes jointly with Prince Charles, letters full of news – brisk and affectionate. But when he writes 'single' letters that are not for Prince Charles to see and sign, he writes more intimately, more earnestly. James writes back, 'God bless thee, my sweet gossip, for thy little letter, all full of comfort,' or thanks 'my sweet Steenie gossip ... for thy kind drolling letter', or tells him, 'Thy single letter was so sweet and comfortable unto me as I cannot forbear to pray God ever to bless and reward thee for it.'

There is a letter in which Buckingham weaves a convoluted conceit about James's generosity, about his heart and 'large bountiful hand', which has been 'but too ready to execute the motions and affections of that kind obliging heart to me'. It could simply mean that Buckingham is grateful for all James's 'bountiful' gifts, but one historian has read it as a veiled allusion to mutual masturbation, and the sexual pleasures the King has given him. It may be so. The passage is deliberately and irretrievably opaque, but certainly the letter seems full of some feeling too powerful and complex for clear expression.

And then there are the simpler declarations. Buckingham is impatient to see the Prince and the Infanta wed, he tells King James, because then he himself 'can make the speedier haste to lay myself at your feet'. He longs for their reunion, he writes, as 'never none longed more to be in the arms of his Mistress'.

Missing his beloved sorely, King James consoled himself with the beloved's family. By the time Buckingham and Charles reached Spain, James had written five letters to Buckingham's wife, Katherine, two to Buckingham's sister Susan, now Countess of Denbigh, and one to Buckingham's mother 'and all with my own hand'. A couple of weeks later Kate and Susan dined and supped with him two days running, 'and so shall do still, with God's grace, as long as I am here'. They brought with them Buckingham's baby daughter Mary, little Mall, to whom James refers as though she were truly of his own family. 'My little grandchild with her four teeth is, God be thanked, well weaned, and they are all very merry.'

He conferred an earldom on Buckingham's brother Kit, with property besides. He busied himself making new land grants to Buckingham and paying his debts. He reported that Katherine had been sick with a headache, but 'after a little casting [vomiting] was well again' and tenderly hoped that she might be pregnant. She wasn't, but all the same he sent her dried plums, and 'violet cakes' and chickens, and plenty of grapes from his hothouses.

He wrote a poem:

> *What sudden change hath darked of late*
> *The glory of the Arcadian state?*
> *The fleecy flocks refuse to feed,*
> *The lambs to play, the ewes to breed;*
> *The altars smoke, the offerings burn,*
> *Till Jack and Tom do safe return.*

The spring neglects her course to keep,
The air with mighty storms doth weep;
The pretty birds disdain to sing,
The meads to swell, the woods to spring;
The mountains drop, the fountains mourn,
Till Jack and Tom do safe return ...

And so on and so forth for eight disconsolate stanzas.

Entrance

ALL Spain, all Europe indeed, was agog at the news that the heir to the British throne had arrived in a foreign capital unheralded, and without any of the pomp and ceremony such a visit required. It was astonishing. It was 'venturous'. It was romantic. It was sensational news.

It was all most irregular, and could not be allowed to continue. The visitors must be invited into the Alcázar, which was a fortress as well as a palace, where their every move could be watched.

The invisibility of Prince Charles continued for a week. He and Buckingham went out with King Philip and his two brothers to the Pardo, where they watched the royal huntsmen using guns (a novelty – this was not yet done in England) to kill 'partridges flying, and conies running'. Within the city, though, they lay low.

There was a solemn procession in celebration of the feast of St Joseph. King Philip ordered his most eminent courtiers to join it, in order to impress the visitors. It was explained to Prince Charles that, although they were there in his honour, he must not openly acknowledge them. He watched from a balcony 'hidden behind a shutter'. His mortal, physical body might have been there, present in Madrid, but for more than a week after that comparatively insignificant part of him had come clattering on horseback up to the door of the House of Seven Chimneys, it had to be kept hidden. His immortal, quasi-divine, monarchical body was deemed not yet to have arrived.

The Council of State met. The court chronicler records that 'since this event has no parallel in history, it was hard to know how to deal with it'. A committee was formed to organise Prince Charles's formal entrance into the city of Madrid. It would take place the following Sunday. No expense would be spared. It would mimic a royal coronation. Olivares, exasperated, agreed that his new sumptuary laws would have to be suspended for the occasion. As James Howell reports, 'the custom of the Spaniard is, though he go plain in his ordinary habit, yet upon some festival or cause of triumph there's none goes beyond him in gaudiness'. The arrival of the Prince was such a festival.

On the Saturday, Buckingham and Charles slipped surreptitiously out of Madrid, preparatory to coming back in the following day. They spent the night at the Royal Monastery of the Hieronymites, outside the city walls, where the kings of Spain slept before being crowned. On Sunday the solemn entrance took place.

Buckingham described the ceremony to King James. First the Spanish grandees, led by the members of the Council of State, came to the monastery to greet the Prince. Then King Philip arrived with his two brothers and their retinue, and, according to Buckingham's letter to King James, 'forced your Baby to ride on his right hand'.

It was a pivotal moment for Olivares. He had been running the country ever since Philip IV succeeded. His exact status, though, remained ill-defined. He had no title commensurate with his power. His position had been fluid; Buckingham's presence in Madrid crystallised it. He had worked in the shadows; Buckingham's arrival forced him into the light. If Buckingham, known in Spain as the King of England's *primo ministro*, could represent that monarch in a way that (to Bristol's chagrin) an ordinary ambassador could not, then someone must be put forward as his equivalent and opposite number at the Spanish court.

In Spain, elders were respected. In the Council of State, Councillors spoke in the order in which they had been appointed. Olivares, thirty or more years younger than some of his fellows, was a long way down the list. So he tended to bypass the Council, and to rule by means of royal decrees, or through privately agreed alliances made in his own chambers or in the privacy of his carriage as it rattled around Madrid drawn by six fine mules. He had little windows cut into the walls of the Council Chamber so that the King, unseen, could hear the debates. As Philip listened, Olivares would be beside him, guiding his responses, cajoling him towards the positions that he – Olivares – wished him to take.

All of this was customary, an established part of the Spanish political process, but it was not overt, not official.

Buckingham's status at the Jacobean court was repeatedly made visible – by his beautiful clothes, by his *primo ballerino* roles in the masques, in his tennis-playing and tilting, and by James's habit of singling him out in public. Olivares's power was never performed in that way. He was said to resemble a scarecrow as he went around the palace with documents stuck in his hat or dangling from his belt. His coach was not furnished with cushions and velvet curtains, but with shelves and cubbyholes for the storage of state papers. When he rode out in it, he wasn't displaying himself. He kept the blinds down and dictated to his secretaries as he went. He might control 'everything', but he was seen, and probably saw himself, not as a glittering courtier but as a titanically assiduous worker, a mighty drudge.

Over the following months the two favourites would repeatedly appear in public, paired. They would ride together only a few paces behind, or be seated together only a few steps down from royalty. When a banquet to welcome the Prince of Wales was given at court, Charles sat with the Spanish royal family on a dais, beneath a canopy of state. Buckingham sat with Olivares at another table, under another canopy. Everyone else, however lofty their station, remained standing.

On the day that Prince Charles formally entered Madrid, Spanish king and British prince rode side by side under a fringed damask canopy, closely followed by Olivares and Buckingham, also side by side. Then, behind these two supremely powerful pairs, rode all the Spanish nobility, 'and they made their entry with as great triumph as could be'.

The procession entered Madrid from the east, and passed all through the city, along the ceremonial route of the Calle Mayor, to the Alcázar, the royal palace, perched on its precipice at the city's western edge. A contemporary engraving shows stages erected along the route for extemporary shows. An amnesty was declared and some 350 prisoners (many of them British, held by the Inquisition and destined for death or the galleys) were released. There were armed men on foot, with lances and halberds. There were grandees in tall plumed hats riding on horses almost as splendidly dressed as they were themselves. There were heralds. There were ambassadors with their trains of servants. There were drummers and trumpeters. There were houses adorned with rich hangings and paintings. There were sceptre-bearers carrying the bejewelled golden insignia of office. There were no women – they didn't attend such public events. 'It was a very glorious sight to behold,' wrote Howell (Plate 15).

The expense was colossal. The Venetian ambassador wrote jocularly that – by making it necessary for the court to drain the Exchequer in order to welcome him 'with all the magnificence that possibly could be devised' – Charles 'had managed to sack the city without an army'.

On arriving at the Alcázar, Charles and Buckingham were presented to Queen Isabella, before the King himself accompanied the Prince to his chambers. Buckingham, by Bristol's account, was 'lodged in a quarter of his own, adjoining to the Prince's Highness, with a very plentiful diet and nobly attended'. He was being treated with extraordinary respect and honour, wrote the ambassador (with what degree of jealousy one can only guess). 'There have been such demonstrations made unto him, both by the King, the grandees and all the court, as I think have never been made to any subject.'

King Philip had chosen sixteen of his own 'privy gentlemen' to form the core of Charles's court-within-a-court. They would surround Charles, protecting him from the world outside, and denying him access to it. He was permitted to choose his own personal servants and Gentlemen of the Bedchamber. (This was seen as a great kindness on King Philip's part.) Buckingham and Bristol became the two first Gentlemen but, since the rest of Charles's own people would not arrive from England for weeks yet, he was served, in the main, by strangers.

He lived according to the conventions governing the behaviour of a royal personage of Spain. When he dined in public, he was required first to dip his hands in water, a ritual as well as an actual purification. He must then take the napkin that was handed to him by his Lord Chamberlain, down on bended knee. As he ate, his entourage watched him silently, standing, their heads uncovered. In Spain a royal personage seldom saw another human being seated. Their subjects addressed them on their knees.

The liberty enjoyed by Tom and Jack Smith was over. Prince Charles and Buckingham had been swallowed up and subsumed into the court of Spain, one of the most rigidly conventional and ceremoniously hierarchical on earth.

Religion

AMONG all the goods and chattels – the jewels and armour and saddles and suits – sent after Charles and Buckingham as necessary to the state of a royal prince, came, as King James put it, 'all the stuff and ornaments fit for the service of God'. There were surplices, copes, candlesticks, etc., etc., and, most importantly, books – Thomas Cranmer's Book of Common Prayer in English and Spanish, copies in English and Latin of the King's own religious treatises – and, along with the rest of the 'stuff', two chaplains. The chaplains were under instructions to conduct themselves, and their services, in such a way as 'shall, I hope,' wrote the King, 'prove decent and agreeable to the purity of the primitive church and yet as near the Roman form as can lawfully be done'.

The hope for a compromise was typical of King James. Theological dispute was one of his favourite pastimes. He had corresponded on questions of divinity with scholars around Europe, most notably the great theorist of the Counter-Reformation, the Jesuit Cardinal Bellarmine. His intellectual duel with Bellarmine, though, had been essentially political, not theological. It was about the Oath of Allegiance that James required his subjects to take, swearing their obedience to him, above all other earthly powers, including the Vatican, and declaring that they 'abhor, detest, and abjure as impious and heretical this damnable doctrine and position – that princes which be excommunicated by the Pope may be deposed or murdered by their subjects'. Not surprising that a king might dislike that 'doctrine'.

But much as he wished to limit the Pope's temporal power, James had no particular hatred of Catholicism. In 1604 he told the English Parliament, 'I do acknowledge the Roman Church to be our mother church,' albeit 'defiled with some infirmities and corruptions'. Later he wrote, 'It hath ever been my way to go with the Church of Rome *usque ad aras* [all the way to the altar].'

King James's 'sweet boys' seem to have been similarly careless of sectarian disputes. Charles was ready to marry a Catholic Infanta. He would eventually marry a Catholic French princess. While he was in Madrid he was to write that he was 'far from plotting anything contrary to the Roman Catholic religion'.

As for Buckingham, he was and always remained Protestant (without ever showing any religious fervour), but two of the most important people in his life were, or had been, or would soon be, Catholic. His wife had grown up a Catholic, abandoning her faith only after much persuasion (after his death she would return to it). His mother was originally Protestant, but in the previous year she had been seeing what John Hacket called some of 'those dangerous and busy flies which the Roman seminaries send abroad'. He meant the Jesuits, the missionary order whose priests had spread across Europe, intent on bringing heretics into the Catholic fold. One of them, writes Hacket, had 'buzzed about and infected' the Countess of Buckingham. Bishop Williams had alerted King James to the danger. James and Buckingham together, both aware what political use the Puritans in Parliament would make of it if the Countess converted, tried to steer her away from doing so. A debate was arranged for her benefit. The Jesuit who established such a hold over her, John Percy, was opposed by William Laud, the future archbishop, already a rising man in the Anglican Church. Laud was judged to have spoken well, but the Countess did eventually join the Church of Rome. Her change of religion had no ill consequences for her (although it would be brought up against her son). She continued to enjoy the King's favour.

Charles and Buckingham alike had lived in a Protestant court where some of the greatest noblemen and highest-ranking officials were papists. Perhaps they were expecting their Spanish hosts to be equally pragmatic, equally easy-going. If so, they were to be surprised.

When the Count-Duke of Olivares woke King Philip IV with the astonishing news that the Prince of Wales had arrived in Madrid, both men immediately assumed that Charles had come to announce his readiness to convert to Catholicism.

Just in case he was mistaken, though, Philip turned to the crucifix hanging above his bed and, addressing it, solemnly swore that he would follow the Pope's ruling on the proposed marriage and 'that I will keep my resolution, even if it were to involve the loss of all the kingdoms'.

During the visitors' first few days in Madrid, Olivares came to the House of Seven Chimneys to pick up Buckingham in his carriage and drive out into the countryside. Alone and unheard, except by Endymion Porter, who was interpreting, they talked about the Match. Olivares suggested that there was no need to wait for the papal dispensation. The marriage could go ahead at once. Buckingham was astonished. How, he asked, had this so suddenly become possible? 'The means', said Olivares, 'is very easy. It is but the conversion of the Prince.' Surely, Olivares went on, this must be imminent. 'We cannot conceive but His Highness intended upon this resolution for his journey.'

Buckingham and Prince Charles were dismayed. They wrote to King James that the Spanish were 'hankering upon a conversion'.

In Madrid, religious ceremony was ever-present. On holy days (and there were many) processions wound through the streets. Arriving towards the end of Lent, Buckingham and Prince Charles were in time to see the awe-inspiring solemnity with which Christ's Passion was celebrated. Hundreds of friars flagellating themselves as they went; massive crosses carried on bleeding backs; dancers; tableaux; chanting; trumpets.

On Maundy Thursday, the two visitors were allowed to watch, unseen behind a screen, as King Philip went through the ritual of feeding the poor and kissing their feet. On Good Friday, barefoot friars paraded through the city, mortifying themselves as they went. Some had smeared their faces with ashes. Some wore crowns of thorns, with which they had scratched themselves so that blood flowed down their foreheads and into their eyes. Charles and Buckingham were invited to watch from a balcony.

To Protestant eyes these spectacles were disturbing. Buckingham was repelled by what he described as 'superstition'. Prince Charles asked permission to withdraw into the countryside for the Easter holiday. No, came the reply from the King's officials. He and his companions must stay in the city, and witness the sombre theatricality of the Easter celebrations. It was hoped this great sequence of ritual lamentations and rejoicings would impress him, and hasten his conversion.

*   *   *

The two chaplains King James had sent over had a hard journey. Richard Wynn reports that one of them was sadly shaken up by his mule, who subjected him to 'infinite bounces beyond his resistance' and eventually threw him.

Their journey was in vain. Olivares called Cottington to see him, and informed him that if the heretical chaplains tried to enter the royal palace, they would be forcibly expelled.

King Philip came regretfully to understand that Prince Charles had not arrived already eager for conversion. He must therefore be led towards it. Olivares pressed the point repeatedly. During his second meeting with Charles, he spoke reverently of the Prince's Catholic grandmother, Mary, Queen of Scots. In repeated conversations with Buckingham, he insisted that Charles must at least listen to arguments in favour of Catholicism. To refuse, he made plain, would be to halt further negotiations over the marriage.

Buckingham agreed reluctantly. On 23 April, St George's Day, the day when King James had imagined they would be impressing their hosts by donning their Garter robes, Buckingham and Charles met with a group of theologians. They were in King Philip's own apartments in the Alcázar, but Philip kept away for fear that he might be obliged to sully his royal ears by listening to heresy.

The discussion did not go well. A Capuchin quoted a verse from the Gospels in such a way as to imply that the Church of England was the work of the Devil – a trap and a delusion from which Prince Charles, once he had been saved himself, would rescue his fellow-countrymen and women. Buckingham left the room and, once safely out of sight of the divines, vented his anger by flinging his hat on the floor and trampling on it.

There were plenty of people in England who would not have been surprised by these attempts to convert the Prince.

In 1621 the Vice Chancellor of Oxford, Dr John Prideaux, told his congregation he was certain that the Pope was the Antichrist, 'seeing horns and marks are so apparently discovered'. Pamphleteers recalled the Catholic conspiracies against Queen Elizabeth, and pointed to the Gunpowder Plot as evidence of 'how insatiable [Rome] hath always been of blood, and English blood'. To such ultra-Protestant thinkers the

Match had always been deplorable, and Prince Charles's riding off to Spain had been dreadful news.

To those so-minded it seemed obvious that Charles would be used as a hostage. 'While our Prince is in Spain,' wrote one English correspondent, 'the Spaniards get what they wish from us.' 'Alas,' wrote another, 'our hands are now bound by the absence of our most precious jewel.'

They felt sure that the wicked Catholics would take advantage of Charles's presence among them. He would be intimidated and brainwashed and made to convert, whether he wanted to or not. The Earl of Kellie wrote to a friend, 'You can not believe such a dead dump it did streak in most men's minds here.' Archbishop Abbot described it as 'the most doleful accident unto us that hath befallen in the later age of the world'.

When James's licensed fool Archy heard of it, he took off his fool's cap and put it on the King's head. Others had the same idea. D'Ewes records a street show – a cage on a cart, and in the cage 'two in splendid apparel resembling the Marquess and the Prince, and an ancient man standing by, in a fool's coat resembling the King for letting them go'.

Courtship

THE Infanta Maria was sixteen, one year younger than the King her brother. Buckingham wrote to King James, 'Without flattery, I think there is not a sweeter creature in the world.' Obliging as always, he was saying the right and expected thing. Prince Charles was besotted: Endymion Porter wrote to his wife, 'The Prince hath taken such a liking to his mistress that he now loves her as much for her beauty as he can for being sister to so great a king.' But her portraits suggest Maria was on the plainer side of ordinary-looking (Plate 17). She was fair-haired. 'She is rather of a Flemish complexion than Spanish,' wrote James Howell. She had a long nose, heavy-lidded eyes and the unfortunate Habsburg mouth. Howell writes diplomatically that a protuberant lower lip 'is held a beauty rather than a blemish, or any excess, in the Austrian family, it being a thing incident to most of that race'. The best that Bristol could find to say about her appearance was that she had nice hands and that she was 'straight and well-bodied', and likely to make the Prince, and all England, happy 'by a plentiful issue'.

She had already been betrothed since childhood, to another of the Habsburg 'race', her first cousin, the heir to the Holy Roman Emperor, but he had died in 1619. In her portraits as an adult (the most notable one being by Velázquez), she looks watchful and serious. She had a discerning eye for art, collecting Spanish and Flemish paintings. She might have made Charles Stuart a good wife.

That prospect, though, didn't please her. In 1622, six months before Prince Charles arrived in Spain, she told Olivares that she was not happy. She probably believed that if she married a Protestant she would have to live with the knowledge that her husband would be consigned to hellfire for all eternity. Worse, so would her children if – as proposed in the original contract – they were to be taken from her and educated within the Church of England once they reached ten years of age. All of this she was prepared to endure if her marriage would induce the King of England to grant the Roman Catholics in his kingdoms freedom of worship. In that case, she would do her duty. Otherwise she would sooner 'enter a convent of barefooted nuns' than be married to his son.

Howell wrote to a friend that 'the people here do mightily magnify the gallantry of the journey, and cry out that Prince Charles deserved to have the Infanta thrown into his arms the first night he came'. The Infanta herself was more wary.

Once the English guests were installed in the Alcázar, the 'wooer', as King James and Buckingham now routinely referred to Charles in their letters, was at least under the same roof as the lady he wooed. Little good it did him.

The palace was immense. It was built around two main courtyards. There stallholders traded, news was passed from mouth to mouth, and suitors and supplicants waited and waited and waited for a chance to present petitions to the great ones passing through.

Within were the chambers of the various councils that administered Spain and its many overseas territories, and the Council of State. King, Queen, Infanta and infantes, each had their own quarters, where they were attended by their own households. The royal family, the ladies especially, lived secluded. They visited each other ceremoniously. People could not just wander about the Alcázar, calling upon whom they pleased.

Prince Charles asked to be allowed to meet the Infanta. He was given no positive answer. He asked again. Again the response was evasive. His dreams of slicing through obstructive ceremonial and laying claim at once to his bride by the sheer power of his loving enthusiasm were not coming true.

On his first meeting with the Queen of Spain (who was French, sister to King Louis and the Princess Henrietta Maria), Prince Charles had offended by some breach of etiquette. Buckingham told King James that there 'grew a quarrel between your baby and the lady for want of a salutation'. Buckingham was inclined to make little of it. 'Your dog's opinion is, that this is an artificial forced quarrel, to beget hereafter the greater kindness.' In Madrid, though, such things mattered. Spanish women were strictly chaperoned. When out and about they went veiled and, according to Howell, 'their habit is so generally alike, one can hardly distinguish a countess from a cobbler's wife'. Charles had somehow transgressed against the code of proper behaviour towards a married queen. A nubile infanta was fenced around with far stricter conventions.

Three weeks after the Smiths had arrived in Madrid, King Philip told his Council that Prince Charles was now demanding, 'with extraordinary force and more than usual fervour', to be permitted to visit the Infanta. A concession was made. The Prince was permitted to glimpse his beloved from behind a screen as she and the rest of the royal family passed through a long corridor to attend Mass in the royal chapel. A Spanish official wrote that Charles should have 'had a very good view of the Lady Infanta, because the procession moved very slowly'. It was something, but not much. Charles asked again for a face-to-face meeting. After further deliberation, King and Councillors together decided that a week later he might actually be allowed to converse with his beloved.

Charles dressed carefully for the occasion. He wore his George, and a garter about his leg. He had diamonds in his hat. All the same, Olivares, checking him over before the event, judged his outfit to be insufficiently splendid and arranged for him to be lent some better clothes.

King Philip attended Mass in his private chapel. Charles, accompanied by Buckingham, met him as he came out and they went together, followed by a train of courtiers and ambassadors in solemn procession, to the Queen's chamber. There the royal personages were all seated in a row in the following order – King Philip, the Infanta Maria, Queen Isabella (placed, in her capacity as chaperone, between the wooer and wooed), Prince Charles. The King's two younger brothers were at the ends of the line. Buckingham stood among the assembled courtiers and ambassadors.

When it was indicated to him that he might speak, Charles stood and paid his respects to the Queen, who rose to reply. He then passed on to the Infanta, seated beyond her. He kissed Maria's hands. He told her – in English – that he had come to Spain 'to make a personal acknowledgement' of the friendship between King Philip, her brother, and King James, his father, and to 'continue and increase' that friendship (the words 'by means of our marriage' being implied but not spoken).

Bristol translated for the Infanta's benefit. She said she valued the Prince's courtesy. Pause for translation. Charles enquired after her health. Bristol translated again. She said, 'Very well, thank you, Your Highness.' Pause for translation.

Charles then attempted some sort of elaborate compliment. Perhaps it was the one his father had suggested to him. King James had sent a jewelled mirror, advising Charles that he might present it to the Infanta, telling her that she had only to look into it to see the most beautiful lady in the kingdom.

Charles, never easy-mannered, embarked upon his lengthy conceit. Bristol toiled on, staunchly translating it. The Infanta stared blankly at her suitor. The court gazette reported that she carried herself 'with much gravity'. Another observer put her po-face down to bashfulness. The Venetian ambassador, who had heard that she was utterly opposed to the marriage, thought she acted with remarkable 'self-control'. Charles returned to his seat.

After half an hour the encounter was over. King and Prince, followed by Olivares and Buckingham, and then by all the other gentlemen, processed back through the palace's corridors to their respective apartments.

Once a week, a troupe of players came to entertain the royal family. This was the golden age of Spanish drama and King Philip enjoyed performances. In the Alcázar he had a *salon de comedias* set up, where 'machine plays' almost as elaborate as those Inigo Jones created in Whitehall were staged. They provided further opportunities for Charles to see his intended bride.

A row of seats would be set up beneath a tasselled and fringed canopy. Again Prince Charles would be placed on the young queen's right, with the Infanta beyond her. Prince Charles would gaze at Maria (the players, apparently, received little of his attention). Olivares thought his gaze was predatory – he watched the Infanta as a cat watches a mouse. To an English observer it seemed his 'thoughtful, speculative' look was kinder than that: he would gaze at the Infanta 'half an hour together', which must surely have been 'tedious, unless affection did sweeten it'.

On other occasions, when she drove out in her carriage, Charles would be positioned in his 'closed coach' to watch her go by. Occasionally they were permitted to converse, but their conversations were neither private nor fluent. They spoke haltingly, while Bristol acted as interpreter and 'the King always sat hard by to overhear all'.

Nor were there smiles or encouraging glances to make up for the awkwardness of their talk. That would not have been Maria's way. The Earl of Carlisle had had an audience with her a few months before Buckingham and Charles arrived. She was seated on a chair of state raised upon a dais. He approached as though to kiss her hand; but she would not hold it out to him. Carlisle was noted for his charm and self-confidence, but even he reported that 'his compliments, motions and approaches could not draw from her so much as the least nod'. She remained, all the while he was in her presence, 'as immovable as the image of the Virgin Mary when suppliants bow to her on festival days'. Poor Charles had no better luck.

Endymion Porter still thought he loved her for her goodness and beauty. Cottington, taking a lustier approach, wrote home that Charles was so excited by Maria 'as without all doubt she will be with child before she get to England'.

Buckingham continued to assure King James that she was a 'sweet creature', but he must have written more frankly about the frustrating courtship to his wife. Katherine Buckingham wrote back jocularly that she was looking out for a good pair of 'perspective-glasses', so that poor Charles could at least see his bride a little more clearly when he peered at her from afar.

Weeks passed.

King Philip took Prince Charles and his friend Buckingham hunting. He told them how much he would like to visit them in London one day. From what observers record, and from the letters that passed between them, it seems that the two royal youths genuinely got on well. Philip was not going to push his sister, of whom he was extremely fond, into a marriage that was abhorrent to her. But neither did he want to distress and humiliate his new friend. Charles couldn't be summarily dismissed. He must be entertained, and loaded with gifts and treated honourably. On the other hand, he had to be manoeuvred into a situation that he himself could see was insupportable.

He must be brought to understand, with nothing explicit said, no overt insult offered, that there was nothing for it but to go home.

Prince Charles was filling the many tedious hours by working on his Spanish. He bought Spanish books, including a popular romance by Fernando de Rojas called *La Celestina*. In it, the young hero reaches his beloved lady by climbing a ladder placed against the wall of a garden in which she is confined.

The Infanta liked to visit a royal summer house in a park across the river. There she and her ladies gathered May-dew (which was purportedly good for the complexion). One morning Prince Charles followed her there, accompanied by Endymion Porter.

They were received into the house, and allowed to go out into the garden, but still they hadn't reached their goal. The Infanta and her companions were in a further enclosure, in an orchard surrounded by a high wall. The gate was bolted on the orchard side. Like the hero of *La Celestina*, the Prince clambered up onto the wall. He saw Maria. The wall was high, but he leapt down, perhaps hoping she would be charmed by the dashing impetuosity of his approach and impressed by his athleticism.

What in his mind was the action of an ardent lover looked to Maria like a threatened assault. According to the Spanish court gazette, she 'did not turn her head nor take any notice, but carried on walking'. According to James Howell, who would have heard the story from Porter, she shrieked and ran away.

The elderly nobleman whose task was to protect the Infanta went down on his knees to the Prince. He implored Charles to leave at once, explaining that 'he hazarded his head if he admitted any to her company'.

The orchard gate was unbolted. The Prince was hustled out. Rebuffed, disappointed and looking foolish, he returned to the Alcázar.

Art

COURTSHIP was frustrating. Diplomacy was baffling. Opportunities for viewing and acquiring art, though, were excellent.

By the end of March, Buckingham's picture man, Balthazar Gerbier, had arrived in Madrid. There was plenty for him to do. Gerbier – who seemed to be able to slither through keyholes, so astonishing was his skill in getting access to the inaccessible – was allowed to visit the Infanta and paint her portrait. Buckingham had intended to send the picture to Katherine, but Prince Charles insisted on having it, and then sent it to King James. (Katherine, who was following the story of the royal wooing with amusement, was annoyed, and insisted Gerbier paint her a copy.)

Gerbier started hunting out artworks for sale. Madrid, unlike London, had a well-developed art market. There were *tratantes en pinturas* (picture dealers) happy to oblige (for a consideration) by putting a would-be collector in touch with an owner ready to sell.

Within two weeks of his arrival in Madrid, Gerbier had acquired for Buckingham a Spanish ebony cabinet and £350 worth of paintings. Within a month he had acquired further paintings valued at double that amount.

Soon, though, Buckingham was obliged to step back. Prince Charles saw what he was doing and wanted to start buying too. When one is travelling with the heir to the throne, one must – however reluctantly – allow him first pick. Graciously, Buckingham invited Prince Charles to make use of Gerbier's expert eye and irresistible powers of persuasion. And so Charles set about expanding what was to become his great collection.

Lope de Vega, the foremost Spanish poet and playwright of the era, wrote five years later that Prince Charles 'was most zealous in having brought to him all the paintings that were to be had; he valued them inordinately and paid excessive prices for them'. The artist Vicente Carducho reports that the collectors of Madrid 'were at great risk when the Prince of Wales was here'. He was forcing up prices. His appetite for artworks was insatiable, 'money being no object in their acquisition'. We hear of him offering to buy 'for any price' one of Leonardo da Vinci's notebooks. Its owner declined. He was luckier when he visited the collection of one Don Funes y Muñoz, and bought eight paintings 'by the greats', as well as weaponry – swords, crossbows and harquebuses (Spanish metalwork was highly prized). He bought ancient busts of Marcus Aurelius, of Apollo and Faustina. He paid 1,100 reales for a *Madonna* by Dürer.

Endymion Porter was helpful to him: when, towards the end of that summer, Diego Velázquez arrived at court, it was Porter who arranged for him to draw Prince Charles (a sketch for a portrait that was never painted). In most of his purchases, though, Gerbier, Buckingham's man, was the Prince's adviser and go-between.

King Philip had resolved that, though they could not have his sister, anything that 'is temporal and is mine' – any of his own possessions – he would willingly give to please his visitors.

He arranged for them to be given guided tours of the Alcázar and its contents, and of the other great royal treasure house, the Escorial. For the first time in their lives, Buckingham and Prince Charles were seeing a great quantity of outstanding paintings. They were not only acquiring possessions, they were getting an education.

The Escorial is a fortress, a monastery, a college, a mausoleum and a palace. Some thirty miles north of Madrid, at the foot of the Sierra de Guadarrama, it was built for King Philip II in the previous century. Philip had asked his architects for 'simplicity in the construction, severity in the whole, nobility without arrogance, majesty without ostentation'. He got it. The Escorial is the biggest Renaissance building in Europe. It is grey, austere and very, very grand.

Seventeenth-century visitors were awed by it. 'What I have seen in Italy and other places are but baubles to it,' wrote James Howell. Howell was struck by the contrast between the 'craggy barren hills' looming around it and its exquisite artificial grounds – 'what grots, gardens, walks and aqueducts there are there, and what curious fountains'. The interior was equally overwhelming. 'To take a view of every room in the house one must make account to go ten miles.' There was not one library, but three. There were statues 'like giants', and 'a world of glorious things that purely ravished me'. Those things included the majority of the royal collection of over two thousand pictures.

Soon King Philip, true to his resolution, was giving Prince Charles some of those marvellous artworks – not minor things he could easily spare, but masterpieces. One of them was Titian's *Venus del Pardo*. When the Pardo palace burnt down in 1603, King Philip III is said to have asked whether the *Venus* had been destroyed. Once told that it was safe, he said, 'I am satisfied, for the rest will be redone.' Only this painting, of all those he owned, had seemed to him to be irreplaceable and unreproducible. Yet now his son gave it away.

Almost more significant, because it carried such a potent symbolic charge, was Titian's portrait of the Emperor Charles V with a hound. Immense dog, gorgeous brocades, prominent codpiece: the picture is a celebration of virility and power. It also carried a dynastic message. Charles V had ruled over the Holy Roman Empire as well as Spain and its American dominions. He was the embodiment of Habsburg supremacy. His titles included 'Monarch of all the World'. In Titian's painting he looks pensive, wary, weighted down with responsibility. He was the patriarch of the two great interlinked ruling houses into which Charles Stuart was hoping to marry. Giving the picture to him, Philip seemed (but only seemed) to be welcoming him into the family.

Advice on Bargaining

HOW TO BEHAVE WHEN NEGOTIATING A DEAL

Act nonchalant. Pretend you are only mildly interested in what
your opposite number has to offer.

When he rejects your proposed terms, turn on your heel.

Do not look back until you hear his feet running after you. Turn
slowly. Act surprised. Return only as though reluctantly to the
discussion.

Act as though the outcome of negotiations is a matter of
indifference to you. Let it be understood that you are
conferring a favour. Hint that you have other prospects in
view.

Never reveal your need, or your desire, or your desperation.

HOW NOT TO BEHAVE IN SUCH CIRCUMSTANCES

Do not lay aside the advantages that your status confers upon
you. If you are Prince of Wales, and heir to two kingdoms, do
not disguise yourself as Tom Smith.

Do not go to your opposite number. Be coy and contemptuous.
Let him come to you.

Do not gallop across Europe and arrive after dark, panting and
eager, declaring that you cannot wait to see and lay claim to
your prize.

Do not declare that you are madly in love with the object you are
hoping to obtain, that you will accept no substitute, that you
must have it or die of a broken heart.

Do not allow your opposite number to keep you waiting, or to
otherwise humiliate you.

Do not go into his house, or take a seat in his shop, or accept gifts
from him, or allow him to do you favours that will put you
under an obligation. Do not accept invitations from him that
will make it hard for you to slip away.

If you fail to observe these rules, you are liable to find that the deal you
thought had been finalised has altered. Further caveats and conditions
may appear on the contract. Even when you have agreed to all these new
terms, you may find your opposite number has reconsidered. Perhaps
he has seen a new prospective buyer approaching. Perhaps he has
decided not to sell after all.

King James understood all this: it was one of the reasons why he had
opposed the adventure. Prince Charles and Buckingham, apparently,
did not.

Mewed Up

On 3 April a ship had set sail from Portsmouth bringing the beginnings of Prince Charles's court in Spain. There were the two chaplains, and Archy, King James's jester. There were twenty Gentlemen or Grooms of the Chamber (including our source Sir Richard Wynn). By the time they landed at Santander five days later it was already clear to Prince Charles that they would not be welcome.

King James had imagined, as Charles must at first have done himself, that the Prince would be given palatial apartments where he could accommodate a proper princely household. James even wrote suggesting he set up an oratory in his quarters, as though he would have rooms to spare. That was not the case. When Charles received news that his courtiers were en route through the mountains of Galicia, he sent urgent orders, commanding the majority of them to turn back.

They were dismayed. 'It struck such a general sadness in us all,' wrote Wynn, 'that for half an hour there passed not a word between us.' They dreaded the return journey. They deduced the business of the Match was going badly. They feared for the Prince's safety. Eventually Wynn and a handful of others received further orders that they were, after all, to proceed to Madrid, but the rest of the Prince's servants turned back for Santander.

Arriving in Madrid, which initially reminded Wynn of Newmarket, 'both for the country and the sharpness of the air', the few who had completed the journey were dismayed to find their Prince living in 'two little rooms'. They kissed the Prince's hands. Wynn was shocked to see him and beautiful Buckingham in 'Spanish habits, such an attire as will make the handsomest man living look like another thing'.

Madrid had only been the Spanish capital for a few decades. 'It is but a village, and lately grown to this greatness,' wrote Wynn. It was a tight-packed, stony place. It had grown upwards, rather than outwards. Six-storey buildings lined the narrow streets and open space was rare within the city walls – the Plaza Mayor, which Wynn called 'the only thing in that town a man would stand and look at', being the only exception. Of the Alcázar Wynn wrote there was 'nothing in it worth much observation'. There the Prince and Buckingham lived 'mewed up'. If they wanted exercise and fresh air, they had nowhere to go but down some stairs into a small garden that Wynn judged 'such a one as hardly deserves the name. So nasty, and so ill favouredly kept, that a farmer in England would be ashamed of such another.'

Wynn and his companions soon found they were redundant, for a courtier is nothing without a court. Worse than redundant, actually not wanted. They were put up for the time being in a nobleman's house, but there was nowhere to accommodate them in the longer term, and no provision for feeding them. Wynn was at once disappointed and relieved when, only a few days later, they were ordered to set off home for England. While they were in Madrid, 'most of our company did nothing but play at cards. For to say the truth, there was nothing to be done else.'

In 1630, looking back seven years, Olivares boasted, 'I alone was the minister who undid' the Match. There were other people involved, other contributing factors, but, broadly speaking, Olivares's claim is true.

Soon after Charles and Buckingham arrived in Madrid, Olivares's agent in the Vatican asked the cardinals to rewrite the conditions upon which the dispensation was to be granted, making those conditions unacceptable to the English.

The cardinals acquiesced. They drafted a new dispensation demanding 'the free and public exercise of the Roman Catholic religion' throughout Britain and 'that this concession be approved' by the English Privy Council and by Parliament.

That – as everyone who knew anything about the English Parliament was well aware – would never happen. The dispensation was designed to be an offer that Buckingham and Prince Charles could not accept.

*   *   *

Buckingham and Charles wrote to King James that, though the dispensation had been granted, they were annoyed by the conditions it was 'clogged with'. They warned the King not to disclose the new demands to anyone in England: 'We beseech Your Majesty to be secret.' They now wrote not about a triumphant return, but about an escape: 'We shall soon get forth of this labyrinth.' They urged him to dispatch a fleet as soon as possible. They hoped they would soon be sailing home. To hurry matters along, Charles asked his father to give him an all-embracing power of attorney.

James was as eager as the two young men were to get the marriage done, and his boys safe home. On 11 May he sent Prince Charles a letter authorising him to agree to whatever terms he judged acceptable. He used the wording Charles himself had proposed: 'We do hereby promise, by the word of a king, that whatsoever you our son shall promise in our name, we shall punctually perform.'

More Advice on Bargaining

Once you have shown that you are weak, that you have more to
gain than you have to offer, that you will draw lines in the sand
only to step over them, your opponents will ask more, and
more, and ever more of you.

If you have external authority – God or Parliament or your kingly
father – to whom you can allude as you explain to your
opponent, 'Unfortunately I cannot concede this point, much
as I would like to oblige you, because He/they/he will never
agree', then it is a bad idea to have in your pocket a letter from
that authority (a letter which may very well have been opened
before it reached you) explicitly agreeing to back whatever
decision you make.

Unhappy

BUCKINGHAM was unhappy. There was a Jesuit, Fray Francisco, who had been appointed spiritual guide to the poor benighted heretics. He wrote that he thought Buckingham had come to Madrid 'with confidence in his power of overcoming all the difficulties in the way of the marriage, merely by the help of courtesy'.

The remark was perceptive. In England Buckingham's courtesy, along with his good looks, had opened palace doors for him, procured honours and wealth for him, brought him power second only to the King's. He had never been given any reason to doubt courtesy's omnipotence. But in Spain it failed him.

In Spain he was not very much liked. He was over-dressed. Once his wardrobe caught up with him, he was a peacock, preening in silk. That sort of look didn't go down well in Madrid. Gerbier noted that 'the nobles of Madrid wear black frieze in the winter; plain taffety in summer'. Another of the English visitors reported that Buckingham's 'French garb' was 'much disrelished by the Court of Spain'.

So was 'the height of his spirit' and 'his over-great familiarity with the Prince'. Olivares might scold his king and overrule him in private, but in public he grovelled before His Majesty. Buckingham, who wouldn't so much as interrupt his game of tennis when his king called him, was not so deferential. Spaniards were taken aback to see him sitting down to dinner with Prince Charles. Equally shocking – he would sometimes keep his hat on while chatting with the Prince.

Later an official Spanish complaint about him was presented to the English. In it he was accused of addressing the Prince of Wales by 'ridiculous names'. He did. To him the Prince was 'Baby Charles'. Together in their rooms in the Alcázar they whiled away the time in dancing. The Spanish observers described this as performing 'grotesque and undignified contortions'. Their behaviour, wrote James Howell, was 'opposite to the way and temper of that grave, sober and wary people'.

Unpopularity made Buckingham tetchy. The man who had always been so modest, so graciously emollient, was now at a disadvantage, and it was having a bad effect on his temper.

He quarrelled with Bristol, whom he accused repeatedly of being 'Hispaniolised', of treacherously failing to press the British case. Howell reports that 'matters stand not right' between the two of them.

He quarrelled with Olivares: it was common knowledge there was 'some darkness' between the two powerful favourites.

Negotiations over the marriage contract stalled.

On 11 May Olivares announced he would consult further with Rome, and Charles should ask for further concessions from King James. Buckingham's hopes for the Match were waning. More experienced diplomats had seen, years earlier, that the Spanish were using it as a piece in a game rather than a real prospect. A Venetian ambassador called their part in the negotiations 'all wind and metaphysics'. A Genoese thought the Match had never been more than a fantasy, 'as pointless as a dog chasing its shadow'. Now Buckingham was coming round to their view.

Far from cutting through the tangle of negotiations, his presence and the Prince's, he could now see, had complicated them. He persuaded Charles that they should leave forthwith for England.

Charles told King Philip that he would need to return home to present the latest Spanish conditions to his father. 'His own presence would be very necessary.' The Spanish summer was heating up. His adventure, which had begun so jauntily, had become tedious and humiliating. King James was writing yearningly to Buckingham. All three of them wanted to be together, in England.

Buckingham decided that they would leave on 13 May. Prince Charles informed King Philip, through Olivares, of their intended departure. King Philip replied that his desire to arrive at a 'better arrangement' on the Match 'obliged him urgently to beg His Highness to be so good as to refrain from taking any resolution in opposition to the plans which had been proposed'. In other words, no. Charles was not free to go home.

Richard Wynn, commenting on the cramped quarters and the tedium he had experienced in Madrid, wrote, 'How wearisome a life this was to those that had lived continually at liberty, you may easily guess.' The word 'liberty' hints at a nagging unease. Buckingham and Charles were about to find that the awkward dependency of a guest with an over-solicitous host shades imperceptibly into the helplessness of the prisoner.

Charles sent Francis Cottington to Olivares, with a second request that the King might consent to his returning to England. Buckingham approached Fray Francisco, asking him to approach Olivares on their behalf. He also asked Gondomar to intercede. No, came the answer again. And again, no. And again, no. Such a departure could not be countenanced. Philip would not hear of it. Prince Charles was not to go back to England.

Buckingham could go. Olivares would have been glad to get him out of the way, but Buckingham flatly refused. It was his duty to stay with Baby Charles.

Finally, it was agreed that Cottington would be the emissary. He set out for England. Buckingham and Charles remained mewed up.

Entertainments were laid on to alleviate the tedium of their confinement. There were more plays in the royal apartments. More visits to the Escorial. More hunting in the Pardo. A bullfight. One night Endymion Porter arranged for the two of them to be taken in a closed carriage to visit a noted musician. They stayed for an hour, listening to the man play duets with his equally gifted daughter.

They were not exactly hostages. No one was using them that way. Not overtly. Not yet.

Refusing to renounce their heresy, the English visitors became less popular. Now the devout were saying that their presence in the Alcázar, within 'those walls which up to that time had been so pure from this contagion', was offensive. It was not only that the building was the home of their Most Catholic Majesties; it was also close to the shrine of the Virgin of Almudena, an ancient statue that had been found hidden in the city walls in the eleventh century, and had been adopted as the patron of Madrid. The proximity of the godforsaken English to such a venerable effigy felt like desecration.

Love Letters

LETTERS went back and forth between London and Madrid. Letters discussing matters of state passed each other on the road, according to John Chamberlain, as regularly as buckets hauled up and down in a well. And alongside them went letters of love. Lord Holland wrote from Madrid to say that 'the Duke sheds tears at his absence from the King'. Buckingham wrote to King James, 'Your baby shall no sooner have her [the Infanta] in his arms but Steenie shall make haste to throw himself at your feet.' Secretary Conway wrote from London to Buckingham, 'Never father loved a son, never master loved a servant, with more tender affection than His Majesty loves Your Grace ... For your absence, he afflicts his blessed heart.'

In May, King James wrote conferring a dukedom on Buckingham. There were no other non-royal dukes in England. Buckingham was now the highest-ranking person in the kingdom outside the royal family. And, best of all, the honour had been given to him spontaneously. Buckingham wrote that James, in the loving letter that accompanied the patent, had 'enriched my cabinet with so precious a witness of your valuation of me as in future times it cannot be said that I rise, as most courtiers do, through importunity'. The dukedom was a token of love.

There were others. Words, thoughts, passionate declarations. King James wrote to Buckingham to say how much he missed him. He wrote, 'My extreme longing will kill me.' He wrote, 'Alas, I now repent me sore that ever I suffered you to go away.'

As from James to Buckingham, so, with increasing ardour and boldness, from Buckingham to James. In his letters from Madrid we hear the voice, not just of a dutifully affectionate subject and grateful recipient of favour, but of a lover. His letters are passionate, yearning. He 'threatens' that 'when he once gets hold of your bedpost again', it will be 'never to quit it'. He writes, 'My thoughts are only bent on having my dear Dad and master's legs soon in my arms.'

King James's were not the only doting letters Buckingham was receiving in Spain. While poor Prince Charles peered at his intended bride through screens or past the interposed body of her sister-in-law as they sat in the royal line-up watching a play, his companion's marriage was thriving. Katherine wrote that no one 'could love you better than your poor, true, loving Kate doth; poor now in your absence, but else the happiest and richest woman in the world'. Their relationship was playful, sensual. She yearned for him. Gerbier, before he set out to Spain himself, wrote to tell him that Katherine 'so greatly deplores your absence that she cannot exist without having your image and shadow before her eyes'. Gerbier is being a trifle self-serving here – the image in question was his own portrait of Buckingham. 'Madame keeps it, as her sweet saint, always within sight of her bed.'

She wrote to him. He wrote back, long affectionate letters for which she thanks him. She writes about their little girl Mall, just beginning to toddle. 'When she is set to her feet and held by her sleeves she will not go safely but stamp and set one foot afore another very fast, that I think she will run before she can go.' Mall dances whenever she hears music. She is full of 'pretty plays and tricks'. She looks just like her father. Kate will send him a picture of her, as well as one of herself. And she has already asked Gerbier to make a copy of a miniature of Buckingham, because she has had to give up the original to the King.

Kate delights, she says, in being 'that happy woman to enjoy you from all other women'. She has no doubt of Buckingham's love and loyalty. 'Everybody tells me how happy I am in a husband, and how chaste you are, that you will not look at a woman, and yet how they woo you.' Endymion Porter wrote to his wife, 'My Lord and I … live very honest and think of nothing but our wives,' and Kate was pleased when Cottington told her Buckingham had vowed not to touch another woman until his return home.

Her father seems not so sure of his son-in-law's chastity. Rutland wrote warning Buckingham to beware of trifling with 'ladies of honour' while in Spain – 'you will be in danger of poisoning' – and if he visits whores, 'you will be in danger of burning'.

*   *   *

We do not know whether Buckingham paid much attention to this advice. Whatever he and Porter told their wives, it is unlikely he was completely celibate through the five months he was in Spain. Gossips, both in Madrid and London, spread stories about his dangerous liaisons there. He was accused of bringing prostitutes into the palace. It was said that he contracted syphilis, that he flirted with great ladies at court, offending them and enraging their husbands. It was even alleged that he had attempted to seduce Olivares's wife.

The Countess of Olivares would have been an improbable partner for him. He liked her. He described her in a letter to King James as being 'as good a woman as lives'. When he was ill with a fever, and too weak to walk, she lent him a sedan chair. But Doña Inés was reserved, devout and rather forbidding. A portrait of her by Velázquez shows her looking thin and wary. Like her husband, she was celebrated for her moral rectitude and piety. She was praised by her confessor as a 'manly woman', by which the priest meant that she was a strong character, capable and commanding, who ran a well-disciplined household.

Clarendon robustly scotches the rumour of Buckingham's alleged liaison with her by saying that she was 'a woman so old ... of so abject a presence, in a word so crooked and deformed, that she could neither tempt his appetite or magnify his revenge'. It is true that Doña Inés was eight years older than Buckingham, and this was an era when women were considered old at forty, but we have only Clarendon's word for it that she was anything less than perfectly presentable. But even if Buckingham did find her attractive, it is most unlikely he would have endangered his mission for her sake.

Strucken

KING James, happily unaware of what was going on in Madrid, was preparing for the homecoming of his son, his new daughter-in-law and his beloved favourite. Back in March, Balthazar Gerbier had offered to paint 'a pretty piece of the return from Spain with the Infanta', to 'immortalise' Buckingham's achievement in having made the match and brought the happy couple home. The picture would make an excellent wedding present for Buckingham to give the royal couple, thought Gerbier. It would show the Prince and the Infanta riding through the waves in a chariot drawn by Neptune's horses, driven by Buckingham 'as Admiral of the Sea'. The waves would be crested with water nymphs, the sky would be full of angels trumpeting the success. 'This would be very beautiful,' says Gerbier. By May 1623 there were other artists in England imagining similar scenes. Inigo Jones and a group of noblemen headed by the Duke of Richmond were sent to Southampton to prepare spectacular ceremonies for the arrival of the Infanta.

Gradually, though, hints percolated through that all was not well. During May the courtiers whom Charles had sent home arrived, by various routes, back in England. The accounts they gave of what was going on in Spain were dismaying. A ballad circulated:

> *Prince Charles can get no victuals there,*
> *Sufficient for his train,*
> *His horses and his trumpeters*
> *Are all come back again.*

Rumours from Spain seeped back to England and spread. It was said that Prince Charles and Buckingham would soon convert. It was said that they had already done so. It was said that Buckingham was a secret papist and that he and Cottington together had conspired to get Prince Charles to Spain so that the Prince would be obliged to go over to Rome once he was there. It was said that Prince Charles was being starved by the Spaniards, and that he was not allowed to see the Protestant chaplains in his train. It was said King James himself would 'make a breach to ignorance and superstition' by adopting the Roman faith. It was said that English Catholics were becoming uppity. The Puritan historian John Vicars called 1623 'the year the Romish foxes came out of their holes'. Another commentator complained about 'impetuous, unbounded' papists who went about declaring 'dangerous and fearful positions, insolently intimating what a golden time they now shall have'.

In St Paul's, the minister prayed that God 'preserve the King and Prince from any that should go about to withdraw them from their love and zeal' for the Anglican Church.

On 13 June, at two o'clock in the morning, the ship bringing Francis Cottington arrived in Dover. A fleet of ten ships commanded by Buckingham's father-in-law, the Earl of Rutland, had been got ready to bring Buckingham, Prince Charles and the Infanta home. Cottington was appalled to hear that it was set to leave for Spain that very day. He sent a message to Rutland telling him he should delay his departure because 'it may be that when His Majesty hath heard me he will resolve on some longer stay of the fleet'. Rutland, as intransigent in this as he had been over his daughter's wedding, refused to listen and gave the order to set sail. Early the following morning, after Cottington had galloped post-haste to London and made his report, King James dispatched a packet boat to intercept the fleet while it was still in the Channel and issue the royal order to turn back.

14 June. Letter from King James to Prince Charles and the Duke of Buckingham.

My sweet boys.
Your letter by Cottington hath strucken me dead.

Charles might still think he was going to be married. Buckingham might still imagine that he could somehow manage things so that he would eventually bring the Infanta home. James was a great deal cannier than either of them. As he read the new Spanish demands, he understood immediately that the adventure of Tom and Jack Smith had been a fiasco, that the Spanish Match was no longer a credible prospect and – worst – that his son, and the person whom he loved more than his own life, were in a trap.

The official letter from Buckingham and Charles brought news bad enough to make King James feel it would 'very much shorten my days'. There was an even more alarming one, also carried by Cottington, addressed to Lord Keeper Williams. This second letter contained an enclosure from Prince Charles with instructions that Williams was to read it to King James in private, and then burn it. In it Charles asked James's permission – should it become necessary – to 'depart from Madrid as secretly as he came hither'.

Rumours that he might do so would shortly be circulating in Madrid. James Howell reported 'whisperings' that Buckingham and the Prince were being held against their will, that they were longing to leave and that if the Spanish authorities prevented their doing so, they would 'go away disguised', as they had come. He writes that someone asked the Prince whether he might soon steal away under cover of darkness, and that Charles had replied, 'If love brought him thither, it is not fear that shall drive him away.'

The word 'fear', once spoken, cannot be unsaid. As they hunted with King Philip in the Pardo, or watched interminable, incomprehensible plays in the Queen's apartments, or stretched their legs in their sorry little yard of a garden, Charles and Buckingham continued to conduct themselves as though nothing was amiss. King James had none of their need to preserve a confident appearance. On reading their news, he felt the fear and poured it out in a passionate letter, begging them to do or say or sign anything – whatever was necessary – to extricate themselves from the web they were caught in and come safely home.

'Come speedily … and give over all treaty … I care for match nor nothing, so I may once have you in my arms again. God grant it! God grant it! God grant it! Amen, amen, amen.'

The End of the Affair

As Buckingham and Prince Charles were trying to leave, their compatriots were still arriving. Gondomar was asked by the Queen of Spain how he had found London. Was it as populous as Madrid? Yes, Madame, he said, usually it was, but 'there's scarce a man left there now but all women and children, for all the men both in court and city were ready booted and spurred to go away' to Spain. The first shipload of would-be courtiers had been followed by others coming out privately, in the hope of adventure or advancement, or profitable speculations. By the beginning of July, writes Howell, a 'confluence of English gallants' had gathered in Madrid.

Not all of them conducted themselves politely. They were as arrogant and boorish as the worst kind of modern tourist. 'I am sorry to hear,' wrote Howell, 'some of them jeer at the Spanish fare, and use slighting speech and demeanour.' They were rowdy and quarrelsome. Gondomar was repeatedly called in to extricate them from trouble; they rewarded him with racist insults. Howell marvelled at his patience 'notwithstanding the base affronts he hath often received of the "London boys", as he calls them'.

Some of the new arrivals were Buckingham's friends. One day Lords Denbigh (his brother-in-law) and Carlisle (his long-term supporter) were in their quarters in the Alcázar. Tobacco-smoking was abhorrent to King James, who called it 'a custom loathsome to the eye, hateful to the nose, harmful to the brain, dangerous to the lungs, and in the black stinking fume thereof, nearest resembling the horrible Stygian smoke of the pit that is bottomless'. In Spain, it was tolerated but discouraged indoors, so Denbigh and Carlisle took their pipes out onto a balcony. Denbigh dropped some smouldering ash onto the parched garden below. The dry grass caught fire. Carlisle's barber courageously jumped down off the high balcony and stamped out the nascent flames. A catastrophe was averted, but the impression that Spain's English visitors were uncouth and careless grew.

In the middle of July, four months after their arrival, Buckingham and Prince Charles resolved to bring matters to a head. They were guests or hostages or prisoners. They were heretics in a city where heretics were frequently put to death simply for being heretic. They were – in Madrid in high summer – hotter than they had ever been in their lives before.

They attended a play, and while Charles sat as usual in the row of royal personages, Buckingham, standing in the audience along with Olivares, pressed the Count-Duke to stop equivocating and to tell him King Philip's final terms. Shortly thereafter, Olivares did so:

1. King James must send a formal written acceptance of the amended articles, which bound him to make sweeping concessions to the British Catholics, suspending all the penal laws limiting their worship. Upon its receipt in Madrid, with his signature appended, the Prince and the Infanta could be betrothed.
2. The marriage could take place in Spain, by proxy if the Prince had already left, at Christmas.
3. The Infanta would remain in Spain for some further months, allowing the Spanish, and the Pope, to observe whether or not King James was carrying out his obligations under the treaty. If he was seen to do so, then the Infanta could go to England to join her husband 'in the spring' (no date specified).

Throughout the night Buckingham and Prince Charles argued back and forth over how they should respond. We do not know what they said. Two possible guessed-at versions of their all-night conversation present themselves.

FIRST POSSIBLE DIALOGUE

Buckingham spells out the reasons why the Spanish offer is unacceptable.

The terms require James, or Charles when he succeeds, to bring in legislation that will never pass through Parliament. In the inevitable event of their failing to give their Catholic subjects the freedoms they have promised, the Infanta will remain in Spain. King Philip and his heirs, under the terms dictated by the cardinals in Rome, will be bound to go to war against England.

If the marriage takes place by proxy, and the Infanta does not then come to England, Charles will be a husband without a wife, 'locked from all posterity'.

Nothing will have been achieved over the matter of the Palatinate.

So many arguments *contra*. Buckingham argues strongly that they must reject the offered terms, abandon hope of the Match and go home.

Charles – according to this imagined version of events – responds by saying that all the arguments *contra* are outweighed by the one argument *pro*. He tells Buckingham (as they will both claim he did) that he is accepting the Spanish terms because he loves the Infanta, and wants to marry her, 'for her respect only'.

Buckingham acquiesces.

Or were the two of them secretly in agreement? Subsequent events suggest that their conversation that night may have gone quite differently.

SECOND POSSIBLE DIALOGUE

Buckingham argues that the Spanish offer is unacceptable, but it is now clear they are never going to get a better one.

They must leave, but they will not be allowed to do so because the Spaniards are still determined to make Charles convert – if necessarily by holding him captive until he does so.

The best way out of the trap is to pretend to accept everything. To sign anything, promise anything, do whatever is necessary, to make it possible for them to get safely away from the hot and hostile city in which one after another of the English visitors is succumbing to fever or sunstroke, and to leave behind them the whole bothersome question of the Spanish Match.

Charles agrees. He and Buckingham will accept the preposterously unrealistic marriage contract. For the rest of their time in Spain – nearly two more months – they will be acting a part.

* * *

There is no way of knowing which of these versions of that night's conversation is closer to the truth. This is why contemporaries thought the whole story a 'labyrinth' and why modern historians still find the episode so mysterious.

On the following day, 17 July, Prince Charles astonished Olivares, King Philip IV and all the rest of the Spanish administration by announcing that – for love of the Infanta Maria – he wished to go ahead with the marriage on the terms proposed.

When the news reached London, King James took an oath, in the presence of Privy Councillors and the two Spanish ambassadors, that he would accept all the Spanish demands and sign the marriage contract. Simonds D'Ewes alleges that as he did so, the King was seen to shake uncontrollably.

His subjects were furious. Spanish Place in Holborn, where the ambassador lived, was 'the only merry street of so spacious a city'. The Spaniards' merriment provoked rage. Spanish visitors to London were accustomed to 'many insolencies of rude and savage barbarism', but that summer it got much worse. Repeatedly, Spanish diplomats found themselves 'besieged' by people who threw stones at their coaches and shouted abuse until they 'dare scarce to go abroad'.

On 25 July, in Madrid, Prince Charles and King Philip both signed the treaty. Its articles provided for 'perpetual toleration of the exercise of the Roman Catholic Religion among private persons' throughout 'England, Scotland and Ireland'.

Buckingham wrote to King James that 'our business here is at an end, all points concluded'. He added that he couldn't wait to be home. And so, at last, the 'betrothing-day' for the Prince and the Infanta was fixed, for 7 September, after which Buckingham and Charles would be permitted to leave.

In the meantime, the order of the royal line-up in Madrid changed so that Prince Charles and the Infanta Maria could be seen side by side. Charles wrote to his father that Maria 'sits publicly with me at plays'. Her position in the pecking order of royal precedence was elevated. She was formally addressed as Princess of England. The Countess of Olivares, who was her lady-in-waiting, told Buckingham that Maria was very distressed to hear that her new fiancé would shortly be leaving. She ordered rich clothes to present to Charles, some made of perfumed leather, others embroidered with gold and silver and embellished with pearls. She began, belatedly, to take lessons in English.

Bonfires were lit. The Venetian ambassador to Madrid records 'universal rejoicing and congratulations'. Courtiers wrote poems in Spanish and Latin to celebrate Charles's wooing. James Howell thought 'the Spaniards generally' still desired the Match, and that 'the bravery' of Prince Charles's journey and 'his discreet comportment' had won approval. 'They confess there was never Princess courted with more gallantry.'

But that was not really what all the celebration was about. The Spanish elation was not so much over a happy couple getting together, as over the prospect of a benighted heretic nation being returned to the Catholic fold by the agency of His Most Catholic Majesty of Spain.

One of the arguments in favour of the Spanish Match had been that it would somehow facilitate the restoration of the Palatinate to Frederick and Elizabeth.

The likelihood of that ever happening was by this time vanishingly small. In February 1623, the Emperor Ferdinand had granted the Palatine Electorship and the territory of the Palatinate to Maximilian, Duke of Bavaria. When King James heard the news, he understood what it meant. He wrote that the Emperor had 'spewed the uttermost of his unquenchable malice' against Frederick.

Prince Charles, though, still believed his marriage could benefit his sister. He demanded an interview with Olivares. He asked about the Palatinate. Olivares gave him some clear, hard answers. The Emperor would not go back on his word to the Duke of Bavaria, nor would his Spanish cousin presume to ask him to do so. There could be no question of Frederick being restored to the Palatinate. Olivares scoffed at such an idea.

Charles was very upset. He told Olivares, 'If you hold yourself to that, there is an end of all; for without this you may not rely upon either marriage or friendship.'

Olivares didn't care. The Spanish didn't value England's friendship all that highly. They had never relied upon the marriage. Far from it.

Late one night, Buckingham visited Olivares to try, yet again, to mitigate the terms of the marriage treaty. He reproached the Count-Duke.

He said that the marriage could have been finalised years earlier if only the Spanish had entered into the negotiations with 'goodwill'. Olivares didn't deny it. Instead he shocked Buckingham by finally telling him the truth. He produced the letter in which King Philip IV told him that neither he nor his father had ever wanted the Match to succeed, and instructed him to 'divert' it.

No wonder the bargaining had been so hard. What Buckingham had to offer, a British bridegroom for the Infanta, was something no one in Spain had ever actually wanted.

Madrid in August. In the heat of the day, nobody stirred. Buckingham and Charles, in their apartments in the Alcázar with its massive stone walls, suffered less than the other British visitors roasting in cramped lodgings around the city, but even for them, the climate was punishing. When Buckingham met Olivares, it was usually around midnight. Buckingham fell ill again.

The British contingent were making themselves increasingly unpopular. As they became more frustrated, more restive and ill-tempered, they gave ugly demonstrations of how deeply anti-Catholic prejudice was entrenched in British culture.

One of Prince Charles's pages had a fever. When he was dying, an English Catholic priest, resident in Madrid, visited him to administer the last rites – 'to tamper with him', as one Sir Edmund Verney put it. Verney saw the priest coming out of the sick man's chamber. 'They fell from words to blows.' Striking a priest was an incendiary act. As Howell remarks, 'the greatest Don in Spain will tremble to offer the meanest of them [priests] any outrage or affront.' Gondomar, the British party's truest friend in Madrid, had to be called in once again to hush up the incident.

The day of the betrothal ceremony was approaching. More rejoicing, more bonfires lit in celebratory anticipation. But then came the news that Pope Gregory XV was dead. King Philip told Prince Charles that he now had to wait for the approval of the new Pope, Urban VIII.

The prospect of further delays was insupportable. Charles told Philip that there was 'a general kind of murmuring in England over his long absence'; that his father was 'old and sickly'; that the fleet was standing by to take him home. Philip gave way. He agreed to 'personate him' in a proxy wedding once the papal permission had come, and afterwards the Prince 'might send for his wife when he pleased'. Charles was effusively grateful.

On 28 August, presents were exchanged. King Philip gave Buckingham twenty horses with saddle cloths of embroidered damask fringed with gold lace, and a diamond-studded hatband. The Infanta gave Prince Charles a pair of gloves. Prince Charles distributed the fabulous store of jewels his father had sent out for this purpose. He gave the Infanta the diamond brooch in the shape of an anchor (the one King James had thought should be given to Buckingham, who had declined it) and a necklace of 276 pearls, weighing eight ounces. 'Spaniards', wrote Howell, 'stood astonished at their beauty.' The Infanta did the proper thing, saying she could not accept the jewels yet, but would entrust them to the Secretary of State, and wear them on her wedding day. Olivares received a jewel set with eight diamonds, including one of 18 carats. King Philip was given a diamond-studded sword that had belonged to Prince Henry. Lesser dignitaries, ladies of honour and grandees, received rings. Howell estimated the value of all this treasure as being some £100,000.

On 7 September the ceremony of betrothal took place. Buckingham, who had a fever again, was not present. The doctors had bled him, leaving him too weak to stand, but two days later the Prince, the favourite and their now extensive entourage were en route for the coast.

King Philip and his brothers accompanied them as far as the Escorial, where they spent two days feasting and hunting. There, according to Ambassador Bristol, 'the former distastes betwixt the Duke and the Conde of Olivares' grew 'to a public professed hatred, and an irreconcilable enmity'. The two had a final meeting during which Buckingham said, 'I tell you very frankly that I shall never be a friend to Your Excellency.'

At the Escorial, Charles signed the document in which he gave his consent to the marriage by proxy, and entrusted it to Bristol, telling him to make use of it as soon as the dispensation from the new Pope came through.

King Philip and Prince Charles, who genuinely liked each other, bade each other goodbye with 'wonderful great endearments and embraces in divers postures'. Philip ordered that a pillar should be erected on the spot to commemorate this momentous parting.

Now that her wooer was gone, the Infanta appeared to be reconciled to the idea of their marriage.

Maria's part in this story is almost entirely silent, and full of pathos. Her courtship had been pleasureless and awkward, but now she appeared to be looking forward to the wedding that would never take place. She had a Mass sung every day, with prayers for Charles's safe journey. She chose the ladies and gentlemen who would accompany her to England to form her court.

Her enormous dowry was to be partially paid in pictures. Prince Charles had asked for all of Titian's *Poesie*, his great series of paintings on tales from Ovid. The painter Carducho saw them 'packed into crates, for shipping to England, these being *Diana Bathing*, *Europa*, *Danae* and the rest'.

Preparations for the proxy wedding proceeded. Bristol ordered thirty outfits for his followers, all of blue velvet 'with silver lace up to the very capes of the cloaks'. A terrace was built, to be draped with tapestry, connecting the royal palace with the church where the wedding would be solemnised. It looked as though the Match might yet be consummated.

That impression, though, was an illusion. The English travellers' next resting place was Segovia. By the time they got there, Charles had decided that he did not, after all, wish to marry the Infanta Maria. Perhaps he had decided it nearly two months ago, on that night in July when he and Buckingham talked till morning.

In Segovia, he wrote a letter to Bristol and entrusted it to one of Buckingham's people, Edward Clerk. Clerk was to return to Madrid and to wait there until the renewed papal dispensation arrived. Then, but not before, he was to give Bristol the letter he carried.

Continuing northwards, Prince Charles and Buckingham passed through Valladolid. There they stayed at the Palacio de la Ribera, where more of the tremendous royal art collection was housed. Prince Charles took away two masterpieces when he moved on, both of which he gave to Buckingham. One was Veronese's *Venus, Cupid and Mars*. It was Gerbier who drew the Prince's attention to the picture. It shows Mars undressing Venus. Her breasts are already bare and presented titillatingly to the spectator, the light full on them. It is clear we are watching the first moves in a seduction, but Gerbier chose to base his description of the picture on a bit of business in the lower right-hand corner, involving Cupid and a spaniel. He describes this lushly erotic work as 'a painting by Paolo Veronese of a boy fleeing from a dog'.

Charles's other acquisition was a more-than-life-size statue by Giambologna of Samson wrestling with a Philistine. Andrés Mendoza notes that Prince Charles declared himself 'much delighted' with the piece, and that 'he was served with it'. One wonders on whose authority these gifts were made, King Philip not being present. Probably Gerbier was party to it. Certainly it fell to him to organise the transport of the colossal statue back to London, where it would find a home, not in a royal palace, but at Buckingham's York House.

They travelled on.

An English gentleman with an injured arm arrived in Madrid. He was Edward Clerk.

He was given a room at the House of Seven Chimneys. He fell ill with a fever. No one knew what he was doing there. 'We fear', wrote Howell, 'that this Clerk hath brought something that may puzzle the business.'

A rumour went round that the papal dispensation had been delivered. Clerk sent a message to Bristol from his sickbed, saying he had something that he must now urgently give to him. Bristol came to his room. Clerk handed over the letter from Prince Charles. It instructed the ambassador that the document Charles had left with him, authorising the proxy marriage, was not, after all, to be acted upon. The Prince had changed his mind. Bristol was to explain to the Spaniards that before he engaged himself further, he must first be given a guarantee that the Infanta would not enter a convent. He would send further instructions from England.

Bristol was appalled. For Charles to withdraw at this late stage would be deeply offensive to the Spanish. Bristol foresaw the 'rupture and utter dissolution' of everything he had so patiently accomplished. He foretold that his own career would be wrecked. He was right.

He asked for an audience with King Philip. He gave Charles's message. And so, as Howell writes, 'that structure which was so many years a-rearing was dashed, as it were, in a trice'.

*   *   *

What was Charles thinking of? Perhaps the given explanation is the true one. Perhaps he thought how sad would be his state if he found himself married to a nun. Perhaps he had been swayed by a letter from his sister Elizabeth, brought by a messenger they met on the way, urging him not to agree to the marriage without extracting a promise that Spain would intervene in the Palatinate.

Most likely, though, he and Buckingham had been deceiving everyone around them for weeks, if not months.

When he was in Segovia, writing to King Philip assuring him of his 'fraternal and sincere friendship' and confirming his 'firm and constant resolution to stand by all my father and I have agreed', the Prince of Wales was – possibly within the next few minutes – about to write his note to Bristol ordering him 'not to deliver my proxy'. When he was in Valladolid, soliciting for more gifts, acquiring his Veronese and the colossal statue he subsequently gave to his dear Buckingham, he had already decided to insult and humiliate his supposed fiancée and betray his kingly host.

The travellers passed through the mountains where Wynn had felt in the deep valleys that he was in a stove, and where the mountainside paths had so terrified him, and where Howell had seen 'two huge wolves, who stared upon us a while, but had the good manners to go away'.

They reached Santander towards the end of September, to find the fleet James had sent for them ready and waiting (Plate 16). On 5 October they were in Portsmouth. The next morning they were in London, breakfasting at Buckingham's York House before riding straight on to Royston. As they were climbing the stairs to the King's chamber, James, still in his nightshirt, came hurrying down to meet them. The two young men fell to their knees. James burst into tears. 'My heart and very soul dances for joy,' wrote Buckingham.

The stages erected along the streets of Madrid so that crowds could watch the Infanta's wedding procession were dismantled. The jewels Charles had presented to Maria, King Philip and other dignitaries were eventually returned. James Howell thought it 'no unworthy thing of the Spaniard to deliver them back'. Prince Charles did not reciprocate by returning the splendid artworks he had been given, but – mercifully for Spanish art lovers – Titian's *Poesie*, not yet shipped, were taken out of their crates and hung back up on the walls of the Spanish royal palace. They would not be seen all together in London until they were united there for an exhibition nearly four hundred years later. Lucian Freud was to describe them as 'simply the most beautiful paintings in the world'.

Three years after Prince Charles failed to marry her, the Infanta Maria was betrothed to her cousin, King Ferdinand of Hungary, brother to her first fiancé. In 1631 she married him. In 1637 she became the Holy Roman Empress.

III

WAR

Jubilation

BEFORE he left Madrid, Buckingham had written to King James, regretting that he would be returning home without the Infanta, 'which hath almost broken my heart, because yours, your son's and the nation's honour is touched by the miss of it'. Perhaps he really supposed that his and Prince Charles's homecoming would be received as a dishonour and a defeat.

Instead they were met with what a contemporary observer describes as 'such unlimitable and violent inundations of joy that the people ... seemed to lose their own being and forget that they were themselves'. 'Men, women and children made but one consort and the music of that consort sounded nothing but "The Prince is come, our Charles is come."' They welcomed Charles's return because he was their prince, but even more they were deliriously happy because the Match had failed. The pamphleteer Thomas Scott spoke for thousands when he exulted because Charles 'returned *alone*, and showed by his single returning *alone* that he loved us ... *God be praised that he is come home ALONE.*'

Arriving on English soil, Charles and Buckingham left most of their entourage behind and hurried ahead, resolving to ride through the night. They stopped at an inn in Godalming, where – in a variation on the ferryman incident back in the spring – they gave away their identity by paying in Spanish coin. The publican's wife, overcome with excitement, repeatedly kissed Prince Charles. Another woman grasped his hand and refused to let it go until he swore he would never go back to Spain. They rode on. By morning they were in London. They were greeted in Lambeth by Archbishop Abbot, for whom the failure of the Match was wonderful news. He escorted them on to York House.

While they paused there for breakfast, the city exploded with happiness.

Bells pealed, guns were fired, bonfires were lit, hats were tossed in the air, drums played and trumpets sounded. So wild, so raucous and enthusiastic were the celebrations that one observer thought the noise of Londoners' 'unspeakable joys and universal acclamation' could surely be heard as far away as Brussels. The weather was 'foul and rainy', but it didn't dampen anyone's mood. There was singing. There was dancing. Seven men and two women, due to be executed at Tyburn that day, escaped, liberated by the crowds. No one did any work. All day long 'the people for joy and gladness ran up and down like mad men'. Old men with tears 'trickling along their cheeks' declared 'such triumphanting they did never behold'.

As darkness fell, fires were lit. Simonds D'Ewes claims to have counted 335 bonfires between Whitehall and Temple Bar. 'So infinite were the fires, so costly and high flaming' that night seemed like day. When firewood ran out, furniture and tubs of lard were burnt instead. There were fireworks. On the roof of St Paul's there blazed as many torches as Prince Charles had years (twenty-three). 'The people were so mad with excess of joy,' wrote John Chamberlain, 'that if they met with any cart loaden with wood they would take out the horses and set cart and all on fire.' Everyone was drinking, the rich dispensing free liquor to the poor. Hogsheads of wine and butts of sack were set out in the streets, 'along with all manner of provisions' for a city-wide celebration. Secretary Conway thought there was not a sober head between Southampton and … well … where? 'God knows where to find one.'

Even after the first hysteria had subsided, the celebrations continued.

'Suddenly, sweetly to our admiration/He came to us, to our hearts' exultation,' wrote John Vicars. Vicars was one of scores of people – playwright Sir John Beaumont and Parliament-man Sir Benjamin Rudyerd among them – moved to express their happiness in poems. Oxford and Cambridge universities both issued volumes of Latin verse. Up and down the country there were formal ceremonies with orations; 5 October became a day of annual rejoicing. Every year until the outbreak of civil war, bells were rung at St Margaret's Westminster on 'that very day which made England most happy and triumphant', which gave 'our royal Charles his second birth'.

All of this, not for a wedding but for the disappointed return of an involuntarily celibate prince. The people gained 'greatest contentment', wrote the Presbyterian minister David Calderwood, from the knowledge that 'the Prince was not married upon the daughter of Spain'. Those delirious revellers were toasting Charles because he had done them the ineffable favour of failing to get married.

Breakfast eaten, Buckingham and Charles hurried on. It would be nice to believe that Katherine and little Mall were at York House that morning – that Buckingham had at least a few minutes with his family – but we have no record of it, and even if he did, there was no time to linger. He and Charles had to go full pelt to greet the King, who was at Royston.

So thickly crowded were the streets with revellers that their carriage couldn't pass. It had to be lifted up and borne shoulder-high through the throng. Charles and Buckingham, still on horseback, rode ahead of it, side by side, the Prince 'not stirring his hat, but waving his hand and smiling', Buckingham bare-headed and bowing right and left, while the people cried, 'We have him. We have our prince again!'

King James had stayed in bed that morning, feeling low. Then came the news he had hoped and prayed and yearned for. His 'ecstasy of joy', wrote Conway, 'has cured the King'.

There was weeping. There were 'embraces and familiarities'. There was 'freedom and love'. Over and over again, during the last seven months, James had ended his letters with a prayer that the Lord would send his 'sweet boys' a 'happy [or comfortable, or speedy] return to the arms of your dear Dad'. And here they were at last and their dear Dad was half-frantic with delight.

John Hacket reports that 'His Majesty in a short while retired, and shut out all but his son and the Duke; with whom he held conference till it was four hours in the night.' There were listeners, as always in a court, straining to hear how this 'conference' went. 'They that attended at the door sometimes heard a still voice, and then a loud; sometimes they laughed, and sometime they chafed.'

Less than a month before, Buckingham had written to James a private letter ('by stealth from your Baby' – this one was not for Charles to see).

In it Buckingham told the King how he longed for their reunion. 'The change will be no less than to leap from trouble to ease, from sadness to mirth, nay from hell to heaven.' Now at last the dog and his master were back together. There were tears, and there would be more, but just for this night, they were all tears of joy.

Honour

WHEN, in October 1622, Endymion Porter had set out for Spain, his mission being to expedite the marriage negotiations and so seal the match that would bind Spain and England in everlasting amity, crowds gathered in the harbour to see him sail. They were not there to wish him success in his peacemaking project. As he boarded ship, a great shout went up: 'Bring us war! Bring us war!'

When, a year later, Prince Charles and Buckingham came home, a large number of those dancing in the streets were jubilant because they believed that now war had come.

The people of England, wrote Clarendon two decades later, were 'naturally enough inclined to war (having surfeited with the uninterrupted pleasures and plenty of twenty-two years peace)'.

There were pacific voices warning against the horrors of conflict. A preacher warned 'Happy Britons ... who sit under our own vines and our own fig trees' to beware the fate of 'other nations ... which do ride up unto their horses' bridles in blood'. In Europe, the chain reaction triggered by the uprising in Bohemia was accelerating. In the realm of the Rex Pacificus, 'there is no rifling of houses, no flying to refuges ... no rapes of virgins, no dashing of babes against stones', but on the Continent all of those horrors were becoming commonplace. Imagine, cried another preacher, 'what it is to see thy house fired, thy goods seized, thy servants fled, thy wife ravished before your face and then hung up by the heels ... thy daughter crying to thee for help in one corner while thy little son is tossed on another's pike and the sword at thine own throat'.

These voices were not heeded. Clarendon, in thinking it 'natural' for those who lived in peace to crave war, understood his own countrymen all too well.

* * *

Three things militated against King James's project of keeping the peace.

First, the English hatred of Spain.

Second, the English Protestant hatred of the Roman Catholic Church. Many considered it their sacred mission to prevent the Most Catholic Kings of Spain from extending their power. The theologian Thomas Gataker warned that if England failed to defend the Protestants of Bohemia and the Palatinate, 'the Curse of Meroz may light upon us; we and ours may be destroyed'.

Third, Englishmen (there is no indication that women thought this way) were afraid that holding back from conflict would be shameful. They would be seen to be weak and cowardly. They would be dishonoured.

King James had done his best to outlaw duelling, but the code of honour that made the practice so hard to eradicate was still strong. Many of his subjects felt that foreign policy should be shaped by it, that a statesman should protect not only his people's well-being, but also their pride. Wars were to be fought about 'reputation'.

The theme rings shrilly through the debates in Parliament over the following year. One speaker after another dwelt on the 'great indignities' that Prince Charles had endured in Spain, how he was 'made cheap amongst them'. Another said that the loss of the Palatinate 'hath made us a scorn to all', and insisted that the only way to recover the world's respect was 'to take the English way to recover what we have lost by the sword'. Yet another declared, 'We have been famous heretofore; now our honour is in the dust.'

Buckingham had been the King's man, the disciple and assistant of the Rex Pacificus. But something had shifted in the months he had been away. King James said Buckingham had 'he knew not how many devils within him since that journey'. Those devils had got into Charles too. Three months after his return from Spain, Charles told Parliament that if they shrank from war, 'it would be dishonourable unto yourselves as well as unto me who am now first entering into the world'.

In November 1623, scarcely a month after the King had welcomed his sweet boys home, shedding tears of joy, they made him cry again.

James had gout, and was in constant pain. He kept away from court. The Earl of Kellie, a trusted member of his household, thought his illness was brought on by anxiety. Buckingham stayed with him. Prince Charles was in London, presiding over Privy Council meetings and, as one Councillor recorded, 'entering into command of affairs ... and all men address themselves to him'. The Venetian ambassador notes that 'while Buckingham remains at Newmarket to prevent any harm, [Prince Charles] stays here to achieve the good. Thus they cooperate towards the same end, with different functions, yet with a good understanding.'

They were political partners now, and loving friends. Those long months mewed up together in Madrid had brought them very close. It was painful to King James that they were working together to oppose his policies. Perhaps he was also jealous of their affectionate intimacy. An observer records that when they were together, Buckingham and Prince Charles 'never go asunder but arm in arm'.

The Spanish Match had not yet been officially abandoned, but soon Prince Charles came down from London to visit his father. With Buckingham backing him up, Charles told the King that he no longer trusted Spain's promises. It was time to halt all negotiations, and to challenge the Habsburg powers over the Palatinate. King James asked plaintively, 'Do you want to commit me to war in my old age and make me break with Spain?'

The answer was that, yes, Charles and Buckingham wanted precisely that. They urged him to summon Parliament. Only Parliament could authorise the raising of enough money to create a fighting force. James raged and called them fools. They persisted. As they pressed ahead with war plans, the Venetian ambassador wrote that King James 'now protests, now weeps, but finally gives in'.

With infinite reluctance, and many warnings about how greatly he and his boys would come to regret it, he summoned Parliament.

Magnificence

CHARLES returned from Spain still single. Buckingham came back to a loved and loving wife. While he was waiting impatiently to leave Madrid, Katherine fell ill. When he heard, he was said to be reduced to 'a brick wall of reflection'. He wrote to her saying he would come at once if she was not yet recovered. She wrote back reassuring him, but saying she thought her illness was caused by grief at his extended absence. 'I hope when once we are together again we shall have no more such partings, for if ever I should be so unfortunate again I am sure it would kill me.' She teased him with a pretended suggestion that he might be looking to replace her, 'Then might you have a finer and a handsomer wife,' before adding, with heartfelt sweetness, 'but never a lovinger wife than your poor Kate is.'

Katherine would soon be pregnant again. King James's demands on Buckingham meant that the couple were together far less than they would have liked, but at least they had plenty of houses to enjoy together.

While Buckingham was in Spain, work on York House had been going forward. Balthazar Gerbier (although frequently absent) was in charge.

The building was being transformed into an Italianate palazzo. Gerbier, keeping his master abreast of the project's development, wrote, 'We have got scaffolds everywhere.' Ceilings were held up with iron braces. Balconies were 'clapt up in the old wall, daubed over with finished mortar'. The house was to be as up to date technically as it was aesthetically. The celebrated Dutch inventor Cornelis Drebbel (whose creations included microscopes and torpedoes, a perpetuum mobile and the world's first navigable submarine) was brought in to work on the plumbing.

Gerbier wrote, 'I shall always prefer the ancient magnificency [by which he meant the neo-classicism of the Italian Renaissance] to that of all other nations.' Accordingly, he had designed two extensions, doubling the size of the building. One (which was never built) was to face the Strand. The other overlooked the river – a long Palladian-style facade between a pair of pedimented projecting wings. King James had given Buckingham 2,000 tons of Portland stone for it. Other dignitaries contributed as well, paying tribute to Buckingham's grandeur. Lord Salisbury sent him a painting. Dudley Carleton sent him several more, as well as a marble chimneypiece and a gateway, also of marble. When Inigo Jones visited the site, Gerbier, always rivalrous in his dealings with Jones, thought him so impressed and envious that 'he was like a person confused and ashamed'.

The chamber where the most important paintings would be displayed 'will be the grandest thing in the kingdom', Gerbier told Buckingham. In the great saloon the wooden floor was replaced with stone. Katherine protested that surely it was not necessary to order quite so many tapestries. (Priced according to the value of their materials – precious silks and gold and silver thread – tapestries were more expensive than even the finest paintings.) Gerbier wrote to Buckingham, 'Monseigneur, beg of Madame that she will be pleased to dress the walls of the gallery' and save those walls from the shame of nakedness.

Gerbier was joking. The walls were sumptuously arrayed. Carpets, and silks for upholstery, arrived from Holland, woven to Gerbier's designs. He bought up the London textile merchants' entire stock of velvet, for curtains and upholstery and for twelve 'sumpters', the magnificent horse trappings that would be proudly displayed in the sumpter room. Cloth of gold was imported from Persia.

The massive statue by Giambologna that Prince Charles had given Buckingham in Spain was set up in the garden in front of the new wing, visible to all who passed along the river. It was the largest and most technically ambitious piece of Renaissance sculpture yet seen in Britain. Arranging its transportation had been a monumental task. Preserving it from the damp and dirtiness of the London air was another. 'It did not moulder when it stood in the garden of the Duke of Lerma,' Gerbier wrote fretfully. It was generally agreed, though, to have merited all the trouble. Henry Peacham, admiring it, wrote that 'the garden will be renowned for as long as John de Bologna's *Cain and Abel* stands erected there, a piece of wondrous art and workmanship'. He was following the common mistake as to the statue's subject matter. Another letter-writer, in 1624, got it right: 'a goodly statue of stone … bigger than life, of a Samson with a Philistine betwixt his legs, knocking his brains out with the jawbone of an ass'.

Buckingham, reports John Chamberlain, 'takes great delight in his building'. He gave a feast there in honour of visiting ambassadors. Chamberlain tells us the bill of fare included 'forty dozen of partridges and as many quails', and the dinner was followed by a masque. The building was a theatre and an exhibition space. It contained rooms fit, wrote Gerbier, 'to entertain foreign princes … according to the dignity of a prime minister of state'. It was a setting for paintings, for music and banquets, for rarities and curios, for jewel-embellished clothes and ancient statuary. It was itself an artwork, an installation piece of which the theme was the greatness of its owner.

Buckingham's power and splendour now seemed so brilliant that people bestowed on him ever more exalted titles. The Bishop of Llandaff dedicated a book to him as 'high and illustrious prince'.

St George on Horseback

It was two and half years since Francis Bacon had been driven out of office. During that time he had completed his *History of the Reign of King Henry VII*. He had translated his thesis *The Advancement of Learning* into Latin. He had written two more volumes of his magnum opus, *The Great Instauration*, which was to be 'a total reconstruction of sciences, arts, and all human knowledge'. He had written essays on vainglory, on anger and on masques. In the last named he had laid it down as fact that 'the colours that show best by candlelight are white, carnation and a kind of sea-water green': it seemed there was nothing on which Bacon did not have an opinion, backed up by observation and experiment. He had written that he preferred 'loud and cheerful songs' to 'chirpings or pulings'. His political career had been destroyed, but he didn't pule. 'Do what we can,' said Prince Charles, 'this man scorns to go out like a snuff.'

For all his ceaseless scholarly busyness, Bacon was also keeping a beady eye on the court from which he had been so cruelly excluded. He was still corresponding with Buckingham. Once again he sent his mentee some advice.

Buckingham had been King James's assistant in peacemaking. Now he had become foremost among those who wanted war. The proverb said, 'A wise man changes his mind, a fool never will,' but in politics, warned Bacon, a turncoat is always suspect.

Buckingham knew it. He had been kept informed as to how, while he was away, his rivals were gathering strength. Hacket writes that he had 'secret intelligencers' left behind in London when he went to Spain 'to be, as it were, the lifeguard of his safety'. These intelligencers, the 'cabinet men at Wallingford House', were warning him that by sweeping into Madrid and taking over negotiations he had offended Bristol. This he well knew, but perhaps he had underestimated the extent of Bristol's influence. The ambassador had 'a great and more powerful party in court than you can imagine'. That party included some influential people. 'Your presence is most necessary here for home affairs,' wrote one of the cabinet men, 'for your absence hath caused too great insolency in the court.'

There were three 'parties', Bacon wrote to him. The first was 'the party of the papists, which hate you'. (While anti-Spanish Protestants suspected Buckingham of having lured Charles to Spain in order to get him to convert, Catholics accused him of having deliberately sabotaged the Match.)

The second party, Bacon went on, was 'the party of the Protestants, including those they call Puritans, whose love is yet but green towards you'. It would take a while for them to believe he was sincere in his new pro-war policy. Their leaders included his first sponsors, Archbishop Abbot, the Earl of Pembroke and the Countess of Bedford. They might support Buckingham pragmatically 'for the breaking of the Match or putting the realm into a war', wrote Bacon, but he must remember that they didn't trust him.

Bacon's third party were 'particular great persons' who were Buckingham's 'reconciled enemies or discontented friends'. One of those 'discontented friends' was Bishop Williams, the Lord Keeper. He had been Buckingham's protégé, but Buckingham knew, through his informants, that Williams had been conspiring against him, and that he now privately called Buckingham 'a man odious to all the world'. Another discontented friend was the Lord Treasurer, Lionel Cranfield, now Earl of Middlesex.

Cranfield had served King James since 1605, holding various finance-related offices, including Receiver General of rents from the royal estates, Surveyor General of Customs and Chief Commissioner of the Navy. He was clear-minded, hard-working and determined. When Buckingham came to court in 1615, Cranfield was soon acting as his financial adviser, assembling a portfolio of properties for him and even lending him money to buy a profitable estate. Buckingham trusted him and made use of him, both for himself and for the country.

Cranfield was the son of a mercer (a cloth merchant) and had been a mercer himself. He was a businessman, one of the middling sort. Noblemen of greatly inferior intelligence looked down on him. When he was appointed Master of Requests, an aristocratic official wrote he was astonished that 'so base a fellow ... should be admitted to such a place'. Buckingham, who suffered from such snobbery himself, recognised his worth and supported him steadily. King James records that the young favourite 'found this man so studious for my profit that he backed him against great personages and mean'. Together the two of them (Cranfield doing most of the work, Buckingham ensuring the King's support) set about putting the country's finances on a sounder footing.

First came the royal household. Cranfield's rigorous economising caused one official to write of his 'scourging and dreadful commission that hath done such wonders'. From there he moved on to the Exchequer, the Office of Ordnance, and then the Navy, cutting costs, reorganising departments, paring down the payroll, eliminating wastage. Buckingham was with him all the way. King James paid tribute to their partnership in 1617, saying, 'Buckingham laid the ground and bare the envy,' while Cranfield 'took the laborious part', and recording that Cranfield 'many a time protested unto me that he had not been able to do me any service if Buckingham had not backed him in it'.

Then Cranfield had valued Buckingham's support, but he was first and foremost a conscientious public servant, who valued his own integrity and competence above his duty of gratitude to a sponsor. He had been working hard for over two decades to restore the country's economy. He deplored the expense of an unnecessary war.

Bacon was right. Buckingham was the idol of the populace, but at court he had enemies and rivals, and he couldn't rely on his friends. Bacon instructed him that he must be ever-wary, trusting no one. He must be supple, now dispensing favours, now acting sternly, 'showing yourself to have, as the bee hath, both of the honey and of the sting'.

In January 1624 Bristol was ordered to return to London from Madrid to testify before a special commission. When he took his leave, King Philip removed a ring from his own hand and gave it to him, along with a chest full of silver plate. Olivares suggested he should stay in Spain, and offered him a home with 'means and honour equal to the highest of his enemies'. Bristol declined. He may have recalled that decision later with regret.

Bristol's loyal support for his king's foreign policy had profited him nothing. When he arrived home in London, he was locked up in the Tower. The fiasco of the failed Match was to be blamed on him.

In February 1624 Parliament assembled. King James attended the opening. In his speech he said how proud and glad he was that for so many years, thanks to his care, his subjects had lived in peace. Now, though, he had 'awaked as out of a dream'. He had hoped for an alliance with Spain but, for all the 'long treaties and great promises ... the business is nothing advanced'. He had no more to say. He would hand over to Charles and Buckingham to 'declare all the proceedings'. He was no longer his people's father, the head of their body. Instead of insisting that Parliament had no right to discuss matters of state, he asked them for their 'honest and sound advice'. His great vision of a European Union had failed. He was giving up.

A few days later the Lords and Commons were invited to the Banqueting House at Whitehall Palace. This was unusual. Some momentous announcement was clearly to be made. Word spread to the streets. Crowds of onlookers pushed past security guards to listen in. The hall had been set up as though for a theatrical performance. Members of Parliament sat on specially constructed stands, looking down on the table around which the Privy Councillors were seated, Prince Charles at its head. Buckingham stood behind the Prince, leaning on his chair.

Buckingham spoke. He was modest and polite. He reminded his hearers 'how unusual it was for him to speak in so great and judicious an auditory'. He delivered a 'Relation', giving an account of negotiations between England and Spain going back ten years, and culminating in the toing and froing during his visit to Madrid.

His speech was fluent and persuasive. What he said was substantially true, but it was not the whole truth. No mention of the fact that the Prince, with his approval, had signed a treaty granting freedom of public worship to English Catholics. No mention of the promise that whatever children Charles might have with Maria would initially be brought up Catholic. Charles and Buckingham had even agreed that members of the Infanta's household would owe their allegiance primarily to the Pope in Rome. The great Victorian historian S. R. Gardiner was to write that in doing so they had effectively 'signed away Britain's ... sovereignty'. Buckingham gave no hint of that. No mention of the lies Buckingham and Charles had told as they professed undying friendship to King Philip and undying love to the Infanta.

Bristol had been recalled, but it would be weeks before he arrived back in England. Now, in his absence, Buckingham claimed that Bristol had known all along that Spain would never agree to the Match. He implied that the 'Hispaniolised' Bristol's sympathies had been with Spain. He showed himself and the Prince, by contrast, as being, each of them, 'a true-hearted Englishman'. He gave Parliament to understand how staunchly and heroically they had refused to accept Spain's terms (terms laid out in the treaty Charles had in fact signed). He presented the Spaniards as being devious and untrustworthy. He stressed how, in his view, Olivares had consistently pretended to encourage the Match while really opposing it. He made it clear that Spain was England's enemy.

No one contradicted him. As Buckingham spoke, Prince Charles sat by him listening. He smiled and assented. He was endorsing Buckingham's account of events. At one point he intervened to say that, when he had feared that the two of them would be held prisoner in Madrid, he had written to King James selflessly asking the King 'to be pleased (for his sake) never to think upon him any longer as a son, but to reflect all his royal thoughts upon the good of his sister'. The sentiment, appealing to chivalric sentiments and anti-papist feeling now concentrated in the person of Princess Elizabeth, went down well.

Buckingham ended by asking whether Parliament believed negotiations with Spain should continue, or whether 'His Majesty were best to trust in his own strength and to stand upon his own feet'. It was clear which option he preferred.

The 'Relation' was widely circulated in manuscript and subsequently in print. Parliament loved Buckingham for it, and so did the public. Newsletter writers called him 'the darling of the multitude' and reported he 'could hardly go or ride or stand in his gates, for press of people to behold him'. He was lauded to the skies.

The Spanish ambassadors were irate. Buckingham's version of events in Madrid offended them greatly. They protested to King James that Buckingham had insulted the King of Spain so vilely that, if a Spaniard had said such things about the King of England in Spain, he would have had his head cut off.

Buckingham – proving himself an adroit player of the Parliamentary game – seized the chance to make himself a hero of the anti-Spanish party. He repeated the ambassadors' complaints to the House of Lords and asked them to judge whether they agreed that he had offended. No, the Lords declared. Everything he had said was 'fit for him to do'. The House of Commons were then invited to comment. They passed a resolution declaring that Buckingham 'hath merited a great deal of thanks of the House and the whole commonwealth'.

The chorus of praise continued. The enemies against whom Bacon had warned Buckingham had been silenced. Sir George Goring thought he had 'given proof of his courage, judgement, religion and true English heart'. Lord Holland concurred, praising Buckingham's 'wisdom and honour', and declaring 'our nation hath cause to reverence and admire him, so careful hath he been to serve, and nobly to serve, his King and country with offices of a true and religious heart'. Sir Edward Coke declared that 'never any man deserved better of his King and country'.

'Never before', wrote Secretary Conway, 'did … one man … have so much love of the King, Prince and people.' Buckingham was 'St George on horseback'.

Which War?

WAR fever descended like a plague. Francis Bacon, astute commentator, wrote that 'many in the House who speak not are as wise as others that do speak'. We cannot know the opinions of that silent majority. Of those who did speak in the 1624 Parliament, though, nearly everyone wanted war. 'War … is England's best prosperity,' said Edward Coke, the veteran Elizabethan who equated Catholicism with treason. Coke also said that the idea of war made him feel seven years younger. But which war? War against whom and to what purpose? With which allies, on which battleground? There was no clear consensus.

The war to which King James was ready to give his reluctant and tearful consent was strictly limited in its scope and its objectives. Its sole purpose would be to restore his daughter and son-in-law to the latter's hereditary lands in the Palatinate.

James did not endorse Buckingham's view that the Spanish had been insincere in the matter of the Match. He had no wish to punish them for its failure. He never broke off diplomatic relations with Spain. He didn't hate Spaniards for being Catholic, and the prospect of a sectarian conflict, 'a mere quarrel of religion', was horrible to him. After all, as he had written to the Pope, Protestant and Catholic alike, they all shared a God.

His preference would have been for a swift, precisely targeted operation that would drive the Bavarian, Imperial and Spanish armies out of the Palatinate and allow the hapless Frederick to reclaim his territories. But there were problems.

Geographical problems. England had ships, thanks in large part to Buckingham's diligence as Lord Admiral, but it had no standing army. The Palatinate, deeply embedded in Europe, had no sea coast. As one pamphleteer wrote sardonically, the only way King James could attack the occupying forces there would be if 'his great fleet could fly thither over land'.

Logistical and diplomatic problems. Short of such a miracle, the only possibility would be to send troops (what troops?) marching through France and into the Rhineland. Supply lines would be extended. To plot a route that didn't pass through Spanish-controlled or Imperial territory would be tricky. And how would France react?

Prince Charles's aims were more diffuse. He had returned from Spain with a personal grudge against his Spanish hosts. Boarding the English ship that brought him home, Charles had said that the Spanish would come to regret their own 'weakness and folly … in that after they had used him so ill, they would suffer him to depart'. He had been rejected as a wooer, and outwitted as a negotiator. He felt humiliated, and, like any seventeenth-century gentleman who issued a challenge to a duel when he felt his honour had been impugned, or any twenty-first-century streetfighter who reaches for a knife when he feels disrespected, he wanted to restore his *amour propre* by picking a fight.

He wanted to teach Spain a lesson. His pretext for the fight would be, he declared, not his own 'dry entertainment' in Madrid, but to 'put an end to the miseries of my sister and her children'. The ex-Electress of the Palatinate was still his damsel in distress. He hadn't seen her for a decade, but back in 1620 he had told Gondomar, 'You must know that at the bottom this concerns my sister.' After the sequence of Frederick's defeats in 1622, a courtier had written that 'this court hath not a man that is Spanish any longer, all resent the injury we suffered', and, most especially that Prince Charles lamented the loss of England's 'ancient honour' and 'designs himself to some brave enterprise abroad, to recover at least what we have lost'. Now he told one of the Spanish ambassadors, 'Nothing occupies my mind more than the affairs of the Bohemians and of my brother-in-law.'

Quite how Spain was to be punished, Elizabeth's exile ended and England's 'ancient honour' restored Charles did not explain.

The war that the most outspoken members of Parliament wanted was a war at sea, against Spain. They hoped it would take the form of raids on the Spanish Atlantic ports, and on the treasure fleet bringing silver and other valuable cargoes back from the Americas.

Several presumptions, of varying degrees of validity, lay behind this preference:

1. Britain was stronger at sea than on land.
   (Correct.)
2. Such a war would benefit the Elector and Princess Elizabeth because the Imperial and Bavarian forces occupying the Palatinate were financed, at least indirectly, by the bullion imported into Spain from the Americas.
   (Not really. It was true that Spanish troops, under General Spinola, had invaded the Palatinate in support of the Imperial forces, but although the Habsburg powers frequently cooperated, their interests were not identical. Spain was not in a position to subsidise Imperial armies.)
3. A war in which Spain was defeated, or at least bothered and weakened, would help Frederick regain the Palatinate by also weakening the Empire, because King Philip IV and the Emperor Ferdinand were cousins.
   (An irrational argument unsupported by any evidence.)
4. An Anglo-Spanish sea war that led to the capture of ships from the Spanish treasure fleet would not only cover its own cost but leave most of the British participants richer.
   (Correct if the British raiders were successful, but – as subsequent events were to prove – that was a big if.)
5. The Spanish were Catholic and so God, being a Protestant sympathiser, would be pleased if they were defeated. God would also be glad to have Protestant Frederick back in power in the Palatinate.
   (Contentious as it may be, this last point was, in the view of many Parliamentarians, the strongest argument for the war.)

The pro-war or Puritan party looked back wistfully to the era of the Elizabethan sea dogs, by this time receding into legend. They dwelt especially on the splendid exploits of Sir Francis Drake. They loved the old stories of his adventures for their swaggering audacity. They liked them even more because they told of victory bought cheap. When Drake made his raids on Spanish settlements in the Americas between 1567 and 1581, he did so as a terrorist or as a 'privateer', a licensed pirate. He was not employed by Queen Elizabeth's government. He bought his own ships with money raised from private investors. He paid his own men, and hoped to make a handsome profit from loot and pillage and the taking of Spanish treasure ships as prizes. His motives were not patriotic but commercial.

When Drake's raids and robberies failed, they could be disowned by the English authorities. When they succeeded, the Queen's officers took a cut for the Exchequer. Following a similar business model, a war at sea against Spain, thought many in the English Parliament of 1624, could be fought very cheaply. It might even make a profit.

They recalled with proud nostalgia Drake's return from his circum-navigation in 1581, the hold of the *Golden Hind* crammed with enough Spanish silver to pay off the national debt. They forgot, or chose to ignore, that that stupendous success had never been repeated, by Drake or anyone else; that the English fleet assembled to defend England against the projected Spanish invasion seven years later had been extremely expensive; that after the Spanish Armada was 'defeated' – or more accurately, thwarted in its aims by bad planning and the weather – the port towns of south-east England had been full of English seamen dying in the streets, filthy, starving and unpaid.

The war Buckingham wanted was not a holy war against a Catholic enemy. It was not primarily an attempt to regain control of the Palatinate. Rather his aim was to contain the power of the Habsburgs. He told Parliament in March 1624 that the Spanish had 'vast ambitions after the western monarchy'. He saw Spain as an arrogant power intent on dominating all Europe. He was attempting to form an anti-Habsburg alliance to prevent them doing so. To that end, he was in communica-tion with the Dutch, with the Danes and the Venetians and the Duke of Savoy (all allies that Parliament would find acceptable). So far these potential allies had temporised, not quite believing that Buckingham could get the King's and Parliament's backing for his alliance, but inclined, if he could do so, to join it.

Much more problematically, Buckingham was hoping to include the Catholic power of France among his allies. Shortly after he and the Prince had returned from Spain, he sent the Earl of Carlisle as his emis-sary to Paris. Carlisle reported that the Queen Mother, Marie de Médicis, 'hath now a clear sight of the pretensions of the King of Spain unto the monarchy of Christendom'. She might be interested in bringing France into Buckingham's projected anti-Habsburg league.

Buckingham wasn't averse to Parliament's idea of sending English ships to raid Spanish ports and shipping, but for him such raids would be one aspect of a larger project. He was thinking not of Elizabethan-style derring-do, but of Europe-spanning alliances, wars fought by proxies, money deployed rather than men.

On 1 March 1624 Sir Benjamin Rudyerd opened the debate. He called upon the Commons and Lords together to petition the King to break off all dealings with Spain, 'for until it be done, his friends will hold him in continual jealousy'. How were potential allies to believe in an anti-Spanish alliance while King James was apparently still courting Spain?

Over the following days the King and his Parliament bargained hard. By mid-April Buckingham had brokered a deal whereby King James bound himself to sever relations with Spain, and Parliament voted to grant him what one historian has called 'the greatest aid which was ever granted in Parliament to be levied in so short a time'.

Buckingham went down to Chatham to review the fleet, and set in train preparations for a naval expedition – to be paid for, since the Parliamentary subsidies would take many months to collect, out of his own fortune. D'Ewes wrote that all men now hoped to see the Palatinate recovered and 'the gospel again settled in Germany by the armies and assistances of the King of Great Britain'.

The Speaker said, 'The true believers at home, and our neighbours and confederates abroad, may rejoice and sing a new song of joy.' King James noted gloomily that the promised subsidies would allow him at least to begin a war, but 'when the end will be, God knows'.

Prophecy

PARLIAMENT rejoiced at the prospect of war. The King allowed himself to be carried along, however unhappily, with Buckingham's plans. Lionel Cranfield held out. As Lord Treasurer he was responsible for the economic well-being of the nation. He saw that this war (whichever war it was to be) would be immensely expensive. He foresaw no good outcome from it. He continued to argue forcefully against it in the Council Chamber.

In April the Venetian ambassador reported, 'The Lord Treasurer is almost openly trying to oust Buckingham, assisted secretly by the Earl of Arundel.' Buckingham had known of Cranfield's opposition for months. It had been reported to him that Cranfield had 'stayed the passing' of measures he was trying to put in place, and he had received a letter from Ireland informing him that military officers and ministers there were being subjected to 'labour and art' designed to 'withdraw their affections and dependencies' from 'St George to Sir Lionel'.

Cranfield was also said to be trying a more personal method of attack. His handsome young brother-in-law, Arthur Brett, was back from his travels abroad and Cranfield was said to be 'bringing him forward'. King James took no notice, but Buckingham was annoyed.

Buckingham resolved to be rid of the long-term ally who had served him so well. His employing the tough-minded, rigorous businessman-turned-economist had been one of the best pieces of work he had ever done for King James. Now he undid it. On 5 April, one of his clients in the House of Commons brought charges of corruption against Cranfield. The Lord Treasurer would be destroyed by the same archaic process that had brought down Bacon – impeachment.

There is no evidence that Cranfield ever acted against the public interest, even if – like Bacon – he had accepted gifts and favours he would have been wiser to refuse. But he was not popular: no cost-cutting treasurer ever is. He was stiff-necked and unattractively sure of his own rectitude. The noblemen in the Lords looked down on him as a jumped-up tradesman. The Commons thought him arrogant. The charges against him were drawn up in the Commons and presented to the Lords, who found him guilty of profiteering, mismanagement and favouritism. He was deprived of his offices and imprisoned in the Tower.

King James acquiesced in his bringing-down. He defended him in the Lords, saying that some of the things of which Cranfield was accused had been performed with 'my knowledge and approbation'. But he could not, or would not, overturn a Parliamentary verdict.

He was not happy about it. He had Cranfield released after only a few days and halved his fine. Allowing Parliament to judge and condemn one of the King's great officers of state seemed to him to establish a dangerous precedent. Clarendon relates that he made two prophecies. To Buckingham: 'You are making a rod with which you will be scourged yourself.' To the future King Charles I: that he 'would live to have his bellyful of Parliaments'.

Ageing

KING James was only fifty-seven when his sweet boys came home from Spain, but he felt himself to be near death.

The illness that confined him to Theobalds throughout November of that year was the latest of many. In the summer he had written to Buckingham and Prince Charles in Madrid urging them to 'come speedily away if ye can get leave ... except ye never look to see your old dad again, whom I fear ye shall never see, if ye see him not before winter'. Two months later he wrote to Buckingham, 'If ye hasten you not home I apprehend I shall never see you, for my extreme longing will kill me.' This last might be lover's hyperbole, but James meant what he said.

He had been unwell for years – with gout, with recurrent fevers, with the consequences of drinking too much, with dreadful stomach upsets that left him shaken and exhausted.

When Queen Anne died in March 1619 he had not been there, either at his wife's deathbed or at her funeral, not because he was uncaring (though he was accused of it), but because he was so ill that he, and all his attendants, believed that he was dying too. His symptoms were alarming – continual high fever, diarrhoea, vomiting, frothing at the mouth, 'fermentation of bitter humours, boiling in his stomach', and bouts of acute pain. The physical torment was accompanied by 'dread' and 'incredible sadness'. Three weeks after Anne's death, Prince Charles, Buckingham and the entire Privy Council were called urgently to Newmarket to hear him deliver his deathbed speech, which, according to the Bishop of Lincoln, deserved to be 'written in letters of gold'. In it James called upon his heir to take to his bosom all those who had served him, 'and that disciple of his whom he so loved in particular ... the Marquis Buckingham'. He also explicitly named

Buckingham as foremost among those Councillors whom Charles should trust.

He passed three kidney stones, an agonising process. Afterwards his condition improved. He was carried in a litter to Theobalds to convalesce. John Chamberlain reports that, 'weak and weary' as he was on arrival, he would not go indoors until some of his deer had been driven past 'to make a muster before him'.

He hadn't died that time, but nor had he fully recovered. In January 1621 he was carried into the House of Lords in a chair, 'being so weak in his legs and feet', writes Chamberlain, 'that it is doubted he will find little use in them hereafter, but be altogether *perdu* that way'. He could ride. In 1622 the Venetian ambassador noted that there was still no surer way 'to divert him from doing anything than to propose hunting', but he was no longer the fearless and tireless horseman he had been. It was said that grooms ran alongside his horse, holding leading reins. In the bitter winter of 1622 he had a frightening accident while out riding alongside the New River near Theobalds. His horse stumbled. The King was thrown off onto the frozen river. The ice broke and 'he fell in so that nothing but his boots were seen'. But for the prompt action of a courtier who leapt in to pull him out, he would have drowned. As he lay on the bank 'there came much water out of his mouth and body'. He remounted and rode home in his sodden, icy-cold clothes, but it was an unsettling reminder of his mortality.

His body was frail. Unkind observers noted that his intellect was weakening too. Count Leveneur de Tillières wrote, 'It seems to me that the intelligence of this King has diminished. Not that he cannot act firmly and well at times and particularly when the peace of the kingdom is involved. But … his mind uses its powers only for a short time … His timidity increases day by day as old age carries him into apprehension and vices diminish his intelligence.' The Venetian ambassador thought he seemed 'practically lost'.

The world had changed around him. The international situation seemed progressively darker and sadder and more alien. A Venetian envoy reported, 'King James seems utterly weary of the affairs that are taking place all over the world at this time, and hates being obliged every day to spend time over unpleasant matters.' He was bothered and upset by 'requests and incitements to move in every direction, and to meddle with everything. He remarked, "I am not God Almighty."'

Once upon a time King James had thought, if not that he was the Almighty, that he was at least the Almighty's earthly representative. No longer.

Throughout the first months of 1624 James was still maintaining diplomatic relations with Madrid as with a potential ally. Buckingham, meanwhile, was calling for war to check 'the vast ambitions of Spain'. For the first time the King and favourite were openly opposed over policy, and working against each other.

They exchanged reproaches. Buckingham wrote that he had, as instructed, informed Parliament that King James had caught 'such a fierce rheum and cough' that he could not address them. He then added sarcastically, 'But I will forbear to tell them that, notwithstanding your cold, you were able to speak with the King of Spain's instruments.' The grateful deference with which the 'humble slave and dog' used to address his master was gone.

There were angry scenes. After one of them King James wrote to Buckingham protesting against his 'cruel Catonic words' and accusing him of deserting his 'maker' to cling to the rising sun, Prince Charles. Buckingham wrote back that the King had 'wilfully and unjustly ... dejected' him. They no longer trusted each other. Chamberlain thought Buckingham guarded James 'like a sentinel', and that he and Prince Charles took pains, 'with great jealousy', to isolate him. 'As though he were in a state of siege, they keep away from him those whom they consider suspect' – in other words, anyone opposed to their plans for war.

In March Buckingham wrote to James, saying he would 'wait upon you oftener', but that their disagreements were now so extreme that their meeting would only 'occasion many disputes'. There was nothing he could usefully say, 'for to be of your opinion would be flattery, and not to speak humbly mine own [opinion] would be treachery'. He ends his letter by writing that he 'will live and die a lover of you', and that he is still James's 'humble slave and dog'. But 'it is of more comfort and ease to you and safer for me that I now abide away'.

For the Spanish ambassador, the Marquis of Inojosa, the rift between King and favourite was welcome. Buckingham was now Spain's enemy. His position must be undermined and his closeness to the King destroyed.

In April 1624 Inojosa requested a private audience with King James. When it was granted he told James – as though giving the King a friendly warning – that Buckingham was a 'dangerous and ungrateful … affecter' of 'greatness and popularity'. Such generalities were constantly being alleged against the favourite, but the ambassador had more precise accusations as well. Buckingham, he told the King, was the mastermind of a 'pernicious plot against his person and royal authority'. He and his accomplices often met and 'consulted in a clandestine way'. He had befriended 'all the popular men of the state and drawn them forth out of prisons, restraints and confinements', as though he was plotting some kind of uprising.

This was alarming enough, but Inojosa also made allegations that touched King James personally.

He told James that Buckingham held him imprisoned. He said he 'bragged openly in Parliament that he had made the King yield to this and that'. Inojosa said that the country was no longer an autocracy, as a monarchy should be, but a triumvirate, and Buckingham was the most powerful of its three rulers.

All this was near enough to the truth to make King James uneasy. He told Inojosa that he had had 'good cause to suspect [Buckingham] of late'. He was troubled by his influence over Prince Charles, who had formerly been 'as well disposed as any son in Europe', but had lately been 'strangely carried away with rash and youthful counsels'.

Inojosa had more to tell him. Buckingham was plotting, he said, to put his own descendants on the throne. He alleged that Buckingham had deliberately obstructed the Spanish Match because he had a secret agreement with the Elector Frederick. The two of them were conspiring to make sure Charles would never marry, and never father heirs. Buckingham's daughter, Mary, would be married to Frederick and Elizabeth's son. Eventually, when Charles died childless, their child, grandchild to Buckingham, great-grandchild to King James, would inherit the throne of England.

James was upset by this allegation – far-fetched as it was. He was even more distressed by Inojosa's report that Buckingham and Prince Charles had agreed that, if James persisted in opposing their policies, they would make him withdraw from public life. 'They would give him a house of pleasure, whither he might retire himself to his sports.' While he amused himself there, Prince Charles 'now of years and judgement fit to govern', would take over the ruling of the country, guided and manipulated by Buckingham.

It is more than likely that Charles and Buckingham had talked about such an arrangement.

In which family, which business, which hereditary monarchy, have the younger members not discussed in advance what is to be done when the patriarch begins to fail? Tillières reports that the King was given to lamenting that 'sickness renders him incapable of deciding anything, demanding only repose and, indeed, the tomb'. James could hardly be surprised if his own complaints had led those around him to prepare themselves for some kind of regency if he became incapable of ruling, as some people thought he already was. Tillières wrote, 'The King descends deeper and deeper into folly every day, sometime swearing, and calling upon God, heaven and the angels, at other times weeping, then laughing, and finally pretending illness.'

To encourage King James, as he became more frail and weary, to live pretty much as he had always preferred to live – away from the capital, in one of the hunting lodges he loved, enjoying 'sports' – might have seemed to those around him a way of ensuring him a contented old age.

Inojosa, though, made it sound like treason and usurpation. Once James was confined to 'his house of pleasure', he suggested, Buckingham and Charles, now the King's political opponents, would be free to pursue their war plans undeterred.

James listened to Inojosa and believed him. He was angry and deeply hurt.

On St George's Day, 1624, the ninth anniversary of the day when he had welcomed Buckingham into his household, King James was sitting in his coach with Prince Charles beside him, ready to drive from Whitehall to Windsor for the Garter feast. Buckingham made as though to join them. King James stopped him, on the pretext of sending him off on some trivial errand. Buckingham burst into tears. He asked to be told what he had done wrong. James wept as well, 'crying out that he was the unhappiest alive, to be forsaken by those dearest to him'.

King and Prince drove away, leaving Buckingham standing alone.

Popularity

INOJOSA had accused Buckingham of 'popularity', a charge he indignantly denied. The meaning of the word has shifted over the last four hundred years. Now, to be 'popular' can be simply to be well liked. In the 1620s the term's significance was more precise, and more political.

Popularity, in a high-ranking member of the government, meant attaching undue importance to the wishes and requirements of the ignorant multitude. Popularity meant giving the people's demands priority over loyalty to one's king. To a monarchist, and especially to a monarch, a great man who wooed popularity was making himself the slave of *hoi polloi*. He was betraying his caste. He was committing the cardinal error of supposing that power and influence was, or should be, conferred upwards, by the election of a few by the many, rather than being graciously dispensed downwards by the head of state. He was as troublesome as the demagogues of ancient Rome, who dared bypass senatorial authority and call upon the people direct, employing what Thomas Macaulay, writing about the Stuart monarchy in the nineteenth century, was to call 'mean arts and unreasonable clamours'. He was ignoble, untrustworthy and craven. He was making the grave mistake of paying attention to public opinion, or 'vulgar opinion', of which one seventeenth-century commentator wrote, 'Nothing is so easily cheated, nor so commonly mistaken.'

In Buckingham's lifetime vulgar opinion was making itself known to an extent unprecedented in British history. A proclamation of 1620 was issued deploring that 'there is at this time a more licentious passage of lavish discourse and bold censure in matters of State' than ever before. The spread of literacy and the new-found intellectual confidence of those known as the 'middling sort' had opened the way for an outpouring of words. 'The inordinate liberty of unreverent speech ... doth daily more and more increase.'

Vulgar opinion was visible in the woodcuts illustrating printed texts, or in drawings nailed to doors and fences. It was audible from pulpits – sermons were often polemics – and in songs whistled in the streets or bellowed in taverns.

Vulgar opinion was legible in books and pamphlets and tracts and libels and flyers and news-sheets and lampoons – most of them unlicensed, most of them anonymous or pseudonymous; many printed, but others handwritten and circulated by hand. In 1620 the first coranto (a printed news magazine) appeared, published in Amsterdam and brought clandestinely into London. Within the next year numerous others arrived from abroad.

Everyone was hungry for news and raring to comment on it. A Londoner wrote in 1620, 'I cannot pass the streets but I am continually stayed by one or the other, to know what news, so that sometimes I am four hours before I can go the length of two pairs of butts.' News could be picked up from the watermen who ferried passengers down and up and across the Thames, and who had as much of a reputation for passing on the latest rumours as taxi drivers more recently did. It circulated in barbers' shops. It went back and forth between merchants and dealers at the Exchange, or between walkers in the green expanses of Moorfields north of the City of London. 'What's the best news abroad?' was a standard greeting. In Lincoln's Inn Fields the lawyers said it in Latin: '*Quid novi*?' 'The world,' wrote Robert Taylor in 1622, 'is now all ear and tongue.'

Many people were just curious, and keen to know the latest. Others were news-gatherers by profession. The country, and especially the capital, was full of 'news-hounds'. Any ambitious country gentleman needed an informant in town. Diplomats, military men, travellers of any kind hired someone to keep them abreast of shifts in policy and power. John Chamberlain was one of many performing the same function. Sir John Scudamore, MP and future ambassador, employed eight such correspondents.

There were no newspaper offices yet in Fleet Street, where they would open in the next century. But across the fetid Fleet Ditch, and just up Ludgate Hill, there was already a mart for news. It was centred on

London's premier ecclesiastical building, St Paul's – the mediaeval cathedral that would be destroyed by fire in 1666. John Chamberlain was there almost every day.

Ever since the advent of printing in the late fifteenth century, St Paul's churchyard had been the heart of the publishing trade. 'Paul's', as it was generally known, was the largest building in London, and surrounded by gardens and graveyards convenient for walking and talking in.

People went there to browse and buy books and pamphlets from the shops and stalls. Having bought, or not, they loitered to talk. And the British weather being what it was (it was colder then), they would often move indoors, into the cathedral. The central aisle, 'Paul's Walk', became their promenade.

Paul's Walk was a thoroughfare. Carters used it as a shortcut, ignoring the regulation barring donkeys.

It was a catwalk. Thomas Dekker wrote that nowhere can you see 'so many fashions, as are to be seen for nothing, every day, in Duke Humphrey's walk'. (Duke Humphrey was the occupant of a notably splendid tomb.) Dekker advised young gentleman of fashion, 'If you determine to enter into a new suit, warn your tailor to attend you in Paul's.' There, 'like a spy', tailor and client can 'discover the stuff, colour and fashion of any doublet or hose'. Young 'gallants' promenaded, their spurs jingling, only to be chased down by the choirboys, who would levy a 'spur-tax'.

It was a marketplace, its chief merchandise being literary. The antiquary and bookseller Ralph Starkey took along texts for sale – tracts too dangerously subversive to be sold in his shop, or verbatim accounts of debates in the House of Commons.

It was a place to stretch your legs. It was a social venue. It was a playground: children came there from all the adjacent parishes to run around until dusk. Men, and some women, gathered there to pass the time of day.

In the previous century Queens Mary I and Elizabeth I had each tried to discourage all these profane goings-on with decrees forbidding the 'making of bargains' and 'making of disturbances', but in vain. According to the playwright William Haughton, in Buckingham's lifetime Paul's Walk was still a kind of 'open house' filled with a 'great store of company that do nothing but go up and down, and go up and down'.

As they went up and down, they talked. The ancient building was 'the ears' brothel'. It was loud with chatter and polemic in a dozen languages. Ben Jonson called it 'a Babel of wild humours'. The cathedral had become 'the synod of all pates politic'.

A courtier, when he was not at court, was to be found, wrote one of them, 'in Paul's with a pick-tooth in his hat'. Lawyers and merchants went there daily. Ships' captains, arrived in the docks, would go straight to Paul's to pass on news of foreign affairs and get updated on news of home.

It was the fashion, wrote Francis Osborne, 'for the principal gentry, lords, courtiers, and men of all professions not merely mechanic, to meet in Paul's Church by eleven and walk in the middle aisle till twelve, and after dinner from three to six, during which times some discoursed on business, others of news'. Not everyone could tear themselves away for the dinner break. There were plenty of the news-hounds who stayed all day. They were said to 'dine with Duke Humphrey'. Not everything they heard there was true. One described the place as 'the general mint of all famous lies'. But Osborne considered the information they picked up in Paul's Walk to be pretty reliable. 'There happened little that did not first or last arrive here.'

As they walked, wrote one observer, the Paul's walkers made a ceaseless 'grumbling together'. The noise was 'like that of bees, a strange humming or buzz, mixed with walking, tongues and feet'. That 'grumbling' was subversive. King James didn't like it. He sensed it was dangerous. In 1610 Francis Bacon had listed political songs and 'false news' among the signs of imminent 'trouble'. The King agreed. He didn't like the wares for sale at Paul's. He disapproved of 'the common printing and dispersing of traitorous and seditious books and of profane and scurrilous pamphlets and libels'. He didn't like the writing and he didn't like the talk. He wrote a rhyme against rhymesters:

> Hold your prattling, spare your pen,
> Be honest and obedient men.

In 1618 a comet passed through English skies. People were afraid. They saw it as an omen, perhaps the sign of God's displeasure, or a presage of the end of the world. King James wrote another poem mocking their fears. There were other things, closer to hand, that were more worth worrying about, he suggested. Anyone who saw the comet as the Devil's work should 'walk Paul's, and meet the Devils there'.

Inojosa had suggested that Buckingham was in league with those devils. In Paul's Walk, 'vulgar opinion' was predominantly pro-war and anti-Spain, and so, now, was Buckingham.

Illness

EARLY in April 1624, Buckingham was reported to be 'ill at ease' and was 'let blood to prevent a fever'. He retired to New Hall, missing an important session in the Commons. He soon returned to court, but on St George's Day, after the King had rejected him and ridden away in his coach with Prince Charles beside him, Buckingham, deeply distressed, returned to Wallingford House and went straight to bed, turning away all visitors.

He was not yet aware of Inojosa's allegations. The next day he went after the King and Prince to Windsor, to plead for forgiveness for whatever it was the King was holding against him. He appeared distraught. He followed James around, 'inseparable as his shadow'. It did him no good. James remained aloof and suspicious. Two weeks later the court returned to Whitehall, and Buckingham took to his bed again.

Opinions differed as to whether it was his heart that was broken or his health. 'The Duke of Buckingham hath been sick above this seven-night of a fever, the jaundice and I know not what else,' wrote John Chamberlain. 'He hath been thrice let blood at least, yet the world thinks he is more sick in mind than body.' Either way, concludes Chamberlain, 'he declines apace'.

On 10 May the King's own physician, Sir Théodore de Mayerne, came to King James to tell him that his beloved Steenie might very soon die.

Théodore de Mayerne was one of the intellectual ornaments of the Jacobean court. A Huguenot born in Geneva, he was physician to King Henri IV of France until his assassination. Cosmopolitan (he studied in Heidelberg, became a feudal baron in Switzerland and married two Dutch wives) and canny in his evasion of anything that might compromise him politically, Mayerne dictated terms to the great. Everyone, he insisted, be they king or duke or archbishop, must address him in his chosen language, French. He was an open-minded rationalist at a time when medicine was a hodgepodge of the scholastically conventional and the wildly visionary. Among the ancients, he admired Hippocrates for his careful observations and ignored Galen's rigid taxonomy. Among the moderns, he took from Paracelsus, respecting his methodology, but remained sceptical of his prophecies.

As a young man, travelling through Europe in the retinue of the Duke of Rohan, he sought out 'learned men', as he later explained, to 'enrich, by their discourse, my modest store of medical knowledge'. He took careful note of machines and devices – fountains, clocks, planetaria, aqueducts and cathedral organs. He went down into a silver mine, descending by ladder and rope (it took an hour to reach the bottom), to explore the labyrinth where over two thousand miners worked daily. In Strasbourg he was impressed by the arrangement of the beds in the well-ventilated hospital. He was a practical man.

He was interested in matter, and its physical properties. At a time when medical practice seemed often to resemble a kind of poetry – medicines being formulated according to complicated symbolic codes – he insisted that bodily illness resided in the body. It was a material phenomenon and he set out to cure it by means of any material substance – animal, vegetable or mineral – that promised to combat the disease. He was thorough and methodical. He kept careful notes on his patients, their symptoms, the remedies he prescribed for them, and the outcomes of his treatment. Every one of his patients was, for him, a research project.

In 1611 he accepted King James's invitation to move to England. He treated both the King and the Queen. Soon he was the man to whom everyone turned. Court ladies bought cosmetics from him – hair-dye and rouge. He supplied the Earl of Carlisle with hand cream and toothpaste. He made the Earl of Somerset a special scent to counter the bad smell that, Somerset complained, his diamonds left on his clothes. He also saved lives.

For all his perfect physique, Buckingham was delicate. Repeatedly, he seems to have succumbed to exhaustion. He was still in his early thirties and famed for his athleticism, but in the early seventeenth century no amount of muscular strength could keep a person safe from disease. And no degree of physical fitness has been enough, in any era, to protect someone treading a political tightrope from panic attacks and nervous collapse.

Back in 1619, after the King's near-fatal illness, perhaps exhausted after attending the royal sickbed night and day, Buckingham had fallen ill in his turn. James, once recovered, visited him frequently. Buckingham got up too soon, and went out running with some of his gentlemen, 'to try his activity', only to succumb to a sequence of fainting fits. The King, reports a courtier, 'gave him a sharp, kind chiding for adventuring himself so much'.

While he was in Spain he fell ill again. Many of the British visitors came down with heatstroke or fevers. Buckingham was among them. In the last weeks he and Charles were in Madrid he kept mainly to his quarters in the Alcázar, going out, if he had to, carried in a sedan chair.

Several observers, after he returned from Spain, commented with surprise on his new-found boldness as a political manoeuvrer, but the strain told on him.

He and Prince Charles were close now. There is no evidence that their relationship was as physically intimate as that with King James had been, but the Earl of Kellie wrote, 'I can see the Prince loves him in an extraordinary degree.' Charles wrote to Buckingham, addressing him as 'sweetheart'. When Buckingham expressed anxiety that some Councillors might lie to discredit him, Charles wrote, 'I cannot think that any man is so mad as to call his own head in question by making a lie against you when all the world knows me to be your true friend.' He pressed Buckingham to 'let me know what I can do in this or anything else to serve thee'. He wrote again, 'The world shall daily know more and more that I am and ever will be your faithful, loving, constant friend.'

But Charles was younger and politically gauche. Buckingham had done well as James's deputy, but now, as the balance of power at court shifted, he was taking the lead. There were signs that it might be more than he could handle.

*   *   *

Whatever laid him low in 1624 – heartbreak, stress or physical illness –
it was debilitating and dangerous. It was also a stroke of great good luck.

King James was moved by suffering. Vulnerability touched him, and
stirred his love. He liked to nurse and to be nursed. He was very interested in plasters and possets and all the paraphernalia of the sickroom.
He liked to try new remedies. He visited the sick assiduously. Once,
when Somerset was still his favourite, James had a bad fall from his
horse. Somerset didn't come to him afterwards. The King remembered,
and one of the reproaches he made when they parted was that the
younger man had neglected to 'comfort' him then, 'though I gave you
far contrary proof after your fall'. He was not one to downplay a physical ailment, or to neglect one in a dear one.

Chance, in making Buckingham seriously ill, had found him the right
road to reconciliation with the King.

When Mayerne told James that Buckingham had been feverish in the
night, that he was passing saffron-coloured 'yellow bile' and his life was
in danger, the King at once forgot all his suspicions, all his resentments.
He went straight to Wallingford House and spent three hours at his
beloved's bedside.

Over the next days, according to Sir John Coke, he 'hath shown great
tenderness over him and sendeth unto him three or four times every
day'. He sent cherries, grapes, peaches and – a more choice gift – the
eyes, the tongue and the testicles of a deer he had killed himself in
Eltham Park. He set a guard on Wallingford House to keep away the
suitors who tried to disturb the invalid's rest. He refused to meet the
Spanish ambassador. 'If I see Padre Maestro,' he explained, 'it will kill
the Duke with grief.' He let Inojosa know that he had found such 'clear-
ness of ingenuity' in Buckingham as to feel entirely sure he was innocent
of everything the Spaniard had alleged against him.

He was ready to compromise, or even to abandon relations with
Spain. He was ready to do much more. He knelt beside Buckingham's
bed, praying to God to cure his beloved, and offering, if this was what
the deity required, to take the illness upon himself.

Out of danger after two weeks, but still drastically enfeebled –
whether by illness or by the doctors' bloodletting, or both – Buckingham
tried to return to work. He was carried in a sedan chair to visit Prince
Charles at St James's Palace. The King took him to Greenwich, helping

him into the royal carriage 'with his own hand', and then escorting him in his own royal barge downriver.

Once there, Buckingham was laid low by fever again and went home, writing to explain to the King that he was exhausted by his suppliants' demands. 'Though your extraordinary care and watchful eye over me would keep them from speaking with me, yet in a court I must needs look many of them in the face.' Accepting that his recovery could not be rushed, he went to New Hall with Katherine and little Mall, and there – slowly, slowly – he recovered his strength.

As well as Mayerne, he was attended by five learned physicians, who diagnosed jaundice. He also sought help from other, less conventional healers.

He called in a local man whose ministrations he found helpful, a Dr Remington of Dunmow. The title of 'doctor' was self-awarded – Remington had had no formal training. He was one of a legion of practitioners of the period operating in the borderlands between medicine, witchcraft and the ancient science of herbalism. He had been recommended by the Earl of Warwick and was trusted by other reputable folk in Essex. His usual treatment for a fever was to give the patient a medicinal drink, or 'posset', and a poultice, or 'plaster', to be tied to the patient's wrist, and so 'communicate their virtues into the heart by those notable arteries'. It seemed an innocuous process, which might do good. Buckingham tried it on himself and would later – with disastrous consequences – recommend it to the King.

Dr Remington appeared to be respectable enough; not so the other person to whom Buckingham turned in his illness. He wrote to James about someone he was consulting, whom he refererred to as 'my devil'. This devil claimed to have found the formula for the philosopher's stone. He also concocted medicines that impressed Buckingham so greatly that he paid the man the large sum of £400 for his services, and sent one of his potions to King James, saying that it would 'preserve you from all sickness ever hereafter'.

The devil may have been an Irishman called Piers Butler, who claimed to have 'strange faculties' and concocted potions out of the 'distilled spirit of toads'. The Venetian ambassador reported that he was a magician and that 'the Duke gives him a handsome salary'. Others described Butler variously as a charlatan or as a witch suspected of 'hidden sorcery and diabolical compact'. He was volatile and by no means a loyal supporter of Buckingham's. He once pulled a bullet from his pocket while drinking in a cellar and announced that he should have used it to kill the Duke. He was also later to boast he had given Buckingham some kind of magical charm or amulet. 'The King and Parliament could do nothing to the Duke,' he said, 'so long as he keeps one thing.'

Or the 'devil' Buckingham was referring to may have been the man known as the 'Duke's wizard', John Lambe.

While Buckingham languished, the King wrote to him repeatedly. 'Alas, sweet heart, thy letter yesternight made my heart to bleed.' 'God bless thee, and all thine, and send thee health and heart, to the comfort of thy dear dad.'

He fussed over him. 'Take the air only discreetly, and piece and piece [a little bit at a time].' 'For God's sake and mine, keep thyself very warm, especially thy head and thy shoulders.' He advised him on his treatment. 'For God's sake be as wary as thou can with drugs and physicians, for they are but for cases of necessity.' He sent him instructions on diet, and on his daily routines of rest and exercise. He sent him partridges and hares. He sent him pears and 'sugared beans' and strawberries and rasp-berries and 'an excellent Barbary melon'. He prayed for his full recovery. 'Let my last compliment stick to thy heart till we may have a sweet and comfortable meeting, which God send, and give thee grace to bid the drugs adieu this day.'

The King's heart was once more entirely Buckingham's. He poured out his love, piling up repeated words in an attempt to convey the inten-sity of his feelings. 'Blessing, blessing, blessing on thy heartroots.' He asked for love in return. 'Love me still and still.' The letter in which he addresses Buckingham as 'my sweet child and wife' was probably writ-ten in this period.

Buckingham's illness had brought James up against the possibility that his beloved might be snatched from him by death. The thought was unbearable. The letter ends with a fervent prayer for the long continu-ance of their happy togetherness. James signed it initially 'your dear dad and master. James R.' Then, on second thoughts, he crossed out 'master' and wrote 'husband' instead.

*   *   *

By mid-June Buckingham was back at court. Sir Thomas Wentworth thought him 'much discoloured and lean with sickness', but however much his health might be weakened, his hold on King James's love was fully restored. As he knelt before James, his hat off and his hands held up as though in prayer, a courtier reports that the King, 'the tears breaking down upon his cheeks while he was speaking', said, 'Steenie I pray God either to recover thee of this sickness or else to transfer the same upon me, as one that would stand in the gap for thee.' Thereafter there were 'one hundred kisses at the least', and the King was 'continually hanging about his neck'.

The irrepressible Arthur Brett made a further attempt to catch the King's eye. When James was hunting in Waltham Forest one day, Brett suddenly stepped out of the woods and grabbed at his bridle. For a King who lived in daily fear of assassination, it must have been a terrifying moment. James spurred his horse and galloped off, then commanded an attendant to remove Brett from the field. Later the importunate young man was arrested.

Buckingham was once more safely enthroned in King James's heart, and in the seat of power. One courtier wrote that summer, 'He knows himself fixed past jeopardy of relapsing.' 'No man goeth free', wrote Archbisop Abbot, 'that doth not stoop sail to that castle.'

As before, James's love for his favourite spilt out over the favourite's family. He wrote to Katherine often, and she wrote what Buckingham calls 'love-letters' to him. In letter after letter, King James enquires after Buckingham's womenfolk. He invites them to meet him in Windsor, bringing their bows, for some hunting. He still calls them 'cunts', but – recoil as modern readers must from such wording – it expressed no hostility on his part. He writes, 'I must quarrel with thee that, though in both my former letters I prayed thee to bring the cunts with thee, thou hast not,' and then, again, 'I would have thee bring all the cunts with thee (I mean thy wife, thy mother and thy sister), that our joy may be the more full at our happy meeting.'

The two men resumed their mutual teasing, Buckingham once daring to suggest that James's 'natural affections and appetite' were those of a toad. Or the scrawled word may even be 'turd'. Either way the joke is earthy and intimate.

Relationships within the little group were protean. Buckingham might be King James's 'wife', but he was also his 'sweet child'. Along with the two of them, the Villiers women made up another idiosyncratic family within which James relaxed, made jokes, felt loved and loving. He was happy again.

A new French ambassador, arriving in London that summer, reported that the King loved Buckingham so dearly that he let him do what he liked, and saw everything through his eyes. Prince Charles likewise looked on him as 'the sole source of his happiness and contentment'. Clarendon was to write much later that, beloved as he was by father and son alike, Buckingham could no more avoid his promotions and titles and wealth 'than a man sitting in the sun in the sweltering dog-days of late summer can help getting warm'. He 'needed no ambition, who was so seated in the hearts of two such masters'.

The French Match

THROUGHOUT the period of his illness and convalescence, Buckingham was working.

He was working as Lord Admiral. He set in hand an ambitious programme of shipbuilding and renovation, to make the fleet ready for action.

He was working as a diplomat, putting together his anti-Habsburg alliance and attempting to persuade the French king to join it.

He was working as a marriage broker. Another future queen had to be found for Prince Charles. She would be the French princess Henrietta Maria, whom Buckingham and Charles had seen dancing when they were en route for Spain.

In the spring of 1624 two British ambassadors went to Paris to prepare the ground for a French marriage and a French alliance.

The first to arrive was Henry Rich, Earl of Holland, described by Balthazar Gerbier as 'a person who from his birth had been fashioned of wax, of silk, and all covered with beauty-patches, dredged with powders, embalmed with perfumes like the concubines of the Kings of Persia'. Holland was 'governed by fops and postboys', but also 'charmed by women'. He was soon having an affair with the Duchess of Chevreuse, head of the French queen's household, one of the most influential people at the French court.

Holland was joined by James Hay, the Earl of Carlisle, husband of Buckingham's probable mistress, the former Lucy Percy. Carlisle was older and cannier than Holland, but he was another fancy dresser (the two ambassadors were described as engaging in a 'fashion war').

Carlisle had once been a favourite of King James's. Holland had reportedly thrown away his chance of achieving that status when he wiped his mouth and spat after receiving one of the King's slobbery kisses. Carlisle had been less fastidious, and after he had been supplanted as favourite he had remained at the centre of the Jacobean court. It was Carlisle who, on meeting the Infanta Maria, had found her as immobile as a plaster saint, and who had nearly started a fire in the Alcázar with the smouldering ash from his pipe.

Holland and Carlisle were both close to Buckingham. When Buckingham began to lay siege to Carlisle's wife, Carlisle seems to have resigned himself to being cuckolded by one who could compensate for the humiliation by advancing his career. In the Privy Council, he invariably backed whatever policy Buckingham was promoting, and during a public quarrel with another courtier he declared his allegiance. Gesturing towards Buckingham, he said, 'I am so much this noble lord's servant that I will perform whatsoever he commands me.'

These two ambassadors were in Paris to negotiate the marriage and alliance that Buckingham wanted. It was the Spanish Match all over again: the princess whose hand could only be bought with the suspension of penal laws against the English Catholics; the English Parliament's inflexible opposition to such a measure; the necessity of a papal dispensation.

This time, though, there was at least some shared ground on which an alliance could be founded. A French minister wrote to the ambassador in London, saying that Louis XIII – like Buckingham – detested the Spaniards (despite being married to one – his queen was the Infanta Maria's sister), and that he aimed to 'restrain their unbridled passion for domination'.

In the early summer of 1624 Count Ernst von Mansfeld arrived in England seeking employment.

Mansfeld was the most feared and admired of the era's mercenary commanders. Europe was by this time engulfed by war, but still few states had a standing army. Wars were fought by ad hoc task forces, by volunteers hoping to make a fortune from looting and hostage-taking, or by troops of mercenaries put together by warlords-for-hire like Mansfeld. His reputation was formidable but grim. An Englishman who served under him in Germany left a journal recording the campaign, including this account of the taking of a town: 'We entered killing man, woman and child: the execution continued the space of two hours, the pillaging two days.'

Military expeditions were undertaken with little thought for logistics. Fighting men 'lived off the land' by stealing peasants' seed corn and driving away their cattle. (And, too often, raping their wives and forcibly enlisting their sons.) Even when troops were comparatively well disciplined, their very presence was destructive. They trampled crops and muddied springs. The arrival of an army was an event to be dreaded. Mansfeld won battles, but at such a cost in terms of farmland devastated and civilians starving, that the Elector Frederick, who employed him for a while, eventually dispensed with his services and begged him to go away.

He had fought for the Bohemian rebels, then for the Emperor against the Bohemian rebels. Leaving the Palatinate, Mansfeld offered his services to the Dutch Republic and fought the Spanish on their behalf in a series of successful actions that made him, by the time he came to London, a Protestant hero (despite his being Catholic).

His visit was seen as a heaven-sent stroke of luck. He was given a hero's welcome. Prince Charles invited him to stay in St James's Palace, in the lavishly decorated rooms that had been prepared for the Infanta, and entertained him with a sequence of feasts. He presented a solution to the conundrum of how exactly the longed-for but ill-defined war was to be fought.

Soon, under intense pressure from Parliament and from Buckingham, King James had agreed to employ Mansfeld to command a force 'for re-establishing the public peace [a brief so capacious as to be meaningless] and recovering the Palatinate [a clearly defined war aim that was almost certainly unachievable]'. It was a triumph for the war party.

Mansfeld's services were expensive. Buckingham's ambassadors in Paris were given new instructions. They were to ask King Louis for immediate aid. Buckingham proposed a Mansfeld-led military operation to drive the Imperial, Spanish and Bavarian forces out of the Palatinate, to be jointly funded by France and England. Mansfeld would be commissioned to raise 12,000 foot soldiers in England. He would cross the Channel to be met by 3,000 French cavalry. The combined force would then proceed through France towards the Palatinate.

King Louis did not leap at this suggestion. It was true that he sought to contain Habsburg ambitions, but his Catholic allies would not like to see him in league with English heretics. He equivocated. Eventually he said he would provide troops and funds for Mansfeld's army, but he would not put his hand to any written agreement.

King James did not find such an arrangement satisfactory. He would not commit himself to an aggressive campaign for which he might be required to foot the entire bill. He threatened to pull out entirely. The Count of Gondomar was coming back to England. Rumour reported that he carried 'peace and the Palatinate' in his pocket. Perhaps the Spanish Match could be revived?

Prince Charles, exasperated, demanded another audience and told his father that he would most definitely never, ever marry the Infanta, and that if his French marriage was to fall through as a result of his father's dithering, he would be left without a suitable bride. James gave in. Preparations for Mansfeld's campaign might proceed.

They did so slowly or not at all. Those who had seen Buckingham as a merely decorative figure were now learning how much depended on his energy and authority. Dudley Carleton's nephew wrote, 'Until he [Buckingham] be well, all business suffers extreme delays.'

In Paris, negotiations continued. In June 1624, King Louis summoned the British ambassadors and stated his terms for the marriage treaty. King James must commit himself to suspend all penal laws against British Catholics. That old story.

Carlisle and Holland replied that King James could make no such promise. King Louis said that without such concessions he had little hope of getting the necessary papal dispensation. Without the dispensation the marriage was off, and so was the alliance.

Impasse. But by this time Buckingham was more practised in the ways of diplomacy than he had been when wrestling with Olivares the previous year. He had learnt there were ways of saying while simultaneously not-saying. He had become acquainted with the concept of deniability. He had been introduced to the usefulness of back channels.

Late in June Tillières, the French ambassador, was recalled to France. He had been, wrote the Earl of Kellie, 'too much Jesuited and not fit for our purpose'. It was to be hoped that the new ambassador, the Marquis d'Effiat, might be more amenable.

Buckingham flattered d'Effiat. He treated him as his dear friend and confidant. He told the ambassador how hard he had worked to persuade King James to cut off relations with Spain, how much he personally longed for the alliance with France, how greatly he hoped that the French would be ready to make concessions so that the treaty could be finalised, how he would do everything he could to bring about that happy outcome.

D'Effiat was dazzled. He wrote to King Louis saying that Buckingham was the unchallenged ruler of England and that the ministers were all his creatures. Louis was impressed. He wrote to Buckingham in his own hand, addressing him as 'mon cousin'.

Holland came over from Paris expressly to report that the French first minister had told him, discreetly and confidentially, that the matter of the English Catholics need not be mentioned in the marriage treaty. All that was required was a letter from King James – to be shown to the Pope – promising that his Catholic subjects would not be persecuted in future. This would be enough to produce the dispensation for the marriage, and once that was secured, the matter could be quietly dropped.

This looked like a way forward.

In July the court left London for the summer. King James went first to Apethorpe, still one of his favourite places to visit while on progress. Over the previous two years a splendid new wing had been added to the house, the King having provided materials and funds for it. As well as a Long Gallery and a Great Chamber, it includes two magnificent bedrooms, both ornamented with marble reliefs and coved ceilings and cornices all lavishly decorated with plaster strap-work and heraldic devices and mermaids and fabulous beasts. Recent restoration work has uncovered a hidden passage-way leading from one room to another. One is the King's Chamber. The other, slightly larger, one is dominated by a carved overmantel featuring a ship in full sail – fit tribute to a Lord Admiral. It is known as the Duke's Chamber. Buckingham would have slept there that summer of 1624, before escorting King James to Burley, only twelve miles off, where the Buckinghams were ready to entertain the court royally, having ordered in a great store of venison and fish, musk melons and Colchester oysters.

Anti-Spanish feeling was becoming fiercer. Thomas Scott imagined Gondomar returning to England and spying out every 'fortification, haven, creek or landing place about the coast', ready for a Spanish invasion. Another pamphleteer described him as sneaking into England, entering the 'cabinet of secrets' like 'an old rat, feeding on a Parmesan cheese'.

In August 1624, Sir John Holles took a boat across the Thames to the Globe Theatre, to see the show that all London was talking about. He found the playhouse 'so thronged that by scores they came away for want of place'.

Written by Thomas Middleton, *A Game at Chess* is a satirical allegory of recent Anglo-Spanish relations. It is crude, salacious, virulently anti-papist. Its humour is savage. The London audiences loved it.

The White House, representing the English, are virtuous. The Black House (Spanish) are corrupt and deceitful. All of the latter are the creatures of Ignatius Loyola, the Spanish-born founder of the Jesuit order. Attended by Error, Loyola speaks a prologue, in which he explains that his emissaries have 'made dark the land like Egyptian grasshoppers'. But they have failed to make much headway in England, a place of light and

'truth and goodness never yet deflowered'. (The Jesuits had been expelled from England four months previously.)

The plot is bawdy. It concerns attempts by a male Black Pawn (cynical and treacherous) to seduce and, when that fails, rape a female White Pawn (pious, naive). What made the play the talk of the town, though, were the comparatively short passages in which the grandees of the two 'houses' come on stage.

The Black Knight is a cruel caricature of Gondomar. He tends to speak directly to the audience, gloating over his villainies. He boasts of having administered 'mortal poison' to gullible members of the White House, 'and what I have done, I have done facetiously, with pleasant subtlety and bewitching courtship'. Gondomar's disability meant that when his pain was at its worst he couldn't sit in a normal chair. The Black Knight was carried on stage in 'an open chair for ease of that part'. Spectators at the Globe found this hilarious.

The White Duke is Buckingham. He and the White Knight (Prince Charles) are both deferential to their king, and generally on the side of honour and honesty, although (in keeping with the generally prurient tone of the play) the White Duke is over-inclined to 'venery'.

For nine days the play was a sell-out success. The Spanish ambassadors protested vehemently. On the tenth day of its run, obeying orders from above, the Lord Chamberlain closed it down.

A Game at Chess would be reprinted three times in the following year. Thomas Scott brought out a new pamphlet in which he hailed Buckingham as a 'noble, wise and a generous prince', whose faithful service had kept Prince Charles safe in Madrid and who was now, deservedly in Scott's opinion, rewarded with 'general love'. In a verse libel, Buckingham was hailed as a new Sir Walter Raleigh and likened to Scipio, the Roman commander who had triumphed over Carthage. The poet addressed King James, urging him to unleash Buckingham:

> Give him but force his own head to maintain,
> And like brave Scipio he will sack proud Spain.

The negotiations for the French Match were almost as frustrating as those for the Spanish Match, but after much coming and going of letters, ambassadors and private emissaries, it became understood by Buckingham and King James on the one hand, and King Louis on the other, that alongside the official treaty of marriage and alliance there would be another, secret agreement. It would be shown to the Pope but its existence would not be made known to the English people, or Parliament, or even the Privy Council.

In December 1624, King James, Prince Charles and Buckingham travelled from Newmarket, where the King was now spending almost all his time, to meet the French ambassadors in Cambridge. There they ceremoniously accepted the marriage articles and there as well they signed the secret document, the *Écrit Particulier*. The business was conducted so surreptitiously that Archbishop Abbot complained there were now two councils in England and 'that of Newmarket was the higher'. 'This makes me believe that the same course goes on now with the French that was concluded with the Spaniard,' wrote the Earl of Kellie. He was right.

The forthcoming marriage between Prince Charles and Princess Henrietta Maria was announced. The organs in London's churches, St Paul's included, were played for two hours 'on their loudest pipes'. Bells pealed out. But Privy Councillors complained that they had been kept so deeply in the dark over the marriage negotiations that when they saw bonfires light up the sky, they had to send out their servants to ask what was being celebrated.

Simonds D'Ewes wrote, 'The English generally so detested the Spanish match as they were glad of any other which freed them from the fear of that.' But for all the public merry-making, 'wiser men feared much danger would ensue to the Gospel and true religion by this marriage'.

Nearly a year earlier, Holland, newly arrived as ambassador in Paris, had watched Henrietta Maria, dressed as a sunflower, dance in a masque to celebrate the arrival of spring and judged her 'a lady of as much loveliness … as any creature under heaven'. Soon, inflamed by Holland's reports, Prince Charles had begun exchanging miniature portraits with her, falling in love with her from afar as he had fallen in love with the Infanta, and gazing at her picture for hours on end, while King James was writing to her optimistically as 'Dear Daughter'.

Now, with the marriage articles agreed, Charles, throwing himself once more into the role of bridegroom, sent one of his gentlemen to France with a love letter and a 'rich and rare jewel' for his bride.

Gerbier in France

BUCKINGHAM would soon be going to Paris to bring home Prince Charles's new wife. Balthazar Gerbier had been reconnoitring the ground for him. Very promising he found it. He wrote back to Buckingham, 'I never could have thought that they had so many rare things in France!'

Through the winter of 1624/25 Gerbier travelled back and forth across the Channel, bearing messages from Buckingham to the new man of power in Paris, Cardinal Richelieu, and gaining entrée to the great Parisian houses. He wrote, 'All the people here are so fine and so gilded and so curious in their homes that Your Excellency will be much pleased.' The apartments of the Bishop of Paris met with his especial approval. 'You will see in what nice order the pictures are arranged and how rich everything is.' He also had good things to say about the house in which Buckingham would stay when he arrived in Paris in his turn. 'Your Excellency will see how at the home of the Duke of Chevreuse the best pictures are over the chimney piece, and will prove what I always said, that one always puts the principal piece there.' Buckingham might be his 'Excellency', but when it came to the acquisition and display of paintings, Gerbier knew best.

As he came and went, often hampered by muddy roads and stormy seas, Gerbier was making some exciting additions to Buckingham's collection. In Paris that winter he bought:

> A *Head of Medusa* (head by Rubens, snakes by Snyders). The Dutch poet and diplomat Constantijn Huygens, seeing this painting in Rubens's studio, had reacted strongly to the 'horror' of the decapitated head, but was also 'moved by the lifelikeness and beauty with which the grim subject is

rendered'. In York House it would be hung behind a velvet curtain to save visitors the shock of coming across it unprepared.

Danae and the Shower of Gold. 'The most beautiful piece of Tintoretto,' wrote Gerbier. 'A naked figure, that flint as cold as ice might fall in love with it.'

A Raphael *Madonna* 'which is repainted by some devil who I trust was hanged, but still it is lovely, and the drawing so fine that it is worth a thousand crowns'.

A *Crucifixion with the Virgin and St John* by Michelangelo (many of Gerbier's attributions have been questioned or disproved by modern art historians). 'It should be seen kneeling ... it is the most divine thing in the world. I have been such an idolator as to kiss it three times.'

A *Pietà* by Andrea del Sarto, now one of the jewels of the Kunsthistorisches Museum in Vienna, where the greater part of Buckingham's collection eventually ended up (Plate 11).

Titian's double portrait *Cardinal Georges d'Armagnac and his secretary Guillaume Philandrier* (see page 127). When Buckingham first saw it, Gerbier found his response disappointing. 'I beg Your Excellency to look at it a little more at your leisure.' Sometimes the master needed guidance from the man.

In general, though, the man was exultant. He wrote to Buckingham from Paris. 'Our pictures,' (note the pronoun – to Gerbier the things he bought for Buckingham were his as well), 'if they were to be sold a century after our death, would sell ... for three times more than they cost.' He was a connoisseur with an excellent eye and he was also a businessman with a sharp nose for a promising investment. And he had only just begun. 'If Your Excellency will give me time to mine quietly, I will fill New Hall with paintings so that foreigners will come there in procession.'

Another of Gerbier's letters, written to Buckingham from France that winter, shows how art might change hands as items of exchange in the entangled systems of finance, politics, favour and corruption.

It is November 1624. Gerbier recounts, helter-skelter in his idiosyncratic French, how he is so excited by his news that he has galloped

through storm and flood 'with all speed' from Paris to Boulogne, intending to find a ship and hurry over to London to deliver his message to
Buckingham in person, but he has been foiled by rough seas and
contrary winds and an upset stomach so ... he's writing, and he wants
... needs ... *must have* ... a 'prompt reply' because there is a certain
person called President Chevalier who has some 'large and rare paintings', and some antique heads in marble and bronze, that the President
has previously had no intention of selling but which Gerbier is
convinced could be obtained with a 'scheme', and he reveals, with
breathless impatience, that he has such a scheme, and 'I have sworn to
myself, as I did about the Prelate of Venice, that we *must* have them or
I lack invention, for as they are the ornament of a handsome house in
France, they *must* be jewels at York House.' So ... the good news is that
a mysterious stranger has called on Gerbier in Paris and has intimated
to him, after a lot of coy circumlocution, that though the President is
not interested in selling, he might perhaps be prepared to *give* his
pictures to Buckingham free of charge – and to throw in 50,000 francs
worth of tapestries designed by Raphael and 15,000 livres in cash – if
Buckingham will only undertake to intercede with the French authorities to drop charges against a certain person – a nobody of a clerk but
one whose case, if too closely looked into, would prove embarrassing to
all sorts of somebodies including the President.

So ... Gerbier, as he explains to his 'sweet lord and more than father',
has of course told the stranger that Buckingham is an 'enemy of all that
is base and low' and not in the slightest bit mercenary, and justice is
justice, and so forth, but, on the other hand, on further reflection, he,
Gerbier, can't help thinking that doing a humble clerk a good turn
would surely not be a sin, and 'no shame attaches to one who intercedes
for a pardon' (which would really be the charitable act of a good
Christian), and, actually, now he comes to think of it, a generous gift
offered as a token of the President's profound admiration and respect
for Buckingham is not really such a bad thing, is it? Because, after all,
'even the gods refuse not offerings'. So ... could Buckingham think it
over and send an answer instructing Gerbier whether to accept the deal
within a fortnight please, or better still much *much* sooner, because
otherwise Gerbier thinks the President's emissary will turn to the Queen
Mother (Marie de Médicis) instead, and that would be a crying shame
because with these extra pictures the walls of York House could be

splendidly 'dressed' – otherwise 'poor blank walls, they will die of cold this winter', despite the fact that Gerbier has bought, in Paris, lots and lots and lots of other artworks.

In other news, Gerbier feels sure that Buckingham has only to ask, and M. de Montmorency will give him two of Michelangelo's slaves. And … and … and there is so much more Gerbier has to say because 'I have not passed one hour without searching out some rarity.' Oh, and, by the way, the 'Secretary of Titian' is already on its way to London, and 'It is a jewel.'

There's a lot that's questionable in this letter, but there is also exuberance and what sounds like the kind of affectionate double-talk that goes with friendship. One of the things King James had first found delightful in Buckingham was the way the young favourite was uncowed by his majesty. One of the things Buckingham in turn enjoyed about Gerbier was the way the picture-hunter addressed him without undue deference, as his partner in the chase.

We do not know whether Buckingham interceded for the clerk, and received the handsome reward Chevalier was offering. We do know that Titian's 'Secretary' is indeed a jewel. Inigo Jones (once more the arbiter) was one of the first people to whom Gerbier showed it and, tetchy and jealous of competition as Jones could be, he almost (according to Gerbier) 'fell to his knees' and worshipped.

The Disasters of War I

THE negotiations over the royal marriage were entangled with those over French participation in Mansfeld's projected military operation. While, in Paris, English ambassadors and French ministers hedged and fenced and wrangled, the summer of 1624 – the campaigning season – passed. All over the war zone prudent military commanders began seeking winter quarters for their armies. The expedition led by Mansfeld had yet to set out. With every month that went by, its chances of success dwindled.

October 1624. King Louis XIII summoned Carlisle and Holland and told them he agreed to the following:

1. That he would pay a half-share of the costs of Count Mansfeld's expedition for six months.
2. That he would give Mansfeld permission to land his troops at Calais or Boulogne.
3. That he would employ Mansfeld solely for the relief of the Palatinate.

(This last clause was necessary, judged the English negotiators, to prevent the French acting like a house owner who, when builders arrive to mend the roof, says, 'And, while you are here, could you just fix the chimney and throw up a new guest wing as well?' thus greatly adding to the final cost and diverting the workers' energies away from their projected task.)

There was no written agreement. There was no formal military alliance. Carlisle was for walking away, but Buckingham overruled him and persuaded King James that King Louis's word was enough. Secretary

Conway wrote to Carlisle and Holland telling them that the British government 'prize words spoken to you equal with letters graven in marble'. The marriage and the Mansfeld expedition would both proceed.

November. The Privy Council wrote to the Lord Lieutenants of all the English counties ordering them to conscript soldiers. They felt it necessary to add that the men enlisted should be 'of able bodies and years meet for this employment'. The trained bands, the nearest thing that England had to a professional fighting force, were not to be called upon, but retained ready to repel a possible Spanish invasion.

December. King James had given Mansfeld funding for his advance expenses. Mansfeld used it to buy arms and equipment, but insisted he was not responsible for the men until they arrived in Dover, the official rendezvous.

Before they had even left their own counties, the conscripts – unpaid and unfed – began to desert. Those who marched off to Dover, escorted like gangs of convicts by the more reliable trained bands, 'straggle up and down,' according to a report to the Privy Council, 'and not only spoil and take what they list, but do also terrify the poorer sorts of inhabitants and molest and offend all that pass upon the highway'.

Mansfeld, and the English officers serving under him, set about the task of transforming these conscripts into soldiers. One observer wondered 'what miracles can possibly be wrought now by them (being untrained and undisciplined) in this rotten time of winter'.

A naval captain wrote that the troops were more troublesome than the notorious pirates of Dunkirk. The people of Kent longed to be rid of them. They asked that they be sent immediately off to sea, and good riddance. But there arose a difficulty.

King Louis had assured the British ambassadors that the task force would be employed only for its designated task in the Palatinate, and that they could land in Calais or Boulogne. He went back on the first of those pledges, asking that before the army set out for the Rhineland it might be used to relieve the Dutch city of Breda, besieged by Spanish troops. King James refused. In that case, said King Louis, going back on his second pledge, they would not be welcome in France. Carlisle wrote furiously to Buckingham about 'the inconstancy and perfidiousness of those with whom we have to do'. Buckingham's anti-Habsburg alliance was falling apart before his expedition even crossed the Channel. Weeks went by.

In January 1625 a number of Councillors had a meeting with Prince Charles. Charles spoke of the great expedition in preparation and asked for their help and support for it. The Councillors listened silently, until the Earl of Arundel spoke up to say that though the Councillors could see what was going on, they didn't know how it had been decided upon. They had not been consulted. Only if they were taken into the Prince's confidence, he said, would they be able to offer advice.

The decision to send Mansfeld and his makeshift army overseas had been made by the favourite, the Prince and the King without any of the normal consultations. The negotiations with France on the alliance and marriage had gone equally unexamined and undiscussed by Parliament, or by the Privy Council.

Buckingham was now more powerful than ever before, but in choosing to rule so high-handedly, bypassing Parliament and Council, he was also on the way to losing power's essential props.

The people were as unhappy as the Councillors. Those Hispanophobe English Protestants who had been, less than a year ago, so eager to trounce the Spanish and regain the Palatinate were having an unpleasant introduction to the realities of military action. One of those realities was how much money it cost. By the end of 1624, nearly a quarter of the generous subsidy Parliament had voted through earlier in the year had already been spent, and Mansfeld's fleet had not even got to sea. Worse – the expedition was not the Anglo-Spanish sea war that Parliament had wanted.

King James received an anonymous letter begging him to revert to his peace policy because 'those very tongues which ... did cry "War! War! War!"' would 'now curse him that urgeth for one poor subsidy to raise a war'.

January 1625. Buckingham wrote to Mansfeld, still in Dover, ordering him to set sail, with or without the French king's permission to land on the other side. 'Provisions are being wasted, and the whole design will go up in a puff of smoke if Your Excellency does not take a decision to leave immediately for Calais.'

Mansfeld would not go. He had received letters from King Louis – his other employer in this venture – expressly forbidding him to land in France. He needed the two kings to reach an agreement. He wrote to Buckingham saying he could not sail up and down the Channel waiting indefinitely until they did so. He could, however, proceed, he suggested, to Holland, helped by the prevailing winds, and land there.

To give up the project entirely would be an ignominious waste of money and men, and a terrible humiliation for Buckingham – 'my industries made vain, my judgement infinitely charged'. And if the troops did not go abroad, where would they go? Publicly Buckingham boasted of their valour. In a private letter he called them 'scum'. He was fully alive to the 'oppression to the country' if they were to be cut loose in Kent. Reluctantly, he agreed to Mansfeld's plan, and talked Prince Charles and the King into doing so too.

At the end of January, in bitter weather, the ships left Dover for the Dutch coast. An English agent travelling with Mansfeld wrote, 'If I understand any thing, this army will come to nothing.'

Some of the troops were allowed to land at Walcheren, in Holland. Others were sent on to Geertruidenberg. There a severe frost made it impossible for the men to disembark. Confined to the ships, hundreds of them died of disease. Their bodies were thrown overboard, washed up on the shore and left to lie in rotting heaps. The stench was appalling. Huge burial pits were dug. Survivors, going inland at last, found that the countryside had been stripped bare by the Prince of Orange's men, passing through it before them. They were cold. They were starving.

Mansfeld was for marching on Breda, as King Louis wished, but King James forbade it. As the great ones dithered and disagreed, the men still living deserted. The army disintegrated, without a blow struck or a battle fought. Dudley Carleton wrote that it had vanished like smoke, 'many being dead, some fled, and a great part of the remainder sick'. An English officer serving under Mansfeld wrote home, 'We die like dogs.'

The expedition that had been designed to show that England was a great and aggressive power again had ended in an inept and ghastly whimper. John Chamberlain wrote that 'it will quite discourage our people to be thus sent to the slaughter, or rather to famine and pestilence … The basest people in matter of courage dare brave and trample upon us now.'

*   *   *

Buckingham's diplomacy had gone almost as badly as his war-making. When King Louis reneged on his agreement, Carlisle and Holland wrote to Buckingham raging against the 'indiscreet and insolent presumption' of France's 'unworthy false ministers'. The French reported that the papal dispensation for the marriage had arrived, but with requests for various amendments in favour of Catholicism and France. The English party disbelieved them – Buckingham having heard from his agent in the Vatican that the Pope had made no such requests. Buckingham was now calling the French negotiators 'shitten mouths'. King James mocked him, asking, 'Where is your glorious match with France? And your royal Frank Monsieurs?'

No Palatinate. No alliance. All the months of scheming and travelling and bargaining had come to just one thing, a wife for Charles. The marriage at least was going ahead.

Buckingham was going to France (without the Prince this time) to stand proxy for Charles at the wedding and to bring home the new Princess of Wales. He ordered sumptuous suits, all of the finest textiles, slashed and puffed and beribboned and decorated with jewels. He sent his coaches to Dover, ready to be shipped. But then came bad news.

The Posset and the Plaster

WHEN it was King James's turn to sign the French marriage articles in December 1624, he was unable to do so, his hand crippled by arthritis, and had to use a stamp instead. Afterwards he left it to his son to entertain the French envoys while he withdrew to his chamber. He was 'ill troubled with a universal pain in shoulders, elbows, knees and feet'.

A comedy that was to have been performed for his entertainment was cancelled. A week later he was still laid up, 'pained with the gout in his hands and arms'. He was reported to be very melancholy. He could not walk unaided. At Theobalds the doors were widened to allow him to hobble through leaning on the shoulders of two servants.

He was in Whitehall Palace for Christmas, as usual, and on Christmas Day he heard Lancelot Andrewes preach, but John Chamberlain reports that he kept to his chamber thereafter and he didn't 'come once to the chapel or to any of the plays'. He went away again – to Newmarket and then to Theobalds – accompanied by Prince Charles. Buckingham stayed in London, trying to manage the debacle that was Mansfeld's expedition and to manoeuvre the French king into a formal alliance. King James didn't write to him – his hands were still useless – but sent messages via Charles. 'He has commanded me to tell you,' wrote the Prince, 'that he is as ill tormented at this time in his right elbow and knee as he was in Cambridge.' He was no longer hunting or taking any exercise. He was drinking heavily, indulging especially in a thick sweet wine he favoured. He vomited frequently. His old kidney trouble was back.

It was a dangerous time. During the previous year a number of people close to James had died, the Duke of Lennox and his brother most prominent among them. (They were King James's cousins and sons to his first great love, Esmé Stuart.) There was an outbreak of 'purple fever' (probably typhus). 'I send you nothing but deaths,' wrote a court correspondent. At the beginning of March the Marquis of Hamilton succumbed as well. At the same time King James came down with a 'tertian ague', a condition so named because sufferers were said to be shaken by convulsions every third day. It was probably a form of malaria, endemic at the period in the fenlands around Newmarket.

On hearing of the King's illness, Buckingham put all preparations for the journey to France on hold and went to him at once. For the next two weeks he shuttled back and forth between Theobalds and London. Playing cards with the ailing king in the one place, attempting to counter the outrage and disappointment over the Mansfeld fiasco in the other.

At first it was assumed that James's illness was no more dangerous than his many previous ailments. One courtier even quoted the cheering adage 'a tertian in the spring is physic for a king'. Chamberlain wrote that the King 'was in no manner of danger if he would suffer himself to be ordered and governed by physical rules [the rules laid down by physicians]'. The difficulty was that there were so many rules, so many physicians. James himself believed in the efficacy of small beer, of which he drank a great deal, and of holding his hands in cold water to bring down his temperature. Some days he seemed to be improving, but then the convulsions came on again and he said despairingly, 'I shall never see London again.'

In February James had asked Prince Charles to tell Buckingham that 'he hopes that you coming merrily hither with the cunts in your company to be his nurses will make him a whole man again'. Buckingham's wife and sister stayed away, but his mother, the Countess, came with him to Theobalds. Buckingham had sent messages to Dr Remington from Dunmow in Essex, the man he had found helpful during his own illness the previous year. Remington sent one of his usual 'plasters'.

The King's chief physician, Sir Théodore de Mayerne, was abroad, but he had left detailed instructions. The first principle upon which he insisted was that no single person should have to bear the responsibility of caring for the monarch. Rather, a carefully selected group of four or five 'experienced men ... who are calm and sociable and committed to the King's well-being' should all be in attendance when the King was unwell. They would consult together and make decisions jointly, any disagreements being discussed exhaustively until a consensus had been arrived at.

No one outside of this group, decreed Mayerne, should administer any kind of treatment. 'The cranks and triflers, the fraudulent parasites of the great' must be kept away, and so must everyone else, 'all amateurs, whether laymen or unqualified doctors'.

Remington's plaster (or poultice) arrived. Without consulting the royal physicians, Buckingham and his mother applied it to the King's wrist, or his chest (accounts differ), so that it could 'eat down into his belly without the least hurt or disturbance of nature'. James's condition became worse. According to one account, he went into a coma. 'He was one hour dead, and two hours more senseless, not knowing anybody,' before being shaken by another fit. The physicians were so alarmed that a surgeon was woken up in the middle of the night to remove the plaster. (A surgeon was a less esteemed member of the medical profession than a physician. He was required to do the hands-on work, but he was seldom asked for an opinion.)

Later Buckingham and his mother applied the plaster, or one like it, for a second time. Buckingham ordered one of his own servants to make a drink, variously referred to as a 'julep' or 'syrup' or 'posset' or 'cordial', probably to a recipe given him by Dr Remington. Buckingham brought it to James himself and persuaded the King to try it. The King took two sips, but refused to drink any more.

The plaster and the drink, wrote the Earl of Kellie to his cousin, were administered 'without the consent or knowledge of any of the doctors'. Buckingham had acted, Kellie thought, 'wishing much the King's health', but his actions were 'here much disliked and I for my self think much mistaken'.

Buckingham and King James were both frequently ill, and they were both interested in illness. Their correspondence is full of news about bowel movements and the colour ('saffron' or 'red like Alicante wine') or smell ('of extreme highness') of their urine. The fruit the King often sent to Buckingham was a gift for his pleasure, but it was also supposed to be salutary. James believed that a proper diet was the key to health, although his views on the subject didn't please his advisers. Mayerne noted unhappily that he did not observe the proper routine 'of receiving meats and drink', eating fruit constantly and 'without order'. Mayerne also complained that 'he laughs at medicine and regards physicians as not only unnecessary but positively useless'. When Mayerne tried to expound contemporary medical theory to him, King James retorted (quite rightly) that most physicians' art 'rests on mere conjectures, which are uncertain and therefore invalid'.

He did not like purges or 'clysters' (enemas). He resisted being bled. He was not an easy patient. It is possible that he preferred his beloved's doctor from Essex, with his less intrusive forms of treatment, to those his appointed physicians offered him. It is possible that he had actually asked Buckingham to call Remington. He must have acquiesced in the application of the plaster – none of those who queried its use ever suggested that Buckingham or his mother had used force, or improper coercion, in fixing it on the King.

All the same, Dr Remington's plaster and posset, administered by Buckingham and his mother without the sanction of the medical team, were in clear breach of Mayerne's rules.

More days passed. The King seemed to be growing more comfortable. Secretary Conway wrote to the Earl of Carlisle, then in Paris, that everyone present had 'great hope of his amendment'. But then, on 22 March, Bishop Williams hurried to Theobalds, having heard that 'His Majesty's sickness' had become 'dangerous to death'. His 'fits' were violent. Secretary Conway, on Prince Charles's instructions, wrote to Carlisle again, asking him to delay the wedding. 'It cannot be suitable with the good nature of a son, in so dangerous estate of his father's health, to entertain such jollity and triumph as duly belong to so acceptable a marriage.' The Prince also asked that, when the wedding took place, the Duke of Chevreuse should act as proxy because it was not 'congruous with the thankfulness and faithful love of the Duke of Buckingham to leave His Majesty in such a condition as he now is'.

Buckingham sent another messenger to Dunmow and on 23 March, Dr Remington arrived in person at Theobalds. He was not welcomed. The dissension between Buckingham and his mother on the one hand and the physicians on the other was becoming heated, and news of it was leaking out. On 25 March a Flemish agent wrote to report 'strange tragedies' at Theobalds involving 'plasters and cordials'. Buckingham was distraught – with grief, or with fury at being accused of endangering the King. His characteristic suavity had completely left him. Kellie wrote to the Earl of Mar that Buckingham was 'so incensed as Your Lordship would wonder'.

One of the physicians, Dr Craig, said, 'That which was given to the King by the Duke was as bad as poison.' Buckingham raged at him. Craig left. A Groom of the Bedchamber, Henry Gibb, said something similar. Later Anthony Weldon wrote that Buckingham tried to kick Gibb; that Gibb had grabbed his foot, and brought him down so that his head hit the floor ('his pate rung noon'); that Buckingham had then 'run to the dying King's bedside, and cried, "Justice, sir, I am abused by your servant, and wrongfully accused"'; that King James, by this time past speaking, 'mournfully fixed his eyes on him, as who would have said, "Not wrongfully."'

There is no reason to suppose that Buckingham wanted to kill James, his lover and benefactor, his 'maker' and his 'dear old Dad'. He could have killed him inadvertently; there is no way of being certain whether the plaster and the cordial hastened the King's death. But whatever they contained, they were unlikely to be more toxic than the substances the official physicians were administering – early-seventeenth-century medicine was often life-threatening. What is certain, though, is that there were ugly scenes around King James's deathbed, accusations and recriminations and furious departures. Those scenes had long-term consequences.

On 25 March, James had a stroke. His jaw lolled open. He was choking on his own phlegm. His tongue was so swollen that he could not speak. He had violent diarrhoea. The physicians' accounts of the stuff he was evacuating are as disgusting as they are pitiful. He was suffering, wrote one, 'in filth and misery'. He was shaken by increasingly violent fits, the final one lasting ten hours, which 'attacked with great fierceness, with both a long and horrible chill and a cruel fire'. Archbishop Abbot ordered that prayers should be said for him in all the country's churches.

At last, on 27 March, according to the physicians' report, 'the most pious soul of the King – the most prudent, the most just, and the most

Christian of all kings – flew away from this earthly prison, not without the greatest grief and the most profuse tears of all his people, towards Jesus Christ the Redeemer and into eternal joy'.

On the day of the King's death, William Laud was officiating in the chapel at Whitehall. Already the news was spreading through the palace. Laud, 'much troubled', rose to preach, but was unable to finish. 'Being interrupted with the dolours of the Duke of Buckingham, I broke off my sermon in the middle.'

Buckingham's noisy grief was genuine. Mourning in the early seventeenth century was often performative, but it seems that Buckingham was truly stricken by his loss. He still loved James. They had had their disagreements. Over the past year there had been plenty of instances when James's refusal to break with Spain had exasperated Buckingham. But there is a difference between reflecting that life will be easier once an elderly and intransigent relative or boss is gone and actually wanting that person dead.

King James and Buckingham were a couple, however odd. 'When I am from you,' Buckingham had written to the King that winter, he felt 'a separating of myself'. Now the dog howled for his master, the creature for his maker, the 'sweet boy' for his 'dear old Dad', the beloved for his lover.

At Theobalds on the day James died, Buckingham 'grieved exceedingly', wrote a court official, 'and fainted twice'. His friends feared that 'his grief and sickness' might 'shorten his days'. Days later, back in London, he was still swooning 'often' and 'like to die from grief'. Conway found him 'sorrow itself'. There was a day when he collapsed again and had to be 'brought very sick from the court to his house', carried in a sedan chair because he was too shaken to stand. There was another day when Charles had to go to him in York House, where he was keeping to his chamber and 'taking physic'. 'I pray God that they have not done some mischief to the Duke of Buckingham,' wrote an observer, 'for methinks he hath not looked well.'

Grief for the old king prostrated him; the love of the new one was his comfort. 'As soon as the father was dead, the son was seen to kiss the Duke with much affection,' noted the Flemish agent. They travelled up to London together in the royal coach. Buckingham spent that night in Charles's apartments, 'as near to the King as with conveniency might be'. The two of them sat up late, alone together, talking seriously for upwards of two hours. The new King Charles told him, 'I have lost a good father and you a good master ... but comfort yourself, you have found another that will no less cherish you.' He gave Buckingham a golden key, signifying that he could enter the royal palaces whenever he wished, and find no room closed to him.

A few years later Sir Henry Wotton wrote, marvelling, about this moment of transition. Usually, thought Wotton, 'the state of a favourite is at the best but a tenant-at-will and rarely transmitted'. Here was an exception to that rule. In this new reign, Buckingham would be as highly

favoured as he had been in the last. Wotton wrote that he had 'now gotten (as it were) two lives in his own fortune and greatness'.

King James's funeral was the climax of a sequence of ceremonies lasting a full month. To John Chamberlain it was 'the greatest indeed that ever was known in England'. On 4 April, James's coffin was taken from Theobalds to London. In every village and town through which it passed people, kept in order by armed officers, stood with uncovered heads to see it go by. The last phase of its journey through the streets of the capital was lit by torches.

At Denmark House, the body lay in state in a catafalque designed by Inigo Jones, 'the fairest and best fashioned that hath been seen' (Previous page). Raised up on a plinth, domed and pillared, the edifice was flanked by statues of allegorical figures and surmounted by seated figures of women, their faces veiled in mourning. It was adorned with pennants and banners, and topped with a carved crown. A life-size wooden effigy of the King, dressed in royal robes, and equipped with a periwig, beard and eyebrows made of real human hair, lay on the closed coffin. Candles burned around it night and day.

On 7 May, 9,000 mourners, to whom black clothes had been distributed, followed the King's last journey in a night-time procession down the Strand and through Whitehall to Westminster Abbey. Stands for spectators had been set up in the tiltyard. All along the route, houses were decorated with the heraldic insignia of the House of Stuart. Three thousand torches blazed. There were drums and trumpets. There were choirs singing as they processed. There was a 'great banner', made of velvet and satin and Naples silk. King James's funerary chariot, drawn by six horses, was surrounded by members of the nobility and Privy Councillors.

Buckingham was there in the midst of his entourage. He was on foot but – in his capacity as Master of the Horse – he led a horse caparisoned in black velvet embroidered with silver and pearls. Twelve more black-draped horses paced behind him, along with knights carrying twelve royal standards.

In Westminster Abbey a statue of King James as Solomon had been set up. Bishop Williams, giving the funeral sermon, paid a nice compliment to the new monarch when he said that, fine as the statue was, he saw a 'like representation of the virtues of King James in the person of

King Charles our gracious sovereign'. He also made mention of 'that disciple of his' whom the late King 'so loved in particular' and whom he had cherished in 'his inward bosom'.

The ceremony over, that disciple, the Duke of Buckingham, was on his way to France, to bring home the new King's Queen.

Clothes

BUCKINGHAM liked to be gorgeous. An anonymous observer reports, 'It was common for him at an ordinary dancing to have his clothes trimmed with great diamond buttons, and to have diamond hatbands, cockades, and earrings, to be yoked with great and manifold ropes and knots of pearl.'

We have a packing list of what and whom he took with him to France. Three coaches lined with velvet, their outsides adorned with 'gold lace all over'; a barge complete with twenty-two watermen; one hundred and sixty musicians; forty-four yeomen; twenty-seven cooks and forty-five other kitchen staff; twenty-four footmen, nineteen grooms, twelve pages, six huntsmen. All his people had smart new clothes, the watermen especially 'suited with sky-coloured taffeta all gilded with anchors and my lord's arms'.

There were also sixteen lords, twenty-four knights and twenty 'Privy Gentlemen', all of whom would be bringing their own pages and footmen. 'The whole train', writes the list-maker, 'will be six or seven hundred persons at least.'

Buckingham's own clothes for the trip were extravagantly beautiful. The suit in which he planned to make his entrance into Paris was of 'rich white satin' and white velvet, 'set all over, both suit and cloak, with diamonds'. With it he would wear in his hat a 'feather made with great diamonds'. His sword-belt, hatband and spurs would also be diamond-studded. The list-maker estimated the value of the outfit at £80,000. Count von Mansfeld charged his employers £20,000 for each month he kept his army in the field. The value of what Buckingham had on his back that day would have been enough to fund a four-month war.

And that was only the beginning. As it turned out, Buckingham was to be in France for less than a fortnight, but he took with him twenty-seven suits, all 'embroidered, and laced, with silk and silver plushes'. (Plushes were breeches.)

For the wedding ceremony, at which he had expected to stand proxy for Charles, he had had prepared a suit of purple satin 'embroidered all over with rich orient pearls, the cloak made after the Spanish fashion'. Another outfit was made of a fabric designed for the purpose by Balthazar Gerbier, patterned with roses and lilies (the emblematic flowers of England and France). 'His suits are all as rich as invention can frame, or art fashion,' wrote the maker of the clothes list.

We can see Buckingham wearing two of those wonderful suits in portraits painted at the time. In both pictures his face is framed by an intricate, stiffened lace collar projecting some ten inches to each side of his small pointed beard. His hair is chin-length, curly and carefully tousled, with miniature ringlets trailing down over his collar. In the portrait by Paul Van Somer (left), he is wearing a rose-pink silk suit, the bands on the doublet and sleeves parting to show an under-layer of glistening gold damask. Michiel Van Miereveld (right) paints him in a similar suit in steel grey – lustrous as silver, imposing as armour – with an under-layer of diaphanous white.

In both portraits Buckingham is festooned with pearls. Pearls in his ears. Tiny pearls strung together to make button loops into which larger pearls could have been inserted, were it not that the scores of pearls with which the suits are decorated are there, not for buttoning, but for display. Ropes and ropes of pearls – so many they form a swag as thick as a horse's tail, worn slantwise across his body and looped through the slashes on the front of his doublet. In Van Miereveld's picture he is belted around the waist with a further six strings of pearls. In Van Somer's his cross-body sword girdle is densely and intricately embroidered with gold thread. In Van Miereveld's he wears instead his sky-blue Garter sash – banded with rows of pearls. He wore pearl and diamond earrings too, but a contemporary observer notes that the earrings 'scarcely showed because his hair was so long and so much curled as to hide it'.

Pearls were fabulous things. Organic and therefore more voluptuous than any mined gemstone. The story of the pearl Cleopatra dissolved and drank at her fabled banquet associated pearls with sexuality and with exorbitant wealth – associations they still held in the 1620s. Since the advent of cultured pearls, the pictures of Buckingham, so adorned, have lost some of their power to dazzle and astonish. To his contemporaries, for whom pearls were obtained half a world away, and only by divers with no breathing equipment going down sometimes hundreds of feet, pearls were precious. Hundreds of people had risked their lives, many of them had probably died, to give Buckingham his subtle sheen.

Clothes mattered. King James disliked dressing up. He sat for portraits reluctantly, though he knew it was part of his job as a king. Putting on the kind of grand garments in which a king should be pictured was irksome to him. When not on show at court he wore old clothes, often shabby, sometimes grubby. He once refused to wear a pair of shoes decorated with large and elaborate rosettes, asking whether his courtiers would have him look like those fancy chickens that have feathered feet. But for all his impatience with the game of dressing, he was said to be particular about the way his attendants were turned out.

Lord Thomas Howard, writing to advise Sir John Harington as to how he could win the King's favour, told him, 'He doth admire good fashion in clothes ... I would wish you to be well trimmed; get a new jerkin well bordered, and not too short; the King saith, he liketh a flowing garment.' It must be colourful. 'Be sure it be not all of one sort, but diversely coloured, the collar falling somewhat down, and your ruff well stiffened and bushy.' Harington might think such things are trivial, but 'we have lately had many gallants who failed in their suits, for want of due observance of these matters'. Fine clothes advertised the wealth and status of the wearer. They also showed his sense of what was seemly, and what was owed to the majesty of the King.

Clothes were works of art. Their materials were precious and exotic. Silks were imported from China, cottons from India. The weavers of old Byzantium created wonderful patterns and textures and the tradition was maintained under Ottoman rule. Textiles from Istanbul passed through the great Italian entrepôts of east–west trade – Venice, Genoa, Pisa, Amalfi, Naples. By the beginning of the Renaissance, Italian weavers were imitating those of Aleppo and Damascus, producing sumptuous damasks and brocades and woven tapestries.

These were valuable artefacts. Cloth merchants (mercers) could make great fortunes. And if the stuff for a suit was valuable, so were the items used for its adornment. When Buckingham faced his first Parliament, one of the criticisms aimed at him was that he had granted one of his half-brothers the monopoly on gold and silver thread. Haberdashery was a very lucrative trade.

King James dreamed of creating a British textile industry to match those abroad. One of his first initiatives as King of England was to encourage his nobility to plant 10,000 mulberry trees to support a new British silk-manufacturing industry. The project was not a success. Four centuries later, some of the trees are still standing, but the silkworms didn't thrive, perhaps simply because the damp climate didn't suit them, perhaps because most of the trees planted were black mulberries, whereas the worms prefer eating the leaves of the white variety. But though the silk industry failed, James's next venture into textile manufacture was a great success. In 1619 he established the Mortlake Tapestry Works. Fifty Flemish weavers were brought over from the Netherlands and set to train boys recruited from London's orphanages and offered seven-year apprenticeships. Their products were soon fashionable as wall hangings and as dress materials. When Prince Charles rode off to Spain in 1623, one of the items King James offered to send after him was 'your tapestry suit from Mortlake'.

To the modern viewer of a seventeenth-century portrait, the clothes are of only subsidiary interest. They are there to make the sitter look good and allow the painter to show off his skill in depicting the richness of velvet, the lustre of satin or the airy transparency of fine gauze. To a viewer of Buckingham's era, though, the painting was the lesser artwork. In many cases, its *raison d'être* was as a celebration of the more precious thing, the sitter's outfit.

There is a portrait of Buckingham painted by Balthazar Gerbier around the time he went to France. He is wearing a suit that is embroidered all over with gold and silver thread in a vermiculate (wormy) pattern. Writhing tangles of glistening metallic lines waver and meander across the black satin ground, shimmering like ripples in a pond. There are deep borders of fine lace on his long gloves and his ruff. His breeches are caught in above his knees, and finished with a fringe of dangling gold and silver toggles that must have chinked and glittered as he danced. He wears white silk hose and his soft knee-high yellow boots are turned down to display the lining of pink silk. He looks gorgeous.

This is not the painting of a man who just happens to be wearing a fine suit. The suit is the thing.

King James's death and funeral postponed Buckingham's departure. He would not attend the wedding after all. All the same, he took his wonderful new clothes with him to France.

The wedding took place before he arrived, in Notre-Dame. Crowds stood in the rain all through the previous night, queuing for places on the wooden stands from which they could view the royal procession. The spectacle was marvellous. The clothes on show were dazzling.

The Duke of Chevreuse, standing proxy for Prince Charles, was dressed in black, as Charles would have been, in mourning for his father, but Chevreuse's suit was so covered in diamonds and gold that onlookers thought that he flashed 'like a living flame'. Henrietta Maria wore a diamond-studded gold crown and a dress of cloth-of-gold and cloth-of-silver powdered with gold fleur-de-lys. It was so metallic that at the end of the day it was found to have been, not crushed or crumpled, but dented. Her train of pale blue velvet was ostensibly carried by four royal princesses of the blood royal, but so heavily encrusted was it with golden embroidery that a man had to walk concealed beneath it, to carry its weight. Beside her walked King Louis XIII, his robes almost entirely covered with jewels. Behind them came the Queen, the Queen Mother, and then a train of court ladies. The cathedral was lit by so many tapers it seemed to one of the English visitors 'like the palace of the sun'. The flames, reflected and refracted by shining clothes, made 'all the place like the heavens sparkle'.

All these gemstones, all this precious metal and fine silk, were speaking eloquently. They said, 'These people are rich. These people shine like gods or angels. These people are superhuman.' And because this was a multinational event, in which English and French participated and competed, the clothes also said, 'My people are even richer and shinier and more godlike than yours.'

Queens

BUCKINGHAM had lived in France in his teens. He must have spoken the language tolerably well. Passing through incognito, en route to Spain, he had been able to bluff his way into the royal apartments. Returning now in all his pearly magnificence, he had reason to feel confident. One thing about the French court, though, was unfamiliar to him. Several of the people who held most power there were women.

There were plenty of ladies at Whitehall, but none of them had access to the higher reaches of government. Queen Anne had kept her own household, with its own distinct culture. She had her own views (militaristic, anti-Spanish), her own religion (possibly crypto-Catholic), her own tastes in art and performance, and her own opinion of her husband's penchant for young men. In all of this, she was King James's opponent, but silently so. She kept her council, cherished her independence and lived apart in Greenwich or Oatlands. She was now six years dead. Princess Elizabeth had left the country for ever before Buckingham came to court.

Buckingham's family life was female-dominated. His father was long dead, his stepfather insane. His mother was his confidante and adviser. His intimate relationships were with her, his wife, his sister and, increasingly, his doted-upon daughter. His public life, though, was lived amongst men.

France was different. There women had a share in power.

By the time Henrietta Maria's betrothal and proxy wedding ceremonies were done, Buckingham was in Amiens, with all his train. She was to travel there from Paris, accompanied by her brother, King Louis, her mother, Queen Marie de Médicis, and her sister-in-law, Louis's wife, Queen Anne. But then, on the morning after the wedding, King Louis had a sore throat. He took to his bed. It rained. The Seine flooded its banks. Henrietta Maria also fell ill. Days went by. It was still raining.

The postponements began to look deliberate and slighting. Charles, back in England, wrote that he was 'dying with impatience and love', but he was being made to wait for his wife in a way that was personally distressing and publicly humiliating. Buckingham had come to France to dazzle Britain's new allies with British wealth and glamour. Now he was being kept hanging around like a supplicant at the gates. He resolved to take action.

Once more the temporising of a royal bride's family and friends drove him to the conclusion that there was nothing to be done but to mount a horse and go and get her. King Louis, still laid up, received a message announcing that the Duke of Buckingham's glittering show was on the road. It would be in Paris by nightfall.

Buckingham's appearance in the French capital made a lasting impression. One of Queen Anne's courtiers described him as 'the best-made man in the world, with the finest looks'. He conducted himself with 'so much charm and magnificence that he won the admiration of all the people. The ladies of the court were filled with joy (and something more than joy); the court gallants were openly envious, and all the husbands at court were consumed with jealousy.' In the short term it triggered a fashion for hats modelled on one he was seen wearing, a style known to seventeenth-century milliners and fashion-watchers as '*un boukinkan*'.

Two centuries later, his visit was still the stuff of legend. Here is Alexandre Dumas, in 1844, introducing him in his historical novel *The Three Musketeers*:

> He passed, with just title, for the handsomest gentleman and the most elegant cavalier of France or England. The favourite of two kings, immensely rich, all-powerful in a kingdom which he disordered at his fancy and calmed again at his caprice, George Villiers, Duke of Buckingham, lived one of those fabulous existences which survive, in the course of centuries, to astonish posterity.

On hearing of his imminent approach, King Louis dispatched the Duke of Chevreuse to meet him. Chevreuse, who had so recently stood proxy for King Charles, was to be his host. So Buckingham was invited into the home of Marie de Rohan, Duchess of Chevreuse (Plate 21).

The Duchess was only twenty-five but she was already married for the second time. Her first husband, the Duke of Luynes, had been childhood companion and favourite to Louis XIII, holding the office of Grand Falconer of France – a title equivalent to Buckingham's position as Master of the Horse. As his wife, Marie, while still a teenager, had lived at the very centre of French monarchical power. When she was twenty-one, Luynes died suddenly. She was soon married again to Chevreuse. The two of them lived in a new-built *hôtel particulier* in what is now the Cour Napoléon of the Louvre.

She was close to Queen Anne. She had been superintendent of the Queen's household until King Louis – blaming her for his wife's miscarriage (the two young women had been running along a corridor together) – banished her temporarily from court. Audacious and wilful, adept as a political intriguer, she was a formidable power behind the scenes of the French court. Along with the Queen, she was at the centre of a faction opposed to the coming man, Cardinal Richelieu. When Buckingham arrived in Paris, she was having an affair with the handsome English ambassador Henry Holland, and was thus a useful conduit between the English visitors and Queen Anne's supporters. She would soon be mischievously fostering the idea of a liaison between Buckingham and the Queen.

The next of the great ladies of France whom Buckingham encountered on this trip was the most formidable of all, the Queen Mother, Marie de Médicis (Plate 19). A daughter of the great Florentine banking family, Marie had ruled France as regent to the child-king, her son Louis XIII, for seven years after her husband King Henri IV's assassination in 1610. Resourceful and subtle, dressed always in black as a reminder that she was widow of the old king as well as mother of the new, she was a formidably effective ruler.

She married her two eldest children to Spanish royalty, as King James had failed to do. Her son, King Louis, longing to escape her dominance, had rebelled against her when he was fifteen. He had her favourite murdered, arrested her and banished her from court. Two years later she had escaped from the Château de Blois, where she was imprisoned, cutting off her skirts and climbing down a ladder to reach freedom, rallying her supporters and raising an army. Two wars between mother and son ensued, but the Queen Mother was not to be long excluded from power. By 1625 she had been back in Paris for three years and had a seat on her son's Council. In her new-built Palais du Luxembourg she presided over a rival court.

Buckingham pleased her. After he left France, she wrote to King Charles assuring him that his envoy had 'conducted himself here in a most worthy manner and given great satisfaction'.

It was in Marie's palace that Buckingham's counterpart in France, Cardinal Richelieu, her long-time adviser and now the young king's all-powerful first minister, gave a great dinner to welcome the visitors.

One of the gentlemen who travelled in Buckingham's train gave an account of the evening. Buckingham was seated at a high table with King Louis, his brother and three queens (Marie de Médicis, Queen Anne of France and the new Queen Henrietta Maria of England). King Louis marked the occasion by giving him 'a hatband of diamonds so ponderously rich that he excused the not wearing of it more than one day because of the weight thereof'. It was one of many gifts Buckingham was to receive in Paris. 'The Queen and the princes of court have emptied their cabinets of all rich pictures and statues to bestow upon him.'

There is a story, told by an eighteenth-century French author, about the entrance Buckingham made that night. Whether it is true or not, it gives a sense of the impression he made in Paris.

He was wearing one of his fabulous suits. As he entered he tugged on a secret thread, loosening the hundreds of pearls stitched onto the lustrous satin.

It is said that when the goddess Aphrodite stepped on the earth violets sprang up wherever her feet touched the ground. Now, as Buckingham walked down the immense room to where the three queens were waiting to greet him, he scattered pearls as he went. The great lords and ladies of the French court dropped to their knees, scrabbling for the little gleaming orbs.

Remarkably, we are told that every pearl was returned to Buckingham. Pearls were valuable, but Buckingham's favour was more valuable still.

*   *   *

It was at that dinner that Buckingham first met Henrietta Maria, the new Queen of England (Plate 22). Things did not go well between them. The Pope had sent his nephew, Cardinal Francesco Barberini, to Paris on diplomatic business. Henrietta Maria had received Barberini, controversially since France and the Vatican were in dispute over the territory of the Valtelline, the strategically vital pass through the Alps between Italy and northern Europe. Buckingham asked her why she had shown the Cardinal such favour, in defiance of her kingly brother's wishes. Henrietta Maria replied that 'it behoved her to treat with respect the representative of the head of her religion'. She was only fifteen, but she had her principles and she was prepared to defend them boldly. An observer thought Buckingham seemed put out. Perhaps, rather late in the day, he was reflecting how troublesome it might be to give the English people, and more particularly the English Parliament, a Catholic queen.

It was Buckingham's meeting with Henrietta Maria's sister-in-law, the Queen of France, though, that fascinated contemporaries and inflamed the imaginations of posterity. Here is Dumas again:

> Sure of himself, convinced of his power, certain that the laws which ruled other men could not touch him, he went straight to the goal he had set himself, even if that goal was so high and so dazzling that it would have been folly for another man merely to conceive of it. It was thus that he came to approach the beautiful and proud Anne d'Autriche, and to make her love him, by dint of bedazzlement.

Although confusingly known to the French as Anne of Austria, the Queen was Spanish, sister to Philip IV and the Infanta Maria whom Charles had tried so hard to wed (Plate 20). She and Philip had been betrothed to Louis XIII of France and his sister Elisabeth when all four were still children. When Anne was fifteen the two juvenile royal couples were married near the Franco-Spanish border in symmetrical ceremonies, the boys returning afterwards to their respective capitals, the girls leaving home and family for ever to go with their new husbands. The French Princess Elisabeth was renamed Isabella and became the young Queen of Spain, whose body Prince Charles had to peer around in order to catch a glimpse of the Infanta Maria. The Spanish Infanta Ana became Anne of Austria, Queen of France.

King Louis was sexually inept – it was said that on their wedding night he urinated on his bride, not knowing what else he might be expected to do. In later life he was more attracted to men. Madame de Motteville, who was to become Anne's lady-in-waiting, conjures up a poignant vision of the newly wed young queen, in a beautiful green dress embroidered in silver and gold, with long trailing sleeves fastened with diamonds and a black heron's feather in her hair, gorgeous but forlorn, sitting alone on a cushion in her quarters in the Louvre.

Buckingham had recently spent five months in Anne's homeland, living in the palace in which she had grown up, repeatedly meeting the brother and sister she would never see again. He must surely have had much to talk to her about. On the other hand, he was in Paris to put the seal on his grand project of reducing the power of the Habsburgs in general and fomenting war against Spain in particular – hardly a policy that was likely to endear him to a Spanish Habsburg princess. Gossips at the time, though, and for centuries to come, ignored their political differences, seeing only two high-placed people – she unhappily married, he away from home – and conjured up a romance.

Once more from Dumas:

> George Villiers thus stood before the mirror … restored the
> waves to his handsome blond hair, twirled his moustache, and,
> his heart swelling with joy, smiled to himself in pride and hope.
>
> At that moment, a door hidden in the tapestry opened, and a
> woman appeared. Buckingham saw this apparition in the mirror.
> He gave a cry: it was the Queen.
>
> Anne d'Autriche was in the full radiance of her beauty. Her
> step was that of a queen or a goddess; her eyes, which gave off
> glints of emerald, were perfectly beautiful, and full at once of
> mildness and of majesty …

And so on and so forth through hundreds of deliciously overheated pages. *The Three Musketeers* made Dumas a fortune. It is still, via film and television adaptations, computer games and strip cartoons, the most popular vehicle for the reimagining of early seventeenth-century France.

Queen Anne was not a goddess. Nor was she radiantly beautiful (she had the lumpen Habsburg nose and the protruding lower lip). It is most unlikely that she ever received Buckingham alone in a tapestry-hung room. Several people who were in a position to observe them, though, believed she was attracted to him, and years later she confirmed it, telling one of her ladies that 'if an honest woman might love someone other than her husband, then he would have been the only one who could have been acceptable to her'.

Buckingham was used to people being struck by his beauty. He probably registered the Queen's interest, and perhaps he played up to it in his usual caressing way.

Madame de Chevreuse (as the Duchess was usually known) and her lover Henry Holland were amused by the idea of a flirtation between Anne and the handsome visitor. Madame de Chevreuse was in the habit of telling Queen Anne titillating stories 'about carnal love' and teasing her about courtiers who might be in love with her.

When Henrietta Maria's escorts were finally ready to move off for the coast, Madame de Chevreuse travelled with Anne in her coach, 'forcing the Queen's thoughts towards Buckingham by perpetually talking about him, and removing what scruples she had by dwelling on the annoyance thus given [by any liaison between her and Duke] to Cardinal Richelieu'.

The journey was a royal progress. 'A countless throng' accompanied Henrietta Maria: 'guards, people of the city, Buckingham and the other English, and all her suite', some four thousand people in all. Carriages were upholstered in red velvet. The ladies wore black silk masks lined with white satin to protect their complexions from the sun. At Compiègne, Louis bade farewell to his sister and returned to Paris. The rest of the party travelled on to Amiens.

It began to rain again. The escort party lingered, awaiting better weather. There was dancing. Buckingham showed the French ladies some English dances in which couples 'touch hands and pass often near each other' (as they did not do in French court ballets), so that eyes, gestures and 'a thousand other intangible things' can convey 'the words that the honour of such occasions forbids'. We know how dazzling Buckingham was on the dance floor. As representative of the King of England, he would have partnered the Queen.

*   *   *

The house in which Queen Anne was staying had a garden running down to the river. She liked to walk there. One evening Buckingham walked with her. The two of them, strolling some distance ahead of the Queen's attendants, turned into a path where they were screened by high hedges from their companions' sight. Something happened in that secluded alley that made Anne cry out. People hurried to her aid and found her looking flushed and agitated, with Buckingham gone.

Perhaps he had kissed her, or tried to and been rebuffed. Perhaps she had permitted a kiss but been shocked when he tried to go further. Perhaps – as she was to insist – he had simply used words that were too passionate to be appropriate. Buckingham had made a declaration of love, she said, but it 'flattered her glory more than it shocked her virtue'.

King Louis was extremely displeased when he heard about the incident. Marie de Médicis was more robust in her attitude. Such things happen to young queens, she said (implying that she was adored once too, and had known how to handle it). After all, Queen Anne had only been out of her attendants' sight for a very few minutes – not enough time for anything truly scandalous to have occurred.

But perhaps the Queen Mother was a little more concerned than she admitted. When the escort party moved off towards Boulogne, Marie declared she was ill and could not travel any further, and wanted her daughter-in-law Queen Anne to stay and keep her company. Before he left, Buckingham climbed into the carriage in which Anne had driven out to see the procession depart. There, screened from prying eyes by the carriage's curtains but chaperoned by Madame de Motteville, he wept and kissed the hem of her gown.

The travelling party arrived at Boulogne. There was another delay. A storm had got up. It was too dangerous to sail at once for England. As they waited for the weather to change, Madame de Chevreuse was still writing to Queen Anne, her letters full of innuendo about Buckingham. A mailboat arrived from England. Buckingham declared that the news it brought made it necessary for him to confer urgently with the Queen Mother, and he galloped back to Amiens.

According to Madame de Motteville, he went straight to Marie de Médicis in her bedchamber. The two of them talked of matters of state. He then went to see Queen Anne, who was also now ill in bed. A lady-in-waiting offered him a chair, but he refused it. Instead he knelt down by the bed, stroking the sheets and speaking 'softly and tenderly' to the

Queen. The ladies protested that such a position was improper. He said it was the English custom to kneel to queens and that he intended to honour the traditions of his own country. He remained on his knees – the Queen not protesting – until he had said enough.

Was he flirting with an attractive woman with whom he had become recklessly besotted? It seems unlikely that he would jeopardise his cherished anti-Habsburg alliance by making up to the Queen and thus, inevitably, antagonising the King for the sake of an erotic adventure with someone he would very likely never see again. It has been suggested that in fact he was cynically working on Anne's emotions, exploiting her obvious interest in him to win her over to operate on his behalf politically. Or perhaps they were both more interested in politics than in flirtation. Perhaps Buckingham was using a fake wooing to mask a political alliance. Perhaps, as he knelt at her bedside, he was murmuring, not sweet nothings, but directions as to how the two of them together might connive against the Cardinal.

Once again, King Louis was displeased.

It was the last time Queen and Duke would see each other, but it was not quite the end of whatever it was that had sparked between them. In January of the following year the Earl of Holland was back in Paris, under Buckingham's orders, to keep pressing for the alliance that Louis continued to evade. Holland wrote reporting on the progress, or lack of it, of his diplomatic mission. Then in a partially encrypted private letter, he turns to more intimate matters. 'I have been a careful spy how to observe intentions and affections towards you,' he tells Buckingham. 'Though beauty and love I find in all perfection and fullness, yet I vex and languish to find impediments.'

This is all vague, but Holland moves on to the specifics. In the next sentence there is a little symbol of the crown – Holland's usual shorthand for King Louis – and a heart symbol which seems to stand for the Queen. 'For [Crown] continues in his suspects, making (as they say) very often discourses of it, and is willing to hear villains say that [Heart] hath infinite affections, you imagine which way.' As to whether there is truth in what these 'villains' say, Holland is evasive. 'You are the most happy unhappy man alive for [Heart] is beyond imagination right and would do things to destroy her fortune rather than want satisfaction in her mind.'

What is Holland saying here? The fogginess of this sentence is probably deliberate. Holland does not want to take responsibility for anything. 'Do what you will. I dare not advise you. To come is dangerous. Not to come is unfortunate.'

Buckingham, whose wife, to his joy and relief, had just given birth to his first son – the long-awaited and longed-for heir to his many titles and honours and magnificent homes – stayed away.

Richelieu

THE host for the splendid banquet in the Palais du Luxembourg, where Buckingham first met the trio of French queens, was Armand du Plessis, Cardinal de Richelieu. In France, wrote one of his rivals for power, Richelieu 'is everything, does everything, has everything'.

Forty years old in 1625, Richelieu had begun his career as Bishop of Luçon (the post was in his family's gift), before becoming Marie de Médicis's almoner. He was the Queen Mother's man, and when she and the King her son were at war, Louis once declared that he 'hated him like the devil'. But times change. The Duke of Luynes, who had been King Louis's favourite and first minister, died suddenly in 1621. The King was left without a mentor he could trust. His regime was shaken, and not only by his mother's hostility. As Richelieu was to write later, 'The Huguenots shared the state with Your Majesty, the *grands* [the dissident nobility] behaved as if they were not your subjects, and the governors of the provinces as if they were sovereign powers.'

If the authority of the Crown was to be restored, it was imperative that royal mother and son work together. A mediator was needed. Marie de Médicis returned to Paris. Richelieu set to work. He had to proceed tactfully. King Louis was twenty-four years old. Like King Charles of England, he had a speech impediment and was embarrassed by it. He was nervous and moody. He was in need of help, but touchily reluctant to admit it.

Richelieu was deferential by cunning design, but also by conviction. He was a sincere royalist. He promised he could make the young king great. He inspired Louis with 'ideas of glory and grandeur for his crown'. When Richelieu was his adversary, Louis had feared his 'proud and domineering sprit'. Now he came to believe that spirit might qualify the

Cardinal to be his right-hand man. For the next eighteen years Richelieu would rule France.

Two years earlier, Buckingham had met and tussled with Olivares. Back then he had been the comparatively young favourite of a shrewd and experienced monarch, and a novice in the diplomatic game. Now, like Olivares, and like Richelieu, he was mentor and executive to an awkward young king. But though Buckingham had learnt many lessons in the intervening two years, he was no match for the Cardinal. Once again, he seems to have been counting on his charm to power his arguments. Once again, it failed.

Richelieu lived close to insanity. His brother believed himself to be God. His sister, who thought herself to be made of glass, didn't dare sit down for fear that she might shatter to pieces. He himself was reported to have 'operated under the delusion that he was a horse'. It

was said that he would howl and foam at the mouth in moments of crisis. Beset by unreason, he treasured reason, which he called '*lumière naturelle*'.

One of his political rivals wrote that he was not happy, even when he had good fortune. 'He is never at rest, because he is always suspended between fear and hope … He loses his temper with people, with events, with fortune, with himself.' His most authoritative biographer has written that he was 'one who could present an ice-cold exterior to the world. But one who also suffered from the most acute hypersensibility; who … was prone to sudden terrifying outbursts of temper; who burst into tears with embarrassing ease, and whose nervous system was so highly strung that at moments of depression he would physically collapse.' Richelieu himself claimed that his apparent volatility was deliberately willed. 'My rages are all inspired by reason,' he wrote. Marie de Médicis believed him: 'He cries when he wants to.'

Whatever inner turmoil he might be shaken by, his manner was frigidly impressive. He looks out of his portrait by Philippe de Champaigne, thin, pale, watchful, long nose pointed, eyebrows quizzically raised. He was a skilled and intimidating negotiator.

Buckingham had arrived in Paris with a number of requests to present to the Cardinal. The two of them met repeatedly. Their discussions were lengthy and, for Buckingham, bitterly disappointing.

Buckingham asked that France join his projected league of anti-Habsburg powers. No, said the Cardinal. It was not that he disapproved of Buckingham's policy. Like Buckingham, Richelieu believed that Spain aspired to 'universal monarchy', and for the rest of his career he was to work to limit Spanish power. But, no, he did not want to commit his country to an alliance with England and its Protestant allies. To do so would alienate the German Catholic princes whom he sought to win over. So, no, France would not be joining.

Buckingham asked that France should at least promise not to make a separate peace with Spain. No, said the Cardinal. That was unnecessary. There were no plans for such a peace. To make such a promise would serve no purpose.

Buckingham asked that France and England might work together on their separate quarrels with Spain – France's over the Valtelline, England's over the Palatinate. No, thank you, said the Cardinal. The

Valtelline problem was close to being resolved without England's help, and he had no wish for France to become embroiled with the Palatinate.

Buckingham asked if Richelieu would like England to act as mediator between the French king and his Huguenot subjects. No, said the Cardinal, he would not. The Huguenots had freedom of worship within their designated enclaves. Their quarrel with their king was not religious but political. They were rebels against royal authority. They must be brought back to obedience. 'For a foreign ruler to intercede on behalf of rebels was to countenance rebellion itself, and this was something that no prince should do.' (This was an argument that King James would have heartily endorsed.)

Buckingham said that the English might be obliged to settle the Palatinate question by making a treaty with Spain from which France would derive no benefit. The Cardinal didn't bother to reply. He said King Louis would honour his agreement to pay his share of Mansfeld's costs until the contracted six months were up, but that was all. No. To repeat … No, France would not be entering Buckingham's anti-Habsburg league.

Buckingham had got Charles a bride, but the alliance that was to have made the marriage politically meaningful had eluded him. For all the gorgeous clothes, the dances and diamonds and royal flirtations, he would be going back to England defeated.

Rubens

THE banquet at which Buckingham made his pearl-scattering entrance was at once the inauguration of the new wing of the Palais du Luxembourg and the unveiling of the great cycle of paintings created for the space by Peter Paul Rubens. It was a signal honour for the English visitor, wrote a courtier, that the Palace, now completed by these stupendous artworks, was to be – as it were – 'devirginalled' by Buckingham.

Back in 1622, Rubens had been approached by Sir William Trumbull, acting for King James, with the suggestion that he might create a set of canvases to adorn the ceiling of the new Banqueting House, then being built to Inigo Jones's design. Rubens was interested. This, he explained, was a project to suit the grandeur of his art. 'Everyone according to his gifts; my talent is such that no undertaking, however vast in size or diversified in subject, has ever surpassed my courage.'

The commission fell through, at least temporarily. Soon, though, Rubens had taken on another one equally suited to the magnitude of his talent and his self-confidence. After her husband's death, Marie de Médicis had begun building herself a palace commensurate with her power as regent, the Palais du Luxembourg. On returning from her exile, she intended to continue the celebration of her greatness by commissioning a series of paintings to adorn the palace's staterooms. Rubens was the chosen artist.

Forty-eight years old in 1625, Rubens was a diplomat as well as a painter. Worldly and sophisticated (he spoke six languages fluently), he had travelled in Italy as a young man, and served the Duke of Mantua as court painter, artistic adviser and political emissary. Moving on to Spain, he established a useful relationship with the Duke of Lerma, whose equestrian portrait he painted. In 1609 he returned to settle in his native Antwerp, where he designed and built himself a beautiful house, and established a workshop from which a formidable volume of work was sent out to patrons around Europe – some actually painted by him, much of it begun by his students and merely 'touched by the master's hand' at a late stage.

He was court painter to the Archduchess Isabella, the Habsburg governor of the Spanish Netherlands. He also served her in less obvious ways. As Gerbier was to Buckingham ('entrusted with secret messages for great men'), so Rubens was to Isabella. An artist, chatting casually with his sitter, could plant ideas that would be instantly repulsed if introduced in a formal audience with ambassadors. An artist could go anywhere without putting his hosts on the defensive: he was just delivering some pictures or taking some sketches for a portrait. He was a harmless sightseer, and in that guise he could see.

It was probably Isabella who had secured Marie de Médicis's commission for him. She was helping him because she was proud to be the

patron of one of the greatest artists of the day. It would also be extremely useful to her to have him living and working for a while at the heart of the French court, and reporting back to her on what he saw and heard.

Rubens arrived in Paris in January 1622, bringing gifts from Isabella to Marie, including a small dog wearing a necklace of twenty-four enamel plaques. He made contact with the French antiquarian who was to be his collaborator in determining the themes of his great painting cycle and who was to write, 'There is no more lovable soul in the world than that of M. Rubens.' The two of them set to work. Rubens stayed for two months, planning the complex scheme of allegories and mythological subjects behind which Marie de Médicis's turbulent career would be veiled. He made preliminary drawings. This was not to be a fresco cycle, painted *in situ*, but a set of twenty-four canvases. Rubens would do the work back home in his Antwerp studio.

Three years later, in February 1625, he was back, ready to begin installing the first cycle, representing Marie de Médicis's life and achievements, in the great gallery on the first floor of the palace's west wing. It had been a struggle to complete the commission in time – Marie was determined the paintings should be in place ready for Henrietta Maria's wedding. 'I am the busiest and most harassed man in the world,' wrote Rubens in January, but he made it to Paris on time.

The room for which the pictures were destined was magnificently proportioned, with tall windows on each side, its walls hung with red velvet. The installation would be tricky, both technically and politically. Rubens was ready for the necessity of retouching. He was also aware that, given the history of conflict between the Queen Mother and her son the King, it was likely that the pictorial representations of turning points in her life story might prove inflammatory. One composition, *The Departure of the Queen from Paris*, showing Marie being expelled from the capital by King Louis, was scrapped entirely. In others, to avoid unpleasantness, Rubens had resorted to obfuscation. Years later he was to admit that the meanings of some of the allegories were so obscure that no one could comprehend them without 'some explanation by the artist himself', explanation that he discreetly refrained from giving.

When King Louis himself came to view the paintings, the abbé of St Ambrose, loyal courtier to Marie de Médicis, acted as guide. 'He served as the interpreter of the subjects,' noted Rubens, amused, 'changing or concealing the true meanings with great skill.'

Rubens was probably not there on the night of the dinner given by Cardinal Richelieu. He was nursing an injury to his foot. One account tells us it had been administered by a clumsy boot-maker. Another that he had broken a bone when the stand from which he was watching Henrietta Maria's wedding procession collapsed under the weight of onlookers. Either way, he was soon back at work, and Buckingham was commissioning him to paint not one portrait of himself, but several.

Buckingham sat for more than thirty portraits in the course of his life. A man who had risen to power largely thanks to his good looks, he was eager to have those looks recorded. He cared about his appearance. In Paris he was so delighted by a hairdresser's work that he paid £100 to buy the man out of his contract with his master, so that he could be carried off back to London in his entourage. Perhaps it was that man who introduced the distinctive feature of the tiny ringlets that hang down on Buckingham's collar in portraits from that year.

Buckingham was not only gaining beauty tips; he was also learning how to make use of his image, to convey a narrative about himself, just as Marie de Médicis, commissioning Rubens, was shaping the way that posterity would see her. His portraits by Van Miereveld and Van Somer, showing the splendour of his wedding suits, were tributes to his personal glamour. Van Miereveld's picture was engraved, and multiple copies of it were in circulation in 1625, spreading the vision of Buckingham's beautiful face, his fabulously expensive clothes. From Rubens, though, he wanted something more. He wanted to be allegorised, to be depicted as a semi-divine hero. Over the next two years Rubens was to paint him several times, all of the compositions being based on drawings made in Paris during Buckingham's visit that spring.

Here are the pictures Rubens made of him that we still have, at least in some form. There were probably several more.

A drawing in red and black chalk. A close-up of Buckingham's face, framed by a wide, starched and lace-trimmed collar. Buckingham's body is turned to the left. He glances sideways as though at the viewer, but his eyes, slightly squinting and unfocused, do not meet ours (Page 10).

The oil painting for which that drawing was the preliminary sketch. Lost for centuries, this portrait was found in 2017, hiding in plain sight but misattributed, in the Pollok House collection in Glasgow (Plate 23).

An equestrian portrait. Visiting the Escorial, Buckingham had seen Titian's portrait of the Emperor Charles V on horseback and had ordered a copy for York House. He had also seen Rubens's portrait of the Duke of Lerma and he had taken the point that a man on a horse is larger, more imposing and more heroic than one standing on his own two feet. He had yet to ride into battle in the real world, but he wanted a picture of himself as a military hero. He asked Rubens to start work on it.

The resulting painting was of grand proportions. 'I confess that I am, by natural instinct, better fitted to execute very large works than small curiosities,' said the artist. It was destroyed in a fire in 1948, but copies survive (Page 108).

The Apotheosis of the Duke of Buckingham. This circular composition was designed for the ceiling of the great hall at York House. It shows Buckingham in a Roman tunic and armour. Viewed from below, he is being swept up into the clouds by Mercury and Athena, who are escorting him in his flight towards the Temple of Virtue.

This painting was lost after the demolition of York House in the eighteenth century, but a sketch in the National Gallery shows how dynamic and theatrical it must have been, how big and grand and splendidly hubristic. Buckingham was using Rubens to celebrate his elevation from King James's minion to King Charles's great minister.

There were reasons why Buckingham might have been a little wary of Rubens. Rubens was the great artist of the Counter-Reformation. Altarpieces emanating from his studio adorned Catholic churches across Europe. Their brilliant colours and dramatic compositions establish a kind of religious drama in which the sensuous and the sacred mingled in a manner wholly inimical to Puritan taste.

And Rubens was the confidential agent of the Habsburg Archduchess, aunt of the Spanish king. He was the protégé and the representative of those Habsburgs whose dangerous power Buckingham was intent upon checking. Portraitist and sitter were on opposed sides. They shouldn't have been friendly. And yet it seems that – up to the point allowed by their respective positions – they were.

Rubens was loyal to his Habsburg protectors and patrons, but he was also open-minded and cosmopolitan. As a Fleming he had been watching, from close up, the protracted and hideously destructive war between the Spanish and the Dutch, who were struggling to break free and establish an independent republic. Lamenting the commercial decline of his once-great home city of Antwerp, he wrote, 'We are exhausted, and have endured so much hardship that this war seems without purpose to us.' His efforts as a diplomat, go-between and undercover agent were all aimed at averting war or keeping peace.

He was to write, 'Surely it would be better if these young men who govern the world today were willing to maintain friendly relations with one another instead of throwing all Christendom into unrest by their caprices.' Those 'young men' were King Charles I of England, King Philip IV of Spain and King Louis XIII of France, all in their early twenties. Rubens was ready to be affable with them all, and with their favourites, to compromise and cooperate and seek common ground with them – as he believed nations should strive to do as well.

He and Buckingham went together to Fontainebleau to view the French king's paintings there. Buckingham was much taken with the *Mona Lisa*, and asked if he might have it. It was not yet the uniquely celebrated artwork it has since become, but Leonardo's paintings were scarce, and all of them highly prized. Buckingham was told that, no, *désolé*, but the King of France would prefer to keep this one for himself. Unaccustomed to having his requests denied, Buckingham was put out, but the day was otherwise pleasant. Tutored by Gerbier, his eyes opened by what he had seen in Madrid and what he was seeing now in France, Buckingham was becoming increasingly knowledgeable. He was not only a collector. He was, by this time, a connoisseur. Rubens would have been able to teach him to be a better one.

As they looked at paintings together, or when Buckingham came to pose in his studio, Rubens allowed the conversation to turn to international affairs. Gerbier, who was always present when Buckingham was engaged in matters artistic, took notes.

Rubens foresaw, he said, that 'great difficulties might arise between the Crowns of Spain and Great Britain'. Those 'difficulties', as Rubens very well knew, were being fomented by Buckingham. Lightly, casually, as though simply making a general observation, Rubens suggested that 'every honest man should do all in his power' to keep the peace. Buckingham reminded him that the Elector Palatine had suffered 'a wrong ... that needed a cure'. Rubens didn't argue, rather he suggested that his patroness, the Archduchess Isabella – who was a neutral observer of that situation – might be willing to help broker an agreement.

The matter was left unresolved, but the Archduchess, on reading Rubens's report, was pleased, and commanded the painter to 'maintain this friendship with the Duke'.

Plague

As Queen Henrietta Maria arrived in England, the plague struck. King James I's coronation had been postponed because of an outbreak of plague. So, now, was his son's.

The horrors of the 1625 plague have been eclipsed in popular memory by the even more devastating outbreak forty years later, but it was, in its time, felt as a calamity of biblical dreadfulness. John Donne preached on a text from the Book of Exodus relating to the seven plagues of Egypt. 'There was not a house in which there was not one dead.' By the end of the year, the death count in London would be close to one in five of the city's total population.

All forms of public assembly were banned. The prohibition was put aside for the day of the King and Queen's ceremonial entrance into the capital, but afterwards reimposed. Streets were deserted, theatres closed; trade was at a standstill. The seventeen-year-old student John Milton wrote a poem lamenting:

> How Death, his funeral torch and scythe in hand,
> Entering the lordliest mansions of the land,
> Has laid the gem-illumined palace low,
> And levelled tribes of nobles at a blow.

It was an inauspicious beginning to the new reign.

Henrietta Maria was fifteen. She was pretty and vivacious. 'She has eyes that sparkle like stars … [she is] in true beauty far beyond the long-wooed Infanta,' wrote a courtier who had seen both princesses.

On first meeting Charles at Dover, she responded joyfully to his embraces. That night Charles turned all the servants out of her bedchamber, ignoring 'much ado' from a lady who had promised Marie de Médicis never to leave her unattended. The King insisted on privacy and locked all seven doors. In the morning he emerged looking pleased.

Endymion Porter sent his wife a pair of Charles's shoe ribbons as a memento of the royal 'lying-together': 'Long may they do so and have as many children as we are like to have.' On their second evening, Henrietta Maria danced a sarabande, a dance that had been banned in Spain for 'arousing tender passions … and disturbing the tranquillity of the mind'. While Charles watched her, Buckingham watched him, and concluded with satisfaction that the King was likely to be busy 'siring children'.

There was more to the new queen, though, than bright eyes and light feet. After her wedding in Paris she had spent some days in a convent, being reminded of her duties as a Catholic queen in a heretic nation. In Amiens, as she travelled towards her new home, the bishop had presented her with a golden rose and a missive from the Pope exhorting her to be like a flower in the thorny thicket of heresy that was England, and to reseed that country with the Catholic faith.

Her mother had added her voice. On bidding her goodbye, Marie de Médicis had handed her a letter of instruction. Henrietta Maria was to obey her husband in all matters where her conscience was not involved, but on questions relating to her faith, 'you need not fear telling him boldly and openly that you would rather die than give way on even the slightest point'. Further, if she should ever consider leaving the Church of Rome, the blessings her mother was now showering upon her would be turned to 'a thousand curses'.

Buckingham and Charles failed to understand the extent to which the young queen took these instructions and admonitions seriously.

When she arrived in England, Henrietta Maria began tactfully. Asked whether she could 'abide a Huguenot', she replied, 'Why not? Was not my father one?' But however flexible Henri IV's faith had been, his daughter's was uncompromising.

Henrietta Maria's spiritual adviser, Father Bérulle, came to England with her as her confessor. He warned her that they were surrounded not only by plague victims but – even worse – by heretics 'infected before God'. Her household in London also included the Bishop of Mende, four almoners, three chaplains, two clerks of the chapel and twelve Oratorians. Her Protestant subjects noticed with distaste that these people 'perambulate the palace in their clerical habits and say Mass daily in the little oratory'. Many of those who had so jubilantly celebrated the failure of the Spanish Match wondered whether the French Match was not just as bad.

King James had governed through his Privy Council, with Buckingham attending Council meetings as his representative. In the new reign, the Councillors, still smarting from the way the French Match had been negotiated behind their backs, found themselves increasingly shut out of decision-making. When Charles first met them as King, the Earl of Arundel asked that 'great businesses' (by which he meant the looming war against Spain) should 'not be managed by so few as hitherto they had been'. He was to be disappointed.

A committee of five was formed, to be known as the 'Cabinet Council'. Buckingham was one of the five. Three of the other members were his loyal supporters. The fifth, the only one with the status and determination to challenge him, was the Earl of Pembroke. Buckingham wooed Pembroke with high offices at court – Lord Steward for himself and Lord Chamberlain for his brother. The Cabinet Council, or the 'quinque-virale', managed everything, and Buckingham was its leader.

Buckingham pressed ahead with his plans for war. 'Now are we blotting out the motto of twenty-two years standing, *Beati Pacifici*,' wrote the Earl of Clare. The debacle of Mansfeld's expedition was discouraging, but a second attempt – thought Charles and Buckingham – would wipe out that unhappy memory.

Buckingham wrote to the veteran commander Sir Edward Cecil to enlist his services. 'It is resolved upon that a fleet of ships may be employed, accompanied with ten thousand land soldiers, which may do some notable effect.' Cecil was to begin preparing for this venture. The opponent, the destination and the nature of the 'notable effect' were unspecified, but Buckingham dropped a few hints. Cecil was to look for officers 'covetous to measure gold by their hats' and 'other spoils by ships' lading'. Only a raid on the Spanish treasure fleet was likely to yield such rewards.

Men were rounded up and dispatched towards Plymouth. Two thousand English soldiers who had been fighting for the Dutch were brought home to train the conscripted rabble.

But how was this new war to be funded? By Parliamentary subsidy, of course.

The new Parliament, Charles's first as King, met in Westminster on 18 June. The Parliament of 1624 had gone well for Charles and Buckingham. Not so this new one. In the previous year they had been heroes, beloved of a large proportion of the people and of the majority of the members of Parliament, because they had failed to bring home a Catholic princess to be England's next queen. Now they had succeeded in doing so. Their popularity, accordingly, leaked away.

The plague was spreading. In Whitehall Henrietta Maria had her own quarters, with an oratory *en suite*. Her bed was elevated on a dais, in French fashion, crowned with white ostrich feathers, and dressed with the hangings she had brought with her, red velvet lavishly trimmed with silver and gold fringes. Very soon, though, these pleasant lodgings had to be left behind. By the time Parliament assembled, hundreds of

Londoners were dying of the plague each week. The mayor fled the city after one of his household succumbed. The King and Queen retreated to Hampton Court.

John Donne preached a sermon the following year looking back on the epidemic. He told Londoners that the ground on which they trod was 'made of the bodies of Christians'; that 'in this lamentable calamity, the dead were buried, and thrown up again before they were resolved into dust, to make room for more'; that the air the living breathed was full of corpse dust. 'Every puff of wind … may blow the father into the son's eye, or the wife into her husband's.'

It was in this time of horror and fear that King Charles's first Parliament met. London that summer, wrote Thomas Dekker, was a 'desolate and forsaken city'. People kept to their homes. 'If one shop be open, sixteen in a row stand shut up together, and those that are open, were as good as shut, for they make no money.' The members came to Westminster through deserted streets.

To Donne, what was most dreadful about the plague was its meaninglessness. It was 'incurable, uncontrollable, inexorable' but also 'unexaminable'. It struck at random, killing indiscriminately.

Not everyone shared that view. Many commentators saw the plague, not as random ill luck, but as God's punishment for humanity's sins.

To others, divine wrath was more tightly focused. It was the King's marrying of a Catholic that had called down this calamity. The plague was a sign that the Protestant God was displeased by the arrival of a French Queen and her popish priests.

The Commons were discontented. Like the Privy Council, and with even better reason, they felt ignored and excluded. They had been generous in the previous year. They had awarded subsidies. They wanted an accounting. They wanted, at the very least, a progress report. Sir Robert Phelips said, 'The promises and declarations of the last Parliament were in respect of a war … we know yet of no war.' Nathaniel Rich agreed. 'There is a necessity that His Majesty should declare the enemy.'

King Charles accepted no such necessity. It was for the King and his Council to decide when and with whom it might be necessary to go to war. These decisions were matters of state – 'arcana imperii' – not to be discussed with the people and their Parliamentary representatives. The

King might explain to Parliament why he needed subsidies, but he would be as economical with such information as he thought fit.

In his opening speech to the two houses, King Charles reminded members that a war had been 'begun by your advice and entreaty'. But Mansfeld's expedition was not the war Parliament had wanted, and anyway it had failed dismally. It was on the day before Parliament assembled that a report from one of Mansfeld's British officers arrived in London, bringing the grim news that of the 12,000 conscripts who had been sent out, only 600 were left alive, and that they had nothing left to eat but cats and horses.

In 1624 Parliament had voted to grant subsidies for fitting out the ships and recruiting the men required for a raid on Spanish seaports, but the money – anyway inadequate, as King James had foreseen – had been collected slowly and late, arriving at the Treasury in dribs and drabs that made coordinated planning impossible. For more than a year Buckingham had been working to get a fleet ready. He had made progress. Ships had been built. Officers had been appointed. Thousands of men were being rounded up, to serve as sailors and soldiers, and were straggling slowly towards Plymouth. Provisions had been laid in. But the fleet was still not ready to sail.

Over the next three years, the pattern would recur: Parliament was asked to vote through subsidies that were urgently required to fund a military and naval operation. Weeks or months went by while Parliament deliberated. The subsidy would finally be voted. The process of collecting money from taxpayers began. It might take months or even years. By the time it finally arrived in the Treasury (if it ever did), the planned campaign would have gone ahead, dangerously underfunded.

By the summer of 1625, the fleet that Buckingham had worked so hard to assemble was at the point of readiness. 'Its designs', Buckingham told Parliament, 'would vanish if it were not speedily set forth.' Meat and beer had been purchased, but as it waited for the fleet to sail, it began to rot. Men were arriving in Plymouth, some 10,000 of them. Money was needed to pay them, to clothe them, to feed them, to find them billets. With every delay, costs mounted.

* * *

Buckingham had other, longer-term, more ambitious plans. He was an energetic Lord Admiral. He was full of ideas. He wanted the militias to be properly armed and trained. He wanted new dockyards to be built in the south and west. He wanted more ships to guard the coasts against pirates from north Africa and privateers from Dunkirk. The fortifications of coastal towns needed to be repaired. He wanted sailors to be better paid, so that recruitment was not just a form of abduction. But none of this could be done because there was no money to do it with.

Mansfeld was still in Holland, still intending to march on to the Palatinate with whatever troops he had left. He wrote demanding funds: 'Unless I have the full amount, I shall be unable to do anything worthwhile ... the furnishing of money in driblets and at long intervals is the surest way to lose and waste it to no purpose.'

There were English troops serving in the Dutch army who had to be paid. There were bills coming in for armaments. A merchant with the monopoly on gunpowder was refusing to provide any more on credit. Buckingham had spent an enormous amount of his own fortune, but still he needed more. That summer the Lord Treasurer revealed that there was only £600 left in the Exchequer. Nothing like enough.

To abandon any further hostilities for the time being would have been the wisest course. Bishop Williams said, 'A king must make himself sure in the love of his own people at home before he bid war abroad to such a rich and mighty nation' as Spain. But Buckingham wasn't about to turn back. He wrote to tell King Christian of Denmark that King Charles would 'soon be able to address his subjects from horseback like a king and not like a beggar on his knees'.

John Hacket wrote that 'to show the greatness of his power', Buckingham 'made haste to destroy himself'.

Only Parliament could authorise the level of taxation which would make up the deficit. But Parliament was not ready to grant anything like as much as was needed. One member proposed one subsidy. Another spoke up, saying that such a niggardly sum would damage the King, both practically and in terms of his 'reputation'. This speaker proposed two subsidies (still not nearly enough).

There were anxious discussions. Buckingham would ride out to Hampton Court after a day in Parliament, to report to the King on the day's proceedings, riding back into the plague-stricken city to meet his

Parliamentary supporters at York House at midnight. One morning very early Sir John Coke came to his bedchamber while he and Katherine were asleep there. Katherine withdrew and Buckingham, still in bed, heard Coke out. There was no time to lose.

Parliament would not be hurried. An enormous amount of money had already been wasted, said MPs, and yet 'nothing hath been done'. In the House of Commons, speaker after speaker made it plain on whom they laid the blame for what they considered a futile, wasteful muddle of a foreign policy.

Said one, 'The office of Lord Admiral is the place of greatest trust and experience,' and in 'former times' it would only have been granted to one who was worthy of it, not 'young and unskilful persons'. Said another, 'How happy is that king who reposeth his counsel upon men of worthiness, and unhappy he who resteth upon one or two who know better how to flatter and to beg of him than give good counsel.' Sir Robert Phelips said, 'In the government there hath wanted good advice. Counsels and power have been monopolised.' Sir Nathaniel Rich asked that 'when His Majesty does make a war, it may be debated and advised by his grave council'. Sir Edward Coke spoke of 'want of providence' and public money squandered on 'vanity and excess in costly buildings, diet and apparel'. No name was being mentioned, but it was clear to all who was being attacked.

By the middle of July, the number of those dying from the plague each week in London had risen from hundreds to thousands.

Parliament was adjourned, in fear and discontent, with no subsidies granted. Three weeks later King Charles shifted his court to Woodstock, and summoned Parliament again, to meet this time in Oxford.

Curiosities

THERE was a new member of Buckingham's household, John Tradescant, celebrated traveller, plant-hunter and garden designer. In 1623 Buckingham had commissioned him to improve the gardens at New Hall. Two years later he invited him to create a cabinet of curiosities, a *Wunderkammer*, for York House.

In July 1625 Tradescant wrote to the Secretary to the Navy. The letter was composed between the two scratchy Parliamentary sessions of that summer. Buckingham – blessedly relieved, however briefly, of the need to attend Parliament daily – seems to have been beside Tradescant as he wrote.

In the early years of King James's reign, Tradescant had been among those responsible for the creation of Lord Salisbury's garden at Hatfield. Working alongside Salisbury's head gardener, Montague 'Mountain' Jennings, and a Dutch hydraulic engineer who designed the fountains, Tradescant filled the space with imported plants. He bought shrubs from Leiden. 'Flowers called anemones', previously unknown in England, came from Haarlem. He bought irises and tulips from elsewhere in Holland. His friend and rival, the keeper of the Jardin des Plantes in Paris, provided cypress trees. He ordered cartloads of seashells with which to line the beds of the artificial streams.

Since then, his researches had taken him to Russia, in the train of the ambassador Sir Dudley Digges. He had joined an expedition against the Barbary pirates, not because he had any relish for violent action, but because going along as a passenger allowed him to explore Algiers, southern Spain and the Balearic Islands, botanising as he went. For Tradescant, gardening – the most rooted and stay-at-home of art forms – was inextricably entwined with journeying to far-off places. The first

task we hear of him performing for Buckingham in 1625 was the management of the baggage train transporting all the Duke's fabulous jewels and suits and accessories to France.

Buckingham had not only been collecting paintings. Busy as he was, he found time to fossick around with antiquarians. The Arthurian legends suggested that palaces and arms and jewels of great heroes lay buried beneath English soil. Buckingham visited a site on Salisbury Plain where a barrow was being excavated. There he found (no doubt with some tactful guidance from the archaeologists) a 'bugle-horn' tipped with silver that he kept ever afterwards 'as a great relic'.

With Gerbier's help, or sometimes without him, he had been picking up bits and pieces – relics, curios, *objets d'art*. Coins. Medals (of which he would eventually have an exceptionally fine collection). Fossils. Carved gems, including precious ancient cameos and intaglios. Feathers. In Paris he had been struck by the 'strange fowls', stuffed exotic birds, proudly displayed by his host, the Duke of Chevreuse. Now he entrusted the task of expanding and curating his collection of relics and curiosities to Tradescant.

Such collections were for display, and also for contemplation. A cabinet of curiosities might look like a mediaeval sorcerer's spell cabinet, but it manifested the stirring of a new interest in the world, not as it might be transformed by magic, but as it actually was. It was evidence of its owner's aesthetic taste and cultivated interest in marvellous things, and of his enlightened interest in 'natural philosophy', the area of knowledge which was newly becoming known as 'science'.

In his letter to the Secretary, Tradescant writes that his master the Duke has commanded him to ask that all seafaring merchants travelling to 'all places, but especially Virginia and Bermuda and Newfoundland' should look out on their voyages for 'all manner of beasts and fowl and birds alive', and should endeavour to acquire them for His Grace. If live specimens are hard to come by, or to bring safe home, they are to collect 'heads, horns, beaks, claws, skins, feathers, flies or seeds, plants, trees or shrubs'.

As the letter goes on, Tradescant and Buckingham's acquisitive vision seems to expand exponentially. Why limit the instructions to merchants travelling to North America? Why not include the southern hemisphere? Tradescant asks the Secretary to likewise instruct those merchants travelling to Africa, to Guinea and the Gold Coast and Senegal. Paragraph by paragraph, more and more of the world becomes Buckingham's hunting ground. Turkey. The Amazon. The East Indies. Europe: 'also from Holland, of storks, a pair or two of young ones, with divers kinds of ruffs'.

Tradescant signs off, and then begins again in a postscript. It is as though, as they draft the letter together, Buckingham keeps thinking of more things he wants, and more, and more, like a child adding demands to a letter to Father Christmas.

The wish list begins in the particular:

Imprimis an elephant's head with the teeth in it very large
One river horse's head the biggest that can be got [a 'river horse' was a hippopotamus]
One sea cow's head the biggest that can be got
One sea bull's head with horns [a sea cow or sea bull was a manatee or dugong]

Having specified these fabulous beasts, Tradescant despairs of being able to itemise everything his master wants and lapses into the general: 'Of all other strange sorts of fowls and birds skins and beaks, legs and feathers that be rare or not known to us. Of all sorts of strange fishes' skins.'

The list grows. 'Shellfishes, shells, of great flying fishes and sucking fishes.' Snakes, 'especially of that sort that hath a comb on his head like a cock'. Human artefacts – weapons and musical instruments, especially 'ivory long flutes'. Trees, beans, dried flowers, fruits. Shining stones. Especially strange-shaped shining stones.

This list could be endless and still never include the very thing most wanted. How can a collector of the unknown know what he is searching for? Curiosities are, by definition, things you've never heard of or even thought of. Things you cannot possibly know that you want because you do not even know they exist. Things that will astonish you. Things that will impress your visitors by demonstrating the immense breadth of your connoisseurship and the openness of your thinking.

Tradescant gives up on listing. What he wants to obtain for Buckingham, he explains, at last becoming succinct after all this welter of body parts, is 'any thing that is strange'.

We do not know for certain what became of the curiosities Tradescant assembled for Buckingham. But we can guess.

After Buckingham's death, John Tradescant took a lease on a property in South Lambeth. There he and his son (another John) created what came to be known as The Ark, a house-sized cabinet of curiosities – what might have later been called a museum of science and natural history. The epitaph on the Tradescants' tombstone (in the graveyard of the church that is now the Garden Museum) pays tribute to their travels through the orb of the earth, and through nature, and to their collections 'of what is rare, in land, in sea, in air'. In those collections, 'as Homer's *Iliad* in a nut', visitors could admire 'a world of wonders in one closet shut'.

In 1638 a visitor to The Ark left a list of the extraordinary things he had seen there. It includes an elephant's head and a sucking fish (both items on Tradescant's wish list for Buckingham), as well as poisoned arrows, the hands of a mermaid and of a mummy, 'the robe of the King of Virginia' (a magnificent deer-hide mantle decorated with seashells that had belonged to Pocohontas's father and that is now in the Ashmolean) and the Passion of Christ 'carved very daintily on a plum-stone'.

Many of those wonders were probably once in York House. One certainly was. 'A beautiful present from the Duke of Buckingham, which was of gold and diamonds affixed to a feather.' When Buckingham rode into Paris in the diamond-encrusted outfit Tradescant had escorted there for him, he wore that feather (an ostrich plume), and the brooch that held it, in his hat.

Jealousies

At the beginning of August, leaving Tradescant and his wonders, leaving Katherine, who was pregnant, Buckingham went down to Oxford for the second session of that unhappy Parliament.

The move was unpopular. No one wanted to travel during an epidemic. It was also pointless. The members coming down from London brought the plague with them. Their discussions took place as it were on a battlefield. The members' anxiety and resentment, palpable in the first session, were increasingly complicated and heightened by mortal fear.

Bishop Williams had warned King Charles that there were members who had 'no other aim but to bring the Duke upon the stage'. Sure enough, in Oxford it was suggested that 'the great Lord who hath been touched may come to clear himself'.

Buckingham accepted the challenge. The members of both houses were summoned to Christ Church Hall on 5 August to hear what he had to say.

The Commons had put forward a petition that 'all the laws now standing in force against Jesuits, seminary priests and … popish recusants be duly executed'. They suspected that Charles had secretly agreed with the French that he would suspend those laws. They were right. He had. But now, in flagrant disregard of the terms laid out in the *Écrit Particulier*, he permitted Buckingham to announce to Parliament that His Majesty granted their request. He was doing so, explained Buckingham, to honour his father's wish: King James had advised Charles to 'show unto the world' as soon as he was married to Henrietta Maria 'that he did not marry her religion but her person'.

In marrying his French wife, Charles had lost the love of the majority of his Parliament. In giving in to Parliament, thereby breaking his promises to the French, he was making it inevitable that he would, sooner or later, lose the support of his French allies.

And so to the broader question of Buckingham's foreign policy. He told the assembled members that all was going splendidly. Britain's new closeness to the French, sealed by the royal marriage, promised great things when English naval power and the French armies co-operated. He, Buckingham, was in close contact with the Dutch and the Venetians. His anti-Habsburg alliance was becoming a reality. He was proud to be able to report that he was bringing about 'a great change in Christendom'.

Parliament was unimpressed. The members were not interested, as Buckingham was, in the balance of power in Europe. If curbing the Habsburgs meant forming an alliance with Catholic France, then it was distasteful to them. The King was asking for vast sums of money to make war, but he would not deign to inform them of his war aims, or even to name his opponent. 'We know not our enemy,' said Sir Francis Seymour. The only kind of war they wanted was a naval attack on Spain. That kind of war had been promised them. They had paid for it. Why had it not yet begun?

The answer was lack of money, said Buckingham, and it was for Parliament to put that right. Parliament had promised two subsidies, and the King was grateful for that grant as 'a matter of custom, to welcome him to the crown', but the members must understand that far more was needed if the fleet was to sail. Buckingham himself had spent his own fortune on refitting the fleet. King Charles, equally, had exhausted his credit. Now it was for Parliament to remedy the lack.

To encourage them, he threw in a promise. If they would 'put the sword' into the King's hands, they would share in the spoils. 'When the enemy is declared, you may have letters of marque.' (These were documents allowing a private person to fit out a ship and operate from it as a 'privateer'.) 'None shall be denied … You yourselves may go and shall have the honey.'

The two houses separated to consider their responses. For days there were mutterings and grumblings. When they reconvened, Francis Seymour 'took off all vizards and disguises in which their discourses had been masked' and named the target.

The Duke of Buckingham was to blame, said Seymour. To blame for the unpopular French marriage; to blame for the way the subsidies granted in the previous year had been frittered away; to blame for the late setting-out of the fleet. 'Then', wrote Sir John Eliot, 'in plain terms the jealousies were expressed.' Member after member spoke up against Buckingham. 'His nearness to His Majesty was too much; his greatness and exorbitance offensive; his power and practice were both doubted and disliked.' All their problems had one root cause. Seymour summed it up. The trouble was that 'the Duke of Buckingham is trusted'.

John Eliot spoke up. Eliot had been one of the Duke's most useful deputies. The two were the same age, and had known each other since they were in their teens. Eliot had travelled abroad and met young George Villiers in France, before inheriting his father's estate in Cornwall and settling to the life of a country gentleman.

Over the next few years, he established himself as a man of substance in the West Country, sitting on commissions, acting as a magistrate, standing for Parliament. In 1623 Buckingham appointed him Vice Admiral for Devon. Devon included the port city of Plymouth, the starting-out point for great maritime expeditions. Eliot was responsible for pressing seamen, overseeing the preparation and provisioning of ships, and repelling pirates. From Devon he wrote repeatedly to Lord Admiral Buckingham. Elected to the Commons again in the plague summer of 1625, he was recognised as being especially 'powerful with the Duke'. In the course of that summer, though, Eliot changed.

He still backed Buckingham's war policy, but the failure of Mansfeld's expedition had shocked him. He said that it brought 'no fruit but shame and dishonour over the world'. And he was infuriated by the incompetence with which the next projected naval operation was being managed.

Eliot was the man on the spot in Plymouth, working to get the fleet ready and away, but all the delays meant that his efforts were going to waste. Speaking to the Commons in Oxford, he said, 'Our land soldiers were pressed in May and our seamen in April, and our victuals prepared.' Keeping all these men waiting for action, 'lying-to this time to no purpose', was bad for their morale and even worse for the nation's finances. 'Why stay here to consume victuals?' He predicted that the dithering and delay would doom the expedition to failure. 'We lose the season of the year.'

While these 'jealousies' were being aired, King Charles was becoming impatient. He sent a message to the Commons, urging them to grant the necessary money at once. Further delay would render the fleet useless. They should reflect that all this time-wasting talk might lead to some or all of them being struck down with plague.

The Commons did not like being hurried. They drew up a 'remonstrance' in which they promised to 'afford all necessary supply to His most excellent Majesty', but only in 'convenient time' and 'a parliamentary way'.

To King Charles, their intransigence was intolerable. The Commons' 'convenient time' was likely to arrive far too late. Buckingham begged the King to be patient, to endure Parliament's scolding until the all-important subsidies were voted through. According to Eliot, who later wrote an account of this Parliament's proceedings, he went down on his knees before the King. But Charles had had enough.

On 13 August, Parliament was adjourned with no subsidies granted.

A pattern had been set. The Parliament of 1625 introduced themes that would be reprised the next year and again in 1628, each time with greater anger, with more at stake: the identification of Buckingham as the root cause of all problems, who must bear the guilt of all that the Crown was doing wrong. The initial hesitancy about naming him and then, at last, the outpouring of fury against him. The remonstrance. The King taking umbrage. Buckingham begging him to allow Parliament to remain sitting. Charles's intransigence.

During that pestilential summer, against the grim background of public disaster, the drama of Buckingham's downfall began.

The Disasters of War II

ONCE again, when the campaigning season was almost over, one of Buckingham's campaigns had yet to begin.

King Charles and Buckingham were looking now for non-Parliamentary funding. The Queen's dowry would have to be spent. Charles persuaded the Dutch to contribute ships.

In September Buckingham went to Plymouth. According to Edward Cecil, he 'played the general' so effectively that preparations that might have taken three weeks were accomplished in one. At a late stage, he decided not to lead the expedition in person but to make Cecil overall commander. On 5 October, the fleet finally sailed out. There were fourteen of the King's ships, thirty merchantmen, twenty Dutch ships and forty Newcastle colliers. These colliers, the heavy-duty hauliers of the seas, were built for cargo, not human passengers. They were sturdy, and useful for coming close inshore, but they were miserably uncomfortable for those carried in them.

A storm got up. Cecil was afraid to risk his ships. The day after it had set out, in a farcical compounding of this story of delay after delay, the fleet sailed back into harbour again. Cecil got a sharp rebuke from the Admiralty. 'If the safety of your ships had been most to be respected, the way had been to keep them at Chatham.' He led the fleet out once more.

The enemy had at last been named and the mission defined. Cecil was to sail south, heading for Cadiz. He was to destroy the Spanish fleet, or whatever part of it he encountered, and take possession of a Spanish port which could form a base from which British ships could blockade the Spanish coast. He was to look out for the treasure fleet, and capture it if he could. He was to take collective decisions in consultation with his council of war, made up of captains and colonels.

This last requirement suited Cecil, who was averse to risk-taking and afraid of incurring blame. It was to prove the venture's undoing.

It was too late in the year. The soldiers were a rabble, and feeble with it. A foreign observer thought them 'raw men and by nature more sickly, even in summer, than any nation in the world'. With no billets ready for them in Plymouth, they had been so scattered across the countryside that it had been impossible to bring them together for training. They had not been allowed to keep their weapons with them – there were well-founded worries that they might employ them for armed robberies – so they hardly knew how to use them. Many of them lacked shirts, shoes, stockings. Some of them had no breeches. Before they had even gone on board, they were underfed.

As Cecil led his fleet over the horizon, the Florentine agent reported that people in England were boasting that 'the great days of Elizabeth had come again'. They were thinking of Sir Francis Drake, of his audacious raids on Spanish settlements in the Americas, and most particularly of the occasion in 1587 when Drake sailed boldly into the harbour at Cadiz 'with more speed and arrogance,' according to a Spanish officer who was there, 'than any pirate has ever shown'. For two days and a night Drake was in the harbour, looting and burning ships, until the 'smoke and flames rose up so that it seemed like a huge volcano, or something out of hell'. Afterwards he delighted his admirers by boasting he had 'singed the King of Spain's beard'.

In Drake's last years he worked with his chaplain Philip Nichols on two books, for private circulation only, recounting his exploits: *The World Encompassed by Sir Francis Drake* and *Sir Francis Drake Revived*. When King James ended the war against Spain, Drake's legend faded. But in 1625, with another English attack on Spain in prospect, *Sir Francis Drake Revived* was published at last.

As Cecil's fleet crossed the Bay of Biscay, they were lashed by storms. Conditions on board were wretched. The ships held together with difficulty. The contractors who had supposedly provisioned them turned out to have been swindlers. One captain reported to Buckingham afterwards, 'We were told (so was Your Grace) that everyone had six months' victuals and good drink fit for the men, but I believe you will find it nothing so.' Another captain recorded that the meat his men were expected to eat was so foul that 'no dog I think will eat it'.

Arriving off the coast of southern Spain, Cecil decided to land first on the northern side of the Bay of Cadiz, to take on fresh water before engaging in any action. He gave no direction as to what was to be done if the fleet encountered Spanish ships.

They sailed into the bay. The Earl of Essex, one of Cecil's deputies, saw a number of Spanish ships lying at anchor – the kind of prey a swift and decisive attacker could have taken or destroyed. Essex changed course and sailed towards them, expecting others to follow. But without clear orders from Cecil, no other commander felt bold enough to break away after him. Unsupported, Essex dropped back and watched the Spanish ships sail away.

Cecil held a council of war. Some military officers urged an immediate assault on Cadiz. The ships' captains, though, preferred to find a safe harbour first. They identified one. A fort guarded its approach. Cecil ordered some Dutch ships and Newcastle colliers to approach the fort by night and bombard it. The Dutch did well, but the colliers hung back. 'Not a collier appeared the whole night through,' wrote Cecil, and in the morning he had 'to force them to it' with 'threatening and cudgelling'.

A raiding party was sent ashore to attack the fort. There was a frantic hunt for the scaling ladders, which were found too late to be distributed to the men. No one knew where the grenades had been stowed. Fortunately, the Spanish troops guarding the fort proved as unenthusiastic about losing their lives as the British collier captains had been about losing their vessels. Ignoring their commander's orders (he had declared he would fight to the death), they waved their handkerchiefs and surrendered.

The British landed. It was hot. The men were thirsty. Before setting out, Cecil had issued instructions that they were to avoid 'the drinking of new wines'. He had foreseen, but could not prevent, what now ensued.

The men scattered, looking for provisions. They came across some farmhouses in which they found great vats of wine. Soon, according to one of the officers, 'the whole army, except only the commanders, was all drunken and in one common confusion'. Drunkenness led on to violence. Groups of men claimed ownership of the wine. Others fought them for it. The supposed attack turned into a nightmarish bacchanal. 'The worser sort set on the rest … No words of exhortation, no blows of correction, would restrain them.' Soon they were shooting each other. 'Such dissolute wretches the earth never brought forth.' They ignored all orders, 'crying out that they were King Charles's men and fought for him, caring for no man else'.

Frenzy gave way to hangover, mutiny to sullen exhaustion. Having got most of his men back aboard, Cecil abandoned the idea of an attack on Cadiz, or anywhere else, and took the fleet back out to sea. They could at least hope to intercept the treasure fleet. They sighted it, but they couldn't catch it. The Spanish ships, with their fabulous cargo, the capture of which would have solved Buckingham's budgetary problems in one stroke, sailed on by to safe harbour.

It was now late in November. Disease was spreading through the cramped ships at fearful speed. Men were dying. Water supplies were running low again. The captains told Cecil that their ships were in no fit state to stay at sea with the winter coming on. Cecil admitted defeat. He gave the order to run for home, each captain to find his own way. By the time his flagship arrived at the Scilly Isles, the ship was too battered and the surviving men too few to make it back to Plymouth. They were swept northward to Ireland instead, and limped into Kinsale, 'not having seamen enough in health to come to anchor without assistance'.

In August King Charles had told Parliament, 'It were much better the Navy should come home beaten by the enemy, and half lost … than not go out at all.'

It was not beaten by the enemy, but it was, indeed, half lost.

Francis Drake's raid on Cadiz was celebrated. That was the kind of daring exploit that Cecil had been expected to deliver. But it had been made possible, not only by Drake's recklessness and skill, but also by his extraordinary good luck with obliging winds. A more useful story for Buckingham to have held in mind in 1625 would have been that of Drake's next visit to Spain, in 1589, in pursuit of those of the Armada ships that had managed to return to Spanish ports.

On that occasion Drake commanded a fleet of 150 ships, crammed with armed troops – this was to be an invasion. They landed at Corunna, where they overran the suburbs. The men ransacked houses, broke open wine cellars and drank themselves stupid, just as Cecil's would do thirty-six years later. For days they were wild and incapable. They burned the countryside for three miles around but failed to take the fortified upper town. They fell ill, initially with a colossal mass hangover, subsequently with typhus and dysentery.

Drake got them off, then bungled an assault on Lisbon, and turned towards the Azores in the hope of meeting the treasure fleet, but didn't find it. There were storms. Drake gave up and went home. Nearly two-thirds of the 18,000 men who had set out with him had died, most of them of disease. He was 'mobbed on his return to Plymouth by the women whom he had made widows', wrote a pamphleteer. Even for a legendary hero, this was what war tended to be like.

Cecil became the Earl of Wimbledon, as Buckingham had promised he would. The men he had led had no such happy reward. As the ships came straggling home, the ports filled up with the wretched survivors. There was no money to pay them or to feed them. The naval commissioners at Plymouth reported that the thousands of men flooding into town in bitter winter weather were 'so poorly clad that they hardly had wherewithal to cover their nakedness'. They were filthy. 'The poor rags they have are rotten ... they stink as they go.' Starving and freezing, they dropped dead in the streets. Sir John Eliot, in Plymouth again, reported that those still on the ships died even faster, their bodies being 'in great numbers thrown overboard'.

Rubens was following the unfolding events from Antwerp, where he was at work on his great equestrian portrait of Buckingham, creating a romantic image of the Duke as a conquering hero atop a big white horse. Magnifying the glory of his clients by creating splendid images of them and their doings was Rubens's highly lucrative business. His private opinions, though, were more critical.

In September, as the British fleet was preparing, he wrote, 'Should the English armada make a single move against the King of Spain, believe me, the world will see a bad game.'

In November, as the British scuttled for home, he wrote, 'The only prudence the English showed in this enterprise was in retiring as speedily as possible, even though with great losses, and in disgrace.'

Later he added, 'When I consider the caprice and arrogance of Buckingham, I pity the young king who, through false counsel, is needlessly throwing himself and his kingdom into such an extremity. For anyone can start a war, when he wishes, but he cannot so easily end it.'

Money

AT the end of the 1625 Parliament, as members prepared to hurry thankfully away from plague-ridden Oxford, John Coke (who often acted as the King's mouthpiece in the Commons) spoke up. He told the House that if the expenses of the imminent war were not to be met by Parliamentary subsidy, then His Majesty would be obliged to raise money by 'some new way'.

There were ways. King James had ruled without Parliament for years on end. He had sold offices and titles. He had sold monopolies. He had fostered trade, and profited by its revenues. But King James had not fought. His peacekeeping had not only saved untold numbers of lives; it had also saved all the money that might otherwise have been squandered on warfare. Now his son, encouraged by Buckingham, was engaging in acts of unprovoked aggression against the greatest power in Europe. They were going to need a very great deal of money.

No money. No money. No money. That was the refrain that would din itself into Buckingham's ears for the rest of his life. If his grand plans were to be consummated, he needed so much. There was none. He was like an impresario determined to realise the splendid spectacle he had planned, even though he had failed to find backers for it. He went ahead regardless. The results were catastrophic.

Mansfeld's expenses were met by money loaned by the City of London merchants, with the Parliamentary subsidies granted in 1624 as surety. By the time those subsidies reached the Treasury, over half the money had already been spent. Henrietta Maria's dowry paid for the disastrous naval expedition to Cadiz, but the King could not get married twice. Almost as soon as the battered ships returned, Buckingham was planning to refit them and build new ones ready for a repeat attack in the following year. But how was such an attack to be financed?

Buckingham and Charles tried numerous ways to find funds. They made use of gold coin taken from French ships in the Channel on the shaky grounds that those ships' owners were suspected of trading with Spain. They borrowed. Charles's intermediary with the city merchants was the Europe-bestriding financier Philip Burlamachi. Italian by descent, brought up in France and English by naturalisation, Burlamachi was financial adviser to the East India Company, as well as to the Crown. Along with his Amsterdam-based brother-in-law and partner Philip Calendrini, he arranged a sequence of enormous loans for King Charles, but even he could not raise enough to fund the wars on which Charles and Buckingham were embarking. Burlamachi's apparently inexhaustible credit would eventually be exhausted: his loan to Charles – never repaid – would bankrupt him.

In November 1625, as – unbeknownst to him – the sorry remnants of his fleet staggered home, Buckingham set out for the Netherlands. He had a number of things to do there. One of them was to pawn the Crown jewels.

In The Hague, Buckingham stayed with ambassador Dudley Carleton. He was received by the Prince of Orange, and also by the Elector Frederick and Princess Elizabeth, still in exile there, whom he was meeting for the first time. The primary purpose of his visit was to chair the conference he had been planning for months, where he would bring into being what he called 'a great union of all the states which are apprehensive about the power of Spain'.

It was less than half-successful. King Gustavus Adolphus of Sweden did not send an ambassador. Nor did the German Protestant princes. King Louis XIII sent messages promising his cooperation, but would not enter into any kind of formal alliance. The Dutch were represented, however, and so were the Danish.

Denmark's King Christian IV, King Charles's maternal uncle, was the veteran of many campaigns. He was commander-in-chief of the armies of a confederation of Protestant princes within the Empire. He seemed like a leader around whom the anti-Habsburg powers could rally. Buckingham offered to back him, promising to subsidise his war effort to the sum of £30,000 a month (where was that to come from?), in the hope that he would drive the Imperial and Catholic League troops out of all the Protestant states, including the Palatinate. The English and Dutch agreed to assist each other in countering the Spanish in the Narrow Seas.

It was something. But without French support it was not very much. Buckingham had planned to move on to France to try once again to persuade King Louis to join his league. Cardinal Richelieu sent word that he was not to come. Louis was still irritated by gossip about goings-on between his Queen and the Duke of Buckingham on the latter's last visit, and he didn't want him back in Paris. Nor were Louis and Richelieu interested in allying themselves with him. They preferred to operate unhampered by treaty obligations to such a weak would-be ally.

Buckingham had meetings with some Dutch financiers to talk about the cash-for-Crown-jewels idea. The financiers told him they were willing to buy his own personal jewellery, so long as he could prove the pieces' provenance. But, no, not the Crown jewels. Not even as a pledge. Those were national assets. They were not his, or King Charles's, to dispose of.

He passed through Antwerp, where he visited Rubens and posed for another portrait. Afterwards Rubens wrote that Buckingham seemed to him like a man walking towards the edge of a precipice.

While Buckingham was still on his travels, a London-based agent of the Archduchess Isabella (codename 'X') wrote to his spymaster in Flanders. In X's opinion Buckingham's position depended upon the outcome of the attack on Cadiz. 'The success of this fleet [should it succeed] shall encourage all good subjects to strip themselves unto their shirts for the maintenance of so glorious an enterprise.' The price of failure, though, would be correspondingly high. Buckingham had taken 'a wolf by the ears, for if the fleet shall not answer the expectation here, his greatness will be in no small danger', for 'many in court begin to weary of his tyranny'.

Buckingham's wider popularity had ebbed away as well. The foreign secretary of the Spanish Netherlands, watching developments in England keenly, thought that if Cecil's fleet failed, 'the rage of the people will be so great against [Buckingham] as he will hardly save himself at the next Parliament'.

*   *   *

On arriving back in England, Buckingham went straight to Hampton Court to make his report to King Charles. An hour later, the Earl of Essex arrived with news of the catastrophic failure of the expedition to Cadiz, of the many dead to no purpose, and of the fleet's miserable return.

Rape

JUNE 1625. Parliament was sitting. The plague was spreading silently and insidiously through London's streets. Dr John Lambe, Buckingham's wizard, once more in trouble with the law, was being held in the King's Bench prison. There, as was normal for those prisoners who could afford it, he was permitted to keep servants and to send out for fresh food.

On the Strand, not far from Buckingham's York House, was the New Exchange, London's premier shopping mall. A handsome colonnaded building, it had been opened with much ceremony and excitement in 1609, with the royal family in attendance. The Grand Duke of Tuscany, visiting a few years later, describes it. 'It contains two long and double galleries, one above the other, in which are distributed in several rows great numbers of very rich shops of drapers and mercers filled with goods of every kind, and with manufactures of the most beautiful description. These are for the most part under the care of well-dressed women.'

Mabel Swinnerton, who lived nearby with her husband, a bricklayer, was one of those smartly turned-out shop assistants. One Friday morning, Mabel's friend Elizabeth Seager came to her house 'in a pitiful manner wringing her hands like a woman overwhelmed with extreme grief, crying out and saying, "I am undone, I am undone."' Mabel asked whether there was bad news of her husband. Mr Seager had been imprisoned for debt, and 'at that time lay very sick to all such as saw him there, thinking him no man for this world'. No, said Elizabeth. It was true her man was desperately ill, but 'her grief was a worse sorrow than that!'

She was so upset she could not bring herself to explain what had happened. She went on wringing her hands, and begging Mabel

Swinnerton to come home with her. Mabel agreed and the two women hurried towards Elizabeth's house in Southwark. As they went Mabel tried to soothe her friend with talk about God's mercy and the power of prayer, but Elizabeth took no notice, repeatedly wailing that she was 'undone'. Then came a variation. It was her daughter, Joan, who was 'undone'. Mabel asked to know more. 'She told me it was that villain Dr Lambe had undone her child, and said she could say no more, her grief was so great. "But ask the girl," said she, "and she will tell you."'

Joan Seager was eleven years old. Mabel questioned her. For a long time Joan was too 'abashed and ashamed' to answer, but eventually she began to tell the story of her ordeal.

Her mother, Elizabeth, sold fresh herbs. John Lambe's servants would visit her to buy greens. On the day before the feast of Whitsun, there was a basket to be carried to Lambe at the King's Bench. Elizabeth Seager's house was full of women, all very busy. Elizabeth asked young Joan to take the basket, and so she did. When she arrived at Lambe's room, she found him there with a serving man, who was scraping plates. Lambe took her basket, and then asked her to play on the virginals.

While she did so, he sent the serving man out, and once the man had gone, Lambe locked the door from the inside. Then, as Mabel later testified in court, he took Joan 'and led her into his closet and made fast that door, and took her upon a joint-stool, and put his tongue in her mouth to kiss her, but she was wondrous fearful of him, and strived with him as much as she could, but he would not let her alone, but strove with her'.

The story is told in a pamphlet published in the following year. At this point in the narrative the anonymous author writes, 'There are certain passages which are upon the records which for modesty's sake are here omitted.' What the author does tell us, though, is perhaps the most poignant part of this painful story. Mabel asked the girl 'why she told it not at the first, and she said she was afraid her Mother would have beaten her'.

Elizabeth Seager didn't blame her daughter, but she and Mabel both knew enough about the world in which they lived to understand that the child was undone. 'She may recover her health of body again, but never her credit, for it will be a stain to her reputation whilst she lives.' They reported the rape. Lambe was tried and found guilty 'of an assault' in the course of which he 'feloniously and violently did ravish, deflower, and carnally know' poor Joan.

A pathetic child ruined by a vicious man. It doesn't speak well of Buckingham's judgement that he had employed such a person as Lambe.

Rape was a capital crime. The rape of a minor was considered especially serious. Lambe was condemned to death. The execution never took place. The pamphleteer reports that 'by His Majesty's especial grace he was pardoned'.

There is no reason to suppose that King Charles had any particular interest in Lambe. It was probably Buckingham who intervened to save him. Certainly the public thought so. From this time forward the association between Buckingham and his wizard – a connection which linked the Duke with black magic, but also now with sexual violence and child abuse – became an insistent theme in the libels and rhymes written by those who sought to bring him down.

John Lambe, alias Dr Lambe,
A Quack and reputed Conjuror.

Coronation

In February 1626 King Charles was crowned. His wife was not present. Henrietta Maria had refused to take part in a Protestant service. Her brother King Louis had approved her decision, writing, 'A heavenly crown is better.' Charles was annoyed. Buckingham advised him not to insist. It might, he pointed out, be better this way. Protestant England did not want to see the coronation of a Catholic queen.

Things were not well between the royal couple. King Charles had written to Buckingham in The Hague to tell him the 'monsieurs', as he called the Queen's priests and other gentlemen, were 'attempting to steal away my wife or ... making plots with my own subjects'. He had given her Denmark House (his mother's old home) and she was making him unwelcome there, rejecting his advances in 'a humour of distaste'. Buckingham soothed him, promising 'kind usages would be able to rectify those misunderstandings', but the French Match, designed to seal an alliance between the two countries, had become a point of irritation. And so, on the great occasion of his coronation, instead of a wife, King Charles had his favourite at his side.

Buckingham was Lord High Constable for the day. In that role he was the master of ceremonies, and Charles's helpmeet and squire. He knelt before the King to hand him his orb and sceptre, then knelt again to fasten his spurs. Later, as they approached the steps up to a wooden platform by Westminster Hall, Buckingham offered Charles his hand. Charles responded by holding out his own hand, saying, 'I have more need to help you than you have to help me.' The two of them were each other's props and stays.

They needed all the support they could give each other. The attack on Cadiz, even though it had never actually taken place, was a hostile act and the Spanish were not likely to let it go unpunished. Rubens, keeping his ears pricked at the Habsburg court in Antwerp, wrote, 'I have no doubt war will follow.' Buckingham was preparing for an imminent invasion. He needed funds. He and the King would once more have to beg for subsidies.

In February 1626, soon after his coronation, Charles summoned Parliament. A royalist member of the Commons wrote optimistically, 'We shall have a tame House and the King will master his own ends without much ado.' He was wrong. The session was to be described in retrospect by Hacket as 'a long discontent of eighteen weeks ... nothing but a tympany of swelling faction and abrupt dissolution'.

La Rochelle

In that busy month between the coronation and the opening of Parliament, Buckingham received a visitor, the Duke of Soubise, the French Huguenot leader who called himself the 'Admiral of the Protestant Church'. Soubise wanted to talk to him about an issue which was not yet at the forefront of Buckingham's mind – the matter of La Rochelle.

La Rochelle was a port city on France's Atlantic coast. Surrounded by saline marshes, it had grown rich trading in salt. In the mid sixteenth century it became a centre of French Protestantism, and in 1568 it declared itself a 'Reformed republic' – a Calvinist free city like Geneva. During the Wars of Religion of the 1570s, it was repeatedly fought over, but in 1573 it was granted special status as one of three French cities in which Huguenots were permitted to worship freely.

For half a century a grumbling peace was maintained, but in the 1620s the aristocratic Huguenot brothers, the Duke of Rohan and the Duke of Soubise, led a rebellion against the French authorities. They aimed to establish a fully independent statelet at La Rochelle, with its own armed forces and its own tax system. Rohan declared that if the Huguenot citizens of La Rochelle 'were threatened in their rights and creeds, they would imitate the Dutch in their resistance to Spain, and defy all the power of the monarchy to reduce them'. His brother Soubise led seaborne attacks on French coastal towns, briefly occupying two islands lying off La Rochelle, the Île de Ré and the Île d'Oléron.

King Louis retaliated. Richelieu declared that 'so long as the Huguenots in France are a state within a state, the King cannot be master within his realm'. La Rochelle was blockaded and besieged. But Soubise still held the islands. The French navy was too small and

Vero disegno della ROCCELLA, piazza fortissima de gli Heretici in Francia; cō le trinciere et forti fatti intorno di essa da sua M.tà Christ.ma Insieme col disegno dell'ISOLA DE RE, e suoi forti; combattuti dall'armata Inglese: quest'anno 1627.

ill-equipped to drive him off them. Early in 1625, King Louis requested the loan of ships from England. King James obliged.

To James, this was a political matter. The Rohan brothers and the Rochelloises were rebellious subjects, and he saw no harm in assisting his French brother-monarch to repress their revolt. To Buckingham, it was an opportunity to establish friendlier relations with the French, whom he hoped to bring into his anti-Habsburg league. Parliament, as they would discover the following year, saw it differently: as a shocking case of their Protestant king and his favourite aiding and abetting an attack on their co-religionists.

In September 1625, the French royal fleet, including thirty Dutch ships and the six borrowed English ships, confronted and defeated Soubise. French troops, commanded by Marshal de Toiras, took the Île de Ré back and set about building forts there, including the massive citadel of Saint-Martin. Soubise withdrew to England, taking his remaining ships.

In February 1626, the Rochelloises signed a treaty with the French which preserved their religious freedom but required them to disband their fleet. There was peace for a time, but in London Soubise was planning further action. And so, shortly after King Charles I of England's coronation, he approached Buckingham.

Nothing came of their contact immediately. Buckingham was otherwise engaged, his mind on the quarrel he had picked with Spain and the
necessity of persuading Parliament to support him in it. La Rochelle was
far from his thoughts, but its fate, and most especially that of the Île de
Ré, would be entangled with his own until the day he died.

Eliot

PARLIAMENT assembled on 9 February 1626. King Charles rode in state to the opening, with Buckingham beside him. Buckingham's bridle was improperly fastened 'and fell quite off, with the plume of feathers, to the ground'. Afterwards people remembered the mishap as an ominous sign that he was perhaps losing his grip.

Buckingham had been working to neutralise his opponents. Back in September he had persuaded Charles to remove Bishop Williams, with whom he was on terms of 'open defiance', from his post as Lord Keeper. In November 1625, he had arranged for six of his Parliamentary opponents to be appointed sheriffs. The post was an honourable one, and could not be refused, but sheriffs were not eligible for election. Those thus eliminated included the redoubtable Sir Edward Coke, Sir Robert Phelips, known to his peers as 'that master of expression', and Sir Thomas Wentworth (the future Earl of Strafford), described by fellow MPs as having a 'strong eloquence', a 'comprehension of much reason' and a 'great reputation'.

With those powerful voices silenced, it was not clear who would be the driver and spokesperson of the party seeking to depose Buckingham. One MP wrote early in the 1626 session that, though there were 'many great and active spirits' among them, they were feeling the lack of a 'good director, such as Edward Coke is, or Sir Robert Phelips'. Soon, though, a new 'director' was to emerge: John Eliot.

In 1624 Sir Francis Nethersole had written to Dudley Carleton, 'There is one Sir John Eliot of our House, a spruce young man and as spruce a speaker,' who had 'provided a wondrous fine speech … fraught with quaint words'. At that time, Eliot had been given, wrote Nethersole, to 'extolling praise of the King, Prince and Duke'. He had proposed that 'solemn thanks' should be conveyed to all three. In Oxford a year later – as we have seen – he was more critical.

Then came the disastrous expedition to Cadiz, recklessly begun – as he had warned – far too late in the year. Then the return of the ships, full of men dead and dying. It was Eliot's job to find billets for the survivors, but there was no money to pay the householders who were ordered to take them in. He found himself duty-bound to enforce measures which seemed to him unjustifiable, with no support, financial or administrative, from a shambolic central government.

He blamed the naval commissioners. He blamed another Cornish grandee, Sir James Bagg, who was 'victualler of the fleet'. He blamed Buckingham.

Once he had been Buckingham's man. Now he was set to be Buckingham's nemesis.

Before Parliament met, Eliot and some like-minded members drew up a document itemising the 'Particular Misdemeanours of the Duke', along with lists of potential witnesses. They were assembling a dossier. It began with the declaration that Buckingham was 'vicious ergo not fit to be so near a king'.

The misdemeanours fell under various headings: 'Bribes and moneys unlawfully taken'; 'Juggling in matters of religion'. Others were more personal. There were allegations about Buckingham's seduction of court ladies; about his having threatened Queen Henrietta Maria; about his 'horrible oppression' of political opponents.

Most incendiary of all, the list included bringing the late King the 'unfortunate posset and plaster after the using whereof [King James] never looked cheerful but said he was killed'.

Eliot and his associates were not explicitly saying 'poison'. They were not saying 'murder'. But they were saying that the sickroom disputes between Buckingham and the doctors, his 'violence in quarrelling' with the King's groom Henry Gibb, his driving Dr Craig away, were evidence of his 'foul and unchristian-like carriage about the King towards his end'.

Parliament assembled. Eliot called for a full inquiry into the Cadiz expedition. He denounced 'misgovernment, misemployment of revenue, miscounsel, misadvising of the King'. Such an abject failure was not to be tolerated. 'Is the reputation and glory of our nation of a small value? Are the walls and bulwarks [meaning the ships] of our kingdom of no esteem? Were the numberless lives of our lost men not to be regarded?' He thundered against the person responsible for the debacle, whoever that person might be. 'Our honour is ruined, our ships are sunk, our men perished.' These disasters had been brought about, 'not by the sword, not by an enemy, not by chance but … by those we trust'.

No one doubted whom he meant by 'those we trust'. He was not attacking the King. That he would never do. He subscribed to a vision of government according to which a monarch – who was above criticism – might be led astray by incompetent or evil advisers. He did not name Buckingham, but the copy he kept of this speech is headed, in his own handwriting, 'Sir J.E. on the first quest. of the D.'

The 'question of the Duke' would dominate this Parliament. The session was to become what participants described as a sequence of 'hot skirmishes' or 'hot wars' between those who supported Buckingham and those who were intent on bringing him down.

No Money

BUCKINGHAM and King Charles had not called Parliament in order to instigate time-consuming inquiries into their past mistakes. All they wanted from Parliament was supply, and they wanted it urgently.

No money. No money. No money.

As Parliament sat, and he was attending sessions daily, Buckingham was struggling to put Britain on a war footing. In his capacity as Lord Admiral, he was sending out letters to his lieutenants day by day. More ships were needed to defend the south coast. None were available. No money. The fishermen of Norfolk and Suffolk begged for escort ships to protect them from pirates. Buckingham asked the Navy commissioner to put in hand the building of six 'tartans' – low-draught vessels suitable for cruising inshore. No money – only two were built.

Mansfeld wrote to say he needed £40,000 if he was to hold his army together any longer. No money. The Danes complained that the funds promised under the Treaty of The Hague had not been paid. No money.

King Christian of Denmark, on being told that the English could not give him what they had promised, made a sensible suggestion. If the King of England could not afford to carry out the war on which he had embarked, then he had better desist from 'annoying' the King of Spain and begin to sue for peace.

The logic is impeccable. But neither King Charles nor Buckingham seemed to be able to hear it.

Sir John Pennington, a captain with the fleet at Portsmouth and loyal supporter of the Lord Admiral, wrote imploring Buckingham 'to take some speedy course for our supply; otherwise we must be constrained to discharge our men and let the ships ride destitute, for without victuals we cannot keep them'. Pennington, with no new ships available, was refitting those that had come home battered from Cadiz. Worse, he was using the same provisions that had already been to Spain and back with Cecil. By this time the food was so rotten that the men fell ill almost immediately upon eating it. No money for fresh provisions. No money for clothes for the men. No money to pay them. Sailors deserted faster than the press gangs could bring them in.

Sir Henry Palmer was Buckingham's commander in the Channel, responsible for protecting the south coast of England from invasion and from pirates. In March 1626 he wrote, 'I have of late suffered more trouble and affliction to keep those men under my charge from dangerous mutinies, for want of victuals and clothes, than I have ever been acquainted with.'

The marauders Palmer was expected to repel included 'Dunkirkers'. They were Flemish warships, privateers with the backing of the authorities in the Spanish Netherlands. After the provocation of Cecil's expedition to Cadiz, they were increasingly numerous, increasingly aggressive. They preyed on English and Dutch shipping in the Narrow Seas. They harassed the fishing fleet. They landed and terrorised English harbour towns up and down the North Sea coast. Officials from East Anglia sent repeated reports to the Privy Council with the 'fearful and troublesome' news of how the Dunkirkers had become 'masters of the Narrow Seas' and 'the daily enemy of these coasts'. Buckingham had estimated seventeen ships were needed to guard the Channel ports alone: only five had been built. No money.

Parliament convened, but the Commons did not immediately authorise subsidies. More time slipped away. Pennington wrote. 'I am heartily sorry that the Parliament is no more sensible of the consequences to this fleet ... considering how patiently our great enemy, the Spaniard, prepares against us.'

But there were those in Parliament who were, in fact, acutely 'sensible of the consequences'. There were people who reflected that Buckingham, in embroiling the country in an unaffordable conflict, had handed them a precious advantage in their struggle to contain and control the monarchy's power. With no Spanish dowry, with King James's careful avoidance of a Treasury-draining war reversed, a monarch, for the first time since James's accession, actually needed Parliament and might be persuaded to make concessions to them.

There were also people who were glad Buckingham had given those who detested him the opportunity to attack him personally.

Evils, Causes and Remedies

WHEN populace and Parliament alike had loved Buckingham for his hostility to Spain John Hacket compared him to Alcibiades. It was an ominous analogy.

Alcibiades was the leader of the Athenian pro-war party at the time of the Peloponnesian War. Restless and ambitious, he proposed to make Athens greater by invading and conquering Sicily. His more circumspect political rival, Nicias, warned, 'Beware of Alcibiades and do not give him the chance of endangering the state in order to live a brilliant life of his own.' No one listened. Alcibiades was appointed general. The people of Athens celebrated him and saw him off on his expedition with trumpets and hymns of praise and libations of wine poured into the sea. That was when they expected him to bring them success. But the Sicilian adventure ended in defeat. An old charge of blasphemy against Alcibiades was revived. He was recalled, and when he declined to return, he was tried in his absence and sentenced to death.

In 1624 Buckingham had been, wrote Hacket, 'the Alcibiades that pleased the commonwealth'. Two years later – after Mansfeld's failure, after the unpopular French marriage, after Cadiz – he was the Alcibiades upon whom the commonwealth turned. Sir Henry Mildmay wrote that there were many at court 'who look upon my lord Duke his proceeding with more than a curious eye'. In the streets people were singing a rude song about 'the Duke of Fuckingham'. In Parliament, wrote a member of the Commons, 'the fire in the lower house ... against my lord Duke groweth into a greater flame every day'.

John Eliot demanded to know what had become of the subsidies Parliament had voted for in 1624. Other MPs clamoured to know that too.

The answer was that the sum had been barely enough to cover the costs of Mansfeld's expedition, of the maritime support promised to the Dutch under the terms of the Treaty of The Hague, of the financial aid granted to King Christian of Denmark under the same treaty. But Parliament wasn't interested in those outlays. They hadn't wanted to pay for an expensive mercenary army, or to see English money paying Danish troops or funding Dutch ships. An inquiry must be made.

King Charles was indignant. The conduct of a war was the monarch's responsibility. To deign to explain and justify himself to his subjects would be undignified, and set a dangerous precedent. A Councillor suggested he had better let the Commons make their inquiry, or he would not get his subsidies. He replied, 'Gold may be bought too dear.'

27 February. Sir John Eliot set out a plan of action.

The Commons must define the evils besetting the nation.

They must identify the causes of those evils.

Finally, they must find a remedy.

A 'Committee of Evils, Causes and Remedies' was appointed, Eliot being one of its members. It would find out how the 1624 subsidies had been spent and what had gone so disastrously wrong.

6 March. Time was slipping by. In the House of Lords, Buckingham's ally Lord Montagu pointed out they had sat nearly a month without considering 'the arduous and urgent business for the defence of the kingdom'. The Lords accordingly drew up recommendations to be made to the Commons 'for the defence of the realm'.

They proposed that a fleet should be dispatched immediately 'against the King of Spain, to annoy him, and to prevent the invasion of this kingdom'. Another must be prepared for coastal defence. Funding must be found for the maintenance of Mansfeld's army and for Christian of Denmark. For all these undertakings, Parliament must authorise supply.

King Charles sent the Upper House his 'very hearty thanks'. He asked them to 'proceed with all alacrity and speed'. The Lords obliged. They delivered their proposals to the Commons. The King asked the Commons 'without further delaying', to determine 'what supply you will give him for these his present occasions'.

The Commons ignored the request for haste. The King needed money in a hurry. His urgent need gave the Commons leverage. The Committee for Evils, Causes and Remedies continued its deliberations.

11 March. Dr Samuel Turner addressed the House of Commons. No one had yet named the person upon whom the blame for the nation's problems was to be laid. Now Turner did so. There was, he said, a '*causa generalissima*' for all the 'evils' besetting the country. That cause, he said, was Buckingham.

Turner listed his specific complaints against Buckingham.

> The parlous state of the nation's finances were his fault. He had grown rich on gifts from the Crown, and he had passed even more riches on to his kindred.
> He had sold honours and offices. Judges, churchmen and ministers had bribed him to install them in roles for which they were not fitted.
> He had taken on many more official roles than he could possibly perform.
> He had fostered and protected Catholics and other recusants.
> He had not led the expedition against Cadiz as a Lord Admiral and General should have done.
> He had allowed England to lose control of the Narrow Seas.

A debate on Turner's charges was scheduled for 24 March.

The Commons assured King Charles that they would 'assist' him with supply, but not until they had investigated 'these great evils which have occasioned Your Majesty's wants and your people's griefs'.

15 March. Kings do not like being asked to wait.

The Commons' committee had declared its intention to question the King's Councillors. Charles told them he would not permit questioning of 'such as are of eminent place and near unto me'. He knew their agenda. 'I see you especially aim at the Duke of Buckingham.'

He reminded them how they had praised the Duke two years earlier in 1624. 'What he hath done since to alter and change your minds, I wot not.' To attack Buckingham would be tantamount to attacking King Charles himself. 'He hath not meddled or done anything concerning the public or commonwealth but by special directions and appointment, and as my servant … I did command him to do what he has done.'

In the past, Buckingham – flexible, accommodating, an increasingly canny political operator – had sacrificed Bacon and Middlesex to placate the Commons, but King Charles – tetchy, proud, maladroit, honourable – was standing by his man.

19 March. An MP wrote to the Earl of Middlesex, 'There are other things against the Duke, Sir John Eliot told me, which are not yet in the House but shall be very shortly.'

24 March. The debate triggered by Dr Turner's speech two weeks previously began.

The Committee for Evils, Causes and Remedies formally presented their findings. Eliot named the 'causing cause'. He confirmed Turner's conclusion. It was the Duke of Buckingham.

The 'evils' listed were effectively the same as those put forward by Turner, but with one addition. The new grievance was about the English ships lent to France, and used against the Huguenots at La Rochelle, for which Buckingham was now blamed. Eliot added the charge to the indictment and alleged that it was because of the loan of those ships that there had not been enough left to guard the Narrow Seas.

Some members protested. The Lord Chancellor said that it 'cannot be made the Duke's fault, the not guarding of the seas'. Public servants should not be blamed for what they are unable do because 'there wants means to perform them'. Buckingham's problem was simple. No money.

Eliot would not believe it. 'We know it too well, there is no want of moneys.' Again he questioned what had become of the 1624 subsidies: 'Massy and great sums of money.'

John Coke was a loyal supporter of Buckingham and one of his deputies in the naval office. He knew how Buckingham had worked to upgrade and modernise the fleet, and how much of his own fortune had gone on the endeavour. Now Coke protested at 'how unjustly these things are laid upon the Lord Admiral'.

Coke was reprimanded for showing disrespect to the committee. To speak up for the favourite was now an offence against Parliament.

27 March. John Eliot summed up. It was because of Buckingham's insatiable 'avarice and ambition', he said, that 'the King's treasures are exhausted, his revenues consumed'.

And so Eliot arrived at his point. To see public funds 'pillaged' could not but 'dishearten' and 'discourage' the King's loyal subjects from voting more subsidies. He told the Commons that Kings Henry III and Richard II had each, in times past, agreed to dismiss ministers when Parliament demanded it, and been rewarded with grants of supply.

The deal was on the table. The Commons would consider offering three subsidies and three 'fifteenths' to the King 'as soon as we have presented our grievances and received the King's answer to them'.

Those grievances all related to Buckingham. If Charles wanted his money, he would have to sacrifice his favourite.

29 March. King Charles was incensed. Parliament, in his view, was not there to 'set the dice and make your own game'. It was there to serve him. The kind of exchange the committee was proposing was 'not a Parliamentary way, and not a way to deal with a king'. He summoned the members of both houses to Whitehall for an audience.

He sat silently, enthroned, while the Lord Keeper, speaking for him, explained how unacceptable both sides of the offered bargain were.

On the one hand, the supply proposed was paltry. The Commons' offer fell far short of what he needed. 'It exposeth him both to danger and disesteem.' They must do better, and they must do it fast. It was now Wednesday. He would expect the new offer by Saturday.

On the other hand, they were wrong about Buckingham. 'His Majesty hath commanded me to tell you that himself doth better know than any man living the sincerity of the Duke's proceeding.' The Commons' criticisms were slanders voiced by those 'whose years and education cannot attain to that depth'.

Two days earlier the MP William Coryton had summed up the House's difficulty. 'We must of necessity lay the fault upon somebody. Upon the King we cannot, seeing his care and great wisdom. And upon the Council we cannot. But on nobody but the Lord Admiral.'

There was still a divinity that hedged a king. A favourite, though, could be a fall guy, a placatory sacrifice. Such was common practice. By such means kings kept their thrones. By such means Charles, fifteen years later, would hope to keep his when he signed the Earl of Strafford's death warrant. But in 1626, he was still too stubborn, too honourable, too confident of his own authority as monarch, or too devoted to his dear Steenie, to play the game.

He was also foolhardy. No one in the Commons was saying directly that they were unhappy with their king. Would they, twenty years before they imprisoned him, twenty-two years before they put him to death, have dared to articulate such a thought in public? Probably not, but Charles did. The Lord Keeper, still speaking for him, told the assembled MPs that His Majesty 'cannot believe that the aim is at the Duke of Buckingham, but findeth that these proceedings do directly wound the honour and judgement of himself'.

Having so dangerously given voice to others' secret thoughts, the King then revealed his own, equally incendiary ones. The Lord Keeper having finished, Charles himself spoke.

He saw, he said, that his Parliament believed that they were indispensable to him. They should remember that 'Parliaments are altogether in my power for their calling, sitting and dissolution. Therefore, as I find the fruits of them good or evil, they are to continue, or not, to be.'

30 March. The Commons met again to reflect on what the King had said. Charles had inadvertently transformed a quarrel over funding into a doomsday battle over the constitution. He had stirred up the Commons to fight for their fundamental rights.

John Eliot spoke. He was solemn and dramatic. 'The matter now to be handled', he said, 'is of the greatest weight that ever came within these walls.' Charles had suggested that they were not entitled to discuss the actions of his Councillors. This was an outrage. It was for the members of Parliament to decide what they were going to talk about, not the King. Their right to free speech was absolute, and fundamental. Without it they could not or would not function. They were asked to debate supply. 'If our privileges be denied we can debate neither this nor anything else.'

Eliot concluded by proposing that the House suspend all further business while they drew up a remonstrance. His proposal was accepted.

* * *

That same morning the Lords and Commons were summoned to assemble in the Painted Chamber. There they were addressed by Buckingham.

Where the King had been peremptory, Buckingham was emollient. This was how it went. The King was inflexible; Buckingham was placatory. The King decreed; Buckingham asked politely.

It was true, said Buckingham, that the grant offered was – unfortunately, regrettably – insufficient, but the King was willing to allow Parliament time to consider how much more they could give him. (No more talk of a Saturday deadline.) Meanwhile His Majesty would permit a committee to examine previous expenditure. Where Charles had haughtily refused to explain where the money granted him in 1624 had gone to, Buckingham – all sweet reasonableness – was happy to make accounts available.

He then went on to answer the complaints against himself. He was 'amazed', he said, by the accusations against him, 'so many and on such a sudden'. But he would endeavour to learn from them. He offered an 'explanation', taking the allegations against him point by point.

> *That he was too sympathetic to Catholics.* Not true, he said. Had he not given evidence of his loyalty to the Anglican faith when, in Madrid, he rejected Spanish demands for freedom of worship for English Catholics? (It was as well for him that his actual agreement to those demands had never been made public.)
>
> *That he high-handedly operated alone, without listening to advice.* On the contrary, he said. Everything he had done was done by order of the King or in consultation with the Council. He had regularly consulted his fellow Councillors in the run-up to the expedition against Cadiz, and in negotiating his alliance with the Dutch and Danish at The Hague. 'I never spake almost of the business but with them [the Council]. I never came to town but I met with them.'
>
> *That he had burdened Britain with impossibly expensive commitments under the Treaty of The Hague.* No, he said. It was complicated, but actually the deal he had agreed was – for this, that and the other reason – far less onerous than it might appear. Anyway, when the French joined the league it would

turn out to have been an excellent bargain. (He did not dwell on the unlikelihood of the French doing so.)

That he had lost command of the Narrow Seas. Not so, he said. The country was far stronger at sea than it had been before he became Lord Admiral. He had cut costs while increasing the number of ships. The coastal defences were as good as he could make them, given budgetary constraints, and he had a fleet standing ready to sail against Spain. He did not believe anyone could have done more.

He ended with a call for unity. The Spaniards were preparing an invasion. 'Gentlemen. It is no time to pick quarrels one with another. We have enemies enough already.'

Those 'who were indifferent or not much his enemies' thought Buckingham had spoken well, but they were in a minority.

Work on the remonstrance continued.

5 April. The remonstrance was presented to the King. Parliament adjourned for the Easter recess.

Poison

In the spring of 1626, while Parliament sat, a pamphlet was published in the Netherlands in Latin, English and German editions. It contained sensational allegations. It was called *The Forerunner of Revenge upon the Duke of Buckingham for the poisoning of the most potent King James of happy memory King of Great Britain, and the Lord Marquis of Hamilton and others of the nobility.*

Its author was a Scottish doctor and polemicist named George Eglisham who had left England in a hurry in 1625, under suspicion of a variety of nefarious activities, including witchcraft and forgery. In April 1626, around the time the English Parliament went into recess for Easter, Rubens bought a copy of *The Forerunner* in Antwerp. By the end of the month the English edition was available in London and an English Catholic named Gabriel Browne was writing to a friend in Spain that as a result of its publication Buckingham was 'the most distasted man alive'.

Eglisham accused Buckingham of multiple murders, including that of the king who loved him. The pamphlet had 'so covered him with the filth' of 'foul crimes', wrote Browne, that 'all the water in the Thames or ocean' would not suffice to wash him clean.

This is the story that *The Forerunner* embellished and retold.

On 1 March 1625, the Marquis of Hamilton, a Scottish relative of King James, died suddenly of a fever. On hearing the news, Buckingham, apparently deeply distressed, went to the French ambassador's quarters. It was late. The ambassador was already in bed. Buckingham burst in, weeping copiously.

King James slept badly that night, and the next day he told one of his gentlemen, 'When the branches decay the tree must follow.' It was as though he saw Hamilton's death as a presage of his own.

By morning, Hamilton's body, and especially his head, was 'exceedingly swollen'. The news-gatherer John Castle heard it was 'full of ulcers; his flesh loose and gangrened'. Others spoke of blisters and bumps and strange spots, of hair and fingernails falling out and the dead man's face turning black. All of these phenomena were taken to be signs that the deceased had been poisoned.

One of Hamilton's doctors was George Eglisham. Soon after Hamilton's death, followed only three weeks later by King James's, Eglisham moved to Brussels. There he found a new employer.

The Count of Gondomar had been on his way to England to try to reopen negotiations with his friend and fellow Diego, King James. After James died, the new King Charles sent word that the ambassador would no longer be welcome. Gondomar went instead to Brussels. His mission was to prepare for the Anglo-Spanish war that now seemed imminent, and to recruit agents for an intelligence-gathering operation in England.

In Brussels he met George Eglisham. Spanish ambassador and unhappy British doctor were useful to each other. It was with the backing and approval of the Habsburg powers that *The Forerunner* was published and distributed in England the following year.

The story Eglisham had to tell was not a brand-new one.

At the time of King James's death people were annoyed, even scandalised, by Buckingham's high-handed flouting of Mayerne's rules. As time went by, and rumours spread, Dr Remington's posset and plaster came to be seen as much more sinister than a breach of medical etiquette.

Only a week after King James had died, a Flemish agent was reporting that there were those 'who will say that the Duke's mother hath poisoned King James and bewitched King Charles'. The agent added that some people said 'a monster' had set up its nest in the bosom of King Charles, and that 'this cankerous weed' must, for the safety of all Christendom, be 'displanted'.

The weed, the monster, the malignant bosom friend was clearly Buckingham. The juxtaposition of the attack on him with the accusation against his mother hinted that he was, at the very least, an accomplice in her supposed crimes.

*   *   *

Eglisham presented himself not as the bearer of an original revelation but as an uncoverer of dangerous truths. Many people, he wrote, knew as much as he did, but they were too afraid to tell. He could speak out boldly only because he was safely away from those 'dominions' where Buckingham 'reigneth and rageth'. All the same, he was risking his life, he wrote, because the Duke, on becoming aware of anyone speaking of these 'heinous murders', would 'send forth a poisoner or other murth-erer to dispatch him and send him after his dead friends'.

In his pamphlet he implores Parliament to take action against the man who by means 'lawful or unlawful, human or diabolic ... tortureth the kingdom'. Buckingham's influence was everywhere. 'All the judges of the kingdom, all the officers of the state, are his bound vassals or allies, or affeared to become his outcasts.'

Eglisham addressed King Charles directly. The King, he wrote, must know 'how insolent, how ingrate an oppressor, what a murtherer and traitor' Buckingham was. Charles must separate himself from this terri-fying person and bring him to justice. Otherwise 'manifest damage approacheth unto Your Majesty no otherways than death approached unto King James'.

Buckingham poisoned Hamilton, alleges Eglisham, then made a 'counterfeited show' of grief. He 'came out muffed and furred in his coach, giving out that he was sick for sorrow', but when he was safely secluded with his sycophants at New Hall, 'he triumphed and domi-neered ... excessively, as if he had gained some great victory'.

The story of Hamilton's death takes up most of Eglisham's pamphlet. To the majority of his readers, though, what made the pamphlet sensa-tional was a further allegation, added on as if a mere afterthought. It appears in a three-page appendix, headed 'Concerning the poisoning of King James'.

Eglisham shapes his story skilfully. While Buckingham was away in Madrid in 1623, he explains, he was disturbed by reports that 'many spoke boldly to the King against him' and, worse, that James listened, and began to 'censure him' too. Feeling that he could no longer count on James's favour, Buckingham turned against him. On his return to England he seized control of policy-making. Whatever King James 'commanded in his bedchamber' Buckingham would countermand in the next room. He received dispatches from foreign princes, and replied to them, without informing the King. He was insubordinate and disrespectful to the point of treason. He wanted to rule supreme, and he needed to seize power quickly, before Gondomar, seconded by the Earl of Bristol, whom James had recalled, could reverse his anti-Spanish policy.

So far, all of this was at least close to being true.

Then comes the shocking conclusion. According to Eglisham, Buckingham resolved to get rid of the King, if necessary by killing him.

As Eglisham tells it, when James fell ill in March 1625 Buckingham seized his opportunity. While all the King's doctors were at dinner, Buckingham gave James a medicinal 'white powder'. The King refused it at first but was eventually overcome by Buckingham's 'flattering importunity' and drank the powder washed down by a glass of wine. Immediately he 'became worse and worse, falling into many soundings and pains, and violent fluxes of the belly', and cried out, 'Oh this white powder, this white powder! Would to God I had never taken it, it will cost me my life!'

A few day's later, Buckingham's mother – again the doctors were out of the room – applied the notorious plaster to the King's chest, 'whereupon His Majesty grew faint, short-breathed and in great agony'. The doctors – returning – 'exclaimed that the King was poisoned'. There were ugly scenes as Buckingham quarrelled violently with them and with servants, even drawing his sword in the King's presence. His

mother, the Countess, complained to James that 'some had had the gall to say that "my son and I have poisoned Your Majesty"'. To which the poor King could only murmur 'Poisoned me!' before he fainted away. Shortly thereafter, he died.

Eglisham, in a reprise of his account of Hamilton's death, goes on to give more horrid details of the posthumous swellings and strangely accelerated corruption of the King's corpse, and concludes with the plea that 'the traitor' should be taken 'without any fear of his greatness'.

To kill by poison was cowardly, and was therefore low, morally and socially. A nobleman killed in the light, proudly flourishing his sword, risking his own life as he took another's. A poisoner, working unseen in the shadows, was furtive, ignoble, 'base' and 'mean'.

Poisoning was intimate. There was something disturbing, the way Eglisham tells it, about the way Buckingham and his mother worked on the King as he lay helpless, naked or wearing only his nightclothes. The vision of the favourite and King together in a bedroom, with something secret and forbidden passing between them, was given a potent frisson by the readers' awareness of the persistent rumours about Buckingham's erotic relations with King James. And if the poisoner and his victim had been lovers, how much more horrifying was the crime. 'The poisoning under trust and profession of friendship is the most heinous,' wrote Eglisham.

Poison was frightening because it was insidious. Sir Edward Coke, prosecuting Overbury's murderers, had said, 'The Devil hath brought many to be very cunning in it, so that they can poison in what distance of space or time they please.' By the time of death the poisoner might be far away. How could one protect oneself against a death that came so silently and stealthily?

Poison was un-English. Its concoction was known as 'the Italian art'. John Webster associates it with the courts of the Duchess of Malfi or of Vittoria Corombona. Laying out the charges against Somerset in 1616, Francis Bacon had said that poisoning was 'a foreign manslayer fetched from Rome ... an Italian revenger, a stranger to the records of England'.

Poison was associated with witchcraft. Many people consulted 'wizards' like Dr Lambe, but they did so suspiciously and in fear. They believed the potions could cure them, but they also believed that similar potions might make them impotent (as the poor Earl of Essex had supposedly been). Medicine might drive them mad. John Chamberlain heard tell that the insanity of Buckingham's brother, John Purbeck, had been brought on by 'powders and potions' given him by his unfaithful wife, who 'did intoxicate her husband's brains'. And witchcraft and poison could come together to kill, as Sir Thomas Overbury had been killed.

Eglisham is one of many of his contemporaries to allege that Buckingham had 'bewitched' or 'enchanted' King James to gain his love. People believed in the efficacy of love potions, and were willing to pay large sums for them. Love potions, poisons: they were both literal, material things, and both witchy. If Buckingham could be suspected of administering the one, then he could, as easily, be believed to have made use of the other.

Uneasiness

14 April. William Laud wrote in his diary, 'The Duke of Buckingham fell into a fever.'

It had happened before that, in a time of crisis, Buckingham's physical strength gave out. When Parliament assembled again after the Easter break, he was too weak to attend.

What was it like to be Buckingham in the spring of 1626?

The Venetian ambassador, after an audience with him soon after Parliament reconvened, reported that Buckingham had confessed his 'mind was tossed by a thousand agitations'. He looked drained. 'The pallor of the Duke's face betrays his deep uneasiness at the embarrassments in which he finds himself.'

He was facing the threat of a foreign invasion, and struggling to put together an army and a fleet fit to repel or pre-empt it. Initially the Commons' grievances and remonstrance must have seemed a mere irritation – an exasperating postponement of the all-important grant of the subsidies. In time, though, the attacks on him began to hurt. The Earl of Clare had a conversation with him during which Buckingham 'discoursed much with me of his Parliament business', complaining that he was being blamed for 'other men's actions', and that the vitriol being directed against him was charged with 'the envy of his fortune'.

He had no fatherly adviser to whom he could turn. In 1624, when he was the people's darling, Francis Bacon had warned him to beware of complacency, to know how much he was hated. But two years later, as Buckingham faced his haters in Parliament, Bacon died.

John Aubrey tells the story. Bacon was on the road near Highgate with a scientifically minded friend. There was snow on the ground.

Looking out at the frozen world, Bacon, his mind whirring as busily as ever, began to speculate. Might it be possible to preserve meat by freezing it? He thought so.

Proceeding according to the principle he had laid down – that truth was only to be ascertained by experiment – he ordered the coachman to stop. Aubrey relates that 'they alighted out of the coach and went into a poor woman's house at the bottom of Highgate Hill, and bought a fowl, and made the woman exenterate [disembowel] it'. Bacon then scooped up some snow in his hands and stuffed the chicken with it. 'The snow so chilled him that he immediately fell so extremely ill, that he could not return to his lodging … but went to the Earl of Arundel's house at Highgate, where they put him into a damp bed that had not been lain in … which gave him such a cold that in two or three days he died of suffocation.'

Bacon was a great loss – to science and to a particularly sophisticated strain of English culture. He was also a great loss to Buckingham, whose first and subtlest mentor he had been.

Impeachment

20 April. The Commons reassemble and resolve to impeach Buckingham, the 'causer of causes'. They will press ahead with their investigation into his 'avarice and ambition', working on it 'forenoon and afternoon, setting all other business aside till that be done'.

21 April. Sir Dudley Digges proposes that a committee of twelve be formed to put together the case against Buckingham.

Digges has sat in every Parliament since 1610. He is an adventurer – he has sponsored voyages to the New World. He is also a thinker – he has written books on *The Worthiness of War* and on trade. He has been ambassador in Muscovy and Holland. He has been a courtier and a Gentleman of the Privy Chamber, unquestioningly loyal to the king, but this Parliament will change him. Later he will write a book on *The Rights and Privileges of the Subject*.

Digges and Eliot are both elected to the committee.

22 April. When Francis Bacon was impeached in 1621, fifty people gave evidence against him. When Cranfield was impeached in 1624, the hearing of witnesses lasted for three weeks. Now, for all Eliot's industry, no one will speak against Buckingham. The King having forbidden the Commons to question Councillors, it is going to be difficult to prove any kind of case against him. King Charles, writes John Hacket, has 'wrapped up the Lord Duke, as it were, in his own royal robe, to preserve him'.

Buckingham, while admitting – in his usual modest way – that he might have committed 'some errors', has protested that he has been 'pressed too far upon common fame'. Secretary Conway has declared it 'unlegal and unparliamentary' to make accusations 'in generality and upon report'.

Now, lacking witnesses or substantial evidence, Eliot calls for a vote on a measure permitting hearsay evidence to be considered during the impeachment process. The vote passes. 'Common fame' is now admissible as evidence.

25 April. The members of the committee agree that Buckingham will be charged with eight 'evils'. The charges include all those named before, with one new one – that Buckingham administered a plaster and a drink that caused King James's death.

Free copies of incendiary libels and pamphlets would often be spread around St Paul's and the Exchange. Eglisham's pamphlet, reported the Earl of Middlesex's agent, 'makes a loud cry'.

Some members of Parliament would have read it. Nearly all would have heard what it alleged. Gabriel Browne, the correspondent who had announced *The Forerunner*'s publication to his Spanish friend, reported gleefully that as a result, the Parliament men were trying 'to tear' Buckingham to pieces, and to eat those pieces 'raw with salt'.

26 April. The Commons' committee begin their hearings in the Court of Wards. For two days they examine the physicians who attended upon King James during his final illness.

They establish that, yes, it is true that Buckingham twice applied a plaster to the King, and gave him a posset or syrup. The royal physicians had not liked him doing so, but they 'would say nothing', according to one of them, 'lest they offend the Duke and the King'. The things had been supplied by a doctor from Essex recommended by Buckingham. One of the physicians testifies that he 'sundry times heard the Duke tell the King that he had used such a plaster which had done him much good'.

The physicians agree that there was no coercion involved. In each case King James took Dr Remington's medicine willingly, even enquiring impatiently 'whether that was ready which the Duke had prescribed him'. Two of the doctors report that they tasted the potion or touched the plaster and suffered no ill effects.

After the second application of the plaster James grew worse. Several of the doctors were angry. John Craig said, 'That which was given to the King by the Duke was as bad as poison.' (It was after he had done so that he and Buckingham had their fierce quarrel and Craig left, ordered away by Buckingham.)

James told another doctor that the drink 'makes me burn and roast'. He was in great pain. Someone heard him say, 'Will you murder and slay me?' Another recalled him saying that what had made him so ill 'was that I had of the Duke of Buckingham'.

One of the King's physicians, John More, was a Catholic. His clients included Count Gondomar, as well as Buckingham and his mother, the Countess. Now the other doctors say More was not properly qualified. He was 'no sworn physician'.

It emerges from the committee's investigations that a day or two after King James's death, Dr More, with Buckingham's approval, produced a list of the ingredients of the plaster and the potion, and a statement declaring that they were harmless. He asked his fellow physicians to sign the statement. They refused. It was true, they said, that the listed ingredients were 'safe and good', but how were they to be sure there was nothing else in the mixture?

Another of those who testify before the committee is one Robert Ramsay, who has things to say about Buckingham's connection with Piers Butler, the 'devil' whom Buckingham had recommended to King James two years before. Buckingham used Butler for 'secret services' and paid him a handsome salary. These secret services were probably intelligence-gathering – Buckingham had a number of agents observing events in foreign courts and reporting back to him – but Butler had an evil reputation. When he travelled to Sweden a Scots gentleman wrote to a Swedish minister warning him of the arrival in his country of a dangerous man, known for his skill in *artibus veneficis*, the art of poison.

None of the physicians accuses Buckingham of deliberately hastening the King's death. All the same, the Tuscan agent reporting on the hearing writes 'there is a whisper of poison'.

27 April. The committee, after deliberating on what they have heard, reports to the Commons that Buckingham's administering the posset and applying the plaster constitutes 'an act of a transcendent presumption' and 'dangerous consequence'.

In the ensuing debate Buckingham's supporters argue that even if it 'was a great indiscretion and rashness of the Duke of Buckingham', it was well meant, and actions 'which seem presumptuous to us, to kings and their near ones are but liberty'.

Both sides seem to be talking, not about murder, but about the shocking intimacy of the scenes around King James's sickbed. Here was the monarch, a person so exalted that no commoner might stand beneath his canopy or set foot on the carpet on which he sat enthroned, and here were Buckingham and his mother making free with his body.

Other voices are more hostile. A lawyer, Edward Littleton, says that 'if a mad man kill the King it is high treason'. Ostensibly Littleton is merely saying that even the unaccountable actions of the insane are subject to the law. The words 'high treason' and 'kill the king', though, worm their way into his listeners' minds.

A vote is called. A majority are for pursuing the matter. Buckingham's 'presumption' and 'dangerous' behaviour around the time of King James's death will be thirteenth on the list of charges to be presented for his impeachment.

There was another threat hanging over Buckingham, in the person of the Earl of Bristol, the former ambassador to Madrid.

Bristol had often been with Buckingham when the Duke was talking with Olivares. He knew what had really gone on in Spain. When, in 1624, Buckingham had given his 'relation' to Parliament of his visit to Madrid, he had omitted many things, including the fact that he and Charles had promised, on King James's behalf, to repeal the penal laws against English Catholics. If those promises became known to Parliament and public, a storm would follow.

Bristol had many reasons to feel hard done by. Buckingham's arrival in Spain had been bad for him on many counts. The silliness of the sudden appearance of the 'venturous knights' had been deeply embarrassing to him as his country's representative. He knew how bizarre and unbecoming the Spaniards thought it. He had worked hard to counter the offence given and to do what he could to restore Prince Charles's dignity.

As Buckingham had come swaggering in, taking the lead in negotiating, Bristol had effectively been demoted. He had lost face. He had been forced to watch while a newcomer with no understanding of Spanish culture or of diplomacy (the whole story of Buckingham and Charles's adventure is evidence of that) undermined all that he had achieved. He had been working for years to realise the Spanish Match. Its failure had been a disaster for his career.

Worse, on his return home he found himself treated as a villain. Buckingham had accused him of conspiring with Gondomar, of serving the Spanish state rather than the English one, of being a traitor.

Buckingham had considered impeaching Bristol. But in justifying himself, Bristol might condemn others. Instead Buckingham had him placed under house arrest, first in London and then in his country estate in Dorset.. And so two years went by.

In April 1626, as the Commons' committee was preparing charges against Buckingham, Bristol submitted a petition to the House of Lords. Since his return from Spain, he wrote, he had been silenced by Buckingham, who was determined 'to keep him from the presence of Their Majesties and the Parliament, lest he should discover many crimes concerning the said Duke'.

He asked to be allowed to take his seat in the Lords. King Charles ordered him to first present himself for trial by his peers.

1 May. Bristol is brought before the House of Lords, and charged with high treason. Buckingham is present. As the indictment is being read out, Bristol interrupts, pointing and calling out, 'I accuse that man the Duke of Buckingham of high treason. And I will prove it.' He is allowed to speak.

He makes twelve charges against Buckingham. He accuses him of plotting with Gondomar and the Pope, of deliberately luring Prince Charles to Spain with the intention of converting him to Catholicism, of having 'perverted the Prince and subverted the true religion established in England'. He says that in Madrid Buckingham avoided Protestant services, instead adoring the blessed sacrament like a papist. He accuses Buckingham of corruption and depravity. He says that Buckingham offered Spaniards gifts and favours 'for the recompense and hire of his lust'. He says that Buckingham's meddling had been 'the cause of the ruin and misfortune' of the Elector Palatine and his family.

He conjures up a vision of what might have been if only Buckingham hadn't disrupted the negotiations over the marriage contract: Charles married to 'a worthy lady whom he loved'; the English Treasury filled by a dowry 'much greater than was ever given in money in Christendom'; the Spanish King intervening to restore the Palatinate to Frederick and Elizabeth. To a Parliament being asked to subsidise what many of them considered a dangerous and unnecessary war with Spain, it was a poignant vision of a happier alternative reality.

Bristol throws another dart. He says that early in 1625 he appealed to King James, who agreed to look into his case. 'I pray God that promise did him no hurt,' Bristol went on, 'for he died shortly after.'

The implication is clear. Bristol is suggesting that, in order to keep him from speaking out, Buckingham might have killed the King.

Buckingham has declared that he will not interrupt Bristol, who 'has been his friend', but at this 'touch upon the late King's death', he protests. The hearing, as described in contemporary newsletters, becomes noisy. Bristol insists that his charges against Buckingham should be considered before the charges against himself. It is eventually agreed that the two cases should be tried together. Bristol is placed under house arrest again, whereupon he bursts out 'into angry passion', saying that since he and Buckingham are both now accused of treason, they should be given equal treatment.

Fair or not, his objections are overruled.

As the Commons' committee are preparing their case for Buckingham's impeachment, he is being accused in the House of Lords of being a Catholic sympathiser, a sexual predator and a traitor to his country. No wonder the Venetian envoy thought he was near to being overwhelmed by 'embarrassments'.

8 May. The impeachment process arrives at its first climax. Representatives of both houses meet in conference in the Painted Chamber of the Palace of Westminster.

In an impeachment, it is for the Commons to present the case against the accused, and for the Lords to assess whether it is valid, and then to judge it. Eight members of the Commons' committee have been appointed to speak.

Their task will not be easy. An impeachment is a criminal trial. It is not clear how many of the charges against Buckingham can properly be considered crimes. Nor is it certain that the Lords will agree as easily as the Commons have done that 'common fame' can be accepted as evidence.

Buckingham's accusers must exert themselves mightily to make their case. They must employ every tool or weapon they have. Those weapons are all drawn from the arsenal of rhetoric.

Oratory

THE speakers chosen to act as Buckingham's accusers were virtuosi in the most respected and influential art of the time – that of the spoken word. Each one of their speeches was a carefully studied performance drawing upon years of training. Any boy destined for a career in public life (and a tiny number of girls with exceptionally enlightened fathers) would have read Aristotle on Demosthenes. They would have studied and parsed and analysed the speeches of Cicero and his dicta on oratorical technique. They (or their tutors and schoolmasters) would have read Thomas Linacre's *De constructionis figuris* and the comprehensive study of the art of speech by Linacre's great student Erasmus, *De copia*.

They would have spent years mastering the rules and practising the skills of the *trivium*, the three ways that had been recognised, ever since the time of Plato, to lead to oratorical mastery: grammar, logic and rhetoric. Grammar for clarity and precision of expression. Logic for reasoning so exact it is impervious to hostile argument. Rhetoric to move and persuade, to carry the speaker's thought into the listener's minds with maximum force, to alter opinion and sway sympathy, to make a theory into a drama; as Francis Bacon put it, 'to apply reason to imagination for the better moving of the will'.

Speakers who had been given such an education found a ready audience, some of whom had had no formal education at all. The great majority of the population was illiterate, but the post-Reformation introduction of services in the vernacular had made resonant words and complex ideas familiar to everybody, regardless of class or gender. Tyndale's Bible, Cranmer's Book of Common Prayer and, more recently, King James's Authorised Version of the Bible were imprinted deeply on the minds and speech patterns of all churchgoers. Memories, trained by an education largely based on learning by rote, were capacious. In the next generation, when orthodox religion was being challenged by a multiplicity of sects, preachers sprang up ready to hold forth with astonishing fluency and eloquence in barns and open fields, or under hedgerows along the roadside, moving their listeners to fury, to wild enthusiasm, or to tears.

This was the great age of English drama, when noblemen and commoners alike (the latter on their feet) listened keenly for hours on end to Latinate blank verse in iambic pentameters. Shakespeare, Jonson, Webster, Middleton, Tourneur – these authors were respected by the court, but their plays were equally enjoyed by the groundlings.

It was the age of the sermon. King James appreciated fine preaching. He listened to three times as many sermons per week as Queen Elizabeth ever had. He slept with a volume of Lancelot Andrewes's sermons under his pillow. He enjoyed a cunningly constructed argument as a sports enthusiast might enjoy a sequence of passes and counter-passes full of surprise turns and opposition-defying twists. He – and a high proportion of his contemporaries – could follow the ins and outs of sophistical theorising and revere the speaker for their ingenuity. He – and a high proportion of his contemporaries – loved to have their emotions stirred.

In 1621 Buckingham had intervened with King James to get John Donne appointed Dean of St Paul's. Donne was a star among preachers. The love poems for which he is now chiefly remembered are exuberant in their passion, tautly controlled in their syntax. Donne's sermonising – although far more verbose and discursive – has the same paradoxical combination of rigour and extravagance. Isaak Walton wrote that he spoke 'like an angel from a cloud, but in none', by which Walton seems to have meant that while his listeners were mesmerised by him, Donne remained lucid.

When Donne preached outdoors, as he often did, at Paul's Cross in the open space next to the cathedral, he could draw a congregation of up to six thousand. No more than a tenth of those people could have heard enough to follow exactly what he was saying, but he worked on the rest of the crowd with his personal charisma, with what Walton calls his 'most particular grace and an unexpressible addition of comeliness'. He used carefully paced histrionics. He sobbed and lamented and threatened. 'The preacher … standeth of no one thing more in need' than 'moving the affections', wrote Andreas Hyperius in 1577. Donne could do it. He manipulated his hearers' emotions until some were carried, so Walton tells us, 'as St Paul was, to heaven in holy raptures'. They would weep. Donne would weep with them.

These extraordinary displays of mass emotion were not spontaneous, They were planned according to the principles of an ancient art. Donne was an outstanding practitioner, but the Parliament-men lining up to accuse Buckingham had all been educated in the strategies he used, and some of them could match his performances. Donne built his sermons, he said, like a 'goodly palace', with a sequence of spaces, of courts in which to pause and look about, and inner sanctums for introspection. He repeated himself insistently, piling synonym upon synonym, belabouring his hearers' ears with multiple variations, with choral reprises. He used exemplary stories, from scripture or from classical mythology. Virgil, Plutarch, the saints were summoned as his witnesses. His sentences rolled musically. He employed dramatic pauses. He varied his tempi. His arguments progressed gradually, two steps back for each step forward. They branched and meandered, allowing his hearers time to reflect, to catch up. But then he would begin his crescendo. He gathered up all he was saying into a ball and tightened it and tightened it and at last flung it heavenwards in a flashing climax.

Many of his listeners brought pen and ink to write down his words.

As in the theatre and the pulpit, so in Parliament. This was – above all – the age of political oratory.

King James had tended to be prolix. His addresses to Parliament were measured in hours rather than minutes. Not everyone enjoyed them. Sir John Eliot judged that 'the long orations of King James did inherit but the wind'. King Charles, hampered and embarrassed by his stammer, spoke more concisely. Eliot writes approvingly of his 'brevity and plainness'.

Like most of his peers, Eliot was a discerning connoisseur of rhetoric, an art in which he himself was generally considered to be a master.

He respected several of his peers for their oratorical gifts, but in this Parliament he would outshine them, or shine in the place of those who had been prevented from standing.

Eliot on Sir Thomas Wentworth (excluded): 'A strong eloquence he had and a comprehension of much reason ... His arguments were weighty and acute and his descriptions exquisite.'

Eliot on Sir Edward Coke (excluded): 'That great father of the law.' Coke's oratorical reputation was so well established that Eliot felt the need to say no more. The savagery with which Coke had torn into Sir Walter Raleigh was notorious. The *gravitas* and argument-proof directness with which he had opposed the King over the commendam had made him an object of reverence.

Eliot on Sir Robert Phelips (excluded): 'There was in this gentleman a natural grace of oratory, a moving and Nestorian way of rhetoric … a choice store he had and elegance of words, readiness and dexterity in fancy and conception, a voice and pronunciation of much sweetness.' His defects were 'a redundancy and exuberance … and an affected cadence and delivery'. Eliot was impressed that Phelips invariably spoke 'extemporaneously'.

Eliot on Sir Benjamin Rudyerd (elected): 'A great artist', but he lacked the confidence to improvise. He 'did speak never but premeditated, which had more show of memory than affection and made his words less powerful'.

Eliot himself wrote his speeches out beforehand (arriving in the Commons with his pockets crackling with paper, carrying many more than he would get the opportunity to deliver). Preparation was necessary, but when the time came to speak, Eliot, unlike Rudyerd, would lay aside his text and speak extempore.

He and all of his fellows in the team assembled to denounce Buckingham knew how to project their voices. They understood pacing. They used sarcasm and pathos and menace. They knew when to coax, when to insinuate, when to rant, when to thunder. They were masters of the spoken word.

Meteor

A MOCK epic – *The Warres of the Gods* – is on sale in London. Apparently composed when King James was still alive, it tells how Great Jove 'that sways the imperial sceptre' has become enthralled by an 'upstart love'. This relationship has set the times out of joint. The 'glorious starry border' of the heavens is disordered.

> *Each planet's course doth alter,*
> *The sun and moon*
> *Are out of tune,*
> *The spheres begin to falter.*

The theme of cosmic disruption is about to be reprised in Parliament.

8 May. The conference in the Painted Chamber begins. Sir Dudley Digges is the first to speak. He is addressing the Lords' chosen representatives, Buckingham among them. Buckingham is sitting directly opposite him, watching him, according to an anonymous diarist 'with a cold and intrepid stare'.

Digges's preamble conjures up a vision, like those presented in court masques, of the 'beautiful composition and fair structure' of the kingdom. Digges is no revolutionary, though he will soon be treated as one. He is pleased by hierarchy. He is a conservative for whom each person's place is preordained and immutable. Like Shakespeare's Ulysses, he believes that a respect for 'degree' is essential to the stability of a society and the happiness of its people.

He describes a universe divided horizontally. He explains that the common people are like the lowest zone – the earth. The higher realms of air and fire correspond to the middle and upper ranks of society.

Above them are the nobility and the high officers of state, equivalent to the celestial planets and the stars. Above all others is the King, the 'one great glorious sun' that lights and heats the whole.

This arrangement is as natural and harmonious as God's creation. But it has been breached. Buckingham, says Digges, in soaring so far above the station to which he was born, is like a comet 'drawn out of the dross of the earth'. He belongs by rights in one of the lower bands. The grace and favour of the sunlike King has lifted him up, but he is a 'meteor' made of 'corruptible matter'. This meteor is unnatural. Its 'irregular motions' and 'prodigious magnitude' are fearsome. It is a sign that the time is out of joint. One of Digges's listeners notes that a prodigy of this kind 'prognosticates the ruin of the commonwealth'.

Having conjured up this vision, Digges previews the charges against Buckingham. Arriving at charge number thirteen, he says it will concern 'an injury offered to the person of the late King of blessed memory that is with God', and that 'you shall anon have further information'. With Eglisham's pamphlet by this time circulating widely, few people can fail to know what he is talking about.

Digges then says something which Buckingham will allege is 'treasonable'.

Over the next few days there will be a great deal of dispute about what Digges's exact words are, and further dispute about what he means by them. A plausible source records that he says that he will be cautious in speaking of the alleged 'injury' because 'I am commanded by the Commons to take care of the honour of the King our sovereign that lives'.

Several people present take that to mean that he is holding back information suggesting King Charles was complicit in the murder of King James.

Buckingham will say later that if he had not been 'restrained by the order of the House', he would have immediately called upon Digges to be 'reprehended'.

After Digges has prepared the ground, the first eight of the thirteen charges are read out. Each one is expounded upon, the Commons speakers taking it in turn.

Buckingham, sitting among the Lords, listens silently. Everyone is looking at him. Everyone is reading his face and body language according to their own preconceptions. One thinks he shows perfect confidence; another sees pride; another sees cheerfulness; another sees scorn. He is being attacked ferociously. His accusers' speeches are unsparing. The Florentine agent describes them as highly coloured and 'without the slightest respect for his person'. To Queen Henrietta Maria's almoner, the Bishop of Mende, they seem 'words more venomous than a viper'. Buckingham hears them without flinching.

At six in the evening, according to one diarist, 'Lords and all in a sweat with heat and thrusting, we could go no further ... so we went all weary home to our lodgings.'

9 May. The conference is suspended because one of the scheduled speakers is ill. The Commons meet to discuss the previous day's progress. The committee's speakers agree that they do not like laying out their charges while Buckingham sits listening to them. They are intimidated by his presence. 'There is such a power in the Duke as cannot be precedented in Parliament.' They consider it 'too much favour' to him that he 'should be suffered to come to affront us who came to accuse him'. He doesn't interrupt, or do anything to prevent them speaking, but it is not fit, they say, 'for us to see him thus outface us'.

The Commons vote by nearly two to one to demand Buckingham's arrest as soon as the charges have been read out.

10 May. The conference meets again and the rest of the charges are read. This time Buckingham stays away.

Article twelve accuses Buckingham of having become too rich by improper means. The Commons' spokesman says, 'Never so much came into any private man's hands out of the public purse.' And yet now Buckingham says he is in debt. 'If this be true, how can we hope to satisfy his prodigality? If false, how can we hope to satisfy his covetousness?' He is being built up into a monster, voracious and predatory.

Article thirteen deals with the death of King James and with Buckingham's plaster and posset. The speaker, Christopher Wandesford, delivers a passionate denunciation of Buckingham's 'boldness' and 'presumption'. A king's body was 'not to be thought upon without reverence, not to be approached unto without distance', but Buckingham, 'transported by the passions of his own will', had had the audacity to interfere with it. Such behaviour has 'ever been decried as leading to ruin and destruction'.

With every charge, Buckingham is becoming larger and more ominous.

Wandesford ends with a classical allusion. He says that King James 'so loved and affected' Buckingham that he must have felt as Julius Caesar did when Brutus stabbed him and he cried out '*Et tu Brute! Et tu fili!*' (And you Brutus! And you my son!).

Wandesford isn't saying explicitly that Buckingham was King James's assassin, as Brutus had been Caesar's, but he is planting that idea in his listeners' minds.

Sir John Eliot is last to speak. He is the orator chosen to synthesise all the charges against Buckingham, and bring the proceedings to a thundering climax.

Taking up the theme of monstrosity, Eliot says that the 'patterns' of Buckingham's mind are so 'full of collusion and deceit' that he is like 'the beast called by the ancients Stellionatus; a beast so blurred, so spotted, so full of foul lines, that they knew not what to make of it'.

That 'beast' was Eliot's own invention. To the Romans, *stellionatus* was not a mythical creature but a crime. The word was used for various forms of fraud that fitted into no other defined category. It conjured up wickedness of an exceptional nature, baffling because so egregious. Using it of Buckingham, Eliot is saying he is a being whose foulness is beyond comprehension.

Eliot goes on to enumerate Buckingham's vices or sins, and the 'evils' or crimes into which they have driven him. He is ambitious, and has got 'the government of the whole into his own hands'. He is a tyrant who has made men and laws 'inferior to his will'. He is greedy, making himself rich by extortion and corruption. He has spent public funds, 'not only to satisfy his own lustful desires but the luxury of others'. He has opened the veins of the state and let its lifeblood run out until the 'body of the kingdom' is now 'in a consumption'. He has had vast sums of money and spent it on 'his riots and excesses' on 'sumptuous feasting and magnificent building'. He is a canker. He is a moth (the kind that destroys precious textiles). His power 'could hardly be paralleled, except perhaps by that of Sejanus, the unscrupulous favourite of the Emperor Tiberius'.

Sejanus

TACITUS described Sejanus as a curse called down 'by the anger of heaven against that Roman realm for whose damnation he flourished and fell'. Beloved by Tiberius, he ruled supreme in Rome while the Emperor secluded himself.

Sejanus was a handsome young man. Tacitus writes that he was 'orderly and modest to outward view, at heart possessed by a towering ambition'. He was impelled 'at whiles to lavishness and luxury', and as a young man he had 'sold his virtue' to a rich patron. But the sins of the flesh were of less interest to Sejanus than power, to the pursuit of which he devoted all of his formidable 'industry and vigilance'.

He first attracted attention when Emperor Tiberius and his guests were dining in a villa built within a great cave. There was a rockfall. People were killed. As everyone searched anxiously for Tiberius, they found Sejanus on his hands and knees, shielding the imperial body with his own.

Soon he had bound Tiberius to him 'by his multifarious arts'. The Emperor was notoriously secretive, but he became, 'to Sejanus alone, unguarded and unreserved'. He delegated far-reaching powers to him. He made Sejanus praetor, an office reserved for the members of the great senatorial families and for which Sejanus, as a mere eques, was not eligible. He ordered golden effigies of Sejanus to be set up and honoured. He approved the construction of an altar to Amicitia (friendship) flanked by statues of Sejanus and himself.

Tiberius receded from public view. Sejanus was more and more visible, more and more powerful. He won around senators with promises of high offices, for which they paid him. He surrounded himself with clients and cronies. He murdered Tiberius's son and drove his grandsons into exile.

The Emperor withdrew to the island of Capri. There – according to Suetonius, the most salacious historian of the ancient world – he amused himself with orgies and 'still grosser depravities that one can hardly bear to tell or be told'. Young men and women, little boys, even babies, were pressed into his sexual service. Meanwhile, back in Rome, Sejanus ruled unchallenged.

Much of this story seemed to Buckingham's critics to have parallels in their own time. The reclusive or elusive prince who withdrew (to Capri – to Theobalds or Newmarket) to pursue private pleasures, rumoured to include transgressive sexual practices, leaving his favourite to rule the roost. The way power shifted from legally sanctioned institutions (the Roman Senate – the English Privy Council and Parliament) to extra-constitutional power-bases (the praetorian guard – the Jacobean bedchamber). The privileging of youthful charisma over legitimate authority. The use of improper influence and the sale of offices to establish a nouveau-riche faction. The infatuated ruler surrendering power to the unworthy object of his love.

Pamphleteers seized on Sejanus to give their attacks on Buckingham a classical gloss. The anonymous author of *Tom Tell Troath* had written that King James risked becoming his favourite's helpless puppet, and then, writes 'Tom', his subjects will 'cry with Tiberius, "O people prepare for servitude."' Alexander Leighton, author of another tract, wrote that a king should have many counsellors, and never 'commit the helm of affairs unto one man's hand'. As an example of the problems that ensue when he does so, writes Leighton, 'take this one of Sejanus, whom Tiberius advanced'.

Sejanus's story does not end well. In 1603 Ben Jonson had written a play about him. It was given again the following year, with Richard Burbage in the lead and with William Shakespeare playing Tiberius. Jonson would have been thinking of Queen Elizabeth's beloved Earl of Essex. By the time the play was republished in 1616, though, it was widely understood to be a coded comment on King James's relationship with Buckingham. It is entitled *Sejanus His Fall*.

Once Tiberius had withdrawn to Capri, Sejanus imposed what Tacitus calls 'a grinding despotism'. He purged the Senate of his opponents. Spies and informers were everywhere. There were show trials, suicides, executions.

Five years after he had left Rome for the last time, Tiberius became alarmed by messages warning him that Sejanus intended to displace him and seize absolute power. He wrote a letter to the Senate. Sejanus came to the Senate House to hear it read out, having been informed that it was full of praise for him. As he listened, the praetorian guards, no longer loyal to him, surrounded the building. Then came the passage in which Tiberius ordered the senators to arrest Sejanus, charge him with treason and put him to death.

He was overpowered and imprisoned. Rome was in uproar. That evening he was taken out and strangled. His body was thrown down the broad steps leading from the Capitoline Hill to the Forum, and left lying there, to be torn to pieces by the mob. Sejanus's friends and supporters were hunted down and killed. His statues were toppled and destroyed. His name was erased from public records. His children were executed, his daughter first being raped because the execution of virgins was forbidden. Even coins bearing his image were defaced.

To liken Buckingham to Sejanus was to warn that he, too, would one day fall.

When Sir John Eliot compared Buckingham to Sejanus, he stressed particular themes. He spoke of the way Sejanus promoted his unworthy friends to high office, noting that Buckingham did so too. He talked of Sejanus's pride and high ambition. He recalled how Sejanus would work together with his imperial master: just so had Buckingham made himself not the King's servant but the King's partner. And there were other parallels, said Eliot, which he would not mention (but mention them he did) – Sejanus's 'salaciousness, his neglect of counsels, his veneries, his venefices'.

'Salaciousness' and 'veneries' – in the list of topics Eliot and his colleagues drew up when they began work on their dossier was a category entitled 'Adulteries and the like'.

Buckingham was repeatedly accused of promiscuity. A poem published while the impeachment hearings proceeded calls him 'England's wanton duke'. No doubt he had affairs, both before and after his marriage. He was an exceptionally good-looking man who was often away from home, living at a court where sexual mores were notoriously lax. Many of the specific accusations, though, are hard to credit: the Countess of Olivares; Anne of Austria; most recently, the Duchess of Chevreuse.

When Madame de Chevreuse came to England with Henrietta Maria in the summer of 1625, Buckingham saw a lot of her, visiting her at Denmark House and spending hours there. They were talking politics, the Duchess briefing Buckingham on Richelieu, and the best ways to handle him. There were rumours that they were also making love, but there are reasons to doubt them: Chevreuse was nearly nine months pregnant, her baby's probable father being Buckingham's friend and supporter Lord Holland.

There were many more such allegations. It is as though any woman whose private life was irregular was imagined to have been Buckingham's lover, his victim or his prey. And there were cruder stories – that he had exposed himself to some nuns in Spain, and that at New Hall he had watched while a man had sex 'with three women one after another', and that his wife Katherine had 'wept for the same'.

These goings-on were not among the impeachment charges. They had no place in the august setting of the Painted Chamber. Eliot does not mention them directly, but in speaking of Sejanus's 'veneries' he allowed a whiff of sexual transgression to enter the debate.

'Venefices' – Eliot's last word was deliberately obscure, but most members of Parliament knew enough Latin to understand it. 'Venefice' means the 'the art or practice of poisoning'.

Eliot doesn't refer directly to the accusations contained in Eglisham's pamphlet. He delivers a contorted sentence in which he hints there is a thing – a weighty, dreadful, important thing – he cannot talk about. 'I fear to speak it, nay I doubt to think it.' But the word 'venefice' is a carefully planted giveaway. What Eliot is saying but not saying is that Buckingham is a poisoner – that he killed the late King.

Eliot's speech was long. Its rhythms were sonorous, its rhetoric vehement. At last he said, 'I have done, Your Lordships', and then finished with a ringing call. 'Know the man. What have been his actions. Whom he is like. I leave him to your judgments.'

The Tower

SOME verses are circulating. There is a 'Buck', a 'King of Game'. He is 'fair in sight'. He is magnificent but destructive. He keeps 'the lesser flocks in fear'.

> *The huntsmen have pursued this deer,*
> *And followed him with full career,*
> *But such his craft and such their lot,*
> *They hunt him oft, but take him not.*

It is hard for them because the 'new Charlemagne'

> *… takes much delight*
> *In this great beast …*
> *And loves too well*
> *His Buck-King-Game.*

The Parliament-men are the huntsmen. But will they be able to bring down the dangerous buck, protected as he is by Charles/Charlemagne?

11 May. The peers who have been listening to the Commons' committee's speeches in the Painted Chamber have been taking notes. King Charles calls upon them to show him their 'table books'. Having read, Charles decides they need his guidance.

Accompanied by Buckingham and some of Buckingham's most loyal supporters – his father-in-law, Rutland, the diplomats Carlisle and Holland – Charles travels by barge the short distance upriver from Whitehall to Westminster.

He addresses the Lords. He has been too forbearing, he says, in allowing this laying of charges against Buckingham to go forward. He has permitted it only because Buckingham wishes to be brought to trial, so that he can 'approve his innocency'. But he, King Charles, needs no such proof. The charges will not stand: 'I myself can be a witness to clear him in every one of them.'

Having made his position clear, the King leaves to spend the afternoon playing tennis.

If Buckingham is a criminal, the King of England is one too. Back in March, Charles had told Parliament that whatever Buckingham may be accused of, 'I did command him to do what he has done'.

It is largely true. If Buckingham lied to Parliament about what happened in Spain, he did so with Charles's connivance. Charles was present in January 1624 when Buckingham gave his relation of events in Madrid to Parliament. As Buckingham delivered his account, Charles nodded and occasionally spoke to confirm what was being said. Now Bristol has cast doubt on Buckingham's narrative. King Charles has said that Bristol's attack is 'as far upon himself as upon the Duke'.

More seriously, if Buckingham poisoned King James, whether deliberately or inadvertently, Charles will be partially responsible. Dr Craig has told the committee that, in the last days of King James's life, he and one of his fellow physicians went to Charles to beg him to intervene. They asked him to 'advise' Buckingham that he should leave the dying King's treatment to the people whom Mayerne had appointed. Charles failed to act on their request. And so the perhaps-lethal plaster was applied to King James's body for the second time.

The Bishop of Mende writes to Richelieu that if Buckingham's name is not cleared, 'the King will look like an accomplice'. The Venetian envoy agrees. If the King dissolves Parliament, he reports, that 'rupture' would be taken to mean he was afraid of an inquiry 'into the causes of the late King's death'.

While the King has been visiting the Lords, the Commons have been hearing, from their eight representatives, how their speeches were received and debating what is next to be done. They arrive at a resolution. A group of members led by Sir Nathaniel Rich crosses the Palace of Westminster to the Lords chamber. Rich has come to deliver the Commons' recommendation: Buckingham – who is present – should immediately be placed under arrest.

The Lords reply that they will first hear him speak in his own defence.

Buckingham agrees to do so. He is rueful, courteous, hurt. He has made mistakes, he says. So have all ministers. 'I am not an angel amongst men.' He is puzzled, he says, as to how he should respond to his accusers. 'If I should hold my tongue it would argue guilt; if I should speak it may argue boldness, being so foully accused.' But he has not deserved the dishonour of the present proceedings. He has never committed, will never commit, or ever even intend to commit, any crime 'as truly deserves punishment from the state'.

He is not arrested.

While he is speaking, the Commons are still in session. That morning King Charles said he had been 'too remiss in punishing those insolent speeches'. Now, in St Stephen's Chapel, the serjeant-at-arms discreetly approaches the two speakers the King had in mind, Sir Dudley Digges and Sir John Eliot. The serjeant tells them that they are wanted in the lobby. They follow him out. A party of royal messengers is waiting for them. They are arrested on the King's orders, taken to the Tower and locked up there.

Their arrest is an outrage against members' rights to free speech and freedom from arrest while Parliament is sitting. It is a shocking breach of their privilege, which must remain sacrosanct if Parliament is to survive the onslaughts of tyranny.

Time passes. It is a while before their fellow members understand where the two have gone. There are whispers, and then a great commotion. People shout 'Rise! Rise!' Every man is on his feet, signifying that Parliament cannot – will not – sit under such oppression. All business is suspended. All the members leave the chamber in protest.

But then, having left their seat of power, where are they to go?

That evening many of them gather privately, in separate groups, to lament, to fume, to plan.

12 May. The Commons reassemble. Sir Dudley Carleton, who has been Buckingham's host in The Hague, with whom he has traded in art and antiquities, is known to be 'a favourite of the Duke'. Now back at court as Vice Chamberlain and an MP, Carleton rises in the Commons. Amid noisy heckling, he sets out to justify the arrests. Digges and Eliot, he says, used 'contemptible terms'. Members shout 'No!' and 'Sit down!'

Carleton presses on. He says that Eliot spoke of Buckingham without due respect, as 'this man' or 'the man', as though he was already stripped of his titles and found guilty.

Worse – Digges spoke of the death of King James in a way King Charles finds highly objectionable. Carleton explains that King Charles thinks that Digges thought that King James was murdered, and that Charles himself was somehow complicit in the crime. This suggestion has made Charles so angry that he is thinking of doing without Parliament altogether and embracing 'new counsels'.

The Commons respond by denying that Digges ever said anything to justify the King's interpretation of his words. They insist that those members of the Commons' committee who were present in the Painted Chamber heard him say nothing exceptionable.

For four days they argue.

King Charles had a tendency, which became ever more marked as his tragic life went on, to rush towards trouble. It wasn't in him to pretend – as a more adroit politician might – not to have heard a muttered insult.

Simonds D'Ewes wrote to a friend that Charles had told the Lords that, in likening Buckingham to Sejanus, Eliot had suggested that he, Charles, was a new Tiberius. In Tacitus's account, well known to seventeenth-century readers, Tiberius is the epitome of a tyrant – cruel by nature, sexually perverse in his private life, autocratic and irresponsible as a ruler. No one was saying that Charles was similarly tyrannical. (If Eliot was implying that anyone was like Tiberius, it would have been, not Charles, but his father, King James.) It was not wise for Charles to be putting the thought into the people's heads. D'Ewes was so shocked by it that he asked the friend to whom he wrote it to burn his letter.

Whatever it was exactly that Digges said in the Painted Hall, he had certainly not said that Buckingham had deliberately poisoned King James with the new king's approval. Even to hold such an idea in one's mind might be treason.

Charles, though, insisted on responding to innuendoes as though they were explicit allegations. In so doing he brought what might have remained an almost unthinkable suspicion, something to be whispered only in the darkest corners, out into the light.

13 May. Buckingham speaks again in the Lords. He says that in all he has done, 'he did nothing but by the King's command'. When he responds to the allegations about the potion and the plaster, he is seen to have tears in his eyes. He says that it is 'an affliction' to him so much as to hear people speak of the death of King James, who was 'so good to me'.

15 May. Digges is released from the Tower. He has apologised for any offence he may have given by saying whatever it was he said, and King Charles receives him 'graciously'. Digges is back in the Commons chamber the next morning.

Sir John Eliot, though, has refused to humble himself. He stands by what he said – Stellionatus, Sejanus and all. The King's messenger tells the Commons that his continued imprisonment is not a breach of his Parliamentary 'rights and liberties'. He is being held (as Edward Coke was back in 1621) because he is under investigation for some unspecified 'things that are extrajudicial to the House'.

His lodgings are searched, his papers examined. He is interrogated by the Attorney General. The line of questioning suggests that he may be a dangerous revolutionary. He is asked what he thinks about kings who

508 W A R

have been 'compelled to give way to the will of the people'. He is asked for his opinion on the deposition of King Richard II. To both questions he replies that he 'detested' such disrespectful treatment of a monarch, as being 'contrary to the laws both human and divine'.

Eliot is speaking the truth. In the course of his speech the previous week in the Painted Chamber he interrupted himself, claiming he heard someone among the listeners say the word 'king'. (During those lengthy Parliamentary speeches, there must have been much muttered commentary.) The word prompted him to say there was something that he had to make plain: in nothing he or any of his fellows had said did they 'intend to reflect the least ill odour on His Majesty or his most blessed father of happy memory'. On the contrary, 'with all honour we do admire them'. They wished only to save the reputation of the kings, 'to vindicate their fames', and draw a distinction between their 'sacred names' and their evil advisers, described by another MP that month as those 'vipers' that give the King 'poisonous information' and 'do us so much harm'.

There is no reason to doubt Eliot's sincerity. Eliot believed, as nearly all of his fellow MPs believed too, that if there was something rotten in the state of England, it was personal, not structural. That rottenness was concentrated not in the King, but in the favourite, the corrupt and corrupting meteor, the Duke of Buckingham.

19 May. The Commons are sitting, but in silence. They have declared that until Eliot is released they will do no business. Among the things they will not be doing is granting the King his supply.

Their silent protest is effective. Carleton tells them that a royal warrant for Sir John Eliot's release is on its way to the Tower.

20 May. Eliot takes his place in the Commons. He is free, but his job as Vice Admiral of Devon has been taken from him, for 'divers [unspecified] misdemeanours'.

In the Lords, Buckingham asks – since he is to be put on trial – for some time in which to seek legal advice. The Lords agree.

Antiquities

FOR nearly a month Buckingham absented himself from Westminster. He was working to prepare a fleet for the projected second expedition to Cadiz, and he was spending time in the most magnificent of his homes.

York House was now a court, with numerous residents. Buckingham had granted Balthazar Gerbier – as the palace's custodian – a house of his own in the grounds. There Gerbier lived with his wife, Deborah, his children and several servants. Gerbier's father-in-law, a Dutchman named Kipp who made fine picture frames, was also one of the resident team working to beautify York House. Another was the painter Orazio Gentileschi (father of the now more famous Artemisia).

Buckingham had met Gentileschi in Paris in 1625, and invited him to London, lodging him in York House with a 'great upper room' to work in. He arrived with a reputation for being 'arrogant and vindictive'. Gerbier was jealous of him, writing tetchily about the large sums of money he had 'squeezed out' of Buckingham. There were squabbles and huffy scenes, but an Italian painter on-site was an asset to cast lustre on any aristocratic household and, for the sake of the splendour of the establishment he supervised, Gerbier choked back his resentment. Gentileschi depicted biblical scenes, with a preference for those that allowed him to show women with their breasts bared. The penitent Mary Magdalene reclining in a desert cave, her eyes turned heavenward as she contemplates her sins while her russet satin drapes slip down around her waist, is a typical production. His main contribution to the decoration of York House was a sequence of panels for the Grand Saloon showing the nine Muses. They are now lost, but in the next decade he would paint a series on the same subject for Queen Henrietta Maria: two of those panels are still in the royal collection. More beautiful topless women.

New works by Gentileschi and other living artists took their place alongside what was now a picture collection impressive not only for its size (over three hundred paintings), but for its quality as well. Gerbier boasted 'he had bought in the space of a few years what it would have taken others a lifetime to acquire'. It was true. By the time his acquisitions in France had been added, the collection included what Gerbier believed to be twenty Titians, seventeen Tintorettos, sixteen Veroneses, two Correggios, one Giorgione, one Michelangelo, two Raphaels, two Leonardos and several Caravaggios. (Not all of these attributions have stood the tests of time and modern scholarship – but a good number have.)

So much for paintings. Now to diversify.

In the autumn of 1624, Buckingham had written to Sir Thomas Roe, the British ambassador in Constantinople, asking him for his assistance in buying ancient artworks. There was a newly thriving trade in Greco-Roman sculpture, most of it passing through the Ottoman capital. Now Buckingham had heard that the local people 'prize not those rarities of art that are of great esteem in other countries' and were therefore ready to dismantle temples and other ancient buildings and sell them off piecemeal. It was true. So much so that John Evelyn would write that the very best rollers for gravel walks could be 'procured from the ruins of many palaces in Smyrna where old columns of antiquities are being sawed off'.

Roe was accustomed to combining his work as a diplomat with that of snapper-up of massive artworks for aristocratic collectors back home. At the time Buckingham wrote, he and the Earl of Arundel's agent William Petty were engaged in trying to remove six colossal reliefs from a triumphal arch erected by Emperor Theodosius in CE 390. Roe and Petty were thwarted by the Sultan's Great Treasurer, who forbade them to take the reliefs because of a prophecy that disaster would befall the city if the sculptures were ever taken down.

Undaunted, the two continued their pursuits: Petty travelled to Smyrna and Philippi, and on through the Greek islands to Athens, ferreting out inscriptions and manuscripts for Arundel; Roe hunted for sculpture for Buckingham.

*   *   *

In July 1626, as he prepared himself for the impeachment hearings, Buckingham was writing to Roe again. He was obliged, he said, 'for your diligence in search of pieces of antiquities', and asked Roe to continue the good work, 'with this caution only, that you lay not out much money upon any alabaster figure pieces, unless they be figures of exquisite curiosity; for your antique master (as I am informed) never wrought upon alabaster'. He had been doing his research, informing himself of the techniques and materials of the artworks he wanted. And he only wanted the best. Arundel might be happy with an object simply because it gave him a connection to the Greco-Roman world. Buckingham wanted more. He wanted 'exquisite curiosity'. He wanted beauty, and he was ready to pay for it. He was not so fond of antiquity, he wrote, 'to court it in a deformed or misshapen stone', but wherever Roe found 'beauty with antiquity together in a statue', Buckingham would buy at 'any cost your judgement shall value it at'.

He had his great houses and his beautiful things. He had his family. He had his heir: in the previous November, while he was in Holland, Katherine had given birth to a son, named Charles after the king who was his godfather. Buckingham had much to enjoy, but he had little leisure to enjoy it, and no peace of mind. It wasn't what he referred to as his 'Parliamentary business' that worried him most. It was the defence of the realm.

Every day the Council of War met, with Buckingham in attendance. The threat of a Spanish invasion was becoming ever more alarming. British agents reported that the Spaniards were preparing to send more than 200 ships and 40,000 men to land in England or Ireland. They might arrive within weeks. The forts on the Thames and along the coast needed to be repaired and manned. The fleet had to be made ready. The need for funds was becoming ever more urgent. And still the Commons would not vote on supply.

Dissolution

WHILE Buckingham and Bristol prepared themselves for their trials, rumours circulated that Buckingham was thinking of fleeing the country. The Bishop of Mende wrote to Richelieu, 'I have learned from secret and reliable sources' that Buckingham 'will be executed, or banished for life on pain of death'.

Preparations for a second raid on Cadiz were going ahead, but with no funding. Without Parliamentary subsidies there was an economic crisis. Secretary Conway wrote at the end of May, 'The Treasury is empty.'

No one was being paid. Not the shipowners who lent their ships for the previous Cadiz expedition: the naval commissioners were harassed by 'the continual clamour of poor men' whom they could not satisfy. Not the angry, hungry sailors who crowded into London in such numbers that the Privy Council closed down the Globe Theatre for fear it might be used as the base for a riot. Not King Christian of Denmark, who bombarded King Charles with letters reminding him he had yet to pay over a single instalment of the promised £30,000 per month. Not the homeowners who were forced to accept troops being billeted on them, and were not being compensated for it. Not those troops who terrorised market towns, stealing food rather than starve. No money, no money, no money. And, unless King and Parliament could agree, no legitimate means of getting any.

Buckingham has been working on his statement with a high-powered legal team. His advisers are the Attorney General, a future Chief Justice, and William Laud.

Laud is Dean of the Chapel Royal. Later he will be the Archbishop of Canterbury and, later still, a martyr. He is the leader of the High

Church movement within the Anglican Church known as Arminianism (viewed with suspicion by Puritans in Parliament as 'but a cunning way to bring in popery'). He is the person to whom both King Charles and Buckingham turn for advice on religious matters. Charles will come to think that Laud's dogmatism and 'peevish humours' stirred up needless controversies, but for now he is still the King's favourite cleric, and he has been closely associated with Buckingham for over two years.

Laud is a small man, even shorter than the King. He is said to prefer cats to women, and perhaps he prefers beautiful men to cats. In 1621 he noted in his diary that Buckingham 'was pleased to enter upon a near respect to me. The particulars are not for paper.' Three years later he records a delicious dream. 'That night in my sleep, it seemed to me that the Duke of Buckingham came into bed to me; where he behaved himself with great kindness towards me.'

8 June. Buckingham presents his reply to the Commons' charges. This is not yet the impeachment process. It is a pre-trial hearing.

A newsletter describes his speech as being 'very modest and void of all bitterness'. He is not angry with the Commons, he explains, only regretful that they should have mistaken 'common fame' for truth.

He says, 'I have been raised to honour and fortune ... (I freely confess) beyond my merit.' But he has worked diligently for his country, to which he has always been completely loyal. 'Could there be the least alienation of my heart from the service of the state, I should be the ungratefullest man living.' He admits he may have made mistakes, but he denies any 'heinous and high misdemeanours and crimes'.

Buckingham is good at this. Where his master King Charles is always tetchily on the lookout for provocation, Buckingham is yielding. He offers modesty, mollification and obligingness.

He takes the charges one by one.

He is accused of pluralism, of having more lucrative jobs than he can possibly perform. He agrees that he has many titles, but he explains that only three of his offices – Lord Admiral, Lord Warden of the Cinque Ports and Master of the Horse – come with real responsibilities. The others are sinecures – 'rather titular and additions of honour' than roles requiring work. (This is one of the things his critics find annoying.)

He is accused of bribing office-holders to give up their positions to him or to his family members. He argues that such arrangements are usual and quite harmless. They allow an 'ancient servant of the Crown, by age and infirmity disabled' to make a little money for his retirement by selling his place.

He is accused of embezzling or extorting money from the East India Company. He says the sum in question was given him by order of King James.

He is accused of failing as Lord Admiral. He gives a detailed summary of what he has achieved, how many ships he has had refurbished or built, how modern and effective the new ships are, how he has initiated negotiations with the Barbary states to curb piracy.

He talks of the ships lent to France and subsequently used against the Huguenots of La Rochelle. He says that they were lent on King James's orders. He is not responsible for the way King Louis has employed them.

And so on and so forth. For each of the 'evils' of which he was accused he has a justification, a refutation or an explanation. He is patient, calm and well prepared.

Even when he comes to the last and most shocking allegation, that he endangered King James's life by giving him unauthorised medicine, he is unruffled. He tells how James expressly asked him to send for the medicine that he, Buckingham himself, had found helpful. He says that he was absent when Dr Remington's plaster and posset were delivered, but that on his return the King then asked him to administer them. Some of the physicians were in the room when he did so, 'in no ways seeming to dislike it'. He relates how later he 'heard a rumour as if this physic had done the King hurt'. He told King James about this rumour, whereupon the King 'answered thus: "They are worse than devils that say it."' He asks the Lords to 'commiserate with him' for his 'sad thoughts' of the death of the King who had loved him, and whom he loved in return.

He ends graciously, acknowledging his 'many weaknesses and imperfections', but asserting again 'his love and duty to his country'.

Many reporters judge his response 'satisfactory'.

9 June. King Charles tells the Commons that he is 'daily advertised from all parts of the great preparations of the enemy ready to assail us'. Parliament must support him in his efforts to defend his country, which is also theirs. Unless they pass the subsidy bill by the end of the following week, he will 'take other resolutions'.

More days pass. The subsidy is no nearer to being granted. The Commons are preparing another remonstrance.

Another rhyme is circulating. It warns that Turner, Eliot and Digges may all be 'scourged like whirligigs' (whipped like tops), but it will do the King no good while he continues to back Buckingham. Parliament, the King's 'wife', may help 'the king to money', but only if 'He will hear her most just groans/And chase from him those busy drones [Buckingham and his friends and relations]/That eat up all the honey'.

12 June. The Commons' remonstrance is completed and read out. It says, 'We protest before Your Majesty and the whole world that until this great person be removed from intermeddling with the great affairs of state, we are out of hope of any good success; and do fear that any money we shall or can give will, through his misemployment, be turned rather to the hurt and prejudice of this your kingdom than otherwise.'

14 June. King Charles is angry. This is not what it ought to be like to be a king. At a meeting of the Privy Council, he says that even if the Lords impeach Buckingham and find him guilty, he will 'raise him up again' as soon as the subsidies are received at the Exchequer.

He goes further. He says he has a mind to dissolve Parliament at once.

Buckingham argues strongly against it. He wants his trial to begin. He believes his name will be cleared, and then he is confident he can win Parliament round. If the war against Spain is to proceed, he says, he must have Parliamentary support and Parliamentary subsidies.

15 June. The King loses patience. He instructs his mouthpiece, Lord Coventry, the Lord Keeper of the Great Seal, to go to the House of Lords to announce the dissolution of Parliament. Coventry, a learned and scrupulous lawyer, dares to argue with him. Charles is adamant. Coventry goes.

In the House of Lords, when Coventry has made his announcement, Lord Montagu, one of Buckingham's clients, proposes 'that the whole House move the King to make a pause of this, for that it may be of most dangerous consequence'. A delegation of four peers, all close to Buckingham, are deputed to try to persuade Charles to change his mind.

On behalf of the Lords, they implore him to allow Parliament to sit for at least a few more days.

'Not a minute,' says the King.

A Whirlwind of Water

In the week of Parliament's dissolution, London was hit by a fearsome storm. Torrents of rainwater ran waist-high through the city streets. Hailstones piled up in heaps so massive that, even though it was midsummer, they took two full days to melt away. Churchyard walls were breached. Graves were opened and their contents set afloat on the racing water. Coffins broke apart, so that the corpses of those who died in the previous year's plague swam through the streets, horribly nudging the living as they struggled to save their children, their shops and their homes.

Parliament-men looking out from the Palace of Westminster saw something strange and terrible manifest itself on the River Thames – something nameless and unprecedented that was like a whirlpool thirty yards in circumference, but also like a 'water-pillar' as tall as a church steeple. It rose up, black and frightful, from the churning flood near Lambeth, sending boats spinning. From there it passed eastwards, enveloped in mist of its own generation, along the south bank of the river past Whitehall Palace.

Somewhere near to where the Royal Festival Hall now stands it swerved, 'very impetuously' according to one observer, and flew 'like an arrow shot' across the river to crash against the pillared baroque water-gate of the Duke of Buckingham's York House. 'It struck upon the garden walls with a great force, and mounted itself as high as an house and so went over the walls and broke down some cherry trees, and from thence ascended up into the air in a twining manner and so vanished away like smoke.'

In the early seventeenth century it was a commonplace of poetry, and believed by at least some of the poets' readers, that monstrous natural phenomena were triggered by political disorder. William Shakespeare had imagined the sheeted dead squeaking and gibbering in the streets before Julius Caesar's assassination, and horses eating each other in the Scottish royal stables as King Duncan was murdered.

The actual storm mirrored the political one. The strange thing – variously named a 'turbo', a 'cataract', a 'mass of crusty matter' or a 'whirlwind of water' – had singled out Buckingham's home. 'Everybody', wrote a diarist that week, 'took it as a judgement against the D.'

Not quite everybody, in fact, was so convinced. To others it seemed as though Buckingham himself had conjured up the prodigy. Another diarist records, 'It was said that there was a spirit at the same time seen upon the water, which did sore affright all beholders.' That spirit had come, not to judge and punish Buckingham, but to serve him. A gentleman was pilloried for saying that 'one of the Duke's devils' had arisen on the thunder on that frightful day.

Commentators, foreign and home-grown, agreed that the dissolution, with no subsidies granted, was a disaster. Flemish agent 'X' noted that Charles had 'hazarded the loss of his own honour and love of his people at home and of his allies abroad'.

Buckingham was blamed. 'The credulous vulgar', wrote the Venetian ambassador, believed it was the favourite's evil magic that had caused this devastating breakdown of relations between Charles and his people's representatives. A Palatine official wrote, 'The young King is as it were kept a prisoner by one proud man, so that those that would give good counsel have no access,' and that there was no hope for the Protestant cause 'if God does not deliver the King of Great Britain from present slavery'.

The Bishop of Mende reported to Richelieu that 'all the talk' is of throwing Buckingham into the river, 'so that his death can give the state life'.

No matter that Buckingham had been willing, even eager, to clear his name by submitting to an impeachment. No matter that he had implored Charles to allow Parliament to continue to sit.

Everything that had gone wrong, and everything that might go wrong in the future, was seen to be Buckingham's fault – never, yet, the King's.

In August Charles told his Privy Council that he would hear no more talk of Parliaments. He did 'abominate that name'.

The Forced Loan

SECRETARY of State Conway wrote to the Elector Palatine, 'We have no money, and no means of finding any … The Duke cannot manufacture money, and his personal credit is exhausted.'

King Christian of Denmark's armies were small, ill-trained and short of all the necessities of war. The £30,000 per month of English money promised him in the Treaty of The Hague might have gone some way towards remedying these problems if it had been paid punctually. It wasn't.

Christian went to war in Germany, regardless, in June 1626. His co-commanders in a three-pronged campaign were Count Mansfeld and the twenty-six-year-old Duke of Brunswick. Mansfeld was defeated by Imperial armies under the Duke of Wallenstein. His men were unpaid and starving. He withdrew into Dalmatia and there he died in October. Brunswick's advance was blocked by Count Tilly – generalis-simo of the Catholic League. Brunswick retreated, and died of disease in his camp. Tilly swept on to confront King Christian, who was retreating northwards.

It was August, but it was raining. The baggage carts and the heavy guns of Christian's army sank into mud or got lost in impassable woods. Tilly caught up. For three days Christian's troops trudged on, while Tilly's troops harassed their flanks and rearguard, capturing artillery, capturing wagons loaded with gold, killing men. At Lutter, only twenty-five miles short of his base, Christian was forced to turn and fight. His troops were surrounded. Four horses were shot under him in the course of the day. He survived, but a third of his men were left dead on the field.

After Lutter, Christian's allies dropped away. The German populace, Protestants included, saw him as a foreign invader. His men, roaming the countryside, starving and desperate, in search of food to steal, were shunned. His intervention in the wars had achieved nothing.

There was a lesson to be learnt from his experience, about the futility of becoming involved in the ghastly sequence of linked conflicts turning the German lands into a slaughterhouse, but Charles and Buckingham were deaf to it.

The news from Lutter reached King Charles on 11 September, two weeks after the battle. At once he abandoned his summer progress and went back to London. He summoned the Danish ambassador and told him, with tears in his royal eyes, that he would do all he could to assist Christian, 'even at the risk of his own crown and hazarding his life'. Fine words, but all Christian wanted or needed was money, the money he had been promised, and if possible a lot more besides.

Having given up on his subsidies when he dissolved Parliament, Charles was exploring other ways to fund his government. In the past he had been able to obtain large loans, promising repayment once subsidies reached the Exchequer. Now, though, his credit was running out. He and Buckingham turned to the City, hoping to raise £100,000. They got £20,000. Not enough.

After Lutter, King Charles needed even more money, even more urgently. Three days after news of the defeat reached him, he asked the Privy Council to propose new ways of raising it.

They tried a variety of expedients.

Previous monarchs had traditionally been granted the right to collect 'tonnage and poundage', a customs duty that was a 'prerogative tax' – one for which Parliamentary approval was not required. Charles's Parliament had yet to confirm his right to make the levy. Now his Council suggested that 'tonnage and poundage' could be collected anyway.

They proposed a 'benevolence', a voluntary tax whereby the counties could demonstrate their love for their king by giving him the money that would have been raised from the subsidies, if only they had been voted through. It turned out the love wasn't there: only four counties complied. The benevolence raised less than one thousand pounds.

They suggested that the coastal towns should pay 'ship money'. The coastal towns – plagued by pirates and impoverished by the collapse of

14. *The Count Duke of Olivares*
Diego Velázquez 1624

15. *Fiesta in the Plaza Mayor to welcome the Prince of Wales*
Juan de la Corte 1623

16. *The return of the Prince of Wales from Spain*
Hendrick Cornelisz Vroom 1623

17. *The Infanta Maria Ana*
from the studio of Velázquez

18. *King Philip IV of Spain*
Diego Velázquez 1624

19. *Marie de Médicis,*
Queen Mother of France
Peter Paul Rubens

20. *Anne of Austria,*
Queen of France
after Rubens

21. *Marie, Duchess of Chevreuse*
as Diana the Huntress
Claude Deruet

22. *Henrietta Maria,*
Queen of England
Anthony Van Dyck

23. *The Duke of Buckingham*
Peter Paul Rubens 1625

24. *The Duke of Buckingham*
Daniel Mytens 1626

25. *The Duke and Duchess of Buckingham and their Children*
Gerrit Van Honthorst 1628

26. *Mercury presenting the Liberal Arts to Apollo and Diana*
Gerrit Van Honthorst 1628

27. *The Duke of Buckingham*
Peter Oliver

28. *Katherine, Duchess of Buckingham in Mourning*
Anthony Van Dyck

29. Lady Mary Villiers, detail from
The Family of the Earl of Pembroke
Anthony Van Dyck

30. *The 2nd Duke of Buckingham and Lord Francis Villiers*
Anthony Van Dyck

the fishing fleet, so many men having being taken away to serve in the King's ships – said they couldn't pay.

They toyed with a scheme to debase the currency and mint quantities of inexpensive coin.

They sold Crown lands.

They demanded loans on the authority of the King's Privy Seal. Again the returns were paltry. 'All such projects', wrote Thomas Fuller, 'to quench the thirst of the King's necessities proved no better than sucking bottles – soon emptied, and but cold the liquor they afforded.'

Fuller was contrasting them with the 'natural' and abundant 'milk of the breast; I mean subsidies granted by Parliament'. But when a Councillor suggested loans, to be repayable next time Parliament assembled, King Charles 'disliked it utterly'. He would recall Parliament, he said, only 'if reduced to extremity and pulled by the hairs of his head'.

Finally, in September, the Council, prompted by Charles, came up with the money-raising mechanism that would become known, and detested, as the 'Forced Loan'.

Buckingham seems to have had little hand in its inception. Preoccupied with preparing the fleet, he spoke seldom in Council that month. All the same, the Forced Loan would come to be seen as his creation.

The idea was simple. In May, Parliament had let the King know that once their grievances had been answered, they would grant him four subsidies. They had never voted the grant through, but never mind that. The King's officers would go ahead and collect a sum equivalent to those subsidies anyway, as though taxation had been authorised. It was a 'loan' not in that it would ever be repaid, but in that Charles's subjects were being required to pay it in advance of Parliamentary approval (which might never come). A royal proclamation of 7 October explained that this unorthodox procedure was 'enforced upon us by necessity' for 'common defence'.

This was no voluntary 'benevolence'. Those who refused to pay the Forced Loan were punished. An MP said afterwards he had paid only 'to escape imprisonment and death'. Peers who refused to pay up (there were fifteen of them) were left at liberty but had their names entered in an ominous 'black book'. A hundred or more leading gentry were imprisoned. Common people who wouldn't or couldn't pay were dragged from their homes and pressed into the army or navy. Some were threatened with hanging from 'the next tree to their dwellings' as 'an example and terror unto others'.

No one likes paying tax, but the Forced Loan was not just unpopular in the ordinary way. It was seen as an act of tyranny, a breach of the people's fundamental rights. It was laid down in Magna Carta that no monarch might take their subjects' property without the subjects' prior consent, as given by their representatives in Parliament. Without that principle, no one could be safe in his own house. Without that principle, monarchs could extort money from their people unchecked. Without that principle, there was no prospect of Parliament ever being called again.

Two knights, Sir Francis Barrington, who was a Parliament-man, and his son-in-law refused to collect the loans. They were imprisoned. Those who paid were required to sign a 'loan book'. Many paid up for fear of reprisals but refused to sign, saying that they would not put their names to an illegal instrument. One of them was the Lord Chief Justice, the venerable Sir Ranulph Crewe. King Charles dismissed him.

The Bishop of Mende reports a conversation with King Charles that summer during which Charles asked him about 'the means used by the Kings of France to rid themselves of Parliament'.

The Disasters of War III

How to defend the realm without enough ships? How to launch a hostile raid with no men? How to feed and clothe and arm and pay an invasion force with no money? These were the questions with which Buckingham wrestled in the summer and autumn of 1626.

The men who had already been recruited deserted. Some of them mutinied, attacking their officers. Crews left their ships and marched on London, 'that their case might truly be known to His Majesty'. Some of them had not been paid for sixteen months. Their wives and children were starving. They did not want 'to perish aboard for want of clothes and other necessaries'.

Buckingham was struggling to hold together the fleet assembled at Portsmouth. The Dutch, with whom it was to join forces, were complaining that they had been waiting long enough, and still there was a dearth of supplies.

Buckingham, whom Eliot had imagined thinking only of sumptuous banquets, was hearing complaints about rotten food and stinking beer. He spent his days writing letters about peas and pork for his troops. He was trying to find quantities of rice and sugar and oatmeal.

He needed thousands of shoes, stockings and shirts, and vinegar for cleaning and disinfecting the ships. He was spending his own money, and so was Sir Allen Apsley, the Victualler of the Navy. But still there were shortages – of sails, of rigging, of anchors. The Treasurer of the Navy estimated he needed £50,000 to pay the sailors what they were owed; the Exchequer could offer only £3,000.

Buckingham was doing his best. The people who worked closely with him recognised it. 'I know no man that loves the King with more zeal-ous affection, or more seriously takes to heart the good of the state, than yourself,' wrote the Master of Ordnance. He could inspire. Sir John

Pennington, one of the naval officers who worked closely with him, wrote, 'I do not only honour my lord, but love him as a young man doth his mistress.'

He was not self-indulgent or idle, as Eliot imagined, but he had set himself, and the country, an impossible task. In beginning a war with Spain, and in trying to continue it, he was disastrously irresponsible.

No money, but also bad management. One captain wrote he 'never did see such confusion of business as is in this'. The people most closely involved did not blame Buckingham. Buckingham himself blamed the naval commissioners' incompetence, but it was hard for the commissioners too. When he ordered them to build pinnaces and fireships, they told him they had laid off the shipwrights, but, yes, if he insisted, they would 'force men to work with threatenings, having no money to pay them'.

The men were angry. The commissioners reported that when they visited the ships in the Thames, they met with 'clamour and danger to our persons'. Mutinous sailors tried to break down the doors of a room in which they were meeting. Hundreds of sailors from Chatham marched into London. In Portsmouth, 500 men, on being offered only one month's wages (a fraction of what they were owed), 'hurried away' and set out for London, shouting, 'One and all, one and all!' The Treasurer of the Navy was at home when 300 unpaid sailors surrounded his house, broke down the gates and 'would have plucked him out by the ears had he not given them fair words'.

Buckingham was a prime target. In October his carriage was smashed to pieces as it waited for him outside the Council Chamber. Men from London's trained bands were set to guard his houses, as well as the court at Whitehall. Even so, a group of army officers who had been serving in Ireland, and had been left unpaid for months, forced their way into his apartment in Whitehall as he was eating dinner. He told them that to invade the court in that way was a capital offence. They said that if they were hanged, there would be many more to come after them, 'and from this proceeded to such uncouth language as His Excellency was fain to yield and to promise them upon his honour they should, and speedily, be satisfied'.

*   *   *

In this atmosphere of desperation and mutiny, the fleet finally sailed. The feared Spanish invasion had not materialised. This was to be another unprovoked and provocative raid.

Back in June Buckingham had told Parliament, as the Commons prepared to present the charges against him, that his greatest regret was that the attempt to impeach him had caused 'the loss of this year for foreign attempts'. At that point he seemed to understand that a naval attack begun past midsummer was doomed. But by October his efforts to send the fleet away had shifted from determination to grim stubbornness. Yet again he had missed the campaigning season, but still, for the third time, he sent out an expedition too late, and therefore with very poor chances of success.

He appointed Lord Willoughby commander and on 13 October he sent him orders almost identical to those he had given Cecil the year before – to cruise off Cadiz, 'to take, spoil, or sink' all Spanish ships in the bay there, and to lie in wait for the treasure fleet and capture some of its ships. Willoughby went glumly, without much hope, but 'resolved to try the event'.

Once more in the Bay of Biscay the fleet was battered by storms. Once more provisions were inadequate, the food rotten. Once more men fell ill. Once more ships that had been repaired and equipped by such desperate efforts were damaged. Long before he had even sighted the Spanish coast, Willoughby turned back.

Buckingham didn't reproach him. Gracious as ever, he wrote to Willoughby, 'It is God's doing and we may not repine at it.' Others disagreed. Hundreds, perhaps thousands, of men had died of disease and hardship on the ships. There were many who thought the futile waste of human lives and material resources was not in fact God's doing. It was Buckingham's own.

Concord/Discord

CHARLES disliked his wife's entourage, those infuriating 'monsieurs'. He felt undermined by them. When the Queen had upset him by refusing to be crowned alongside him, he asked her to watch the coronation procession from the apartments of the Countess of Buckingham, the Duke's mother. On the day of the coronation it rained. Henrietta Maria didn't want to get her shoes muddy crossing the courtyard when she could see the procession perfectly well from her own apartments, and she told Charles so. He was annoyed.

Henrietta Maria told the French ambassador about the argument. He advised her to obey her husband, so she did. This only irritated Charles further – it showed she cared more for the Frenchman's opinion than she did for her husband's wishes. Another blow to Charles's self-esteem. Another instance of the monsieurs' undue influence over her. He longed to be rid of the whole lot of them. He felt he would never be master in his own marriage, as he thought a man should be, until the monsieurs (and mesdames) were gone.

Five months later, shortly after he had dissolved Parliament in June 1626, King Charles visited his wife's apartments. Henrietta Maria and her ladies were dancing in a way he didn't like. He grabbed her hand, pulled her into an adjoining room and locked her in. He then ordered her attendants out into the garden. There he told them he was of a mind to have them all sent home. Henrietta Maria, watching through a window and seeing her ladies crying, 'grew very impatient and broke the glass windows with her fist'.

Charles didn't carry out his threat immediately, but in August Buckingham received this letter from him.

I command you to send all the French away tomorrow out of the town. If you can by fair means. But stick not long in disputing; otherwise force them away, driving them away like so many wild beasts until ye have shipped them. And so the Devil go with them.
  Let me hear no answer but of the performance of my command.

'The French' were Henrietta Maria's household. She was left with two priests, a cook, her musicians and her dressmakers, which seemed to her a pitifully small following for a queen. Instead of her own compatriots, she was now surrounded by Buckingham's women. His wife, mother, sister and niece were all among her ladies-in-waiting. Henrietta Maria knew she was being watched and controlled, and she did not like it. She told the Bishop of Mende she was 'like a prisoner who cannot talk to anyone', and that she called upon God 'to have pity on a poor oppressed princess'.

It was not a good way to improve Anglo-French relations. Unfortunate because Buckingham was still clinging to his vision of an anti-Habsburg alliance, and without France that vision could not be fully realised.

Richelieu's grip on the government of France was tightening. An English report of 1626 notes that 'the Cardinal keeps the King in his power', and that under the Cardinal's influence Louis was so 'overawed with the fear of damnation' that he had become newly determined to quell Protestantism.

In the summer of 1626, Richelieu took for himself the post of Admiral of France and began to build up a French fleet to rival the English one. He needed ships to subdue the Huguenots who were defying the power of the French monarchy from La Rochelle. It seemed to the Bishop of Bordeaux, and to many in England, that he was intent as well on 'lowering the pride' of the seafaring Protestant nations, Holland and England.

Dudley Carleton wrote to Buckingham that this was something 'not to be neglected'. The Council of War agreed. Richelieu's maritime plans, they decided, were aimed at 'the usurping of an absolute or equal dominion with His Majesty upon the British ocean, to the great prejudice of His Majesty's regality and the ancient inheritance of his imperial crown'.

Buckingham had no desire, yet, to challenge France. He sent representatives to Paris to try again to persuade the King and the Cardinal that their first preoccupation should be with the Spanish menace, 'a girdle of mischief and offence encompassing France'. His arguments went unheard.

To the French, England was neither a force to be feared nor an ally to be coveted. The Bishop of Mende told Richelieu, 'There is nothing to fear from England, the King lacks the wherewithal to fit ten boats.'

On 27 September 1626 a new French ambassador arrived in London, the Marshal de Bassompierre. His mission was to persuade King Charles to allow some of Henrietta Maria's household to return. Buckingham seized upon his coming as a new opportunity to reach an accord with France. On the very night of his arrival, he drove over to greet him. The following day he received Bassompierre at York House. Observers reported that the two men were in 'close and constant contact'. On one occasion Buckingham took his little daughter Mall along with him, as though visiting an intimate family friend.

King Charles was not so friendly. He was determined not to see the 'monsieurs' return. Many hours of negotiation ensued. On one occasion the debate grew so heated that Buckingham had to step between King Charles and Bassompierre to pacify them. But eventually, after many weeks of toing and froing, it was agreed that a bishop and twelve further priests might be readmitted to Henrietta Maria's household.

On 5 November Buckingham celebrated with a great feast at York House. The King and Queen attended. Guests were entertained with a masque. It celebrated Marie de Médicis, mother to the King of France, mother-in-law to the kings of Spain and England and to the Duke of Piedmont. Buckingham was suggesting that Marie represented, in her own person, a happily united Europe. Seated high above the performance space, surrounded by gods and goddesses, she addressed all her royal children and their spouses, and Frederick and Elizabeth of the Palatinate. She called upon them 'to put an end to all the discords of Christianity'.

It was a vision King James would have approved of. But it was very far from truthfully representing what was going on in the world outside the glowing, picture-hung and tapestry-clad walls of York House.

*   *   *

English naval officers were under orders from their Lord Admiral Buckingham to intercept ships (of whatever nationality) trading with Spain. On several occasions during 1625 and 1626 they captured French ships. French authorities retaliated by confiscating the trade goods or ships of British merchants in France. These tit-for-tat seizures escalated. In November 1626 the stocks of all English merchants in Rouen were seized. In December Buckingham instructed his captains to arrest all vessels belonging to France or carrying French goods.

The British wine fleet was in the harbour at Bordeaux. The French seized 200 ships. The Venetian ambassador reported that in London merchants were 'practically frantic' as a result. In response Buckingham ordered Vice Admiral Pennington to destroy French vessels at Le Havre. Pennington declared himself delighted to let 'the Frenchmen know that their insolencies are not well taken, neither shall pass unrevenged'.

So much for Marie de Médicis's happy family and the end of discord in Europe.

Still Buckingham believed that he and Bassompierre had arrived at a friendly agreement. In late December the ambassador set out for home. The weather was wild – 'a tempest of wind and rain as the like is not recorded in the memory of our age'. Bassompierre was delayed in Dover. Buckingham caught him up there. He had resolved, once again, to go to Paris to see if he could prevail upon King Louis to join his league. In Dover Castle, as the two of them waited out the storm, Bassompierre spoke frankly. He finally admitted to Buckingham that there was no prospect of an alliance between their two countries. He told him that he must on no account go to Paris. King Louis would not welcome him there.

There is an awful repetitiveness to Buckingham's story in the last three years of his life. Motifs recur. The insistence on marrying Charles to a Catholic princess despite the force of British public disapproval. The attempted raids on Cadiz, leading to humiliation and the deaths of thousands, followed by the return to England of desperate men. The attempts to woo France into a relationship the French showed no sign of wanting. The naval-military operations undertaken with no clear idea of what advantage they might serve, or how they were to be financed.

Buckingham was flexible and adroit in his dealings with others – always ready to give ground, to accommodate and bend. At court, he was catlike, unruffled, persistent but tactful. In his policy-making, though, he was mulishly stubborn. If at first he didn't succeed, he wouldn't do the sensible thing – re-examine his goals and his strategy and consider modifying them – he would try and try and try again.

There was, besides, something he did not know which made all his wooing of France futile. In early August 1626 King Louis of France had contacted King Philip of Spain through back channels, proposing that they should set aside their differences and act in concert. They might even, suggested Louis, consider a joint attack on England. King Philip, provoked by the previous year's English raid on Cadiz, and with the prospect of another one imminent, responded cordially.

Nothing was formally agreed, but far from untying the girdle of Habsburg power, France was inching towards an alliance with Spain. The prospect that King James I had worked so hard to avert – of Europe divided along sectarian lines, with a coalition of Catholic powers menacing England – had become a real threat.

An anonymous libel was published about Buckingham's aborted trip to Paris. It begins by asking why people had been elated to hear a rumour that he had 'run away' to France.

> Why did the sailors and their wives
> Hope for fresh meat and merry lives?

It imagined knights and squires keeping open house in celebration, Parliament's benches being brushed ready for a new session, and soldiers carousing happily in inns. But then comes the turnaround.

> The Duke's returned, these hopes are vain ...

It was true there was foul weather as he set out for Dover.

> But ah, poor wretches, did you think
> Your admiral so soon would sink?

It was not to be.

> *Although some fondlings idly say*
> *The wind his periwig blew away.*

As he passed through Canterbury, as the libeller tells it, Buckingham met another kind of storm, being set upon by the furious wives of the men who had served in his two expeditions to Cadiz.

> *With knitting needles, and with ladles,*
> *Spits, fire-forks, and legs of cradles,*
> *The women whose friends were yet unpaid*
> *The coaches of the Duke assayed.*

Buckingham got away, and went back to London. The rhyme tells all those who have suffered for him that

> *… Though your wives have sharped their nails*
> *To scratch his face, that project fails;*
> *He is guarded by the city Swisses,*
> *And whilst you scold, he hugs his blisses.*

Envy

YORK House, as remodelled for Buckingham by Gerbier, centred on a great square hall. The ceiling was lined with canvas panels painted by Rubens. They were lost when the house was demolished in the eighteenth century, but we have Rubens's sketch for the central roundel, known as *The Apotheosis of the Duke of Buckingham*.

It shows Buckingham ascending, not to heaven (he was not dead yet, nor was there any reason to suppose he soon would be), but to the Temple of Virtue. His guests, gazing up, would have seen him being wafted skywards through billowing draperies and golden-glowing clouds. Dressed and armoured in a baroque version of Ancient Roman costume, he is seen from below, his celebrated legs elegantly breeched and booted. Three naked Graces wave him on. Adoring winged babies trumpet his triumphs or hold out wreaths of bays. Helmeted deities assist him. Above, Virtue, a shadowy figure, awaits him in the portico of a temple. Down below, a contorted creature, its evil designs against him frustrated, writhes and grimaces. This ugly being is the spirit of Envy.

Three years before Buckingham first came to court, the translators of the King James Bible declared in their preface, 'This will easily be granted by as many as know history ... that Envy striketh most spitefully at the fairest, and at the chiefest.' Always fairest of face and body, and now chiefest in power, Buckingham was, and acutely felt himself to be, Envy's target.

Francis Bacon wrote an essay on the topic, so apposite to Buckingham's case that he could have had Buckingham in mind as he composed it. He notes that 'persons of noble blood are less envied in their rising' than upstarts like Buckingham, 'for it seemeth but right done to their birth'; that those who rise '*per saltum*', by great leaps, are especially resented; that the greater the envied one's 'glory or triumph', the more bitter the envy. All true of Buckingham.

There were stories about his arrogance. It was said that he had been carried in a litter to St James's to play tennis while the King walked beside him, as though Charles was the footman and Buckingham the potentate. It was said that when he arrived late for the performance of a play, the players started all over again from the beginning even though the King had already sat through the first act. It was said that one day the two of them were playing bowls. Buckingham had his hat on. There were onlookers (a king was never alone). A Scotsman stepped forward, snatched off Buckingham's hat and threw it to the ground. Buckingham 'then offered to spurn him; but said the King, "George, let him alone; he is drunk."' The Scot protested he was sober and said, 'A subject I thought he had been.' The point of the story was that no subject should keep his head covered in the presence of the monarch.

As the year 1627 began, the Venetian ambassador noted Buckingham 'is universally detested, his measures, whether good or bad, do him equal harm, envy assigning evil consequences to every event'.

Insignificant Persons

AT the beginning of 1627, after that stormy night in Dover with Bassompierre, Buckingham did an abrupt about-face. During January he agreed with the Huguenot champions, the brother-Dukes of Soubise and Rohan, that he would send an English fleet, carrying an army, to assist the Huguenots of La Rochelle in defending themselves against any possible future attack by the French royal forces.

He wrote to Richelieu. He said that since King Louis refused to endorse the friendly agreement he had drafted with Bassompierre, he no longer considered England to be tied by any obligations to France.

Here is a nineteenth-century historian's account of his motives. Frederick Fairholt, writing in 1850, explains that Buckingham 'took mortal offence at the court of France, which threw obstacles in the way of his journey to Paris, where he anxiously desired to go again to throw himself at the feet of Anne of Austria. In his rage, he conceived the idea of visiting France as an enemy, and urged the King to war in favour of the Rochellers, whom he had before endeavoured to crush.'

A thwarted romance between a handsome duke and a lonely queen; a petulant rage; a capricious change of policy from crushing Huguenots to favouring them: it's a cluster of motivations that feels more fit to drive an operatic plot than to explain real-world events. The truth is, though, that Buckingham's policy shift, from seeking an alliance with France to going to war with that country, was based on a plan barely more rational than the story according to Fairholt.

It appears that he still aimed to make King Louis agree to join his anti-Habsburg league; that he blamed Cardinal Richelieu for having set the King against an alliance with a Protestant nation; that he believed that by offering assistance to the French Huguenots he would bring about Richelieu's downfall (how?); that he counted on Louis, once separated from the Cardinal, deciding he wanted an Anglo-French alliance after all (why?); that he thought by making war on France he – Buckingham – would thus have won France's friendship.

It's a line of thought that has been bewildering interpreters for four centuries. If historians have failed to make much sense of it, it is not because they lacked knowledge or understanding; it is because it was never sensible in the first place.

Later in 1627 Sir Isaac Wake, the English ambassador to Savoy, was asked by other members of the diplomatic corps in Turin to explain Buckingham's foreign policy. Wake simply couldn't do it. He had sought in vain for a way of making sense of what Buckingham was up to. He admitted to being 'as ignorant of the affairs of England as of those of Nova Zembla'. Meanwhile, in Madrid, the Venetian ambassador reported that his French counterpart 'asked me repeatedly what reasons the English adduce for the rupture with France'. Like Wake, he was baffled. Only one thing seemed clear to him, that Buckingham was to blame. But still he could not imagine 'on what frivolous pretext' the Duke had decided on his reckless attack.

Buckingham's letter to Richelieu was carried to Paris by Balthazar Gerbier. It was a prelude to war-making, but Gerbier was also working, along with his friend Rubens, to try to make a peace. The two of them were corresponding about artworks Buckingham had bought from Rubens. Their letters were largely about methods of payment, about packaging, about the procurement of ships. In among discussion of these practical topics, though, were passages dedicated to international politics.

The fighting in Germany was a vortex into which more and more European powers were being sucked. Rubens and Gerbier thought they could arrest the dreadful escalation of destruction and violence. From Paris, Gerbier travelled on into the Spanish Netherlands.

Rubens had proposed that his patroness, the Archduchess Isabella, might act as mediator in negotiations between King Charles of England and her nephew King Philip of Spain. Gerbier passed on the message to his master. Buckingham was interested. Gerbier was carrying a letter from Buckingham for the Archduchess.

Buckingham told her that if she was authorised by King Philip to negotiate a truce between Spain and the Treaty of The Hague confederates – England, Denmark and the Dutch Republic – then he, Buckingham, would welcome it. He would do his best to persuade his allies to join with him in talks designed to bring about 'suspension of arms' for perhaps seven years, 'restoring commerce to its original footing as in times of peace, during which time an accommodation may be treated for'. The Archduchess approved the plan.

It was a promising development, a glimmer of hope in a period when war was engulfing more and more of Europe. Nothing came of it.

Buckingham complicated the negotiations by insisting that any agreement must provide 'satisfaction' for the Elector Palatine. It was as though he still had not understood that Spain would never take sides against the Holy Roman Empire, nor that the Palatinate was not in Spain's gift. The Spanish king, he wrote, must use his power to restore Frederick to his throne. Without that, no truce.

It was not only Buckingham's stubborn insistence on a lost cause that put a stop to the artists' plan. Rubens travelled to Madrid, carrying the Archduchess's letters to King Philip. Philip did not at all like this way of doing diplomacy. He wrote back to his aunt, 'I am displeased at your mixing up a painter in affairs of such importance. You can easily understand how gravely it compromises the dignity of my kingdom, for our prestige must necessarily be lessened if we make so insignificant a person the representative with whom foreign envoys are to discuss affairs of such great import.'

Philip was not unappreciative of art, but he would have been deeply shocked could he have foreseen that he would, four hundred years later, be remembered chiefly for having repeatedly modelled for that other 'insignificant person', Diego Velázquez.

His snubbing of the Anglo-Spanish peace plan concocted by Rubens and Gerbier, though, was not really about the undesirability of discussing serious matters with mere artists. He had no interest in befriending England and its allies. On 10 March 1627, shortly after he received the Archduchess's letter, Philip finally signed a treaty of alliance with France. Buckingham wouldn't know it for several months, but he was now confronting two great Catholic powers, newly united against him.

All the letters passing between Gerbier, Rubens and their patrons in the course of these abortive negotiations were coded and deeply confidential. But there is no such thing as a secret.

Rumours about Buckingham corresponding with Spain began to spread. Princess Elizabeth heard them in The Hague and wrote to her ambassador in London, Von Rusdorf. Von Rusdorf talked to his contact Archbishop Abbot. Abbot began to refer to Buckingham furiously as 'ce mignon' and shared the rumours with his friends and fellow papist-haters.

Buckingham can be justly accused of terrible things – of causing thousands upon thousands of deaths by his reckless war-making – but the allegations against him current in the spring of 1627 were unfounded. As he prepared to fight the Catholic nation of France in defence of French Protestants, talk spread about his being pro-Spanish, and therefore pro-Catholic. A rhyme appeared. It called him

> An agent of the Spanish state;
> The Romist's friend, the gospel's foe,
> The church and kingdom's overthrow.

He was said to be planning to make himself 'the head and protector of the Catholics, because his greatest hindrances proceed from the Puritans'. He was suspected of being ready, as Lord Admiral and Lord Warden of the Cinque Ports, to admit a Spanish invasion force into England. He was said to be a black-hearted traitor.

In January 1627 Buckingham gave orders that the best twenty ships in the English Fleet should be made ready for action by the end of February. He was planning an expediton to La Rochelle. Soubise and Rohan's representative Saint-Blancart (Rohan himself being at sea) were often with him. The Venetian ambassador reported that the task force would 'be commanded by the Duke in person'.

Quite why he did all this remains a mystery.

Perhaps he simply wanted to prove he wasn't a Spanish agent or 'the Romist's friend', to be hailed as 'St George on horseback' once more. He told a fellow Councillor that he wanted to 'win back the affection of the common people'. He was said to be confident he would soon be as adored as the Elizabethan Earl of Essex had been after his successful raid on Cadiz in 1596. Perhaps he just wanted to be loved.

Babies

In November 1625, while Buckingham was in Holland attempting to pawn the Crown jewels and setting up his league in The Hague, his first son was born. Named Charles, the baby was welcomed with delight, because every child is a blessing, but also because he was male. Only a boy could inherit Buckingham's titles and perpetuate his glory. The womenfolk around Buckingham may have felt differently about it – his mother who had asked to be a countess in her own right and declined to share the title with her husband, his wife who was her father's sole heir – but to all male observers it seemed obvious that Buckingham must exult in being at last the father of a boy. On returning from the Netherlands, Buckingham rode with all speed to Burley, to be with Katherine and the new baby. The news, wrote John Chamberlain, was 'no small joy'.

In March 1627, when he was sixteen months old, little Charles died. We do not know how or why. The deaths of infants were so common that his needed no explanation. Because Buckingham was in Spain for six months near the beginning of his daughter Mall's life, we have Katherine's letters to him about her – doting proud-mother letters in which she writes about the baby's first tooth, her first steps, the way she 'dances' in her cradle. There are no such letters about Charles. His life began and ended unrecorded by written words. There is no portrait in which he appears as a bundle in his mother's arms.

A king was his godfather. A future archbishop, William Laud, conducted his funeral. He was buried in Westminster Abbey. A grand ending to a pitifully brief life.

Déjà Vu

IN February 1627 Buckingham had all the loops and ropes and swags of pearls cut off the gorgeous suits he had taken to Paris less than two years earlier. Back then, all a-glimmer in gold damask and rose-pink or silver-grey silks, he had been intent on cementing a lasting union with the French monarchy. Now that union had changed to enmity.

He had been accused in the previous year's impeachment hearings, and would be accused again, of stripping the Exchequer bare to fund his extravagances. It was true that he never clearly distinguished between his private indulgences and his official spending. He took, but he also gave.

Now, if he was to go to war again, England needed an army, a navy and a fleet. No use looking to the Lord Treasurer for the necessary funds. So Buckingham sold his pearls. He put Wallingford House up for sale. He offered to rent out his apartments in the Palace of Whitehall. He sent all his jewels, but for a few favourite pieces that reminded him of King James, to Amsterdam for pawning. All this for the Navy. He had amassed a great fortune. He declared it was all his country's. Everything the two kings who loved him had ever given him, he said, would be seen transmuted into ships, afloat in the King's service.

It was not enough. Nothing like. Trinkets, even those as magnificent as Buckingham's, are not as expensive as men and materiel. The dismal old refrain started up again. No money.

He sent Sir Henry Mainwaring 'to go presently aboard [the ships] for His Majesty's present fleet and to hasten by all possible means the fitting, furnishing, arming, victualling and full manning of every one of them'. But how was it to be done?

The shipwrights had not been paid for months. They would have to be given what was owed them before they would set to work. No money.

The Victualler of the Navy could not or would not equip and provision those ships until his arrears had been paid, so that he could, in turn, pay off his debts to suppliers. No money. The Privy Council agreed to find funds, but the only way to do so would be by selling Crown lands. No money now and even less in the future. Buckingham could, at a pinch, have fourteen ships by the end of March. But only if money was forthcoming immediately. No money.

The ghastly sense of déjà vu grows stronger. Buckingham's inability to learn doomed him, and all England with him, to endure the peculiar torture of going through the same pain over and over again. Each time it was worse.

The country was in turmoil. Men who had suffered on the ships sent to Cadiz, or who had worked in the shipyards at home and never been paid for it, were no longer prepared to endure such hard labour or to give their lives for nothing. Angry people, desperate from hunger and from watching their children go hungry too, were on the roads. The dockworkers from Chatham, unpaid for a year, had 'forsaken their works and ... gone in great numbers towards London to demand their said arrearages'.

Some five hundred mutinous sailors walked from Portsmouth to the capital. They went to the house of Sir William Russell, Treasurer of the Navy. Russell was absent, but they smashed the windows. Another mob massed in the streets outside Whitehall Palace. King Charles spoke to them from a balcony. He told them if they removed themselves to Tower Hill they would be paid the following day. They went. At the Tower, a boy climbed up onto the scaffold and announced that unless they were paid 'on the morrow', they would cut off the Lord Admiral's head. A guard was set outside York House. More angry sailors rioted there and threatened to pull the house down unless they were paid.

The authorities responded sternly – meeting misery with repression. The counties' Lord Lieutenants were given 'commissions of martial law' greatly expanding their powers to fine and imprison. King Charles authorised the trained bands to 'use all means of force, as shot or other offensive ways' against 'mariners and other loose people'. The Privy Council appointed provost marshals (equivalent to modern military police) to assist the sheriffs and constables. Buckingham asked a judge what action could legally be taken against deserters. The answer was whipping (a whipping could leave a man close to death) and ducking (near-drowning). He ordered that four deserters should be brought to the gallows and made to play dice for their lives. The loser was hanged.

For two years Buckingham had been trying to create a fleet of ships built for combat and ready for use whenever required. He had been weeding out 'the slothful, negligent, mutinous and insufficient' commanders. He wanted a navy that offered a regular career for officers, and therefore attracted better candidates. He was building a dry dock in Portsmouth (previously all shipbuilding and repair facilities were along the Thames, where ships could be trapped by contrary winds). His ideas were sound. He worked hard to realise them. His letters reveal how industrious he was, how meticulous his attention to detail. That spring he wrote to the Lieutenant of Dover Castle asking 'how many tons of beer you have ... how long your beer hath been brewed ... whether the cask be butts or pipes or hogsheads ... And likewise whether the beef be dry-salted or pickled and whether cut in 2 or 4 lb pieces ...' And so on and so on and so on. How many pounds of bacon? How long will the biscuit last? Are the casks new-dried?

Buckingham's critics thought he was a self-indulgent flibbertigibbet. They had no idea how hard he worked. Captain Richard Gifford, one of his supporters in the Naval Office, wrote, 'You have taken more pains and care to have all things reformed concerning the Navy as never was the like done by any Lord Admiral.'

But, repeatedly, his sensible long-term plans were disrupted by his impetuously undertaken adventures. He had appointed a special commission to look into naval administration. But in spring 1627 he suspended its inquiry. Reform would have to wait while he pulled together his expedition to La Rochelle.

There came an extraordinary stroke of luck. Buckingham had instructed Pennington to 'intercept and take ... all French, Dunkirkers and Spanish ships and goods as shall come out of the Low Countries for the use of the French king'. Pennington reported that it couldn't be done: the ships he had were 'not capable to do service', and most of his men were 'rogues taken up in the streets, that hath neither clothes nor knows anything'. He had no oars. He had no compasses.

Buckingham took action. He stirred up the commissioners. The oars and compasses were found. Pennington led his ships out and captured prizes worth £70,000. It was a wonderful respite from the dreary no-money theme. But was it legitimate? Were these ships hostile warships? Or harmless merchants?

Buckingham put pressure on Sir Henry Marten, who presided over the Court of Admiralty, to rule that they were all 'good prizes'. Marten thought they were not. He resigned rather than find against his conscience. Buckingham didn't hold it against him. Marten was restored to his post a few weeks later. Meanwhile Buckingham kept his booty. The expedition to La Rochelle could go ahead.

In April the Florentine ambassador noticed that Buckingham had a new outfit – 'a military costume … with an immense collar and a magnificent plume of feathers in his hat'. The ambassador took it as a sign. 'People now begin to believe that … he will command in person.' It was true. Buckingham asked the naval commissioners to add to the long list of his requirements 'silk flags and pennants suitable for a Lord Admiral of England'. He was going to war.

His personal preparations were lavish. An eighteenth-century engraving based on a lost image by Buckingham's contemporary Renold Elstrack (previous page) shows him stepping out in a fantastically ruffled and scalloped and embroidered outfit, a lustrous silk banner billowing behind him. He was taking a velvet-upholstered coach and a retinue of servants dressed in richly embroidered clothes. He was taking a barge decorated in scarlet and gold. He spent thousands of pounds on linens and silks and on gold and silver buttons. He was taking a number of suits in satin and velvet (some of which went astray – presumed stolen – in Portsmouth). He was taking a harp and a musician to play it, and £50 worth of books. However hungry his men were going to be, he would be eating well. He was taking ample wine and groceries and 'living provisions' – oxen, cows, goats and chickens. One historian has calculated that what he spent on equipping himself and his household would have maintained an entire regiment for six months.

He was harrying and pushing the commissioners to get the ships ready. 'It much imports His Majesty's service to have all the fleet to be instantly at sea.' He commanded surgeons to be ready at Portsmouth and Plymouth for the returning wounded, and ordered drugs for them. He recruited chaplains for each of the ships – one of them was the poet Robert Herrick. At last all was ready.

Always delicate, Buckingham tried to forestall any physical collapse. He took purges, and passed some days in bed to gather his strength. He prompted Bishop Laud to compose a prayer, to be read in churches throughout England, asking for God's blessing on the expedition. He gave a farewell feast at York House. The King and Queen were guests of honour. He entertained them with a masque in which he played the central role. 'First comes forth the Duke; after him Envy, with divers open-mouthed dogs' heads representing the people's barking; next came Fame; then Truth.'

On 5 June, the King left for Portsmouth, to see the fleet away, taking the Duke of Soubise with him in his coach. Buckingham was to join them within days. The expedition was ready to leave at last.

Buckingham's bid for popularity had partially succeeded. An observer commented that 'by his real setting of sail' he had 'converted many men's curses into prayers'. But plenty of others still looked sceptically on him and his adventure. Some of them, like the author of this libel, still wished him dead.

> *Rejoice brave English gallants,*
> *   Whose ancestors won France;*
> *Our Duke of Buckingham is gone*
> *   To fight and not to dance.*
> *Believe it, for our ladies*
> *   His absence greatly mourn;*
> *And swear they'll have no babies*
> *   Until he doth return*
> *...*
> *His army was twelve thousand,*
> *   Well numbered on our shore,*
> *Besides his pasties and baked meats,*
> *   Which were as many more.*
> *...*
> *But now he is at sea,*
> *   Where he commands amaine,*
> *Whence all true Englishmen do hope*
> *   He'll ne'er come back again.*

Married Love

BUCKINGHAM didn't go with the King to Portsmouth because he intended to visit his wife. It was three months since they had lost their baby son and in that time they had seldom been together. Katherine was in the country, feeling unwell. She hoped she was pregnant again. Buckingham had written to tell her that he would be going to La Rochelle – the first time he had gone into battle himself, a dreadful moment for a wife. He promised that he would come to her before he set sail.

The day after King Charles left London, a fleet of ships was sighted in the Channel and thought to be the long-dreaded Spanish invasion force. Buckingham rode at once to Dover and led all the English ships there out to sea. The fleet was actually made up of Dutch merchantmen. Buckingham called off the pursuit, but the false alarm had eaten up a week. Meanwhile the King was growing impatient. Buckingham wrote to tell Katherine he would not be able to come after all. He had to go directly to Portsmouth. He wouldn't see her again before sailing, which meant he might never see her again. She wrote him a long, sad, furious letter back.

She writes that she had always feared he would command the expedition himself. She sees the necessity of it. 'There was no other likelihood … but you must needs go.' But it is terrible for her, and it prompts her to look back on so many, many other times when he left her – for court, for King, for Spain, for Council or for Parliament. 'I have been a very miserable woman hitherto, that never could have you keep at home.' She had counted on at least seeing him one more time, but now 'I do plainly see you have deceived me.' She is miserable, and she is angry. 'Never while I live will I trust you again.'

She apologises for writing so desperately. She tells him to burn the letter and forgive her, 'but my heart is so full I cannot choose'. She thinks she is the 'unfortunatest of all other, that even when I am with child I must have so much cause of sorrow as to have you go from me'.

She has loved him. She has counted herself the happiest wife alive. But now she writes, 'I pray God never woman may love a man as I have done you, that none may feel that which I have done for you.'

She says that 'if any pains or any suffering of mine would do it', she would endure anything 'to fetch you off this journey with your honour'. But he has made his choice. 'You have sent yourself,' and 'there is none more miserable than I am now'.

The Disasters of War IV

IN Portsmouth Buckingham made his will, with a preamble explaining that he was intending 'a voyage to sea' and was conscious of 'the many casualties and dangers that the life of man is subject unto'. He hoped that Christ would save his soul, and asked that his body be interred in Henry VII's chapel in Westminster Abbey.

On Midsummer's Day, 24 June, he went aboard his flagship, the *Triumph*. He had ninety ships, 3,000 sailors and 6,000 soldiers. On the 25th he went back ashore to round up deserters. He found a number of army officers hiding in their lodgings, and drove them on board.

On the 26th a favourable wind got up, and he led out his fleet.

By 30 June they were off the island of Ushant. There was a violent storm. The *Triumph* was driven into shallow waters and almost foundered. Buckingham showed no sign of fear, but he called the crew together in prayer. The chaplain would have continued to cry out to God for mercy until the ship was righted, but Buckingham cut him short, saying, 'It is not long prayers that doth it.'

On 10 July, the fleet was finally at anchor off La Rochelle.

Back in London, Soubise and Saint-Blancart had assured Buckingham that the Rochelloises would welcome him as their liberator and gladly rise up, with his support, against the might of royal France. That was not what happened.

On 11 July, Buckingham sent Sir William Beecher ashore to deliver a message to the mayor and council. The mayor and council sent word that they were observing a fast, and they could receive no one. Beecher was not invited to enter the city.

The following day Buckingham sent Beecher again, this time accompanied by Soubise and Saint-Blancart. The mayor met the visitors at the city gates. He reminded Soubise how dreadfully his people might suffer if he allowed the English forces to enter. He begged them to go away.

During the past decade the people of La Rochelle had been repeatedly defeated by the French royal forces. They cared, or many of them did, about their religious freedom and political independence, but they also cared about the harvest and about trade. They had been grateful for the period of peace they had enjoyed since the failure of Soubise's rebellion two years previously. They had observed Richelieu's programme of shipbuilding and understood that it meant the 'Admiral of the Protestant Church' could no longer be sure of protecting them from possible blockade. They did not share the heroic ambitions of the Rohan brothers. They had no desire to provoke the might of France.

Soubise's mother, the dowager Duchess of Rohan, was living in La Rochelle. Hearing that her son was being prevented from entering the city, she went down to the gates, took Soubise's arm and walked with him into the town, his companions following. The mayor, defied by such a great lady, felt unable to stop them. They walked through the streets to her house, where Soubise summoned the town council to a meeting. Beecher addressed them, reading out the manifesto Buckingham had written. King Louis, he explained, had fallen under the influence of a 'Jesuit and Spanish faction' (meaning Richelieu), and intended the destruction of the Huguenots. King Charles of England, responding to appeals from Rohan and Soubise, had sent this force to offer them assistance, on condition they would join him in the fight.

Beecher then asked the Rochelloises whether they would accept the English offer of help. If so, Buckingham would send his troops into the town. They must decide promptly.

English observers thought the people of La Rochelle seemed ready to welcome them, but the Councillors were wary. A group of them were rowed out to the ships to speak with Buckingham. They could not make up their minds as swiftly as he wanted, they said. First they must consult with other Huguenot communities elsewhere in France. This might take weeks.

This cautious response was depressing. Buckingham knew too much about ships and sailors and the diseases they carried to think he could keep his men on board while the Rochelloises deliberated. He proposed to his officers that they should land on the Île de Ré, a narrow, low-lying island of sand and salt pans and windswept vineyards, nineteen miles long and three miles wide, that overlooked the seaward approaches to La Rochelle, its easternmost part divided from the mainland by less than two miles.

There was a French garrison on the island, commanded by the Marshal de Toiras and based in the formidable new citadel at the island's main town of St-Martin. Any vessel approaching La Rochelle had to pass beneath their guns. None of the English knew for certain what kind of defences the French had on the island or how many troops were stationed there.

Soubise begged Buckingham to postpone the landing. There was a world of difference – diplomatically speaking – between the English lending support to an uprising of the Huguenots of La Rochelle and the English landing on French soil uninvited. The Rochelloises would come round, thought Soubise. They had been caught off guard by the English fleet's unforeseen arrival. They needed time. Buckingham told him that there was no time to spare.

His plan was adopted. His soldiers would go ashore the very next day. The place chosen was a narrow peninsula, the Pointe de Sablanceaux, at the easternmost point of the island. The English ships would surround it, while landing craft carried the men into shallow water from which they could wade ashore. If French forces attempted to drive them back, the English ships would fire on them.

Buckingham was about to invade France.

Before dawn the next morning he received the sacrament. He spoke with Soubise, who was returning to La Rochelle to make a further attempt to stir up the townspeople. Saint-Blancart, as dubious about the proposed landing as Soubise was, nonetheless elected to stay and take part in the day's action.

While it was still dark, Buckingham sent a boat carrying a few musketeers and a local boy over to the point. The boy slipped into the water and swam ashore. He ran about a mile inland. He saw no mass of troops, but he was spotted by three French scouts on horseback who chased him back into the sea. He swam back to the boat and was taken to Buckingham to report.

Buckingham got into his red velvet-lined barge and was rowed from ship to ship, issuing instructions. Returning to the *Triumph*, he climbed to the top of the mainmast (something few other officers, let alone an admiral, would do). From there he saw a large body of French troops drawn up a mile away from the landing place. He ordered his ships to fire on them. He returned to his barge and joined the landing party.

Putting an expeditionary force ashore on a coast where enemy troops are ready to repel them is a brutal business. The first soldiers to disembark from the landing craft had fought in Holland and were thought to be reliable, but what they were being asked to do was more than they had courage for. They lingered in the water. One observer initially thought they found it refreshing after three weeks on board, but this was not a pleasurable dip in the ocean: between thirty and forty of them drowned that day.

Buckingham, seeing the men floundering fearfully among the waves, had himself rowed among them. One of his officers describes how he 'thrust himself upon the revolters ... railing and threatening'. He seized a cudgel and helped to drive those within reach ashore. At last about a thousand Englishmen made it onto dry land. They were hastily drawn up ready to face the imminent attack.

The fighting was close up, brutal and bloody. The French cavalry swooped down 'with all speed, furiously'. The English were driven back into the sea. Buckingham led them back up the beach. 'They followed slowly', but 'the most of them leapt out of the water, and upon the General's words, thrust themselves forward, as if they would have fought bravely'. The English lines re-formed, creating a barricade of pikes through which a second French cavalry charge couldn't pass. Then up came the French infantry, firing muskets, and when they got close enough 'fell to it with swords and push of pike until they were breathless on both sides'.

The English pikes were longer than the French ones, so the French tossed theirs away and drew back, throwing stones. 'But ours', wrote one English participant, 'beat them out with stones and made them fly away very disorderly.' The French commander, Marshal de Toiras, whose brother was among the numerous French officers killed, ordered his men to withdraw to the island's main town of St-Martin, where they took refuge in the citadel.

It was Buckingham's first battle. An English officer wrote home, 'Our General hath behaved himself so courageously and nobly that his very enemies speak well of him.' In the aftermath he acted, as usual, with gracious good manners. The French were permitted to bury their dead unharassed. When three captured French noblemen asked to be allowed to return to the mainland to have their injuries attended to, he sent them away in his scarlet-lined barge, with musicians to ease their pain.

Fourteen of his officers were dead, including his master of ordnance, as was Saint-Blancart, his chief point of liaison with the Rochelloises. These losses would be painfully felt.

For two days the English busied themselves with putting up palisades to protect against further attacks as the rest of the men came ashore.

On 15 July the English army moved off the beach. Buckingham rode at the head of the mile-long column, with Soubise beside him. That night it rained heavily – a foretaste of what was to come. Buckingham slept on a camp bed, covered only by his cloak. Come morning, he led his sodden troops across the island to St-Martin. The citadel was a massive edifice on the waterfront. To avoid its guns, Buckingham entered the town from the furthest side. The townspeople promptly surrendered, their representatives meeting him with a flag of truce.

So far all was going moderately well for the English. Buckingham called a council of war to consider what was next to be done.

Sir John Burroughs, Buckingham's senior military officer, gave his opinion that the citadel was impregnable. Burroughs's advice was that Buckingham should take his army over to the undefended nearby Île d'Oléron, where he could await the Huguenots' decision.

Buckingham disagreed. The capture of such an imposing stronghold would be the kind of impressive success he wanted. The English sat down before the citadel's walls.

The Duke of Rohan wrote afterwards that the English landing on the Île de Ré had caused a great stir at the French court, and that 'there was every probability of a great change in the face of affairs', by which Rohan meant the downfall of the Cardinal. The Venetian ambassador in Paris agreed. He reported, 'There is no Frenchman who does not rejoice at the success of the English against this country, such is the universal detestation of the government.'

Richelieu saw the danger. He called upon all the captains of French ships to come up with stratagems for getting food and munitions into the besieged citadel of St-Martin, and he persuaded King Louis to write to Toiras promising him unsparing support. Buckingham, far from aiding the people of La Rochelle, had stirred up the might of the French monarchy against them.

Buckingham was expecting 4,000 further troops to reinforce his army – King Charles had promised them to him before he left Portsmouth. Surely, he thought, their arrival would cause the French garrison to despair and surrender. Surely the Rochelloises, and their fellow Huguenots, would soon rally round him, seeing the citadel fall.

How did Buckingham imagine those 4,000 extra troops would be found? And the ships to carry them, and the beer and the flour and the lard to sustain them, and the clothes and weapons necessary to transform them from desperate ragamuffins into an effective fighting force? He knew how this went. No money. No money. No money. He had been living with that for years. Yet somehow, the excitement of action and the hope of a glorious victory dulled his common sense and erased his memory of what it was like to conjure up an army. He chose to believe King Charles's promise.

It was 17 July when Buckingham made himself master of the town of St-Martin. Back home the 'inferior orbs', wrote Sir John Coke, would have been ready to start recruiting, but 'money, the *primus motor*, doth retard us all in our ends'. It was no good Buckingham sending to England for immediate reinforcements. The levying of troops – likely to take weeks or even months – had not even begun because cautious officials preferred not to embark on such a troublesome and expensive task until 'we shall hear of the success of the fleet'.

Buckingham acted as though there were men and supplies and weaponry waiting to take ship as soon as he called for them. On 18 July he sent Sir William Beecher back to England to hurry them along. He needed them soon, before Richelieu could move against him.

They were not ready, nor would they be until a further four months had gone by.

As the English troops laid siege to Fort St-Martin, they were afflicted by trials to rival Job's, thought one, or the seven plagues of Egypt, thought another.

The rain fell unremittingly throughout that unseasonably cold summer. Night after night the men were wet. Buckingham ordered them to dig trenches encircling the citadel on its landward side – exhausting work with inadequate tools. Day after day, standing for hours in the rapidly flooded trenches, they were still wet. They fell ill with 'catarrhs, diseases of the lungs, burning fevers and dysenteries'. Some of them died.

The Île de Ré, low-lying and marshy, was home to virulent mosquitoes, so many of them that the people made trousers to protect their donkeys' legs (four hundred years later, the donkeys still wear them, though mostly now for the amusement of tourists). The local women's bonnets had long flaps to cover their necks and shoulders. The English, without such protective clothing, suffered grievously.

Where there were mosquitoes, there was malaria. More men fell sick. More men died.

The English were as hungry as the French they were attempting to starve out. They had not come prepared for a long-drawn-out campaign. They had expected the Rochelloises to feed them.

Buckingham wrote, 'Our provisions grow low and our men decrease.' More deaths.

Driven by hunger to forage for what they could find, the men ate unripe grapes, which brought on diarrhoea. An officer estimated, a few weeks into the siege, that a third of his men were sick 'and the disease runs on so violently as worse is daily to be feared'.

Weeks went by. Not enough food. Not enough men. Some of the soldiers had to be stationed along the island's coastline, ready to repel any French landing party that might appear. Still waiting in vain for reinforcements, Buckingham decided to retrain some of the sailors as infantry. This caused resentment on both sides. 'The land commanders, especially the younger ones, took it in great snuff,' reported one of them. Buckingham was obliged to give up on the project, and return the sailors to the ships.

He was losing control of his force. He ceased to summon councils of war because, explains one of his officers, 'the Duke finds them other than he expected or because in this state of affairs there is little use for them'. He preferred to 'do all his business on the spur', without consultation. His officers did not like him for it.

Buckingham's strategy depended on keeping French supply boats away from St-Martin, but even with the English ships drawn up in an arc around the fort, small vessels slipped through under cover of darkness.

Buckingham's engineers tried to exclude them with a sequence of ineffective constructions.

A floating island. Formed of upturned boats lashed together, this was to be a kind of gigantic seafaring armoured vehicle from which English gunners and bowmen could fire on any approaching French vessel. It was expected to be 'of great moment in keeping the enemy from our shore'. Such hopes were disappointed. 'It being bruised and shattered with the winds and force of the waves, it came to nothing.'

A stockade made of masts and other timbers fastened together with chains, its ends embedded in the shore on either side of the fort, its length swung out to loop round, forming a half-moon-shaped enclosure anchored to the seabed. In mild weather it could have been an effective barrier, but the sea was being churned up by storms. Too rigid to endure battering waves, the stockade was torn apart.

A floating barrier – more mobile and seaworthy than the stockade – formed of a number of ships and small boats and barrels linked by stout cables. Once it was in place, Buckingham declared that only birds would be able to pass into the fort. The storms continued. The floating barrier was driven towards the remainder of the English fleet, threatening to crash into the ships. Having laboured so hard to construct it, Buckingham's men – working in circumstances of great danger and difficulty – scrambled to take it apart.

Months went by. The men on the Île de Ré felt abandoned and angry. They take themselves, wrote an officer, 'for men neglected and forgotten'. Another wrote home to his father, a Privy Councillor. 'Winter comes on; our men will fall sick, but if we lose this island it shall be your faults in England.'

Buckingham wrote repeatedly to Beecher, still in England, urging him to 'use some diligence in your solicitation of supplies, both of men, monies and munitions'. But even the King could not conjure up funds or fighting men where there were none to be had. No money. No money. No money.

Charles wrote to the Lord Treasurer, 'If Buckingham should not now be supplied, having so bravely and (I thank God) successfully begun his expedition, it were an irrecoverable shame to me and all this nation.' But what was the Lord Treasurer to do? The Exchequer was empty, he said. 'Buckingham had taken all the money to Ré.'

While in England the monarch ineffectually pleaded with his officials, in France the monarch moved.

Buckingham's attack was an impertinence that could not be ignored. In August, the French royal army under the Duke of Angoulême began to encircle La Rochelle. This campaign against the Huguenot stronghold was to be given the highest priority. Over the ensuing months Cardinal Richelieu and King Louis himself would, in turn, command the besieging troops.

As he waited for support from England, Buckingham was in contact with his opponent, Marshal de Toiras. Courtly as ever, he sent Toiras a dozen melons. Toiras reciprocated with a gift of a dozen bottles of orange-flower water and some boxes of Cyprus powder (a kind of incense).

Buckingham sent the fragrances home for his wife, but she was afraid to use them – with good reason. A French deserter arrived in the English camp. He was found to be carrying a dagger. He was tortured, and confessed that the blade was envenomed, and that he had been sent, on Toiras's orders, to use it to kill Buckingham. Toiras swore with 'deep oaths and imprecations' that the allegation was untrue, but for all the courtesies and pretty gifts, he and Buckingham were at war.

The besieged French were suffering even more than the English besiegers. Buckingham's men burnt their windmills and poisoned their wells, depriving them even of bread and water. Inside the citadel they had as little protection from the rain as the English did. For all the grim grandeur of its massive walls, the fort was open to the sky. The huts were knee-deep in liquid mud. Buckingham ordered that all the local women whose husbands were among the fort's defenders were to be driven out of their homes in the town and left, in noisy distress, by the gates of the citadel. The French let them in, and – as Buckingham had intended – the difficulty of feeding these extra mouths made their situation more desperate.

For Toiras, as for Buckingham, the struggle for the citadel was becoming too costly. Toiras sent to Paris asking for permission to negotiate. Richelieu told King Louis to hold firm. If Buckingham wants to talk about peace, he said, 'it is a sign that he does not feel himself strong enough to make war'. The siege of Fort St-Martin went on.

Early in September came reinforcements at last, but also an escalation. Two and a half thousand troops arrived from Ireland to support Buckingham. Not enough, but a substantial help. On the mainland, as hostile French troops gathered around their walls, the people of La Rochelle at last accepted the English offer of support, not realising how little the English, now fully engaged on the Île de Ré, could do to help them. A week later the Rochelloises fired on the besieging French troops for the first time. Buckingham's expedition, previously a piratical raid on an isolated fortress, was now part of a conflict with a national army that vastly outnumbered the little English expeditionary force.

Richelieu laid aside his cardinal's robes. He left Paris booted and spurred and went south to join Angoulême's army. This was Richelieu's country – he had grown up not far from La Rochelle. He went to Sables-

d'Olonne on the coast some twenty-five miles north of the Île de Ré.
There he assembled a flotilla of thirty-five shallow-draughted boats.

On 23 September Beecher finally arrived back from Engand, bringing
with him, not the thousands of troops and ample provisions
Buckingham had hoped for, but just 400 men, and disappointingly
small quantities of food and money and ammunition. But then, two
days later, came a breakthrough.

A steady stream of French deserters were leaving the Fort St-Martin.
Perhaps despairing at seeing the British reinforcements arriving, Toiras
sent to Buckingham, asking on what terms he would accept the garrison's surrender.

This was a great opportunity. Had Buckingham seized it, perhaps he
could have come away from the Île de Ré with a success to boast of, but
he hesitated, and the opportunity was lost. He asked Toiras's messenger to return on the following day. When he did so Buckingham said
he would prefer Toiras to propose his own terms. Another day passed.
And that night, tide, wind and current at last came together to favour
the flotilla at Sables-d'Olonne. Richelieu's boats set out for the Île de
Ré.

It was a dark night, too dark for the English to see the approaching
vessels. Buckingham had belatedly received intelligence of their coming,
but he expected them to land on the western tip of the island and had
sent troops there to repel them. Instead the French boats, crammed with
men and food, made straight for St-Martin, slipping between and
beneath the tall English ships, whose guns were aimed too high to hit
them.

All night Buckingham struggled to prevent the French relief force
unloading their cargoes. He led a group of small boats, in an attempt to
head off the French ones, but the sailors were not trained to fight and
had no stomach for it. According to one of the officers, 'Many of them
did very ill perform their duty.' Twenty-nine of the thirty-five French
boats made it ashore alongside the citadel. A fireship was prepared. The
Frenchmen ashore were able to push it back out to sea with long poles.
The provisions were unloaded and carried into the citadel.

As day broke, the English – close to starvation – saw the French
defenders taunting them by waving chickens and hams, turkeys and
tongues and loaves of bread, impaled on their pikes and flourished from

the parapets. The fort that had so nearly been Buckingham's two days previously was no longer in a surrendering state of mind.

It was a bitter blow. With the French army massing on the mainland beyond La Rochelle, Buckingham's officers advised him to leave for England while it was still possible to do so. He refused, too proud to accept defeat, too dogged to lift his siege.

For another month he remained on the Île de Ré. A French observer wrote, 'The soldiers themselves do pity him. He is commonly every night in the boats or in the trenches till midnight.' Several times he seemed ready to pull out, but then would come a message from Soubise or Rohan or the Rochelloises, assuring him of support, and he would agree to wait a little longer. News came that his friend the Earl of Holland would soon be leaving Portsmouth with more men, and more supplies. Again Buckingham postponed his departure.

Back in England the usual muddle. No money. King Charles was doing his best, but the naval commissioners – their inertia, their ponderous bureaucracy, their time-wasting – got the better of the monarch's good intentions. The Lord Treasurer was waiting upon some tax-farmers who were so 'scrupulous and dilatory' that the Exchequer's business was at a standstill. Buckingham had been spending his own money to pay the troops, and borrowing from his wife and mother. The latter told him she feared that no one in England, where 'all is merry and well pleased', cared about his tribulations.

There were people at court who did not want Buckingham to succeed. His friend the Earl of Dorset wrote to complain of those 'diabolically disposed to hinder and distract these courses'. But bigger problems than diabolical hindering were inertia and incompetence. To many of Buckingham's friendly correspondents, it seemed that without his energy and determination, the will to make things happen was lacking. 'Your being here would breathe new life into most men.' In his absence, 'there is a kind of languishing in all proceedings here'.

At the end of October, French troops landed on the Île de Ré. The English, sick, hungry and now outnumbered, were unable to drive them back. For Buckingham to keep his men there any longer would be to see them massacred. Four months after he had arrived, he prepared to take them off the island and back to England. But he wouldn't simply accept that he had failed and get out as best he could. He would defy fate and make one last bid for glory. He would lead his exhausted troops in storming the citadel of St-Martin.

The story of Buckingham's assault is ghastly.

Four cannon shot gave the signal to advance. The English troops sang a psalm: 'Let God arise, and let his enemies be scattered'. They drove the French back from the defensive outworks. They reached the citadel and swarmed down into its defensive ditch. They reached the foot of the massive walls. They set up their scaling ladders.

The ladders were too short.

The English soldiers climbed up those ladders to their deaths. Clinging on precariously, unable to reach the parapet and force their way into the fort, unable to go back down for the press of their fellows climbing behind them, they were stuck. A French eyewitness describes their plight. 'When they attained the height of their ladders, and had no further means to go on, casting their threatening eyes about they remained unmovable till they were shot and tumbled down.' The fortress's star shape allowed French musketeers to pick them off from points alongside and behind them, while those on the parapets above pelted them with logs of wood or barrels full of stones.

It was two hours before Buckingham called a halt. His men lay dead in heaps around the citadel's walls. As the survivors pulled back, the French garrison opened its gates and sallied out to drive them off the island.

In Roman times the Île de Ré was not one island but three. Over the centuries the sea level had fallen and salt marshes had filled in the gaps between the three land masses. By Buckingham's time those original islands were linked by causeways, to either side of which lay marshes – quaking and unstable, not safe to cross. The English ships were waiting off the middle island, the Île de Loix.

Retreating from St-Martin, Buckingham's men reached the beginning of the causeway to Loix – five hundred feet long and just four feet wide. They jostled their way onto it, tightly packed. Some way along the causeway the French had left an overturned cart, over which the retreating English had to clamber. Only about half of them had made it across when French troops came crowding up behind them. The English stampeded, pushing and struggling with each other. Hundreds were shoved off the causeway and fell into the marshes, to be thrust underwater by French pikes, or hacked to pieces by French swords, or shot by French muskets, or simply to struggle in the swamp until they sank.

Buckingham was already on the beach at Loix. The English ships were anchored in deep water. Small boats were coming ashore to collect the men. Seeing the disaster unfolding, he ordered the boats back to the ships to avoid a panicked rout. By the time the French poured off the causeway, he and his officers had got the men drawn up ready to repel them. A hard and horrible fight ensued before the French were driven back and Buckingham's men, those that remained alive, could be taken off to the comparative safety of the ships.

Forty British officers had been killed and twenty taken prisoner. Over 500 soldiers had died in the fighting. The same number again had drowned.

Still Buckingham lingered. He could not face up to his own failure. He sent a message offering to take his troops to La Rochelle. The Rochelloises didn't deign to answer. Food and ammunition they might have welcomed, but hungry men they did not want. Buckingham waited a week, hoping for their reply, but then, at last, with winter coming on and no sign of the promised provisions, he turned for home. There were storms in the Channel. Some of his ships foundered. His men were starving. One of his officers, lying sick in his cabin, wrote, 'My soul even melts with tears to think that a state should send so many men and no provisions at all for them.'

In fact, far too late, the state had bestirred itself. By a bitter coincidence, Holland, bringing the reinforcements and supplies Buckingham had so desperately needed, set out from Portsmouth on 8 November, the very day that Buckingham left the Île de Ré to sail home in defeat.

Of the 6,000 men who had gone out with him initially, and the 2,000 troops from Ireland who joined him in September, fewer than 3,000 survivors returned. For Buckingham, the expedition to La Rochelle had been a failure. For the majority of his men it had been a nightmarish ordeal that ended with their deaths.

'This only every man knows,' wrote Sir Thomas Wentworth, 'that since England was England it received not so dishonourable a blow.'

Hated

BUCKINGHAM knew how many enemies he had at home. When he had come close to shipwreck en route for La Rochelle, he said coolly, 'There's nothing grieves me in all this but that the rascals in England will say, "It was the just judgement of God upon him."'

He had hoped to win the people's love by going to aid La Rochelle. On his return, his wife wrote sadly, 'By his action he is not any whit the more popular man than when he went.' It was an understatement. He was hated.

William Fleetwood, who described himself as 'an unfortunate Commander in that untoward service', wrote an account of the expedition in which he hoped that Parliament 'will send [Buckingham] to hell without any more ado'. Simonds D'Ewes wrote that his 'coming safe home occasioned almost as much sorrow as the slaughter and perishing of all the rest'.

He was jeered at as a craven courtier, pampered and feeble.

> So, stay at court then, and at tennis play;
> Measure French galliards out, or kelligray [a card game].

One of his own officers accused Buckingham of being slow to embark at the outset of the expedition because he was 'fearing some miserable death' or reluctant to be 'estranged from his effeminate pleasures here at home'. On his return, a libel addressed him:

And art returned again with all thy faults?
Thou great commander of the All-go-naughts,
And left the isle behind thee? What's the matter?
Did winter make thy teeth begin to chatter?
Could not the surging and distempered seas
Thy queasy stomach, gorged with sweetmeats, please?

He was derided for his mistakes, which were all too real. He was vilified for his supposed betrayals, which were imaginary, but widely believed.

These things have lost our honour, men surmise –
Thy treachery, neglect and cowardice.

Rumours circulated.

Rumour said that Buckingham (as a supposed secret Catholic) had deviously planned the expedition in order to call down the wrath of the French king on the Huguenots of La Rochelle.

Rumour said that Sir John Burroughs, who had been shot dead by a French musketeer, was too effective a commander, and that Buckingham was so determined that his expedition should fail that he had ordered Burroughs's murder.

Rumour said Buckingham had weakened the besieging force by withdrawing two regiments to serve as his personal bodyguard.

Rumour said that he had sent a double into battle dressed exactly like himself, while he hid, gibbering with fear, in a boat.

Rumour said that he had lied to his officers before the assault on the Fort St-Martin, telling them that most of the garrison had covertly withdrawn and that the suicidal attack he had ordered was therefore likely to succeed.

Rumour said that he had given up too soon and run for home 'for want of wenches' to satisfy his lust, or because he was afraid the handsome Earl of Holland might supplant him as royal favourite, or because he was worried that in his absence the Earl of Bristol would turn King Charles against him.

Rumour said that Buckingham had been working with Toiras – the two of them co-conspirators in a popish plot.

Rumour said that the plot had been exposed and on his return Buckingham had been arrested and imprisoned in the Tower.

*   *   *

Buckingham was not in the Tower. King Charles's love for him was unshaken. 'With whatsoever success ye shall come to me ye shall be ever welcome,' wrote Charles, 'one of my greatest griefs being that I have not been with you in this time of suffering, for I know we would have much eased each other's griefs.' It was not Buckingham who had failed. 'I must say this with my own hand that in this action you had honour. All the shame must light upon us here remaining at home.'

On the island Buckingham had felt abandoned. In July King Charles had written to him, 'No man ever longed so much for anything as I do to hear some good news from you.' But Buckingham had no good news to give, and he came to doubt the King's patience. He told his secretary that 'the great business of a fleet, of an army, of a siege, of a treaty, of war, of peace, both on foot together and all of them in his head at a time' came close to overwhelming him, but that nothing caused him so much anxiety as his fear 'that some at home ... of whom he had well deserved, were now content to forget him'.

Charles wrote to reassure him: 'No distance of place nor length of time can make me slacken, much less diminish my love to you.' He told him that disagreement 'cannot fall between us'. He advised Buckingham to count his blessings, in particular that of 'True friendship ... the greatest of riches, and now hardest to be found'. Charles himself, in the loneliness of his royal childhood, had never had an affectionate companion. But with Buckingham he had found friendship at last, and he would never let it go. He was, he told Buckingham, and always would be, 'your loving, faithful, constant friend'.

The King's constancy, though, could not protect Buckingham. When he landed on his return from the Île de Ré, he was informed there was a plot to murder him as he rode towards London. From that time onward, he lived in the knowledge he might at any moment be killed. Basil Feilding, his sister Susan's nineteen-year-old son, who had been his aide on the Île de Ré, volunteered to be his stand-in. He asked Buckingham to lend him his coat and blue ribbon (the Garter) and said he would 'muffle up himself in his hood, as the Duke's manner was to ride in cold weather', so that any would-be assassin would kill, not the famous uncle but the self-sacrificing nephew. Buckingham, deeply moved, declined.

The story is told as evidence of young Feilding's nobility, but it is a reminder that Buckingham would now forever be a target. The next stranger who stepped out of the crowd with hostile intent towards him was likely to do more than knock off his hat.

Five Knights

WHILE Buckingham was absent in France the King's commissioners were still active across the country, attempting to collect the Forced Loan. Opposition to it grew. There were ways of avoiding paying. Many people left the county in which they were registered – moving temporarily to another where they would not be pursued. Christopher Wandesford, MP, hid repeatedly in a priest-hole when the commissioners came round. Others pleaded poverty or promised to pay later, and the commissioners – who were in many cases doubtful of the loan's legitimacy – could be lenient and leave them alone. Those who were detained were either too poor and ill-connected to take evasive action, or they were defiant. They were the ones who wanted to challenge the loan in court and prove that it contravened their rights.

In the spring of 1627 some hundred gentlemen-refusers were being held in London. Initially they were imprisoned, but as months passed the prisons became too full to hold them, so they were released on parole, obliged to report every three days to the Council. They were not brought to trial. Councillors and judges alike seem to have felt that the legality of the loan had better not be put to the test in courts of law.

The refusers' presence in the capital was disruptive. There were demonstrations in their support. In June, as the fleet sailed to France, they were sent down into the shires separately, escorted by sheriffs, to live under house arrest in their homes. A number of them refused to go and challenged the Council to justify their being deprived of their liberty. They were given no answers. Some were locked up again in the Fleet Prison.

In October 1627, a few weeks before Buckingham brought his defeated fleet home, a group of the loan-refusers, known to history as the Five Knights, petitioned the Lord Chief Justice 'that counsel might be assigned them to plead for their relief out of prison'. The judges asked the King for guidance. Charles allowed the case to proceed.

The hearing was in Westminster Hall, which was crowded for the occasion. The Five Knights (actually only four by this time – one had withdrawn his case) were not wild revolutionaries. They were serious men, pillars of their communities – described by one historian as 'gentlemen of probity, property and Protestantism, who paid their debts, fed the poor of their parishes' and were admired as conservative defenders of fundamental constitutional rights against newfangled absolutism.

The King could imprison a subject on suspicion – that was not contested. But on suspicion of what? Counsel for the Knights invoked Magna Carta and the ancient writ of *habeas corpus*. They claimed that detention 'without cause given' was unlawful. A news-writer reports that they spoke to 'great applause, even of shouting and clapping of hands, which was unusual in that place'. The Attorney General counter-argued that in cases involving matters of state the King could imprison without showing cause. He won his case. The Lord Chief Justice was now Nicholas Hyde, who owed his promotion to the fact that (unlike the previous incumbent) he was ready to enforce the loan. Hyde invoked a precedent from 1594 establishing that when someone was imprisoned at the King's command, 'cause for committal need not be shown'.

The Crown had prevailed, but at great loss to its popularity and prestige. The Knights remained in prison until January 1628, when all the loan-refusers were released. Two months later twenty-seven of them, including the Five, stood for election to the House of Commons. They all won their seats.

As an exercise in fund-raising, the Forced Loan had been successful – £260,000 reached the Exchequer. Its political consequences, though, would be dire.

Beauty and Home

In January 1628, ten months after his little Charles had died, Buckingham's second son and eventual heir was born, and named George. If Buckingham's public life was now all effort and turbulence, he had at least a fruitful domestic life, and magnificent homes in which to enjoy it.

Father now of two living children, he was thinking about education. He had been to school at Angers, where he learnt ancient and modern languages, as well as how to dance and fence and manage the great horse. In his twenties he had been taught statecraft by Francis Bacon and by wily, learned, disputacious King James. He was sneered at as an empty-headed fop, but not many scions of the great aristocratic families were so well educated.

Buckingham was traditional enough in his world view to accept without apparent resentment that those scions were born to power, but he was also progressive enough to think that they should be trained ready for a life of public service. He made plans for the establishment of an academy for the 'children' (by which, for all his affection for his daughter, he meant boys) of the ruling class.

As for girls, they must be well married. He arranged for five-year-old Mall to be betrothed to Lord Charles Herbert, a seven-year-old boy who was heir to both his uncle, the Earl of Pembroke, and his father, Lord Montgomery. Thus Mary was promised a likely future as the chatelaine of Wilton, one of England's most beautiful houses, while her father strengthened a useful bond with Pembroke, who had been first his sponsor, then his formidable opponent, and who was now once more his ally.

* * *

An immense consignment of modern paintings and ancient sculptures had arrived at York House.

In Paris in 1625, chatting while he sketched Buckingham's head for a portrait or while they rode out to Fontainebleau together, Peter Paul Rubens had mentioned his collection of Greco-Roman sculpture. It included a batch of statuary he had bought from Dudley Carleton ten years earlier, after Carleton's intended buyer, the Earl of Somerset, was imprisoned in the Tower. Since that time Rubens had accumulated many more pieces. They were a valuable resource. He used them as models for his mythological compositions, full of Olympian gods and ancient heroes. Now, though, always a shrewd businessman as well as a creator, Rubens was ready to part with them for the right price. Buckingham was interested. He wanted the antiquities and he wanted more of Rubens's paintings. He instructed Balthazar Gerbier to negotiate a deal.

Later that summer Gerbier visited Antwerp to view the collection on his master's behalf. Then, when Buckingham was in the Netherlands in November 1625, he was able to see for himself what Rubens had to offer. Months passed. Letters went back and forth. The selection was made. Early in 1627 Rubens crated up his antiquities and set out for Paris to meet Gerbier there. After forty-eight hours they had agreed a price of 100,000 florins for them, along with thirteen paintings by Rubens's own hand (no fobbing them off with studio assistants' work). Further months went by while Gerbier wrestled with the task of transporting such bulky and precious things to London at a time when – thanks to his master's stirring – French and English ships were harassing each other in the Channel. At last, in September 1627, the fabulous consignment arrived. When Buckingham came home from the wars, he could admire his new possessions and work with Gerbier to plan the best way for them to be displayed.

By this time York House was, as Gerbier had promised it would be, an art gallery to which foreigners came 'in procession' to marvel. An inventory from the next decade lists 330 paintings and ninety pieces of Roman sculpture. It was also a museum with rich and varied contents. There were all the curiosities Tradescant had accumulated. In Holland in 1625 Buckingham had bought a number of rare manuscripts 'exquisitely written in Arabic' that had been 'sought in the most remote parts' and acquired by the celebrated traveller and Orientalist scholar Thomas

Van Erpe, known as Erpenius. (Robert Ashley, traveller and translator, wrote in 1627 that the Escorial contained a 'glorious golden library of Arabic books'. Buckingham must have seen them and decided he would like some of his own.) Henry Wotton sent him gilded leather hangings from Venice. He had collections of cameos and incised gems, some new-made, some by Renaissance masters, some from ancient Rome. He liked exquisite small things as well as massive and imposing ones.

In the last winter of his life he was thinking about the defence of the realm, about oatmeal and stockings and billets for the wretched survivors of his expedition to the Île de Ré, and about raising money and recruiting men for his next campaign, but there was also room in his life for his wife (only months after George's birth Kate became pregnant again), for his baby son, for his little Mall, for poring over Islamic calligraphy, for toying with cameos cut in the time of the Roman emperors. He played bowls and tennis and cards, recklessly placing large bets and losing as often as he won. He took part in tournaments, his armour and accoutrements all intricately decorated with mother-of-pearl and precious metals. When he ate, he did so to the sound of trumpets or of fiddles. When he rode into a town, he liked to be greeted with peals of bells.

He was a dilettante and an amateur, not in the derogatory modern sense of those words, but in their original meaning – he was one who delighted in and loved beautiful things.

Anger

SHORTLY after Buckingham left the Île de Ré, Spanish ships began arriving there, ready – had he not already gone – to support the French by driving him away.

At the beginning of 1628 a French envoy travelled to Madrid to draw up plans for a concerted invasion of England.

Buckingham had annoyed the Spanish. He had annoyed the French. They were bound to retaliate. In the Privy Council he urged King Charles to use the winter months to build up a navy ready 'to scour the seas, to defend the coasts of this kingdoms against the attempts of his enemies, and to assist his friends and allies'. In particular, he still wanted to assist the Rochelloises. Shortly after he returned from the Île de Ré, Charles had written to him that they must try again. 'You and I are young enough to redeem this misfortune.'

Once more, Buckingham was set upon compounding a failure by repeating it. Again that nightmare of circularity, of a disaster ending only to begin again.

How was a second expedition to be mounted? How was it to be paid for?

The survivors of the 1627 expedition were dying in Portsmouth and Plymouth almost as fast as they had died abroad. 'The winter will eat out more of them than the enemy unless better provision be made for clothes for them,' wrote one of Buckingham's officers. Another warned that sailors were planning to 'forsake their ships and march up to the court'.

And with the men he already had in such dire condition, Buckingham was asking for more to be found. An officer whom he had ordered to begin recruiting wrote, 'I humbly pray Your Excellency to take into consideration how hard a business it will be for me to procure men without pay.'

* * *

To read about Buckingham's preparations is to be numbed again by the stubbornness of his perseverance. Everything was as it had been the year before, and the year before that, and the year before that. Sailors and soldiers unpaid. Their wives and children starving. Nothing to keep the men who were expected to give their lives for England from the winter cold – no suits, no shirts, no stockings, no hammocks, so that they slept, if they could sleep at all, on bare boards. Their food rotting. Fresh provisions unobtainable because there was no money to pay for them. Wounded men put ashore and sent to houses where nobody cared for them, where they were left, said a visitor, 'their toes and feet rotting from their bodies, and so smelling that none are able to come into the rooms where they are'.

Impossible to recruit new men, even by force. Hard to keep those already pressed into service. Mutinies. Mass desertions. Crowds of desperate men on the road to London intent on making their anger felt. In Plymouth, gallows erected for the execution of a mutineers' leader torn down by a mob of furious sailors and thrown into the sea.

The rich, having reluctantly paid the forced loans, felt the anger of those gulled by extortionists. The middling sort, seeing the roads clogged with sullen pressed men and the countryside infested with bands of deserters, felt the anger of those who no longer felt safe in their homes. The poor, whose menfolk were forced to fight in Buckingham's futile wars, felt the anger of the directly injured.

In February a band of sailors assaulted York House, breaking down the gates. Buckingham came out to remonstrate with them. He offered them 'promises', but they wouldn't listen. So menacing and disrespectful were they, he was obliged to draw his sword to 'repel their audacity'.

Another rhyme about him concluded

> *And now, just God!*
> *I humbly pray*
> *That thou wilt take that slime away.*

The peace that King James had given England was past. The time of mulberry trees and tapestry works and great state-funded literary endeavours was over and gone. King Charles, with Buckingham's support, was putting the country on a war footing.

Charles ordered a muster of the county militias. For infantry, he had the survivors from the Île de Ré, who had at least, however unsuccessfully, seen action. Cavalry, though, was almost entirely wanting. He urged his courtiers to get ready to use their experience of tournaments and stag-hunting in combat, filling 'places of charge and command in horse troops'. He sent two emissaries to Germany to buy weapons and hire a thousand mounted men. In February Buckingham decreed that English ships should abandon the practice of firing salutes. Gunpowder and shot had to be conserved. The Council of War met three times a week.

Buckingham, as Lord Admiral, had been nominally responsible for the fleet for over a decade, but he had worked through the Naval Commission. Now the King stripped the commissioners of their powers and responsibilities. Their administrative methods might suit times of peace, but they moved at 'a slower pace than the activeness of these times of war and danger ... will safely permit'. The drastic change was presented, in a way reassuring to conservatives, not as an innovation, but as a return to an 'ancient manner and institution'. The Lord Admiral and his staff would henceforward work unhindered by tiresome modern bureaucracy. They would take back control and get things done.

Yet still the dismal chorus continued. No money. Buckingham wanted a hundred ships for his navy, but when east-coast fishing fleets asked for ships to guard them as they set out for the Icelandic fishing grounds, he was unable to send them even four.

What was to be done? The Councillors discussed taxing beer and wine, but agreed that such a tax was unthinkable – the people would never stand for it. Historically, the ports and coastal towns had been called upon to pay 'ship money' to fund the building of the ships that guarded them. Ship money was not subject to Parliamentary approval. The King could raise it on his own authority. Charles and Buckingham extended the demand for it to the whole country.

Over the next decade Charles would ask for ship money repeatedly. Each time he did so he became more unpopular, and each time his opponents seized upon his demand as further evidence of the illegitimacy of his rule. Buckingham saw the danger, but the Crown had no further resources, and so, Buckingham told Charles, 'I see no other way but this.'

No other way, that is, except for the obvious one – but the King was inflexibly opposed to that. In December the Earl of Westmorland had declared, 'A Parliament must of necessity be called, and that, I think very speedily.' Buckingham agreed. He is reported to have gone down on his knees before the King and begged him to issue the summons. Charles refused. In January he said that Parliament would waste time with their grievances and protestations. 'The occasion will not let me tarry so long.' And so he tarried, repeatedly postponing the unwelcome moment when he would have to face his subjects' representatives.

Weeks went by. Two months went by. Already, again, one of Buckingham's warlike ventures was going to be crippled before it began by the lateness of its preparation. Sir John Coke records that the entire Privy Council could witness that Buckingham 'was the first mover and persuader of this assembly of Parliament'. Still Charles dithered and havered. He summoned Parliament. He changed his mind and postponed its assembly until after his demands for ship money had been met. He changed his mind again, withdrew the demand and once more summoned Parliament.

He had accepted the inevitable. In the middle of March, Parliament assembled.

Ghost

ONE dark night a gentleman employed in the King's wardrobe at Windsor Castle was terrified by the sudden appearance at his bedside of an elderly man. Clarendon tells the story.

The apparition asks the gentleman whether he knows him. The gentleman, 'half dead with fear and apprehension', is at first unable to reply but, on the second time of asking, he manages to stammer out that, yes, he recognises his visitor as being Sir George Villiers, the Duke of Buckingham's father, by this time long dead, whom the gentleman knew when he himself was a schoolboy. The old man tells him he is right, and that he must 'go from him to his son and tell him, if he did not do somewhat to ingratiate himself to the people ... he would be

suffered to live [but] a short time'. He then vanishes. The gentleman tosses and turns until morning, when he tells himself he has simply had a bad dream.

A few nights later, the late Sir George visits him again at the dead of night and gives him 'very sharp reprehensions'. Again, come morning, the gentleman tells himself he must have been dreaming. Again he decides to do nothing.

In tales like this, things tend to occur in triplicate. And so, of course, 'the same person appeared to him a third time, with a terrible countenance, and bitterly reproaching him for not performing what he had promised to do'. The gentleman pleads, in mitigation, that he doesn't know the Duke, and that even if he could pass on the ghost's message, he would undoubtedly be thought to be mad. Not so, says the dead-alive father, who then tells him two or three secret 'particulars' that he is to repeat to Buckingham.

So the gentleman goes to London, where his contacts are actually somewhat better than he has given the ghost to understand. He has a friend, Sir Ralph, whose wife is a distant connection of Buckingham's. Sir Ralph speaks to Buckingham. Buckingham, whose 'graciousness and condescension' are well known, is obliging. He will be going hunting with the King the following day. His horses will be brought to meet him at Lambeth Bridge. He himself will be arriving there by water at five o'clock in the morning. 'If the man attended him there at that hour, he would walk, and speak with him.'

And so it comes about that the nameless gentleman has a private audience with the most powerful person in the land. No one is about but Sir Ralph and the Duke's servants. In the early morning gloaming, Buckingham and the gentleman walk a little way off. As they talk, Sir Ralph, who cannot hear what they are saying, observes that Buckingham 'spake with great commotion'.

The interview over, Buckingham rides off. The gentleman tells Sir Ralph that when he passed on the secret 'particulars', the Duke went pale and 'he swore he could come by that knowledge only by the Devil'.

All that morning Buckingham rides 'with great pensiveness, and in deep thought, without any delight'. He slips away from the chase early and goes to his mother's apartments in Whitehall Palace, staying for two or three hours, 'the noise of their discourse frequently reaching the ears of those who attended in the next rooms'. (At court there were always ears pricked in the next room.) When he leaves, the Countess is 'overwhelmed in tears' and the Duke appears 'full of trouble'.

A few months later, so Clarendon has heard, Buckingham's mother will receive the news of his death with extraordinary calm, 'as if she had foreseen it'.

Liberty

FOUR days before the opening of Parliament, Buckingham's most determined critics met at the house of the historian and manuscript collector Sir Robert Cotton. They resolved that, rather than infuriating the King by reviving the impeachment proceedings against the Duke, they would concentrate their energies instead on defining and defending 'the liberties of the subject'.

The Forced Loan and the consequent imprisonments without trial had been flagrant attacks on citizens' rights. The principles enshrined in Magna Carta had been violated. That was the Parliamentarians' main concern. The Venetian ambassador reports that they therefore agreed that 'nothing shall be said about Buckingham'.

The King ordered that those imprisoned for refusing to pay the Forced Loan should be released. But his leniency was conditional. He issued a declaration. 'If you make this present supply we will then go on with our Parliament, if not then we must think of a more speedy way.'

At the opening, on 17 March 1628, Buckingham walked immediately behind the King, followed by his father-in-law, the Earl of Rutland, carrying the Sword of State. The first speeches set out the royal agenda. Charles was blunt: 'I think there is none here but knows what common danger is the cause of this Parliament, and that supply at this time is the chief end of it.' He was prepared to 'forget and forgive what's past', but if Parliament would not oblige him by granting him money, he would 'use those other means which God has put into my hands'. Everyone present understood those means would include the dissolution of Parliament.

The Lord Keeper, speaking for the King, expanded on the theme of the 'common danger'. The Pope and the House of Austria, he said, were making themselves 'masters of Spain and Italy and the great country of Germany'. France had been 'drawn to their adherence'. Therefore (this is always the most questionable part of the argument) it was imperative to attack France, and to do so swiftly. 'We may dandle and play as we will with the hour-glass that is in our power, but the hours will not stay for us.'

The Commons were not impressed. What did any of these shifts in the European power balance matter to England? They had another agenda. Twenty-seven of the members had been among those imprisoned for refusing to pay the Forced Loan, and only very recently released. They were there to ensure their rights would never again be so trampled upon.

Sir Edward Coke was back in the House. Seventy-six years old, renowned for his courage, his formidable knowledge of the law and his fierce temper, Coke had come intent on speaking truth to power once more. He declared, 'I fear not foreign enemies. God send us peace at home.' Speaker after speaker echoed him. Sir Robert Phelips: 'I more fear the violation of public rights at home than a foreign enemy.' Sir Edward Kirton: 'We are told of dangers abroad. We have as great at home.'

The dominant theme of seventeenth-century English history was announcing itself loud and clear. This Parliament was to be a tussle between monarchy and the royal prerogative on the one hand, and the rights of the subject as protected by the law on the other.

Day after day went by. Members had grievances to air, about the way soldiers were being billeted on private citizens, about the imposition of martial law in peacetime, about the imprisonment of those who would not pay the Forced Loan.

The King's supporters tried to shift the discussion back to supply. Sir John Coke laid out the royal requests. Thirty ships to guard the English coasts. Ten to succour La Rochelle. An army of 10,000 infantry and a thousand cavalry for service overseas. Six thousand men to assist Denmark's fight for Protestantism in Germany. Long-term funding for a modernised and much enlarged navy. Without them, he said, 'every day we run into more danger'.

Some influential members were persuaded. Sir Robert Mansell, whom Buckingham had succeeded as Lord Admiral, urged his fellow

Parliamentarians not to allow their concern for the 'sufferings of the commonwealth' to make them forget 'His Majesty's necessity'. Even Edward Coke agreed that the people's representatives should assist the Crown against a 'common danger' (though he would not support any overseas war). But before they would do so, said Coke, certain resolutions must be accepted and given the force of law.

The resolutions were drafted. They were succinct. That no one was to be imprisoned, even at the King's command, without cause shown. That habeas corpus must be respected. That no tax, loan or benevolence was to be levied without Parliamentary consent.

Four members, including Sir Edward Coke and Sir Dudley Digges, presented the resolutions to the House of Lords. Coke spoke passionately. 'The greatest inheritance that a man hath is the liberty of his person,' he said. His listeners knew he spoke from experience. Many of them had been in the House in 1621 when he had presented his remonstrance to King James I asserting the primacy of the law over the royal prerogative, and defending the same rights that he was fighting for again now. Then Coke had been imprisoned in the Tower without trial for nine months. Now he said, 'A prison without a prefixed time is a kind of hell.'

The Lords listened. They would deliberate over their response.

While they did so, on 4 April, the Commons turned at last to the question of supply. They resolved that five subsidies should be voted – not immediately, but in due course, once they had a satisfactory response to their resolutions.

When John Coke brought Charles the news, the King said he had once 'been a liker of Parliaments', that he had lost his liking for a while, but now 'I am where I was. I love Parliaments. I shall rejoice to meet my people often.'

The Disasters of War V

As the Commons debated citizens' rights, Buckingham's mind was still on La Rochelle. He asked the Duke of Soubise to assume command of a fleet of English ships. When Soubise learnt how small and ill-prepared the fleet was, he declined. The thankless task passed to the Earl of Denbigh.

Denbigh was Buckingham's brother-in-law. As William Feilding, son of a family from the same social stratum as the Villierses – minor provincial landowners – he had married Buckingham's elder sister, Susan, in 1606, years before anyone could have foreseen how high young George might rise. The Denbighs rose with him. Susan was always close to Buckingham, becoming a great lady in royal circles and lady-in-waiting to Queen Henrietta Maria. William was given a place at court as Master of the Wardrobe, and became Earl of Denbigh in 1622. He followed Prince Charles and Buckingham to Madrid in 1623, and in 1625 he was one of the vice admirals in the disastrous raid on Cadiz.

Amid all the vitriol poured out on the hated Villiers 'kindred', Denbigh largely escaped attack. He was mocked for claiming to be a Habsburg by descent, which he wasn't, but no particular wrongdoing was alleged against him. Nor did he distinguish himself. After Buckingham's death he went as ambassador to the court of Persia, and afterwards visited India to inspect the East India Company's settlements. He is now best remembered for the engaging portrait Van Dyck painted of him on his return, showing a florid-faced Englishman, untidily dressed in red-and-gold-striped silk kurta-pajama that don't exactly fit him, strolling through the artist's vision of an Indian landscape, complete with palm tree, parrot and turbaned pageboy. He looks genial but a little lost.

Buckingham was frequently accused of over-promoting his family members. His giving Denbigh command of the fleet in 1628 seems to bear out the charge.

Preparations were bedevilled by the usual problems. Inadequate provisions. Disaffected sailors. Buckingham sent his servant Edward Clerk, who had useful Huguenot connections, to Plymouth to accompany the fleet. Clerk reported that of the promised thirty ships only fifteen were manned, the crews were mutinous and supplies intended to feed the starving people of La Rochelle were 'so poor as will hardly prove one month's provisions for the town'. Was it even worth sending out such a poor excuse for a fleet? Buckingham thought it was. Denbigh was ordered to sail as soon as possible. At the end of April, he led out his ships.

They came within sight of La Rochelle, but Denbigh found the French blockade was impenetrable. A sea captain who was with him told Buckingham later that there was 'no such difficulty in the relief of that place as it seems was pretended'. All that had been needed was a commander 'capable of the affair ... one whose spirit and judgement must sway without fear in the greatest distress'.

Denbigh was not such a captain. He made no contact with the people of La Rochelle, and could find no way of delivering the provisions he had brought for them. After eight days he gave up and took his ships home.

The Crisis of Parliaments

THE resolution the leaders of the Commons had made in Sir Robert Cotton's house before Parliament opened – that no word should be said about Buckingham – was proving hard to keep.

Preaching in April, Puritan minister Jeremiah Dyke reminded his hearers of the tempest that had churned up the Thames just before the dissolution of the 1626 Parliament, and sent a pillar of water crashing into Buckingham's garden. 'God gave us fair warning,' said Dyke. It was time to act on that warning, and to save the land from what Dyke called 'judgements coming'.

A week later Robert Melvin, a Scotsman who admitted to being drunk at the time, was heard in a tobacco house on the Strand saying 'foul and undutiful things' about the Duke. He was imprisoned, but the allegations he had made were soon circulating among the news-writers. He said Buckingham met every night with a secret council of Jesuits and Scotsmen; that he was plotting to have Parliament dissolved; worse, that Buckingham and King Charles, at the head of 'a great army of horse and foot', would make war on the English Parliament. The 'enemy' (Spain and/or France) would invade in their support because 'the kingdom is already sold to the enemy by the Duke'.

25 April. The Lords had taken nearly a month to reflect upon the Commons' resolutions. At last they presented their much milder version. Each resolution was tempered and modified. Each paragraph began by asking 'that His Majesty would be graciously pleased to grant' this or that right.

Edward Coke raged against the new wording. Graciousness had nothing to do with the matter. 'When the King doth a thing "of grace" it implies that it is not our right.'

The Lords asked the King to ratify his subjects' 'just' liberties, but who was to decide which liberties were 'just'? The right to liberty was absolute.

The Lords allowed the King to imprison a subject 'without cause shown' if he judged it necessary for 'matters of state'. This was in flat contravention of Magna Carta. There it was written, 'No freeman shall be taken or imprisoned or be disseised [deprived] of his freehold or liberties but by lawful judgment of his peers or by the law of the land.'

This sentence lay at the heart of English common law. It was non-negotiable. To admit of exceptions would be to open the way to tyranny. 'Matters of state' were 'matters in the clouds, where I desire we may leave them'. 'Reason of state', said Coke, 'lames Magna Carta.'

John Selden supported Coke. 'There is not one of these five propositions fit to be desired and asked.' The Commons rejected the Lords' draft. Back to work.

28 April. King Charles was becoming impatient. He had made it plain what this Parliament was there to do – to grant him supply – and they hadn't done it.

He came to the Lords, and summoned the Commons to stand at the Bar. He had heard that Parliament's delay in granting his wishes was due to a debate about the liberty of the subject. He hoped to speed things along by explaining his position. He listened while the Lord Keeper delivered his promise to 'maintain all his subjects in the just freedom of their person and safety of their estates'. He assured them that Magna Carta and other statutes fundamental to English law were 'all in force'. He told them, 'You shall find as much security in His Majesty's royal word and promise as in the strength of any law ye can make.' He asked them to 'proceed to his business'.

For the Commons, his promises were not enough. They wanted a bill to give those promises the force of law. 'Nothing else will enable them cheerfully to serve His Majesty.'

King Charles was irritated. He gave notice that he would be suspending Parliament on 13 May, two weeks away. That would not allow enough time for the Commons to bring in their bill.

*   *   *

As Parliament convened that spring, Robert Cotton had written that the King would need to mollify his subjects by practising a 'gracious yielding'.

Gracious yielding was Buckingham's forte. As right-hand man to two monarchs who believed passionately in the royal prerogative, he had learnt by long practice how to bend and accommodate and adapt his plans to the requirements of an autocratic master. He was a courtier. When he was crossed, he was still always amiable, even-tempered, obliging.

For King Charles, though, gracious yielding did not come easily. It was contrary to his nature, which was anxious, proud and stubborn. It was not consistent with his sense of his kingly role as head of the body politic, arbiter of all matters of state. He had not learnt (nor would he ever learn) that it is sometimes wise to accept a compromise. Had Charles been better at gracious yielding, the history of his country over the next three decades might have taken a different turn. It was his inability to yield graciously that began and prolonged the Civil Wars, and that lost him his kingdom and his head.

Now his refusal to allow time for his subjects' rights to be fixed in law infuriated the Commons. Edward Coke, whose understanding of legal process was unrivalled, suggested another, speedier way. He proposed that they draw up a petition listing the King's illegal actions (the Forced Loan, the imprisonment of the refusers) and asking for confirmation that these actions would not be repeated.

This was not a Petition of Grace, a humble request for concessions to be granted as favours by the King. It would be an affirmation of rights long established, a complaint that they had been violated, and a demand that they be respected in future. It would be a Petition of Right.

The petition was drafted. Edward Coke, who was its chief author, read it out to the Commons. It was brief and peremptory and legally watertight. No pussyfooting about His Majesty 'graciously enacting'. 'Be it enacted,' wrote Coke.

Day after day, for eight days, the Commons debated the draft. As they did so they received repeated messages from the King, delivered sometimes by John Coke, sometimes by the Speaker. Charles wanted to know whether they would 'rest upon' his royal word. He told them he would tolerate no 'encroachings upon that sovereignty or prerogative which God hath put into his hands'. He reminded them that he was in a hurry.

Anxiety possessed the Commons. Even the most resolute wavered: to defy a King went against their deeply engrained conditioning. There were times, after receiving one of Charles's messages, when they sat in dead silence, afraid to say a word. To contradict or disobey the monarch was treason. Supposedly, they were protected by Parliamentary privilege, but they looked at Dudley Digges, at John Eliot, at Edward Coke, all of whom had been taken from the Chamber to the Tower, and they feared imprisonment or worse.

Was there no other way but this petition? the moderates asked. The stalwarts told them, no, there was not.

Sir Robert Phelips: 'To speak in plain language, we are now come to the end of our journey.'

Sir Benjamin Rudyerd: 'This is the crisis of Parliaments. We shall know by this if Parliaments live or die.'

8 May. The petition was ready. The Commons had given the draft their unanimous approval. Sir Edward Coke presented it to the Lords in the Painted Chamber.

Buckingham went back and forth between King and Lords and Commons. None of these Parliamentary wrangles were of much concern to him. A softened phrase here, a less absolute prohibition there, he thought, and the petition could pass and the King receive his subsidies and a 'right understanding between the King and his people' be established. He was not interested in constitutional rights: he simply wanted to clear the way for his next expedition to La Rochelle.

The case for his impeachment had not been revived. His name had still not been spoken during this session by anyone in the Commons. He did not know how much it was on the members' minds.

12 May. The Lords' and Commons' representatives met in conference. The Lords said they assented to the substance of the petition, but still they wondered 'whether there might not be some words altered, or put in to make it more sweet', so that it might be acceptable to His Majesty?

As they discussed this, the Lord Keeper brought another message from the King. Charles would have them know that he would not relinquish his right to imprison without cause shown. To do so would 'soon dissolve the very foundations and frame of our monarchy'. He was announcing his rejection of the Petition before it had even been presented to him.

The Lords continued their deliberations.

13 May. The date on which the King had threatened to suspend Parliament came and went. The members were now on borrowed time. At any moment the King might dismiss them.

15 May. The Lords returned the petition to the Commons. They had added a paragraph in which they assured the King of their 'due regard to leave entire that sovereign power wherewith Your Majesty is entrusted'.

So this was what the Lords meant by 'sweet words'. To the Commons those words were bitter as gall. They nullified the entire petition. One after another the House's most eloquent speakers rose to denounce them. Eliot, Digges, Pym, Wentworth: they all categorically rejected the Lords' addition. 'What is this "sovereign power"?' 'We cannot admit the words with safety.' 'Let us give that to the King the law gives him, and no more.' 'If we do admit of this addition, we shall leave the subject worse than we found him.'

Edward Coke: '"Sovereign power" is no Parliamentary word. Should we now add it, we shall weaken the foundation of law and the building must fall.'

For five days the Lords clung to their 'sweet words'. Two more chivvying messages arrived from the King. The Commons leaders argued and pleaded. At last the Lords succumbed. The offending paragraph was deleted.

28 May. The petition was given three readings in each of the two houses of Parliament, and formally approved by them.

A deputation from both houses carried it to King Charles in Whitehall, inviting him 'to give his assent in full Parliament'.

Buckingham was glad. 'There is now likely to be happy agreement between the King and his people,' he wrote.

He felt so confident that the subsidies would at last be granted that he sent a succession of messengers galloping through France to inform the Rochelloises that the King of England was ready to send 'a greater force' to relieve the besieged city. He thought his troubles with this most troublesome of Parliaments would now be over. He was wrong.

2 June. King Charles came to Westminster and sat enthroned, the Lords seated and the Commons standing before him. He said tartly, 'I have not taken so many days in answering the petition as ye have spent weeks in framing it.'

The petition was read aloud.

There was a proper way for a Parliamentary petition to be presented. There was a proper way for it to be received and accepted by the monarch. If all was done in this proper and time-honoured manner, then the principles asserted in the petition would have the force of law.

What the King was required to say, to signal that the petition was granted, were the 'law-French' words '*Soit droit fait comme est désiré*' ('Let right be done as it is desired'). Those were the words the Commons were waiting for. As soon as those words were uttered, their battle would be won.

Lord Keeper Coventry spoke first. Charles, hampered by his stammer, preferred to keep his own speeches as brief as possible, allowing the Lord Keeper to amplify them with a prologue or epilogue, or both. On this occasion, Coventry began by announcing that the King had come to 'strike a league' with his people. He went on to make a highly questionable twinned assertion: that those people's 'liberties are an ornament and strengthening of His Majesty's prerogative, and his prerogative the defence of their liberties'.

The Commons listened in stony silence. They were there assembled to ask that the King should desist from using his prerogative to override the law. These were not congenial ideas.

At last King Charles spoke. He didn't utter the six expected old-French words.

He said, 'The King willeth that right be done according to the laws and customs of the realm ...'

So far so unexceptionable.

'... and that the statutes be put in due execution ...'

Yes, no one would disagree with that.

'... that his subjects may have no cause to complain of any wrongs or oppressions contrary to their just rights and liberties ...'

Exactly what Parliament was asking too, except for that ominous qual-ifier 'just'.

'... to the preservation whereof he holds himself in conscience as well obliged ...'

This was all wrong. The people's Parliamentary representatives wanted their rights to be preserved by the law, not to be dependent upon the workings of the King's conscience.

'... as of his prerogative.'

The stinger. The last word negated all that had seemed promising in the preceding words. So the King's respect for his people's rights and liber-ties would always be balanced, and might be outweighed, by his respect for his own prerogative, the 'divinely given' privilege that entitled him to act 'subject to no restriction or interference' and 'out of the course of common law'.

That was all. The longed-for words were not spoken. Charles had made another promise which – conditional as it was on his regard for his own prerogative – was valueless.

The King might think he had accepted the Petition of Right. To the House of Commons it was clear that he had not.

3 June. The Commons met. They had set great store by their petition. They had thought it would be transformative, but the King had batted it away. As they assembled the next day, they were frustrated, angry, humiliated by their own impotence.

Sir John Eliot spoke. He had of late, he said, had 'many a sad thought, in respect of disasters abroad and disorders at home'. Cadiz, the Île de Ré, Crown lands sold, Crown jewels pawned, the Treasury empty, soldiers and sailors starving in the streets. He had asked himself repeat-edly what was the cause of all these disasters, who was responsible for the 'waste of our men and ships and navy'.

He did not give himself an answer. He continued to observe, for the time being, the agreement made in Cotton's house that a certain name should not be spoken, but everyone in the chamber, remembering his coruscating attack on Buckingham two years previ-ously – that furious and fantastic speech in which Eliot called Buckingham the spotted monster, the Stellionatus – knew what that answer would be.

Some members were anxious. If it was true that a foreign invasion was imminent – as Buckingham and the King seemed to believe – surely this was not the time to sow dissension? Sir Humphrey May, a Privy Councillor, tried to stop Eliot. Members shouted 'Go on! Go on!' May said, 'If he goes on, I hope that I may go out.' Shouts of 'Begone! Begone!'

Eliot went on. The King, he said, seemed not to know what was being done in his name. It was the duty of Parliament, 'the great council of the kingdom', to open his eyes. They must draw up a remonstrance and present it to King Charles.

Then spake Sir Edward Coke. If Eliot was the swordsman of the anti-Buckingham faction, Coke was its heavy artillery. He agreed with Eliot. If he thought that the King already knew 'the true cause of our dishonours and disasters', then he, Coke, would have no part in the proposed remonstrance. 'But he knows not the true cause, which we know.'

Still the taboo held. The name had not been spoken. But it was now clear to the entire Commons that the 'remonstrance' would be a denunciation of Buckingham.

By this time rumours were swirling around England, and abroad as well, about Buckingham's supposed treachery. People found it hard to believe in his devotion to the cause of the Huguenots of La Rochelle. It seemed so inconsistent with his previous policy, so baffling strategically – if he wanted an alliance with France, why make war on the French king? To explain the perversity of it, theories were mooted. It was said that he was a 'Spanish agent', that he was secretly in the pay of King Louis. Elizabeth of the Palatinate, still in The Hague, discussed the theory with the Venetian ambassador and said 'she believed the worst'.

4 June. The Commons began to draft the remonstrance.

King Charles was still waiting impatiently for his subsidies to be voted through. He was receiving reports of what was being said and done in the Commons. He understood that in drafting the remonstrance, the members would be raking over all their old grievances against Buckingham. It was just as he had feared it would be, just as it was in 1626. All he asked of his Parliament was that they should do their appointed job, and authorise their monarch to raise taxes. But always they would be meddling – impertinent and interfering. Always they would insist on this futile, time-wasting attempt to discredit his great minister, whom he would never forsake.

He sent a message to the members informing them that the Parliamentary session would end within a week and ordering them not to begin 'any new matter, which may exceed time'.

5 June. The members of the House of Commons were in a state of extreme tension compounded of fear, hopelessness and heroic resolution. The King's latest message seemed to them a clear defiance of Parliamentary privilege.

Another royal message arrived, reiterating the message of the previous day and expanding it. The members of the Commons were forbidden to lay 'scandal or aspersion on the state or the ministers thereof'.

It was a fundamental condition of British Parliamentary democracy that members enjoyed absolute freedom of speech while the House was sitting. Whatever they said in the Commons chamber, they said with impunity. King Charles's order was an outrage. But to disobey a royal command was a kind of treason, and treason was a capital offence.

The crisis had come.

Sir Robert Phelips spoke. His tone was one of biblical lamentation. His voice was breaking. 'If ever my passions were wrought upon, it is now … We came hither full of wounds, and we have cured what we could. Yet what is the return of all but misery and desolation?'

Sir John Eliot rose. Again, everyone knew what he would say, whom he would accuse. Everyone knew he was fearless, that the threat of the Tower would not silence him.

The Speaker, Sir Heneage Finch, stopped him.

The Speaker was the mediator between King and Commons. His loyalties were divided. He could not ignore a royal command. Finch said that he was obliged to interrupt any member who was intent upon casting aspersions on a minister. A contemporary news-sheet tells us that as he affirmed the royal gagging order – as he was bound to do – Finch shed tears.

John Eliot sat down.

A pause.

Dudley Digges said, 'Unless we may speak of these things in Parliament, let us arise and be gone, or sit in silence. We are miserable. We know not what to do.'

'Hereupon', wrote the Parliamentary reporter, 'there was a deep silence in the House for a while.'

The fear that had made the Commons' representatives so distressed at having to accuse Buckingham to his face in 1626 had seized them again. Twenty-seven members had been imprisoned in the last year for refusing the Forced Loan. Everyone present remembered Edward Coke's long imprisonment. They remembered that Eliot and Digges had both been hauled off to the Tower at the end of the last Parliament. They didn't know how much more severe King Charles was likely to have become. They were afraid, but many of them were convinced that this was a pivotal moment, that this time they must not fail.

The silence was broken by Sir Nathaniel Rich. He reached, as they all did in moments of high solemnity, for the language of the Bible and the liturgy.

'We must speak now, or else for ever after hold our peace. Shall we now sit still and do nothing and so be scattered?'

Uproar.

A contemporary news-sheet describes the scene. 'On that black and doleful Thursday' there followed 'such a spectacle of passions as the like had seldom been seen in such an assembly, some weeping, some expostulating, some prophesying the fatal ruin of our kingdom'. Some members seemed frozen, 'their great griefs making them dumb and silent'. More stalwart spirits 'bore up in that storm and encouraged others'.

Grave men of dignity and substance, middle-aged or elderly, sturdy pillars, most of them, of their communities – justices of the peace, squires, merchants, clerics – dissolved into floods of tears. Another news-writer reports, 'I have been told by a Parliament-man that there were above a hundred weeping eyes.'

John Pym tried to speak, but even he, redoubtable Parliamentarian that he was, broke down sobbing.

Edward Coke rose, but he too was 'forced to sit down when he began to speak, through the abundance of tears'.

* * *

The House resolved to go into 'Committee of the Whole'. According to Parliamentary convention, when the House meets as a Committee of the Whole, the Speaker absents himself, the doors are locked and members are forbidden to leave. Speaker Finch went out. Everyone knew he must go straight to King Charles. He might return with orders for an immediate dissolution. They had perhaps an hour. They did not know when, if ever, Parliament would meet again.

Sir Edward Coke composed himself. This was his moment. He had worked all his life – patiently, pedantically, fearlessly – to make the law strong enough to survive any tyrannical attempt to undermine it. He was ready. 'God has laid this upon us', he said, 'because we have hood-winked ourselves and have not spoken plainly.' He was old. He had been imprisoned for defying a king before and was not afraid of the prospect. If he must die in the Tower, then so be it. 'And therefore, not knowing if I shall ever speak in this House again, I shall now speak freely.'

One man was to blame. 'Let us set down the causes of all our disasters and they will all reflect upon him.' That man was 'the grievance of griev-ances'. They must make the King understand so much, or 'we shall never sit here or go hence with honour'.

Coke would prevaricate no more. The name must be uttered. 'The Duke of Buckingham is the cause of all our miseries.'

'When one good hound recovers the scent,' wrote one member after-wards, 'the rest come in with a full cry.' In saying the unsayable, Coke had set on the pack. Voice after voice joined the chorus.

William Coryton: 'This Duke is the great enemy of the kingdom.'

Edward Kirton: 'He has gotten all our ships, our forts in his hands … [He] makes us all slaves.'

Christopher Sherland: He is 'a Spanish agent'.

Benjamin Valentine: 'This great man has soldiers every place to cut our throats.'

John Selden summed up. There was no need for further enquiry or discussion, or for the appointment of committees, he said. It was enough 'to express the cause'. The cause was 'the Duke'.

The Death of Dr Lambe

ONE night that week, while the Parliamentary pack was baying after his patron in the House of Commons, Dr John Lambe walked out to see a show at the Fortune Playhouse in the fields to the north of London.

Founded in 1600 by the actor-manager Edward Alleyn, and only recently rebuilt after a fire, the Fortune was one of the rougher and rowdier of the London theatres. Grand events, like a performance attended by the Count of Gondomar in 1621 and followed by a banquet given by Alleyn in his honour, alternated there with less decorous occasions. Mary Frith, alias Moll Cutpurse, alias 'the roaring girl', had appeared at the Fortune, cross-dressed as she habitually was in doublet and breeches, singing and playing a lute and exchanging backchat with the audience. The Fortune's post-performance 'jigs', which saw audiences and actors joining in raucous knees-ups, were considered so dangerously disorderly that the city authorities decreed they must cease, for fear of fisticuffs and thefts. At least one murder had taken place at the theatre, and in 1626, two years before Lambe's visit, a constable was set upon by a mob of sailors – presumably some of those hungry wretches, victims of Buckingham's underfunded war-making, who walked to London in great angry processions to demand their pay.

At the Fortune, Lambe was recognised. The show ended and he got ready to leave, but according to an anonymous account published that same year, 'the boys of the town and other unruly people' surrounded him and 'began in a confused manner to assault him, and offer violence'. He tried to escape across the fields to the city. Once more there were sailors in the area. Lambe appealed to a group of them, and offered them money to protect him. 'But so great was the fury of the people,

who pelted him with stones, and other things which came next to hand, that the sailors (although they did their endeavour for him) had much ado to bring him in safety as far as Moorgate.'

Inside the city walls things got worse. 'The rage of the people increased so much that the sailors, for their own safety, were forced to leave him.' Alone once more, Lambe was hunted through the narrow streets by the pack of tormentors. He banged on doors, begging to be taken in, but no one dared open to him. His persecutors chased him down Coleman Street and through Old Jewry into Poultry, where at last four constables managed to stay the mob long enough to drag him into the comparative safety of the Counter prison. Too late. 'For before he was brought thither, the people had had him down, and with stones and cudgels and other weapons had so beaten him that his skull was broken, one of his eyes hung out of his head, and all parts of his body bruised and wounded so much, that no part was left to receive a wound.' A surgeon was sent for, but Lambe died before morning.

A bill was posted on a column in the City.

Who rules the Kingdom? The King.
Who rules the King? The Duke.
Who rules the Duke? The Devil.
Let the Duke look to it, for they intend shortly to use him
worse than they did his doctor, and if things be not shortly
reformed, they will work a reformation themselves.

A couplet was chalked up on a wall near St Paul's:

Let Charles and George do what they can,
Yet George shall die like Doctor Lambe.

Remonstrance

6 June. With the Commons in a passion, King Charles set about courting the House of Lords, where Buckingham was in daily attendance. Charles invited several peers who had previously displeased him – including Archbishop Abbot and the Earl of Bristol – to kiss his hand as a token of reconciliation. He sent the Lord Keeper to the Upper House to inform them how pleased he had been 'all the time of this Parliament' by the Lords' 'dutiful and discreet proceedings'.

7 June. Dutifully and discreetly, and coaxed along by the ever-placatory Buckingham, the Lords made a suggestion. Still dutifully and discreetly, they asked whether the King might like to reconsider his answer to the Petition of Right?

Buckingham approved. He told the Lords, 'Since you think these distractions [he meant the wild scenes in the Commons chamber] have arisen from this answer [the King's first unsatisfactory response to the petition], I am glad you are fallen upon this way.' A delegation of peers, including Buckingham, went to Whitehall Palace to make their suggestion to the King and Privy Council.

It can't have been an easy meeting. They were telling God's anointed that he had made a mistake. Worse, they were asking him to admit his error. 'Gracious yielding' was once again being asked of Charles, and once again he found it hard. Six hours went by in argument and persuasion.

At last Charles gave in. Word was sent to Westminster that the King would come to meet his Parliament and make a second answer to the Petition of Right. The Commons gathered behind the Bar in the Lords chamber.

He came. He yielded, though not altogether graciously. People had been saying that his first slippery answer had been composed for him by Buckingham as part of the Duke's dastardly plan to cause dissension between the King and his people. Now Charles set out to refute that rumour. The wording of his first response had been the creation, he said, not of a single adviser but of a collective. It had been drafted and approved 'by the judgement of so many wise men' that he 'could not have imagined' it would have failed to satisfy Parliament. However, now he had learnt that the members were not content with 'substance'. They insisted on 'words as well'. And so, to pander (so he seemed to imply) to their tiresomely pernickety insistence on an archaic formula, he would give them those words.

He did not speak the words himself. Perhaps he could not bear to utter them because they represented a submission, on his part, to his no longer subservient Parliament. Perhaps, once again, he was afraid that his speech impediment would make him stumble. He instructed the clerk to read them out. '*Soit droit fait comme est désiré.*' The petition passed into law.

From the Commons, standing behind the Bar, there went up a great roar of triumph. The news spread into the streets around the Palace of Westminster. It was carried along the Thames to the City by the boatmen, who were London's most efficient distributors of information. 'It broke out', wrote a Privy Councillor, 'into ringing of bells, miraculously.' That night there were as many bonfires lit as there had been to welcome Charles and Buckingham on their return from Spain, back in the time – less than five years ago – when the two of them were the people's darlings.

The Commons were still at work on the remonstrance. Edward Coke had said that they must 'present' Buckingham to King Charles, showing him in all his iniquity, so as to protect His Majesty from the danger of association with him. Now Coke insisted again that it was Parliament's duty to 'free' the King.

Buckingham's accusers ploughed up all the same ground covered in the impeachment, with particular stress laid on his favouring Catholics, and with more grievances added. Here are the new allegations:

That he had brought troops over from Ireland, and billeted them
in the coastal towns. In the event of an invasion by a Catholic
power, these Irishmen 'may unite with the popish party ... and
join with an invading enemy to do extreme mischief'.
He had appointed Catholics to command the King's ships. It was
because they were disloyal, not being of the 'true religion', that
those captains had failed to defend the English against raiding
Dunkirkers.
He had proposed the 'strange and dangerous purpose' of hiring a
thousand German horsemen and bringing them into the
country with the intention of using them to enforce the
imposition of an illegal excise.
He was General 'of an army in the land in the time of peace'.

The implication behind all these new charges was that Buckingham was
engaged in 'some secret and strong cooperating here with the enemies of
our religion abroad', and that, along with them, he was preparing some
kind of armed coup aimed at 'the utter extirpation' of Protestantism.

Finally, the authors of the remonstrance urged King Charles to ask
himself whether so much power should be put into 'the hands of any
one subject whatsoever'. And to consider whether 'it be safe for Your
Majesty and your kingdom to continue him either in his great offices or
in his place of nearness and counsel about your sacred person'.

When the remonstrance was presented to him, Charles said that he was
astonished at the Commons' temerity in presuming that they knew
more than he did about matters of state. He refused ever to discuss the
remonstrance, 'for I am sure no wise man can justify it'. He probably
didn't even read it. 'It is certain', wrote an MP despondently, 'that His
Majesty's favour to the Duke is no way diminished.'

The following week, the long-awaited subsidies having finally been
voted through, King Charles appeared unexpectedly in the Lords chamber, and sent for the Commons to hear him there. He told his Parliament
that he had come 'so suddenly' because he had been informed that
another remonstrance (this one about tonnage and poundage) was
about to be presented to him. 'Being not willing to receive any more
remonstrances to which I must give a harsh answer,' he said, 'I am
forced to end this session.'

Parliament was dismissed. A member wrote, 'The ill will of the people [towards Buckingham] is like to be thereby much increased.'

Family Portrait

WHEN Balthazar Gerbier was in the Netherlands with Rubens in 1627, he became interested in another painter, Gerrit Van Honthorst.

Honthorst was a Dutchman from Utrecht who had spent several years in Rome, learning from Caravaggio and becoming celebrated for his dramatically lit interiors. Returning to Holland, he made a good living. Dudley Carleton, still ambassador to The Hague, was impressed by his work and recommended him to the Earl of Arundel. Elizabeth of the Palatinate commissioned him to paint her portrait, and employed him as drawing master to her children. He became friendly with Rubens, entertaining the Flemish master to dinner and including a portrait of him in one of his history paintings.

It was inevitable that Gerbier, who made it his business to be au fait with all the latest art news, would meet Honthorst, and equally inevitable that Gerbier would want to acquire some of his work for Buckingham's collection. No way was Gerbier going to allow the Earl of Arundel to acquire a piece by this fashionable new painter before his own master did. In 1628 Honthorst came to England. That summer he painted Buckingham twice.

The first painting is a formal family group (Plate 25). Honthorst (known in Italy as Gerardo delle Notti, Gerrit of the nights) has lived up to his reputation. The background is dark – dimly visible trees silhouetted against a dusky sky. In the foreground brilliant light falls on the Duchess. Katherine is wearing a golden dress, brocaded and slashed and puffed and decorated with ribbons and an enormous diamond brooch and ruffles of gauzy lace. Her distinctive face – the low brow, the Roman nose – is pearly-pale.

Both she and Buckingham, seated to her left in a lavishly silver-striped black suit, gaze seriously out at the viewer. Their stillness holds the composition, while to their right it is delightfully disrupted by their children. Little George, shortly to become the 2nd Duke, is wriggling on Katherine's lap. He is reaching out for the flowers (emblems of nature's abundance but also of life's brevity) that his sister, Mary, in a carnation-coloured dress as gorgeous as her mother's, is holding up in her apron. Mary, unsmiling, looks past him.

George junior is a bonny baby, not yet able to stand on his own, but strong enough to stamp and bounce on his mother's thigh as she holds him up. He looks at least seven months old. He was born in January, so this portrait would have been made after the dissolution of Parliament, after George senior had been identified as 'the grievance of grievances'. The Duke holds a piece of paper in his hand. It seems to be a map of La Rochelle.

Father, mother, baby, second child – the composition is that of a Holy Family with St John, but this is not a joyous nativity scene. It is an engaging picture, solemn with a touch of sweetness, but, for a depiction of a loving family, it is peculiarly melancholy.

Soon the portrait would be hanging in King Charles's bedroom in Whitehall Palace, a memento of the man Charles and his father had both loved.

The Disasters of War VI

ALL that summer, as Buckingham sat in the House of Lords or at meetings of the Privy Council, he was listening with only half an ear. Letters were arriving from his deputies, who were struggling to assemble men, money, food and armaments ready for another expedition to La Rochelle. Buckingham would lead the fleet himself again. He was determined to be away as soon as the subsidies were voted through. He had new ideas, new strategies. His head was full of fireships and floating mines. Another Councillor noticed how his attention was distracted by letters from Portsmouth. He read those letters hungrily but 'by pieces, as the debate gave him leave'.

Word came from La Rochelle that the starving citizens could not hold out much longer without relief. Three thousand English troops were straggling towards Portsmouth. Buckingham was hurrying the supply ships anchored in the Thames Estuary – without which the expedition would be futile – out to sea to join the fleet.

The men were mutinous. Denbigh, in Portsmouth, wrote complaining of 'their refractory and disobedient manner'. Desertions were ceaseless. Even those men already embarked found ways of slipping ashore and vanishing. Buckingham gave orders that a watch should be kept along the coast to ensure 'that no seamen or mariners be suffered to land'.

Buckingham received threats – death threats, threats that his house would be pulled down around his ears. Attempting to answer his critics using their own medium, he had a notice pinned to a pillar in the Royal Exchange.

I have done more for you than ever my predecessors did. I
procured the increase of your pay to a third part more than it
was. I have parted with mine own money to pay you ...

It was not enough.

John Rous wrote in his diary that 'the Duke was gone to the Tower,
and the King accompanied him for fear he should be thrown over the
bridge or knocked on the head'. It was not only King Charles who feared
for Buckingham, noted Rous. 'Some of his friends had advised him how
generally he was hated in England, and how needful it would be, for his
greater safety, to wear some coat of mail, or some secret defensive
armour, but the Duke said, "It needs not – there are no Roman spirits
left".'

Many were saying otherwise. A numerological fortune-teller declared
that Buckingham's name, read according to certain arcane principles,
added up to 1628.

> Thy numerous name with this year doth agree,
> But twenty-nine, Heaven grant thou never see.

Another piece of popular doggerel asked

> Hath no witch poison?
> Nor no man a dagger?

A widely credited prophetess, Lady Eleanor Davis, predicted repeatedly
that before the end of August, Buckingham would be dead.

By the 14th of that month he was in Portsmouth, and had established his
headquarters in the Greyhound Inn. Katherine was there with him. The
inn was full, day and night, with officers hoping for a word with their
general.

The city was crowded. The atmosphere was volatile. The King arrived
and set up his court at Southwick, a gentleman's manor house a few
miles outside town.

On the 17th some two hundred sailors surrounded Buckingham's
coach outside the Greyhound as he set out to visit Charles, shouting that
they wanted their pay. One man tried to drag him from the coach.

Buckingham leapt out and overpowered the attacker, marched him into the inn and ordered the innkeeper to hold him prisoner until he returned. He then drove off to Southwick to keep his appointment with the King. In his absence, sailors surrounded the inn, threatening to pull it down unless their comrade was released. By the time Buckingham returned, the innkeeper, fearing for his home, his livelihood and even his life, had let the prisoner go.

The man was captured again. Buckingham summoned his officers together to form an impromptu military court. He tried the sailor for mutiny and condemned him to death.

One of the officers of the guard reports that 'the sailors in great multitudes drew together with cudgels and stones, and assayed with great fury' to drag the prisoner away from the constables. The officer ordered his men to fire their muskets – but not to shoot to kill, 'because I had no order'. He was reinforced by a party of ships' captains 'who banged and slashed' the mutineers with their swords. Finally, Buckingham and some of his officers came up on horseback and charged into the crowd with swords drawn. They 'drove all the mariners before them in a most furious manner, killing some two of them and wounding divers'.

The sailors were chased back onto their ships. The man was hanged by one of his fellow mutineers, who bought his own reprieve by the act, while Buckingham looked on.

The force assembled in Portsmouth was not a happy band setting out, hearts aflame, to save their Protestant brethren. It was a reluctant, miserable, rebellious rabble.

Scapegoat

THIRTEEN years later, in 1641, the Earl of Strafford, who was King Charles's right-hand man as Buckingham had once been, was executed. The King had promised to save him, but Parliamentary leaders were clamouring for his death. The Earl of Essex said he would accept no lesser punishment for Strafford's alleged treasons: 'Stone dead hath no fellow.' Oliver St John said Strafford was a dangerous animal who must be 'knocked on the head'. Charles signed the death warrant in despair, saying the condemned man was happier than he was.

To many people, then and ever after, Strafford's execution was a turning point. To historians, with the advantage of hindsight, it is the moment when King Charles's inability to control his Parliament and his country was made unmistakably clear. Strafford's death leads on to Charles's own – a story trundling inexorably towards its tragic conclusion. To people at the time it was equally crucial, but in a quite different way; it was the moment when the evil counsellor who was leading their king astray was removed at last, clearing the path for happier relations between the monarch and his people. Even Strafford, in his last letter to Charles, referred to himself as an 'unfortunate thing' blocking the way towards the 'blessed agreement' which his death 'God, I trust, shall for ever establish between you and your subjects'.

Strafford, like Buckingham, was the 'grievance of grievances', the root cause of all that was wrong in the kingdom. Cast him out, thought the discontented, and all would be well.

But that is not really the way history works. Sir Philip Perceval, an Anglo-Irish landowner who had served Strafford, wrote after his death, 'I remember I was in England when the Duke of Buckingham fell, whom many men thought the only cause of all the evils; but those that were of that opinion did not find it so afterwards.'

* * *

One of the sharpest contemporary critics of the early Stuart kings was Francis Osborne. Osborne was a Parliamentarian and a republican who was to argue, after the execution of Charles I, that monarchy was inevitably subject to corruption. But hostile as he was to kingship, he had some interesting things to say about its functioning.

He approached it obliquely, by considering the Ottoman Empire (which he had never visited). There, there was no hereditary aristocracy monopolising places at court. Instead the highest offices in the land were held by slaves. The Sultan's ministers were janissaries, non-Muslim men who had been abducted from their homes as children and brought up to serve the Sultan and be loyal only to him. They had no land, no inheritance, no families, but they were paid salaries, and could become very rich.

Like Somerset, like Buckingham, the janissaries were their master's creations, people who might hold immense power, but whose greatness could be dissolved by one royal (or Sultanic) frown.

The great advantage of such an arrangement, wrote Osborne, was that the Sultan could deflect all his subjects' complaints onto his ministers. If those ministers failed to find a solution for the difficulty, the Sultan would sacrifice them to the anger of the people. They would be demoted, imprisoned, executed. The people would rejoice at the downfall of the designated culprit, while the Sultan still 'appears before his people like the Sun'.

Francis Bacon, in the letter of advice that he wrote to Buckingham at the beginning of his career, says something along the same lines. He warns that some kings have used their favourites as dispensable baggage to be tossed to the wolves. So Buckingham had better take care. The favourite's place is of 'much danger, if not wisely discharged'. He must remember that 'the King himself is above the reach of his people, but cannot be above their censures, and you are his shadow'. If the King makes a mistake, and blames it on his ministers – as kings tend to do – 'you are the first in the eye'. So perhaps the 'shadow' will be 'offered as a sacrifice to appease the multitude'.

He is confident, says Bacon soothingly, that in Buckingham's case the King has no intention to 'interpose you between himself and the envy of his people'. But King James had in fact had a similar thought about his favourites. He compared them to burning-glasses (lenses that could be used to concentrate light and start a fire) 'interposed between him and the subjects'. To the public it seemed that they were 'multiplying the heat of oppression'. From the monarch's point of view, though, they acted as screens saving that heat 'from reflecting upon the Crown'.

In the summer of 1628 it was being said, both in Westminster and in the country at large, that the Duke of Buckingham was an 'evil spirit that walketh between a good master and loyal people'; that it was through his 'ill offices' that the King was so recalcitrant, so unmindful of his subjects' rights; that Buckingham was dividing 'the King from his people, and them from him'.

The first citation for 'royalist' in the *Oxford English Dictionary* dates from 1642. Fifteen years before that there was no need for such a word. No one was a 'royalist', because almost everybody was. In April 1628, even as they struggled against his illegal tax-raising, the Commons assured King Charles that they loved him, that he was 'the breath of our nostrils and the light of our eyes … nothing is or can be more dear to us'. They flattered, of course – this was an age when flattery was an expected part of social discourse – but they also meant it. Even Sir John Eliot, who had spoken so furiously against Buckingham, was still unquestioningly loyal to Buckingham's master. 'It is our King we serve,' he wrote. 'We wholly rely on his goodness, and on none else.'

And yet this good and beloved King was presiding over bad and hateful policies. How was a subject to react? By finding a surrogate, a whipping boy, upon whom to lay the blame for all that had gone so terribly wrong.

Buckingham had seen how a person could act as a lightning rod, attracting anger away from its true target. Bacon, who had warned that a favourite might be used that way, had himself been driven into the political wilderness loaded with others' sins – the sins of greed and corruption associated with the monopolies, the sin of homosexuality. The sins had been the King's, and the King's favourite's, but those two were untouchable, so Bacon, at the time of his downfall, wrote gnomically about making an 'oblation' of himself for the King's sake. He understood that he was being 'offered as a sacrifice to appease the multitude', as he had warned a favourite might be.

Dr Lambe's gruesome death was another instance of such displaced punishment. It's not recorded what motivated the 'unruly people' who lynched the Duke's wizard. It was generally assumed, though, that it was not for sexual violence against a child, or for conjuring up devils, that the mob became so furious with John Lambe that they smashed his skull and tore out his eye. They hated him for being the Duke of Buckingham's man. It was for Buckingham's transgressions, not his own, that he was set upon so ferociously.

Bacon had thought about the way public hostility to an individual might mask a more fundamental discontent. In his essay on envy, he writes, 'This is a sure rule, that if the envy upon the minister be great, when the cause of it in him is small ... then the envy (though hidden) is truly upon the state itself.'

King Charles understood that. Every criticism levelled at Buckingham, he said, was really an attack on the monarchy. Every accusation made against Buckingham was tantamount to an attack on himself. Buckingham was a human shield who interposed his body between the sacred person of the King and the slings and arrows of his furious subjects. As the fleet assembled at Portsmouth in the summer of 1628, King Charles issued a proclamation in which he said that 'he saw himself wounded through the Duke's sides'.

Buckingham had made decisions that resulted in the deaths of thousands and the destitution and misery of tens of thousands more. He was not a blameless sacrificial victim, but he served that function. He was a scapegoat.

Assassination

WHEN King Charles, with his second answer to the Petition of Right, seemed at last to have accepted the will of his people, Londoners celebrated long and loudly. They exulted in having bent the King to their will. Some of them exulted as well – prematurely – in being rid of his favourite. Surely, they thought, their king had seen the light and would repudiate his evil genius.

A group of boys pulled down the scaffold on Tower Hill, saying that they would soon be building a new one for the execution of the Duke of Buckingham.

Those boys were wrong. Buckingham was as much loved and honoured by the King as he had ever been. From Portsmouth, he would frequently ride out to Southwick. Sir John Oglander describes one such occasion when 'the King looked out of a window a whole hour, expecting his coming, before he came'. When Buckingham was at last seen approaching down the road, the King 'and all … went down into the base court to meet him, as if he had been the greatest prince in the world'. A few days later Buckingham was ill, and stayed in bed. King Charles came to visit him at the Greyhound, and as he was leaving the two of them embraced 'in a very unusual and passionate manner'.

The remonstrance had done nothing to lessen Charles's affection for his dear Steenie, or his dependence on his first minister. But that is not to say it had no effect.

John Felton came from Suffolk. His family were country gentry, neither rich nor influential. Felton was a Calvinist, serious and devout. Henry Wotton calls him 'a younger brother, of mean fortune, by nature of a deep, melancholy, silent, and gloomy constitution'. He spoke little but read a great deal. He became a soldier, and fought for Buckingham as a lieutenant on the Île de Ré. He was wounded, coming home with one useless arm.

In England, he had to wait and wait and wait for his pay, becoming hopelessly entangled in debt as a result. Twice he asked to be promoted to captain. Twice his request was denied. It is unlikely Buckingham had any knowledge of Felton at all, but as Lord Admiral he was ultimately responsible for all promotions: Felton blamed him for his rejection.

The text of the remonstrance was printed and readily available in London. Felton came across a copy in one of the print shops around St Paul's where he went to pick up news. In it he read that Buckingham was 'the chief cause of these evils and dangers to the King and kingdom'. He had already read Eglisham's *Forerunner*, which, as he later explained, made Buckingham 'one of the foulest monsters upon the earth'. It came to him that 'by … killing the Duke he should do his country great service'.

He bought a knife for ten pennies from a cutler's shop on Tower Hill. He sewed its sheath into his pocket in such a way that he could carry it concealed but then, when his opportunity came, draw it out easily with his one good hand. He wrote out a gnomic short statement and stitched the piece of paper into the lining of his hat. He set out for Portsmouth, travelling a large part of the seventy-odd miles on foot because he could not afford a horse.

On the morning of 23 August, Buckingham rose, according to James Howell, in 'a well-disposed humour'. He left Katherine in bed. There were people milling around his chamber as he was shaved. (Privacy was rare at court – in the crowded quarters of an admiral about to lead his fleet to war it was non-existent.) One of the bystanders was John Felton, leaning against a windowsill, watching for his moment.

Buckingham went down into the parlour of the Greyhound. The room was thronged with his senior officers and supporters, including several French Huguenots accompanying the Duke of Soubise. Soubise told Buckingham that La Rochelle had been relieved. It hadn't – Soubise was misinformed – but Buckingham, whose dancing had once dazzled the court and bewitched a king, was so 'jocant and well-pleased' that he amused onlookers in the Greyhound by 'cutting a caper or two'. He ate breakfast – quick and impatient – then called for his carriage. Several of his gentlemen were already mounted, ready to ride with him to Southwick to share the glad tidings from France with King Charles.

At the door leading from the parlour into the wide hall of the inn one of his colonels, Sir Thomas Fryer, approached him with a question. They spoke briefly. As they parted, Fryer bowed and Buckingham, ever graceful, ever courteous, bowed as well. As he straightened up, John Felton reached over Fryer's still-lowered shoulder and stabbed the Duke of Buckingham in the heart.

Buckingham shouted 'Villain!' or 'Traitor thou hast killed me' or 'God's wounds, the villain has killed me'. In that crowded place no one could hear or see clearly what was going on. The knife was still in his chest. He tugged it out. He staggered a few steps, trying to draw his sword, before collapsing. There were so many people crowded together in the hall that he fell not to the ground but into the press of bodies. It seems that no one had actually witnessed the blow. People 'guessed him to be over-swayed with some apoplexy'.

Felton withdrew, no one noticing him. Blood was now gushing from Buckingham's wound and from his mouth. The author of the epitaph on his monument claims piously that 'at the moment of death' he 'poured forth these prayers: Let me receive thy blood, my Jesus, while the wicked feast upon mine'; but nobody present heard him say any such thing. Minutes later he was dead.

The attack had happened in full sight of dozens of people, but so bewildered and distraught were all the onlookers that Felton came near to escaping. John Rous reports that 'with a shouting shriek, everybody withdrew, and none knew who killed him'. Buckingham's old friend Sir Dudley Carleton wrote to Queen Henrietta Maria later that day. 'Madam, you may easily guess what outcries were then made, by us that were commanders and officers there present, when we saw him dead in a moment and slain by an unknown hand.' Some rushed to bar the gates, others ran to the ramparts around the town to see if the murderer was already on the road. As they went out, Carleton reports that 'a multitude of captains and gentlemen' came pressing in, 'crying out amain, "Where is the villain? Where is the butcher?"'

Kate Buckingham heard the uproar from her bedchamber. She and her sister-in-law, Kit Villiers's wife, stepped out onto a gallery that ran around the hall. They looked down. Beneath her Katherine saw her beautiful husband, who had danced for joy that morning, laid out on a table, dead.

'Ah poor ladies,' wrote Carleton to the Queen, 'such were their screechings, tears and distractions that I never in my life heard the like before, and hope never to hear the like again.'

Felton was hiding in the inn's kitchen when he thought he heard people calling his name. In fact they were yelling 'A Frenchman!' because everyone at first assumed the murderer was an enemy agent. He could easily have slipped away, but thinking that he was discovered, or perhaps just wanting to lay claim to his deed – the 'great service' to his country that he had performed – Felton stepped forward, saying, 'No villain did it but an honourable man. I am the man. Here I am.'

He was nearly killed immediately. The inn was full of armed men in a state of shock. Carleton and some other officers intervened, and with 'much trouble and difficulty' kept him clear of those who wanted to run him through with their swords on the spot. Felton might be only one of a number of conspirators. (It was twenty-three years since the discovery

of the Gunpowder Plot, but its memory still shaped British politics and nightmares.) It was essential that he be arrested and then tried by law. At last a troop of musketeers arrived to escort him to the Governor's house, where he was questioned by the Lord Chamberlain.

The piece of paper in his hat read, 'That man is cowardly, base and deserveth not the name of a gentleman or soldier, that is not willing to sacrifice his life for the honour of his God, his King and his country. Let no man commend me for doing of it, but rather discommend themselves as the cause of it, for if God had not taken our hearts for our sins, he would not have gone so long unpunished.'

As Felton was led away, someone, probably Carleton, galloped to Southwick. King Charles was attending morning prayers. Clarendon writes that when the messenger whispered the terrible news to him, he 'continued unmoved, and without the least change in his countenance, till prayers were ended; then he suddenly departed to his chamber, and threw himself upon his bed, lamenting with much passion and with abundance of tears'. John Oglander reports that he 'came not out in two days'.

Two processions set out from Portsmouth for London. The first was Buckingham's. It was grand and solemn. The coffin-bearers who carried his corpse through the streets were chosen from among his colonels. They were followed by all the noblemen present in Portsmouth (there were many assembled there for the setting-out of the fleet). As they reached the long line of waiting coaches, guns thundered from the waterfront and from the ships in the harbour. 'I never heard a braver peal of ordnance in my life,' wrote one witness. Only months before, Buckingham, to preserve ammunition, had banned the firing of ceremonial salutes, but the sorrowing King was determined to pay him all possible honour.

Arriving in the outskirts of London a week later, as darkness fell, the cortège was met by the chief officers of the court. Lit by flaming torches, led by heralds, they escorted the Duke's body home to Wallingford House. For two weeks it lay in state there. Charles called for a splendid monument to be erected, but he was persuaded against the idea. It would be improper for the King to commemorate his friend before he had commemorated his father, said the Lord Treasurer. Also, it would be prohibitively expensive. The usual problem. No money.

Buckingham was buried in Westminster Abbey, in Henry VII's chapel, a resting place hitherto reserved for monarchs and royal princes. The funeral took place at night. Crowds came out to watch the procession pass, but the Venetian ambassador thought their murmurs 'sounded more like joy than commiseration'. The trained bands kept up a loud drumming as they marched behind the hearse. It was noticed that, instead of trailing their pikes as a sign of grief, as was customary, the men carried them upright on their shoulders. Perhaps the departure from tradition marked the men's refusal to mourn. Or perhaps their officers had decided they needed their weapons at the ready in case a hostile crowd attempted to disrupt the ceremony. It was rumoured that, for the same reason, Buckingham's body had actually been interred the previous night, and that the coffin so solemnly escorted from Whitehall to Westminster was empty.

The night's proceedings ended in confusion. An observer reports that the honour guard who were supposed to fire a salute as Buckingham's hearse arrived at the Abbey 'ran away without giving any volley of shot at all and so left him to be buried in the dark, everyone running away with his torch'.

With Buckingham dead, many of those who had not previously dared to speak out against him did so, pouring out their pent-up anger in anonymous verse.

> *Where's thy ambition, policy and hate,*
> *Thy pleasures to the soul incorporate?*
> *Thy curious fare? Unlimited excesses?*
> *The splendour of thy ivory palaces?*
> *...*
> *For all thy quondam power, thy name shall be*
> *For ever hateful to posterity.*

The second procession was John Felton's. He had walked most of the way from London to Portsmouth, carrying his knife. Now he walked all the way back again under guard, to be interrogated, tried and executed.

As he was being taken off for questioning, he had shouted out, 'In your hearts you rejoice at my deed.' It was not true of Buckingham's supporters at the Greyhound, but in the country at large Felton was a hero. In Portsmouth, on the day after Buckingham's death, Sir Francis Nethersole reports that 'the base multitude in this town drink healths', and that there were 'infinitely more cheerful than sad faces'. Felton's long march was supposed to be punitive and humiliating. In fact he was celebrated as he went. People called out 'The Lord comfort thee', or 'God bless thee, little David' because he had slain a man who loomed over the state like the giant Goliath. Poets composed verses in his honour.

> Live ever, Felton; thou hast turned to dust,
> Treason, ambition, murder, pride and lust!

He was taken to the Tower, and locked in the cell where Sir John Eliot, Buckingham's Parliamentary nemesis, would later die. He was questioned by the Privy Council who, according to John Rushworth, 'pressed him to confess who set him to work on such a bloody act, and if the Puritans had no hand therein'.

No, he said. No one had 'set him to work'. He had acted on his own initiative, prompted by his own sense of what was right. The Councillors were frustrated. One of them, perhaps William Laud, perhaps the Earl of Dorset, threatened him with the rack. Felton, demonstrating that he was uncowed by his grand inquisitors, replied, 'If it must be so, he could not tell whom he might nominate in the extremity of torture, or which of Their Lordships he might not name.' He might even, in his agony, he said, identify the lord who ordered the torture as his co-conspirator. It was a defiant and witty answer. Torture was not legally sanctioned, but it was often threatened, and still sometimes used in the course of interrogations. Some historians credit Felton with having helped to hasten its decline.

He was returned to the Tower, outside which crowds gathered to pray for him. In September, the fleet finally sailed from Portsmouth. King Charles was there to see them off, and made an encouraging speech. When he finished, the men shouted out to him, audaciously asking him 'to be good to John Felton'. A few weeks later, a clergyman was convicted in the Star Chamber of drinking a health to Felton and saying he envied the murderer the 'honour of that brave action'. The clergyman lost his ministry and was stripped of his degrees and ordered to pay a large fine. He would have had one ear cut off had his father not had influence at court.

More songs circulated.

> *The Duke is dead, and we are rid of strife …*
> *A rotten member, that can have no cure,*
> *Must be cut off to save the body sure.*

Felton himself, though, lost faith in his mission. Imprisoned, he came to believe it was the Devil who had prompted him to kill. He declared his crime was 'abhorrent'. He said, 'I have much dishonoured God in it.' Perhaps he came to see the irrationality of the Puritans' hatred of Buckingham. As the Duke's epitaph correctly points out, 'While he was waging war against the papists [he] was accused of papacy: while promoting the Protestant cause, [he] was slain by a Protestant.'

In his remorse, Felton turned the deadly anger he had felt for Buckingham against himself. Tried before the King's Bench, and confronted with his knife, still smeared with Buckingham's blood, Felton pleaded guilty and asked that the hand with which he had held that knife be cut off. The judges refused his request, but condemned him to death. He was executed two days later. His body was taken back to Portsmouth and hung up in chains outside the city gates.

Afterwards

'IN one moment', wrote the Venetian ambassador, 'is this great colossus overthrown, and the greatest and most remarkable favourite whom the world has seen for many centuries dies instantaneously.'

All England – all Europe – waited to see how the political landscape would shift to accommodate the downfall of such a gigantic figure. Many hoped that Buckingham's elimination would make way for a new and happier era to begin.

On the Parliamentary side, Sir John Eliot expressed his belief that once Buckingham was out of the way, the goodness of King Charles, 'like the glory of the sun, not capable in itself of any obscurity or eclipse', would shine again. At court, as well, it was expected that the sun would come out. Pembroke (Buckingham's sometime ally) wrote to Carlisle (his loyal follower) that since the death of the controversial favourite, 'the King our master begins to shine already, and I hope this next session to see a happy agreement between him and his people'.

Buckingham was popularly understood to have been running the country. When he sailed for La Rochelle, the year before his death, a libel had asked how King Charles would manage without him.

> O who shall then his sceptre sway
> And kingdoms rule when thou art gone away?

More astute commentators thought otherwise. A month after his death one news-writer wrote to his client, 'Whereas it was commonly thought he ruled His Majesty, it was clear otherwise, having been His Majesty's most faithful and obedient subject in all things.'

Sir Thomas Wentworth wrote that it was only in his role as scapegoat that Buckingham would be missed. 'It is said at court there is none now to impute our faults unto.'

The fleet that Buckingham was to have led sailed to France under another commander. It achieved nothing. A month after Buckingham's funeral, La Rochelle fell. Richelieu was to cite the English attack on the Île de Ré as an example of how King Louis was so 'manifestly blessed by God that even setbacks and reverses are converted into an occasion for glory', because it had ended in the destruction of the Huguenot opposition. In April 1629 a peace treaty was signed between England and France.

In the following year a similar agreement was made with Spain, returning relations between the two nations to more or less what they had been under the treaty King James had signed in 1604.

So many lives lost as a result of Buckingham's aggressive foreign policy; so much money squandered, to achieve nothing.

During the last year of Buckingham's life, the marriage between King Charles and Henrietta Maria, which had begun so irritably, was growing happier. While Buckingham was on the Île de Ré, Charles had written to him, 'My wife and I were never better together; she ... showing herself so loving to me ... that it makes us all wonder and esteem her.' The rapprochement was slow and tentative, but, deprived of his favourite, Charles looked around for another person to depend upon, and fell conveniently in love with his wife. Their first baby was born nine months after Buckingham's murder.

Katherine Buckingham posed for her portrait in deep mourning, wearing a miniature of her husband hanging around her neck on a black ribbon (Plate 28). In 1634 she erected a magnificent tomb to him in Westminster Abbey sculpted by Hubert Le Sueur in black marble and gilded bronze. It declares that she 'honoured the most sweet memory of her dearest husband with all possible piety and respect'.

The following year she remarried, and moved to Ireland as the Countess of Antrim. King Charles had once promised that, should Buckingham be killed at La Rochelle, he would be a 'husband to his duchess, a father to his children, a master to his servants and an executor to pay his debts'. He was as good as his word, untangling

Buckingham's convoluted financial affairs and satisfying his creditors. On Katherine's remarriage, he took her two sons – George, the 2nd Duke, and Francis, the child she was carrying when Buckingham died – into his own household. They were brought up alongside the young princes, Charles and James, as almost-brothers to two future kings.

Van Dyck painted the Villiers boys (Plate 30), not in the boldly unconventional way he had painted their father, but in one of his tenderest celebrations of aristocratic childhood – dark solemn eyes, rosy lips, plump young bodies clothed in lustrous silks.

He also painted their sister Mary, Buckingham's little Mall (Plate 29). She stands at the centre of his superb death-haunted group portrait at Wilton, a pale child bride. She was eleven at the time, and about to marry Pembroke's fifteen-year-old heir. The young husband died a year later. Mary was married again twice, to the Duke of Richmond, and then to one of the Howard family. She had two children but no grand-children.

Francis inherited his father's looks. Clarendon said he was a 'youth of rare beauty and comeliness', and Andrew Marvell praised his 'inimitable handsomeness'. He was killed fighting for the King at the age of nineteen.

George fought in the Civil Wars too, taking part in his first battle when he was fifteen. He survived and went into exile with King Charles II.

He became a prominent but controversial figure at the Restoration court. His estates were returned to him, making him one of the richest men in England, and he built himself a great house at Cliveden (of which only a colonnaded terrace remains). Charles II appointed him a Privy Councillor. He became first minister, but he is chiefly remembered for the scandals surrounding his name. Notoriously promiscuous, he attempted to seduce two of the King's sisters in turn. He had an affair with the Countess of Shrewsbury, killed her husband in a duel and then moved 'the widow of his own creation' into his home, having packed his wife off back to her father. He attacked the Marquess of Dorchester in the House of Lords, pulling off Dorchester's periwig in an undignified brawl. He was also a poet, an alchemist and a dramatist (his play *The Rehearsal* is still sometimes performed). John Dryden (who had a grudge against him) described him as

Stiff in opinions, always in the wrong,
Was everything by starts and nothing long;
But, in the course of one revolving moon
Was chymist, fiddler, statesman and buffoon.

He died in 1687, from a chill caught out hunting, lamenting on his deathbed that he was 'despised by my country and I fear forsaken by my God'. He had no legitimate heirs, so all his father's titles died with him.

In 1643 a committee of the House of Commons ordered the seizure of the contents of Queen Henrietta Maria's chapel in Somerset House. The main altarpiece, by Rubens, was thrown into the Thames.

The art collections amassed under the early Stuarts – Arundel's, King Charles's, Buckingham's – were hateful to Puritans. They stood for excessive wealth and extravagant spending. They represented a Europe-facing, cosmopolitan culture in which Roman Catholicism was tolerated. They spoke of luxury, of physical beauty, of sensual delight. Paintings showed scenes from pagan mythology, setting up heathen idols. Even worse – others depicted biblical scenes, reducing the sacred word of God to pretty pictures. In 1643 William Dowsing, appositely nicknamed 'Smasher', was appointed 'Commissioner for the destruction of monuments of idolatry and superstition'. The Dean of St Paul's writes of how Dowsing 'goes about the country like a Bedlam breaking glass windows', defacing carvings and burning pictures.

Amidst this storm, Buckingham's great art collection survived, if scattered. In 1640 the Earl of Northumberland (brother to Buckingham's mistress Lucy Carlisle) rented York House, and lived there for the next seven years surrounded by the things Buckingham had owned. Northumberland supported the Parliamentary cause, but he was no Puritan. He was an art-lover and a connoisseur.

He lent the Parliamentary regime a large sum of money. In 1645 Parliament declared that Buckingham's collection, being the 'property of a delinquent', should be sold, the proceeds going to the Treasury, or – in the case of 'superstitious' works – destroyed. Northumberland stepped in. He told the Parliamentary authorities he was prepared to forgive their debt to him in exchange for what he called a few of Buckingham's 'family portraits' of 'no value'. These supposedly value-less pictures included Rubens's equestrian portrait, described by a twentieth-century art historian as 'the greatest of all baroque portraits of an English sitter', for which Buckingham had paid the enormous sum of £500. Also among the 'family' pictures Northumberland took for himself were Titian's double portrait of Cardinal Armagnac and Philandrier, two depictions of the Madonna and Child by Andrea del Sarto, a set of miniature paintings of saints by Elsheimer and a view of the interior of a cathedral by Hendrick Van Steenwijk, all now in Alnwick Castle or Petworth House.

Having taken his pick of the collection, Northumberland helped his landlord, the still teenaged 2nd Duke of Buckingham, to save the rest. Before the young duke went into exile in 1648, they secretly shipped sixteen crates full of paintings from York House to Antwerp. There they were bought by the Archduke Leopold, Habsburg governor of the Spanish Netherlands and an avid snapper-up of the treasures washed his way by the wreckage of the English Royalist cause. Leopold sent them to Prague, where Hradčany Castle's walls had been stripped bare by the Swedish army. Buckingham's Tintorettos and Titians, his Rubenses and Bassanos, hung there for a while, before being moved to Vienna, where they now form the core of the Kunsthistorisches Museum's collection of Italian and Flemish art.

Balthazar Gerbier was employed by King Charles, who sent him to Brussels as resident agent. There he became involved in a conspiracy to overthrow the Spanish governors, in which he was simultaneously conniving with the conspirators and selling their secrets to Spain. On his return to England, King Charles made him his Master of Ceremonies. During the Civil Wars and Commonwealth he did this and that – banking in France, gold-hunting in Guiana, running a painting school in Bethnal Green and – ever the opportunist – currying favour with the republican government by writing a book called *The Pernicious Effects of Wicked Favourites and Great Ministers of State.*

On the day after Buckingham's death, Sir Francis Nethersole wrote, 'The stone of offence now being removed by the hand of God, it is to be hoped that the King and his people will come to a perfect unity.' It was not to be.

In January 1629 Parliament reassembled. To the King's displeasure, the Commons refused to allow the reading of a proposed bill authorising the collection of tonnage and poundage. Instead they debated, angrily and at great length, the 'subtle and pernicious spreading of the Arminian faction', Arminianism being the King's preferred brand of religion.

In February King Charles ordered them to adjourn until the following week. When they returned they received another message ordering them to adjourn again. The Speaker prepared to leave. Two members dragged him back and held him forcibly in his chair: so long as the Speaker sat, the House was still formally in session. The doors were locked on the inside. The King's messengers beat on them, while within, MPs yelled at each other and grabbed at their sword hilts. For two hours the Speaker was held down while a defiant protestation was composed. Afterwards nine MPs were arrested, including Sir John Eliot, who was imprisoned in the Tower until he died three and a half years later.

Simonds D'Ewes described the 'tumultuary' scene as 'the most gloomy, sad and dismal day for England that happened in five hundred years'. Sir Thomas Roe thought that 'the zeal of the Commons was vented with more passion than wisdom' and had 'shipwrecked all'. King Charles dissolved Parliament. It would not meet again for eleven years.

Two months later a paper was passed around in Paul's Walk. It was an address beginning, 'Oh King, or rather no King, for thou hast lost the hearts of they subjects', and went on to declare that Charles was 'therefore no king, nor they any longer thy subjects ... That relationship now ceaseth, violated on thy part.'

In fact King Charles I ruled undisturbed for another decade. At peace with France and Spain, freed of the impossible requirement to make war with no money, he presided over a decorous and cultured court.

Then the Civil Wars began.

In February 1648, nearly twenty years after Buckingham's death and twenty-three years after King James's, the House of Commons issued a Declaration. Royalist newsletters called it a 'masterpiece of treachery'; another said it scourged King Charles 'with scorpions'; a third described the Parliament-men who had written this 'Hellish Westminsterian lie' as a 'viperous generation of cruel and inhuman cannibals'.

King Charles was a prisoner in Carisbrooke Castle on the Isle of Wight. Just under a year later he would be tried for high treason, found guilty and killed, but his death would not be lightly accomplished. The Declaration made Parliament's case for his execution and, to strengthen that case, it included what a Venetian report calls 'old and almost forgotten charges' that 'His Majesty hastened the death of his father by poison', or that Buckingham had done so, with Charles's consent.

A Royalist newsbook published an answer to the Declaration with new testimony from Buckingham's barber, John Baker. Baker related how King James (not Buckingham) had ordered him to go to Dunmow to fetch Dr Remington. The doctor was ill in bed, but he wrote out a prescription. Baker had it made up by a local apothecary and rode back to Theobalds. There Baker himself – watched by the assembled physicians, drank a dose of the posset, and ate a piece, about the size of a walnut, of the plaster. He suffered no ill effects. Two Gentlemen of the Bedchamber, both 'aguish', tried the posset and reported that they were cured by it.

The newsbook went on to an account of King James grasping Buckingham's hand at the point of death. One of the Bedchamber men, Sir James Palmer, asked Buckingham to close the King's eyes. Buckingham, overcome by tears, could not do it. So Palmer took his hand and helped him 'close the eyes of the best master in the world'.

In 1650, the year after King Charles's execution, a book called *The Court and Character of King James* was published. It was attributed to Sir Anthony Weldon, then two years dead, who had been a minor official at the Jacobean court, but had been dismissed, and had become, in the last years of his life, a zealous republican. According to the book, 'None was great with Buckingham' but 'bawds and parasites and such as humoured him in his unchaste pleasures, so that since his first being a pretty harmless, affable gentleman, he grew insolent, cruel and a monster not to be endured.'

Throughout the 1650s pamphlets and newsbooks piled invective on Buckingham. He was lustful, a raper of virgins. He was friend to witches. He was friend to Catholics. He and Charles together killed King James. The Puritan anti-royalist author Lucy Hutchinson wrote that King James's court was full of 'fools and bawds, mimics and catamites'. Buckingham was the epitome of that depraved society. He had reached the 'pitch of glory ... upon no merit but that of his prostitution'.

The Bishop of Gloucester, Godfrey Goodman, had been Queen Anne of Denmark's chaplain, and flourished under King James and King Charles. When he read Weldon's book, he was so indignant about what he saw as its misrepresentations that he wrote a book of his own in reply. He concluded that 'there never lived a better-natured man than Buckingham'.

Endymion Porter died in 1649. In his will he had written that he wished his children and his children's children to 'observe and respect the children and family of my Lord Duke of Buckingham, deceased, to whom I owe all the happiness I had in the world'.

On Buckingham's tomb in Westminster Abbey there is a lengthy inscription. It describes him in a series of paradoxes. He 'was all things, yet had nothing'. He was 'named his country's father and its foe'. He was 'both the delight and the plaint of Parliament'. He was one 'whom kings loved deeply, whom the nobility held in honour, whom the church lamented, whom the multitude loathed'.

He was 'the riddle of the world'.

Mercury

GERRIT Van Honthorst was still in England when Buckingham's body was interred in Westminster Abbey, still at work on the second picture he made of the Duke that year.

Honthorst's second piece is much more ambitious and inventive than the family group he had painted a month or two earlier. There Buckingham was a father, a sumptuously suited grandee, a mortal. In this new picture (Plate 26) there are wings on his hat and on his sandals. He is otherwise dressed only in a billowing blue silk scarf and a crimson tunic, hitched up above his knees, that leaves half his chest bare. Instead of looking gravely out at the viewer, he is gazing upwards, open-mouthed, in profile, all his attention on the two deities seated on a cloud at the top left-hand corner of the picture space.

He is Mercury, one of the immortals, and he is leading the Liberal Arts out of the cave in which they have been imprisoned. The couple in the sky are King Charles and Queen Henrietta Maria in the guise of the divine twins, Apollo and Diana. They float high above the ground, as the gods and goddesses in a masque would float on clouds created for them by Inigo Jones. Female figures (representing Muses but recognisably portraits of real-life court ladies) stand behind them, craning over their shoulders to see what is happening below.

The seven Liberal Arts, named by Pythagoras and endorsed by Plato, formed the basis of ancient Athenian education. The word 'liberal' meant suited to a free person. The arts did not include manual skills, like painting or sculpting in marble: those were for the enslaved. The Liberal Arts were the arts of the mind. They fell into two categories. First, the three arts of the word – grammar, rhetoric and logic (or dialectic). Then the four arts of measure – arithmetic, geometry, astronomy and music.

The Liberal Arts became a favourite subject for artists. They were generally pictured as beautiful young women, holding identifying symbols (a lute for music, a pair of compasses for geometry). Often they were being presented to an aspiring scholar by some kind of intermediary, Prudence or Wisdom or Lady Philosophy. Buckingham, in commissioning Van Honthorst's painting, was inserting himself into a well-established tradition. But he was not claiming to be a personified virtue. He was merely Mercury, the go-between of the gods.

In the angry months that had just passed he had been seen by his Parliamentary opponents as 'the man of separation', who came between the King and his subjects. But he saw himself quite otherwise. Mercury was the patron of trade and of free communication. Adopting his persona, Buckingham was presenting himself as one who made connections and fostered exchange. He had repeatedly been accused, that summer, of arrogance, but in Van Honthorst's painting he is not self-assertive, but an obliging subordinate who brings his master the great gift of culture.

He is carrying a caduceus, as Mercury usually does. With it he points at Grammar, kneeling beside him, her naked bosom forming the focal point of the crowded composition. (The picture's structure is very similar to that of Titian's *Ecce Homo*, which Van Honthorst could have studied in York House.) Grammar's head is thrown back as she looks up at the royal couple, so that her face is only partially visible to us, but she is generally and credibly believed to be Buckingham's Duchess, making this the second time Katherine had bared her breasts for art. She carries a book, Grammar's identifying object, and also a golden key, because grammar – the proper understanding and use of language – is the key to all intellectual endeavour.

Behind her come crowding the other arts with their attendants, their attributes and their fantastic hats (Astronomy's blue-and-white-swathed-cartwheel style is especially striking). Mercury is leading them all out of the darkness where they have been held by the giant Ignorance, who is being skewered in the bottom left-hand corner by some ferocious children. In the centre foreground another little boy is ramming a stave into the anus of a goat (traditionally associated with lust and other bestial appetites).

The inscription on Buckingham's tomb tells us he was 'most famous in the arts; he was a magnificent patron of letters and literary men; of inexhaustible generosity to any worthwhile project'. King James had been a scholar and an author, but not an artistic connoisseur. Under King Charles, the English court was newly set to become a centre of excellence in the visual arts.

Van Honthorst's Mercury is Buckingham as he would like to have been remembered: not as the despoiler of the kingdom; not as the libertine wasting the nation's wealth on superfluous feasts; not as the instigator and loser of futile wars; but as a benign impresario, self-effacingly enabling his king to preside over a modernised, enlightened and newly civilised court.

The painting hangs now in Hampton Court. Buckingham never saw it complete. Mercury is the Roman equivalent of the Greek Hermes. Hermes was a teasing trickster of a god, but there was one role in which he was solemn. In a reversal of the way, in Van Honthorst's vision, Buckingham is escorting the Liberal Arts out into the light, Hermes/Mercury would escort the newly dead down into the underworld, into the dark and silent realm of non-being into which Buckingham had gone.

Acknowledgements

The enormous debt I owe to other writers, alive and dead, is acknowledged in the Bibliography and Notes.

My first thanks are to my daughters, Mary Franklin and Lettice Franklin, who read this book with care and commented on it with kindness and acuity. I have learnt that they are nearly always right.

I am grateful as well to my agent Felicity Rubinstein and to her American counterpart Kim Witherspoon, to Nicholas Pearson, who published my previous four books and commissioned this one, and to Louise Haines – another person who is always right – who has seen it through to publication. Among her colleagues at Fourth Estate who have worked on it I am especially grateful to Julian Humphries, Patrick Hargadon, Matt Clacher, Alex Gingell and Victoria Pullen, to copy-editor Tim Waller and proof-reader Martin Bryant. Thank you to Millicent Bennett and her colleagues at HarperCollins USA.

The following people have shown me their houses or their pictures, allowed me to read their theses, suggested sources I should explore or books I should read, lent me books or given me books, told me things I didn't know or prompted me to think differently about things I already knew, read and commented on early drafts of this book, argued with me, encouraged me or otherwise helped me. I am grateful to them all: Rupert Christiansen, Diana Dethloff, Lord and Lady Egremont, the Countess of Euston, Jonathan Keates, Simon Loftus, the staff of the London Library, Andrew Loukes at Petworth House, Shana Kilbee at Euston Hall, John McCullough, Niko Munz, Ian Patterson, Baron Jean Christophe von Pfetten, Lady Victoria Percy, Thomas Rose, Francis Russell, Nicholas Stogdon, Jane Swadling at New Hall School, Daniel Watkins at Alnwick Castle.

Finally I thank my husband, Dan Franklin, my prop and stay.

Notes

IN most cases the sources of quotations are made clear in the text. With the help of the bibliography, interested readers will be able to trace them. The following notes are intended to help where sources are not self-evident.

In writing this book I have depended gratefully on the scholarly work of my predecessors. I am particularly indebted to the late Roger Lockyer. My vision of Buckingham, my priorities and my narrative strategy all differ widely from Lockyer's, but his comprehensive biography of Buckingham, published in 1981, has been an essential resource in the writing of this one. Quotations that are otherwise unattributed, either in my text or in these notes, are taken from it.

Among more recent historians I have benefited especially from the work of Thomas Cogswell, writing solo or in partnership with Alastair Bellany. I thank them both.

In writing about events that took place four hundred years ago it can be hard to arrive at a definitive chronology. In instances where historians disagree, I have followed Lockyer.

In quoting from letters between King James and Buckingham I have used Bergeron's edition.

PART I: PEACE

St George's Day – pp. 17–26
  Description of St George's Day ceremonial and Lady Anne Clifford in Sharpe (2010). King James's letter to Somerset in Akrigg. The dubbing of Villiers described by Abbot in Ashton. 'His carriage is ungainly …', Fontenay in Ashton. Abbot's account in Ashton. 'I know what becomes …', Venetian State Papers in Ashton. 'Many for shame …', Weldon. 'Those ordinary ceremonies …', Sir Roger Wilbraham in Ashton. 'King James …

loved best …', Sir Robert Moray in Cogswell (2017). 'An able woman …', Desmarets in Young.

King James: Fear – pp. 27–32

In this chapter and the next I have drawn extensively on Alan Stewart's *The Cradle King*. Otherwise unattributed quotations are from that book. 'The true bird …', Buchanan in Fraser. 'Very difficult for a foreigner …', Wotton in Ashton. 'Pistol-proof', Weldon in Ashton. 'This promised land …', Fraser.

King James: Love – pp. 33–39

'Strange, extraordinary affection', Thomas Fowler in Young. 'It is thought …', quoted in Somerset. 'Fierce and gentle …', Fraser. 'If any mischance …', Bergeron. 'And to that end …', Weldon in Ashton. 'With whom the King …', Foscarini in Bergeron. 'No man should marvel …', Chamberlain.

Dancing – pp. 40–48

In writing this chapter I have drawn extensively on books by Hille, Howarth, Orgel, Parry and Strong, and on the essay by MacIntyre, as well as on sources cited in the text. 'The gentleman waiters …', Goodman in Ashton. 'From the nails …', Bergeron. 'It is a true old …', *Basilikon Doron*. 'Naturally he did not …', Wilson in Ashton. 'God's wounds …', Fraser. 'I will have no coach …', Sharpe (2010). For James's first opening of Parliament, see Parry. 'The streets seemed …', Dekker in Parry. Busino's report in Ashton. 'High dancers …', MacIntyre.

Exit Somerset – pp. 49–57

In writing about Somerset's marriage and downfall, and the murder of Sir Thomas Overbury, I have drawn extensively on Anne Somerset's book, which is the source for all otherwise unattributed quotations in this chapter. King James's letter in Akrigg. Howard's letter in Stewart. 'Submitted entirely …' and 'a jolly sire …', Young. 'I desire to be your friend …', Weldon. 'Beauty of the greatest magnitude …', Fraser. 'Inflaming eyes …', Donne, Eclogue, 26 December 1613. 'Were so poor and idle …', Stewart. 'An anti-monarchist', Weldon. For the diamond necklace, see Stewart. 'Whether you loved me …', this, and all other letters between King James and Buckingham quoted in this book, are from Bergeron.

Showers of Love – pp. 58–61

'Went daft …', Fraser. 'A small kind of giddy …', Cornwallis in Brotton. 'The delight of mankind …' and 'even in the midst …', Brotton. 'Under the canopy …', Wake in Howarth (1997). 'Exceedingly rich …' quoted in Fraser. 'The king's affection …', Sherburne in Ashton.

Older Women – pp. 62–67

'The same naughty boy …', Lockyer. 'Her ragged habit …' and 'should appear with …', Roger Coke in Lockyer. Donne on Lucy Bedford in Rundell.

Sex – pp. 68–74

In writing this chapter I have drawn extensively on Michael Young's *King James and the History of Homosexuality*. All quotations otherwise unattributed here or in the text are from that book. Letters between King James and Buckingham from Bergeron. Roger Coke in Somerset. Edward Coke on sodomy in Young. 'Never regards …', Young.

Favourite – pp. 75–85

'No suit, no petition …', Sparke in Bergeron. 'What a delicious heaven …', Marston, *The Favourite*, quoted in Lockyer. 'But why do I presume …', Ben Jonson, *The Gypsies Metamorphosed*, in Parry. Abbot's account of his promotion of Buckingham in Ashton. Story of pike in Newbery. Abbot's character described from various sources in Nicolson. Abbot's letter to Buckingham in Goodman. Bacon's character and household in Aubrey. Harvey and Herbert in Aubrey. Quotations from Bacon in this chapter are from his *Letter of Advice* and *Essays*. 'Men of noble birth …', Bacon, *Of Envy*. 'Endure that one born …', Lando in Bergeron. 'The King spent all …' and 'if it shall daily run out …', Young. 'Their master's spaniels …', Christopher Neville in Chamberlain.

Bedchamber – pp. 86–89

Much material in this chapter has been drawn from essays in Starkey (1987), especially from 'The Revival of the Entourage' by Neil Cuddy.

Loving Buckingham – pp. 90–99

'Jesus Christ did the same …', King James addressing the Privy Council in 1617, as reported by the Spanish ambassador, in Stewart. 'A day of oblation …', Lockyer. Fenton, Sherburne, Gerrard and Lando in Young. 'Sole monarch …', Wilson. 'Short of sending his heart …', Lockyer. 'A university man …', Nicolson. Barlow in Nicolson. 'The best tutor …', Lockyer. My understanding of the concept of *amicitia*, and of male friendship and same-sex love in the 16th- and 17th-century Britain, has been refined and extended by John McCullough's writings on the subject. Otherwise unattributed quotations in this chapter are from his thesis of 2005.

Peace – pp. 100–105

'It is an unchristian …', Young. '*News from the New World*', Parry. King James's procession through London in Parry. 'A secure and honourable …', Cogswell (1989). King James's 'Christian League', Malcolm. 'Says aloud, she hopes …', Young. Prince Henry's Barriers described by John Stow in Parry. 'The Prince performed …', Orgel (1975). Archy's taunts, Francis Osborne in Ashton. 'Up then, brave Prince …' and 'Live to march …', Parry.

Horses – pp. 106–109

The principal source for this chapter is Peter Edwards's *The Horse Trade of Tudor and Stuart England* (2004).

The Arts of Peace – pp. 110–120
  For Gerbier, see Betcherman (2010). Otherwise unattributed quotations
  relating to him are from that book, or from his own *To All Men that Loves
  Truth* (1646). For the Earl and Countess of Arundel, see Howarth (1975). For
  King James's ambassadors, see Jackson. 'If it were not for ambassadors …',
  Howell in Jackson. For Wotton, see Logan Pearsall Smith. For Roe, see
  Michael Strachan. For Carleton, see Howarth.

Work – pp. 121–127
  'Keeping my back unbroken …', Cogswell (2017). 'Those formalities of state
  …', Wilson in Ashton. 'Adore their sovereigns …', Molin in Ashton. 'The
  throng at court …', Wilbraham in Ashton. 'Shows him everything …',
  Gondomar in Lockyer. 'You are the truest …', Bacon in Lockyer. All other
  quotations from Bacon in this chapter are from the *Letter of Advice*. 'I beg
  Your Excellency …', Gerbier in Betcherman (2010).

The Law – pp. 128–135
  In writing this chapter I have drawn extensively on Catherine Drinker
  Bowen's biographies of Bacon and Coke. 'The best orator …', Hulme. 'Made
  four of her creatures …', Chamberlain.

Young Women – pp. 136–139
  Anonymous pamphlet, Hutchinson, Harington, Clifford, all in Somerset.
  'He looks upon the whole race …', Ashton. For Lucy Percy, see Betcherman
  (2005).

Hunting – pp. 140–148
  I am grateful to Thomas Rose for allowing me to read his thesis on James I
  and hunting. 'Beagles, spaniels …', Cogswell (2017). 'Easily satisfy him …',
  Stewart. 'Some goodly horses …', Nicolson. 'He loves the chase …',
  Fontenay in Ashton. 'Houses, castles, forests …', Wilbraham in Ashton. For
  Theobalds, see Leith-Ross. 'Health and welfare …', 'than other kings …',
  'We are all become wild men …', all in Stewart. My account of the stages of
  the hunt is based on Turberville. 'On Saturday last …', Stewart. 'Noble and
  magnificent …', Rose. 'King James loves to be merry …', Hille.

Family – pp. 149–163
  The account of the feast at Wanstead is from Thomas Lorkin in Nichols.
  'Above in the skies …', Chamberlain. 'I was alone …', Bergeron. 'Treat her
  as …', Young. 'No good can come …' and 'There is nothing but lurking
  hatred …', both in Stewart. For James's relationship with his children, see
  Stewart. 'I thank God, I carry …', Stewart. 'I pray you …', Prince Charles in
  Ashton. Waterspout incident in Stewart. For Lady Compton's abandoning
  her husband and coming to court, see Goodman. For her 'meddling in state
  affairs', see Gardiner. 'They drink and play …' and other rhymes in Fairholt.
  'Brought the Earl about …', Hacket. Rutland's letter and Buckingham's reply

in Goodman. 'Children are so much the goods …', Stone (1977). Buckingham's letter to Rutland in Goodman. 'Lechery' and Katherine's letter in Goodman. 'Piques himself …', Young.

Portraits of a Marriage – pp. 164–169
For Van Dyck, see Blake.

The Spanish Match – pp. 170–173
In writing about the Spanish Match I have been greatly helped by the information and insights offered by Glyn Redworth. Otherwise unattributed quotations in this chapter are from his book. 'Two Diegos', Carter. 'What ballads and pasquils …', Howell.

Magic – pp. 174–180
I am indebted to Tracy Borman's book on witches. Otherwise unattributed quotations in this chapter are from it. 'Man that offered him …', Bellany & Cogswell. For Lambe, see Anon., *A briefe description*.

Apocalypse – pp. 181–184
Herbert, Abbot and *The Messiah Already Come*, all in Adams.

Corruption – pp. 185–193
My account of the proceedings of the 1621 Parliament is based on Lockyer. Otherwise unattributed quotations are from that book. King James on Parliament – quotations in Lockyer (1998). 'Very cheerful …', Healey. 'God bless ye …', Bowen (1985). 'Discontented persons that cannot fish …', Cogswell (2017). 'Wrangling lawyers' and 'It makes my hair stand upright', Bowen (1985). 'If I were to imitate …' and 'I never had a bribe …', Bowen (1985). 'Hog well fed …', Healey. 'Not to take any notice of him …', Bowen (1985). 'Offered as a sacrifice …', Bacon's *Letter of Advice*.

Ganymede – pp. 194–197
'The case remains …', Conrad Russell in Young. Tillières and *Tom Tell Troath* in Young. *The Warres of the Gods*, Hille. Simonds D'Ewes in Bellany & Cogswell. Marlowe in Hille. 'Thou wilt be pleased …', Young.

Despenser – pp. 198–203
Bacon's dismissal in Bowen (1963), with additional detail in Bowen (1985). For proceedings in Parliament, see Lockyer, from which otherwise unattributed quotations are taken. For Edward II and his favourites, see Orgel (1996). 'Boys and base fellows …', Bowen (1985).

Houses – pp. 204–209
For Burley-on-the-Hill, see Leith-Ross. For Whitehall, see Sharpe in Starkey (1987). For New Hall, see Lockyer, Orgel (1975) and Leith-Ross. For negotiations over York House, see Lockyer. 'Where my father died …', Lockyer.

Matters of State – pp. 210–218

I have followed Redworth's account of diplomatic negotiations and of Bristol's tour. Otherwise unattributed quotations on the subject are from his book. 'The King trusted no one so entirely …', Gondomar in Redworth. For proceedings in Parliament, I have generally followed Lockyer, from which otherwise unattributed quotations are taken. For Coke's speech, the petition and his imprisonment, see Bowen (1985).

Gerbier in Italy – pp. 219–223

Quotations from Gerbier's letters in Betcherman (2010). Arundel's offer for *Ecce Homo* in Gardiner. 'Obnoxiously snobbish tradition' – e.g. David Howarth.

Effeminacy – pp. 224–232

In this chapter I have drawn extensively on Michael Young's book, from which otherwise unattributed quotations are taken. 'His subjects were as dear …', King James in Fraser 'If I were not so certain …', Gondomar in Redworth. King James's letter to the Pope in Patterson. 'A Golgotha …', Ergang.

Prince Charles – pp. 233–237

'Was exceedingly feeble …', Brotton. 'The best and surest …', De Lisle (2018). 'The gallantry of Henry's spirit …', Hamon l'Estrange in Brotton. 'Who was far quicker …', Molin in Ashton. 'Must not expect …', De Lisle (2018). The lost ring, Sherburne in Stewart. 'Kiss his arse', De Lisle (2018). 'True and worthy son', Gardiner. 'A danger for some other …', Salvetti in Lockyer.

PART II: SPAIN

The Plan – pp. 241–244

Valaresso in Jackson. Cogswell in Redworth. For the inception of the plan and the scenes between James, Charles and Buckingham, see Clarendon.

The Match – pp. 245–248

Otherwise unattributed quotations are in Redworth. 'The decision has already been made …', Gondomar in Redworth. 'General voice runs …', Howell in Redworth. 'This prince has offered …', Gondomar in Gardiner. 'Intended to take his friend …', Gardiner.

The Codpiece Point – pp. 249–250

Lando in Gardiner. 'Were it not for the sin …', Gardiner. 'Danced as well …', Bristol in Redworth. 'You wonder how …', Brotton.

Companions – pp. 251–256

The prime source for this chapter is Clarendon. Otherwise unattributed quotations are from his book. D'Ewes in Bergeron.

Chivalry – pp. 257–259
'To give a final end …', Lockyer. Middle Temple oath in Ellis. 'In my opinion …', Junius in Hitchens (https://www.theatlantic.com/magazine/archive/2004/04/reactionary-prophet/302914/).

The Journey – pp. 260–269
The prime source for this chapter is Wotton (1642), from which all otherwise unattributed quotations are taken. 'The coming of the illustrious …', Brotton. 'Dark rumours …', Howell. 'Has the King of England …', Redworth.

Olivares – pp. 270–277
For this chapter I have drawn extensively on Elliott (1986). Otherwise unattributed quotations are from that book. Backstory of negotiations over the Match in Redworth. 'Professeth an extraordinary desire …', Patterson. 'Understood, and so treated …' and 'satisfaction to the King …', Redworth.

Invisible – pp. 278–280
All quotations from Buckingham's letters to King James.

Separation – pp. 281–285
Beecher in Lockyer. Gerbier in Bergeron. 'One historian …', Young.

Entrance – pp. 286–289
'Hidden behind a shutter', Redworth. 'Since this event …', Spanish court chronicles in Jackson. 'All the Spanish nobility …', Howell. 'Lodged in a quarter …,' Bristol in Lockyer.

Religion – pp. 290–294
'Far from plotting …', Patterson. 'I will keep my resolution …', Redworth. 'Hundreds of friars …', Wynn. Dr Prideaux, pamphleteers, Kellie and Abbot, in Cogswell (1989). 'While our Prince …' and 'Alas, our hands …', Cogswell (1989).

Courtship – pp. 295–300
Otherwise unattributed quotations in this chapter are from Redworth. 'Thoughtful, speculative …' and 'the King always sat …', Howell. 'His compliments …', Betcherman (2005).

Art – pp. 301–303
Lope de Vega, Carducho and information on Prince Charles's art purchases in Madrid in Brotton.

Mewed Up – pp. 306–308
In tracing the complexities of the negotiations in Madrid I have followed Redworth.

Unhappy – pp. 310–312
Again I have followed Redworth, from whose book otherwise unattributed quotations are taken. 'With confidence in his power …', Redworth. 'French

garb …' and 'the height of his spirit …', Howell. 'Happy agreement …',
Lockyer.

Love Letters – pp. 313–315
Katherine's letter in Lockyer. Gerbier in Betcherman (2010). Rutland's letter
in Lockyer. The Countess of Olivares in Elliott (1986).

Strucken – pp. 316–318
'Make a breach …', 'impetuous, unbounded …' and 'preserve the King …',
Cogswell (1989).

The End of the Affair – pp. 319–329
'There's scarce a man …', Howell. 'Many insolencies …', Cogswell (1989).
The Infanta taking English lessons in Howell. 'Universal rejoicing …',
Lockyer. 'If you hold yourself …', Lockyer. 'Personate him …', Howell. 'The
former distastes …', Patterson. 'I tell you very frankly …', Lockyer. For
Carducho and the *poesie*, see Brotton. 'A painting by Paolo Veronese …',
Brotton. Clerk's arrival with letter, all from Howell.

PART III: WAR

Jubilation – pp. 333–336
In writing this chapter I have drawn extensively from Cogswell (1989).
Otherwise unattributed quotations are from that book. 'Such unlimitable …'
and 'Men, women and children …', Sharpe (1992). Scott in Young. 'Not
stirring his hat …', Bergeron. 'Embraces and familiarities …', Bergeron.

Honour – pp. 337–339
Again, otherwise unattributed quotations are from Cogswell (1989). 'He
knew not how many …', Lockyer. 'It would be dishonourable …', Young.
'Entering into command …', 'While Buckingham remains …', 'Do you want
to commit me …', all in Lockyer.

Magnificence – pp. 340–342
'Then might you have …', Lockyer. Gerbier's letters and details of the decor
of York House in Betcherman (2020). Henry Peacham in Brotton. 'High and
illustrious prince', Lockyer.

St George on Horseback – pp. 343–348
For Bacon, see Bowen (1963). 'Secret intelligencers …', Lockyer. Bacon's
letter in Lockyer. 'Means and honour …', Howell. 'Awaked as out of a
dream …', Patterson. Buckingham's 'Relation' in Bellany & Cogswell. Coke
and Conway in Lockyer.

Which War? – pp. 349–353
In unravelling the complex and contradictory views of those who wanted
war in 1624, I have been helped by Sharpe (1978). Bacon and Coke in Sharpe
(1978). 'A mere quarrel …', Patterson. 'His great fleet …', Cogswell (1989).

'Weakness and folly ...' and 'dry entertainment ...', Lockyer. 'For until it be done ...', Adams in Sharpe (1978). 'The greatest aid ...', Ruigh in Sharpe (1978). 'The true believers ...', Patterson. 'When the end ...', Lockyer.

Prophecy – pp. 354–355
Otherwise unattributed quotations are from Lockyer.

Ageing – pp. 356–360
For King James's illness in 1619, see Stewart. 'Grooms ran alongside ...', Cogswell (2017). 'There came much water ...', Stewart. For Inojosa's allegations, see Howell and Stewart. 'Good cause to suspect ...', Lockyer. Tillières in Stewart. 'Crying out that he was the unhappiest ...', Stewart.

Popularity – pp. 361–365
Otherwise unattributed quotations in this chapter are from Cogswell (1989). 'Nothing is so easily ...', OED, s.v. *opinion*. Dekker in Rundell. 'Dine with Duke Humphrey', 'grumbling together ...' and King James's rhyme in Healey.

Illness – pp. 366–373
'Inseparable as his shadow', Stewart. For de Mayerne, see Trevor-Roper. 'Try his activity' and 'sharp, kind chiding ...', Lockyer. 'I cannot think ...', Lockyer. For Dr Remington and Pierce Butler, see Bellany & Cogswell. Wentworth in Lockyer. 'The tears breaking down ...', Bellany & Cogswell. 'He knows himself ...' and Abbot in Lockyer.

The French Match – pp. 374–381
In unravelling the negotiations over the match I have mostly followed Lockyer, from which otherwise unattributed quotations are taken. Holland and Carlisle in Betcherman (2005). 'We entered killing ...', Wedgwood. 'An old rat ...', Jackson. Scott in Bellany & Cogswell. 'Give him but force ...', Bellany & Cogswell. 'A lady of as much loveliness ...', De Lisle (2022).

Gerbier in France – pp. 382–385
Gerbier's letters in Betcherman (2010). 'If your excellency ...', Hille.

The Disasters of War I – pp. 386–390
Otherwise unattributed quotations in this chapter are from Lockyer. 'My industries made vain ...' and 'If I understand ...', Bellany & Cogswell.

The Posset and the Plaster – pp. 391–399
In narrating events around King James's death I have generally followed Bellany & Cogswell, from which otherwise unattributed quotations are taken. 'I shall never see London ...', Stewart. 'Being interrupted ...', Bergeron. 'The fairest and best ...', Howarth (1997). Bishop Williams's sermon in Ashton.

Clothes – pp. 400–405
'It was common …', Fairholt. Packing list in Hille. 'Scarcely showed …', De
Lisle (2022). Howard to Harington in Ashton. The proxy wedding in De
Lisle (2022).

Queens – pp. 406–415
A full account of Buckingham's visit to Paris is in De Lisle (2022), from
which otherwise unattributed quotations are taken. 'The best-made man …'
and 'conducted himself here …', Lockyer.

Richelieu – pp. 416–419
Otherwise unattributed quotations in this chapter are taken from Elliott
(1984).

Rubens – pp. 420–426
Otherwise unattributed quotations in this chapter are from Lamster.

Plague – pp. 427–434
'How Death …', translation by William Cowper of Latin poem by Milton.
Otherwise unattributed quotations relating to Henrietta Maria are from De
Lisle (2022). 'Now are we …', Bellany & Cogswell. Donne's sermon in
Rundell. In narrating proceedings in Parliament I have followed Lockyer,
from which otherwise unattributed quotations are taken.

Curiosities – pp. 435–439
Otherwise unattributed quotations are from Leith-Ross.

Jealousies – pp. 440–443
'No fruit but shame …', Bellany & Cogswell.

The Disasters of War II – pp. 444–449
Otherwise unattributed quotations are from Lockyer. For Drake's 1589 raid,
see Hughes-Hallett (2004). Rubens in Lamster.

Money – pp. 450–453
Otherwise unattributed quotations are from Bellany & Cogswell.

Rape – pp. 454–456
This chapter is entirely based on Anon., *A briefe description …*

Coronation – pp. 457–458
'A heavenly crown …', De Lisle (2022). 'I have more need …', D'Ewes.
Otherwise unattributed quotations are from Lockyer.

La Rochelle – pp. 459–461
In this chapter I have drawn largely on Elliot (1984), from which quotations
are taken.

Eliot – pp. 462–464
Otherwise unattributed quotations are from Hulme. 'Vicious ergo …',
Bellany & Cogswell. 'Sir J.E. on the first …', Bellany & Cogswell.

No Money – pp. 465–467
>   Otherwise unattributed quotations are from Lockyer.

Evils, Causes and Remedies – pp. 468–475
>   Otherwise unattributed quotations are from Lockyer. Day-by-day
>   chronology of the Parliament based chiefly on Hulme. 'Duke of
>   Fuckingham', Jackson. Mildmay in Bellany & Cogswell. 'There are other
>   things ...', 'whose years and education ...' and 'The matter now to be
>   handled ...', Hulme.

Poison – pp. 476–481
>   In this chapter and the next I have drawn extensively on Bellany & Cogswell,
>   from which otherwise unattributed quotations are taken.

Uneasiness – pp. 482–483
>   Laud in Lockyer. Bacon's death in Aubrey.

Impeachment – pp. 484–490
>   Otherwise unattributed quotations are from Bellany & Cogswell. 'An act of a
>   transcendent ...' and 'to keep him from the presence ...', Lockyer.

Oratory – pp. 491–494
>   Comments on Donne in Rundell. Eliot's judgements on other Parliamentary
>   speakers in Hulme.

Meteor – pp. 495–498
>   *War in Heaven* in Hille. Digges's speech in Hulme. 'Prognosticates the ruin
>   ...' and 'restrained by the order ...', Bellany & Cogswell. Florentine agent
>   and Mende in Bellany & Cogswell. 'Lords and all ...', Hulme. 'There is such
>   a power ...', Lockyer. Eliot's speech in Hulme.

Sejanus – pp. 499–502
>   Eliot's speech in Hulme. *Tom Tell Troath* and Leighton in Young. 'With
>   three women ...', Bellany & Cogswell.

The Tower – pp. 503–508
>   Otherwise unattributed quotations are from Bellany & Cogswell. 'King of
>   Game ...' Fairholt. King Charles's speech of 11 May in Lockyer, Hulme and
>   Bellany & Cogswell. Letters to Bishop of Mende and Venetian ambassador
>   in Lockyer. For Eliot in the Tower, see Hulme.

Antiquities – pp. 509–511
>   Gerbier in Betcherman (2010). Gentileschi in Wood. For Buckingham's
>   correspondence with Roe, see Howarth (1985).

Dissolution – pp. 512–516
>   Otherwise unattributed quotations are from Bellany & Cogswell. 'Was
>   pleased to enter ...', Laud in Hunneyball. 'Could there be ...' and 'many
>   weaknesses ...', Lockyer. 'Not a minute', Lockyer.

A Whirlwind of Water – pp. 517–518
  Descriptions of the storm in Bellany & Cogswell. Otherwise unattributed quotations in this and the next three chapters are from Lockyer. 'Abominate that name', Healey.

The Forced Loan – pp. 519–522
  'Even at the risk …', Cust. Fuller in Bowen (1985). 'Enforced upon us …', Cust. 'To escape imprisonment …', Healey. 'The next tree …', Cust. Abbot and Mende in Cust.

The Disasters of War III – pp. 523–525
  Otherwise unattributed quotations are from Lockyer.

Concord/Discord – pp. 526–531
  For conflict between Charles and Henrietta Maria, see De Lisle (2022). 'There is nothing to fear …', Elliott (1984) 'Why did the sailors …', Fairholt.

Envy – pp. 532–533
  Bacon, On Envy. 'Then offered to spurn …', Rous.

Insignificant Persons – pp. 534–537
  Isaac Wake in Jackson. For Gerbier and Rubens's plan, see Lamster.

Déjà Vu – pp. 539–544
  'Rejoice brave English gallants …', Fairholt.

Married Love – pp. 545–546
  Otherwise unattributed quotations are from Lockyer.

The Disasters of War IV – pp. 547–560
  'The land commanders …', Herbert. 'For men neglected …', Sharpe (1992). For the assault on Fort St-Martin, see Loftus.

Hated – pp. 561–564
  Fleetwood in Loftus. 'Fearing some miserable …' and 'estranged from …', Loftus. Rhymes and libels in Fairholt. 'No man ever longed …', and 'No distance …', Sharpe (1992).

Five Knights – pp. 565–566
  For Wandesford, see Kishlansky. 'That counsel might be …', Cust. 'Great applause …', Bowen (1985).

Anger – pp. 570–573
  'And now just God …', Jackson.

Ghost – pp. 574–576
  This chapter is entirely based on Clarendon.

Liberty – pp. 577–579
  'If you make …', Cust. 'The greatest inheritance that a man hath …' and 'A prison without a prefixed time …', Bowen (1985).

The Crisis of Parliaments – pp. 583–593
   Dyke and Melvin in Bellany & Cogswell. For the debates in the Commons in May, I have followed Bowen (1985), from which otherwise unattributed quotations in this chapter are taken.

The Death of Dr Lambe – pp. 594–596
   Based on Anon., *A briefe description …*

Remonstrance – pp. 597–600
   Otherwise unattributed quotations are from Lockyer. 'It broke out …', Bowen (1985).

The Disasters of War VI – pp. 603–605
   'Thy numerous name …', Healey. 'Hath no witch poison …', Fairholt. 'The sailors in great multitudes …', Oglander.

Scapegoat – pp. 606–609
   Perceval in Lockyer. King James in Osborne.

Assassination – pp. 610–617
   All poems and songs in Fairholt. Dudley Carleton's account in Fairholt. 'Ran away without giving …', Loftus. 'If it must be so …', Loftus.

Afterwards – pp. 618–625
   'In one moment …', Jackson. 'Like the glory …', Hulme. 'Whereas it was commonly thought …', Stuteville letter in Sharpe (1992). Rubens altarpiece thrown in the Thames in Brown. For Northumberland's role in saving Buckingham's collection, see Wood (1994). 'The greatest of all baroque portraits …', Howarth (1997). 'The zeal of the Commons …', Sharpe (1992). 'Oh King, or rather no King …', Healey. For the 1648 Declaration and contemporary comments on it, see Bellany & Cogswell.

Select Bibliography

Place of publication is London unless otherwise specified.

Anon., *A briefe description of the notorious life of John Lambe, otherwise called Dr Lambe. Together with his Ignominious Death* (1628)

Anon., Preface to the King James Bible (https://www.ccel.org/bible/kjv/preface/pref1.htm)

Anon., *Tom Tell Troath* (1621) (https://mpese.ac.uk/t/TomTellTroth1622v2.pdf)

Adams, Simon, 'Foreign Policy and the Parliaments of 1621 and 1624', in Sharpe (1978)

Akrigg, G. P. V. (ed.), *Letters of King James VI & I* (1984)

Ashton, Robert (ed.), *James I by his Contemporaries* (1969)

Aubrey, John, *Brief Lives* (https://www.gutenberg.org/files/47787/47787-h/47787-h.htm)

Bacon, Francis, *A letter of advice written by Sir Francis Bacon to the Duke of Buckingham, when he became favourite to King James* (https://quod.lib.umich.edu/e/eebo/A28255.0001.001)

—, *The Essays* (https://www.gutenberg.org/files/56463/56463-h/56463-h.htm)

—, *On Envy* (https://olearyzone.com/classes/philosophyS2/readings/bacon/Envy.pdf)

Barton, Anne, *Ben Jonson, Dramatist* (Cambridge, 1984)

Bellany, Alastair, *The Politics of Court Scandal in Early Modern England: News Culture and the Overbury Affair, 1603–1660* (Cambridge, 2002)

Bellany, Alastair, and Thomas Cogswell, *The Murder of King James I* (2015)

Bergeron, David M., *King James and Letters of Homoerotic Desire* (Iowa, 1999)

Betcherman, Lita-Rose, 'The York House Collection and its Keeper', *Apollo*, 92 (1970)

—, *Court Lady and Country Wife* (Chichester, 2005)

—, *Buckingham's Man: Balthazar Gerbier* (2010)

Blake, Robin, *Anthony Van Dyck: A Life* (1999)

Boneham, Luke, 'The Politics of Desire: George Villiers, James I and Courtly Entertainment' (https://medium.com/@LukeBoneham/the-politics-of-desire-george-villiers-james-i-and-courtly-entertainment-1ba33106b69a)

Borman, Tracy, *Witches: James I and the English Witch Hunts* (2014)

Bowen, Catherine Drinker, *Francis Bacon: The Temper of a Man* (1963)

—, *The Lion and the Throne: The Life and Times of Sir Edward Coke* (1985)

Bray, Alan, *Homosexuality in Renaissance England* (1982)

—, *The Friend* (Chicago, 2003)

Brotton, Jerry, *The Sale of the Late King's Goods: Charles I and His Art Collection* (2006)

Brown, Jonathan, *Kings and Connoisseurs: Collecting Art in Seventeenth-Century Europe* (1995)

Carter, Charles H., 'Gondomar: Ambassador to James I', *Historical Journal* 7.2 (1964)

Castiglione, Baldassare, *The Book of the Courtier*, trans. George Bull (2003)

—, *The Book of the Courtier*, trans. Sir Thomas Hoby (1561)

Chamberlain, John, *The Letters of John Chamberlain*, ed. Norman McClure (Philadelphia, 1939)

Churchyard, Thomas, *A Sparke of Friendship* (1588)

Cicero, *De amicitia* (https://oll-resources.s3.us-east-2.amazonaws.com/oll3/store/titles/544/0267_Bk.pdf)

Clarendon, Edward Hyde, Earl of, *The History of the Rebellion and Civil Wars in England* (Oxford, 1849)

Cogswell, Thomas, *The Blessed Revolution: English Politics and the Coming of War, 1621–1624* (Cambridge, 1989)

—, *James I: The Phoenix King* (2017)

Coke, Roger, *A Detection of the Court and State of England* (1696; https://quod.lib.umich.edu/e/eebo/A33686.0001.001?view=toc)

Cuddy, Neil, 'The Revival of the Entourage', in Starkey (1987)

Cust, Richard, 'Charles I, the Privy Council, and the Forced Loan', *Journal of British Studies* 24/2 (1985)

Davies, Randall, 'An Inventory of the Duke of Buckingham's Pictures, etc., at York House in 1635', *Burlington Magazine* 10/48 (1907)

De Lisle, Leanda, *White King: The Tragedy of Charles I* (2019)

—, *Henrietta Maria: Conspirator, Warrior, Phoenix Queen* (2022)

D'Ewes, Sir Simonds, *The Autobiography and Correspondence of Sir Simonds D'Ewes, Bart.*, ed. James Orchard Halliwell (1845)

—, *The Diary of Sir Simonds D'Ewes (1622–1624)*, ed. Elisabeth Bourcier (Paris, 1974)

Dumas, Alexandre, *The Three Musketeers*, trans. Lord Sudley (1982)

Edwards, Peter, *The Horse Trade of Tudor and Stuart England* (Cambridge, 2004)

Eglisham, George, *The Forerunner of Revenge upon the Duke of Buckingham, for the poisoning of the most potent King James* (1626; https://quod.lib.umich.edu/e/eebo/A21195.0001.001?rgn=main;view=fulltext)

Elias, Norbert, *The Court Society*, trans. Edmund Jephcott (Dublin, 2005)

Eliot, Sir John, *Negotium posterorum* (1881)

Elliott, J. H., *Richelieu and Olivares* (Cambridge, 1984)

—, *The Count-Duke of Olivares: The Statesman in an Age of Decline* (1986)

Ellis, Henry (ed.), *Original Letters, Illustrative of English History* (1824)

Ergang, Robert, *The Myth of the All-Destructive Fury of the Thirty Years' War* (Pocono Pines, 1956)

Fairfax, B., *A Catalogue of the Curious Collection of Pictures of George Villiers, Duke of Buckingham* (1758)

Fairholt, Frederick (ed.), *Poems and Songs relating to George Villiers, Duke of Buckingham; and his Assassination by John Felton* (1850)

Forster, John, *Sir John Eliot: A Biography, 1590–1632* (1865)

Fraser, Antonia, *King James VI of Scotland, I of England* (1974)

Fuller, Thomas, *The Worthies of England*, ed. John Freeman (1952)

Gardiner, S. R., *History of England from the Accession of James I to the Outbreak of the Civil War*, 1603–1642 (1883–1896)

Gerbier, Balthazar, *To All Men that Loves Truth* (1646; https://quod.lib.umich.edu/e/eebo/A85934.0001.001?view=toc)

Goldberg, Jonathan, *Sodometries: Renaissance Texts, Modern Sexualities* (Stanford, 1992)

Goodman, Godfrey, *The Court of King James the First* (1839)

Granville, Sir Richard, 'A True and exact Journal, or Diary, of the most material Passages, happening at, and after our Landing, at the Isle of Rhee, Anno 1627', in *Two Original Journals of Sir Richard Granville* (2023)

Guy, J. A., 'The Origins of the Petition of Right Reconsidered', *Historical Journal*, 25/2 (1982)

Hacket, John, *Scrinia Reserata: A Memorial offered to the Great Deservings of John Williams, D.D.* (1693)

Halliwell, James Orchard (ed.), *Letters of the Kings of England, Now First Collected from the Originals* (1846)

Hart, Vaughan, *Art and Magic in the Court of the Stuarts* (1994)

Healey, Jonathan, *The Blazing World: A New History of Revolutionary England* (2023)

Held, Julius S., 'Rubens's Sketch of Buckingham Rediscovered', *Burlington Magazine*, 118/881 (1976)

Herbert, Edward, Baron Herbert of Cherbury, *The Autobiography of Edward, Lord Herbert of Cherbury*, ed. Sidney L. Lee (Cambridge, 2013)

Hille, Christiane, *Visions of the Courtly Body: The Patronage of George Villiers, First Duke of Buckingham, and the Triumph of Painting at the Stuart Court* (Berlin, 2012)

Holles, John, *Letters of John Holles, 1587–1637*, ed. P. R. Seddon (Nottingham, 1975)

Howarth, David, *Lord Arundel and His Circle* (New Haven, 1985)

—, *Images of Rule: Art and Politics in the English Renaissance, 1485–1649* (Basingstoke, 1997)

Howell, James, *Epistolae Ho-Elianae* (1892)

Hughes-Hallett, Lucy, *Heroes: Saviours, Traitors and Supermen* (2004)

Huizinga, Johan, *The Waning of the Middle Ages* (1924)

Hulme, Harold, *The Life of Sir John Eliot* (1957)

Hunneyball, Paul, 'Archbishop Laud's secret "misfortunes": Decoding sexual identity in the seventeenth century', historyofparliamentonline.org

Hyde, Edward, see Clarendon

Jackson, Clare, *Devil-Land: England under Siege, 1588–1688* (2021)

Jonson, Ben, *Works* (https://www.hollowaypages.com/Jonson.htm)

Kantorowicz, Ernst, *The King's Two Bodies: A Study in Mediaeval Political Theology* (Princeton, 1998)

Kenyon, J. P., *Stuart England* (1978)

Kishlansky, Mark, 'Tyranny Denied: Charles I, Attorney General Heath, and the Five Knights' Case', *Historical Journal*, 42/1 (1999)

Lamster, Mark, *Master of Shadows: The Secret Diplomatic Career of the Painter Peter Paul Rubens* (New York, 2009)

Laud, William, Diaries (https://quod.lib.umich.edu/e/eebo/ A67908.0001.001?view=toc)

Leith-Ross, Prudence, *The John Tradescants: Gardeners to the Rose and Lily Queen* (1984)

Lockyer, Roger, *Buckingham: The Life and Political Career of George Villiers, First Duke of Buckingham, 1592–1628* (1981)

—, *James VI and I* (1998)

Loftus, Simon, *The Digressions of Memory: Offcuts from the Family Scrapbook* (Bulcamp, 2013)

Macaulay, Catharine, *The History of England from the Accession of James I to the Elevation of the House of Hanover* (1769–72)

MacIntyre, Jean, 'Buckingham the Masquer', *Renaissance and Reformation*, 34/3 (1998)

Malcolm, Noel, *Useful Enemies: Islam and the Ottoman Empire in Western Political Thought, 1450–1750* (Oxford, 2019)

—, *Forbidden Desire in Early Modern Europe: Male–Male Sexual Relations, 1400–1750* (Oxford, 2024)

Markham, Gervase, *Country Contentments* (https://quod.lib.umich.edu/cgi/t/ text/text-idx?c=eebo;idno=A06913.0001.001)

McCullough, John, 'Burning His Letters: King James and Buckingham's "scandalous doings" in Thomas Middleton's "A Game At Chess"' (unpublished thesis)

—, 'Disputable Friends: Rhetoric and Amicitia in English Renaissance Writing, 1579–1625', PhD thesis, University of Sussex (2006)

Middleton, Thomas, *A Game at Chess* (1624; Oxford, 1990)

Millar, Oliver, *The Age of Charles I: Painting in England, 1620–1649* (1972)

—, 'Charles I, Honthorst, and Van Dyck', *Burlington Magazine*, 96/611 (1954)

Montaigne, Michel de, *Shakespeare's Montaigne: The Florio Translation of the Essays* (New York, 2014)

Morgan, Nicholas, *The Perfection of Horse-manship* (1609)

Morrison, Kathryn, ed. *Apethorpe: The Story of an English Country House* (2016)

Motteville, Françoise de, *Mémoires de Madame de Motteville* (Paris, 1886)

Newbery, F. (ed.), *The Biographical Dictionary; Or, Complete Historical Library* (1780)

Nichols, J. (ed.), *The Progresses, Processions, and Magnificent Festivities, of King James the First, his Royal Consort, Family, and Court* (1828)

Nicolson, Adam, *When God Spoke English: The Making of the King James Bible* (2011)

Norman, Jesse, *The Winding Stair* (2023)

Oglander, Sir John, *A Royalist's Notebook: The Commonplace Book of Sir John Oglander*, ed. Francis Bamford (New York, 1971)

—, *The Oglander Memoirs*, ed. W. H. Long (1888)

Orgel, Stephen, *The Illusion of Power: Political Theater in the English Renaissance* (Berkeley, 1975)

—, *Impersonations: The Performance of Gender in Shakespeare's England* (Cambridge, 1996)

Orgel, Stephen, Roy Strong and John Harris, *The King's Arcadia: Inigo Jones and the Stuart Court* (1973)

Osborne, Francis, *Historical Memoires on the Reigns of Queen Elizabeth, and King James* (1658)

Palme, Per, *Triumph of Peace: A Study of the Whitehall Banqueting House* (1957)

Parry, Graham, *The Golden Age Restor'd: The Culture of the Stuart Court, 1603–42* (Manchester, 1981)

Patterson, W. B., *King James VI and I and the Reunion of Christendom* (Cambridge, 1997)

Peacham, Henry, *Minerva Britanna* (1612)

—, *Peacham's Compleat Gentleman, 1634* (Oxford, 1906)

Philip, I. G., 'Balthazar Gerbier and the Duke of Buckingham's Pictures', *Burlington Magazine*, 99/650 (1957)

Prynne, William, *Histriomastix* (1632)

Pursell, Brennan C., 'The End of the Spanish Match', *Historical Journal*, 45/4 (2002)

Redworth, Glyn, *The Prince and the Infanta: The Cultural Politics of the Spanish Match* (2003)

Roe, Sir Thomas, *Travels in India in the Seventeenth Century by Sir Thomas Roe and Dr John Fryer* (1873)

Rose, Tom, 'Hunting in Early Stuart England: Status, Sociability, and Politics', unpublished PhD thesis, University of Nottingham (2020) (https://eprints. nottingham.ac.uk/60951/)

Rous, John, *Diary of John Rous, 1625–1642* (1856)

Rundell, Katherine, *Super-Infinite: The Transformations of John Donne* (2022)

Rushworth, John, *Historical Collections*, vol. 1 (1721)

Russell, Conrad, *The Crisis of Parliaments: English History, 1509–1660* (Oxford, 1971)

—, *Parliaments and English Politics, 1621–1629* (Oxford, 1979)

Sanderson, William, *A Compleat History of the Lives and Reigns of Mary Queen of Scotland and of her Son and Successor, James* (1656)

—, *Aulicus Coquinariae, or a Vindication in Answer to a Pamphlet* (1650)

Schwoerer, Lois, *Gun Culture in Early Modern England* (Charlottesville, 2016)

Sharpe, Kevin, *The Personal Rule of Charles I* (New Haven, 1992)

—, *Image Wars: Promoting Kings and Commonwealths in England, 1603–1660* (New Haven, 2010)

—, 'The Image of Virtue: The Court and Household of Charles I, 1625–1642', in Starkey (1987)

— (ed.), *Faction and Parliament: Essays on Early Stuart History* (Oxford, 1978)

Sinfield, Alan, *Cultural Politics – Queer Reading* (1994)

Smith, Bruce R., *Homosexual Desire in Shakespeare's England: A Cultural Poetics* (Chicago, 1991)

Smith, Logan Pearsall, *The Life and Letters of Sir Henry Wotton*, two vols (Oxford, 1907)

Somerset, Anne, *Unnatural Murder: Poison at the Court of James I* (1997)

Sparke, Michael, *The Narrative History of King James, for the First Fourteen Years* (1651)

Starkey, David (ed.), *The English Court: From the Wars of the Roses to the Civil War* (1987)

Stewart, Alan, *The Cradle King: A Life of James VI & I* (2004)

Stone, Lawrence, *The Crisis of the Aristocracy, 1558–1641* (Oxford, 1965)

—, *The Family, Sex and Marriage in England, 1500–1800* (1977)

Strachan, Michael, *Sir Thomas Roe, 1581–1644: A Life* (Salisbury, 1989)

Strong, Roy, *Splendour at Court: Renaissance Spectacle and Illusion* (1973)

Stuart, James, King James I of England and VI of Scotland, *The Political Works of James I* (1616, reprinted 1918)

—, *Daemonologie* (1597)

—, *Basilikon Doron* (1599)

Tillières, Comte Leveneur de, *Mémoires Inédits* (Paris, 1863)

Trevor-Roper, Hugh, *Europe's Physician: The Various Life of Sir Theodore de Mayerne* (2006)

Tuckwell, Tony, *New Hall and its School* (2006)

Turberville, George, *The Noble Art of Venerie* (1575)

Wedgwood, C. V., *The Thirty Years War* (1938)

Weldon, Anthony, *The Court and Character of King James* (1650)

Wilson, Arthur, *The History of Great Britain, Being the Life and Reign of King James the First* (1653)

Wood, Jeremy, 'Van Dyck and the Earl of Northumberland: Taste and Collecting in Stuart England', *Studies in the History of Art*, 46 (1994)

—, 'Orazio Gentileschi and Some Netherlandish Artists in London: The Patronage of the Duke of Buckingham, Charles I and Henrietta Maria', *Simiolus: Netherlands Quarterly for the History of Art*, 28/3 (2000–2001)

Wotton, Sir Henry, *A Parallel between Robert late Earl of Essex, and George late Duke of Buckingham* (1641)

—, *A Short View of the Life and Death of Geo. Villiers, Duke of Buckingham* (1642; https://quod.lib.umich.edu/e/eebo/A67129.0001.001/1:3?rgn= div1;view=fulltext)

Wynn, Richard, 'A Brief Relation of what was Observed by the Prince's Servants in their Journey into Spain, in the Year 1623', in *Historia Vitae et Regni Ricardi II*, ed. Thomas Hearnius

Young, Michael B., *King James and the History of Homosexuality* (2016)

List of Illustrations

PLATE IMAGES:

Index

Catholic princes, 210, 418; German Protestant princes, 101, 170, 181–4, 210–11, 451–2; and occupation of Palatinate (1620–2), 182–4, 210–14, 227, 229, 349–50, 351, 353, 451–2, 536; outbreak of Thirty Years War (1618), 181; prince-electors, 210–11; and Spain, 210, 303, 351, 536

Holyrood, Palace of, 30, 31

Homer, 196

homosexuality, 13, 19, 23, 54, 56, 68–9, 70, 77; attacks on James for, 72, 73–4, 148, 194–7; Bacon's 'Ganymedes and favourites', 194, 197; 'catamites', 70, 196, 197, 227; classical/Renaissance thinking on male friendship, 97–9; and *Corona Regia*, 73–4, 195; of Edward II, 77, 200–2; and familial happiness, 163; Ganymede tale, 195–7, 224–5; and James's pacifism, 226–9; language about, 70, 72, 73–4, 196, 224–5, 283–4; love and pedagogy, 97; pederasty, 73, 97; sodomy, 70, 72, 73–4, 195, 197, 202; speculation about King, 71, 84–5; Yelverton's accusations, 199–200, 201–3

horses, 18, 102, 106–9, 140, 141, 148, 357; Buckingham's horsemanship, 20, 22, 106–7, 109; at Burley-on-the-Hill, 204; Charles's horsemanship, 235; Master of the Horse, 90–1, 106–8, 112, 140, 148, 205, 398, 513

Howard, Frances, 19, 52–4, 55, 56, 136, 156–7, 165

Howard, Lord Thomas, 38, 49, 72, 402–3

Howard, Sir Robert, 135

Howard family, 38, 49, 64, 72, 80, 93, 135, 136, 402–3, 620; and Catholicism, 19, 113–14; Frances and Somerset, 19, 52–4, 55, 56, 136, 156–7, 165

Howell, James, 296, 297, 300, 318, 323, 325, 328; on British behaviour in Madrid, 311, 319, 324; and Charles's formal entrance to Madrid, 287, 288–9; and Charles's rejection of Infanta, 327; description of the Infanta, 295; as diplomat in Madrid, 3, 115, 173, 245, 268, 269; on the Escorial, 302; and male friendship, 98; on Paris, 264; in Portsmouth (August 1628), 3, 611; on the Pyrenees, 267, 328

hunting: at Burley-on-the-Hill, 204–5; Castiglione on, 141; hunting lodges, 54–5,

122, 147; James's fondness for, 18, 20, 30–1, 34, 104, 106, 140, 141–7, 206, 226, 357; and Queen Anne, 142–3; rituals and ceremonies, 144–6; in Spain, 279, 283, 286, 299, 312, 318, 325; *Venus and Adonis* story, 168–9

Huntly, Earl of, 35–6

Hutchinson, Lucy, 136, 624

Huygens, Constantijn, 382–3

Hyde, Nicholas, 566

Hyperius, Andreas, 492

Île de Ré, 459, 460, 461, 548–52, 572, 611, 619; French troops land on (October 1627), 558–9; siege of Fort St-Martin (July 1627), 552–8

India, 119, 403, 580

Inojosa, Marquis of, 358–60, 361, 365, 366, 369

intelligence/espionage: and ambassadors, 116; Buckingham's agents abroad, 112–13; Elizabeth I's spies, 34, 35–6; Gerbier as agent abroad, 112–13, 382, 421, 425, 535, 536, 622

Isabella, Archduchess, 421–2, 424–5, 426, 452, 535–6

Isabella, Queen of Spain, 289, 296–7, 319, 410–11

Italy, 40, 114, 215, 219–21

Jahangir, Mogul Emperor, 119

James I, King of England (James VI of Scotland): aids Louis XIII at La Rochelle, 459–61, 471, 514; baby Henry sent to Stirling Castle, 150–1; *Basilikon Doron* (1599), 70, 129, 144, 224; bawdy/dirty talk of, 24, 104; boyhood love for Lennox, 33–5, 150, 201; and British textile industry, 403; Buckingham accused of poisoning, 180, 477, 478–80, 481, 485–7, 489, 496, 497–8, 502, 504, 506–7, 624; and Buckingham's family, 64, 134, 149–50, 153, 160–1, 284, 372–3, 392; at Buckingham's 'Friend's Feast' (June 1618), 149; and Buckingham's ill health (spring 1624), 366, 369–72; and Buckingham's influence over Charles, 358, 359; and Buckingham's marriage, 159–61, 165–7; childhood ill health, 28; congenital weakness of the legs, 18, 357; Cranfield's financial reforms, 344–5,

Presbyterianism, 29–30, 33–4, 35
Prideaux, Dr John, 293
print journalism, 12, 362, 363, 364
Privy Council, 75–6, 86, 89, 90, 124–5, 130,
131, 356–7, 431; Buckingham admitted to,
92, 125, 429; and Buckingham's murder,
616; and Charles and Buckingham's
secret mission (1623), 257; Charles's
'Cabinet Council', 429, 431–2; Coke
expelled from, 217; and Coke marriage
dispute, 134; 'Forced Loan' policy, 521–2,
565–6, 577, 578, 592; and the French
match, 381; James's long absences from,
143; and Mansfeld's force, 387, 388;
Prince Charles presides over, 339; and
'ship money', 572; and shortage of money
(1626–8), 520–2, 540, 572; and the
Spanish Match, 274
Protestantism: anti-Spanish party at court,
19–20, 80, 101, 104–5, 181–3, 186–7, 227,
293–4, 344, 537; Book of Common
Prayer, 290; and Buckingham's marriage,
157–8; Calvinism, 29–30, 73, 79, 104, 119,
610–11; and English hostility to
Catholicism, 171–3, 211–15, 293–4, 322,
324, 338, 344, 349–53, 429–31, 440–2, 529,
537, 598–9; Frederick's bid for power in
Bohemia, 181–2, 210, 211; French Match
blamed for plague, 431; Henry VIII
severs links with Rome, 115; High Church
movement, 512–13; Huguenots in France,
416, 419, 459–61, 471, 527, 534–5, 537,
547–9, 590; James's 'Christian League'
proposal, 101–2, 182, 213; Parliamentary
support for war on Spain, 351–3; princes
in Holy Roman Empire, 101, 170, 181–4,
210–11, 451–2; services in the vernacular,
491–2; translation of the Bible under
James, 79–80, 491, 532; Tyndale's Bible,
491
Prynne, William, 13
public opinion, 12, 150, 361–5
publishing trade, 363
Puritans, 11, 13, 24, 41, 70, 104, 136, 200,
317, 344, 583; and early Stuart art
collections, 621; 'effeminacy' as
abhorrent to, 224; hatred of Church
hierarchy, 213; in Parliament, 188, 212,
213, 215–16, 291, 351–2, 513
Pym, John, 139, 587, 592
Pyrenees, 267–8, 328

Pythagoras, 626

Raleigh, Sir Walter, 39, 91, 104, 119, 137, 152,
174, 380; trial of, 129, 494
Ramsay, Robert, 486
Raphael, 219, 383, 384, 510
Ravaillac, Francois, 32
Remington, Dr, 370, 392–5, 463, 477, 479,
485–6, 504, 507, 514, 624
Renaissance thinkers, 40, 97, 98
Reni, Guido, 219
Rich, Barnaby, 224
Rich, Sir Nathaniel, 431, 434, 504–5, 592
Richard II, King of England, 77
Richard III, King of England, 75
Richelieu, Armand du Plessis, Cardinal de,
408, 452, 502, 534–5, 619; Buckingham's
letter to (1627), 534, 535; expands French
fleet, 527–8; Gerbier as Buckingham's
messenger to, 382, 535; gives dinner at
Palais du Luxembourg (1625), 409, 416,
420, 423; as guide/chief executive to
young king, 78; and La Rochelle
rebellions, 459–60, 527, 534, 552, 555–8;
mental health of, 417–18; negotiations
with Buckingham (1625), 418–19; rise to
power of, 416–17; and siege of Fort
St-Martin (July 1627), 552, 556–8
Richmond, Duke of, 316
Richmond, Mary Stewart, Duchess of
(Mall, daughter of Buckingham), 162,
236, 314, 370, 528, 538, 569; betrothed to
Lord Charles Herbert, 567, 620; in
Honthorst portrait, 602; Van Dyck's
portrait of, 620
Rizzio, David, 27
Roe, Sir Thomas, 118–19, 510–11, 623
Rohan, Duke of, 367, 459–61, 534, 537, 552,
558
Rojas, Fernando de, 300
Rous, John, 4, 604, 612
royal prerogative, 130, 131–2, 216, 217–18,
578, 579, 583–92
Royston, hunting lodge at, 54–5, 122, 328,
335
Rubens, Peter Paul, 169, 196, 382–3, 476,
601, 621; and the Arundels, 113, 114, 115,
164, 221; background of, 420–1, 424–5;
and the Banqueting House, 420; on
Buckingham, 448–9, 452, 535; equestrian
portrait of Buckingham, 109, 424, 448,